Human DNA: Law and Policy

International and Comparative Perspectives

Human DNA: Law and Policy

International and Comparative Perspectives

Editor
Bartha Maria Knoppers
Professor and Senior Researcher,
Centre for Public Law Research (CRDP)
Faculty of Law, Université de Montréal, Montréal, Canada

Associate Editors
Claude M. Laberge
Professor of Medicine and Pediatrics
Laval University, Québec, Canada
President, Québec Network of Applied Genetic Medicine

Marie Hirtle
Attorney, Research Associate
Centre for Public Law Research (CRDP)
Faculty of Law, Université de Montréal, Montréal, Canada

KLUWER LAW INTERNATIONAL
The Hague • London • Boston

Published by Kluwer Law International,
P.O. Box 85889, 2508 CN The Hague, The Netherlands.

Sold and distributed in the U.S.A. and Canada
by Kluwer Law International,
675 Massachusetts Avenue, Cambridge, MA 02139, U.S.A.

In all other countries, sold and distributed
by Kluwer Law International,
P.O. Box 85889, 2508 CN The Hague, The Netherlands.

Library of Congress Cataloging-in-Publication Data on File

ISBN 90-411-0361-9 (hardcover)
ISBN 90-411-0452-6 (paperback)

Kluwer Law International incorporates the publishing programs of
Graham & Trotman Ltd, Kluwer Law and Taxation Publishers,
and Martinus Nijhoff Publishers.

CONTENTS

ACKNOWLEDGEMENTS

This book contains the proceedings of the *First International Conference on DNA Sampling & Human Genetic Research: Ethical, Legal and Policy Aspects* held in Montreal, Canada, on September 6-8, 1996. The conference was under the direction of Bartha Maria Knoppers, Claude M. Laberge and Gerald Robertson and was jointly organized by the Center for Public Law Research/Centre de recherche en droit public (CRDP), the Quebec Network of Applied Genetic Medicine and the Health Law Institute.

Under the coordination of Marie Hirtle, many individuals worked towards the preparation of the conference and the conference proceedings. We would like to extend special acknowledgements to Sébastien Lormeau who conceived and prepared the comprehensive materials distributed at the conference and to Catherine Mosco who completed the often tedious technical editing with an everlasting good humor. We also wish to thank Catherine Bouchard, Marie-Angéle Grimaud, Lori Luther, Sandrine Pascal-Rossi and Denise Tremblay for their contribution to the conference materials as well as all those who volunteered their time during the conference. Special thanks also go to Samaa Elibyari, Cécile Dubeau, Cécile Bujold, Giséle Chabot and Nina Hawkins for the invaluable secretarial and administrative support.

Many thanks to the speakers and authors of conference papers as well as to the chairs of the plenary sessions and the rapporteurs who masterfully translated the thrust of the conference discussions for the conclusions of each chapter of this book.

Finally, the Conference that led to this book was made possible by the generous support—financial or technical—of a number of governmental and private organizations that we wish to acknowledge: the Canadian Genome Analysis & Technology Program, the Quebec Network of Applied Genetic Medicine, the Centre de recherche en droit public, the Health Law Institute, The Hospital for Sick Children Foundation, the Canadian Breast Cancer Research Initiative, the U.S. Department of Energy and National Center for Human Genome Research, the Inter-University Institute of Calgary, Algéne Biotechnologies, Bio-IMRM R&D inc., and finally, McMaster Meighen, Barristers and Solicitors.

Lastly, we wish to thank DSKY for graciously contributing his artwork towards what we renamed "The DNA Quilt" and which appears on the cover.

B.M.K., C.M.L., M.H.

CONTRIBUTORS

Prof. Lori B. Andrews
Chicago-Kent College of Law
Illinois Institute of Technology
565 West Adams
Chicago, Il. 60661
USA
FAX: 1-312-906-5280

Dr. Christopher P. Austin
Merck Research Laboratories.
WP26A-3300
P.O. Box 4
West Point, PA 19486
USA
FAX: 1-215-652-2075

Prof. Ségolène Aymé
INSERM SC 11
16 Ave. Paul-Vaillant-Couturier
F-94807 Villejuif Cedex
France
FAX: 33-1-45-595 250

Prof. Patricia Baird
Department of Medical Genetics
University of British Columbia
#226 Westbrook Building
6174 University Boulevard
Vancouver BC Canada, V6T 1Z3
FAX: 1-604-822-3565

Prof. Zbigniew Bankowski
Secretary General
CIOMS
CH-1211 Geneva 27
Switzerland
FAX: 41-22-791-0746

Prof. Antonio Cao
Inst. di Clinica e Biologia
Univ. degli Studi di Cagliari
Via Jenner/Casella Postale 251
I-09121 Cagliari Italy
FAX: 39-70-503 696

Prof. Timothy A. Caulfield
461 Law Centre
Health Law Institute
University of Alberta
Edmonton, Alberta
Canada T6G 2H5
FAX: 1-403-492-4924

Prof. L. Luca Cavalli-Sforza
Genetics Department Rm 346
Stanford University
Standford CA 94305-5120
USA
FAX: 1-415-725-1534

Prof. Ruth F. Chadwick
Centre for Professional Ethics
University of Central Lancashire
Preston, United Kingdom
PR1 2HE
FAX: 44-1772-892942

Ms Kathy Cherniawsky
de Villars Jones
300 Noble Building
8540-109th Street
Edmonton, Alberta
Canada T6G 1E6
FAX: 1-403-433-9780

Prof. Joe TR Clarke
Division of Clinical Genetics
Elm Wing, Room 9142
Hospital for Sick Children
555 University Avenue
Toronto, Ontario
Canada M5G 1X8
FAX: 1-416-813-5345

Prof. Maurice A.M. De Wachter
Avenue de L'Été, 74
B-1410 Waterloo
Belgium
FAX: 32-2-354-0218

Prof. Jean-Louis Dhondt
Laboratoire
Hôpital St Philibert
Lomme 59462 Cedex
France
FAX: 33-3-20-22-50-11

Prof. Bernard M. Dickens
Faculty of Law
University of Toronto
84 Queen's Park Cr.
Toronto, Ontario Canada, M5S 2C5
FAX: 1-416-978-7899

Prof. Rebecca S. Eisenberg
Law School
University of Michigan
439 Hutchins Hall
Ann Arbor, MI 48109-1210
USA
FAX: 1-313-763-9375

Prof. Jean Christophe Galloux
Université de Versailles
Saint-Quentin-en-Yvelines
3 rue de la Division Leclerc
78280 Guyancourt France
FAX: 33-1-46-22-78-31

Prof. Sjef Gevers
University of Amsterdam
Academic Medical Centre
Institute of Social Medicine
Meibergdreef 15
1105 AZ Amsterdam
The Netherlands
FAX: 31-20-696-2316

Dr. Kathleen Cranley Glass
Assistant Professor, Department of Human Genetics
Biomedical Ethics Unit
McGill University
3690 Peel St.
Montreal, Quebec
Canada H3A 1W9
FAX: 1-514-398-8349

Ms. Béatrice Godard
Centre de recherche
Pav. Marie de la Serre
Hôtel-Dieu de Montréal
3850 St. Urbain
Montréal, Québec
Canada, H2W 1T8
FAX: 1-514-482-4010

Prof. Henry Greely
Law School
Standford University
Crown Quad, 112
Stanford, CA 94305
USA
FAX: 1-415-725-0253

Prof. Judith G. Hall
Clinical Genetics Unit
Grace Hospital
4490 Oak Street
Vancouver, BC Canada V6H 3V5
FAX: 1-604-875-2890

Me Marie Hirtle
Centre de recherche en droit public
3101 Chemin de la Tour
C.P. 6128, Succ. Centre-Ville
Montreal, Quebec Canada H3C 3J7
FAX: 1-514-343-7508

Prof. Helena Kääriäinen
Family Federation of Finland
Dept of Medical Genetics
University of Helsinki
Väestölitto,Kalevankatu 16A
FIN-00100 Helsinki
Finland
FAX: 358-0-645018

Prof. Douglas T. Kinsella
Office of Bioethics
Heritage Medical Res. Center
Room 93
3330 University Drive NW
Calgary, Alberta Canada T2N 4N1
FAX: 1-403-283-8524

Prof. Bartha Maria Knoppers
Centre de recherche en droit public
3101 Chemin de la Tour
C.P. 6128, Succ. Centre-Ville
Montreal, Quebec
Canada H3C 3J7
FAX: 1-514-343-7508

Prof. Claude Laberge
CHUL #9355
2705 boul Laurier
Ste-Foy, Quebec
Canada G1V 4G2
FAX: 1-418-654-2748

Prof. Moe Litman
461 Law Centre
Faculty of Law
University of Alberta
Edmonton, Alberta
Canada T6G 2H5
FAX: 1-403-492-4924

Prof. Margaret Lock
Social Studies of Medicine, Room 416
McIntyre Medical Sciences Bldg
McGill University
3655 Drummond Street
Montreal (Quebec) Canada H3G 1Y6
FAX: 1-514 -398-1498

Prof. Peter J.M. Lown
Director
Alberta Law Reform Institute
402 Law Centre
University of Alberta
Edmonton, Alberta
Canada T6G 2H5
FAX: 1-403-492-1790

Me Lori Luther
Centre de recherche en droit public
3101 Chemin de la Tour
C.P. 6128, Succ. Centre-Ville
Montreal, Quebec
Canada H3C 3J7
FAX: 1-514-343-7508

Mr. Darryl Macer
Institute of Biological Sciences
University of Tsukuba
Tsukuba, Ibaraki 305
Japan
FAX: (81-298) 53-66-14

Mr. Randy Marusyk
Marusyk, Bourassa, Milton
100 Sparks St. 1000
Ottawa, Ontario Canada K1P 5B7
FAX: 1-613-563-7671

Prof. Noël-Jean Mazen
2 bis rue du Capuert
21 800 Quetigny
France
FAX: 33 80-46- 90-24

Prof. Jean McEwen
Boston College Law School
885 Centre Street
Newton, MA 02159
USA
FAX: 1-617-552-2615

Prof. Victor A. McKusick
Center for Medical Genetics
The Johns Hopkins Hospital
Blalock Bldg, Room 1007
600 N Wolfe Street
Baltimore MD 21205
USA
FAX: 1-410-955-4999

Dr. Bent Nørgaard-Pedersen
Satens Seruminstitut
5, Artillerivej
DK-2300 Copenhagen S.
Denmark
FAX: 45-32-68-3878

Attorney Els Olsthoorn-Heim
Health Council of the Netherlands
PO Box 1236
2280 CE Rijswijk Netherlands
FAX: 31-70-340 75 23

Me Isabelle Panisset
Centre de recherche en droit public
3101 Chemin de la Tour
C.P. 6128, Succ. Centre-Ville
Montreal, Quebec Canada H3C 3J7
FAX: 1-514-343-7508

Prof. Alain Pompidou
Fac. de Médecine Cochin Port-Royal
Laboratoire Histologie-Cytogénétique
24 rue de Faubourg-Saint-Jacques
75014 Paris
France
FAX: 33-1-40-51-09-46

Dr. Octavi Quintana
Adjunto a la Director General
Insalud
Alcalá, 56
28071 Madrid
Espana
FAX: 34-1-338-07-07

Prof. Gerald Robertson
461 Law Centre
Health Law Institute
University of Alberta
Edmonton, Alberta
Canada T6G 2H5
FAX: 1-403-492-4924

Prof. Patricia Roche
Health Law Department
Boston University School of Public Health
School of Medicine
80 East Concord Street, A-509
Boston, Massachusetts
USA 02118-2394
FAX: 1-617-638-5299

Prof. David J. Roy
Center for Bioethics
Clinical Research Institute of Montreal
110 Ave des Pins ouest
Montreal, Quebec
Canada H2W 1R7
FAX: 1-514-987-5695

Prof. Elizabeth Thomson
NCHGR/NIH
Assistant Director, Clinical Genetics Research
Building 38A, Room 617
38 Library Drive, MSC 6050
Bethesda, MD 20892-6050
USA
FAX: 1-301-402-1950

Dr. Marja J. Verhoef
Department of Community Health Sciences
3330 University Drive NW
Calgary, Alberta
Canada T2N 4N1
FAX: 1-403-270 7307

Prof. Ishwar C. Verma
Professor of Pediatrics
Genetic Unit, Department of Pediatrics
AIIMS, New Delhi
India
FAX: 0091-11-685-4434

Prof. Robert Weir
University of Iowa
College of Medicine
Program in Biomedical Ethics
106 Medical Education Bldg
Iowa City, IA 52242-1000
USA
FAX: 1-319-335-8515

Dr. Ellen Wright Clayton
Dept Pediatrics
Vanderbilt University
TVC 3963
Nashville, TN 37232-5577
USA
FAX: 1-615-343-0829

PREFACE

To venture forth into the international nether world of "DNA Sampling" in order to distil the ethical, legal and social policy aspects is to risk losing one's way in a maze of conflicting and differing positions and attitudes. The status of DNA, its protection, its transfer and ultimately its use(s) and transformation reflect how we view ourselves, our body, its parts and cells, what they reveal and even more importantly, how we feel about our families and the health of others in society.

While not as emotive an issue as the creation and use of the human embryo, the information DNA reveals is nevertheless highly personal, familial and socially sensitive information. The fact that it can be immortalized through the creation of cell lines and used beyond one's lifetime makes the issue of the conditions of procurement and storage and possible commercialization all the more crucial.

Collections of human DNA once considered "*res derelictae*", abandoned and available to all for research - no questions asked - have begun to acquire value. This value may be highly personal, human genetic material being considered by law as part of the person as in France, or as property in the United States under the proposed Genetic Privacy Act, as requiring a unique and separate legal status (*sui generis*), or finally, as a gift to the furtherance of research for the advancement of our understanding of disease for the betterment of humanity.

While at first glance the debate may seem to be purely academic, the increasing "commodification" of the sample under either a prohibitive legislative approach with its procedural encumbrances, or, a property approach with its possible commercialization, transforms the DNA into the person and so reduces the person to the DNA.

Yet irrespective of the approach taken, there is no doubt that consent to research has expanded to include an array of choices that reflect fundamental, personal and societal values. Will these choices follow the sample? What if the person has died and cannot consent? Will these choices be respected? Are the choices offered pertinent and realistic or irrelevant and needlessly constraining? It would well be that with DNA sampling, we have reached the epitomy (if not the epiphany) of the informed consent process. We are in danger of losing sight of the larger goals of medicine and of public health. Offering increased choices and control respects the contribution of the person, but where will it end? It could be argued that at a minimum access by family members constitutes a necessary recognition of genealogical, "blood" relatedness — the last vestige of "connectedness". Should a more precise diagnosis of the samples become possible one day, who, if anyone owes a duty (if any) to warn such at-risk relatives, or even, to retest stored samples so as to offer such a diagnosis? Bankers of human DNA also may unwittingly have responsibilities beyond the patient or research participant. This uncharted territory constitutes the biggest challenge to human genetic research and requires more than the current incremental and haphazard approach devoid of a coherent, public debate.

Epidemiological studies, essential prerequisites of public health and prevention programs to say nothing of state health planning and surveillance, have long operated in relative "anonymity" with legislative backing and recognition of their importance. The use of registries and population studies are all the more important as genetic research moves from sequencing to functional genomics and specific gene location. Discussions of the issues then move to another level of complexity. Indeed, the polarized property-person debate acquires new contours that defy linear, monogenic models. A more epigenetic, dynamic understanding is required, an approach that reflects the multifactorial nature and the role of genetic factors in most common diseases, to say nothing of the variability and complexity of the human person.

Legitimate concerns for the protection of privacy or for possible stigmatization that accompanies gene identification with particular populations, regions or ethnic groups, require valid and workable responses that do not undermine the possibility of undertaking genetic epidemiology but instead recognize the specificity and the need for this research. Informatics could well play an important protective role here with the coding or anonymizing of samples before their entry into the Health care system and this all the more so in commercially sponsored research.

Particular attention should be paid to how different cultures and populations view genetic research. Prior consultation and communication are essential considering the sensitivity and cultural values of "interesting" isolates and sub-populations as illustrated by the controversy surrounding the proposed human genetic diversity project.

Other vulnerable populations include newborn and carrier screening programs. The classical, pediatric parameters of the former are being challenged because of the easy accessibility of newborn blood spots. The entire population of the future could be studied and research conducted on "left over" spots. The limitation to only testing for immediately treatable disorders, for conditions of a certain incidence with tests of certain specificity and sensitivity, that is, to finding the asymptomatic, at-risk newborn in the general population for treatment for his own benefit, may well give way. There are pressures to test new technologies on these "spots". Paradoxically, because of the concomitant rise of parental "rights" to consent (or not), is also undermining these programs and would leave the newborn population to their statistical, genetic risk. Similarly, carrier testing programs traditionally limited to well-known ethnic communities or populations and often initiated at their request or even run by such communities, now see their rationale tested by the advent of different and new populations at-risk for genetic factors in common diseases such as breast cancer and hereditary hemochromatosis or hypercholesterolemia or fragile-X. Will, or should, the same rules apply?

Finally, a more "nefarious" actor has been let loose in the system. The devolution of government sponsored research towards private corporate funding is beginning to leave its mark on the process of DNA sampling. Speculative bids for possible patents on anonymous sequences of unknown function have repeatedly had a chilling effect on international collaboration and cooperation. The gold-rush for patent applications has put increasing pressure on ensuring either "waivers" of the potential property interests by DNA "sources" or the granting of (in all likelihood) fictitious future percentages of possible royalties. The resulting commodification of the person and commercialization of research will harm the physician-patient (researcher-participant) relationship. The legitimacy of the traditional patent system should be underscored, informed consent and refusal and choice are essential. Bargaining for future worth in one's DNA is not.

This also creates confusion in the public since it appears that researchers are seeking to patent "persons", or parts, or elements thereof. Researchers also find themselves in contractual situations that impede the sharing of information with other scientists and even with the public. Perhaps, little can be done to change the market system that even government seems to have embraced but the ethical and legal rules need to be clarified and made transparent. Hence, this first international Conference bringing together over 200 participants and experts from around the world - the issues not being limited to any one country or population. Only an international gathering of the "facts" and only a "humanistic" understanding of the reasons for differing approaches can serve to begin the necessary debate.

Bartha Maria Knoppers
Conference Chair
Montreal, March 1997

DNA SAMPLING: WHAT WOULD OSLER SAY?

VICTOR A. McKUSICK

University Professor of Medical Genetics, Johns Hopkins University

Physician, Johns Hopkins Hospital, Baltimore, Maryland USA

"What would Osler say?" is a point of departure for discussing the present and future impact of the New Genetics on medicine. Canada-born and educated, William Osler (1849-1919) was at the peak of his career in 1896. He was arguably the best known physician of his day. As Sigerist pointed out, others wrote as good or better textbooks and certainly others contributed more importantly to both the scientific base of medicine and the application of science in the practice of medicine. But like Hippocrates (who was probably not one man), Osler represented the ideal physician of the time. He gave his name to Oslerian medicine in the way that Victoria gave her name to an era. How does the New Genetics change Oslerian medicine?

Osler was a professor in four universities in three countries on two continents: McGill, University of Pennsylvania, Johns Hopkins and Oxford. We are meeting in the city where Osler got his professional start and evolved the autopsy based type of clinical medicine for which he was known. Imagine the DNA testing that he could have done with pathological samples today. The longest segment of his professional career, 1889 to 1905, was spent at Johns Hopkins. In a new institution where he was the first physician-in-chief, he grew in reputation along with the institution. As the seventh in the succession of physicians-in-chief at Johns Hopkins 1973-1985 and with perhaps more than the usual interest in medical history, I find the topic " What would Osler think?" a challenging one.

Since Osler's day, medicine, while keeping an Oslerian base in morbid anatomy (now done more in the MRI laboratory than in the autopsy room), has added successively a base in pathophysiology, in biochemistry, and in recent times in genetics. The incursion of genetics into both the science and the practice of medicine is a leading phenomenon of the last 50 years.

The Evolution of Genetics in Medicine

It was not until 1956, forty years ago, that we knew that the correct number of chromosomes in the human is 46, not 48 as previously thought. In 1959 the first chromosome aberration was found, the extra chromosome in Down syndrome. After that, studying chromosomes, in cells of the blood, for example, under the light microscope, became rather routine.

In the 40 years between 1956 and now, we have gone from getting the chromosome count right to a point where the human genome project is well along in its goals to map all the genes on those chromosomes and determine their complete chemical structure (sequence of DNA nucleotides).

The ability to study the chromosomes with relative facility from the late 1950s, gave medical genetics as a clinical speciality an anatomic base, gave medical genetics its organ, just as cardiology had the heart and ophthalmology the eye. Acquisition of other procedures and clinical diagnostic and counselling skills requiring special training led, by 1990, to full status for medical genetics as a clinical subspecialty, with all the professional appurtenances, including the American Board of Medical Genetics (the 24th in the family of speciality boards) and the American College of Medical Genetics.

Mapping Genes to Discover the Cause of Genetic Diseases

The linear array of genes and DNA units on our chromosomes is part of our anatomy. Gene mapping on chromosomes started in earnest about 1970 and molecular genetic analysis of the human genome, so-called sequencing, from the early 1980s have provided a new anatomic base, not just for the speciality of medical genetics, but for all of clinical medicine. Map-based gene discovery, technically known as positional cloning, has become a leading paradigm in contemporary biomedical research. Starting in 1986, 10 years ago, most specialities of medicine have used this approach to study their diseases in which the basic biochemical defect was unknown. The way it works is that the disorder is mapped to a particular chromosome region, usually by linkage studies in families, showing that particular DNA markers are located close to the region of the mutant gene causing the disorder. Isolating the gene involves walking down the chromosome from the markers or walking in from flanking markers until the gene is found. Once the defective gene is isolated and the defect in the structure of the gene defined, specific DNA-based diagnosis can be designed and potentially therapy can be improved through better understanding of the disease mechanisms that connect the abnormal gene to the clinical problems.

The list of disorders elucidated by map-based gene discovery includes the most frequent form of muscular dystrophy, cystic fibrosis, familial polyposis of the colon, Marfan syndrome, polycystic kidney disease, Huntington disease and on and on. Scarcely a week passes now that discovery of the gene for at least one mystery disease is announced in *Science* or *Nature* with simultaneous, if not prior report, in the *N.Y. Times* or *Wall Street Journal*. Cancers such as colon cancer and breast cancer, which usually are not inherited, have also yielded to this approach, reminding us that whatever the initiating factors may be, such as cigarettes or radiation, cancer is, in the final analysis, a genetic disease. Change in the genome is required for the uncontrolled growth of cells and other characteristics of aggressive cancer such as metastasis. Map-based gene discovery is also helping sort out the genes that contribute to susceptibility to disorders of complex causation such as hypertension, diabetes and mental illness.

In his writings on hereditary chorea and in his famous textbook of medicine, Osler called attention to the report of George Huntington in 1872 and helped put Huntington disease on the map.

Huntington disease is in many ways a prototype of the mystery diseases that have been elucidated by map-based gene discovery. It illustrates the usefulness of gene mapping, as well as some of the practical problems of applying the information obtained by gene mapping. Huntington disease is a serious neuropsychiatric disorder with onset at 35-40 years of age. In 1983, it was discovered that the Huntington disease gene is located at the tip of the short arm of chromosome 4 because in family studies the disorder showed linkage to DNA markers known to be on that chromosome. Even before the gene itself was isolated, the closely situated markers could be used for prenatal and presymptomatic diagnosis by testing DNA from multiple family members. When the gene itself was isolated, 10 years later in 1993, by "walking in on the gene" from the flanking markers, it was possible to make the diagnosis of Huntington disease with essentially complete confidence, going directly to the gene to demonstrate the unusual and specific change in the patient's DNA, and not needing to rely on family DNAs for linkage studies. Huntington disease illustrates, however, the fact that the Human Genome Project increases the gap between what we know how to diagnose and what we know how to treat. Unfortunately, we have no way to ward off the Huntington disease or treat it when it develops. Nonetheless, Osler would marvel at the recent work and would recognize the potential for early diagnosis and perhaps prevention or therapy in the future.

The Human Genome Project

Map-based gene discovery, the cloning of the genes that are mutated in these mystery disease, is aided greatly by the Human Genome Project. It is part of the spin-off that justifies the HGP for public funding. But the HGP has a specific goal: complete sequencing of the 3.0 billion chemical units (A,C,G,T) in the chromosomes and identifying the 75,000 or so genes distributed through that sequence. The molecular genetics revolution and the informatics revolution are combined in the HGP and make it possible.

The HGP was proposed in 1985, was formally initiated October 1, 1990 and was projected to take 15 years. It now looks as though it might be finished sooner than 2005, perhaps by the year 2003. When it is finished, what we will have is a source book for biology and medicine to study and refer to far into the future. We will have the infrastructure for working out how the mind/brain works, how development and differentiation work, and basic causes and mechanisms in the whole range of pathology and predisposition to disease. We will also have the means for working out the genetic basis of normal physical and behavioral characteristics. Note, however, that when the HGP is completed in 2003 or whenever, we will not know the function of all those 75,000 genes individually, let alone in concert. We will not know the variation in those genes among the six billion persons who will inhabit this globe by that time, and we will not know the relationship between variation in genes and variation in phenotype, that is, variation in how genes express themselves. As someone has said, "as the radius of knowledge elongates, the circumference of the unknown expands".

The HGP and Map-based Gene Discovery

Map-based gene discovery, positional cloning of genes involved in simply inherited genetic disorders, was underway before the human genome project and has been and will continue to be greatly aided by the infrastructure provided by the HGP. The complete sequence will be necessary for finding all the genes. Sequence-based gene discovery is increasingly taking over. Furthermore, attention is extending beyond gene discovery to analysis of the function of those genes (witness the large amount of work on transgenic and "knockout" mice and in expression systems in yeast, insects or bacteria). In the case of genetic diseases, there is some shift from a focus on etiology (identification of the precise causative mutation) to pathogenesis (the mechanism by which the genetic change leads to the abnormalities of phenotype). Understanding disease mechanisms is particularly important in medicine because therapy often can be directed at the steps connecting gene with phene. Unravelling the mysteries of development and differentiation and the workings of the mind/brain will be greatly aided by the availability of the genomic infrastructure provided by the HGP.

Complex traits are beginning to yield to these approaches: disorders such as diabetes, asthma, hypertension and mental illness. These are multifactorial, for the most part, with multiple genetic and environmental factors collaborating in causation, along with chance (accidental or stochastic events).

The single mutations in classic mendelian inborn errors of metabolism such as albinism or PKU involve enzymes at one site in a metabolic pathway. In such genetic disorders, there tends to be a relatively direct relationship between genotype and phenotype. The multiple mutations involved in polygenic disorders are likely to be polymorphisms in enzymes and other proteins at multiple sites in a developmental and metabolic nexus. It is the combination of particular variations at the several sites that adds up to a particular susceptibility. This consideration indicates the necessity to know the "normal" variation as background for genetic epidemiology. This is the type of information that the Human Genome Diversity Project (HGDP) aims to collect. It seems evident that for maximal benefit to be derived from the HGP, information on DNA variation in health and disease will be essential. The potential problems in the sampling and screening of DNA in individuals, family members and populations are the topic of this conference.

What Would Osler Say?

In 1888 while still in Philadelphia, Osler gave the first description of hereditary angioedema. Striking in paroxysmal manner, the disorder causes edema in the upper airway which sometimes leads to death by suffocation. The gene that is mutant in this disorder has been cloned, and mapped to chromosome 11. This was not an instance of map-based gene discovery because the protein affected in the condition, complement component-1 inhibitor, was already known; the gene was isolated by so-called functional cloning, not positional cloning. Once the gene was isolated, specific mutations were found therein responsible for disease in affected persons. Certainly Osler would be impressed by the predictive power and preventive benefit provided by this new knowledge.

In 1901, while at Johns Hopkins, Osler described familial recurrent epistaxis, a disorder that later became known as hereditary hemorrhagic telangiectasia (HHT), following the lead of a Johns Hopkins resident, Frederick Hanes. This is a disorder of small blood vessels in the skin and mucous membranes that break and bleed at mucosal sites such as the nose and stomach. Communications between arteries and veins (arteriovenous fistulas) may develop in the lungs. Map-based gene discovery (positional cloning) has demonstrated at least 2 different genes, one on chromosome 9 encoding endoglobin that is important to endothelial development and integrity, and one on chromosome 12 encoding activin-receptor-like kinase, another protein important to endothelium. There appears to be a third form of hereditary hemorrhagic telangiectasia unlinked to either chromosome 9 or chromosome 12. Various causative mutations have been found in the chromosome 9 or chromosome 12 genes in persons affected by this disorder. Pulmonary arteriovenous fistulas seem to be much more frequent in the chromosome 9 form. Again, Osler would be impressed with the ability to identify affected family members and to practice at least secondary prevention of the serious complications that develop in the second decade or later.

Osler was a notorious therapeutic nihilist. He said that "if most of the drugs in the pharmacopeia were dumped into the sea, it would be all the better for humanity and the worse for the fishes". However, the possibilities for effective and specific therapies resulting from the HGP would surely change his views. With the HGP, medicine will become much more predictive and preventive than it now is, but diagnosis and therapy, the traditional turf of medicine, will also become powerfully more specific and effective. George Poste predicts, perhaps with excessive enthusiasm, that by the year 2000 50% of pharmaceutical research will be genome based. This prediction is reflected in the heavy investment in genome research by large firms such as Smith Kline Beecham, Merck and Glaxo, and in the development of smaller biotech companies with names such as Genome Therapeutics. Sequana Therapeutics, Mercator Genetics (an obvious allusion to mapping), and Darwin Molecular. Again, Osler would be tremendously impressed by the new therapeutic possibilities. His therapeutic nihilism derived from the realization of how ineffectual were the medicines of his day.

The New Genetics and Medicine in the Future

Thanks to the HGP, we can be certain that in the next 50 years, medicine will become more predictive and preventive, as a result of the ability to recognize particular predispositions and susceptibilities in the DNA of the individual. It has been fantasized that newborns might in the future have a complete gene screen that would be incorporated in a credit card size electronic record available to health care providers. The physician in the future will be involved in the interpretation of genome findings and in the design of programs to optimize the health of the individual in the light of those findings. Competence in such matters will be necessary for all health care providers; there cannot possibly be enough genetic counsellors and board certified medical geneticists to fill the need. Genetics, genomic medicine, will need to be an integral part of the warp-and-woof of all clinical medicine.

At the same time that medicine becomes more predictive and preventive, diagnosis and treatment, the traditional turf of clinical medicine, will become powerfully more specific and effective. In cancer diagnosis, DNA testing of tumor tissue will supplement and in some instances replace histological and cytologic examination. The background provided by the HGP will be useful, indeed absolutely essential, for gene therapy. For the near future in the therapeutic area, however, the HGP will have its main impact on the design of drug and other therapies through identification of target molecules, intercellular messengers, transcription factors, and, in general, through knowledge of how expression of specific genes is regulated.

Because of the potential for misuse of information concerning the genome of individuals and population groups, the HGP has paid unprecedentedly early and intensive attention to ELSI, ethical, legal and societal implications of the HGP. There have been concerns, for example, that genetic information would be used for discrimination in employment and insurance, used for stigmatization of individuals or groups.

As already noted for Huntington disease, the HGP increases the gap between what we can diagnose and what we can treat. There is also a risk that it will increase the gap between what we *think* we know and what we *really* know; or between what the public thinks science knows and what is really known.

There is considerable diversity in the human genome, not enough to confound the mapping of the chemical units, the sequencing, but enough to lead to problems from the ELSI point of view. Genome diversity is such that associations may be found between a particular genetic make-up and certain behavioral traits, cognitive ability, criminality. (See earlier discussion of the nature of the genetic variation underlying complex traits.) Some of these associations may turn out to be spurious and others, even though they are statistically significant, may be blown out of all reasonable proportions, to the detriment of individuals and groups.

A concern is that DNA diversity revealed by the HGP, without proper understanding, will aggravate the divisiveness among us along the lines of that nasty book of Hernstein and Murray, *The Bell Curve* - a nasty book in its conclusions and recommendations. We must remember:

1. That genetic diversity is a strength of the human species (and of any species);
2. That there are many priceless heritable qualities that are not measured by the I.Q. test;
3. That to thrive maximally, a complex society requires a diversity of qualities and capabilities; and
4. That equality is a legal, political and moral principle, not a genetic parameter. Our society should not abandon a fundamental dedication to the principle of equality, which is quite unrelated to genetic diversity, and should promote that principle worldwide. In my view, the sooner it is possible to define and understand human diversity in full, the better it will be.

What would Osler say? A notable essayist, Osler would certainly have expressed himself thoughtfully and eloquently on both the medical and societal implications of the New Genetics.

September 1996.

Related Readings

1 Cushing H., *The Life of Sir William Osler*, (Oxford: Clarendon Press, 1926). A biography by a leading physician and neurosurgeon, Harvey Cushing.

2 Collins F.S., "Ahead of Schedule and Under Budget: The Genome Project Passes its Fifth Birthday" (1995), 92 (Review) *Proc. Nat. Acad. Sci.* 1082; Guyer N.S., Collins F.S. "How is the Human Genome Project Doing, and What Have we Learned so Far?" (1995), 92 (Review) *Proc. Nat. Acad. Sci.* 10841. Two reviews from the National Center for Human Genome Research of the NIH outlining the first 5 years of the HGP and making projections for the future.

3 McKusick V.A., "Mapping and Sequencing the Human Genome". (1989), 320 *New Engl. J. Med.* 910. A review of the discussions that went on, 1985-1990, leading up to the HGP.

4 Lander E.S., "The New Genomics: Global Views of Biology" (1996), 274 *Science* 536. A vision of post-sequence biology.

INTERNATIONAL ETHICS GUIDELINES AND GENETIC EPIDEMIOLOGY

ZBIGNIEW BANKOWSKI

Secretary General

Council for International Organization of Medical Sciences (CIOMS)

I am deeply conscious of the honour that the Organizing Committee has conferred upon me, and upon the C.I.O.M.S. (Council for International Organizations of Medical Sciences), in inviting me to give one of the two keynote addresses at this important conference.

I see two ways of interpreting and dealing with the theme I have been given. One is to discuss the applicability and adequacy of current international guidelines on ethics in relation to DNA sampling and genetic epidemiology. I refer specifically to those guidelines issued by the Council for International Organizations of Medical Sciences (CIOMS) on the *Ethics of Biomedical Research Involving Human Subjects* (1982 and 1993), and on *Ethical Review of Epidemiological Studies* (1991), and to the *Declaration of Inuyama on Human Genome Mapping, Genetic Screening and Gene Therapy* (1991).

The other approach is to discuss the meanings and implications of the terms and concepts "international" and "guidelines" in relation to the process of drawing up and establishing international guidelines and in relation to the substance of the guidelines. This also requires some consideration of the continuing evolution and present state of medical, or biomedical ethics.

There is little that needs to be said about the first approach to the theme. To the extent that the CIOMS Guidelines are valid for biomedical research and epidemiological studies, they are valid for DNA sampling and genetic epidemiology. But when they were being prepared, the Human Genome Project and molecular genetics had not advanced sufficiently to be considered and they therefore do not deal with the new or more complex ethical issues being raised by medical genetics in general at the present time. Nevertheless, one can apply the experience gained in their development and establishment as "international" and "ethical" to some aspects of drawing up international guidelines on the ethics of genetic epidemiology.

International

Some of the meanings and implications of "international" in this context may be clarified by distinguishing between "international" and "universal". "International" can refer to a few or many, or even all, nations but should not be confused with "universal". In important respects related to morality or ethics or concepts of "person", indeed to human relationships and behaviour in general, human cultures differ considerably, and it would be impossible or extremely difficult to reflect all such cultural variation in international guidelines. Only "universal" guidelines would accommodate such variation. Well known international codes of medical ethics, such as the Nuremberg Code and the Declaration of Helsinki, are considered by many to be expressions of Western culture, for instance. Nevertheless, as stated by Angell[1] (1988), "there must be a core of human rights that we would wish to see honoured universally...the right of self-determination, on which the doctrine of informed consent is based, is one of them". International guidelines should strive to encompass as much universality as would be practicable but then provide for the means of recognizing and accommodating cultural variation among and within nations.

To ensure the validity of international guidelines as "international", it is necessary to provide explicitly, as regards process and content, for the reasons for which international guidelines are considered necessary, and for all parties to whose interests and obligations the guidelines are to be directed, for example, scientific investigators, health policy makers, ethical review bodies, all who have to deal with ethical issues that arise, in the present case in genetic epidemiology, on an international scale. Hence the need to represent in the process, in a meaningful way, multiprofessional and lay interests from different nations and cultures. Process in this respect includes the preparation and establishment of international guidelines and their monitoring and revision over time. The aim must be to protect from harm and exploitation populations and groups in all nations and to assure their rights to self-determination, so as to prevent the imposition of dominant technological cultures on more traditional cultures.

"International" has special significance in relation to informed consent, a crucial ethical issue in regard to DNA sampling. The purpose of informed consent is to show respect for persons, but because of substantially different perspectives of the nature of "person", internationally and interculturally, it is impossible to provide a definition of informed consent that would be universally applicable, across different nations and cultures. While informed consent may be the most contentious ethical issue, it exemplifies a more general conflict between those who hold that all research should be carried out in accordance with universally applicable standards and those who accept that some standards are universal but contend that others must be adapted to the mores of particular cultures. International guidelines must provide for this conflict and procedural approaches have been proposed. The approach adopted in the CIOMS international guidelines has been the constitution of research ethics committees, ideally based in the population in which research is to be conducted, and the recommendation of ways in which such committees would be formed and function. Another proposal has been for an international ethical review body to advise national bodies on this matter. There is, thus far, little information on the practicality or implementation of guideline recommendations in this respect, but no guidelines that are claimed to be international can avoid this issue.

A particular requirement in an international perspective is the use of clear, unambiguous language that will retain its intended meaning across international boundaries and facilitate translation, as to language and concepts, into languages other than the original. It is not only professionals, who may share a common technical language internationally, who must be considered. The democratization or laicization of biomedical ethics internationally, in developed and developing countries, requires careful attention to the language of ethical concepts and guidelines and to its comprehension on the part of the public and its leaders. The core values of professions as expressed in their ethical codes should be comprehensible not only to their memberships internationally but also to an educated public. This applies in a special way to genetic technology, which is advancing so rapidly that it is feared that society is unable to control it and its effects. The function of international guidelines in providing models for national guidelines also requires the careful use of language.

"International" also implies that technologically developed nations recognize, in practice, that their values and ethical standards must not be imposed on less technologically developed nations and that they do not exploit lax standards or laws or policies that would not be considered ethical in the nations sponsoring the research.

Another implication of "international" is that developing countries receive their due share of the benefits that ensue from the Human Genome Project. At the same time, as we ponder the potential of genetic research and genetic medicine and technology for the prevention or reduction of genetic diseases, and we consider also the heavy burden of common diseases of largely non-genetic or environmental or social etiology which developing countries, especially the so-called least developed countries, carry and which are not being controlled, we must question the value to those countries and even the feasibility of the technologies of genetic medicine and epidemiology for well into the future. "Health for all" is still a distant dream for many countries, even with respect to their present preventable and treatable diseases. Though less developed countries may provide fertile ground for genetic research, its benefits are more likely to accrue, in the medium term at least, to the populations and research interests, perhaps even the commercial interests, of the richer countries.

For a variety of reasons, therefore, not comprehensively covered here, the formulation of international guidelines requires perspectives that are not normally associated with national guidelines on ethics, and that may be overlooked in regard to ethical codes of professional associations.

Guidelines

International guidelines are to be distinguished from more formal international statements or "instruments" for regulating human behaviour, safeguarding human rights, and protecting vulnerable or exploitable individuals or populations. They do not have the force of, for example, United Nations Recommendations, Covenants, Declarations or Conventions, which when ratified by the requisite number of governments are expected to be incorporated into national policies and laws. Neither do they have the force of codes of ethics adopted by professional bodies and expected to be observed by the professions concerned.

Guidelines are typically the level at which non-governmental organizations deal with moral/ethical issues, but on condition that they be established by an authoritative body with credibility and competence. Guidelines have moral, not legal, force. By virtue of the authority and competence of those who establish them they should command very wide respect. Guidelines are not rules; they guide, leaving room for judgement in their application, but without compromising on the ethical principles that they are designed to uphold.

Ethics

Two of the issues that appear to be pertinent in relation to DNA sampling and genetic epidemiology are: the nature of the bond or implied contract between the physician and the individual who provides the DNA sample; and the extent to which the metamorphosis of medical ethics[2] should be reflected in international guidelines on genetic epidemiology.

According to Knoppers and Laberge,[3] DNA sampling "is primarily a medical act that involves the confidential examination of a person's genetic structure and thus the creation of a physician-patient bond, with all the obligations and protections such a bond entails". Many persons who will be subjected to DNA sampling will not be "patients" in the strict sense of the word but may become patients as an effect of the DNA sampling. Is DNA sampling largely a form of screening and ethically subject to the obligation that sample donors or the genetically defined groups that they represent receive an appropriate element of beneficence in return for their participation? How feasible is it, or will it be, in many populations to provide the beneficence indicated by the nature of any genetic disease or predisposition to disease revealed by DNA sampling?

The movement away from the Hippocratic tradition of medical ethics, with its exclusive concern for the good of the individual patient and its medical paternalism, to biomedical ethics, or bioethics, and recognition of the social and population dimensions of ethics, made guidelines on ethics necessary. It may also be said that the dominance of principle based ethics has made guidelines possible or at least relatively easy to formulate, provided their theoretical or philosophical basis is not seriously questioned. Typically, guidelines in this context are now derived from an analysis of the *prima facie* principles:

autonomy (respect for persons), beneficence, nonmaleficence, and justice.[4,5] However, well-recognized limitations of the four-principled approach, and criticism by philosophers and others, have resulted in an erosion of the approach; alternatives are being advocated in the form mainly of theories of virtue, care and casuistry, designed to complement or even to supplant principle-based biomedical ethics. How or to what extent will this unstable state of biomedical ethics, largely a North American phenomenon at present, complicate the formulation of international ethical guidelines on genetic epidemiology? If it is possible to keep DNA sampling and genetic epidemiology strictly in a medical or health care frame of reference, concerned with basic questions of the good of patients and the control of disease in populations, it may be possible to establish guidelines that will not be significantly affected, for some time at least, by the current and cross-currents that swirl around ethics at the present time.

Endnotes and References

1 Angell M., "Ethical Imperialism? Ethics in International Collaborative Research." (1988), 319 *New Engl. J. Med.* 1081.

2 Pellegrino E.D., "The Metamorphosis of Medical Ethics: A 30-Year Retrospective" (1993), 269 *JAMA* 1158.

3 Knoppers B.M. and C.M. Laberge, "DNA Sampling and Informed Consent" (1989), 140 *CMAJ* 1023.

4 Ross W.D., *The Right and the Good.* (Indianapolis, Ind. Hackett Publishing Co. Inc., 1988) at 19.

5 Beauchamp T.L. and J.F. Childress, *Principles of Biomedical Ethics*, 3rd ed., (New York: Oxford University Press, 1989).

STATUS OF HUMAN GENETIC MATERIAL: INTRODUCTION

GERALD ROBERTSON (CHAIRPERSON)

Professor, Faculty of Law

University of Alberta

This plenary session focuses on the legal status of human genetic material. This includes not just the genetic material itself, but also the information contained within it. The primary objective of the session is to provide a comparative overview of the different legal approaches adopted in various countries to the classification of human genetic material, and to discuss the legal, ethical and policy implications of these approaches.

Professor Mazen (France) will focus on the legislative approach adopted in France, while Professor Chadwick (U.K.) will add to this a comparative overview of the position in other European countries, including the notion of "common property" suggested by the U.K. Royal College of Physicians' report in 1991. Professor Litman (Canada) will discuss, from a common law perspective, the implications of a property law regime, and in particular will argue in favour of a *sui generis* approach. Professor Roche (U.S.A.) will provide an analysis of a proposed Genetic Privacy Act, focusing in particular on the reasons underlying the rules governing individually identifiable DNA samples.

This comparative overview of the legal positions in various countries will facilitate a discussion around the overall theme of the session: given the legal, ethical and policy implications of these different legal regimes, what is the most appropriate juridical approach to protecting and balancing the diverse (and often competing) interests involved in human genetic material.

THE LEGAL STATUS OF GENETIC MATERIAL*

MOE M. LITMAN

Professor and Chair, Health Law Institute

Faculty of Law, University of Alberta

Introduction

What is the legal character of human genetic material? In law is it property, an extension of its human source, or is it some other legally recognized interest? The answers to these questions are vitally important. Not only does the juridical character of genetic material have symbolic and psychological significance, but from a purely legal perspective its legal nature makes an enormous and very practical difference. Private property, common property,[1] confidential information, and persons, each of which may capture some of the legal essence of genetic material, are regulated by different prescriptive and proscriptive rules. Property, for example, can ordinarily be sold. Persons cannot. Many of the theft provisions in the Criminal Code of Canada only apply to property. They have no application to persons or information.

Legal taxonomy is purposive.[2] Objects are treated as property, for example, not because they have some intrinsic or objectively measurable characteristic that identifies them as property, but rather because labelling them as property, and thereby subjecting them to property law, best effectuates a broad range of social, philosophical, psychological, and economic goals. Accordingly, legal classification is the antithesis of a technical or objective exercise. It is a normative process.[3] It is rooted in value judgements and entails making fundamental policy choices. This is demonstrated by the unremitting refusal of the legal system to characterize foetuses as persons.[4] This unwillingness stems from the perceived (negative) consequences of such a characterization, and not from any particular scientific notion of what constitutes a person.[5]

This chapter canvasses the various alternatives for legally characterizing genetic material. Such material may be regarded as private property, common property, person, or information. My view is that it would be a mistake to conceptualize genetic material as fitting solely within any one of these traditional legal categories. It is both possible and advisable to characterize human genetic material as a hybrid of all of these categories.

The Legal Nature of Genetic Materials

In Canada, the legal status of genetic material has not yet been determined. Neither case law nor legislation adverts to this issue. In the United States, proposed genetic privacy legislation characterizes "individually identifiable" human genetic material as "property " of its "source".[6] Setting aside the wisdom of labelling human genetic material as property, it is readily apparent that this legislation does not establish the legal character of non-identifiable human genetic material. While the legislation is not explicit on this matter, it seems to imply that non-identifiable human genetic material is something other than property. Given the breadth and diversity of issues surrounding human genetic material, it is very doubtful, if not inconceivable, that legislation would for all purposes characterize human genetic material as either property or person or information. There are a wide variety of policies implicated by genetic material and information, and none of the traditional classifications can alone advance all of these policies.

The current situation is that Canadian courts may, without legislative guidance, be called upon to classify human genetic material. Even if legislation is enacted, which for certain purposes settles the legal character of this material, it may still be necessary for the courts to legally characterize the material in relation to matters not addressed by the statute. Moreover, even if a legislature were ambitious enough to attempt to comprehensively characterize human genetic material, it is not at all obvious how it would regard such material. My analysis counsels against the standard approach of labelling "objects" as "person" or "property". Animating the legal personality of genetic material requires a much more flexible approach. Given the dearth of judicial and legislative opinion on the legal status of this material, first principles, particularly policy, and analogous case law, provide useful guidance for the resolution of this novel and important legal issue.

The Possibilities

A) THE MATERIAL ITSELF

A property lawyer might be forgiven for characterizing genetic material as property. After all, though sub-cellular and therefore invisible to the naked eye, genetic material has a physical existence. Almost all tangible things, other than human beings, are property. And, at least in theory, there are very sound reasons for this being so. The legal institution of property exists for an indeterminate number of reasons. It exists to encourage productivity, to reduce conflagration, to enhance autonomy, to provide for sustenance, security, and privacy, and for numerous other reasons.[7] In principle, therefore, the more objects of property, the better. Economists tell us that universality, in the sense of everything "out there" being part of the property law system, is one of the hallmarks of an efficient property system.[8] Exceptions to the "rule" that tangible things are property exist, but in fact are very few. Non-human living things, some of which share as much as 98% of the DNA found in human beings, are not exempt from being property.[9] Both domesticated and wild animals, including pets, and of course plants, are regarded as property. Light and air, on the other hand, though tangible, are not property.[10] Interestingly they are referred to as "common property". Common property is really the antithesis of property. It is owned by no one.[11] In law, property necessarily entails a right of exclusive control,[12] a right which does not apply to light and air which are found at large.[13] The term "common property" reveals, I think, the tendency to characterize any tangible object as property, even when it is not.

The problem with the property lawyer's intuitive response is that it assumes the very point at issue; namely, that human genetic material, once separated from its human host, is transformed into a non-human entity. It is certainly possible for the law to regard such material as an extension of its human source, even if it is not *per se* a human being. Human genetic material emanates from, and is integral to human beings. It is also of profound importance in the biological process of constituting human beings. Accordingly, it would not be illogical to legally characterize genetic material as "person" rather than "property".

B) THE INFORMATION

There is another layer of complexity which the foregoing analysis has failed to address. It is true that genetic material is tangible, but such material also has an incorporeal side. Genetic material contains information, indeed vital, profound, very personal, but also pedestrian information. This information is encoded, in part, by gene sequences which perform a variety of functions, some of which our scientists understand, but most of which have not yet been discerned.[14] Just as information contained in a book can be severed from and exist independently of the book, so can genetic information be severed from and exist independently of its human source. The capability of human genetic information to exist independently of its host, compels separate consideration of its legal status.

Under existing Canadian law, most information is regarded as common property; that is, "property" belonging to no one.[15] Accordingly, data, knowledge, and ideas are generally "available for the taking". They may be "borrowed", almost without restriction. Information is routinely appropriated for purely prurient interests, and is routinely discarded, improved, modified, criticized, approbated, and sometimes even worshipped. The legal system has a strong commitment to the free circulation of ideas.[16] Societal progress and welfare is regarded as being dependant, in no small part, on the free movement of ideas and information. It is true that in Canada and the U.K., and to a much greater extent in the U.S., there are cases which regard confidential information as property.[17] But in the Commonwealth these cases are very much in the minority, if not discredited.[18] Information, including genetic information, which has been patented is undoubtedly private property, although of a very special type. It is intellectual property. However, this does not mean that unpatented genetic information is private property. Indeed the essence of the patenting process is to confer proprietary status on something which is not otherwise property.

An important and pertinent exception to the rule that information is unprotected, applies to private or confidential information. It is indisputable that sensitive information of this type is protected, not as property, but simply as an interest worthy of legal protection.[19] This type of protection is accorded to confidential information which has been transmitted to persons in the "helping professions" such as physicians, and, also, most probably, to persons working for or under these physicians.[20] Confidences may also bind others to whom they have been transmitted in the expectation that privacy will be maintained.[21] Given that genetic material is replete with exceedingly private and confidential information, it is virtually indisputable that some or all genetic information will be protected as confidential information. It may even be that in exceptional circumstances persons other than the human sources of the genetic information, such as family members or First Nation polities, would be regarded as having a sufficient privacy interest to enforce confidentiality.[22]

C) CHOOSING AMONGST POSSIBILITIES: THE USE OF POLICY & CASE LAW

How does the law decide whether genetic material and information is protected or unprotected property, an extension of the person, or protected or unprotected information? Given that Canadian law has yet to address this issue, let alone provide a definitive answer, there is little doubt that both policy analysis and analogous case law will be of central importance in making this determination. Policy considerations underlie all questions of law, but are particularly important, indeed most important, when new and novel questions are involved.[23] Analogous case law exists, and provides a helpful insight into judicial thinking about the legal character of human biological material. This case law is concerned with the issue of what is the legal status of human body parts and derivative materials, such as embryos, fetuses, gametes, blood, and even human waste products.[24] My assessment of both policy and the case law is that each supports the conclusion that in law human genetic material is *sui generis*, that is legally unique. Its legal uniqueness emanates from the fact that this material is unique in its social implications. It is my view that human genetic material is best classified as a flexible legal hybrid with the character of a number of traditional juristic categories, including property and person. The information itself, at least the sensitive and private part of this information, is clearly confidential information. Improperly divulging confidential information without proper consent or other justification in law may lead to liability for breach of fiduciary duty or breach of confidence.

The issues and policies implicated by human genetic material and information are profound and diverse. Accordingly, the legal status of genetic information must be sufficiently flexible to accommodate a wide variety of issues, which occur in a wide variety of fact situations, and which raise a wide variety of important policies. It would, in my view, be a mistake of considerable magnitude, to situate human genetic material in only one of the traditional categories of property or person. Concluding, for example, that this genetic material is property confers enormous protection to its human source, but may seriously imperil research and development. For this reason, as well as others, the majority of the Supreme Court of California in the case of *Moore v. Regents Of the University of California* rejected the notion that property principles could be utilized to protect the interests of Mr. Moore whose spleen had been surgically removed for therapeutic reasons.[25] Mr. Moore had not been told of the research and commercial interests that his physician and others had in his spleen.

1. Policy

At first sight the debate about whether genetic and other human biological material is person or property seems somewhat ephemeral. Both property law and the law of persons[26] serve very much the same societal ends, including the promotion of autonomy, dignity, and the privacy of individuals.[27] Both the law of persons and property law are pervasive in their protection of persons and property. Property cannot, at least ordinarily, be appropriated without the consent of its owner, and similarly the appropriation of bodily tissue requires consent, indeed informed consent, of the party involved. Where a fiduciary, such as a lawyer, acquires the property of a person - for example, a client - to whom a fiduciary duty is owed,[28] there is a presumption that the property was acquired in breach of duty.[29] Similarly, under the strict precepts of fiduciary law, fiduciaries, such as physicians, who acquire the bodily tissue of patients for any reason - disposal, research, or therapy -, must make full disclosure of any personal interest that may be served by such acquisition.[30] In general, almost anything "untoward" done in relation to either person or property may be remedied in law. Accordingly, whether genetic material is property or is regarded as an extension of the person, it will receive ample protection. So why does it matter whether human biological material is person or property?

The short answer is that the consequences of regarding human biological material, including genetic material, as property are considered by many to be contrary to the interests of society, and even dangerous Both scholarly and judicial opinion warn that treating human beings or their body parts as mere objects of property has the effect of commodifying or objectifying human beings.[31] As Justice Broussard stated in *Moore v. Regents of the University of California*: "Does it uplift or degrade the "unique human persona" to treat human tissue as a fungible article of commerce?"[32] The thrust of this concern is the symbolic and psychological effect of treating bits and pieces of human beings as property. Legal commodification of human beings, it is feared, will lead or contribute to the erosion of the sanctity of human life,[33] thereby endangering the physical and psychological integrity of human beings, and their autonomy, privacy, and dignity.[34] Related fears include the commercial and research implications of commodification. Is it in society's interest to permit body parts, or even microscopic genetic samples to be sold? What are the implications to the health of Canadians and the "inviolable" principles of Canada's health system of setting market forces loose on genetic material? Will the treatment of genetic material as property of its host, and in some circumstances the researcher, impede important scientific research and progress?

Setting aside the validity of these aforementioned concerns,[35] what, if anything, is to be gained by treating human genetic material as property? Given the symbolism at play when human biological material is treated as property, and the fact that the law of persons provides extensive protection for human beings, why not regard human genetic material as simply an extension of its host, and, therefore, protected by the law of persons? This appears to have been the thinking of the majority of the Supreme Court of California in the *Moore* case. In rejecting Mr. Moore's property theory, the Court was both sensitive to the symbolism involved,[36] and took pains to explain that the alleged wrongs suffered by Mr. Moore could be rectified by non-property principles.[37] Both the law of informed consent and breach of fiduciary duty were held to be available to Mr. Moore in his law suit against his physician and the various other plaintiffs.[38]

The Supreme Court's decision in *Moore* had the effect of overturning the majority decision of the Court of Appeal which had earlier subscribed to the property theory. In a very strong statement, Justice Rothman, who formed part of the appellate court's majority, warned:

> A patient must have the ultimate power to control what becomes of his or her tissues. *To hold otherwise would open the door to a massive invasion of human privacy and dignity in the name of medical progress.*[39] [emphasis added]

Surprisingly, this warning was given creditability by the majority of the Supreme Court itself. Notwithstanding that it overruled the appellate court's decision, it explicitly, though tentatively, opined that property law might, in some circumstances, be available to redress wrongful appropriation of or interference with human biological material.[40] Given that on the facts of *Moore* the property theory was rejected with considerable conviction, this qualification is somewhat curious. It may merely be an expression of an abundance of caution, but I would suggest that more than circumspection is involved. The law of persons, like any other body of law, has its limits. There are circumstances in which non-property theory would be incapable of assisting individuals whose biological materials have been misappropriated or otherwise interfered with. Had Mr. Moore donated his spleen to a research laboratory on a pure research, non-commercial basis, and had the spleen been stolen from the laboratory by a biological thief bent on profit, neither the law of informed consent nor fiduciary law could have provided Mr. Moore with a remedy.

The law of persons has a holistic conception of what constitutes a human being. Its supposition is that human beings are not fragmentable, and its rules and principles reflect this assumption. The law has been steadfast in its refusal to classify anything other than post-birth intact entities as persons.[41] This is abundantly clear in the cases pertaining to embryos and fetuses where the Courts have been far more willing to state what these products of conception are not, than what they are. What they are not is persons.[42] Property law, on the other hand, regards objects of property as divisible.[43] Its doctrines have evolved in response to the portability and divisibility of property, particularly personal property. In the law of property, the fact that an object of property has been divided and some of its parts moved, does not, ordinarily, diminish the level of protection accorded to the property owner, and does not deprive the remnants of the object or its parts of the status of property. For this reason alone, at least in some circumstances, property law can remedy wrongs relating to human biological material that cannot be remedied by the law of persons. Accordingly, there are some circumstances in which property law principles are useful, appropriate, and, indeed, the only principles which can accord protection to persons whose biological materials have been misappropriated. These principles should be applied notwithstanding the unfortunate symbolism. To permit concerns about commodification to undermine substantive protection of human beings would be self-defeating. What is important is the protection of human beings, and not some reified notion that they and their severed parts are persons or property.

It may be that a strict application of property principles to genetic material would impede research and development of genetic diagnostic tools, therapies, and technologies. *Bona fide* researchers acting in good faith, but working unwittingly with stolen biological materials might violate some very strict precepts of property such as those found in the very technical law of conversion. The potential liability of innocent researchers was a matter of considerable concern to those judges in the *Moore* case who rejected Mr. Moore's property theory.[44] It is not at all clear, however, that property law would be applied as unyieldingly as these concerns presuppose. Good faith, though not per se a defence to a conversion action, is an important factor in determining liability.[45] Given the novelty of the situation, the equities involved, the fact that genetic material has no economic value per se, the public interest in medical advances, the enormous financial and non-financial incentives for research, and the desirability and possibility of developing effective and appropriate protocols to protect researchers from this form of liability, it is unlikely, I would suggest, that the spectre of liability would significantly impede research or related commercial activity. And even if it did, many would argue that this is a price that needs to be paid in order to preserve the autonomy, dignity and privacy of individuals.[46]

Accordingly, in most circumstances the principles of the law of persons can adequately protect the fundamental interests of individuals implicated by their genetic material. In rare cases property principles might be needed to provide this protection. In yet other circumstances, where, for example, an individual has donated a genetic sample for research, portions of the sample might properly be regarded as part of the common interest of humankind - common property - and therefore, not subject to ordinary legal claims for exclusive possession and control. On the other hand researchers themselves require security and integrity of the supply of samples, and may need the assistance of property law to protect their enterprise.

It is readily apparent that the legal category into which genetic material is attributed, must be sufficiently flexible to allow courts to make assessments on a case by case basis. Traditional categories are simply not up to the job. As one writer has put it:

> The classic distinction between the subject of property, the person, and the object of property, the thing, proves inadequate in the face of today's new scientific realities.[47]

The legal flexibility that is required is best accomplished by classifying human genetic material as an object *sui generis*. This classification frees the law of pre-conceptions, proprietary and otherwise, about how this material should be treated.[48] Traditional classification harbours these pre-conceptions. Classifying genetic material as *sui generis* can provide the legal system with sufficient flexibility to direct that some or all commercial profits spawned by a genetic technology be paid to an individual who has not consented to commercial exploitation of his or her genetic material. It could also enforce strong expectations of privacy which surely exist when genetic material is donated or provided for research or diagnostic reasons. From a jurisprudential perspective, it could provide courts with time and experience with genetic issues, and thereby reduce the chances of the development of ill conceived doctrine, informed by context specific considerations, about the true legal nature of genetic material.

The analysis of the legal status of unpatented genetic information is more straightforward. Like other information which is not subject to any intellectual property regime, it is part of the common heritage of humankind.[49] Legally treating genetic information as "common property" facilitates, but, of course, does not guarantee, the sharing of genetic information so necessary for scientific progress. On the other hand genetic information which is private and confidential, *and* which can be linked to an individual (and, perhaps, to an identifiable group),[50] is protected under standard principles of private law. Such information is essentially of the same nature as sensitive medical information which has been recognized as being the subject matter of a duty of confidence.[51] Conferring confidential status on genetic information which can be linked to an identifiable person, and perhaps group, is critical. There are vital employment and insurance interests at stake, and profound social and psychological implications which can flow from breach of confidence. A person's interest in genetic privacy is so strong that it may well justify a right to personally not know of a genetic condition. However, in extreme circumstances this right not to know may be overridden by the interests of progeny not yet born.[52] Similarly, in some circumstances, the right of an individual to genetic privacy may be subjected to the interests of third parties who or whose progeny would, without the genetic information, be at serious, material, and, perhaps, imminent risk.[53] That rights of privacy protected by the law of confidentiality may be diminished by a compelling public interest, is part of the standard law of confidentiality.[54] The fact that genetic information is replete with private and confidential information should not in practice be an impediment to research. Protocols have already been developed which make the likelihood of a genetic sample being linked to a particular individual extremely remote.[55]

2. Case Law

Analogous case law relating to both human biological materials and the protection of confidential information supports the views advocated in this chapter. These cases suggest, that left to their own devices, judges are likely to characterize genetic materials as objects *sui generis*, and confidential genetic information as confidential information protected by relational wrongs such as breach of fiduciary duty and the law of informed consent, as well as the law of breach of confidence. Legislatures enacting laws relating to genetic material would be wise to do the same.

(a) The Case Law Pertaining to Human Biological Materials. There are a minority of cases which have characterized human materials such as blood or waste products as property,[56] and, numerous cases which have refused to characterize fetuses *in utero* and pre-embryos as "persons" in law.[57] As noted previously the cases pertaining to fetuses tell us what fetuses are not, rather than what they are. However, the emerging and very distinct trend in the cases is to characterize human materials as *sui generis*. This characterization is well established in respect of corpses,[58] and has recently been utilized in several cases involving disputes over human reproductive materials such as frozen embryos and male gametes.[59] The better reasoned of these cases evidence extensive, albeit context specific, policy analysis. In a dispute by a divorced couple over cryogenically preserved pre-embryos produced through a successful *in vitro* fertilization process, the Supreme Court of Tennessee in the case of *Davis v. Davis* concluded that "preembryos are not, strictly speaking, either "persons" or "property", but occupy an interim category that entitles them to special respect because of their potential for human life."[60] In the result the Court held that the couple did not have a "true property interest," but had "... an interest in the nature of ownership, to the extent that they have decision-making authority concerning disposition of the preembryos."[61] In the *Moore* case, an *obiter* opinion of the California Supreme Court suggested that fetuses ought to be regarded as "objects *sui generis*".[62] In *Hect v. Superior Court (Kane)* the California Court of Appeal concluded that cryogenically preserved sperm was a "unique" category of "property", which properly formed part of a decedent's estate and over which the decedent had an interest in the "nature of ownership".[63] Accordingly, the sperm could be given away in accordance with the dispositive direction expressed by the decedent in his will.

The body parts cases, and in particular the leading case of *Moore v. The Regents of the University of California*, are not part of this trend. It will be recalled that the majority of the California Supreme Court did not characterize Mr. Moore's interest in his surgically removed spleen as *sui generis* or anything else. Perhaps wisely, the classification issue was sidestepped. The Court indicated that Mr. Moore could rely on legal principles regulating relational wrongs, principles which do not depend upon legal classification of Mr. Moore's interest in his spleen.[64] However, it is important to note that the judges who supported Mr. Moore's property theory, the minority judges at the Supreme Court, and the majority of the judges on the Court of Appeal, implied that Moore's property interest in his spleen may not be an ordinary property interest. Given that the final ruling in the Moore case left open the possibility that property analysis might be utilized in future human biological material cases, this implication warrants attention.

The implication is clearest in the judgement of Justice Rothman of the California Court of Appeal who cautioned that his finding that Mr. Moore has a property interest in his spleen should not be construed as an opinion on "whether use of human tissue or body parts ought to be "gift based" or subject to a "free market".[65] This statement suggests that in the Justice Rothman's view, Mr. Moore's property right may not include the right to sell his spleen, even absent legislation which prohibits such a sale. When property owners cannot sell that which they own, their interests can be and typically are described as "quasi-property".[66] Quasi-property means that the object in question is property for some purposes, but not for others. Such objects do not spawn the whole array of property rights ordinarily associated with property.[67] In other words, such objects are legally unique, or *sui generis*. It may well be, therefore, that the body parts cases will ultimately be supportive of the trend to characterize human biological materials as objects *sui generis*.

(b) The Case Law Pertaining To Confidential Information. That genetic information must as a matter of law be maintained in confidence is virtually certain.[68] Health professionals such as physicians, nurses, psychotherapists, and medical counsellors are bound by ethical, contractual, statutory, tort law, and other private law obligations not to disclose information pertaining to their patients and clients.[69] One source of this duty is the law of fiduciary obligation which requires that persons who have in some manner undertaken to act in the best interests of others, discharge their undertakings diligently and selflessly.[70] The law insists on very strict observance of fiduciary undertakings. The undertakings of health care providers include a promise of confidentiality which may only be lawfully departed from in extreme cases where "... the safety of individuals or of the public, physical or moral, would be sufficiently cogent to supersede or qualify the obligations *prima facie* imposed by the confidential relationship[s]."[71] The duty of confidentiality not only binds health professionals who have a direct relationship with a patient or client, but most probably also those who work under the direction and authority of these professionals.[72] On this basis alone many genetic researchers and counsellors would be legally bound by a duty of non-disclosure.

Moreover, recent developments in the law of confidentiality suggest that a duty of confidence may arise anytime sensitive or private information has been transmitted in circumstances in which there is a reasonable expectation of privacy.[73] Given the exceedingly private nature of genetic information, the duty of confidence would seem to apply to an extremely broad range of circumstances covering the entire chain of collection and transmission of genetic information. Whether this duty would be extended to a wrongdoer who has acquired confidential genetic information through a unilateral act of misappropriation is not clear. In my view it would, despite the fact that a breach of confidence action "normally" requires that "information must have been *imparted* in circumstances importing an obligation of confidence".[74] [emphasis mine] The act of transmission by the supplier of the genetic sample or any other person is not, I would suggest, indispensable to the existence of this duty.[75] The duty of confidentiality springs from the reasonable expectation of privacy, and transmission which imports an obligation of privacy is merely a factual touchstone of this expectation.

Conclusion

The profoundly personal nature of genetic information and the far reaching consequences of disclosure of such information, warrant a rigorous application of the standard rules of confidentiality to genetic information. It has already been suggested that genetic information is so private that "... courts are unlikely to grant a broad discretion to physicians [and others] to disclose genetic data to biological relatives or reproductive partners, and the courts are even less likely to impose liability on physicians [and others] for refusing to disclose this information."[76] Whether this restrictive view of the privilege and duty of disclosure turns out to be correct, it is clear that genetic information is highly protected as confidential information.

As to genetic material itself, it is unique, not because of its physical qualities, but rather because it has distinctive, profound, and far-reaching social, psychological, scientific, and economic implications. These implications are best regulated through the collective efforts of a variety of areas of law. Neither property law, nor the law of persons, can alone adequately meet the challenge of genetic material. Genetic material is complex and multifaceted in its social, scientific, philosophical, and economic implications. Legally characterizing this material as unique, that is, *sui generis*, will permit courts, on a case by case basis, to choose and fashion appropriate legal rules to resolve a very wide variety of disputes. First principles and case law suggest that this is both possible and desirable.

Endnotes and References

* Parts of this paper are based on ideas explored in earlier works published by myself and Professor Gerald Robertson. These works are "Reproductive Technology: Is a Property Law Regime Appropriate?" in Royal Commission on New Reproductive Technologies, *Research Studies (Volume 3): Overview of Legal Issues in New Reproductive Technologies* (Ottawa: Supply and Services, 1993) 233 at 259, and Litman M. and G. Robertson, "The Common Law Status of Genetic Material" in Knoppers B.M., T. Caulfield and D. Kinsella, eds., *Legal Rights and Human Genetic Material* (Toronto: Emond Montgomery, 1996).

1 This term refers to "property" owned by no one. See text below.

2 Litman M. and G. Robertson, "Reproductive Technology: Is a Property Law Regime Appropriate?" in Royal Commission on New Reproductive Technologies, *Research Studies (Volume 3): Overview of Legal Issues in New Reproductive Technologies* (Ottawa: Supply and Services, 1993) 233 at 259.

3 In *Tremblay v. Daigle*, [1989] 2 S.C.R. 530 at 552-53, the Supreme Court of Canada addressed the issue of whether a foetus is a person for the purposes of the *Quebec Charter of Human Rights and Freedoms* in the following terms: The task of properly classifying a foetus in law and in science are different pursuits.
Ascribing personhood to a foetus is a fundamentally normative task.

4 Supra note 2 at 235.

5 Ibid., at 235 and 259.

6 *Genetic Confidentiality and Non-Discrimination Act of 1996*, s.1898, proposed November 15th, 1995. Second Reading June 24, 1996, s.104.

7 Supra note 2 at 250.

8 Posner R.A., *Economic Analysis of Law*, 4th ed. (Little, Brown & Co., 1992) at 32.

9 Pollack R., *Signs of Life: the Language and Meanings of DNA* (New York: Houghton Mifflin Company, 1994) at 160. See also, Dawkins R., *River Out of Eden: A Darwinian View of Life* (New York: Harper and Collins, 1995) at 42; Relethford J.H., *The Human Species: An Introduction to Biological Anthropology*, 2nd ed. (Toronto: Mayfield Publishing Company, 1994); and Leakey R. and R. Lewin, *Origins Reconsidered: In Search of What Makes Us Human* (Toronto: Doubleday, 1992).

10 Raushensbush W.B., *Brown on Personal Property* (Chicago: Callaghan & Co., 1975) at 8.

11 Ziff B., *Principles of Property Law*, 2nd ed. (Scarborough: Carswell, 1996) at 7.

12 Cohen F.S., "Dialogue on Private Property", (1954) 9 *Rutgers Law Rev.* 357 at 374.

13 Supra note 2 at 251.

14 See generally the various texts referred to in note 9.

15 Litman M. and G. Robertson, "The Common Law Status of Genetic Material" in B. Knoppers, T. Caulfield, and D. Kinsella, eds., *Legal Rights and Human Genetic Material* (Toronto: Emond Montgomery, 1996) 51 at 81.

16 Ibid.

17 See the cases cited by Justice Lamer, as he then was, in *R v. Stewart* (1988), 63 C.R. (2d) 305 at 314 (S.C.C.).

18 Ibid., and supra note 15. See also *Lac Minerals v. Int'l Corona Resources*, infra note 73 at 75 where Justice Sopinka of the Supreme Court of Canada states that the theory that confidential information is property is "tenuous".

19 Supra note 15 at 55 and 81.

20 Ibid., at 55.

21 See discussion of *Lac Minerals Ltd. v. Int'l Corona Resources* infra notes 73 and 74 and accompanying text. See also Litman M. and G. Robertson, supra note 15 at 57.

22 This conclusion follows as a matter of logic in respect of studies which focus on families or First Nations, rather than individuals. It is interesting to note that the policy of the Human Genome Diversity Project is that consent to the taking of samples must be provided by both the individual being sampled and the First Nation of which the individual is a member. See Greely H., "The Ethics of the Human Genome Diversity Project: The North American Regional Committee's Model Ethical Protocol" in this volume at 239.

23 If, as I claim, policy is the most important dynamic in this inquiry, one would expect the case law to be full of policy analysis. Much, if not most, of it is. See Litman M. and G. Robertson, supra note 2 at 252 for a brief discussion of this point. See also *Moore v. The Regents of the University of California*, 249 Cal. Rptr. 494 (Ct. App.1988), rev'd in part 271 Cal. Rptr. 146 at 164-65 (Sup. Ct.), petition for writ of certiorari denied 111 S. Ct. 1388 (1991). Moore was a case of first impression in which the courts considered whether the claimant, Mr. Moore, had a property interest in his surgically removed spleen. In rejecting Mr. Moore's property theory Justice Panelli of the California Supreme Court stated at p.160 that "...the **novelty** of Moore's claim demands express consideration of the policies to be served by extending liability." (emphasis added)

24 Supra note 2, where this case law is reviewed in detail.

25 Supra note 23. The Court permitted Mr. Moore to prosecute his case on his non-property grounds.

26 By this I mean the body of law which protects human beings on the basis of principles other than property law principles. The distinction between the law of persons and the law of property is an artifice, and ultimately a false dichotomy. Though the area of inquiry of each area of law is different, both serve the same ends. See infra note 27 for elaboration.

27 Property law does so more indirectly than the law of persons, but it nevertheless is concerned with these and other fundamental human interests. For this reason, property has been referred to as a "human right". See Levy L.W.A., "Property as a Human Right" (1988), 5 *Constitutional Commentary* 169. See also supra note 2 at 252.

28 A strict duty of fidelity in which the fiduciary is required to look after the interests of the beneficiary of the relationship. Beyond benefits "inherent" in the relationship for the fiduciary, the fiduciary must act selflessly.

29 See Ellis M.V., *Fiduciary Duties in Canada* (Toronto: Carswell, 1993) at 1-3 where the reverse onus is described in the following terms: In equity the Courts will jealously protect the interests of the party entitled to the fiduciary's loyalty. In keeping with the strictness[,] illustrated by the Court's disinterest in the fiduciary's motivation (i.e.. good faith does not validate breach)..., the fiduciary is subject to a reverse onus whereby a presumption of undue influence is automatically extant and must be overcome by rebuttal on the party of the fiduciary.

30 Ibid., at 1-5 where it is stated that "[i]n his fidelity, the fiduciary is responsible for complete disclosure of any material information, materiality being governed by the principle that only a fully informed beneficiary can adequately advise the fiduciary..."

31 For scholarly opinion see, for example, Lavoie J., "Ownership of Human Tissue: Life After *Moore v. Regents of the University of California*" (1988), 75 *Virginia Law Rev.* 1363 at 1367; Hardiman R., "Toward the Right of Commerciality: Recognizing Property Rights in the Commercial Value of Human Tissue" (1986), 34 *U.C.L.A. L. Rev.* 207 at 224; and with regard to the "commodification of reproduction", see Overall C., "Pluck a Fetus from its Womb": A Critique of Current Attitudes Toward the Embryo/Fetus" (1986), *24 Univ. W. Ont. L. Rev.* 1. See the text immediately following for an example of judicial opinion.

32 294 Cal. Rptr. 494 (Ct. App. 1988), rev'd in part 271 Cal. Rptr. 146 at 164-65 (Sup. Ct.).

33 *Moore v. Regents of the University of California*, supra note 23 (Sup. Ct.) at 164 where Justice Arabian rejects Mr. Moore's property theory in the following rather strong and colourful terms: He entreats us to regard the human vessel - the single most venerated and protected subject in any civilized society-as equal with the basest commercial commodity. He urges us to commingle sacred with the profane. He asks much.

34 See Knoppers B.M., "Conclusion: Human Genetic Material- Commodity or Gift?" in *Legal Rights and Human Genetic Material*, supra note 15 at 171. See also Balmaseda M.A.E., "The Legal Role of Biological Proof and Refusal to Undergo Testing in Investigations of Paternity" (1995), 3 *Law & Human Genome Rev.* 43 at 54.

35 It is beyond the scope of this paper to do an evaluation of the commodification arguments. I must say, however, that I am not convinced that the application of property principles to human beings will lead to erosion of the protection presently accorded to human beings by law.

36 Supra note 23 (Sup. Ct.) at 164 per Arabian J.

37 Supra note 23 (Sup. Ct.) at 158 where Justice Panelli states that: One may earnestly wish to protect privacy and dignity without accepting the extremely problematic conclusion that interference with those interests amounts to a conversion of personal property. Nor is it necessary to force the round pegs of "privacy" and "dignity" into the square hole of "property" in order to protect the patient, *since the fiduciary-duty and informed-consent theories protect these interests directly by requiring full disclosure.* [emphasis added]

38 Ibid.

39 Supra note 23 (Ct. App.) at 508.

40 Supra note 23 (Sup. Ct.) at 160 where the Court states: *While we do not purport to hold that excised cells can never be property for any purpose whatsoever,* the novelty to Moore's claim demands express consideration of the policies to be served by extending liability. [emphasis added]

41 Supra note 23 at 54 and 74.

42 Supra note 2 at 242.

43 Ibid., at 245.

44 Supra note 23 (Sup. Ct.) Justice Panelli at 162 expresses these concerns as follows: If the use for cells in research is a conversion, then with every cell sample a researcher purchases a ticket in a litigation lottery.

45 Klar L., *Tort Law*, 2d ed. (Scarborough: Carswell, 1996) at 76. See also Prosser W.L., "The Nature of Conversion" (1956-1957), 42 *Cornell L. Quarterly* 168.

46 See text accompanying note 39.

47 da Silva P.M., "Genes and Patents: Will Traditional Law Become Outdated?" (1995), 3 *Law & Human Genome Rev.* 143 at 147.

48 Supra note 2 at 247-48.

49 See text accompanying and following note 15.

50 See note 22 and accompanying text.

51 *McInerney v. MacDonald* (1992), 93 D.L.R. (4th) 415 at 427-28 (S.C.C.).

52 In effect, this point has been doubted by W. Flannigan in "Genetic Data and Medical Confidentiality" (1995), 3 *Health L.J.* 141 at 285. He concludes at 286 that because there is no risk of immediate or serious harm to another, it is unlikely that physicians can justify a breach of confidentiality for the purposes of disclosing a genetic risk to a reproductive partner of a patient who has undergone genetic testing. See also Miller J., "Physician-Patient Confidentiality and Familial Access to Genetic Information" (1994), 2 *Health L. J.* 141 and Ngwena C. and Chadwick R., "Genetic Diagnostic Information and the Duty of Confidentiality" (1993), 1 *Med. Law Int.* 73.

53 With respect to disclosure to reproductive partners see the previous endnote. Professor Flannigan, ibid., is more open to the argument that physicians may lawfully breach their duty of confidentiality by disclosing genetic risks to biological relatives. At 285 he elaborates on the circumstances in which such disclosure may be justified. These include that the risk would not likely be discovered by other means and that disclosure has utility in the sense that it would permit the relative to seek help or to avoid an environmental trigger of the genetic condition.

54 Supra note 51 and 52 at 269 and 274.

55 See, for example, Knoppers B.M. and R. Chadwick, "The Human Genome Project: Under an International Ethical Microscope" (30 Sept. 1994), 265 *Science* 2033.

56 Supra note 2 at 250 and 255. With respect to waste products see *R. v. Welsh* [1974] R.T.R. 478.

57 Ibid., at 235.

58 Ibid., at 246.

59 Ibid., at 258 and 268.

60 *Davis v. Davis*, 842 S.W. 588 at 597 (Tenn. 1992).

61 Ibid.

62 Supra note 23 at 156 (Sup. Ct.).

63 20 Cal. Rptr. 2d 275 at 281 and 283 (Ct. App. 1993).

64 Supra note 37.

65 Supra note 23 at 504 (Ct.App.).

66 Supra note 2 at 246.

67 Ibid.

68 See endnotes 49-55 and the related text, and particularly *McInerney v. MacDonald*, supra note 51.

69 Supra note 52 at 270.

70 In *Guerin et. al v. The Queen* (1984) 20 E.T.R. 1 at 31 the majority of the Supreme Court of Canada emphasized that undertakings were at the heart of fiduciary obligations, whether the undertakings arose out of "agreement", "perhaps unilateral undertaking" or whether it was imposed by statute. In the most recent Supreme Court of Canada case on fiduciary obligation, *R. Hodgkinson v. Sims*, [1994] 9 W.W.R. 609, the Court occasionally referred to the undertaking as the source of fiduciary obligation. See pp. 645-50 and particularly 646. The discussion of these pages suggests that an undertaking may be actual or constructive (imputed to a party by law). It can arise when one party lets down his or her guard in reliance or reasonable expectation that another will safeguard his or her interest. See also Bryant M. "Crown-Aboriginal Relationships in Canada: The Phantom of Fiduciary Law" (1993), 27 *U.B.C.L.R.* 19, where he also adopts the view that "undertaking" is at the heart of the assumption of fiduciary responsibility.

71 *McIrnerney v. MacDonald*, supra note 51.

72 First principles suggest that absent explicit terms to the contrary in a contract of agency or employment, the duty of an agent or employee is informed by the duties of the principal. This approach helps facilitate accomplishing the goals of the agency and employment.

73 *Lac Minerals Ltd. v. International Corona Resources Ltd.*, (1989), 61 D.L.R. (4th) 14(SCC), at 20 and 35-6 (per La Forest J.) and 69-75 (per Sopinka). La Forest at p.20 quotes from *Coco v. A.N. Clark (Engineers) Ltd.*, [1969] R.P.C. 41 at 47 (Ch.), a judgement of Justice Megarry, who sets out the standard requirements for an action for breach of confidence. They are: the information must itself be confidential, it must be transmitted in circumstances "importing an obligation of confidence", and it must have been used without authorization to the prejudice of the party communicating it.

74 Ibid.

75 It is important to observe that Justice Megarry, ibid., stated that "normally" an action for breach of confidence lies when the three elements he sets are established. To permit a wrongdoer to avoid liability because genetic information has not been voluntarily transmitted, would be to permit the wrongdoer to gain advantage from his or her wrong.

76 Flannigan W., supra note 52 at 287.

CAVEAT VENDITOR: PROTECTING PRIVACY AND OWNERSHIP INTERESTS IN DNA

PATRICIA (Winnie) ROCHE

Health Law Department

Boston University

On September 19, 1996, New Jersey Governor Christie Whitman conditionally vetoed the toughest genetic privacy legislation in the United States.[1] The Governor's objection to the bill, unanimously passed by the New Jersey Legislature to make it unlawful for insurers to discriminate on the basis of genetic testing or information, is based on the inclusion of a provision that establishes an individual's genetic information as personal property. At the urging of the members of the biotechnology industry, who did not participate in the legislative debates, the Governor is now concerned that inclusion of this provision would have the unintended effect of forcing pharmaceutical companies (and other researchers) into sharing royalties with research subjects and requiring that researchers obtain the consent of subjects before DNA samples can be used in experiments.[2]

The conflict over property rights, however, is just part of the broader competition between the privacy interests of individuals and the interests of researchers, as well as insurers and employers in the exploitation of DNA. The omission of a property interest in DNA from the New Jersey legislation may appeal to some as the obvious way to achieve balance between these competing interests. Denying individuals a property interest in DNA is not advisable, however, if protection of genetic privacy as well as support for legitimate research and commerce is a primary legislative goal. For any legislation to effectively serve individual interests, it must address privacy concerns not only in insurance and employment, but in every context in which individually identifiable DNA samples are collected, analyzed and stored and in which private genetic information is created and disclosed.

The purpose of this paper is to describe a proposal for comprehensive federal legislation, entitled the Genetic Privacy Act, which was specifically designed to protect individual interests in DNA and private genetic information.[3] It argues that particular provisions, including the recognition of a property interest in DNA samples, are necessary so that control over DNA, and consequently the information that can be derived from it, is placed with the person who has the most intimate connection to, and the highest interest in benefiting from, the information contained in it - the individual who is the sample source. Designation of the sample source as the person with primary control over DNA is not incompatible with support for the interests of others, particularly medical researchers and developers in the biotechnology industry. Although the New Jersey bill may override currently used consent forms which generally set no limit on a sample's use in clinical trials[4], all this means is that researchers will have to provide more information to individuals before enrolling them in trials and perhaps negotiate for unlimited uses of DNA samples. From the individual's perspective, such requirements are reasonable and warranted by the unique qualities of DNA and genetic information.

A Special Category of Sensitive, Personal Information

The decision to regulate activities involving DNA samples and genetic information presupposes that DNA is unique in a way that merits special protection. Three features of DNA support this presumption. First, DNA samples can be analyzed to predict the likelihood that an asymptomatic individual may suffer from a variety of conditions in the distant future. In this sense it has been characterized as a coded probabilistic future diary.[5,6] Awareness of such predictive information, which may only be possible through decoding of the individual's DNA sample, can impact on a person's self-perception and affect major life choices in regard to educational pursuits, career selection, marriage, reproductive decisions, and even retirement planning.

Secondly, decoding a person's DNA can also divulge information about that person's genetic relatives. Consequently, obtaining genetic information can influence the perceptions family members have of one another and alter their relationships. Lastly, the creation and disclosure of genetic information stands apart from other personal information because of the use that governments and others who control resources can make of such information. Genetic status has historically been used as the basis for categorizing members of society as undesirable or unfit and therefore the targets of vicious discrimination.

Every DNA sample extracted from an individual contains all of his or her genomic information. Consequently as our knowledge of the function of various genes increases, stored samples can provide more and more information about the sample source. If we are to achieve the goal of protecting individual privacy in regard to genetic information, we must address the risks to individual privacy and autonomy that are presented by the storage of samples that can be analyzed and decoded in the future.

With these concerns in mind, the Genetic Privacy Act (GPA)[7] was crafted as a proposal for federal legislation, and to serve as a model for state law and rules that could be voluntarily adopted by those engaged in the collection, storage and analysis of identifiable DNA samples. The overarching premise of the Act and its comprehensive set of rules is that no stranger should have or control identifiable DNA samples or private genetic information about an individual, unless that individual has specifically authorized the collection of DNA samples for the purpose of genetic analysis, has authorized the creation of that private information, and has access to and control over the dissemination of that information.

Core provisions of the GPA

The core provisions of the Act are that:

- no collection of DNA for analysis is permissible without an informed and voluntary authorization by the individual or his or her legal representative;
- those conducting DNA analysis are prohibited from doing so unless execution of written authorization by the individual or legal representative has been verified;
- analysis must not exceed the scope of the written authorization;
- DNA is the property of the individual from whom it is obtained;
- DNA samples must be routinely destroyed once the authorized analysis has been completed;
- anyone who holds private genetic information in the ordinary course of business must keep such information confidential and is prohibited from disclosing it unless the disclosure has been authorized in writing by the individual or legal representative.

These rules govern all circumstances in which individually identifiable DNA samples are collected for analysis. Collection and analysis of DNA without prior authorization is permissible only for law enforcement identification activities when otherwise authorized by federal or state law[8] and for the identification of dead bodies, provided that the kind of analysis that is conducted is limited to DNA typing.[9] Such profiling analysis results in information useful for identification but which is otherwise without meaning. It is similar to fingerprinting in that it involves unique individual markings that reveal no informative details about the individual who is source of the fingerprint. Use of DNA typing for identification, therefore, does not result in the creation of the kind of genetic information which needs protection.

Prior authorization from the individual is also not required when DNA is collected pursuant to a court order, provided that the order is drafted according to the statutory specification.[10] This exception could be applicable in cases, such as paternity actions, where the genetic condition of a party is at issue. In such cases, however, identity is at issue and the genetic analysis that is permissible in those circumstances is not likely to result in the creation of any private genetic information.[11]

These prohibitions and restrictions on collection and analysis of DNA apply to activities involving *identifiable* DNA samples[12], including research. Consequently, enactment of these rules would not effect use of non-identifiable

DNA samples for research because there are no privacy issues involved when samples are not and can not be linked to an individual.

Procedural Requirements and Authorization

To facilitate informed decisions regarding DNA analysis, the GPA prescribes several verbal disclosures that must be made before written authorization is obtained.[13] Requiring verbal disclosures which include the potential benefits and risks of proceeding with an analysis provides an opportunity for individuals to ask questions and to obtain additional information that they deem necessary. In addition to receiving such verbal disclosures, before deciding whether to proceed with the collection and analysis of DNA, individuals must be provided with a notice of rights and assurances. A written notice which fulfils this requirement, for example, informs or reminds the individual that the sample will only be used as authorized, that he or she is the owner of the DNA sample, and that civil remedies for violation of rights created by the GPA are available.[14] The final procedural requirement before collection and analysis of a sample can legally proceed is the execution of a written authorization, and the information that must be included for such authorization to be valid is described in detail in the Act.[15] For example, the purpose of the analysis and the identification of the entity that will perform it must be explicitly stated in the authorization.

What all these rules are about is control - control of individually identifiable DNA samples and control of private genetic information. Placing primary control with individual sources of samples and information cannot be accomplished with any one rule or regulation. Instead, it requires a comprehensive set of rules that not only grants basic rights to individuals, but institutes clear mechanisms and procedures that facilitate the exercise of those rights.

Protecting Individual Interests Through Property Rights

Section 104(A) of the GPA which states "[a]n individually identifiable DNA sample is the property of the sample source" has several implications for individuals since the concept of ownership under United States law includes not one right but an aggregate or bundle of rights, powers and privileges.[16] The right of ownership that is perhaps most familiar and relied upon by individuals is the right of exclusive possession and enjoyment of the property. In regard to DNA samples, this right of exclusion simply reinforces the reality that the sample source is the person in whom this special item originates.

Ownership also encompasses the power to control use of the property by others. The owner of an item, like a book or a watch, can, for example, lend that item to another person for a period of time or for selected purposes without all incidents of ownership being transferred to the borrower. This ability to control use by others without fearing loss of ownership enables both the owner and others to reap the benefits an item has to offer and promotes efficient use of resources. With regard to DNA, it means that permitting the collection of a DNA sample for storage or analysis would not be sufficient for transferring ownership interests to the person or facility conducting those services. Individuals could take advantage of developments in genetic testing without having to choose between the benefits such tests might offer and relinquishment of all property interests in their DNA samples.

The power of ownership can also extend beyond the individual's lifetime since an owner can devise personal property thereby transferring all or some of his or her property interests after death to a designated beneficiary.[17] As the owner of a DNA sample, an individual could transfer some or all interests in the sample to a beneficiary through a will or other legal instrument. Descendants who are the recipients of DNA samples could thus benefit from future developments in genetics which require analysis of DNA from multiple generations. Until the entire human genome is mapped and sequenced, exercise of this right can therefore promote participation in linkage analysis and the development of information that can be of potential benefit to family members and society.

Finally, a property owner has the power to alienate his or her property interests to another.[18] This basically means that property can be donated or sold, at the owner's discretion. Gifts, donations and sales of DNA samples could be made during the lifetime of the sample source to anyone of that person's choosing. Such transfers, like devises of DNA, could be of all or some interests in the sample.

Granting legal recognition to individual ownership interests in DNA would thus promote individual choices in decisions regarding DNA samples. It is also the better response to individuals such as those who recently testified at a public forum in Massachusetts[19] about the issue of protecting genetic privacy in that state. As several witnesses stated to the lawmakers who convened the public meeting, "individuals ought to own all of their genetic information."[20] From the perspective of protecting genetic privacy, it may be more effective to recognize ownership in regard to DNA samples, however, and not simply focus on the information derived from them. Rather than deter individuals from participating in research, particularly when it has commercial objectives, a recognized property interest in one's own DNA sample could give individuals an incentive to participate in research and experiments that would otherwise be of no possible benefit to them and ultimately benefit research and industry.[21]

Enactment of a law protecting individual ownership in DNA would furthermore avoid bizarre results like the case of *Moore v. Regents of the University of California*.[22] John Moore, a patient at UCLA Medical Center in 1976, underwent a splenectomy as part of treatment for hairy-cell leukemia. His physician, Dr. Golde discovered that Mr. Moore's spleen cells produced blood products that could be commercially valuable. Without revealing his commercial interest in harvesting additional samples of John Moore's body products, Dr. Golde had his patient return to the Medical Center over a seven year period and provide numerous bodily samples to Dr. Golde and his research associates. In

1984, when John Moore discovered that Dr. Golde had entered into a contract with Genetics Institute for at least $300,000 in exchange for development of the cell line and products derived from John Moore's cells, he sued to recover what he claimed to be his fair share in Dr. Golde (and the University's) profits. One of the theories he based his suit on was that the defendants were liable for conversion - an interference with his possessory and ownership interests in personal property, i.e. his human cells. The California Supreme Court rejected that claim on several bases, including its application of prior case law, public health codes and a fear that to do otherwise would have a chilling effect on the biotechnology industry. As a result, anyone could have a legally protected ownership interest in John Moore's cells except the source of those cells, John Moore.

In declining to set precedent in this area of property rights, the Court in *Moore* stated that problems in this area were better suited to legislative resolution. The current debate over protection of genetic information presents an opportunity for legislators to resolve this property issue in a more equitable manner and to establish clear rules for researchers and others who are involved with the collection and analysis of DNA samples.

If individuals are to effectively exercise rights, including any ownership rights, established under the GPA (or any legislative resolution), the sample source must know where individually identifiable samples are located. Compliance with the procedural rules in the GPA would ensure that individuals have the information needed to exercise true dominion over their own samples. These procedural rules include the disclosures that must be made prior to execution of the written authorization[23], the inclusion of certain details in the written authorization, the obligation to provide the person with a copy of the authorization, and the notice requirements for storage facilities that intend to transfer operations.[24] In effect these provisions create a "chain of custody" of identifiable samples and serve the individual's interests.

As significant as these property interests are, legally protecting DNA as the personal property of the sample source is neither sufficient for protecting genetic privacy nor should it be seen as the catalyst that places responsibility on those who engage in the collection, storage and analysis of DNA samples to respect individual interests. Researchers (and others) who want to use any previously collected and individually identifiable DNA sample for a purpose not previously authorized by the sample source should refrain from doing so until that source authorizes such use. This restraint could be based on a desire to avoid liability for infringing on the person's property interests. However, even in the absence of a property right in DNA, such restraint would be necessary out of respect for the individual's privacy interests. Obligating researchers and others who collect, store and analyze individually identifiable DNA samples to practice this restraint and act responsibly (as the GPA does) would not disproportionately burden them when the risks that individuals face from unauthorized use of DNA are considered.

Fair Information Practices

In addition to equitably addressing the interests of individuals and others in DNA samples, comprehensive legislation must also protect private genetic information. The GPA does this by requiring that any one who maintains such information in the ordinary course of business (rather than friends or relatives with whom the person might share this information) to adhere to specific informational practices. Those provisions:

- require written authorization by the individual or legal representative before disclosures can be made[25];
- limit disclosures of the specific information described in the authorization to those named in the authorization and for the purpose noted in the authorization[26]; and,
- grant individuals the right to inspect and obtain copies of records containing their private genetic information.[27]

Consistent with the notion that disclosures of private genetic information can have consequences for the individual that may differ in kind or severity than disclosures of other medical information, execution of a general authorization for release of medical records is not sufficient for release of private genetic information.[28] Disclosure of private genetic information without prior authorization can only be compelled in limited circumstances, such as suits in which the genetic condition of a party is at issue or when the person maintaining the information is the subject of a criminal investigation in regard to such activity.[29]

Conclusion

All the benefits and risks from decoding the entire human genome are as yet undetermined and unrealized. What is clear however is that the private information obtained from DNA analysis will have a profound impact on how individuals view themselves and others. The GPA is an attempt to establish rules for the protection of individual privacy as curiosity about perhaps the most private and sensitive information - genetic information - is driven by the piece by piece decoding of the genome and as special interest groups stake claims on that information. Because the GPA concentrates on privacy and confidentiality of information, it does not address all the policy issues involved in the creation of genetic information. For instance, prohibitions against use of genetic information so as to avoid harm to other individual interests are not included, but have been addressed in other proposals, including the New Jersey bill that is currently undergoing revision. Legislative action to regulate the use of genetic information is both desirable and compatible with the provisions in GPA. For all such proposals, however, major difficulties are presented in regard to defining precisely what activities and information are to be regulated and striking an equitable balance between individual and societal interests in exploiting DNA. The GPA presents one comprehensive legislative response to these issues. As

New Jersey's experience illustrates, consensus may be arrived at in regard to some limitations on the uses of genetic information, but we are still a long way from consensus on who should ultimately control DNA: the individual or others who also stand to gain from genetic information. Senator Jack G. Sinagra, the prime sponsor of the New Jersey legislation, summarized his concerns this way: "There is a down side when it comes to genetics- the potential Pandora's box we open when it comes to discrimination. I think we ought to start with one premise, that this is our property".[30]

Endnotes and References

1 1996 NJ S.B 695, entitled the "Genetic Privacy Act".

2 Livio S.K., "Attempt to Shield Privacy Flawed?" *Asbury Park Press*, Aug. 7, 1996, at Sec.A, p.1.

3 Annas G.J., L.H. Glantz and P.A. Roche, *The Genetic Privacy Act and Commentary.* (Boston University School of Public Health, Boston, MA, 1993) (available by request from the Health Law Dept, 80 East Concord St., Boston, MA 02118, and also available at http://www.busph.bu.edu/Depts/HealthLaw/). A report that was funded by the Ethical, Legal & Social Implications of the Human Genome Project, Office of Energy Research, U.S. Dept. of Energy No. DE-F602ER 61626 with additional support by Boston University School of Public Health. Although the New Jersey Bill also bears the title "Genetic Privacy Act", these are two distinct proposals and "GPA" refers to the Annas, Glantz, Roche version.

4 Supra note 2.

5 Annas G.J. and S. Elias, eds, *Gene Mapping: Using Law and Ethics as Guides* (New York: Oxford University Press, 1992) at 9.

6 Annas G.J. "Privacy Rules for DNA Databanks: Protecting Coded Future Diaries" (1993), 270 *JAMA* 2346.

7 Supra note 3.

8 Ibid. at Sec. 122.

9 Ibid. at Sec. 121.

10 Ibid. at Sec. 123.

11 Annas G.J., L.H. Glantz and P.A. Roche, "Drafting the Genetic Privacy Act: Science, Policy, and Practical Considerations" (1995), 23 *J L Med. & Ethics* 360.

12 An identifiable sample is one that is linked to any individual identifier "such as name, address, Social Security number, health insurance identification number or similar information by which the identity of a sample source can be determined with reasonable accuracy, either directly or by reference to other available information." *Genetic Privacy Act*, PA Sec. 3 (h) and (i).

13 Supra note 3 at Sec. 101(b).

14 Ibid. at Sec. 105.

15 Ibid. at Sec. 103(a).

16 *Restatement of Property*, §§ 5-13 (St. Paul : American Law Institute, 1936).

17 Ibid.

18 Ibid.

19 Saltus R., "Laws Urged to Prevent Genetic Bias" *Boston Globe*, Oct. 8, 1996 at p.1.

20 Ibid.

21 Lin M.M., "Conferring a Federal Property Right in Genetic Material: Stepping into the Future with the Genetic Privacy Act" (1996), 22 *Am. J L & Med.* 109.

22 *Moore v. Regents of the Univ. of Cal.*, 793 P.2d 479 (Cal. 1990), cert. denied, 499 U.S. 936 (1991).

23 Supra note 13.

24 Supra note 3 at Sec. 162.

25 Ibid. at Sec. 111.

26 Ibid. at Sec. 112.

27 Ibid. at Sec. 113.

28 Ibid. at Sec. 112(f).

29 Ibid. at Sec. 115.

30 Supra note 2.

HUMAN DNA ON TRIAL IN FRENCH LAW

NOËL-JEAN MAZEN

Associate Professor of Law, University of Burgundy, Dijon

Attorney G.I.E. Coopers & Lybrand

In its attempt at creating the laws which apply to the human body and the use of its parts as "products", the French legislature has managed to generate a multitude of reports, study projects, and commissions.

This approach has lead to the adoption of the so-called "bioethics laws" of July 29, 1994. Very much influenced by pressures from the medical and scientific communities, these laws were intended to create a basis for a legal code regarding the human body. These laws were essentially limited to establishing a number of principles which had already been accepted in regulating certain practices by health practitioners, as well as by members of the legal profession. Notably, they had brought to bear solutions to problems arising from questions of paternity as a consequence of artificial insemination, recognizing and establishing certain rights and privileges between the infant and the couple who had used medical techniques of reproduction.

French legislators also put in place a veritable arsenal of penal and administrative sanctions which underscores the importance it accords matters in its purview.

One might assume that the question of the legal status of the human body, its organs, elements, so-called products or cells is definitively regulated by French law.

In reality, the legislation carefully avoided any truly definitive pronouncement on this matter, preferring to restrict itself to establishing indispensable technical regulations. As a result, it is very difficult to untangle the true juridical choices that lie behind a terminology which is often ambiguous, especially with regards to the legal status of the embryo and the legal strictures surrounding a donation of human material.

The laws relating to bioethics have not dealt with DNA in any special way. They consider the human body as a whole and they regulate the conditions for disposing of, distributing, utilizing human organs, body parts, products or cells, gametes (reproductive cells) and embryos. Only a few legal pronouncements have been specific to the use of genetic material and even the more comprehensive laws of 1994 had become outdated by scientific advances before ever being put into effect. By May 1996, a new legislative act became necessary.[1]

I. The Original Legislation Concerning DNA

DNA is seen objectively as a physical and tangible object and the information it carries is a biological image.[2]

Certain French writers, for philosophical or religious reasons, have tried to enshrine genetic potentiality and attribute to it a kind of intermediary status, describing it in various ways: i.e. "genetic forces, "potential person", etc...[3]

This is not compatible, however, with the two divisions in French law, where everything belongs in one of two categories: either as persons or as things.

Conditions under which DNA may be procured are governed by two guiding principles:

a) the obligation to have the consent of the individual before any genetic material is taken; and

b) the prohibition of any remuneration for this transaction.

A) OBTAINING THE CONSENT OF THE DONOR

The obligation to secure the consent of the donor is based on two fundamental rights of the individual: the prohibition against conducting a procedure on an individual without his prior consent, which is to say, the inviolability of the human body and the prohibition against consenting to a physical intervention which has not been recognized by law.

1. The need for consent

The legislation appears to place the interests of the individual concerned ahead of all others. He/she alone may authorize an invasion of his/her physical integrity.

Currently, this principle is dictated by the *Civil Code*[4] as well as the *Public Health Code*.[5] The importance given to the wishes of the individual is echoed by the fact that this consent in therapeutic matters[6] as well as in the case of a donation[7], is revocable at any time.

This latter requirement "a priori" remains obligatory and the patient or his legal representative must give an authorization as prescribed by French law, even when it is a matter of taking DNA material from waste matter.

The recovery of DNA from a deceased person is subject to two laws. When DNA is taken from bone marrow or from an organ, the recovery of this matter is free of constraint except where the individual had previously expressed his refusal in an explicit manner.[8] The conditions for recovering the DNA when it is taken from tissue or cells as well as from various parts of the human body or products must be in accordance with the decrees of Le Conseil d'État (the French Council of State).[9]

The obligation to secure a prior consent is expressly required within the framework of taking genetic profiles or examining the genetic characteristics of an individual.[10] It is a question of targeting the procedures which provide information about a particular disease, actual or potential, hereditary or not, which the individual may be carrying. Since the performance of such examinations or the taking of profiles may eventually have an effect on the private life of the individual, it is essential that the individual be informed and give his authorization.

Although the rationale behind the necessity for a given consent seems fairly general, the modalities by which such authorization may be given certainly lack any kind of uniformity.

In reality, French law places very little importance on the wishes of the individual, in spite of a well-intentioned approach. The laws are imprecise, include significant exceptions, and present various conflicting measures.

2. Subordinate place of consent

The legislation has provided for an explicit authorization requirement regarding the use of an individual's genes. In actual practice, however, a legal authorization is rarely requested,[11] whether it is a therapeutic matter or in the area of research.[12]

Individuals, therefore, may not be informed in advance of the subsequent recovery and use of genetic material whether it be the donation of an organ, bone marrow, cells, products, other body elements or human blood.

Contrary to the principle enunciated in Article 16-10 para. 2 of the *Civil Code*, the law even permits the option of not informing the individual when genetic profiles or examinations are made, with the intent to protect the interests of the patient by keeping any knowledge of the diagnosis of the disease from him. This is true even when the patient is participating in a biomedical research protocol,[13] or when he has authorized various previously identified donations in the course of treatment which is in the domain of public health.[14]

It may be noted that, contrary to the principle initially stated, the recovery of DNA is often undertaken without the consent of the interested party. Such a situation, of course, would be difficult to resolve if there were a right to compensation for the procedure. However, this problem does not arise in France because the legislation dictates that DNA donation be gratuitous.

B) THE ABSENCE OF REMUNERATION FOR THE DONOR

The uncompensated use of genetic material appears to be confirmed in the declaration of two principles: exclusion from patrimony (which is to say, the totality of economic rights), of the human body, its organs, elements, products and cells, and the corollary, their non-monetary value in law.

1. The exclusion from patrimony of genetic material

Genetic material is considered an element of the human body. Therefore, according to principles stated in the *Civil Code*, it cannot be a matter of a pecuniary transaction ... *"the human body, its elements and its products may not be the subject of patrimonial rights."*[15]

> "Any agreements which would result in placing a patrimonial value on the human body, its elements or its products are hereby null and void."[16]

The postulation of exclusion from patrimony implies logically that the agreement to which it applies may not be the object of any pecuniary transaction, whether it be gratuitous or for monetary value.

A certain number of interpretations derived from the text, as well as from the terminology employed,[17] leads us to suppose that the real goal here is not so much to place the human body, its elements or its products, outside pecuniary considerations as it is to reject entirely all forms of such transactions for financial consideration.

So then, in bioethics law, what must be confirmed is the essentially gratuitous nature of these legal transactions and not that they do not exist, nor that they might not have had any prior legal existence.[18]

One has to question the effectiveness of these principles, however, in light of the significant grey area surrounding their interpretation.

2. Relative values in the principle of gratuitous gift

A gift is considered gratuitous when there is an absence of any kind of financial arrangement in exchange for the recovery of genetic material.

According to the terms of Article 16-6 of the *Civil Code*, "no remuneration may be allotted to anyone who permits an experiment on his bodily person, who permits the recovery of bodily elements or its products." Various sanctions cover these declarations. There are fines and jail sentences[19] imposed on individuals who have obtained products, elements, etc. from a human body for payment. Additional penalties are imposed on physical persons who have carried out or have tried to commit or have contributed to infractions of this law.[20]

The *Public Health Code*, however, provides several exceptions to this rule. Article L. 665-13, after reaffirming that no payment may be made to anyone who permits the recovery of elements of his body, or of it products, goes on to state that the person "may, where there are costs, be reimbursed for incurred expenses."

At the same time, according to parts of Article L.209-8 of the *Public Health Code* "biomedical research does not authorize payment of any kind of financial compensation, direct or indirect, to persons who agree to research, except for reimbursement for incurred expenses". Article L.209-15 of the same code specifies that "in the case where there is research without direct personal financial gain to the individual involved, the researcher 'may make payment' to that individual of an indemnity as compensation for any liability to which they may be subject". The maximum for such an indemnification was limited to 25,000 FF. by decree of 21 February, 1994.[21]

Contradictions between the measures enunciated in the *Civil Code* and those of the *Public Health Code* are apparent. According to the *Civil Code*, only eventual remuneration of individuals is intended. According to the *Public Health Code*, only the reimbursement of incurred expenses is authorized. These two kinds of stipulations seem to be operating at cross purposes.

Genetic material may also be obtained from entities who are authorized to recover such material or to preserve it. Preservation, however, may require certain techniques that are more or less costly. It has already been established that compensation may be possible where gametes and blood products are recovered and preserved. Of course its not a question of the "price" placed on this material, but on the reimbursement of costs involved in the process of preservation.

Nevertheless, the "final product" is never free of charge. Thus, with regards to blood products, French legislators have enacted national guidelines in harmony with European norms that establish a distinction between the blood product itself and whatever may be developed from it. Thus, Article L.666-3 of the *Public Health Code* declares that no remuneration may be paid to a blood donor; but according to Article L.666-9 of the very same code "a decree by the Minister in charge of health and the Minister in charge of social security, after consultation with the French Blood Agency, establishes rates for transferral of blood products."

A similar proposal has recently been adopted concerning products derived from genetic material: under certain conditions, they are now covered by the laws relating to drugs,[22] which certainly implies that they will be given a pecuniary value. Beyond the market value which now is associated with products derived from genetic material, there are also questions concerning their legal status.

II. DNA Product Development

When genetic engineering first appeared 15 years ago, it opened up the possibility for man to have an impact on human beings through the modification and transmission of genes. The so-called "inventions" which resulted from this development have created a multitude of problems.

In its bioethics laws, French legislation did not try to respond to these problems. The laws were limited to prohibiting genetic therapies where the transmission of genetic material is involved while leaving the door open to "research leading to the prevention and treatment of genetic diseases."[23]

It did not provide a definitive solution to questions concerning the licensing or issuing of patents for products derived from: a) genetic material or b) their use.

A) LICENSING GENETIC MATERIAL PRODUCTS

All products developed by industry, and especially in the area of high technology, understandably require a considerable investment in research. In order to protect their financial investments, corporate investors have claimed protection for their discoveries by means of patents which assign exclusive rights to the owner of the patent.

Animals as well as plants whose DNA has been transformed have been recognized as eligible for patent coverage in the United States as well as in Europe. What, then, is the legal status of DNA?

1. Principle of bioethics laws

The law states: the human body, its elements and products, as well as the knowledge of the total or partial structure of the human gene, may not *in and of itself* be subject to a patent.[24]

This somewhat convoluted formulation adds nothing constructive since, according to French patent law, the inventor cannot ask for any protection unless he can demonstrate a genuine act of invention. There are three criteria for according a patent: 1) its innovative character, 2) the fact of an act of invention and 3) the possibility of an industrial application.[25] Any product resulting from DNA would be patentable therefore, if it was brought to public consciousness for the first time, and if securing the patent would result in the development of a new technique and could be reproduced commercially without much difficulty.

As a consequence, French law would permit the processing of a request for a patent concerning products developed from genetic material. Only the identification and classification of genes are excluded from patent eligibility.

2. Principles drawn from the European Law of Patents

For pseudo-moral reasons, the usual assortment of parties in the European Community succeeded in 1995[26] in postponing a vote on a resolution similar to the French laws passed in 1994.

The phrase "in and of itself" constituted one of the major obstacles to the adoption of the draft resolution referred to above, and in its place "a natural state" was substituted. According to Article 3 of the European Community proposal "...the human body and its elements, *in their natural state*, may not be considered as a patentable invention." This statement inferred that in order to be patentable, a sequence of genomes or genes must have been subjected to some kind of modification. The technical intervention by man must necessarily take place prior to any request for a patent. A request like the one made by Craig Venter - based on partially decoding 3,000 sequences of a genome - therefore could not be considered under the accepted EC law.

In line 2 of this same Article 3 however, some modifications are added to the established principle. In effect "...the object of an invention for which there may be an industrial application and which rests on involving an element isolated from a human body or is otherwise a product of a technical procedure, is patentable, even if the structure of this element is identical with a similar element in nature". The criteria which predominates in the question of patentability is the existence of an industrial application. A sequence of genomes or genes may be patented if it leads to an original industrial application.

The European Office of Patents recently handed down a decision in this matter. It had to decide on the validity of a patent covering a fragment of DNA code with respect to a substance called "relaxine".[27] One of the arguments advanced by the opponents to the patent was that "relaxine" was not an invention but a discovery for it existed previously in the body of pregnant women. For the European Office of Patents, though "... the simple fact of finding a substance in nature does not constitute an invention", it may however be considered an invention if it satisfies certain criteria. "[I]t must have a technical character: it must involve a technical solution to a technical problem, it must have an industrial application, and be reproduced without excessive effort." Thus a molecule of DNA is patentable, *per se,* inasmuch as it conforms to certain other requirements for patentability:[28] innovation (completely acceptable by EC law), the possibility of concrete application, and the existence of an innovative application or activity.[29]

This first series of questions shows us what the difficulties are in this matter. What is needed is the resolution of a fundamental problem with regard to the necessary development of these new technologies: the regulation of products derived from genetic material. This question concerns the law of patents in the most profound way since the qualification of drugs derived from DNA products leads to more precise legal protections. Thus we may extend the protection derived from an existing patent - thanks to a supplementary certificate of protection - where the duration of the extension is calculated from the filing of the request for the patent to the first authorization allowing the product to be put on the French market.[30] Furthermore, it may be possible to request a patent covering a second described use as a drug.[31]

B) THE REGULATION OF PRODUCTS DERIVED FROM GENETIC MATERIAL

Products which are developed from genetic material, currently designated as "genetic therapy products", are, for the most part, designed to be used therapeutically. It would appear to be logical that they be given legal status as a drug.

The resolutions adopted by legislation in 1994, far from resolving the problem, introduced significant complexity to this area. Recently adopted rules attempt to unify, to some extent, the regulations governing genetic therapeutic products.

1. Gaps in bioethics laws

The laws governing bioethics do not seek to establish any legal status for products resulting from biotechnology. Their function is to deal with the legality of acts which dispose of organs, elements and products or cells of the human body.

According to the terms of Article L.672-11, the rules applicable to genetic therapeutic products derived from human tissues or cells depend on the products use as a drug,[32] or by rules determined by the Conseil d'État when these products do not qualify as a drug.[33]

The genetic material may be extracted from a number of organs which have been identified since the passing of the laws of 1994, as well as from bone marrow. The regulations with respect to tissues and cells do not apply to bone marrow. Products developed from genetic material originating in bone marrow or from some other organs are subject to a special regulation.

The French political system has a predilection for multiple commissions; five such organizations have been given authority in the control of manufacturing genetic therapeutic products: Commission on Genetic Engineering,[34] Commission to Study the Dissemination of Products Derived from Biomolecular Engineering,[35] Drugs Agency,[36] Consultative Committee for the Protection of Persons Who Agree to Serve in Biomedical Research,[37] and the Group for Viral Safeguards.[38]

The difficulties derived from this almost burlesque situation have not escaped certain parliamentarians who developed a legislative program aimed at simplifying and unifying the regulation of genetic therapeutic products.[39] The resulting legislation of 1996, however, only reaffirms habitual timidity.

2. Contribution of the Law of 1996

Two Senators, Mr. Huriet and Mr. Descours managed to secure the vote necessary to pass four amendments unifying the statute concerning genetic therapeutic, as well as cellular products.[40]

The text is a model of its kind. Quite simply it refuses to identify genetic therapeutic products as drugs, and prefers to group them together in their own *sui generis* category "biological products having therapeutic effects."[41] These latter products which are not being termed drugs, are subject only to certain laws governing drugs. Their distribution must be authorized by the French Drugs Agency and when it is a question of certain specific pharmaceutical items, authorization is given. But in other instances the decision is made by the Minister with the advice and counsel of the Agency.[42] (Subject always, alas, to the busy schedules of both the Minister and the Agency.)

In this typically traditional development on the subject of health, French legislation establishes a quasi monopoly in favour of certain authorized organizations. Only they may guarantee the preparation, distribution, importation or exportation of genetic therapeutic products. The competent authority stands guard over the respect for the laws of good practice, general principles which apply to the donation and use of elements and products of the human body, pursuant to the declarations of the law of 1992 controlling the use and distribution of organisms which have been genetically modified.[43]

Products of genetic therapy will no longer be regulated on a case by case basis, as a function of their origin, but rather in a more simplified manner according to how they are to be distributed.

This kind of classification will allow inventors of genetic therapy products to benefit from a protection reinforced by the certificate of protection supplementary to the patents on drugs.

It is one means of guaranteeing respect for the code of good practice in the manufacture, in the quality of the products used, in the care given to various stages of fabrication, in the serious evaluation of risks involved in the use of the final product and in the respect of all criteria so as to receive the authorization required to commercially market all drugs. It also carries with it the assurance that toxicity is monitored thanks to pharmaceutical vigilance.

The European Community itself has established a specific procedure concerning several products where the drugs result from DNA technology and the use of genetic codes.[44] They may not be distributed in the European Community if their manufacturers have not previously obtained a European "Authorization to Market". This requirement provides an additional guarantee as to the reliability of products developed from DNA. It also puts in question the judicial character of the declarations adopted by the law of May 28, 1996, which group, under certain conditions, genetic therapy products with drugs insofar as it concerns the Authorization to Market. Was this formality really essential in the face of the European Community proposals?

We can only hope that the High Commission on Genetic and Cellular Therapies[45] working with the Prime Minister to suggest various approaches in this matter will continue to study these issues.

The development of genetic therapy product regulations would be better served within a text both specific and complete, not through the means of some proposals contained in a law of general principles. Would it not be preferable that the legislation reduce the number of committees instead of creating new ones? Would it not be preferable to simplify both quantitatively and qualitatively the process rather than oblige researchers to increase the number of their requests for authorizations to place their products on the market?

In response to scientific and industrial pressures, the French legislation has tried to resolve a certain number of technical problems without really coming to grips with the essential prerequisite of developing a solid legal and unified statute for DNA and its products.

Endnotes and References

1 Law 96-452, May 28,1996, J.O.R.F., lois et décrets, May 29, 1996, at 7915.

2 Mazen N.J., "Réflexions juridiques sur le matériel génétique de l'homme" in Drai R. and M. Harichaux, eds., *Bioéthique et droit* (Paris: Presses Universitaires de France, 1988) at 194. See also, Galloux J.C., "Essais de définition d'un statut juridique pour le matériel génétique" (Thèse Bordeaux, 1988). See also, Loquin E., "Les incidences juridiques éventuelles de la procréation médicalement assistée", Vièmes journées d'expertise et de responsabilité médicale, June 14-15, 1989, No147, (Masson: Alexandre Lacassagne, 1990) at 171. See also, Mémeteau G., "L'embryon législatif"(1994), *Chronique* 355.

3 Kayser P., "Les limites morales et juridiques de la procréation artificielle", D.87 *Chronique* xxxv 189. See also, Cornu G., *Droit civil, introduction, les personnes, les biens*, 6ième édition, (Paris: Dornat Montchrestien) at 167.

4 Articles 16, 16-1, 16-3.

5 Article L.665-11 of the *Public Health Code* (Code de la Santé Publique).

6 As established by French jurisprudence.

7 This principle is enunciated only in the *Public Health Code* at article L.665-11.

8 Article L.671-7 of the *Public Health Code.*

9 Article L.671-6 of the *Public Health Code.*

10 Article 16-10 para.2 of the *Civil Code.*

11 The European Patent Office brought up the issue of express consent in the taking and the use of an individual's genes in the *Relaxine* case, O.E.B. (EPO) August 12, 1994, D.1996, 3ième cahier, jurisprudence p.44, note J.C. Galloux.

12 The recent *Relaxine* decision, however, considered the importance of the consent of an individual from whom DNA was taken. Galloux makes a comparison with the facts of the *Moore* case.

13 Article L.209-9 of the *Public Health Code*.

14 Article L.40-5 para.7 of the *Public Health Code*, Law 78-17, January 6 1978 as modified by the Law 94-548, July 1,1994, J.O.R.F., lois et décrets, July 2 1994. See also Mazen N.J., "Tests et empreintes génétiques: Du flou juridique au pouvoir scientifique" (1994), No Spécial Bioéthique, 149 *Les Petites Affiches* 70.

15 Article 16-1 para.3 of the *Civil Code*.

16 Article 16-5 of the *Civil Code*.

17 Taglione C., "L'Aménagement des droits du donneur de matériel génétique", (Mémoire du D.E.A. Dijon, 1994-1995) at 28.

18 Thouvenin D., "La personne et son corps: Un sujet humain, pas un individu biologique", (1994), No Spécial Bioéthique, 149 *Les Petites Affiches* 28. See also, Thouvenin D., " Les organes, tissus et cellules prélevés sont-ils la conséquence d'un don?", in "Les lois No94-548 du 1er juillet 1994, No 94-653 et No 94-654 du 29 juillet 1994 ou comment construire un droit de la bioéthique",A.L.D. 1995, 18ième cahier, commentaire législatif, at 171.

19 Article L.675-3 of the *Public Health Code* and articles 511-2, 511-15, 511-45, 511-9 of the *Criminal Code* (Code Pénal).

20 Articles 511-26 to 511-28 of the *Criminal Code* (Code Pénal).

21 J.O.R.F., lois et décrets, March 30, 1994.

22 Law 96-452, May 28 1996, J.O.R.F., lois et décrets, at 7915.

23 Article 16-4 of the *Civil Code*.

24 Article L.611-17 of the *Intellectual Property Code* (Code de la Propriété Intellectuelle).

25 Article L.61-10 of the *Intellectual Property Code* (Code de la Propriété Intellectuelle).

26 Bulletin UE, 3-11995, at 16.

27 Supra note 11.

28 Ibid.

29 Mazen N.J., "Problèmes juridiques liés aux applications médico-industrielles de la carte génétique humaine" (1991), 2 *Droit Prospectif* 365.

30 Article L.611-12 and 611-3 of the *Intellectual Property Code* (Code de la Propriété Intellectuelle).

31 The Cour de Cassation, contrary to the EPO (O.E.B. May 12, 1984, Dossiers brevets 1984, vi, 6 Bulletin de documentation de la propriété industrielle 1985, 111, 146) avoided this possibility (Cass. com. October 26,1993, JCP, IV, 2716).

32 Article L.672-11 para.2 of the *Intellectual Property Code* (Code de la Propriété Intellectuelle).

33 Article L.672-11 para.3 of the *Intellectual Property Code* (Code de la Propriété Intellectuelle).

34 This Commission is responsible for evaluating the risks associated with genetically modified organisms, the engineering process used as well as the dangers associated with the use of the genetic engineering techniques.

35 This Commision is in charge of environmental risk evaluation.

36 A team of experts from this Agency must study the files relating to the development of genetic therapy products.

37 All research protocols involving humans must be submitted to this Comittee for approval.

38 All trials of products that have not been previously evaluated must be submitted to this Group.

39 Law 96-452, May 28, 1996, J.O.R.F., lois et décrets, May 29 1996, p.7915-7920.

40 Adopted on the second reading in the Senate and National Assembly and finally adopted on March 9, 1996.

41 Article L.665-10 Para.2 & 3 of the *Public Health Code.*

42 Article L.676-3 of the *Public Health Code.*

43 The Drugs Agency when the gene therapy products are pharmaceutical specialties or other industrially manufactured drugs, the minister of health under advisement of an *ad hoc* commision in other cases. See Article L.676-2 of the *Public Health Code.*

44 Regulation CEE No2309/93, July 7 1993, J.O.C.El., No 214 , August 8 1993.

45 Supra note 39, article 19 at 7916.

THE STATUS OF HUMAN GENETIC MATERIAL - EUROPEAN APPROACHES

RUTH CHADWICK

Centre for Professional Ethics

University of Central Lancashire

Introduction: Preliminary Classifications

In thinking about the status of human genetic material there are three preliminary points of clarification to be made. The first question to address is how 'genetic material' is to be defined. Broadly, the question of the status of human genetic material in Europe, as elsewhere, may be divided into two different issues: the status of the genetic material itself and the status of the information contained in that material. The two issues, however, are quite difficult to distinguish: partly because the definition of 'gene' itself tends to combine the two. It has been claimed that "in the history of biology there are few concepts more problematic than that of the gene".[1] Nelkin and Lindee have drawn attention to its status as a cultural icon, used as a metaphor for personhood and identity among other things.[2] As a biological entity, however, it is commonly defined as a segment of DNA that codes for a protein. This definition, with slight variations, is to be found in many contexts in Europe. France is relatively unusual in recognizing in a document of the Comité consultatif national d'éthique[3] both the wider cultural significance to which Nelkin and Lindee have alluded and the dependence of genes both on other genes and on environment:

> "...le mythe du gène, support de programme de la vie, est tel que cela conduit à l'illusion qu'une connaissance parfaite du génome d'un individu donnerait accès à la réalité et au destin de la personne."

and,

> "Un gène correspond à un facteur de détermination biologique dont l'expression et la signification fonctionnelle dépendent souvent de l'influence des autres gènes et de l'environnement."

The biological definition in terms of a stretch of DNA that codes for a protein brings out both the physical and informational aspects of genetic material: the stuff of DNA on the one hand and the code i.e., the information, on the other. While it may be difficult to differentiate between the two, when questions of ownership arise it is crucial to be clear about this.

Issues about the physical material raise questions about attitudes towards the human body and body parts. In some countries, there is no explicit regulation of genetic material itself - rather, attitudes towards genetic material have to be deduced by analogy with the law on the body and bodily parts.

The informational issue, similarly, is linked to prevailing attitudes towards medical information generally, for example as to whether genetic information is considered to be essentially different from or the same as other kinds of medical information.

This article will deal primarily with the conceptual frameworks that are in use in Europe to address the issues. My analysis will take as its starting point a project funded by the European Commission in 1992, which surveyed philosophical approaches to the human genome, body, identity and property in Belgium, France, Germany, Greece, the Netherlands, Spain and the UK.[4] Through the EUROSCREEN network on ethics of genetic screening, which I coordinate, I have attempted to establish what developments have taken place since then and also to explore the situation in additional countries, including Austria, the Czech Republic, Finland, Hungary and Ireland.

The second point of clarification is to ask what is the point of the question: why is the status of genetic material important? There are both metaphysical and ethical dimensions to the question. The metaphysical ones concern what kind of stuff genetic material fundamentally is, and how it is related to the nature of the human person. The ethical ones concern what framework will best satisfy the competing interests that might be at stake with regard to genetic material: who ought to have control over material extracted from human persons and who ought to have access to the information therein. For present purposes, it is the latter question that is important, though our ethical views will inevitably be informed by our more fundamental metaphysical beliefs.

The third and final preliminary point follows naturally from this: while there may be a degree of consensus on certain points in European countries, nevertheless in the light of varied legal systems and philosophical traditions, the underlying justifications used by different parties to the consensus may be widely divergent.

Ownership and Property

The question as to whether individuals can be said to own their genetic material is not a simple one. The ambiguity in the concept of 'genetic material' has already been noted, but there is a further conceptual unclarity in 'ownership'. A full right of ownership would include rights of disposal and sale. The European project mentioned above distinguished between a full and limited sense of ownership as follows:

> ...ownership (or limited property rights) of genetic material would be possible. Self-ownership is clear. If an individual is

> regarded as a self-owner, this implies the right to decide for himself what to do with his body material. A legal prohibition on the sale of his body material would not be justified. ... A limited property right... does not in itself reveal which rights should be included.[5]

The report found full ownership in no country, and this is one point on which there remains consensus. In several countries the sale of bodily parts is expressly forbidden e. g., Belgium, Greece and the UK.

Arguments against full ownership may be of different kinds. For Kant, there is a logical contradiction involved in the idea:

> Man cannot dispose over himself because he is not a thing, he is not his own property; to say that he is would be self-contradictory, for in so far as he is a person he is a Subject in whom the ownership of things can be vested, and if he were his own property, he would be a thing over which he could have ownership. But a person cannot be a property and so cannot be a thing which can be owned, for it is impossible to be a person and a thing, the proprietor and the property.[6]

To others, however, the essential argument may be connected not with contradiction but with the preservation of human dignity or with concerns about the potential consequences, in facilitating exploitation, of allowing ownership of human material.

The report by de Witte et al.[7] brings out the point that to speak of limited ownership is of little value - further arguments are required to establish in what way ownership should be limited and why. De Witte et al. also concluded that the concept of ownership is not often used in Europe with regard to body material, and that Germany was unusual in employing it in the constitution with regard to the body.

There is support for varying degrees of control by the individual over the body and bodily parts, without necessarily using the language of ownership. Indeed, in the light of the above comments it might be asked what further purpose the language of ownership would serve, over and above a specification of the type of control envisaged. The situation, however, is not always clear-cut. Spain is interesting in so far as it has employed a distinction between ownership and possession: we can possess many things that we cannot own, that is, possession includes the legal right to use something without it necessarily being our property.[8] English law, similarly, uses a concept of possession with regard to the dead body.[9]

The EUROSCREEN group has found a variety of views: that in the Republic of Ireland bodily parts appear to be construed as a unique kind of identifying personal property and consent of the individual is required in order for others to put them to use, that in the Netherlands, there is no consensus at the present time. The individual remains in some sense the owner of material in a cell bank but is nevertheless described as the 'donor'.[10]

Genetic Information

In the case of genetic information, as opposed to genetic material, the concept of ownership is very rarely used. Information tends to be protected by existing guidelines, whether or not in specific legislation. Discussion tends to focus on whether or not genetic information is regarded as a special case: whether it should be treated in the same way, or differently from, other kinds of medical information. Most countries apply concepts of confidentiality and/or privacy to genetic information, but some would want to argue for special protection in the case of genetic information, while there are some arguments for weakening the presumption of confidentiality in this context.

General norms are said to apply, for example, in the Czech Republic and in Hungary.[11] Suggestions that there should be stricter control for genetic information have been considered in Germany and in the Netherlands.[12] This may be either because the information is said to be qualitatively different from other types of medical information (e.g., in its predictive capacity) or on account of the potential social uses of the information (e.g., in employment and insurance) with the possibility of their adverse consequences for individuals.

Common Property

In the United Kingdom, on the other hand, it was suggested in a Royal College of Physicians report in 1991[13] that "genetic information about any individual should not be regarded as personal to that individual, but as the common property of other people who may share those genes."

The argument from common property is used to weaken arguments for autonomy and confidentiality in the genetic context. Thus the report suggests:

> ...reasons for reconsidering whether, in certain limited cases, the usually accepted rights of patients and others to autonomy and confidentiality should be reconsidered. These cases concern (a) the special connection of genetic with decisions about having children, and (b) problems with what might be called the ownership of genes.[14]

The arguments for weakening confidentiality, then, do not arise simply from considerations of ownership but also make reference to the interests of other family members, including future people. The arguments based on the interests of other people are not exclusively found in the Royal College of

Physicians report, but are also found in other documents such as the Nuffield Council on Bioethics report on Genetic Screening.[15] They say:

> [t]here would be a stronger case for overriding individuals' objections [to disclosure] where the information would influence a decision having potentially damaging rather than merely inconvenient consequences for other family members.

In other words, it is not sufficient that there are competing interests: the competing interests have to be compelling.

The idea of common property in genes, however, is not one that has proved popular in other European countries. In the UK itself, although there have been other arguments for limits to individual control over genetic information, this has largely been on the grounds of the strength of competing interests of other affected parties, rather than on ownership grounds *per se*.

The argument concerning ownership is fleshed out as follows:

> Because of the nature of genes, it may be argued that information about any individual should not be regarded as personal to that individual, but as the common property of other people who may share those genes, and who need the information in order to find out their own genetic constitution. lf so, an individual's prima facie right to confidentiality and privacy might be regarded as overridden by the rights of others to have access to information about themselves, rather as rights to privacy in the home presumably do not extend to denying access to other people whose property is being held on the premises.

This quotation makes clearer the type of ownership in question. Despite the analogy with home ownership, it does not appear to be the right to transfer and sell that is under consideration. Rather, the analogy is with privacy in the home. Ownership is construed as the ability to control access. Where ownership is shared, other people also have rights of access. Common property, however, is normally construed as 'no ownership' rather than as 'shared ownership'.[16]

What is slightly odd about the argument in the above quotation is the assumption that seems to be made that *the case for* confidentiality and privacy depends on considerations of ownership. Instead, the case may depend on considerations of quite another sort, such as autonomy, self-determination, or even utilitarian considerations.

In fact, the de Witte report concludes:

> ...arguing by analogy from ownership of the human body to ownership of body parts to ownership of genetic material seems invalid. Genetic information (recorded in medical files) cannot be said to have 'belonged' to the body. Therefore, genetic

> information must be protected by another concept than property, or the validity of the concept of property must be justified by another argument.[17]

It is not clear what the argument might be, and why we should need to appeal to a concept of common property.

There is another concept, however, which is increasing in importance in Europe, and that is solidarity. It is conceivable that an argument for common property could be based on solidarity, although that was not used as the basis for the Royal College of Physicians argument.

Solidarity is an aspect of the new communitarianism, which is increasingly challenging an approach based on autonomy and individual rights. Rather than rights, responsibilities are emphasized. There are arguments for a responsibility to share genetic information with genetic relatives. Kare Berg, for example, has suggested that this is a highly ethical act of solidarity with the group.[18]

Other countries that have introduced legislation have tended to emphasize the control of individuals over their genetic information. For example, in Austria, it is provided that if the person investigated requires it, full information on all her data had to be given to her, and data may only be given to persons to whom that person consents (apart from persons directly concerned with collection, analysis or computation of data and the doctor requesting the analysis or treating the persons concerned).[19]

Tony McGleenan[20] has argued that considerations of solidarity, among others, provide reasons for opposing the protection of genetic information via a genetic privacy act. The concept of privacy is not well developed either ethically or, in the UK, legally, but he argues that solidarity, rather than a development of privacy law, may be better protection than privacy against such threats as, genetic discrimination.

Conclusion

It was stated above that the point of elucidating the status of genetic information is to establish what framework will best satisfy the competing interests at stake. Hence, it seems preferable to adopt the type of approach that McGleenan takes, of asking what are the threats against which safeguards are needed.

It seems clear that a notion of common property will not do the job, just as it seems fairly clear that a concept of individual ownership will not provide what is required. This is because the concept of ownership is itself in dispute; and as far as common property is concerned, it is not clear what the practical applications might be. One question that a notion of property, or ownership, in genetic information seems quite unable to deal with is the issue of a right *not* to know genetic information. If we say that there is individual ownership, then how is the right not to know supposed to work? For the right not to know only arises when another person A has information about B which B does not have and which B does not want. B's right of ownership, however, seems useless in protecting B from this information.

In the case of common property, suppose that there is some information available about both A and B which A wants and B does not, but that A knowing it will inadvertently give B the information. It is not clear how, if at all, a conceptual framework of property could resolve this issue.

To conclude, then, there is a fair degree of consensus in Europe against allowing full rights of ownership where body parts are concerned. The extent to which it is possible to argue from this by analogy to genetic material is not always clear. Some countries allow a limited concept of ownership over the body or parts of the body but it is quite unhelpful because the limitations need to be not only specified but also justified.

As regards genetic information, countries are distinguished according to whether they treat genetic information as the same as or different from other medical information. In so far as they regard it in the same way, concepts of confidentiality and privacy are used. In so far as they regard it differently, some want special protection because of the particular threats that genetic information can pose. Others want to weaken it. Of most interest here is the concept of common property. But it is better argued for on the basis of solidarity, which is in tension with privacy, confidentiality and autonomy.

Endnotes and References

1 Nelkin D. and Lindee M.S., *The DNA Mystique: The Gene as a Cultural Icon* (New York: W. H. Freeman, 1995).

2 Ibid.

3 Comité consultatif national d'éthique, Avis No. 46: *Génétique et médecine; de la pédiction à la prévention* (Paris: Comité Consultatif National d'Éthique, 1995).

4 de Witte J., et al., *Human Genome, Body, Identity and Property: Philosophical Issues* (EC Project PL 9101027), (Nijmegen: Katholieke Universiteit, Department of Ethics, Philosophy and History of Medicine, 1992).

5 Ibid.

6 Beck L.W., ed., *Immanuel Kant: Lectures on Ethics*, translated by Louis Infield, (NewYork: Harper & Row, 1963).

7 Supra note 4.

8 Ibid.

9 Skegg P.D.G., *Law, Ethics and Medicine: Studies in Medical Law*, rev. edn., (Oxford: Clarendon Press, 1988).

10 Responses from EUROSCREEN participants to questionnaire.

11 Ibid.

12 Ibid.

13 Royal College of Physicians, *Ethical Issues in Clinical Genetics: A Report of a Working Group of the Royal College of Physicians Committees on Ethical Issues in Medicine and Clinical Genetics* (London: Royal College of Physicians, 1991).

14 Ibid.

15 Nuffield Council on Bioethics, *Genetic Screening Ethical Issues* (London, 1993).

16 Litman M. in this volume at 17.

17 Supra note 4.

18 Berg K., "The Need for Laws, Rules and Good Practices to Secure Optimal Disease Control" in *Ethics and Human Genetics: Proceedings, 2nd Symposium of the Council of Europe on Bioethics*, Strasbourg 1993, (Strasbourg: Council of Europe Press, 1994).

19 Hauser G., Presentation on legislation on genetics in Austria, Euroscreen plenary (York, November, 1995).

20 McGleenan T., "Rights to Know and not to Know: Is There a Need for a Genetic Privacy Law?" in Chadwick R., M.A. Levitt and D. Shickle, eds., *The Right to Know and the Right not to Know* (Aldershot: Averbury, 1996).

THE STATUS OF HUMAN GENETIC MATERIAL

TIMOTHY CAULFIELD

RAPPORTEUR

Research Director, Assistant Professor, Health Law Institute

Faculty of Law, University of Alberta

Introduction

Does the use of a property regime in relation to human genetic material create a powerful protection of individual rights or merely hasten the commodification of a substance that is uniquely human? Does property law have qualities which are inherently harmful as to make its use untenable or are there mechanisms within this area of law - such as the notion of gift - which can be appropriately utilized in order to protect the interests of all concerned? The panel on the Status of Human Genetic Material, which typified both the international nature of the debate and the breadth of the views, did more to articulate the nature of the essential issues than resolve any of the principal questions. Nevertheless, as we will see below, themes did emerge.

The following is a brief review of the presentations by Ruth Chadwick, Moe Litman, Noël-Jean Mazen, Thomas Murray, Patricia Roche and, the Chair of the session, Gerald Robertson. Rather than focusing on the details of the presentations, information which can be obtained from the presenter's papers, I hope to convey a sense of the debate and of the basic issues which emerged.

Framing the Debate

The legal characterization of human genetic material has both a practical and symbolic significance. For example, as we have seen from the relevant case law, property principles have the potential to serve as a mechanism for the resolution of disputes concerning the control of genetic material. On a more fundamental level, it has been suggested that property law may operate as an effective means of ensuring that individuals are not exploited or, at least, that their participation will be an essential ingredient in any decision making process involving the use of an individual's genetic sample.

But the concept of property comes with a good degree of conceptual baggage. Indeed, it is inextricably tied (for good reason) to notions of commodification and commercialization. The negative implications of these forces in the sphere of health care are not trivial (e.g., erosion of the patient/physician relationship, creation of conflicts of interest, etc.) and, as such, we should, arguably, proceed cautiously in the adoption of property principles. These concerns, while likely largely founded on the symbolic weight of property language, are particularly relevant to genetics where the degree of research investment - in both time and money - is matched only by the potential for financial gain. In addition, property rights are predominantly perceived as individual. Therefore, if property rights emerge as the governing regime, we will once again be emphasizing autonomy and the individual over solidarity and the community. Given the nature of human genetic material, is such an approach appropriate?

It is within the boundaries of these concepts - the use of property as a protective mechanism versus the unresolved negative implications - in which the presentations and discussion took place.

The Current Characterization

All panel members, either explicitly or implicitly, recognized that the legal character of human genetic material remains, at best, uncertain. For instance, in Canada, as noted by Professor Litman, we can draw upon common law cases for guidance but the nature of genetic material has not been directly addressed and, as such, we can only speculate on how it would be treated by our judiciary. Likewise, Professor Roche's call for the implementation of a *Genetic Privacy Act* underscored a perceived need in the United States to clarify who controls a given identifiable genetic sample. In Europe, we see jurisdictional variation in the approach to genetics, ranging from what Professor Chadwick termed "weak" to "strong" genetic property. Even in France, which, as explained by Professor Mazen, has an extensive bioethical regulatory scheme, the debate concerning the legal status continues.

Despite this lack of a distinct, universally accepted characterization, all seem to agree that genetic material is either itself unique or that our dealings with genetic material warrant unique consideration. Throughout the presentations and in the discussion that followed, we continually returned to issues of human dignity, ownership of the body, commodification and threats to "genetic privacy" Although these concepts were often used in differing manners to buttress conflicting ideas (e.g., human dignity was used as both a reason for and a reason against the use of a property principles), their presence in the debate illustrates the scale of the issues at hand. Rightly or not, genetic material is clearly viewed as more than mere "biological stuff." So, while a concrete characterization of genetic material remains elusive, the need for a unique approach seemed to be accepted by all.

Approaches to Characterization

There also appeared to be general agreement among the panel members concerning the nature of the principal issue. This was articulated by Chadwick as follows: *What conceptual approach best protects the interests at stake?* However, views on how best to address this issue (and whose interest should be protected) differed greatly.

For example, Litman argued that if genetic material were characterized as *sui generis* (that is, unique), common law property principles could provide a variety of useful safeguards while remaining flexible enough to respond to the various policy issues. By applying property principles in the case by case manner, the factors critical to each particular circumstance could be examined and weighed within the relevant context.

In contrast to Litman, Roche articulated the need for a more concrete and immutable property right as a means of ensuring that individuals maintain control over their genetic material. Indeed, she argues that, in this context, property rights are essential for meaningful privacy protection. In particular, she advocates the implementation of a *Genetic Privacy Act* (GPA) which would make "an individually identifiable DNA sample the property of the sample source." By doing so, it would ensure that the sample source, who has the highest interest in the genetic information, would be involved in an extensive and ongoing consent process. It should be noted that this approach seems directed at the individual - both in the sense of whom it seeks to protect and with whom the GPA vests the power of control.

But is a property approach needed in order to create these protections? For Chadwick, the use of "property language" would likely be viewed as unnecessary. These "weak" property rights - such as the need to obtain consent - can be secured without the trappings of property law (e.g., by the use of private consent law or within a statutory framework which avoids the language of property law). Likewise, she suggests that property approaches are perhaps too centred on the individual and thereby stress only individual exclusionary rights (as opposed to an individual's duty to third parties). Chadwick seeks an approach which embraces the notions of solidarity and the community, thus emphasizing a responsibility to share the information. She recognizes, however, that given the current emphasis placed on autonomy it may be difficult to impose a duty of solidarity on an individual.

Murray, in his oral presentation, took a different approach. While maintaining the language of property law, he too emphasized broader social obligations. Arguing that there are only three ways to characterize a transfer of human genetic material (either as a sale, an abandonment or as a gift), he noted that if the exchange were treated as a gift, the recipients (e.g., the scientific community) would have certain "profound obligations." Generally, in our society, the acceptance of a gift brings reciprocal duties - such as a responsibility to act responsibly upon the receipt of the gift. Thus, the unique nature of the relationship between gift giver and recipient will reflect, and sustain, the moral and social significance of the "gift" of genetic material. In addition, by characterizing the transaction as a gift it removes it from the "sphere of markets" and places it in the "sphere of gifts", thereby helping to mitigate the concerns associate with commercial forces. As noted by Mazen, the gratuitous nature of the donation of genetic material is also emphasized in the French approach.

So, on the one hand, we have an embracing of property law as a protector of individual interests (e.g., Roche) and, on the other hand, we have the outright rejection of the very notion of "genetic property" (e.g., Chadwick). Since all presenters seem to agree on the goal - the protection of relevant interests - why the stark contrast in approaches? I would suggest there are, at least, two reasons. First, those who accept property law as an appropriate protective mechanism seem to consider the interest of the individual as paramount. Second, the two "camps" place differing weight on the importance of the numerous corollary, and adverse, implications of the use of a property regime in the context of human genetics (e.g., commodification).

Because property law is clearly capable of serving as one possible protective mechanism, future debate on this issue should avoid revisiting basic property law theory and concentrate on the policy concerns which are causing the schism. Should we adopt an approach that emphasizes individual rights over the interests of the community? Are concerns regarding the adverse implications of a property approach justified? Of course, how such questions are answered will depend greatly on the society in which they are asked. Indeed, in America - arguably the most individual centred society in the world - property law stands a much stronger chance as emerging dominant than in most European jurisdictions. As a result, a simple and uniformly accepted approach to the legal status of human genetic material may be difficult to achieve as this issue is, ultimately, tied to the basic ideology of nations or cultures.

Conclusion

In the final analysis, it can be said that all participants agreed that individuals should be afforded certain legal protections in association with their genetic material. These "protections" can be expressed as property rights - such as a limited right of control as manifested in the consent process - but may not need to be framed in such a manner.

As noted by both Litman and Murray, whatever approach is adopted, it should be flexible enough to accommodate the different issues that seem inextricably linked to human genetics (e.g., issues of privacy, discrimination, etc.). Does property law provide such as scheme? It certainly seems to have the flexibility necessary, particularly if genetic material is characterized as *sui generis*. Likewise, it has sufficient historic and legal teeth to provide individuals with a significant degree of protection. However, while property rights may serve some of the desired protective goals (e.g., an individual right of control) they don't meet others (e.g., the emerging right not to know). More importantly, however, property law has a variety of symbolic and substantive traits which many consider threatening to broader social goals.

In this increasingly commercial climate which has fostered the encroachment of market forces into almost every aspect of health care and science, the linking of human genetic and legal property seems particularly worrisome. And while the adoption of a property regime would not, by itself, create an environment of exploitation and commodification, it would, at the very least, make a fundamental tool of exploitation more readily available.

CONSENT AND CONFIDENTIALITY: INTRODUCTION

BARTHA MARIA KNOPPERS (CHAIRPERSON)

Professor of Law, Senior Researcher

Public Law Research Centre (CRDP), Université de Montréal

The issues of consent, confidentiality and access with regard to human genetic material cannot be answered without having examined the status of such material. Yet, paradoxically, whether property or person, or *sui generis*, the real issue is that of consent with regards to various choices to be made concerning the control of genetic material and information. These choices include the question of consent to diagnosis for a specific disease or other diseases or even for use in anonymized studies. Once having made these disease-specific choices, others have to be taken with regards to use by different researchers in or outside of the country, to say nothing of the creation of permanent cell lines to be shared or not, and this, beyond the lifetime of a person.

Increasingly, the scientific literature as well as codes of practice and ethical guidelines distinguish between retrospective and prospective research. Retrospective research involves looking back at samples already collected. Can stored "leftover" samples be used at will? Samples may include for example, residual samples removed during "consented-to" medical care, samples removed for specific research purposes, archived pathological samples, or samples for which different research is proposed.

There is absolutely no doubt, that in the absence of prospective choices, new consents must be sought for different research protocols or for new uses of the same sample. While research protocols are slowly adjusting to the multiplicity of choices to be offered and followed, less attention has been paid to the impact of the recent trend towards the "sacralization" of the sample, on public health and surveillance or epidemiological studies using samples collected during routine care. Traditionally, these studies (usually performed on a population basis) anonymized samples so that the "source" could not be identified. However, the expansion of the requirements of consent to include already stored samples where the person has long left medical care or has died, raises new ethical issues. To recontact former patients or to contact family members of a dead person could well be more intrusive of privacy then using anonymized samples without an explicit, written consent. Moreover, hastily drafted legislation, often in reaction to imagined fears of "gene banking information thefts" has served to undermine public confidence in research whereas it is the whole general area of medical confidentiality that requires revisiting. Legislation requiring informed, written consent for any research on stored samples collected during routine care (and this even into the grave), may effectively close down essential public health and epidemiological studies or make them extremely difficult.

European approaches to this issue reflect a greater preoccupation with the role of the citizen in public health concerns and with the need for the acquisition of fundamental data (incidence, prevalence, frequency, etc.) through epidemiology in order to provide a specific, scientific basis for genetic or other medical studies. Some countries suggest an opting out mechanism whereby patients are informed that materials collected during routine medical care will be anonymized and used for research unless they refuse. This respects individual values, allows the citizen to participate for the public good, and, furthers necessary research that will benefit all.

Finally, in the rapidly evolving areas of human genetic research diagnosis, and treatment, storage of DNA samples permits looking back and looking forward and even "sideways" to at-risk family members and to future generations. But where to draw the line in terms of obligations, be they legal, ethical or moral? If there were to be such obligations, to whom would they be owed, and within what time frame?

Currently, the delimitation of possible avenues for communication on incidental findings, on the availability of new or more refined tests with clinical significance or, on risks for other family members, draw by analogy on the infectious diseases model, the mental health model, or, the HIV model. Distinctions and refinements however, must be made between these models and human genetic research and medicine.

The position(s) adopted will largely reflect both how this field of scientific endeavour and medicine is seen in society and whether the interests of public health or of family members (as distinct from other third parties) in knowing or not, or, in accessing genetic material and information, are legitimate exceptions to the autonomy and privacy of the individual. Genetic material and information are by their very nature personal, familial and social. At a minimum, patient and research participants should be warned about this characteristic of genetic information prior to testing or participation in research. Refusal by the person to warn family members may in certain situations, create new professional duties. Furthermore, would such refusal to provide access to information be binding from the grave?

Prospective genetic counselling and consent forms which concern yet to be defined, future discoveries and situations with no means of ascertaining changes in personal values or lifestyle since the original time of sampling as well as choices concerning communication with family members, make these "applied forward-backward-sideways" banking questions as probabilistic and problematic as human genetics and human relationships themselves.

CHOICES, CONTROL, ACCESS - THE CANADIAN POSITION

BERNARD M. DICKENS

Professor of Law, Faculty of Law, Faculty of Medicine and Joint Centre for Bioethics, University of Toronto

Introduction

Canada has no legislation that is designed specifically to govern human genetic material or information. However, many concerns that arise with respect to such material and its specific uses fall under the scope of general legislation and judge-made law. Legislation and judgements of courts apply at different levels of abstraction. For instance, the law on informed consent to medical treatment has an overarching application, and is designed to govern a comprehensive range of interactions between health service providers and recipients of treatments. At the other extreme, judicial decisions on public authorities' access to tissue samples for forensic testing, including materials from which genetic data may be obtained, govern a limited but critical number of agencies and interactions.

Codes of ethical conduct and policies relevant to genetic practices, such as the *Policy Statement Concerning DNA Banking and Molecular Genetic Diagnosis* issued in 1991 by the Canadian College of Medical Geneticists,[1] Canadian research ethics guidelines and international frameworks such as the *International Ethical Guidelines for Biomedical Research Involving Human Subjects*, produced in 1993 by the Council for International Organizations of Medical Sciences in collaboration with the World Health Organization, have legal significance. Although prepared as ethical and policy statements, these may be used by courts as evidence of what standards of conduct are expected of practitioners and institutions when courts have to determine negligence and the discharge of professional, employee and institutional contractual, fiduciary or other undertakings. The tendency of courts to hold professionals and employees to the standards and practices they expressly or impliedly undertake to observe gives ethical and policy guidelines a potential for legal enforcement.

Criminal Law

Criminal law has at most an indirect influence on genetic practices in Canada. The Supreme Court of Canada has held that information itself is not amenable to theft,[2] although improper removal of materials through which data are recorded obviously may be. Accordingly, obtaining unapproved access to private genetic information and violating the confidentiality of health records and, for instance, genetic data banks, will not constitute theft. This central area of criminal prohibition does not secure the exclusivity of a lawful possessor's information, such as against unauthorized copying. Crimes concerning mischief to property[3] may also be inapplicable since data themselves are not considered property, although the records containing data and means of access to them may be protected. For instance, section 430(1)(c) of the Criminal Code of Canada defines mischief to cover wilful obstruction, interruption or interference with the lawful use, engagement or operation of property, and subsection 430 (1.1) applies equally to data, which includes a computer service or system.[4]

The capacity of genetic evidence not only to inculpate the guilty but also to exonerate the innocent was demonstrated in the case of Guy Paul Morin when, with the concurrence of the prosecution, the Ontario Court of Appeal in 1995 allowed his appeal and acquitted him of a 1985 murder of which a jury had convicted him. Subsequently available DNA evidence had shown him not to be the assailant. Nevertheless, Canadian courts have developed strong safeguards against police seizing tissue samples amenable to genetic and other analysis for use in criminal proceedings other than by strict adherence to due process of law. The Supreme Court of Canada conditioned the judicial environment in which public authorities' access to identifiable individuals' tissue samples is to be considered in the 1988 case of *R. v. Dyment.* [5] The Court invoked the celebrated 1967 book by Professor Alan Westin, *Privacy and Freedom,*[6] to establish that privacy is at the heart of liberty in a modern state, and is essential for the well-being of the individual. The Court observed that "[t]he restraints imposed on government to pry into the lives of the citizen go to the essence of a democratic state."[7]

The Court in *Dyment* was considering blood sample evidence of a motorist's alcohol consumption. The danger to human life and health posed by impaired driving was recognized as a matter of major public concern to which the law should be responsive, but protection of personal privacy against improper governmentally-authorized search, and against seizure of blood or other bodily substances made available to others for medical purposes, was also seen as of major public concern. The Court considered that the purposes of justice were best served by requiring governmentally-authorized searches and seizures to conform strictly to legal procedures, and by protection of medically-procured tissue samples against informal seizure by and surrender to police or other state agencies. In Canada, public hospitals are not considered to be agencies of government,[8] but public health officers are analogous to police officers and act on the basis of public health legislation historically dependent on governmental policing power. The Court's strict view of the control the law must exercise over governmental access to tissue samples and personal data for purposes of criminal law enforcement has been consistently emphasized since the *Dyment* ruling in such cases as *R. v. Dersch* [9] and *R. v. Colarusso.*[10]

The federal government of Canada has recently proposed that a genetic data bank of serious offenders, particularly dangerous sexual offenders, be established, in order that repeat offenders be more promptly identified by genetic testing of tissue samples such as blood and semen found at the sites of serious crimes and recoverable from the bodies of victims. Identification would also serve the purpose of reducing suspicion that might otherwise fall of past offenders by showing genetic differences between their samples and those so found and recovered. Creation and management of a forensic genetic databank or tissue bank would raise major constitutional and legal concerns on such issues as how banked samples or data were obtained, whose genetic information was liable to be banked, how long information would be retained, the purposes for which it might be used, which agencies would have access to such information and under what circumstances, and which agency would be responsible for collecting, maintaining and releasing banked material and/or data.

Provincial Law

I) CONSENT

Canadian law on health care of patients falls within a framework familiar in North American and West European jurisdictions.[11] The doctrine of informed consent was embraced by the Supreme Court of Canada in 1980,[12] leading Canadian law away from its roots in English law[13] towards U.S. jurisprudence where, for instance, Australian law has followed.[14] The benefit of this doctrine is that its focus is not on what health care professionals are accustomed to telling patients, but on what disclosures are material for patients to receive in order for them to make decisions according to their own wishes and their perceptions of their interests. A patient's consent operates in law to negate a health professional's liability for battery, meaning unauthorized touching, even if the consent is inadequately informed. However, the professional's failure to make due disclosure of information may lead to liability for negligence if injury results to the patient. This liability transcends battery since it applies both to touching patients and to management of their concerns when no touching is involved, including when, through inadequate disclosures, they decline treatments from which they would have benefited.

Material information that health care professionals may be obliged to disclose to patients includes future uses to which their stored tissue samples and genetic information may be put. Disclosure includes uses that professionals know is intended or likely, and uses that are less probable but of special concern or sensitivity to the patient. An unresolved issue is whether disclosure is required of uses of data or of tissues for epidemiological studies. These are frequently authorized by legislation. When the conditions set by such legislation are observed and no more tissue is taken than is required for legitimate diagnostic, therapeutic or monitoring purposes in the patient's interest, it may be that no specific disclosure is required, even when an investigator may have access to the patient's identity. Legal consent in such studies may be found in the legislature's approval and protection of the public's and patients' interests assured by the executive branch of government. It is less likely that non-disclosure can be justified or excused by the legal doctrine of therapeutic privilege, which allows non-disclosure of information that would be counter therapeutic to give. Criminal courts have noted that patients may harmfully forego indicated diagnosis and care if they fear knowledge of their genetic or other medical status coming into the possession of police or other government agencies,[15] but it is not evident that reaction to knowledge of epidemiological studies would present comparable harm.

When health care providers know that research is intended on patients' data or tissue samples that falls outside the scope of statutory authorization, they or others responsible for such studies seem legally obliged to inform patients and to seek their prior consent. Patients' refusals of consent may impair the scientific validity and integrity of studies, but that is a burden investigators bear since their legitimate interests and goals, and their claims to academic freedom, do not necessarily justify violation of patients' interests in privacy and confidentiality. It has been seen that the courts hold these interests in high regard as an important safeguard in modern society. If studies are truly of social importance, it may be expected that they will be authorized by legislation, such as that authorizing the operation of some provincial cancer registries. Even when non-consensual access to identifiable genetic or other data is so authorized, investigators may be required to satisfy a suitable research ethics board that their access without patients' informed consent is ethically appropriate. It is not a satisfactory answer to the question why the investigator considers non-consensual access to be ethical that such access is lawful, since it is not invariably ethical to employ a power approved by law.

The Supreme Court of Canada has recently afforded patients further protection in health care professionals' management of their data. In *McInerney v. MacDonald*[16] the Supreme Court of Canada recognized physicians' fiduciary duties owed to patients in their possession of information derived from patients.[17] This duty requires physicians to follow patients' directions on disclosure of patients' health information, but also requires physicians both to employ such information on their own initiative to advance patients' interests, and to refrain from uses that would compromise or defy patients' interests. The obligation is not necessarily to make decisions that prove beneficial in effect, but to exercise conscientious and prudent judgement, directed to patients' well-being and advantage. Releases and protection of genetic information must be guided by this beneficent motivation.

II) PRIVACY AND CONFIDENTIALITY

Privacy and confidentiality are sometimes treated as a single concept and their descriptions as synonymous and interchangeable, but a growing practice is to recognize them as separate though closely related concepts. In presenting its Consultation Paper on *A Legal Framework for Health Information* in June 1996, the Ministry of Health of the government of Ontario explained that:

> There is a difference between privacy and confidentiality. Privacy involves the right to limit access to one's health information, while confidentiality comes into play after the information has been obtained by another person or agency. In that context, people give up some privacy in order to receive health care and other services, and they are not directly involved in the day-to-day management of health information. It is important to patients that their information is kept confidential and secure, no matter who holds it, and used only for agreed purposes.[18]

Privacy is voluntarily surrendered not only in patients' revelations to health care professionals but also in their discussions with family members and others, and for instance in presenting themselves where others can see them and draw conclusions, correct or incorrect, about their health and well-being. Privacy is also removed or compromised when health care professionals are under legal duties or exercise legal powers to make patients' health information available to others, such as by reporting patients' notifiable diseases, whether or not genetically related, to others such as public health authorities. The significance of the surrender or compromise of genetic privacy is that patients may supply more information than they realize or intend, because recipients may gain an understanding of what the information portends for patients' futures that the patients themselves do not share or appreciate. In Ontario, for instance, cancer patients' privacy is limited by legislation that set up a register of patients and authorizes investigators' access to it for *bona fide* epidemiological and related research without patients' consent or knowledge.

Recipients of health information who are health care or related professionals owe duties of confidentiality in their management of information that may be enforced directly by law, such as by claims for breach of contract or of fiduciary duty, or indirectly by professional disciplinary proceedings for professional misconduct. This is so whether they received the information when patients made it available to them or others voluntarily, or when legislation compelled its delivery to them. That is, even if their receipt of the information illustrated the patient's lack of privacy, they still owe the patient the duty to manage the information confidentially.

Federal Law

Dating back to 1983, the federal government of Canada's *Privacy Act*[19] gives effect to international standards that regulate collection, use and disclosure of personal information by governments and governmental agencies. The *Act* applies to about 150 federal government institutions and agencies, but the Supreme Court of Canada has held, in the slightly but not necessarily very different context of the Canadian *Charter of Rights and Freedoms*,[20] that public hospitals are not governmental institutions or agencies.[21] The *Act* sets out principles often referred to as "fair information practices."

The principal elements of such practices are that:

i) No personal information shall be collected by a government institution unless it relates directly to an operating program or activity of the institution;[22]

ii) A government institution shall, wherever possible, collect personal information...directly from the individual to whom it relates except where the individual authorizes otherwise...;[23]

iii) A government institution shall inform any individual from whom the institution collects personal information about the individual of the purpose for which the information is being collected;[24]

iv) Personal information...shall not, without the consent of the individual to whom it relates, be used by the institution except (a) for the purpose for which the information was obtained or compiled by the institution or for a use consistent with that purpose...;[25]

v) Personal information...shall not, without the consent of the individual to whom it relates, be disclosed by the institution except in accordance with [the detailed provisions of section 8 of the *Act*];[26]

vi) A government institution shall take all reasonable steps to ensure that personal information that is used for an administrative purpose by the institution is as accurate, up-to-date and complete as possible;[27]

vii) Personal information that has been used...shall be retained...for such period of time after it is so used as may be prescribed by regulation in order to ensure that the individual to whom it relates has a reasonable opportunity to obtain access to the information;[28] and

viii) An individual regarding whom personal information has been collected by government may if a citizen or a permanent resident of Canada, obtain access to such information on request,[29] object

> to the accuracy or completeness of such information, request correction,[30] require that a notation be attached to the information reflecting any correction requested but not made,[31] and require that any person or body that received disclosure of the information in the previous two years before the request for correction be notified of the correction or notation of an uncorrected objection, and, where disclosure was to a government institution, that such institution make the correction or notation on any copy of the information under its control.[32]

The *Privacy Act* defines "personal information" to include "information relating to the...medical...history of the individual...,[33] and governs such information whether held by a government institution in isolation or in a personal information bank, unless the institution is exempted from having to afford rights of access to individuals, and respect their related rights described in (viii) above, by the Governor General of Canada,[34] which in effect means by the federal Cabinet. The *Act* governs refusals of disclosures on such grounds as injury to Canadian international affairs and defence,[35] and to law enforcement and related investigations.[36] Further, in a more general provision, section 28 of the *Act* provides that:

> The head of a government institution may refuse to disclose any personal information requested under subsection 12(1)[37] that relates to the physical or mental health of the individual who requested it where the examination of the information by the individual would be contrary to the best interests of the individual.

An individual who has been refused access to personal information requested under subsection 12(1) of the *Act* may complain to the Privacy Commissioner whose office was created by the *Act*, and thereafter to the Federal Court's Trial Division.[38]

Recommendations of the Privacy Commission of Canada

In its terms, the *Privacy Act* makes no mention of genetic data or tissue samples. Data will constitute "personal information" governed by the *Act*, but it is not clear that tissues from identifiable individuals that are amenable to genetic testing are subject to the *Act*, although information includes "information about an identifiable individual that is recorded in any form."[39] The Privacy Commissioner of Canada published a Report in 1992 entitled *Genetic Testing and Privacy*, which observes that:

> The *Privacy Act* is the focus of this report's efforts to prevent genetics from spawning another nightmare in our surveillance society. The *Act*, however, is simply not up to the job... One must torture its provisions almost to the breaking point to offer any meaningful privacy protection to Canadians... existing laws

> will not prevent realizing our worst fears about privacy abuses through genetic testing.[40]

The Report requires adoption of much more precise legal controls, while recognizing that public discussion, education and explicit expectations of genetic privacy must be generated to support such controls, since law alone cannot ensure that genetic technology is used only for acceptable ends. The Report formulates 22 recommendations, some of which are reinforcements of existing provisions of the *Privacy Act* but many of which would require its amendment and strengthening.

Opening with a recommendation for governmental study of practice of collection, use and accessibility of genetic data in the public and private sectors, the Report addresses the reasonable expectation of genetic privacy in proposing that:

> There should be no mandatory genetic testing at the behest of the state (except in strictly limited circumstances in criminal investigations) or the private sector.
>
> Governments and the private sector should not oblige persons to learn their genetic traits or disorders.[41]

The Privacy Commissioner's recommendation regarding private sector conduct raises the issue of legal means of enforcement. The Canadian constitution is applied to give provincial governments ascendancy in health matters, but the federal government can claim a residual or marginal shared legal competence in the area of health services. For avoidance of doubt, however, a federal government disposed to give effect to the Privacy Commissioner's recommendation could invoke its undoubted and exclusive criminal law power. Use of this power would be supported by language the Supreme Court of Canada has used to emphasize the high democratic and public purpose that privacy serves.

The following recommendation addresses prohibitions on employers, with no distinction between those in the public and private sectors. Employers are recommended to be prohibited from collecting job applicants' personal genetic information through mandatory or voluntary genetic screening. However, applicants are not to be restrained from offering such information, and employers are recommended to be permitted to screen employees or applicants who volunteer for screening if the employees or applicants retain absolute control over the genetic samples and any related personal information. Recommendation 4 repeats the previous recommendation regarding mandatory or voluntary genetic monitoring of employees.

The next recommendation is expressed in three clauses. The first identifies the general principle that there should be no denial of services or benefits to a person who refuses to undergo genetic testing to obtain the service or benefit. Justifiably required information may be provided through any available option of testing other than genetic testing. It is recognized, however, that genetic information or means to gain such information may be refused, but at the risk of the resulting loss of the service or benefit for which genetic information may justifiably be required. The second clause of Recommendation 5 calls for strict control of the type of information from genetic testing that providers of services or benefits may gather. In particular, no new types of information from genetic testing should be collected without a thorough review of the ethics and human rights implications of the additional collection. The third component of the recommendation is that providers of services or benefits should be permitted to collect and use only the genetic information needed to tell whether the person meets the required standard.

The next series of recommendations is directed to governmental institutions. The first of these is that they should generally not collect, use or disclose personal genetic information relating to human reproduction, whether through mandatory or voluntary genetic screening.[42] The Report records the historical Canadian experience of genetically-based sterilization, including non-consensual sterilization, and places the recommendation in a context that distinguishes appropriate from inappropriate governmental initiative and reaction, leading to the subsequent recommendation that information relating to reproduction that government institutions providing medical care collect should be used only to inform a person's own reproductive choices. The Report discusses the use of genetic testing to identify fetal sex, but takes no position on this, deferring to the then-awaited Report of the Royal Commission on New Reproductive Technologies. Following that Commission's Report, the government of Canada in the middle of 1996 has proposed new legislation, in Bill C-47, that would impose unusually heavy penalties on the supply of genetic diagnosis of the sex of a fetus unless related to a sex-linked genetic disorder.

Beyond the field of reproductive choice, the Report of the Privacy Commissioner addresses normal medical care, where genetic testing can improve both diagnostic accuracy for genetic diseases where symptoms exist, and prediction of later-onset genetic diseases. Mandatory collection of such data by government institutions is prohibited by the *Privacy Act*, but collection of information from voluntary testing is not. The relevant recommendation expresses the limit, however, that personal genetic information collected by government institutions or private physicians providing ordinary (that is, non-reproductive) medical care should be used only to inform a person's own medical choices.

The Report's recommendation on forensic uses of genetic tests balances the need for individual privacy from state intrusion against the public interest in the due administration of criminal justice. It reflects the judicial view expressed in Supreme Court of Canada judgements that unauthorized police searches for and seizures of genetic evidence be disapproved, and that due process of law be observed under perhaps reasonably accommodating legislation. The legal basis for the issue of a search warrant to extract evidence such as a tissue sample from a living person's body for genetic testing is unclear in Canada. Statutory authority to support the practice, such as by minimally invasive recovery of blood or hair samples, from persons convicted of past offences and those under strong suspicion of involvement in a recent, unresolved incident, may seem tolerable.

The Privacy Commissioner's recommendation is that in criminal investigations, suspects should be compelled to provide genetic samples only if specific statutory authority authorizes mandatory recovery and collection. Collection would be restricted to those suspected of a specific crime, and they would have to be suspected on reasonable grounds. For instance, indiscriminate screening of an entire population of an area, such as on grounds of their sex, age-range and ethnic origins, would not be permitted. A related recommendation is that, whether by forensic DNA analysis or genetic screening, mandatory analysis of a suspect's genetic sample should be limited to suggesting or confirming the identity of a suspect, or exonerating the suspect. Genetic screening should not be used to suggest the suspect's psychological characteristics.

It is not uncommon among law-enforcement agencies for a considerable momentum to develop to establish genetic databases and banks of genetic samples to advance crime control by allowing more immediate identification of recidivist offenders. Incentives are particularly strong when brutal crimes are publicized that implicate past offenders and randomly selected victims. The Report cites advocacy in the United Kingdom, for a DNA database on an entire population, regardless of criminal suspicion directed at any member and of any particular offence or type of offence having been committed that might justify a population-wide genetic survey.[43] Arguments in support of a national, regional or local population genetic database include its value not simply for criminal detection and for prompt exoneration of persons whose genetic information differs from that found at the scene of a crime, but for identification of accident victims, demented persons found wandering and, for instance, those found unconscious without identification. These positive benefits could be offered, however, on a voluntary basis, the presumption of innocence protecting those who decline to volunteer.

The Privacy Commissioner's Report considers the potential for intrusions on privacy from mandatory genetic databases (which collect genetic information) and genetic databanks (which collect actual tissue samples amenable to genetic analysis) to be highly damaging to social functioning, and highly objectionable. Addressing genetic information from populations both of persons unsuspected of any crimes and of convicted offenders, Recommendation 11 of the Report states that:

> Governments should not establish banks of genetic samples of convicted persons or of the general population for criminal justice purposes. Governments should not establish genetic databases of the general population for criminal justice purposes. Genetic databases containing identification about

> persons convicted of crimes involving serious violence should not be assembled for criminal investigations or prosecutions without (a) further study of the privacy and other human rights implications and (b) specific authorizing legislation, if the study finds the database to be acceptable.
>
> If genetic databases are to be found acceptable, they should be used only for identification. The information contained in a genetic database and any genetic samples related to the crime should not be used to try to identify other characteristics that may have a genetic link, such as personality.[44]

Research uses of genetic information clearly transcend forensic investigation. The Report recognizes the desirability of using genetic data for population studies of an epidemiological nature, and appears concerned not to compromise necessary studies, but also to maximize protection of individual identities. Observing that "Research is fundamental to progress in the science of genetics", the Report identifies the key issue as "the extent to which personal genetic information should be permitted to be used in research."[45] Its response is formulated in its mildly expressed Recommendation 12, that:

> Wherever possible, genetic research should use anonymous, unlinked genetic samples or information to preserve anonymity.[46]

The Report's discussion of the issue contains the balancing perception that the use of nominal data or samples, should, except in compelling circumstances and with the authority of a governmental or governing body, occur only with consent. Consent is accordingly expected for research access to identifying (that is, nominal) data or samples, coming either from the individual concerned or from a governmental or governing body that bears political and/or legal responsibility for its grant of authorization of access without the concerned individual's consent.

The Report endorses the principles of fair information practices on which the *Privacy Act* is based.[47] A set of recommendations elaborates, refines and supplements provisions of the *Act*, beginning with Recommendation 13, which observes that governmental institutions should generally collect personal genetic information only if specific authority for collection has been legislated by statute. This rule is proposed to apply whether the information becomes available through mandatory testing or voluntary surrender or submission to testing. The following Recommendation requires more than the *Act* offers individuals, since it requires government institutions to tell persons why their personal genetic information is being collected, even if they have no enforceable right under subsection 5(2) of the *Privacy Act* to be told. Similarly, a strict time limit on the retention of data and samples is recommended, and, when exceptionally prolonged retention is justified, extraordinary care to ensure that use is only for the purpose for which collection was justified, or for a consistent purpose.

Recommendation 16[48] addresses quality control of genetic data, to enhance the accuracy and completeness of personal genetic information. Its concerns are, for instance, that only qualified persons conduct genetic tests and interpret their results, and that test results be periodically reviewed to determine whether techniques applied and interpretations proposed some time before remain valid in light of subsequent developments and understanding. Inaccurate and outdated data should be so noted, and where possible corrected, and individuals may need to be asked to allow retesting. The following Recommendation emphasizes the requirement of section 5(1) of the *Privacy Act* that genetic information be collected directly from the person concerned and not, for instance, through the test of a person thought to be a genetic relative. If such indirect testing is the only practicable means of data acquisition, however, it should be clearly explained as such, with details of the beliefs supporting the opinion that the data from the source relate to the person they are claimed to affect.

The three Recommendations beginning at 18 address governmental administrative accountabilities. The first proposes that if data collected for one use are to be subject to a different but "consistent use",[49] that decision shall require the personal approval of the head of the institution and not be delegated. Recommendation 19 similarly requires the institution head's personal consent for specified disclosures of personal genetic information, as a matter of policy. The *Privacy Act* is subject to the ordinary rule of statutory construction that it is superseded by any later conflicting legislation to the extent of the conflict, but the *Act* also provides that it is "subject to any other Act of Parliament",[50] making it subordinate as well to any earlier Act. Accountability of the institution head for compliance with other Acts introduces some degree of rigidity in operation of the *Privacy Act*. Recommendation 20 is that individuals entitled to access to their personal genetic information should also have access to the genetic sample from which such information was derived. The government institution that authorized the original test should bear the cost of retesting and, by implication, be responsible for proper preservation of genetic samples from which it authorizes tests.

The final Recommendations address the private and provincial sectors, and are necessarily tentative because they bring the federal government of Canada close to the limits of its constitutional authority. The penultimate Recommendation 21 depends for its operation on goodwill between the public and private sectors, and between federal and provincial levels of government. It provides that the federal government should explore, with the private sector and with other levels of government, the implementation of policies or laws to improve privacy protection in the private sector. The reference to "other levels of government" clearly applies to provincial and territorial governments, but may also apply to municipal government. Municipalities may operate public health services that use genetic data, for instance in epidemiological studies, and provide clinical health services. However, municipal governmental powers are derived from the authority of provincial government to enact legislation, so that provincial governments can regulate practices of municipalities. Nevertheless, collaboration with municipal government on issues of genetic privacy appears prudent.

The concluding Recommendation 22 similarly urges federal and provincial governments and the private sector to work towards explicit privacy protection, in the form of a right to privacy, in the Canadian *Charter of Rights and Freedoms*, review and reinforcement of the *Privacy Act*, regulation of specific aspects of genetic testing such as forensic DNA analysis, legal and policy regulation of private sector intrusions into genetic privacy, and generally fostering respect for genetic privacy. The extent to which collaboration and common enterprise are needed to this end is shown in the paucity of prevailing protections of genetic privacy under provincial laws.

Provincial Laws

Provincial laws in Canada are not particularly advanced or sensitive on protection of genetic information.[51] Most developed on protection of health information in general are the laws of Quebec.[52] Article 3 of the *Civil Code* of Quebec recognizes that everyone holds personality rights "such as...the right to the inviolability and integrity of the person, and the right to the respect of his name, reputation and privacy." The application of this right is universal, but not absolute, since Article 7 provides that "No right may be exercised with the intention of injuring another or in an excessive and unreasonable manner which is contrary to the requirements of good faith." The duty to act in good faith may limit patients' rights to withhold use of their genetic data that may alert family members to implications of their genetic inheritance and their genetically-conditioned susceptibilities to environments, diets and other potential causes of harm to them or their children.

Article 22 of the *Civil Code* allows research on human tissues, but only with consent of the source, raising questions about the legality of epidemiological studies, including those involving anonymous tissues.[53] The Article provides that:

> A part of the body, whether an organ, tissue or other substance, removed from a person as part of the care he receives may, with his consent or that of a person qualified to give consent for him, be used for the purposes of research.

Although Article 7 limits individuals' ability to deny consent in a way that is excessive or unreasonable and "contrary to the requirements of good faith", it does not appear to justify not requesting consent, as indicated by Article 22, on the ground that it would be unreasonable and a breach of good faith to withhold it.

Two chapters of Quebec legislation have particular significance for management of personal information, namely Chapter A-2.1 concerning public bodies, analogous in part to the federal *Privacy Act*, and Chapter P-39.1 applicable to the private sector. The former, described as *An Act Respecting Access to Documents Held by Public Bodies and the Protection of Personal Information*, applies "whether the documents are recorded in writing or print, on sound tape or film, in computerized form, or otherwise."[54] It therefore governs computerized medical records, but appears limited to recorded documents, so that it may not apply to tissue samples *per se*, whether or not genetic analysis has been undertaken of them. The *Act* provides for individuals' access to documents held by defined public bodies, including health and social services institutions, but section 87.1 allows refusal to afford a person access to information "where, in the opinion of his attending physician, serious harm to the person's health would likely result." In such a case, the section provides that "the public body, on the recommendation of the attending physician, shall determine when the information may be released and inform the person concerned." This allows the person to be appropriately counselled in preparation for gaining access to the information. The *Act* creates the *Commission d'accès à l'information* to administer the *Act*'s provisions on requests for access to information, refusals of requests, appeals, corrections of and, for instance, refusals of corrections of information.

Chapter P-39.1 is more immediately concerned with health information, since hospitals and health care professionals operate in the private sector. Described as *An Act Respecting the Protection of Personal Information in the Private Sector*, the *Act* governs information that relates to an identifiable natural person. It contains provisions to regulate private sector databases and individuals' means to know of their existence, objects, use, locations and the sources of their information, and to achieve correction. Means of securing information confidentiality must be established and notified. Section 13 provides that:

> No person may communicate to a third person the personal information contained in a file he holds on another person, or use it for purposes not relevant to the object of the file, unless the person concerned consents thereto or such communication or use is provided for by this *Act*.

However, no consent is required to communicate necessary information to a person under "the urgency of a situation that threatens the life, health or safety of the person concerned."[55] Information may similarly be given to a person authorized to use it for study, research or statistical purposes in accordance with section 21 of the *Act*, which sets conditions for the Commission established under Chapter A-2.1 on public bodies to approve private sector research.

The *Act* contains provisions on persons' access to information collected concerning themselves, but, with special significance to genetic information, adds in section 31 that:

> The spouse and the direct ascendants or descendants of a deceased person are entitled to receive...communication of information relating to the cause of death contained in the person's medical file, unless the deceased person recorded in writing, in his file, his refusal to grant such right of access.
>
> Notwithstanding the first paragraph, the blood relatives of a deceased person are entitled to receive communication of the information contained in that person's medical file to the extent that such communication is necessary to ascertain the existence of a genetic or family disease.

The *Act* duplicates in the private sector provisions in Chapter A-2.1, section 87.1 on denial or postponement of a person's access to information on advice of that person's attending physician, but conditions refusal on offering the person the possibility of disclosure of information to a health care professional whom that person designates.[56] As under Chapter A-2.1, the Commission constituted by that *Act* has general supervisory jurisdiction on issues of access to information, refusals of access, appeals, corrections of and, for instance, refusals of corrections of information governed by this *Act*.

No other Canadian jurisdiction has legislation of the sophistication and detail of Quebec's measures. Access and privacy legislation of a general nature exists in Alberta, British Columbia, Ontario and Saskatchewan, and Manitoba, New Brunswick, Nova Scotia and the Yukon have legislation on access to personal information. Newfoundland has legislation on privacy. Administrative guidelines on protection of personal information exist in several jurisdictions that may indirectly be given legal effect, such as by expressly or impliedly becoming terms of contracts. However, even in Quebec, no jurisdiction has enacted legislation that deals specifically with health care information. Manitoba and Ontario have recently issued papers on the topic, namely Manitoba Health's Discussion Paper of May 1996 *Privacy Protection of Health Information*, coupled with Manitoba Culture, Heritage and Citizenship's Discussion Paper *Access to Information and Privacy Protection for Manitoba* of the same date, and the Ontario Ministry of Health's June 1996 Consultation Paper *A Legal Framework for Health Information*. These papers pay little if any specific attention to genetic information and sampling.

The Supreme Court of Canada's 1992 judgement in *McInerney v. MacDonald*[57] elaborated on the physician-patient relationship, and securely established its fiduciary character in law. This means that patients have rights to know the significance of medical information regarding themselves, and although they do not have a legal right of direct access to the medical record itself and to read the raw, uninterpreted data it contains, the physician bears the burden of justifying any denial of direct access. Protection of the patient's interests appears the only credible ground of refusal of direct access. Offering to submit the full record to a health professional designated by the patient to interpret it according to the patient's wishes and interests is often a reasonable middle path between outright refusal and complete surrender of possibly counter therapeutic or dysfunctional information. How far the judgement extends to health care practitioners beyond physicians is unclear and, for historical reasons, its application in Quebec may be questioned. However, in light of Quebec's specific legislation, it is improbable that a patient would have to invoke or rely on this judgement.

A further aspect of the fiduciary duty is its application to regulation of disclosures of patients' health information. In posing a trustee-beneficiary relation between physician and patient,[58] the Supreme Court may have recognized physicians' duties or at least their powers to use patients' health information in patients' best interests, and requirements that, in the absence of explicit instructions, they exercise discretion in good faith. Accordingly, a physician may act in apparent breach of confidentiality but in good faith by disclosing, for instance to a patient's sister or brother, the likelihood of the latter conceiving a child with a genetically-related disability, on the basis of genetic information obtained from the patient and evidence of strong emotional family ties. Confidentiality arises at common law as an implied term of a contract or as a standard of care in negligence law, but fiduciary duties are historical creatures of equity. Equity is founded on good conscience, and when provisions or applications of common law and equity are in conflict, equity prevails. Further, a patient's refusal to permit information to be communicated to another person knowing that communication could assist that other or prevent his or her misfortune may dispose a court unsympathetically.

Research

The particular provisions of Quebec's Civil Code accommodate research interests, although it has been seen that uncertainty concerns non-consensual use of patients' tissues for research.[59] In other jurisdictions, research falls under the general law, and ethical codes have legal force when incorporated as terms, usually implied rather than explicit, of agreements such as between research funding agencies and recipient investigators and/or their employing institutions, and between investigators and their institutional employers or grant-managers. In March 1996, a draft *Code of Conduct for Research Involving Humans* was presented for public discussion by the three Canadian federal research funding councils, namely the Medical Research Council of Canada, the Natural Sciences and Engineering Research Council of Canada, and the Social Sciences and Humanities Research Council of Canada. The draft document has received widespread attention, and the Tri-Council Working Group that prepared the March 1996 draft was reconvened, with slightly changed membership, to prepare a new draft by June 1997 that takes account of comments made in response to the initial draft.

The draft *Code* deals with such obvious issues as consent, privacy and confidentiality and access to personal records, but also contains two features of particular concern to DNA sampling and genetic information. It has a section devoted entirely to Human Genetic Research that includes issues of relations between individuals and their families, genetic stigmatization and discrimination, genetic counselling, gene therapy and particularly banking of genetic data, blood and other tissues. Further, the draft *Code* addresses research that involves not only individuals, but groups or collectivities of people. The concern is not so much with statistical or demographic groups constructed by investigators for purposes of study, but with groups that exist self-consciously, independently of any intention to study them. In Canada, aboriginal bands exist and closed communities of often religiously devout historical immigrant populations exist, such as Hutterites and Doukhobors, that have distinctive genetic characteristics. They may also bear genetic consequences of long traditions of marriage and reproduction within restricted family groupings. Some of these populations may be sensitive to genetic studies that make public findings about them as groups, and to their dependence for future health on genetic services offered by institutions that want to investigate them as case-studies in population genetics.

Delicate issues arise for these groups as such and for their individual members, and also for potential investigators, their institutions, research funding agencies and members of research ethics review boards. They concern such matters as group representatives' involvement in research planning, design and execution, collective and individual consents and refusals to research proposals, confidentiality of research data, interpretations of data particularly when investigators and group members do not participate in a common culture and share perspectives and means of comprehension, and publicity of research conclusions. Negotiation and resolution of these issues can be of legal concern, since ethical codes and ethical processes of research protocol review may indirectly be legally enforceable within various funding agency and institutional relationships. Concerns in genetic research with population groups are not unique to Canada, of course, and Canadian responses may not prove to be specially innovative. However, how Canada resolves issues of genetic research with its particularly distinctive populations may contribute experience to other countries as they grapple with their own concerns.

Endnotes and References

1 (1991), 14 *Clinical Investigative Medicine* 363.

2 *R.v. Stewart* (1988), 41 C.C.C.(3d) 481 (S.C.C.).

3 Criminal Code, R.S.C., 1985, c.C-46, s.430.

4 Ibid., ss.430(8) and 342.1.

5 *R.v.Dyment* (1988), 55 D.L.R.(4th) 503 (S.C.C.); see also *R.v.Pohoretsky* (1987), 39 D.L.R.(4th) 699 (S.C.C.).

6 Westin A. F., *Privacy and Freedom* (New York: Atheneum, 1967).

7 Supra note 5, at 513.

8 *Stoffman v. Vancouver General Hospital* (1990), 76 D.L.R.(4th) 200 (S.C.C.)

9 (1993), 85 C.C.C.(3d) 1 (S.C.C.).

10 (1994), 110 D.L.R.(4th) 297, (S.C.C.).

11 Leenen H., S. Gevers and G. Pinet, *The Rights of Patients in Europe* (Deventer: Kluwer, 1993). See also, Giesen D., *International Medical Malpractice Law* (Tübingen: Mohr (Paul Siebeck)), 1988).

12 *Reibl v. Hughes* (1980), 114 D.L.R.(3d) 1 (S.C.C.).

13 *Sidaway v. Board of Governors of the Bethlem Royal Hospital and Maudsley Royal Hospital*, [1985] 1 All E.R. 643 (H.L.).

14 *Rogers v. Whitaker* (1992), 109 A.L.R. 625 (H.Ct.Aust.).

15 Supra note 5, at 522.

16 (1992), 93 D.L.R. (4th) 415 (S.C.C.).

17 Dickens B.M., "Case Comment on *McInerney v. MacDonald*" (1994), 73 *Canadian Bar Review* 234.

18 Government of Ontario, Ministry of Health, *A Legal Framework for Health Information: Consultation Paper*, (Toronto: Ministry of Health, 1996) at 2.

19 R.S.C., 1985, c.P.-21.

20 R.S.C. 1985, Appendix II No.44, enacted by the *Canada Act 1982* (U.K.), c.11.

21 Supra note 8.

22 Supra note 19, at s.4.

23 Ibid., s.5(1).

24 Ibid., s.5(2); subsections (1) and (2) do not apply where compliance may result in inaccurate information or defeat or prejudice the purpose of collection.

25 Ibid., s.7.

26 Ibid., s.8(1).

27 Ibid., s.6(2).

28 Ibid., s.6(1).

29 Ibid., s.12(1).

30 Ibid., s12(2)(a).

31 Ibid., s.12(2)(b).

32 Ibid., s.12(2)(c).

33 Ibid., s.3.

34 Ibid., s.18.

35 Ibid., s.21.

36 Ibid., s.22.

37 See text at note 29 above.

38 Supra note 19, at s.41.

39 Ibid., s.3.

40 Privacy Commission of Canada, *Genetic Testing and Privacy* (Ottawa: Minister of Supply and Services Canada, 1992) at 3.

41 Ibid., Recommendation 2, at 31.

42 Ibid., Recommendation 6, at 39.

43 Ibid., at 46-48.

44 Ibid., at 50.

45 Ibid.

46 Ibid., at 51.

47 See text above between notes 21 and 32.

48 Supra note 40, at 68.

49 See text above at note 25, regarding the *Privacy Act*, s.7.

50 Supra note 19, s.8(2).

51 See generally, *Legal Rights and Human Genetic Material* Knoppers B.M., T. Caulfield and T.D. Kinsella, eds., (Toronto: Emond Montgomery Publications Ltd, 1996).

52 Hirtle M., "Civil Law and the Status of Human Genetic Material", ibid. at 85-116.

53 Ibid., at 93.

54 Chapter A-2.1, s.1.

55 Chapter P-39.1, s.18(7).

56 Ibid., s.37.

57 Supra note 16.

58 Supra note 17.

59 Supra note 52.

DIFFERING PERSPECTIVES ON CONSENT, CHOICE AND CONTROL

ROBERT F. WEIR

Program Director in Biomedical Ethics and Humanities

University of Iowa College of Medicine

The interim report of the Task Force on Genetic Testing, a task force of the National Institutes of Health/Department of Energy Working Group on the ethical, legal, and social implications (ELSI) of human genome research, states at one point that "the ethical propriety of not informing people about anonymous use [of stored DNA samples] in situations in which the specimen is going to be collected for another purpose is currently being debated outside the Task Force".[1] With that simple statement, the Task Force pointed to an important debate that has been taking place in the United States in recent years regarding the issues of consent, choice, and control over stored DNA samples.

In terms of consent, the debate has focused on questions related to the disclosures that should be made to patients and participants in research studies in order for these persons to be able to give informed consent to the use(s) of their stored biological materials, including (1) blood and other tissue samples and (2) possibly an immortalized cell line made from an original tissue sample. Should such persons, for example, be told about the common scientific practice of secondary use of stored DNA samples, the practice mentioned by the Task Force?

In terms of choice, the debate has featured differing perspectives related to whether patients and research participants should be given an opportunity to express preferences about the use(s) of their stored DNA samples. For instance, should these persons be given options regarding (1) the anonymization of their DNA samples, (2) the scientific purpose(s) for which the tissue sample or cell line can be used, and (3) future access by third parties to the personal information that may be gained from their stored biological materials and placed in a DNA databank, or should scientific investigators continue to make these decisions about DNA samples in their labs?

In terms of control, the debate has demonstrated varied positions regarding the legal and moral status of stored DNA samples. For example, do DNA samples remain the property of the individual source of the tissue samples, even though the samples reside in one or more forms in one or more scientific laboratories? Or do DNA samples become the property of the investigator, university, or company carrying out the scientific studies with the samples, thus enabling genetics researchers to determine the length of time the DNA samples will be stored and the scientific purpose(s) for which they will be used? Or is it preferable to divide control in some manner between the parties (the individual source of the DNA sample and the investigator(s) working with the sample), in terms of sequential ownership or conditional gifts?

My purposes in this paper are threefold. First, I will present the origins of this recent debate in the U.S.A. Second, I will describe the major positions in the debate and several of the significant developments to date. Third, I will use two empirical studies as examples to show why the issues of consent, choice, and control need to be given more attention by investigators and participants in genetics studies using stored DNA samples.

Origins of the Debate

The debate over the appropriate use of stored tissue samples has been simmering for a number of years and has revealed several different positions regarding the questions of consent, choice, and control.[2] The media in the United States has tended to focus on parental disputes over cryopreserved pre-embryos in assisted reproduction programs, the use of stored neonatal blood spots for anonymous epidemiological studies of HIV prevalence, and the federal government's requirement that military personnel provide blood samples and cheek swabs for military identification purposes to the Department of Defense's DNA databank.

However, for biomedical scientists and for government-mandated committees established to protect the interests of participants in research studies, the important implications of the debate over stored tissue samples were first seen most clearly in an otherwise noncontroversial series of studies carried out by the Centers for Disease Control and Prevention (CDC). Since the 1960s, more than 70,000 persons have participated in the National Health and Nutrition Surveys (NHANES). The third National Health and Nutrition Survey (NHANES III) is different from the previous two surveys in that it is the only national survey in which physician examinations are performed to measure an individual's health. Beginning in the 1980s, NHANES III had multiple purposes: to provide a natural history of diseases in the population, to give an accurate description of the distribution of diseases in the country, to monitor changes in the health of the population, to study the etiology of diseases, and to establish empirical data for recommended changes in health policy (e.g., unleaded gas).

The NHANES III methodology consisted of identifying 40,000 sample persons in 26 states; selecting high sample rates for certain groups (e.g., children, older adults, racial minority groups); interviewing 30,000 of the persons regarding nutrition, reproductive health, physical activity, mental health, and health habits; giving them an extensive physical examination with multiple lab tests of blood and urine; doing a home study examination regarding socio-economic status, demographic information, and environmental influences; and promising a long-term follow-up ("After several years, we will check back with you to note any changes in your health."). All of the medical and health data was linked to other personal information to facilitate the multiple purposes of the study and to make long-term follow-up more valuable. By the mid-1990s, the CDC scientists had also produced an archive of approximately 17,000 tissue samples, including immortalized cell lines from approximately 9,000 persons.

To meet the ethical and legal requirements for informed consent, the NHANES III administrators, working with the Institutional Review Board (IRB) at the CDC, initially prepared a very detailed and technical statement on consent to be given to prospective participants in the study. That document was later judged to be too technically difficult, and it was replaced by a simple 6-page booklet with pictures. The only language in the booklet that pertains to informed consent for banked samples is a one-sentence, descriptive statement: "A small sample of your blood will be kept in long-term storage for future testing".[3]

In early 1994, some officials at the CDC faced a major problem. On the one hand, they possessed an invaluable "national treasure chest" of health information on a cross-section of the U.S. population and an unmatched archive of DNA samples for biomedical research. On the other hand, they wondered (in the light of recent professional literature on molecular genetics and ethics) if the CDC scientists had adequately informed the sample population regarding the planned storage and scientific uses of their blood samples, if persons in the study population had understood themselves to be consenting to long-term research on their banked blood samples (given the single sentence statement buried in 6 pages of descriptive text and pictures about NHANES III), and if the CDC would need to get additional, more specific consent (at an estimated cost of $2 million) from these persons before carrying out the planned research with the stored samples.

Because of this concern at the CDC, a meeting was held at the National Institutes of Health (NIH) in July, 1994, to address questions related to "Informed Consent for Genetic Studies Using Stored Tissue Samples." The meeting was jointly planned by representatives from the CDC and the National Center for Human Genome Research (NCHGR) at the NIH. Several persons invited to participate in the meeting had previously received funding from the ELSI (ethical, legal, and social implications of genetics) branch of the NCHGR. The planned purpose of the meeting was to produce a consensus statement regarding informed consent and the use of stored tissue samples in genetics, whether at the CDC or elsewhere. An initial version of the statement was drafted by a small group under the leadership of Ellen Wright Clayton, M.D., J.D., who chaired the meeting. However, the desired "consensus" proved difficult to accomplish, with the group expressing important differences over traditional research uses of stored tissue samples, the meaning and necessity of informed consent in the context of archival samples, the ownership and control of stored samples, the impracticability of recontacting persons for consent to anonymize stored samples, and the limits to be placed on the use of anonymized samples. As it turned out, this group discussion at the CDC/NIH meeting foreshadowed much more specific positions in the debate that appeared the following year.

Positions in the Debate about Consent, Choice, and Control

In early 1995, George Annas, J.D., along with Leonard Glantz, J.D., and Patricia Roche, J.D., began distributing a model piece of legislation that had been drafted with ELSI funding through the Department of Energy. Called "*The Genetic Privacy Act*" (GPA), the model Act is intended as a proposal for federal legislation, although it could be, and has been proposed as well for state legislation.[4] The GPA is based on four premises: genetic information is different from other types of personal information; the genetic information contained in DNA is like a "coded probabilistic future diary"; this information can be accessible to many parties in the era of molecular biology; and, because of the highly personal nature of the information and its accessibility, individually identifiable DNA samples need to be protected by law. Consequently, the overarching premise of the GPA is that "no stranger should have or control identifiable DNA samples or genetic information about an individual unless that individual specifically authorizes the collection of DNA samples for the purpose of genetic analysis, authorizes the creation of that private information, and has access to and control over the dissemination of that information" (**emphasis** added).[5]

The proposed GPA frequently addresses the questions of consent, choice, and control, with most of the proposed legislation's answers to these questions depending on the identity status of stored DNA samples: whether the samples are identified to an individual source, linkable to that source, completely anonymous as to individual origination, or anonymized after collection. The central claim in the GPA is that individually identifiable DNA samples are the property of the person from whom they come (identified as the "sample source"). Therefore, if tissue samples will be individually identifiable, the Act states that the sample source must grant advance authorization in writing to the collection, storage, and proposed use(s) of the samples, as well as to the possible disclosure of private genetic information gained from genetic analysis. In addition, the sample source (or that person's representative in the event of incompetence or death) has a number of rights: to revoke consent to genetic analysis at "any time prior to the completion of the analysis," to inspect records that contain information derived from a genetic analysis, to prohibit the use of the DNA sample for research or commercial purposes "even if the sample is not in an individually identifiable form," to consent (with 45 days advance notice) to the transfer of a DNA sample to other scientists for secondary research purposes, and to order the destruction of the DNA sample upon the research study's completion or the withdrawal of the sample source from the study.

By contrast, the GPA would permit anonymous tissue samples to be used for research purposes if such use was not previously prohibited by the sample source. The authors emphasize: "Nothing in this Act shall be construed as prohibiting or limiting research on a DNA sample that cannot be linked to any individual identifier".[6] Moreover, research by pathologists, geneticists, and other medical investigators can be done on archival tissue samples, even if the stored samples are individually identifiable, as long as the samples were stored "prior to the effective date of this Act." However, no individually identifiable genetic information may be disclosed without the authorization of the sample source's representative.

In late 1995, two published papers staked out additional positions in the developing debate. The first paper was a position statement of the American College of Medical Genetics (ACMG), written by John Phillips, M.D., and other members of the ACMG Storage of Genetics Materials Committee.[7] Emphasizing the importance of informed consent, the authors make several recommendations regarding the storage and use of genetic materials that are obtained for clinical tests. They recommend that patients be informed about the purpose and possible outcomes of the genetic test, the anticipated use of the blood or other tissue sample (including whether the sample will be stored for additional scientific purposes), and their options regarding future access to the genetic information and the possibility of subsequently requesting that the samples be destroyed. They also recommend that if samples are going to be stored, patients should be asked for permission to use the samples and the derivative genetic information in counselling and testing their relatives, and for permission to anonymize the samples for the purposes of additional scientific research.

In terms of tissue samples that are obtained for investigation purposes, the ACMG committee recommends that potential participants in research be informed about the purpose and possible outcomes of the current research study, the investigator(s)' policy regarding the length of storage time for samples and subsequent destruction of samples, and the possibility that the research may lead to the development of diagnostic tests having several related issues (e.g., the possible need to disclose personal genetic information in a family setting, and the remote chance that diagnostic tests will be commercially profitable). They also recommend that research participants be asked for permission to anonymize their tissue samples for other types of research, and to recontact them for additional consent for (currently unknown) future research efforts with their stored samples. As to research on archival samples, the committee simply points out the inherent conflict between the desirability (in terms of ethics and law) of recontacting individuals to secure their informed consent for ongoing research studies and the impracticability (in many research settings) of recontacting persons from whom samples were previously collected, but makes no specific recommendations regarding how this conflict can or should be resolved.

The second paper, the report coming out of the CDC/NIH meeting, was controversial before and after its publication. Written by Ellen Wright Clayton and several other persons with diverse professional backgrounds, the paper "Informed Consent for Genetic Research on Stored Tissue Samples" was supported by most of the individuals who attended the 1994 meeting.[8] However, portions of the paper were unacceptable to some geneticists at the meeting who work with archival tissue samples, and they refused to be signatories of the document.

The Clayton et al. document emphasizes the importance of conducting research with stored tissue samples within the ethical and legal framework provided by federal regulations for the protection of human subjects, and by local review by IRBs. The document addresses a range of situations and questions pertaining to genetic research on stored tissue samples: (1) whether anonymous samples for research are exempt from federal regulations regarding informed consent, (2) whether removing identifiers from existing samples can be done without the consent of the individual "source" of the sample, (3) whether limits (related to the preferences of sources, or the psychosocial risks of the research) need to be placed on the use of linkable or identified samples for research, (4) whether genetic research can be done on samples (in pathology or elsewhere) obtained from persons who subsequently died, (5) whether tissue samples from children can be used in genetic research, and (6) whether public health investigations involving genetic studies can be done without the consent of the tissue sources.

The consensus document makes several specific recommendations. In terms of tissue samples that have already been collected, the document emphasizes the distinction between anonymous samples and samples that are identifiable or linkable at the time a research project is proposed. Samples that are already anonymous (e.g., anonymous pathological samples that might be used for a genetics study) do not require informed consent for the obvious reason that it is impossible to identify the individual source directly or indirectly. Even genetic studies with anonymous samples, however, should be reviewed by IRBs, at least in part to determine if the desired scientific information could be obtained in a protocol that allows individuals to consent. By contrast, stored samples that are currently identified or linkable to the individual source (e.g., samples originally obtained for diagnostic purposes, numerous kinds of pathological samples) require informed consent by that person if investigators plan to do genetic studies on the samples without anonymizing them.

What about the fairly common practice whereby investigators take existing identified or linkable samples and make them anonymous for use in research by removing all identifiers or linking codes? Current federal regulations permit this practice of anonymizing samples without the consent of the individual source. For the writers of this document, this practice is problematic, sometimes disingenuous, and occasionally deceptive when, for example, clinician investigators obtain a tissue sample for diagnostic purposes, know that they plan later to anonymize the sample for research purposes, do not convey that information to the source of the sample, and subsequently remove the identifiers without consent. Consequently, the writers recommend that this practice be curtailed by changing the federal regulations and by having IRBs weigh the benefits of any such proposed research with to-be-anonymized tissues against the difficulty of requiring the investigators to recontact the individual sources for their consent for such anonymization.

In terms of collecting samples in the future, the document is quite clear about the questions of consent and choice: "People should have the opportunity to decide whether their samples will be used for research."[9] In clinical and in research settings, information about possible research studies with tissue samples should be provided to individuals when their tissue samples are collected. Whenever individuals agree to such research use of their tissues, the writers of this document recommend that they be given the following options: (1) whether they are willing to have their samples used in identifiable or linked research (with appropriate information about confidentiality, psychosocial risks, and possible withdrawal from the study) and (2) whether they prefer or are willing to have their samples stripped of identifiers and linking codes for use in research (again, with appropriate information about the investigators' personal interests, possible commercial benefit, and so on). Additional recommendations involve giving research participants other choices about the research use of their tissue samples: whether they are willing to have their tissues shared with other scientists for secondary research purposes, whether they want to limit their tissue samples to certain kinds of research studies, and whether they want to restrict their tissue samples from being used in scientific studies they do not want to support.

Critical responses to the Clayton et al. consensus statement began even before the paper was published. Wayne Grody, M.D., Ph.D., wrote a sharply critical editorial in Diagnostic Molecular Pathology about the consensus statement when the paper was still in final draft form, arguing that the traditional practices ("as long as anyone can remember") of pathology were threatened by an undue ELSI emphasis on informed consent.[10] Stating incorrectly that the paper had been written by members of the ELSI Working Group, a group "too heavily weighted toward the ethicists and lawyers at the expense of the views of working geneticists," he said that the recommendations of the consensus document "would severely restrict access to archival clinical specimens for molecular genetic research and other purposes."[11] The recommended choices to be given patients about the uses of their tissue samples would require "a multitiered consent form with more options and permutations than an airline frequent-flyer program." Moreover, the same lengthy consent form would have to be administered to patients in all sorts of settings: "every phlebotomy, urinalysis, sputum collection, and even haircut." If actually put into practice, "these restrictive and burdensome policies would seriously impede, or completely block, a major proportion of molecular research on human disease, especially impacting those research questions that can be addressed in no other way than through retrospective study of large numbers of archival specimens."[12]

Soon thereafter, a "Rapid Action Task Force" (RATF) of the American Society of Human Genetics (ASHG) circulated a draft proposal regarding "Informed Consent for Genetic Research."[13] Chaired by Edward McCabe, M.D. and comprised of ten members (including John Phillips and Wayne Grody), the

RATF draft criticizes the Clayton et al. document by affirming the "traditional research practices in human genetics" and calling for the development of consent forms that are "as clear and brief as possible." Accepting virtually all of the consensus statement's recommendations regarding prospective genetic research, the RATF's important differences with the earlier document pertain to archival samples, such as those contained in pathological laboratories and newborn screening laboratories.

Like the earlier document, the RATF draft endorses "the use of anonymous samples for genetic research, subject to institutional review." Like the earlier document, the RATF draft says that consent should be obtained for research involving samples that retain identifiers. But unlike the earlier document, the RATF draft proposes to maintain the traditional practice of anonymizing existing tissue samples without consent. For the RATF group, it is important to be able to do genetic research on both (1) anonymous samples ("biological materials that were originally collected without identifiers and are impossible to link to their sources") and (2) anonymized samples ("biological materials that were initially identified, but have been irreversibly stripped of all identifiers and are impossible to link to their sources [but may be linkable] with clinical, pathological and demographic information [gained] before the subject identifiers are removed"). They state that the practice of anonymizing samples without consent has two important benefits: it reduces the "chance of introducing bias" in a study by means of an incomplete study sample (some persons may refuse to consent, and others may be impossible to contact for additional consent), and "importantly, making samples anonymous will eliminate the need for [investigators to] recontact [sources] to obtain informed consent."[14]

In January 1996, additional concerns were expressed by some geneticists and pathologists attending a meeting convened by the NCHGR on "Genetics Research on Human Tissues: Conflicting Implications for Scientific Discovery, Informed Consent, and Privacy." As Richard Lynch, M.D., observed at the meeting, the role of pathologists as legal custodians of stored diagnostic tissue samples largely involves noncontroversial investigations of anonymous, anonymized, and identifiable tissue samples, with biomedical benefits arising from each kind of research. He commented: "99% of what pathologists do with stored tissues is just aimed at better characterizing a lesion that already exists and has been excised by the surgeon."[15] But as pointed out by privacy advocates at the meeting, problems arise when the tissue samples are subjected to genetic tests that may reveal personal genetic information that was neither known nor anticipated by the patient, the surgeon, or the pathologist, and that may now involve substantial psychosocial risks for the source of the tissue sample and relatives of that person.

Alternative Solutions

What should be done regarding the questions of consent, choice, and control of stored tissue samples? What possible solutions are available that can help us manage the complexities and conflicts over stored tissue samples in the era of molecular genetics?

As indicated by the chronological developments and positions just described, six possible solutions have been suggested and/or tried. One possible solution is to retain as many traditional research practices as possible, especially regarding retrospective research on archival samples. As illustrated by Wayne Grody's editorial and by the RATF proposals to the ASHG, there are some pathologists and geneticists who want to downplay the importance of informed consent with stored tissue samples and thereby to continue traditional research practices, especially the practice of anonymizing samples in pathology laboratories and newborn screening laboratories. The RATF proposal, while emphasizing the importance of informed consent in prospective studies, clearly favours placing greater weight on traditional research practices than on considerations of informed consent when the stored samples in question are samples that have been, and could continue to be, anonymized without the consent of the sample sources, their relatives, or surrogates.

The RATF proposal contains suggested guidelines for the need to obtain informed consent in genetic research, organized by the level of anonymity in a research study. The guidelines indicate that no informed consent is needed for retrospective studies using anonymous samples, or anonymized samples, or even identifiable (or linkable) samples whenever a waiver of federal consent requirements is secured for studies involving minimal risk to the research participants.[16] Although the guidelines state that "consent must be obtained for all new projects" using existing samples, they immediately point out that investigators can apply for a waiver under the National Research Act for studies involving minimal risk to participants. They do not point out that the "minimal risk" language in the federal regulations was written years before concerns were expressed about the psychosocial risks connected with genetics studies.

As to the practice of anonymizing existing samples without consent, the RATF proposal strongly supports the practice. The RATF group makes only a passing comment about the appropriateness of IRB review of studies using anonymized samples, and then only "when there is available medical intervention for the disorder being tested, or if there is a finite sample quantity."[17] No mention is made of possible ways of anonymizing samples in an expanded context of informed consent, either by (1) recontacting the still-identifiable adult sources before anonymizing the samples (as had been discussed in the CDC/NIH meeting and Clayton et al. paper) or (2) initiating a request to an adult sample source (or the parent(s) of a neonatal sample source) for consent to anonymize samples for research purposes before the samples gain the status of "existing" or archival samples.

A second possible solution is to recommend new professional society guidelines that can update and change professional practices in the light of new technological developments and new ethical and legal concerns about stored samples. The strongest feature of this possible solution is the importance placed on self-governance and change from within professional ranks, with the hope that choosing to adopt peer-influenced change will preclude imposed change from forces outside the profession (e.g., by law, federal regulations, or patient-advocacy groups).

Thus the Storage of Genetics Materials Committee produced a position statement for the that briefly interpreted the concept of informed consent in the context of stored tissue samples, and then gave a series of recommendations regarding the collection of tissue samples for prospective genetic tests in clinical and research settings, and the currently acceptable uses of stored DNA or genetic materials. Likewise, the Rapid Action Task Force made a proposal to the American Society of Human Genetics regarding the application of informed-consent considerations to genetics studies using prospectively collected samples and retrospective studies of existing samples. Both documents may turn out to be helpful resources for updated information and recommended change. However, both documents have serious flaws: the ACMG document fails to make several needed recommendations pertaining to DNA banking and informed consent, and the RATF document seems, at least on the issue of anonymized samples, to be a proposal that is primarily protective of the research interests of some of its authors. The published version of the RATF document, as revised by the Board of Directors of the American Society of Human Genetics, is even more protective of the research interests of investigators who use anonymized samples without consent.[18]

A third possible solution is to try to arrive at consensus about acceptable research practices through special meetings of interested parties who have conflicting interests and concerns about stored DNA samples. This is the solution currently favoured by the NCHGR at the NIH, as illustrated by the multidisciplinary meetings it planned and hosted in July, 1994, and January, 1996. In the first of these meetings, representatives from the CDC and NCHGR met with invited genetics investigators, ethicists, attorneys, and patient advocates in the hope of reaching agreement on whether the CDC could proceed to do research on its 17,000 tissue samples, or whether investigators at the CDC and elsewhere need to gain more specific consent of individual sources before carrying out research on identifiable and/or anonymized tissue samples. In the 1996 meeting, several leading pathologists were invited to meet with NCHGR representatives, ELSI representatives, advocates for physicians and biomedical investigators, and patient advocates in order to enable the pathologists to express professional concerns over the issue of informed consent and stored tissues. Neither meeting resulted in unanimous agreement of the participants, but both meetings were educationally and politically beneficial. Both meetings also ended with a renewed sense that compromise was possible on at least some of the issues in question, with several participants voicing hope for soon achieving a reasonable balance between the rights of individual patients and research participants, and the practices and interests of biomedical professionals. How much compromise is actually achieved remains to be seen, given the vested interests and high stakes involved in the debate.

A fourth possible solution is to recommend changes in the federal regulations and IRB review practices pertaining to genetics studies using human participants and stored tissue samples. The clearest example of this approach is the Clayton et al. paper published in JAMA. This document states that the authors place considerable weight on the federal regulations regarding the protection of human subjects (and related publications by the federal Office for Protection from Research Risks) because the regulations "are legally enforceable and because they are the embodiment of an attempt to strike a balance between the desire to increase knowledge and the protection of individual interests."[19] The document therefore quotes the federal regulations at numerous places in the text and sometimes goes to considerable lengths to show how the regulations can and should apply to some important research issues that have developed since the regulations were written, namely the emerging questions about the collection and use of stored tissue samples.

Nevertheless, this proposed solution depends not merely on professionals in multiple fields being able to know, interpret, and apply the federal regulations to state-of-the-art concerns about the collection and use of stored DNA samples, but more importantly being able to bring about changes in the regulations (and their use by IRBs) so that they will continue to balance the competing interests of scientific investigators and individuals (and families) who participate in research studies. Therefore the Clayton et al. paper indicates several ways in which the regulations need to be updated, clarified, and changed to provide needed guidance for investigators and the IRB members who review their research proposals: the appropriate limits to be placed on genetics studies with anonymous samples, IRB review of studies using anonymous samples, the practice of anonymizing existing samples, the limits of impracticability in securing consent, and the degree of deference to be given to individuals' preferences not to have their tissue samples used for specific types of genetic research.

A fifth possible solution is to produce updated consent forms in clinical and research settings that more accurately describe current research practices with stored samples and more adequately enable individuals to make informed choices about how their DNA samples (and personal genetic information contained therein) are to be used. The ACMG committee, the Clayton et al. group, and the RATF group all seem to assume that most of the conflicts over stored samples can be addressed by means of (1) more appropriately worded consent documents and (2) improved IRB review of research protocols using identified, linkable, anonymous, or anonymized tissue samples. The catch, of course, is whether updated consent forms will be more protective of the rights of individual sources to make informed-consent choices about their banked tissues, or of the professional interests of biomedical investigators. The challenge will be to see if multidisciplinary interests can be reflected in updated consent documents that contain workable compromises, such as including modest amounts of information to patients about pathological research practices in surgical consent forms before any biological samples are collected as part of the surgery.[20]

The sixth possible solution is to mandate by law the changes in the era of genetic medicine that are necessary to protect individuals from unauthorized analysis of their DNA samples, unauthorized disclosure of personal genetic information resulting from genetics studies, and unauthorized transfer of their stored biological materials to other investigators. The clearest and most comprehensive attempt to work on this solution is the proposed GPA written by Annas, Glantz, and Roche. According to this model piece of legislation, an individual "sample source" has property rights to his or her DNA samples and therefore can determine who may collect and analyze a blood or other tissue sample, limit the purposes for which a DNA sample can be analyzed, know what information can reasonably be expected from the genetic tests, order the destruction of stored DNA samples, delegate authority to a surrogate to order the destruction of stored DNA samples, prohibit even the anonymous use of their samples in research, refuse to permit the use of the DNA sample(s) for research or commercial activities, and inspect (and obtain) copies of records containing information derived from genetic analysis of the DNA sample(s).[21]

This proposed solution is, of course, quite different from the other strategies. Rather than relying on peer-influenced change, consensus-driven change, or updated changes in regulations and consent forms, this approach would force change through the power of law and the threat of legal penalties. Thus the proposed GPA has a section on civil remedies according to which a person (e.g., a clinician, a biomedical investigator, a professional in a biomedical lab) who violates the provisions of the GPA through negligence would be liable for a $25,000 fine plus other monetary damages, and a person who wilfully violates the GPA would be liable for a $50,000 fine plus other monetary damages.

As with the other proposed solutions, it remains to be seen whether this proposal will actually work. At the present time, the GPA remains a controversial proposal for a model law that has been frequently discussed, widely praised, and occasionally rejected as unnecessary and counterproductive to biomedical progress.[22,23,24]

Two Studies of Consent, Choice, and Control in DNA Banking

Two studies conducted in the United States in recent years have focused on the issues of consent, choice, and control in the context of DNA Banking. Both studies involve consent forms developed for genetics research. One study examines a number of actual consent documents used by genetics investigators to see what information research participants are being given about DNA banking with their tissue samples, including information related to choices they may have and the control and ownership of their samples. The other study involves a model consent document and the attitudes of possible participants in genetics research to see what they think about the content of the model form, including content related to the issues of choice and control.

The first study was carried out under my direction in 1994 by persons in the ELSI core of the Cooperative Human Linkage Center at the University of Iowa. The study involved the collection and analysis of numerous consent documents from genetics investigators in 47 states and the District of Columbia, with some of the consent documents coming from a randomized survey and other documents coming from nonrandomized requests for consent forms from university-based investigators in three states. The randomized survey produced 79 usable consent documents, with documents being supplied by 50 investigators in 25 states and the District of Columbia; the nonrandomized phase of the study resulted in 24 usable documents. The survey therefore produced a total of 103 consent documents. Of these 103 consent documents, 23 documents explicitly asked potential research participants for consent for planned DNA banking or contained language informing potential research participants that the investigators wanted to have permission to store their tissue samples or transformed cell lines for subsequent research.[25,26]

We subsequently analyzed these 23 consent documents for content using the standard of a "reasonable person" (or, more correctly, a combination of reasonable persons) whose consent is being sought by a genetics investigator for a research project that will include the long-term storage of biological materials. What kinds of information would a reasonable person want to have about the planned DNA banking before he or she agrees to supply a tissue sample? What kinds of concerns or questions would a reasonable person have regarding the storage of blood or other biological materials from his or her body for a period of years in a genetics laboratory? In particular, what kinds of questions might a reasonable person have regarding the issues of informed consent to participate in the research study, personal choices related to the handling and scientific use(s) of the stored biological materials, and control of the biological materials and genetic data derived from them once the samples are in a genetics lab?

We concluded that a reasonable person in this kind of situation would likely ask some or all of the following questions:

1. Will information about my banked sample (or my DNA) get into the wrong hands?
2. It is my banked sample (or my DNA), right?
3. Can I withdraw my banked sample from this research project at any time?
4. How long do you plan to keep my banked sample (or my DNA)?
5. If you find out something important about me from my banked sample, will you tell me? What if I don't want to have that information?
6. Will other people in the future have access to genetic information about me?

7. Will other scientists do experiments with my banked sample (or my DNA) for other purposes?[27]

We proposed that these items of concern represent seven "categories of content" that should be present in all documents seeking consent for DNA banking. All of the categories of content involve concerns about choices and control that prospective participants in genetics studies might reasonably be expected to have. In particular, such individuals are likely to have concerns related to personal choice, as indicated by the questions seeking information about how long the biological samples will be stored, the disclosure of personal information to the sample source that might have clinical significance, and the exercise of the right to withdraw from the scientific study (questions 3-5). Such persons can also be expected to have concerns related to control, as indicated by the questions seeking information about the confidentiality and privacy of the stored samples and derivative data, the ownership of the banked sample, the future access of third parties to the personal genetic data, and the possible use of the stored biological materials for scientific purposes other than the purposes for which they were originally requested (questions 1-2, 6-7).

Unfortunately, the Iowa study demonstrated that many of the consent documents currently being used by genetics investigators do not provide this kind of information to potential participants in the research. The large majority of the 23 documents (ranging from 13 documents to 21 documents, depending on the item being analyzed) fail to provide sufficient information about planned DNA banking to enable a reasonable person to make an informed decision about participation in such a study. The result is that many genetics investigators seem to be asking individuals to agree to participate in their research studies without adequately addressing (and often, even mentioning) these areas of concern about choice and control in the consent documents they use in connection with those studies. To do so seems to reserve all of the control over the banked samples and most of the choices about the banked samples for the investigators themselves.[28]

The second study was carried out in 1996 by Jon Merz, Pamela Sankar, and other persons affiliated with the Center for Bioethics and a developing DNA Bank at the University of Pennsylvania. In contrast to the Iowa study, this study of DNA banking and informed consent explores the attitudes of a group of lay persons to the possibility of donating blood samples to a DNA Bank funded in part by a pharmaceutical company. The methodology used in the study consists of developing a model consent document, using a questionnaire with several groups to test the language and content of the model document, and having a group of volunteer lay persons read the model document, fill out the questionnaire, and thereby provide information regarding the views that donors to the developing DNA Bank might be expected to have about several items of choice and control related to their stored DNA samples.[29]

The model consent form has a 9th grade reading level. The document begins with fairly simple but potentially quite helpful information about genes, the benefits of research with genes, and the DNA Bank at the Hospital of the University of Pennsylvania. The document then provides information about the physical risks of a blood draw, the voluntariness of supplying a blood sample to the DNA Bank, the planned anonymity of the blood samples in the bank, the confidentiality with which the samples and their derivative genetic data will be maintained, and the joint funding of the DNA Bank by the University of Pennsylvania and a pharmaceutical company. Regarding items of choice, the only option the model form offers is a choice about being contacted in the future by genetics investigators for additional information or participation in specific genetics studies. In terms of the issue of control, the model form is very specific: blood samples will be regarded as gifts, the stored samples and derivative genetic data will be the "exclusive property of the hospital", donors will not get any financial compensation if "commercial uses or products" result from the research, the DNA Bank will be able to destroy the stored samples and derivative data "at any time without notice" to the donor or the donor's family, and any future effort by the donor or the donor's family to have access to the stored blood samples and derivative data may or may not be possible because "genes may be lost, ruined, or used up."[30]

After some preliminary testing, the model document and questionnaire were first used with a group of 99 prospective jurors at the Philadelphia County Courthouse. The questionnaire largely consists of a series of 21 yes/no and true/false questions testing comprehension and understanding of the consent form. However, the questionnaire goes beyond the model form by also seeking information about some possible choices that prospective donors to the DNA Bank might have with a revised or different form: the choice of anonymized or coded samples, the choice of restricting research on a donated sample(s) to certain diseases and conditions, and the choice of preventing pharmaceutical companies from using a donated sample(s) in their studies. Moreover, the questionnaire asks if these prospective jurors (and possible donors) would be offended if their donated samples were used by investigators to "patent inventions resulting from this research," or if they think they would "deserve a share of the profits" from any successful products resulting from research with their donated samples.[31]

The results from the questionnaire are interesting, especially in terms of what they say about informed consent, choice, and control. In terms of the consent document itself, the prospective jurors indicate that they found the model form relatively easy to understand, but thought the 3-page form provided them with too much information. As to matters of choice, 60% of the prospective jurors indicate that they would choose, at least hypothetically, to donate to the DNA Bank. Of those choosing to donate, 84% state that they would agree to be contacted again in the future. Regarding other choices, the prospective jurors are evenly split regarding having their blood samples anonymized or coded, and most of them indicate that they would not want to limit the scientific use of their donated samples to certain diseases, that they are not bothered by the potential commercial aspects of this research, and that they do not think they would deserve a share of any profits resulting from the research. As to the issue of control, most of the prospective jurors in this study are apparently not concerned about their donated samples becoming the property of the university, the possible commercial profits that might result from the research, or their own limited access in the future to the samples and personal genetic information stored in the DNA Bank.

In conclusion, the debate over informed consent, choice, and control of stored tissue samples continues in the United States. A number of professional groups and individuals have taken positions and advocated certain policy directions, but no consensus yet exists. Moreover, the two studies of consent documents described above do not point in the same direction. The first study contends that questions related to choice and control of stored tissue samples are necessary components of adequately informed consent, but the second study suggests that these questions are not particularly important, at least to the lay persons in the pilot run of the study. Whether this difference is substantive, or simply the result of methodological differences is unknown. What is known is that several differing perspectives on consent, choice, and control currently exist in the United States, with no resolution of these differences in sight.

Endnotes and References

1 National Institutes of Health/Department of Energy Task Force on Genetic Testing, "Interim Principles", unpublished document, p. 27.

2 Some of this material also appears in a longer, different version of this paper. See infra, note 29.

3 Centers for Disease Control and Prevention, Department of Health and Human Services, "National Health and Nutrition Examination Survey III," January 1994, p. 3.

4 Annas G.J., L.H. Glantz and P.A. Roche., "The Genetic Privacy Act and Commentary," unpublished model law, February 1995.

5 Ibid.

6 Ibid.

7 American College of Medical Genetics Storage of Genetics Materials Committee, "Statement on Storage and Use of Genetic Materials" (1995), *57 Am. J Hum. Genet.* 1499.

8 Clayton E.W., et al, "Informed Consent for Genetic Research on Stored Tissue Samples" (1995), 274 *JAMA* 1786.

9 Ibid.

10 Grody W.W., "Molecular Pathology, Informed Consent, and the Paraffin Block" (1995), 4 *Diagnostic Molecular Pathology* 156.

11 Ibid.

12 Ibid.

13 American Society of Human Genetics Rapid Action Task Force, "Report on Informed Consent for Genetic Research," unpublished document, 1995.

14 Ibid.

15 Stephenson J., "Pathologists Enter Debate on Consent for Genetic Research on Stored Tissue" (1996), 275 *JAMA* 504.

16 Supra note 13.

17 Ibid.

18 American Society of Human Genetics, "Statement on Informed Consent for Genetic Research" (1996), 59 *Am. J Hum. Genet.* 471.

19 Supra note 8.

20 Supra note 15.

21 Supra note 4.

22 Clayton E.W., "Panel Comment: Why the Use of Anonymous Samples for Research Matters" (1995), 23 *J L Med. & Ethics* 375.

23 Holtzman N.A., "Panel Comment: The Attempt to Pass the Genetic Privacy Act in Maryland" (1995), 23 *J L Med. & Ethics* 367.

24 Reilly P.R., "Panel Comment: The Impact of the Genetic Privacy Act on Medicine" (1995), 23 *J L Med. & Ethics* 378.

25 Weir R.F. and J.R. Horton, "DNA Banking and Informed Consent-Part I" (1995), 17(4) *IRB* 1.

26 Weir R.F. and J.R. Horton, "DNA Banking and Informed Consent-Part II" (1995), 17(5-6) *IRB* 1.

27 Supra note 25.

28 Supra note 26.

29 Merz J.F. and P. Sankar, "DNA Banking: An Empirical Study of a Proposed Consent Form" in Weir R.F., ed., *Ethical and Legal Implications of Stored Tissue Samples* (forthcoming).

30 Ibid.

31 Ibid.

DNA SAMPLING: DUTCH AND OTHER EUROPEAN APPROACHES TO THE ISSUES OF INFORMED CONSENT AND CONFIDENTIALITY

SJEF GEVERS

Professor of Health Law, University of Amsterdam

ELS OLSTHOORN-HEIM

Legal Adviser, Health Council of the Netherlands

Introduction

The DNA of an individual contains unique information about his or her genetic make-up, including information on future health risks. Analysis of DNA may also provide data on blood relatives. The fact that genetic information is 'hidden' in a DNA sample and needs to be 'decoded' to become available, does not render it less sensitive. Therefore, it is not surprising that the call for protection of the individual with regard to DNA sampling makes itself felt, the more so since the possibilities of genetic testing are increasing and the importance of DNA as a source of personal medical information continues to grow.

Although there is sufficient reason to look at DNA sampling as a matter of ethical concern and as a potential subject for legal regulation, it is impossible to set it apart from related problems. First of all, genetic information may not only become available as a result of DNA analysis, but also in other ways. This means that if one wants to protect the genetic privacy of the individual, DNA sampling is only one of the issues to be addressed, be it an important one. Secondly, since DNA is to be extracted from substances of the human body (blood, tissue or other biological specimens), an attempt to provide protection with regard to DNA sampling must take into account standards concerning the use of human tissue in general. Finally, one should realize that there are also other types of analysis of human substances which may produce sensitive health information (e.g. HIV testing).

From a legal and ethical point of view, the issues raised by DNA sampling are basically similar to those raised by the collection and analysis of human tissue in general. To mention just a few of them: who is entitled to carry out such analyses? which safeguards are there with regard to quality and safety? what about property rights, commercialization and patenting? This paper is concerned with the protection of the individual who is the 'source' of the DNA: what are his or her rights with respect to information, consent and confidentiality, not only in the stages of collection and storage, but also in that of analysis for different purposes. Its main objective is to survey to what extent and how this question has been addressed in Europe, and in particular in the Netherlands, against the background of the emerging debate on the appropriate use of human tissue in general.

In giving this survey, we will first have a look at the guidance developed by international organizations at the European level. The following part deals with the Dutch approach to the use of human tissue, and of DNA samples in particular. The subsequent section provides information on some of the other European countries. Finally, the results of the survey will be briefly discussed.

Principles Developed at the European Level

At present, there is no body of rules adopted at the European level which deal in a more or less comprehensive way with the use of human tissue in general, or with DNA sampling in particular. Apart from a few more specific provisions embodied in Council of Europe Recommendations (see below), reference can only be made to some general principles concerning the control of patients over the use of tissue and other substances of the human body.

As to these general principles, first of all the Declaration on the promotion of patient's rights in Europe should be mentioned. This declaration has been developed by the WHO's Regional Office for Europe and was adopted at the European Consultation on the Rights of Patients, held in Amsterdam, 1994.[1] According to section 3.8, the consent of the patient is required for the preservation and use of all substances of the human body. Consent may be presumed when the substances are to be used in the current course of diagnosis, treatment and care of that patient.

It is to be noted that this principle does not make any distinction, for example between different substances, different purposes of further use (treatment of other patients or research, for instance), or between identifiable substances on the one hand and substances which have been made anonymous after being removed from the body on the other. This may have to do with the very general nature of the Declaration and the fact that qualifications and exceptions have been kept out of the text in order to state the proposed rights as clearly and simply as possible.

A similar principle can be found in the Convention on human rights and biomedicine, which was adopted by the Committee of Ministers of the Council of Europe in November 1996, and is now open for signature by individual countries.[2] Article 22 of this Convention deals with disposal of a removed part of the human body. It states that, when in the course of an intervention any part of the human body is removed, it may be stored and used for a purpose other than that for which it was removed, only if this is done in conformity with appropriate information and consent procedures.

The Explanatory Report refers only indirectly to DNA analysis where it states that this provision is necessary "in particular because much information on the individual may be derived from any part of his body, however small." The report further explains, that information and consent procedures may vary according to circumstances, thus allowing for flexibility. Sometimes, it will not be possible, or very difficult, to find the persons concerned again in order to ask their consent. In some cases, it will be sufficient for a patient or his representative, who have been duly informed (for instance by means of leaflets handed to the persons concerned at the hospital), not to express their opposition. In other cases, depending on the nature of the use to which the removed parts are to be put, express and specific consent will be necessary, in particular where sensitive information is collected about identifiable individuals, thus the Explanatory Report.

Further guidance is hardly available at the European level. There is a Council of Europe Recommendation on human tissue banks,[3] but since it deals with tissue donated for therapeutic use in other patients it does not contain provisions on the control of donors over stored tissue. As far as the rights of the 'source' are concerned, it only states that the source of retrieved tissue must remain identifiable, but that access to data concerning the donor should be restricted to the extent necessary to protect confidentiality of information and individual privacy.

Good practice of tissue banks is also a matter of voluntary regulation. At the European level, the European Association of Tissue Banks is developing a code of conduct. In addition to provisions relating to quality, safety and non-commercialization, the draft code provides that the surgeon who removes tissue must inform the 'donor' about the possible use of that tissue before the latter gives consent to removal.[4]

More relevant to DNA sampling is the Recommendation of the Council of Europe on genetic testing and screening for health care purposes.[5] According to Principle 8, the collection and storage of substances and of samples, and the processing of information derived therefrom, must be in conformity with the Council of Europe's basic principles of data protection and data security. In particular, in genetic screening and testing personal data may be collected, processed and stored only for the purposes of health care, diagnosis and disease prevention, and for research closely related to these matters. Indirectly, the latter provision also limits the purposes for which DNA may be sampled and analysed. Furthermore, the recommendation contains provisions on self-determination, but these are not specifically elaborated with a view to the collection and storage of DNA samples.

The Dutch Approach

Until now, in the Netherlands there is hardly any statutory regulation concerning the use of substances of human origin. Apart from the Act on blood transfusion (1988) and the Act on organ donation (1996), there is no legislation which clarifies the legal status of human tissue or sets standards concerning the protection of the person from whom it was removed. The only exception to this is a provision (incorporated in the Civil Code in 1995 as part of the law on the medical contract) which states that the use of anonymous human tissue (obtained during treatment) for the purpose of medical research is allowed unless the patient has made an objection to this (opting-out system). *A contrario*, informed consent of the patient is required in the same situation if the tissue is identifiable. There are no statutory provisions on identifiable body substances, however, and no more on the (further) use of (left over) tissue for other purposes than research. The same holds for DNA sampling.

Over the last years, there has been considerable discussion about the ethical and legal aspects of the use of human tissue in medicine. The most important single result of this has been a report of the Health Council of the Netherlands on the use of human tissue (1994). This report provides guidance to health professionals and hospitals, *inter alia* concerning the rights of the patient in this domain. The Dutch government is now considering whether the recommendations laid down in it should lead to (further) legislation.

The 1994 report was preceded by another one on genetics (published by the Health Council in 1989), in which ample attention is paid to storage and use of cell samples. The latter subject is also dealt with in the Guidelines of the Dutch Association for Health Law on Genetic Testing (1991), which by and large reflect the guidance provided by the Health Council.

Below, we will summarize the two Health Council documents, starting with the report on human tissue; although it is not specifically related to DNA sampling, it has a direct bearing on the collection and storage of human substances for the purpose of genetic analysis.

The 1994 report[6] begins with the observation that human substances which have become available in the course of diagnosis and treatment of patients, may be used for various other, secondary purposes (e.g. research and teaching, quality control, treatment of other patients). The aim of the report is to set standards for 'good practice' concerning decisions on that 'further' use, including the need of somehow involving the person from whom the tissue was taken in such decisions.

As to the latter point, according to the report, as the medical scope for using human tissue has grown, people have come to realise that respect should be shown for the autonomy of the 'donor' when material secreted from the body is put to further use, even if it was not obtained through a physically invasive procedure. The respect owed to the individual and, by extension, to the material obtained from a person's body would confer a certain right on that person to determine what happens to the material he or she has donated or bequeathed. The rules to be developed in this respect, however, should be practicable and not unduly impede the many valuable activities where use is made of bodily material and which are common practice in contemporary medicine.

According to the report, there are a number of additional factors to be taken into account in developing standards for good practice:

- whether the material is identifiable or not;
- the nature of the material involved (one type of material may be perceived as being more sensitive than another);
- the possibility that further use will lead to new findings which are of importance to the 'source' of the material.

One of the main proposals is the provision of general information about storage and use/further use in individual institutions and the code of practice observed there. As an overall guideline, in the case of identifiable material, the persons concerned should first be consulted so that they can be duly informed, give consent and indicate what should be done with any new information that is relevant to them. The possibility of new findings is a cogent argument in favour of this line of approach. Consent usually would need to be given only once and apply to one or more instances of use, whether or not known in advance. If the circumstances require this, the doctor in question should add to the general information, so as to enable the patient to give more specific consent.

The privacy of those whose material is put to further use must always be respected and protected. In the case of non-identifiable material (which should be used wherever possible in preference to identifiable material) it is sufficient that the persons concerned did not object to its use when told by the institution in general terms about the possibility that human tissue might be stored and put to further use. Finally, the Committee of the Health Council which drew up the report states, that medical ethics committees can play an important additional role by offering their advice where appropriate and by assessing controversial research projects in advance.

The approach adopted in the aforementioned report towards the control of the 'donor' is in line with the flexible approach to information and consent procedures to be found in the recent Council of Europe Convention on human rights and biomedicine (see above). When applied to the collection and analysis of DNA, in particular the emphasis on the relevance of the possibility of new findings is important: especially in the case of genetic material, it is to be expected that analysis may lead to new and sensitive information, not only relating to the 'source' of the material, but also to his or her relatives. Therefore, in that case, information and consent procedures should be more elaborate and specific than in general would be required for other cases.

How these procedures could look like had already been elaborated by the Health Council in its 1989 report on genetics.[7] According to this report, 'donors' of cell samples usually deposit the material with the information on them intending it to be stored, first of all with a view to genetic testing for their own benefit and secondly for their relatives. Another current use of DNA stored in a cell bank is for scientific research. Under the law as it stands in the Netherlands, material deposited in a cell or tissue bank, including any new material that may be derived from it, remains the property of the depositor, unless ownership is transferred, by explicit agreement, to the bank. However, irrespective of the question of property, once material has been placed in a bank, the rules of information, confidentiality and privacy apply: 'donors' have the right to be informed on data obtained from genetic testing and the right not to know if they wish so, as well as the right of non-disclosure of such data to other parties.

The Health Council is of the opinion, that prior to DNA banking specific, written agreements are needed, in which the 'donor' states whether he or she:

- wishes to receive all information, both now and in the future;
- consents to the use of the material for counselling relatives, both now and in the future;
- consents to the use of material for research (when the research requires traceability, the material must be used anonymously, with only the counsellor originally approached knowing the identity of the source).

According to the report, those operating cell banks must ensure that 'donors' have given their informed consent to the taking of cell samples; to do this, they must provide complete information on the nature and purpose of the procedure, on the type of results which could emerge from analysis of the material, and on the uses that will be made of both the material and the results. The purpose of the cell bank itself must be made clear, as well as the purposes for which such material can be used. With this information, 'donors' can reach a well thought out decision on whether or not to consent to storage, analysis and further use of the material. They must also be informed about their rights to change their mind, and to have the material destroyed, and how to exercize these rights. Finally, cell bank operators must ensure that the material is stored with adequate attention to security. The protection of data obtained from analyses must also be regulated by the rules of privacy and confidentiality.

The Health Council recommends that the necessary safeguards be ensured in the first instance through self-regulation; legislation could be considered if self-regulation proves to be unsatisfactory. As already stated, so far no legislation specifically relating to DNA banking has been adopted nor is any legislation intended at present.

Other European Countries

Information on the developments in other European countries is only available to a limited extent. Apart from a few reports of national advisory bodies, national legislation which has been made available internationally, and some articles by individual authors published in international journals, there is hardly any material on the ethical and legal developments concerning the use human tissue in general or DNA sampling in particular. One of the few exceptions is the report from the European Workshop on the further use of human tissue, held in The Hague on November 21, 1994. The Workshop brought together members of the medical profession and of the medical industry, and specialists in the area of ethics and health law to explore the possibilities of achieving a proper balance between the rights of patients and the interest of public health. Participants came from about 15 countries. Before the workshop started, a questionnaire was distributed among them enquiring about the state of the art in their country.

From this enquiry,[8] it appears that in most countries the debate on the (further) use of human tissue is limited to the medical profession and advisory boards. To the extent that the debate has resulted in some form of regulation, the use of tissue would seem to be rather a matter of voluntary than of statutory regulation. With some exceptions, the debate has not yet reached the parliamentary level. Furthermore, some of the purposes of further use receive more attention than others. The focus has mainly been on medical research, teaching and (commercial) production. Where rules on (some aspects of) the use of human tissue have been adopted, they are often part of legislation on organ and tissue donation.

Controversies seem to have been limited to the use of blood for HIV seroprevalence studies, and sometimes the commercial use of placentas. In many countries, the use of foetal material caused concern; in some cases this has resulted in guidelines for the use of this kind of 'sensitive material'. The legal position of human tissue (in particular whether or not tissue would come under the law of property and ownership) is generally unclear. This does not necessarily mean, that the 'source' of the tissue would have no control over its use; the legal basis for this control needs clarification, however. The appropriate form of control by the individual over further use of his or her tissue, either in the form of explicit consent or at least in the form of an opting-out system, has not yet been definitely elaborated, it would seem, in the countries where the matter is debated. The debate is complicated by the fact, that a clear distinction is not always made between informed consent as a requirement for the removal of tissue on the one hand, and involvement of the 'donor' in decisions concerning its further use on the other.

The need for the protection of the privacy of the 'donor' and of the confidentiality of data obtained by analysis of human tissue is generally adhered to, but usually not further elaborated. One of the main conclusions from the enquiry is, that there is a clear need for the further identification of relevant aspects, discussion and exchange of views at the international level.

Although it is impossible to provide a comprehensive account of the developments per country, in some instances more specific information is available. In order to illustrate the general findings of the enquiry, I will try to give at least an impression of national developments in some other European countries, drawing both on the report of the European Workshop and on additional sources.

In Finland, rules have been developed for the use of some kinds of human tissue. In 1990, the Finnish National Board of Health issued general guidelines on the use of human tissue residues, placentas and aborted fetuses. The informed consent of the donor is required, and in the case of fetal tissue, the hospital's ethics committee must consider the matter.

Switzerland and Austria have adopted - or are in the process of adopting - legislation on genetic testing. In Switzerland, a draft federal Act on human genetic analysis (1994) states that samples taken for the sake of genetic analysis cannot be used for other purposes without the consent of the person involved. An exception is allowed for research, provided that the material is made anonymous.

The Austrian Act on genetic technology, enacted in 1994, has a similar provision concerning research. According to Section 66, genetic analysis of human DNA samples for research purposes can only take place with the explicit, written consent of the individual involved, unless the sample is made anonymous. A DNA sample is not only considered anonymous when the individual is unidentifiable, but also if it is coded and intervention of the institution where the sample was taken is needed to identify the 'source'.

In France, the Bioethics Laws (adopted in 1994) contain some general principles which are of relevance to the collection of human tissue, and to DNA analysis in particular. As to the latter point, the Act on respect for the human body provides, that the analysis of DNA samples to study the genetic make-up of a person is only allowed for medical or research purposes, and provided that the person concerned has given his or her previous consent.

On October 30, 1995, the National Ethical Consultative Committee presented an Opinion on "Genetics and medicine: from prediction to prevention" which provides further guidance on DNA sampling.[9] In addition to guidelines on information, consent and confidentiality in the case of genetic testing, the opinion also addresses the issue of DNA banking. It recommends that the storage of biological samples that might subsequently be necessary for the implementation of diagnostic or control tests must be assured in order to satisfy the requests of the persons tested. If research is extended to an area that was not foreseen at the time a sample was taken, further consent must be requested. If biological samples are collected as part of a research program, it is the duty of the persons initiating the research to ensure that it is carried out with the available resources and under the conditions indicated at the time that the individuals from whom the samples were taken gave their consent.

In Denmark, the Danish Council of Ethics issued a report on the protection of sensitive personal information (1993).[10] In the chapter on the registration and storage of such information, attention is also paid to banks containing biomaterial, i.e. potentially sensitive information available in indirectly accessible form. The Council is of the opinion that there is a great need to clarify the law on the collection and storage of biomaterial and recommends statutory regulation in this field, all the more so since the information embodied in collections of biomaterial may be of an extremely delicate nature. The general principle proposed is, that biomaterial should be stored only when informed consent has been obtained in advance. The consent requirement should only be waived in exceptional situations, e.g. when storage and analysis is needed to combat an epidemic, life threatening disease.

According to Nielsen,[11] the report was widely debated, in particular with respect to the proposed consent procedure, involving explicit and specific consent to further use. Some critics saw this as a threat to the existing possibilities for medical research. She refers also to a joint recommendation of the Danish Supervisory Data Authority and the Central Scientific Ethical Committee. That recommendation seems to be less stringent. It suggests that a section on the use of biomedical data and blood and tissue samples for research purposes be included in hospital leaflets to inform patients and their relatives on such further use and to explain its importance for the development of medicine. Analysis of samples performed in an ongoing research project would always require previous consent of the patient. Use of stored samples for later research projects should be reviewed in advance by ethics committees.

The United Kingdom is one of the few countries where the ethical and legal issues concerning human tissue have been the subject of a major report, issued by the Nuffield Council on Bioethics in 1995.[12] It states that there is an urgent need to clarify and, where necessary, strengthen the ethical and legal framework within which the clinical and research uses of human tissue take place. The emphasis in the report is less on the role of patients' consent as a mechanism for control, and more on procedures used to organise and regulate the removal, storage and further use of human tissue. There is a key role in these procedures for 'medical intermediaries', for instance the medical professional in charge of a tissue bank. They are the proper custodians both of patients' rightful expectations of tissue being treated with appropriate dignity and respect and of patients' rights to confidentiality.

According to the Nuffield Council, when a patient consents to medical treatment involving the removal of tissue, the consent should be taken to include consent also to the subsequent disposal or storage of the tissue and to any further acceptable use, provided that this is regulated by appropriate ethical, legal and professional standards. As an aid to ensuring that consent to treatment is properly informed, it recommends that institutions responsible for consent procedures should consider whether any additions to their explanations or forms are needed to make it clear that consent covers acceptable further uses of human tissue removed during treatment. In general, the use of left over tissue for research would not require approval of an ethics committee. Only where it might prove to be of special interest, referral to such a committee is recommended.

The framework proposed by the Nuffield Council is a general one. It leaves room for more stringent requirements in special circumstances. DNA sampling is not discussed in the report, but it might well be a situation in which the 'appropriate ethical, legal and professional standards' would require more in terms of patient control. More stringent guidelines with regard to the analysis of identifiable DNA samples for research purposes have been proposed by Harper.[13] He observes that successive phases of research may use the same sample and that at a later stage, implications for the use of samples may exist that were not present or even thought of initially. When samples taken from families with genetic disorders are to be stored and used for future tests, new consent should be obtained if the implications for the person at risk resulting from the new research are considerably different, for example if mutations are to be looked for rather than a general linkage analysis. Furthermore, if the possibility of identifying defects in people is foreseen and inevitable then such samples should be coded and made anonymous for the purpose of these tests, unless the person concerned has specifically requested - on the basis of adequate information - that relevant information should be disclosed. Finally, according to Harper, ethical committees reviewing DNA research projects should pay at least as much attention to the consequences of a sample being taken as to the risks attached to the sampling procedure.

Discussion

In the above survey, ample consideration has been given to the emerging standards relating to the (further) use of human tissue in general. Basically, all human tissue is a potential source of DNA and may serve as material for genetic analysis. Therefore, in the last resort an effective protection of the individual cannot be achieved without the development of a general framework concerning the collection, storage and analysis of substances of the human body. Furthermore, as already stated in the introduction, since in a certain sense DNA itself is also such a substance, in regulating DNA sampling, sooner or later one must take into account the standards developed (or to be developed) for the use of human tissue in general. With due regard to the specific privacy hazards inherent in the use of DNA, more stringent standards could then apply to situations in which genetic analysis is the direct purpose of the removal of tissue, or in which tissue originally removed for conventional forms of testing is used as material for DNA analysis.

In Europe, such a general ethical and legal framework for the use of human tissue has not yet been elaborated, neither at the European, nor at the national level. Only in some countries a more comprehensive body of standards has been proposed, but even there, the issues associated with the collection and storage of tissue have not yet been definitely resolved. If one looks at the debate and the emerging standards, basically two approaches can be distinguished:[14] a patient-oriented approach which relies on patient involvement as the main mechanism for control and which would require informed consent for (further) use in some cases, and at least an opportunity to opt out in others; and a procedure oriented approach which would emphasise and build on already recognised professional responsibilities and rely on intermediaries such as the physicians involved, hospitals and research ethics committees as the custodians of legitimate patients' interests.

The first approach would seem to prevail, for instance, in the Dutch report on the use of human tissue (1994), the second one in the report of the Nuffield Council in the United Kingdom (1995). It should be noted, however, that the two approaches do not exclude each other, and as a matter of fact, in each of the reports at least some elements of the 'other' perspective are included. A similar conclusion was reached at the European Workshop on human tissue. According to the summary of the discussion,[15] the two approaches should be regarded as complimentary: some patient involvement was considered imperative for some situations, irrespective of the approval of an ethics committee etc. One of the factors which in particular would make explicit consent necessary would be the chance that further use would generate new, sensitive information (e.g. genetic research, or the testing of material for transmissible diseases prior to use for treatment purposes).

This brings us to the ethical and legal issues concerning DNA sampling. In Europe, the previous informed consent of a person before his DNA is analyzed in such a way that the results can be traced back to him, is generally considered imperative. Given the particularly sensitive nature of genetic information, this would also apply to further use of DNA not related to the original request of the patient. There is also consensus on the need of stringent safeguards concerning the confidentiality of the data resulting from DNA analysis. At this basic level, the approach in Europe is not different from the one adopted across the Atlantic.[16]

Most of the information on national developments concerning DNA analysis presented in the preceding section, relates to the use of DNA for research. This information indicates, that patient involvement going beyond general information and implicit consent is considered necessary prior to such use, in particular if the samples are identifiable. New consent has to be obtained if the sample is used outside the scope of the original consent. An example of this is when a patient has agreed to analysis of the sample in the context of a particular kind of research and it is used for a different form of research (in terms of the implications for the persons involved resulting from the new research).

What all this implies for the standards and procedures applying to the banking of DNA has not yet been completely elaborated, although in some countries attempts to this effect have been undertaken. It is obvious that as the practice of storing human substances for the purpose of DNA analysis proceeds, and the amount of personal information that may result from DNA analysis is growing, further guidance is needed, in particular (but not only) concerning the information to be given to individuals and the agreement to be reached with them before DNA samples are stored for future use. The approaches developed so far for obtaining consent prior to DNA banking (not only within Europe,[17] but also abroad[18]) can serve as useful models for this purpose.

Endnotes and References

1 WHO, *A Delaration on the Promotion of Patients Rights in Europe* (Copenhagen: Regional Office for Europe, 1994).

2 Council of Europe, Directorate of Legal Affairs, Strasbourg, November 1996.

3 Recommendation No.R (94) 1, Strasbourg, 1994.

4 Beaumont P., "EATB: Statement of Principles and Ethical Code for Tissue Banking: Final Proposal" (May 1994), *Bull. Med. Eth.* 10.

5 Recommendation No.R (92) 3, Strasbourg, 1992.

6 Health Council of the Netherlands, *Proper Use of Human Tissue* (The Hague: Health Council of the Netherlands, 1994).

7 Health Council of the Netherlands, *Heredity: Science and Society* (The Hague: Health Council of the Netherlands, 1989).

8 See the summary of the results in the special issue of the European Journal of Health Law devoted to the workshop. See Markenstein L.F., "An Analysis of the State of the Debate on the Further use of Human Tissue in Various European Countries" (1995), 2 *Eur. J. Health Law* 125.

9 The recommendations have been published in english in (1996), 47 *Int'l. Digest Health Legisl.* 263.

10 Danish Council of Ethics, *Ethics and Mapping of the Human Genome: Protection of Sensitive Personal information* (Copenhagen, 1993).

11 Nielsen L., "Legal and Ethical Aspects of Further use of Human Tissue" (1995), 2 *Eur. J Health Law* 109.

12 Nuffield Council on Bioethics, *Human Tissue: Ethical and Legal Issues* (London, April 1995).

13 Harper P.S., "Research Samples from Families with Genetic Diseases: A Proposed Code of Conduct" (1993), 306 *BMJ* 1391.

14 See for this distinction: Markenstein L.F., Summary of the discussion (of the European Workshop on the further use of human tissue), supra note 8 at 137.

15 Supra note 14.

16 See e.g., American Society of Human Genetics, "DNA Banking and DNA Analysis: Points to Consider" (1988), 42 *Am. J Hum. Genet.* 781. See also, Annas G.J., "Privacy Rules for DNA Databanks; Protecting Coded 'Future Diaries'" (1993), 270 *JAMA* 2346. See also, Gostin L.O., "Genetic Privacy" (1995), 23 *J Law & Med. Ethics* 320.

17 Supra note 7 at 110.

18 Knoppers B.M. and C.M. Laberge, "DNA Sampling and Informed Consent" (1989), 140 *CMAJ* 1023. Also Knoppers B.M. and C.M. Laberge, "DNA Banking/Collecting: A Canadian 'Sample' of Consent Forms" in B.M. Knoppers, Caulfield T. and Kinsella T.D., eds, *Legal Rights and Human Genetic Material* (Toronto: Emond Montgomery Publications Ltd, 1996).

LOOK-BACK: THE DUTY TO UPDATE GENETIC COUNSELLING

JOE T.R. CLARKE

Division of Clinical Genetics, Departments of Pediatrics and Genetics

Hospital for Sick Children, Toronto

PETER N. RAY

Department of Pediatrics, University of Toronto

Introduction

The general standards of practice related to the collection of blood or tissue samples, laboratory testing, and reporting of results to the attending physician and patient in the course of routine diagnostic investigation, are well established and are founded, in part, on the principles of competency, consent, confidentiality, and disclosure. The capability to add to information extracted from biologic specimens by the application of new laboratory tests on stored material is not new. However, what makes the application of genetic laboratory techniques so powerful is (a) the enormous scope of the information that is accessible through further analysis, (b) the technical ease of extracting it, (c) the rapidity with which the precision of genetic testing in general is evolving and improving, and (d) the implications of such testing for relatives of the individual originally providing the blood or tissue specimen. It has become customary for samples of DNA, collected for diagnostic testing, to be stored for indefinite periods for other purposes, including the development of new tests that would enhance or modify counselling based on the original testing.

Technologic advances in clinical genetics are occurring so rapidly that the genetic risks, estimated from the results of newer techniques, are often significantly different than those calculated on the basis of original testing. That is, the re-calculated risk is sufficiently different from the original risk to change personal planning and reproductive decisions. In addition to the need to keep up with technologic advances, geneticists and the directors of genetics diagnostic laboratories are increasingly having to face difficult counselling issues, such as when, on whom, and under what circumstances should "look-back testing" be carried out, and how should the information about the availability and results of testing be communicated to the consultand.

A recent judgement against two Canadian family physicians has served to focus attention on the issue of whose responsibility it is to ensure that genetic counselling is updated subsequent to new developments in diagnostic technology.[1] During the interval of several years between initial counselling and a woman's first pregnancy, major improvements had occurred in the identification of carriers of Duchenne muscular dystrophy (DMD), the disease that had caused the death of the woman's brother. The court ruled that the woman had a right to expect to be referred for updating of the original genetic counselling in the light of these improvements.

In this paper, we explore the issue of "look-back", the notion that genetic information that might be beneficial to an individual or his or her relatives might only come to light after retesting samples of DNA some years after the samples were collected.

Existing Guidelines Relating to Retesting

Although there is general concern in the clinical genetics community relating to "look-back testing", and various centres are working on policies and approaches to dealing with them, there has been little discussion at a national level, and whether or not there is any consensus among clinical geneticists is unclear. Guidelines specifically relating to the conditions under which DNA samples obtained from individuals for genetic diagnostic purposes should be stored have been developed by American Society of Human Genetics (ASHG), the Clinical Genetics Society (U.K.), and the Canadian College of Medical Geneticists (CCMG) (TABLE 1). The guidelines developed by the ASHG[2] emphasize the role of health care professionals in the relationship between individuals or families and DNA banking facilities. The primary goal is clearly to protect the rights (privacy, autonomy, etc.) of the depositor, the individual from whom DNA was collected for banking. The guidelines are less helpful in defining the responsibility, if any, for recalling depositors for retesting in the event that a specific advance in diagnostic technology presents an opportunity to improve significantly on genetic counselling based on older techniques. They identify a need for maintaining contact between the depositor and the DNA bank, implying a potential for retesting and updating of genetic counselling. However, the recommendations regarding the matter are more permissive than prescriptive, and there is no comment on whose responsibility it is to initiate the contact or how it is to be done.

The guidelines developed by the Clinical Genetics Society (U.K.) are more explicit in acknowledging the need to anticipate the potential for more sophisticated genetic testing of banked DNA samples in the future, and the need to recall and review families previously counselled on the basis of the results of older diagnostic techniques.[3] They include the identification of a need to plan to store samples of DNA for several decades, under secure conditions and with appropriate administrative arrangements, particularly by

Regional Genetics Services, to ensure their accessibility for use in future counselling. However, like the ASHG guidelines, the U.K. guidelines stop short of assigning specific responsibility for initiating the retesting or recall of individuals previously tested and counselled, and the terms upon which it is done.

TABLE 1. Sample guidelines relating to the banking of DNA and the duty to update genetic counselling.

Sponsoring Society	Comments	Ref.
American Society of Human Genetics, Ad Hoc committee on DNA Technology (USA)	• health care professionals should serve as intermediates in relationship between individuals or families and DNA diagnostic laboratories, concerning both testing and reporting • banked DNA is the property of the depositor, i.e., the individual from whom the sample was taken • recommendation with regard to retesting at a later time is permissive, rather than prescriptive • no comment on responsibility to update information or recall individuals for retesting	2
Clinical Genetics Society(UK)	• Regional Genetics Services assigned a key role in recalling and reviewing families previously seen, but no explicit recommendations • specific concern expressed regarding importance of anticipating the future service needs of families • emphasis on technical aspects of DNA storage, including documentation and information retrieval • identification of the need to plan to store samples of DNA for several decades, with appropriate administrative and security arrangements	3
Canadian College of Medical Geneticists (Canada)	• health care professionals should serve as intermediates in relationship between individuals or families and DNA diagnostic laboratories, concerning both testing and reporting • recommendation for storage for 100 years (approximately four generations) • no comment on responsibility to update information or recall individuals for retesting	4

The policy statement of the CCMG concerning DNA banking and molecular genetic diagnosis resembles the guidelines developed by the

ASHG.[4] It focuses primarily on measures to protect the privacy and autonomy of individuals from whom DNA has been collected and the security of the storage facilities and procedures of DNA banks operating in Canada. The guidelines have little to say explicitly about a responsibility for recalling individuals to obtain consent for retesting, or recalling them for updating of counselling in the light of technologic advances in genetic diagnosis. However, the recommendation that samples of DNA be stored for at least 100 years, i.e., about 4 generations, implies a responsibility to relatives of an individual long after the information obtained by genetic testing would be of any value to the individual providing the original DNA sample.

A recently published analysis of responses from 96 of 148 DNA diagnostic laboratories surveyed in the U.S. showed that DNA banking is growing rapidly, particularly in academic settings. However, few have written policies or written agreements with sample depositors to guide their activities, particularly regarding possible disputes between family members over banked DNA, but also involving procedures designed to maintain contact with depositors and the duty to recall for retesting.[5] Fewer than half of the labs involved in DNA banking required signed documentation defining the rights and obligations of the laboratory and of the individual from whom the sample was taken. Only 13% of labs banking DNA had written internal policies regarding procedures for maintaining contact with depositors of DNA samples, and in only 10% was the internal policy communicated to the depositors in the form of a written agreement. Fewer still spelled out the conditions under which the banking laboratory had a duty to recall the depositor for retesting in the event that a new or improved test, or new genetic information relevant to the purpose for the original testing, became available. Only one out of 84 labs banking DNA incorporated a statement into a written agreement with depositors specifying whether the lab has a duty to re-test. "[Depositors of DNA samples] have a right to know the conditions, if any, under which they will be recontacted with relevant new information regarding their samples, how long they can expect their samples to be maintained, and what will happen to the sample in the event of particular future contingencies."[6]

At least one widely discussed DNA sampling and storage consent form and its successors, developed by Knoppers and Laberge,[7] albeit primarily for use by research laboratories, includes questions formally acknowledging that genetic information pertaining to an individual may be of value to family members, even after the death of the individual. The consent form specifically solicits authorization to carry out new or additional genetic tests on stored samples of DNA, and seeks consent to communicate those results, and relevant counselling, to the individual from whom the DNA was obtained. The consent form is more complete in this regard than those developed by most DNA banking agencies that have bothered to produce formal policies on the matter. It explicitly assigns responsibility to depositors for ensuring that the DNA banking facility has a means for contacting them should technologic advances in DNA diagnostics provide the opportunity to improve on genetic counselling. On the other hand, it places on the storage facility the responsibility for determining the point at which a change in a genetic risk based on older techniques "becomes significant because of new findings".

Unresolved Issues

Under what circumstances should individuals, who have been counselled previously, be contacted to update genetic counselling on the basis of new knowledge about a disease or advances in genetic testing? Although it is widely regarded to be appropriate to recontact individuals when technologic advances are considered important enough to have a *significant* impact on the calculated genetic risk for which the individual originally sought counselling, the judgement of what is significant is generally made by the geneticist, though the primary care physician might be expected to assume a greater role in this. Factors commonly taken into consideration are (a) the extent to which the risk of a particular outcome would be changed by application of the new testing, (b) the seriousness of the condition for which testing was originally undertaken, (c) the anticipated reproductive plans of the consultand based on their age, (d) changes in possible options for intervention, such as prenatal diagnosis, and (e) the resources available to recontact the consultand and undertake the testing. However, the rights of the individual seeking genetic counselling are conventionally regarded to include the right to judge, for themselves, the significance of any genetic risk they may face.[8] To assign to geneticists or DNA banking facilities the responsibility for determining the significance of any change in genetic risk for the purposes of recalling individuals for renewal of genetic counselling is inconsistent with the commitment to this principle of autonomy.

To what extent does the responsibility extend to the notification of family members who might be affected by the results of further testing of DNA from the individual undergoing the original testing? In principle, any information derived from genetic testing on an individual is considered to be the property of that person. Whether the information is shared with family members is regarded as the right of that individual, a notion supported by the commitment to the principles of privacy and confidentiality, and imbedded in various consent forms which have been developed for use by geneticists. In practice, information from studies on family members for which explicit consent has not been obtained is commonly used in counselling individuals. How this information is handled is not limited to the issue of look-back testing and is still a matter of debate. The situation is even less clear after the death of the consultand.

The number of individuals who have undergone genetic counselling on the basis of molecular testing, and from whom DNA samples are in storage, is growing extremely rapidly, and there is no obvious practical limit at which it might reasonably be expected to stabilize. Advances in DNA testing technology which might be expected to modify risks calculated on the basis of previous testing are also occurring at a very rapid rate. Taken together, these factors are likely to place enormous pressure on geneticists and DNA diagnostic laboratories.

The rate with which new knowledge is accumulating and the number of individuals seeking genetic counselling is growing is very rapid, making it increasingly difficult for the individual geneticist to assume unshared responsibility for keeping consultands and family members, who may never have been counselled in the first place, abreast of technologic developments affecting previous counselling. Geneticists and consultands have always shared this type of responsibility in practice; however, the principles determining the distribution of responsibility have not been clearly defined.

To the extent that the ability to cope with the rapidly mounting pressure to recontact, re-test, and counsel individuals previously tested is related to the resources available for the task, society itself must share in the responsibility for the quality of genetic counselling available to its citizens.

Shared Responsibility

What is emerging among geneticists in this country is a conviction that the responsibility for remaining abreast of developments in genetic testing, arranging retesting and counselling as appropriate, and ensuring that the resources available are adequate to do it, is a shared responsibility. Individuals seeking genetic counselling, along with geneticists, primary care physicians, diagnostic laboratories, and the state, are required to participate.

THE MEDICAL GENETICIST

Geneticists and genetic counsellors are central figures in most of the formal guidelines that have been developed regarding DNA testing and banking. These professionals, with specific expertise in medical genetics, are generally accepted to be the ones to determine who is to be tested in the first instance, what testing is to be done, and how the results of the testing are communicated and interpreted to the consultand. The responsibility to recall, re-test, and re-counsel individuals as advances occur in diagnostic sophistication is a natural extension of the original responsibility to the consultand. In most discussions of the need to recall individuals for retesting, the responsibility is generally assumed to reside with the geneticist. However, this creates some problems, both in principle and in practice.

To vest in the geneticist the responsibility to recall individuals for retesting and recounselling also assigns to him or her the right and responsibility to determine when and under what circumstances renewed contact is made. The geneticist is required to decide, on behalf of each consultand, what potential change in risk would be significant enough to merit further testing and counselling. This is inconsistent with one of the major principles of genetic counselling, which requires the geneticist to provide consultands with sufficient information for them to make decisions for themselves with respect to the significance of any risk and the choice of options to deal with it.[9] The geneticist is commonly faced with the dilemma of determining whether the ultimate potential impact of communicating new genetic information to the consultand is positive or negative. Considerable formal and anecdotal information exists to indicate that what the medical geneticist might judge to be significant may be perceived by the consultand as inconsequential, and *vice versa*.[10] The disability caused in some circumstances by the anxiety generated may be far greater than additional or re-calculated risk of a particular genetic disorder. However, the geneticist is required, in principle, to communicate *any* additional risk, or change of a pre-existing risk, to the consultand, no matter how small or apparently trivial, and to explain the change and options for dealing with it in sufficient detail to enable the consultand to make appropriate choices for themselves.

The practical problem relates to the potentially enormous resource requirements for the geneticist to maintain sufficiently current information on previously counselled individuals to recall them, not to mention the need for the personnel and facilities to do the recalling, retesting, and recounselling. Some consent forms for DNA testing and banking include a commitment on the part of the consultand to maintaining contact with the geneticist for the purposes of retesting. However, the responsibility is generally limited to providing the geneticist with a current address. The implied responsibility for re-initiating contact with the consultand for updating still resides with the geneticist.

The consultand might reasonably be expected to assume a much more active role in the look-back process (*vide infra*). However, if they are to be expected to assume significant responsibility for staying abreast of advances in genetics that may be relevant to their own situation, they must be provided with the means to determine when and how to access the information. At the very least, many medical geneticists now advise consultands to stay in contact with the genetics centre on a periodic basis, usually annually, to be re-counselled, particularly if advances in relevant genetic technology are deemed to be imminent. In addition, however, the CCMG requires Fellows "[to] encourage any reasonable effort to extend and improve the education of the public on medical genetic matters", which could be interpreted to include providing information to the public in a manner that would help individuals to determine on a continuing basis when and how they should seek counselling with regard to pre-existing, as well as new, genetic risks. The full implications of this undertaking have not been discussed. Public education, including continuing education of colleagues in family practice and other medical specialties, is an area in which medical geneticists might reasonably be expected to play an increasingly important role.

THE PRIMARY CARE PHYSICIAN

For the purposes of this discussion, the primary care physician is the one with whom the consultand has contracted to provide general medical care, including reproductive care. In Canada, he or she would most often be a family physician. However, specialists consulted as part of the medical care of the patient automatically become partners in the management of the genetic, as well as other, aspects of care, and for the purposes of this discussion, are included as part of the primary medical care team.

Primary care physicians might be expected to recognize genetic high-risk situations, particularly pregnancy, and to appreciate that advances in human genetics in general are occurring so rapidly that genetic counselling that might have been acceptable in the past might not still be appropriate. In such circumstances, their responsibility might be expected to extend no further than referral of the patient to an appropriate specialist in clinical genetics, such as a genetic counsellor, for detailed counselling. The extent to which primary care physicians are expected to remain sufficiently abreast of the details of new developments in genetics, and to know the patients they may have seen in the past well enough, to recall patients for updated counselling for specific genetic disorders is not yet clear. Whatever the case, specialists in medical genetics might reasonably be expected to assume considerable responsibility for helping primary care physicians keep abreast of advances in medical genetics relevant to their practice.

THE RESPONSIBILITY OF THE DNA DIAGNOSTIC LABORATORY

Most of the published guidelines dealing with the potential for recall and retesting for genetic diseases are directed specifically at DNA diagnostic laboratories and DNA banking facilities, and these have already been discussed. An issue that merits further discussion is the responsibility of DNA laboratories arising out of their pursuit of technologically improved testing methods independent of the testing and counselling of specific individuals. Most DNA diagnostic laboratories are involved in developmental research on ways to enhance the reliability of genetic testing. There are at least two ways in which these activities are directly relevant to individual consultands: (a) stored samples of DNA are commonly used anonymously for developmental research unrelated to the genetic disorder for which the original DNA sample was obtained, and (b) developmental research, undertaken on DNA from individuals previously tested for the same condition by less sophisticated techniques, commonly produces results that change the estimated risk of the disorder for which the DNA was collected in the first place.

In the first case, existing published guidelines for DNA diagnostic laboratories and banking facilities include the requirement for obtaining consent from depositors, i.e., the individuals from whom the DNA was obtained, for the use of the material in this type of research, on the condition that their identity is protected. To the extent that the guidelines are observed, and anonymity of the DNA samples used in the research is ensured, the potential for recall for revised counselling is negligible.

The situation with regard to research developments specifically retesting a class of patients from whom DNA samples have been stored is different. For example, what is the responsibility of the laboratory with regard to individuals who have had DNA stored in the course of testing for a particular condition, such as DMD, by linkage analysis when the potential for carrier detection is enhanced significantly by the application of specific mutation analysis? Is the laboratory automatically obligated to apply the new, more accurate, mutation analysis to stored samples of DNA from individuals previously tested by linkage analysis? If retesting is done, which samples should be tested, and when and how should the results be communicated to the consultand?

Some of these questions are anticipated in the model consent form proposed by Knoppers and Laberge.[11] The requirement for consent to be contacted, and the responsibility of the consultand to maintain contact with the testing laboratory, are formally acknowledged. However, the extent of the obligation of the laboratory to re-test stored DNA samples is not stated. In this respect, the consent is permissive, rather than prescriptive. And how the contact with the consultand is to be made is not clear; the consent form places responsibilities on the laboratory which might be more appropriately responsibilities of the medical geneticist and the consultand.

THE CONSULTAND

Much of the attention on the relationship between depositors and DNA banks has focused on the issue of the rights of the depositor, the right to privacy and the right to physical security of the sample and future access to the DNA.[12] Those involved in DNA banking are also beginning to acknowledge a need to develop mechanisms for updating information on genetic risks on the basis of advances in diagnostic technology, though few centres have actually developed procedures for recalling previously tested individuals. There has been much less formal discussion of the responsibilities of the depositor, particularly in the context of the apportionment of responsibility for staying abreast of new developments potentially affecting the assessment of their own genetic risk. However, it is not unreasonable to expect individuals to assume some defined responsibility for ensuring the counselling they receive is current. This is particularly true if the consultand is expected to retain the right to *refuse* retesting, which is implicit in the concept of autonomy.

No one has as much invested in the accuracy of their counselling as the consultand, and no one is as competent as the consultand to judge the significance of retesting to that individual. It vests in the consultand much more control over the recall process, supporting his or her autonomy. Finally, assigning some responsibility to the consultand for initiating retesting and associated counselling decreases and redistributes the cost of genetic surveillance with respect to individual consultands. The principle of formally involving consultands in the responsibility for keeping abreast of developments in the genetics of their particular disorder is now being proposed for inclusion in the formal professional and ethical guidelines of the CCMG: the responsibilities of Fellows of the College to patients include "[to] inform patients that *it is their responsibility* [emphasis added] to maintain contact with the genetic centre in order to stay informed about the current status of their genetic disorder". This is the only reference in the proposed guidelines to the issue of recall and retesting.

THE ROLE OF THE FAMILY

The implications for family members of an individual undergoing genetic testing are enormous. Most of the discussion on the rights and responsibilities of family members have had to do with measures to safeguard the privacy and autonomy of adults and the safety and long-term security of children. Many of the difficulties associated with the potential for the inadvertent loss of autonomy or breaching of confidentiality through genetic testing have been anticipated and addressed in consent forms, at least to the extent that consent forms are used. The rights and responsibilities of family members in the context of look-back testing have not received the same attention, though the requirement to save samples of DNA, for example, implies that the genetic information they contain may be useful to family members even after the death of the depositor. Questions that have not been addressed include: Who in the family should have access to genetic information extractable from biologic samples, including DNA, obtained from individuals after the death of the depositor? To the extent that genetic information is familial, and information on one individual automatically discloses information on blood relations, grounds may exist for limiting access to DNA testing on deceased members of a family. That being the case, what limits should be placed on the type of testing done on the samples, and who should be responsible for controlling access to the samples, the type of testing done, and how the information is interpreted and communicated to relatives of the deceased?

THE RESPONSIBILITY OF THE STATE

The primary role of the state with regard to the handling of genetic information has been more restrictive than prescriptive. The state has, in some cases, placed statutory restrictions on the storage of and access to such information to protect individual citizens, particularly with regard to genetic discrimination and health insurance.[13] It would appear, at first glance, to have little, if any, role to play in recalling individuals for updating of genetic counselling, an activity which is arguably appropriately covered by existing regulations concerning the practice of medicine. However, in countries like Canada, where the bulk of genetics laboratory services, especially DNA diagnostic testing, are carried out in laboratories funded, directly or indirectly, by government, the state would appear to have some responsibility for ensuring that the facilities provided are adequate to deal with the service load generated by the obligation to re-test DNA samples for the purposes of updating genetic counselling. For example, is it reasonable for a society to require laboratories that are part of a government-funded health care system to store samples of DNA for extended periods of time, under specific conditions, without providing the financial resources to do so? The question is not qualitatively different from many similar issues concerning health care resources, and it is not likely to be answered adequately until the more general issue is resolved.

Conclusions

The pressure created by the rapidity of developments in genetics has created new problems for geneticists, particularly with respect to the need to update genetic counselling in the light of new advances in diagnostic technology. Existing guidelines for the handling and storage of samples by DNA diagnostic and banking facilities anticipate the potential future importance of retesting DNA samples from individuals who may have undergone genetic testing in the past, by requiring that samples be stored under secure conditions for long periods of time. The guidelines also stipulate what measures must be taken to ensure that the identity of the depositor is protected. However, the guidelines are less helpful in establishing the assignment of responsibility for determining what samples should be re-tested, when it should be done, and how new genetic risk information can be generated and the significance of the information established without compromising the autonomy of the depositor or consultand. What is emerging is the concept of shared responsibility involving the medical geneticist, the primary care physician, the laboratory, and the consultand. Having been appropriately advised of the importance of doing so, and on condition that suitable mechanisms are developed by geneticists and primary care physicians to enable the individual to know when recounselling would be appropriate, the consultand should be expected to assume significant responsibility for initiating the process, either through contact with their primary care physician or a specialist in clinical genetics. Acceptance of such a principle places enormous pressure on geneticists to ensure that individuals and their primary care physicians are equipped with information appropriate to make such decisions.

Acknowledgements

We are grateful for discussions with Dr. Dorothy Wertz.

Endnotes and References

1 Stern L., "Mother of Terminally Ill Boys Wins 'Wrongful Birth' Lawsuit" (June 12, 1996), *The Toronto Star* A12.

2 Ad Hoc Committee on DNA Technology of the American Society of Human Genetics, "DNA Banking and DNA Analysis: Points to Consider" (1988), 42 *Am. J Hum. Genet.* 781.

3 Yates J.R.W., S. Malcolm and A.P. Read, "Guidelines for DNA Banking. Report of the Clinical Genetics Society Working Party on DNA Banking" (1989), 26 *J Med. Genet.* 245.

4 Hall J., J. Hamerton, D. Hoar, R. Korneluk, P. Ray, D. Rosenblatt and S. Wood, "Policy Statement Concerning DNA Banking and Molecular Genetic Diagnosis" (1991), 14*Clin. & Inv. Med.* 363.

5 McEwen J.E. and P.R. Reilly, "A Survey of DNA Diagnostic Laboratories Regarding DNA Banking" (1995), 56 *Am. J Med. Genet.* 1477.

6 Ibid.

7 Knoppers B.M. and C.M. Laberge, "DNA Sampling and Informed Consent" (1989), 140 *C MAJ* 1023. Also Knoppers B.M. and C.M. Laberge, "DNA Banking/Collecting: A Canadian 'Sample' of Consent Forms" in B.M. Knoppers, Caulfield T. and Kinsella T.D., eds, *Legal Rights and Human Genetic Material* (Toronto: Emond Montgomery Publications Ltd, 1996).

8 Fraser F.C., "Genetic Counseling" (1974), 26 *Am. J Hum. Genet.* 636.

9 Ibid.

10 Emery A.E.H. and I.M. Pullen, *Psychological Aspects of Genetic Counselling* (London: Academic Press, 1984).

11 Supra note 7.

12 Hannig V.L., E.W. Clayton and K.M. Edwards, "Whose DNA Is It Anyway? Relationships Between Families and Researchers" (1993), 47 *Am. J Med. Genet.* 257.

13 Hudson K.L., K.H. Rothenberg, L.B. Andrews, M.J.E. Kahn and F.S. Collins, "Genetic Discrimination and Health Insurance: An Urgent Need for Reform" (1995), 270 *Science* 391.

THE GENETIC INFORMATION SUPERHIGHWAY: RULES OF THE ROAD FOR CONTACTING RELATIVES AND RECONTACTING FORMER PATIENTS

LORI B. ANDREWS

Professor of Law and Norma and Edna Freehling Scholar

Chicago-Kent College of Law

Research Fellow, American Bar Foundation

Should legal policies facilitate (or even force) our ride along the information superhighway that is contained in our genes? American courts have only recently begun to address the issue of whether physicians must breach a patient's confidentiality and warn his or her relatives about genetic risks; courts have yet to grapple with whether physicians must recontact a patient when new information is discerned about him or her from existing genetic information or samples. Whether the law will evolve in the direction of greater disclosure will depend on the value assigned to genetic information. In a culture such as the United States in which the benefits of genetic information tend to be assumed or exaggerated, and the potential harmful impacts ignored (such as the impact of genetic information on self image, personal relationships, and relationships with social institutions), we may see increasing attempts to push the law towards a disclosure model. Nevertheless, the potential impact of genetic information cautions against such a model.

The Impact of Genetic Information

The question of whether legal policies will develop to foster the spread of genetic information will depend on a society's implicit or explicit assessment of how useful and beneficial such information is thought to be in an individual's personal decision making and how likely it is that the individual will learn about that information in other ways. As these assessments are undertaken, we need to be aware that the types of genetic information available and their potential audiences have changed markedly in the past two decades. Genetic testing such as carrier testing and prenatal testing used to be available to people who could identify themselves as being in high risk groups, such as people whose family history or ethnic background suggested that they might be at higher than average risk for a given genetic mutation, or women whose advanced maternal age put them at a higher than average risk of giving birth to a child with Down syndrome. In many instances, the person who was being offered testing knew someone with that disorder (since others in their family, or ethnic group, or age group may have been affected). Now, however, wider scale population screening is being advocated, so that more people can be tested for more things. Some geneticists[1] and policy analysts,[2] for example, foresee a time when the entire Caucasian population of childbearing age will be tested for the cystic fibrosis gene. Thus, while in the past, individuals may have known that particular types of genetic information might be relevant to them, that may be less true today. An argument could consequently be made that, since people may not know when to seek genetic information, genetic information should seek them.

There are several developments that caution against an unabashedly pro-disclosure policy that provides unasked-for genetic information to individuals, however. The first is that the types of genetic information that are available, and the significance of such information, have changed markedly in the past two decades. Initially, there was a societal consensus that disorders being tested for were serious (for example, Tay-Sachs disease, Down syndrome, and sickle cell anemia). This has changed; now, for example, there are a variety of prenatal tests available for what are considered to be less serious conditions, for disorders that can be ameliorated after birth (such as phenylketonuria), for disorders that will occur later in life (such as breast cancer), and for conditions that may not even be viewed as medical disorders (such as sexual preference). These types of genetic information may be less central to most individuals' decision making process than information about, for example, Tay-Sachs disease, which presents a fatal, imminent threat to infants.

Even conditions which were considered serious when genetic testing was first introduced may be viewed differently today. The disability rights and independent living movement has created a different perspective on the value of life with Down syndrome, spina bifida and other physical or mental disabilities. At the same time, better treatments have enhanced the quality of life and life span of people with conditions such as sickle cell anemia and cystic fibrosis. For those reasons, there may be less consensus among people that it is desirable to learn about their own or their offspring's genetic risks.

Even in situations in which genetic information might arguably be material to an individual's personal or medical decisions, people may choose not to seek the information because of potential negative psychological or social impact. Learning genetic information about oneself or one's children can cause anxiety,[3] can cause one to have a negative view of *other* aspects of one's health,[4] can negatively influence one's relationship with one's spouse,[5] and can change the way one experiences pregnancy.[6] Even when the results of genetic testing reveal that a person does *not* have a genetic mutation, the results may cause psychological harm to her. Some people experience "survivor's guilt", similar to that of soldiers whose buddies have died in war, as they wonder why they have been spared when other family members tragically have inherited the gene.[7] Of people who undergo genetic testing for Huntington's disease and learn that they do *not* have the gene, 10% experience severe psychological problems as a result.[8] In addition, learning they do not have the gene radically changes their self-image.[9] One woman said, "If I'm not at risk - Who am I?"[10] The generation of genetic information can also lead to stigmatization and discrimination. Insurers and employers may discriminate against an individual based on his or her genetic status.[11] In the United States, unlike countries with national health insurance, people are penalized for knowledge. If they know they will later become ill, they must disclose that fact (if asked) to insurers, who may then drop then from health insurance coverage.

Because of the potential impact of genetic information, there are a growing number of situations in which even if people are aware of the availability of genetic tests, they may decide that they do not want to receive the genetic information that is potentially available. Fewer than 15% of people who are at risk of having the gene for Huntington's disease request testing to learn if they have the disease.[12] In one study, in which members of the general population were offered cystic fibrosis carrier testing free of charge, only 4% sought testing when the offer came by letter, and only 24% sought testing when the offer was made when they were at the healthcare facility for other purposes.[13] And when pregnant women were tested without their knowledge for sickle cell carrier status, although all those who tested positive with positive spouses sought amniocentesis, none of the couples who learned their fetuses would be affected with sickle cell anemia aborted based on that genetic information.[14]

In summary, while genetic information is *potentially* relevant to a wider *range* of people, there are many people who do not want genetic information or who do not view such information as relevant to their personal and medical decision making. In addition, the existence of genetic information can cause certain psychological, social, and financial risks. This would argue against routinely disclosing unsought genetic information to patients or their relatives.

The Legal Context

The foundation for the legal policies governing disclosure of genetic information is found in court cases from the late 1970's and early 1980's. This was an era when the disorders for which genetic testing was available were generally considered to be serious. Moreover, with the recognition in 1973 of women's constitutionally protected right to an abortion, couples who did not receive information about the availability of genetic testing could claim that they had been harmed by not receiving information that would have been material to their decision about whether or not to continue a pregnancy.

A federal court case, *Lifchez v. Hartigan*,[15] held that, since people have a fundamental right to privacy to make reproductive decisions, they have a fundamental right to information upon which to make those decisions. Wrongful birth cases have been brought based on physicians' failure to advise a person he or she was in a high risk group for passing on a genetic or chromosomal defect (due to being a member of a particular ethnic group or being past a certain age) and that a test was available for that defect. For example, actions have been brought for wrongful birth for not advising a woman over 35 of the availability of amniocentesis.[16] Lawsuits have been brought for not properly diagnosing a genetic disorder in a first affected child in time to prevent the conception of a second affected child.[17]

Thus far, courts have found a duty on the part of physicians to offer testing only for serious disorders.[18] In addition, at least one court implied that, unless it is obvious that the patient is in a high risk group or the patient alerts the health care provider that he or she is in a high risk group, the provider does not have a duty to provide information about testing that is potentially applicable.[19]

The wrongful birth cases have dealt with plaintiffs who sought health care (primarily pregnancy related services) and were not told that there are tests available which could provide genetic information that might be relevant to their decisions about the condition for which they were seeking care. This is distinguishable from instances in which an individual is not a patient and is not currently seeking health care information.

Contacting Relatives

Telling *patients* who have sought health care services about their own genetic risks or the availability of means to obtain genetic information is a different matter than telling *non-patients* that their relative's genetic status indicate that, they, too, may be at genetic risk. U.S. law currently provides very little basis for a duty on the part of a patient's physician to inform relatives. In the legal cases dealing with confidentiality of medical information, if a physician does not have a relationship with the relative (or other third party), the physician may breach a patient's confidentiality only if the patient, by his or her action, will potentially present a risk of serious, imminent harm to the relative or other third party.

A duty to breach confidentiality has been found in psychiatric cases in which the patient disclosed to a mental health professional that he or she was going to commit violence against a particular individual.[20] Not every potential risk triggers a duty to disclose, just those which present serious, imminent harm to an identifiable person.

Courts have also ruled that physicians are privileged to breach a patient's confidentiality, if they wish, to warn family members or other individuals who are likely to be exposed to a patient's serious infectious disease.[21] In a few cases, the courts have gone further and actually found that the physician had a duty to warn and that the relatives or other third parties could sue physicians for not warning them. In some instances, the court indicated that the duty could be met, not by actually warning the relative or third party, but by warning the patient of the risks to the relative or other third party.[22]

There are few cases dealing directly with the issue of whether health care providers have a duty to breach confidentiality and warn relatives of a genetic risk. In a 1995 Florida case, *Pate v. Threkel*, a daughter whose mother was diagnosed as having a genetic disease, medullary thyroid cancer, sued the mother's physician for not warning her that she, too, might be at risk.[23] The court held that even if the prevailing standard of care required disclosure of the genetic nature of a condition, the physician had no duty to warn the daughter, but should have told the mother that the condition was genetic. The court ruled that a state law protected patients' confidentiality, that patients could be expected to pass on the warning, and that "requir[ing] the physician to seek out and warn various members of the patient's family would often be difficult or impractical and would place to heavy a burden upon the physician."[24] A 1996 New Jersey case, *Safer v. Estate of Pack*, took a different approach, however. In that case, a doctor had treated a man for retroperitoneal cancer, ulcerative adenocarcinoma of the colon and adenomatous polyps.[25] Twenty six years after the man died, his daughter learned she had cancer of the colon and multiple polyposis. She sued, claiming that her father's doctor had breached a duty to warn of the hereditary risk to her health and thus deprived her of the chance for monitoring, early detection, and early treatment. The trial court judge dismissed the case because there was no physician/patient relationship between the doctor and the daughter and because genetic disease was distinguishable from infectious disease since "the harm is already present within the non-patient child as opposed to being introduced, by a patient who was not warned to stay away."[26]

The appellate court, however, eschewed the need for a doctor-patient relationship. Because of the procedural posture of the case on appeal, the court was required to accept as true the daughter's expert's assertions that it was the prevailing standard of care at the time of the father's treatment to "warn of the known genetic threat."[27] The appellate court pointed out that genetic risks are as foreseeable as infectious ones and "[t]he individual or group at risk is easily identified, and substantial future harm is easily identified or minimized by a timely and effective warning."[28] Applying an infectious disease precedent, the court held that there can be a duty to warn relatives and remanded the case for trial for a determination of whether that duty was breached in this case. The court noted that the trial court would need to take a number of things into account, such as the extent of the daughter's risk, what the costs of monitoring would have been as compared to the expenses associated with the breach of duty, and whether - if the father had instructed the doctor *not* to disclose to his daughter - that request should have been honoured.

Despite the fact that *Safer* applied infectious disease precedents, cases dealing with warning people about genetic risks are different than those dealing with violence or infectious disease since there are already established social policies embodied in laws that are aimed at preventing violence or contagion. Thus, breach of confidentiality furthers an established social policy that has been subject to legislative debate. In contrast, society's position on genetic disease is not so clear cut. For example, no laws have been adopted to prevent the birth of children with genetic disorders.

The cases involving infectious disease and violence could be interpreted as offering no precedent for a privilege or duty of health care providers to breach confidentiality to warn relatives of a genetic risk. As the trial court in *Safer* noted, in the genetics context, the patient is not *causing* the relative to have the gene at issue.[29] Warning siblings or cousins about genetic risks will not prevent them from having the gene (that has already been programmed in at birth), although it might prevent a particularly risky gene/environment interaction. Warning them about their genetic risk may prevent them from conceiving a child with the gene (but such a future risk is not the type of serious, imminent harm about which the cases have generally required disclosure).

In all of the infectious disease cases where disclosure was permitted or required, there was something that the relative or other third party could have done to prevent infection or to prevent serious physical harm from occurring. These precedents suggest that, with respect to genetic diseases, there would not be a privilege or a duty to warn of an untreatable or unpreventable disorder. Thus, there would not be a duty to warn relatives that they were at risk of Huntington's disease, or that they might have a genetic or chromosomal abnormality that could lead to bearing a child with a genetic disorder.

Because the purpose of disclosure would be to protect the relative from harm, policy makers should also consider the potential harms to the relative from disclosure. If the relative is given new risk information, she would have to disclose that on insurance applications. She would also have to adjust psychologically to that information. The potential psychological harms might vary depending on whether there is a definitive test she might take to learn of her actual risk. For example, it could be problematic to inform a person that he or she is at risk of a particular type of cancer when there is no definitive test yet. While the person might undergo more frequent monitoring, the person might not actually need it and might be subject to increased worry and unnecessary procedures without sufficient benefit.

Similarly, consideration should also be given to the eugenic symbolism of breaching confidentiality to warn relatives. The Committee for the Study of Inborn Errors of Metabolism of the National Research Council cautioned that allowing a breach of confidentiality to warn relatives without consent implies "a medical-social judgement that genetic 'normality' is a prime childbearing goal for society to follow."[30]

Recontacting Patients

With respect to contacting relatives, there are important policy reasons not to require disclosure of genetic information to relatives,[31] including the negative impact that such a breach of confidentiality will have on patients' willingness to seek genetic testing in the first place; the potential negative social, psychological, and financial impact that such information will have on the relative who receives the information; and the eugenic message that is conveyed by mandating such disclosures. Similar cautions are appropriate with respect to recontacting patients when new genetic information is available about them.

Thus far, no U.S. court has found a duty to recontact a former patient to provide new genetic information (in contrast to a duty to continuing patients to advise them of new medical developments that might affect their care). The duty to recontact patients has been found in circumstances in which the physician has undertaken an intervention in a patient (such as by administering a drug or inserting an intrauterine device) and that particular intervention is later discovered to have risks about which the patient should be warned.[32] Such a duty is related to the physician's duty of informed consent and duty not to abandon the patient. In *Taber v. Riordan*, a case in which a patient suffered a non-negligently inflicted complication from surgery, the court pointed out that "[t]he duty to inform of possible complications before an operation or course of treatment can be analogized to the duty to inform the patient afterwards of complications that have arisen."[33] When a duty to recontact has been found, it has not mattered that the physician's initial relationship with the patient was fleeting or that much time had passed since the physician rendered the services. A physician was held to have a duty to recontact a patient about newly discovered risks of a Dalkon shield IUD, even though the physician had seen the patient only once.[34] In another case, approximately two decades had passed between the contact with the patient to prescribe a drug and the subsequent duty to disclose.[35]

Questions about recontacting former patients with *new* genetic information might arise in two different situations. In the first scenario, a new genetic test might be undertaken on the patient's previously collected tissue sample. Subsequent genetic testing on existing samples without a patient's knowledge and consent is not uncommon, and when patient identifiers are included, the researcher or clinician who undertook the testing may wonder if he or she should contact the patient with the new information. In one such instance a pathologist, without informing the patient or asking her permission, tested tissue left over from her biopsy for the gene for breast cancer. The pathologist then called the patient and told her she had the genetic mutation.[36]

In the second scenario, no new testing is done. Instead, the existing genetic information based on a consented-to test, takes on a new meaning.[37] To give a recent example, numerous people have undergone testing for apoE4 to determine if they are at a higher than average risk for heart attacks. Subsequently, some evidence emerged that apoE4 was associated with a higher than average risk of Alzheimer's disease. The physicians wondered whether they should now recontact the heart patients and tell them of their increased risk of Alzheimer's disease.[38]

The legal contexts of these two situations are quite distinct. There is a growing recognition that genetic testing should not be undertaken on a patient's sample without his or her advance, informed consent, because the generation of genetic information may cause physical, psychological, or financial harm to the patient. Recently, a variety of individuals and groups have suggested guidelines that should govern genetic testing on previously collected tissue samples.[39] These include an American College of Medical Genetics Committee (ACMG), an American Society of Human Genetics Committee (ASHG), the National Institutes of Health/Department of Energy Working Group on the Ethical, Legal and Social Implications of the Human Genome Project (ELSI Working Group) and a group of scientists, ethicists, lawyers, and consumers convened jointly by the National Institutes of Health (NIH) and the Centers for Disease Control and Prevention (CDC). Courts, too, have turned their attentions to the rules that should govern the collection and subsequent use of tissue.[40] The consensus of these groups in the United States, as well as the requirements of the federal regulation on human research,[41] is that informed consent of the patient is necessary before patient-identified testing is undertaken on samples collected for other purposes. Consequently, there are likely to be fewer circumstances in which physicians "discover" new genetic information about a particular individual by undertaking new testing on the patient's sample. Moreover, there is a growing consensus that a patient should be specifically asked in advance of collecting a tissue sample whether he or she wishes to be recontacted with test results.[42]

The situation in which the original consented-to test reveals new genetic information requires a different analysis, however. Here, the information has not been generated by any subsequent action that the physician undertook on the patient's sample; consequently, there is not the same opportunity to seek consent as there would be when a new test was necessary to generate the information. Nevertheless, the new information may be unwanted by the patient. In the case of apoE4 testing, people's interest in receiving information about their risk of heart disease may be quite different than their interest in receiving information about their risks of Alzheimer's disease. The people who seek apoE4 testing in the cardiac context generally have high cholesterol levels and thus already know that they are at higher than average risk for heart disease. They may feel there are actions they could take (such as diet, exercise, and other strategies) to prevent heart attacks. However, people may feel differently about receiving information about their risks of Alzheimer's disease. The information may be traumatic to them, since it is unexpected. Moreover, since there is no therapy to prevent Alzheimer's disease, fewer people may want that information than want information about heart disease. As noted earlier, fewer than 15% of people at risk seek testing for Huntington's disease, which, like Alzheimer's disease, is an untreatable late-onset disorder. Moreover, learning that one is at increased risk for Alzheimer's disease can be disruptive to one's life. Each time the person misplaces car keys, or forgets the name of a colleague, the person might nervously assume that he or she is symptomatic for Alzheimer's disease.

The interrelationships among certain genetic facts require a rethinking of the type of informed consent that is obtained in advance of *any* type of genetic testing. It may be necessary to inform patients that the results of tests they are considering undergoing may not only provide the immediate sought after information, but may also later be discovered to indicate risk factors for late onset disorders or for giving birth to a child with a serious genetic disorder. The fact that not everyone will want this secondary information should caution physicians about their decisions to employ genetic testing in the first place. They should ask themselves (and discuss with the patient) whether the information that is generated by the genetic test will have any impact on their clinical management of the patient. They should also ask the patient in advance of collecting the initial sample whether the patient wishes to be recontacted with new information about the following kinds of disorders: treatable versus untreatable disorders; early onset versus late onset disorders; disorders affecting the patient versus disorders that could affect potential offspring. Patients should be allowed to refuse or approve being recontacted in all circumstances or only for a subset of disorders.

Conclusion

As we embark on the information superhighway, we need to consider whether people want or need as much information about their internal worlds as they do about the external world. There is no question that the United States is an information seeking society, but the act of seeking genetic information is much different than going on the Web to get information for a term paper, read a movie review, or arrange a date. Studies of genetic testing reveal that certain information (about carrier status for particular disorders or about genetic mutations for late onset disorders) is not routinely sought by people who are informed of its existence. Research also shows that genetic information carries certain psychological, social, and financial risks. Such findings suggest that policy makers should rarely, if ever, encourage the provision of unasked for information by finding a duty to contact relatives or a duty to recontact patients.

Endnotes and References

1 Kerem B., J.M. Rommens, J.A. Buchanan, D. Markiewicz, T.K. Cox, A. Chakravarti, et al., "Identification of the Cystic Fibrosis Gene: Genetic Analysis" (1989), 245 *Science* 1076.

2 Office of Technology Assessment, U.S. Congress, *Cystic Fibrosis and DNA Tests: Implications of Carrier Screening* (Washington, D.C.: U.S. Government Printing Office, 1992).

3 Childs B., et al., "Tay-Sachs Screening: Social and Psychological Impact" (1976), 28 *Am. J Hum. Genet.* 550.

4 Marteau T. M., "Psychological Implications of Genetic Screening" (1992), 28 *Birth Defects: Original Article Series* 185 at 185.

5 Quaid K.A. and M.K. Weeson, "The Effect of Predictive Testing for Huntington Disease on Intimate Relationships" (1994), 55 *Am. J Hum. Genet.* 1728.

6 Katz Rothman B., *The Tentative Pregnancy* (New York: Viking, 1986).

7 Quaid K.A., et al., "Knowledge, Attitude and Decision to be Tested for Huntington's Disease" (1989), 36 *Clin. Genet.* 431; Wexler N., "Genetic Jeopardy and the New Clairvoyance" (1985), 6 *Progress in Medical Genetics* 277.

8 Huggins M., et al, "Predictive Testing for Huntington Disease in Canada: Adverse Effects and Unexpected Results in Those Receiving a Decreased Risk" (1992), 42 *Am. J Med. Genet.* 508 at 508.

9 In one case, a man whose parent had Huntington's disease assumed he would get the disease as well. He lived his life on the assumption he would die early. He engaged in dangerous sports and did not save for the future. When he was tested and learned he did not have the gene, he ended up embezzling from his company. Ibid., at 512.

10 Supra note 8 at 510.

11 Andrews L. B., "Prenatal Screening and the Culture of Motherhood" (1996), 47 *Hastings Law Journal* 4. See also, Holtzman N. A., *Proceed with Caution* (Johns Hopkins University Press, 1989) at 195. See also, Billings P.R., M.A. Kohn, M. deCuevas, J. Beckwith, J.S. Alper and M.R. Natowicz, "Discrimination as a Consequence of Genetic Testing" (1992), 50 *Am. J Hum. Genet.* 476. See also, Hudson K. L., K.H. Rothenberg, L. B. Andrews, M.J. Ellis Kahn and F. S. Collins, "Genetic Discrimination and Health Insurance: An Urgent Need for Reform" (1995), 270 *Science* 391.

12 Bloch M., M. Fahy, S. Fox, and M.R. Hayden, "Predictive Testing for Huntington Disease: II. Demographic Characteristics, Life-Style Patterns, Attitudes, and Psychological Assessments of the First Fifty-One Test Candidates" (1989), 32 *Amer. J. Med. Genet.* 217.

13 Tambor E.T., B.A. Bernhardt, G.A. Chase, R.R. Faden, G. Geller, K.J. Hofman and N.A. Holtzman, "Offering Cystic Fibrosis Screening in an HMO Population: Factors Associated with Utilization" (1994), 55 *Am. J Hum. Genet.* 626.

14 Rowley P.T., S. Loader, C.J. Sutera and M. Walden, "Do Pregnant Women Benefit from Hemoglobinopathy Carrier Detection?" (1989), 565 *Ann. N.Y. Acad. Sci.* 152.

15 735 F.Supp. 1361 (N.D. Ill. 1990).

16 *Becker v. Schwartz*, 46 N.Y.2d 401, 386 N.E.2d 807, 413 N.Y.S.2 895 (1978).

17 *Schroeder v. Perkel*, 87 N.J. 53, 432 A.2d 834 (1981) (cystic fibrosis).

18 Most wrongful birth cases have involved serious illness, and in wrongful life cases, courts have recognized a distinction between seriousness and non-seriousness. See *Turpin v. Sortini*, 643 P.2d 954, 962-63 (Cal. 1982) (footnote omitted) in which the court reasoned "[i]n this case, in which the plaintiff's only affliction is deafness, it seems quite unlikely that a jury would ever conclude that life with such a condition is worse than not being born at all. Other wrongful life cases, however, have involved children with more serious, debilitating and painful conditions."

19 *Munro v. Regents of the University of California*, 215 Cal. App. 3d 977, 263 Cal. Rptr. 878, 885 (1989).

20 *Tarasoff v. Regents of University of California*, 131 Cal. Rptr. 14, 551 P.2d 334 (1976).

21 *Simonsen v. Swenson*, 104 Neb. 224, 177 N.W. 831 (1920).

22 *DiMarco v. Lynch Homes-Chester County*, 583 A.2d 422 (Pa. 1990).

23 *Pate v. Threlkel*, 661 So.2d 278 (Fla. 1995).

24 Ibid., at 282.

25 *Safer v. Estate of Pack*, 291 N.J. Super. 619, 677 A.2d 1188 (1996).

26 Ibid., at 624.

27 Ibid., at 625.

28 Ibid., at 626.

29 In the infectious disease cases, if the third party would have gotten the disease anyway, there was no duty to warn. See *Skillings v. Allen*, 148 Minn. 88, 180 N.W. 916 (1921); *Britton v. Soltes*, 563 N.E.2d 910 (Ill.App. 1990).

30 Committee for the Study of Inborn Errors of Metabolism, National Research Council, *Genetic Screening: Programs, Principles, and Research* (1975). Troy Duster, in his testimony before the Institute of Medicine's Committee on Assessing Genetic Risks on September 17, 1992, made the point that the existence of a genetic screening test "communicate[s] that the screened for characteristic is undesirable." Requiring disclosure would even further underscore the undesirability of the characteristic.

31 For a more extensive discussion of this topic, see Andrews L.B., "Gen-etiquette: Are There Moral and Legal Responsibilities to Share Genetic Information Within Families?" in Rothstein M., ed., *Genetic Secrets* (Yale University Press, forthcoming).

32 See, for example, *Tresemer v. Barke*, 150 Cal. Rptr. 384 (Ct. App. 1978).

33 403 N.E.2d 1349, 1353 (Ill. App. Ct. 1980).

34 *Tresemer v. Barke*, 150 Cal. Rptr. 384, 389 (Ct. App. 1978).

35 *Mink v. University of Chicago*, 460 F.Supp. 713, 715 (N.D. Ill. 1978).

36 Andrews L.B., "Genetics and Informed Consent" (1996), 271 *Science* 5254.

37 For example, a physician may undertake a diagnostic test on a patient that indicates that a *high* level of an enzyme indicates that the individual is a carrier for a particular genetic disorder. Subsequently, it may be learned that a *low* level of the enzyme indicates carrier status for another disorder. Does the physician have a duty to recontact the individuals whose initial tests had revealed a low level of the enzyme and tell them about the new meaning? Andrews L.B., "Torts and the Double Helix: Malpractice Liability for Failure to Warn of Genetic Risks" (1992), 29 *Houston L. Rev.* 149.

38 Kolata G., "Gene Test Poses Dilemma for Alzheimer's Experts" (October 26, 1995), *International Herald Tribune*.

39 Wright Clayton E., et al., "Informed Consent for Genetic Research on Stored Tissue Samples" (1995), 274 *JAMA* 1786. See also, American College of Medical Genetics Storage of Genetics Materials Committee, "Statement on Storage and Use of Genetic Materials" (1995), 57 *Am. J. Hum. Genet.* 1499. See also, Andrews L.B., "Genetics and Informed Consent" (1996), 271 *Science* 1346; American Society of Human Genetics, "Statement on Informed Consent for Genetic Research" (1996), 59 *Am. J. Hum. Genet.* 471.

40 *Moore v. Regents of the University of California*, 51 Cal. 3d 120, 271 Cal. Rptr. 146, 793 P.2d 479 (July 1990).

41 45 C.F.R. § 46.101(b)(5) (1994).

42 See, for example, supra note 39.

DNA SAMPLING AND DUTIES TO RELATIVES LOOKING BACK: EUROPEAN APPROACHES

MAURICE A.M. DE WACHTER

Consultant in Bioethics, member of the IRB at the Brussels Sint Jans Clinic

President of EACME, the European Association of Centres of Medical Ethics

European Approaches: Focus on Informed Consent

Informed choice in health care has been acknowledged as a major expression of individual self-determination. Western society in general and many European nations in particular subscribe to this principle. The latest Draft of the so-called Bioethics Convention of the Council of Europe says in article 5 that "an intervention in the health field may only be carried out after the person concerned has given free and informed consent to it."[1] In 1992, the Committee of Ministers of the same Council of Europe issued a Recommendation stating that self-determination guaranteed by express, free and informed consent is basic. The Ministers recommended special safeguards for minors, for persons suffering from mental disorders and adults placed under limited guardianship. Nevertheless, in the context of genetic testing, they also said that "testing of these persons for diagnostic purposes should be permitted only when this is necessary for their own health or if the information is imperatively needed to diagnose the existence of a genetic disease in family members."[2]

The exponential growth of knowledge and know-how in the field of genetics, particularly the use of blood and tissue samples expands the horizons of informed consent, privacy and confidentiality. Back in 1989, the Health Council of The Netherlands had already stated that "cell banks should require a code of behaviour which, on the one hand, does justice to the donor's rights and, on the other hand, does not impede unnecessarily the use of material for the benefit of others or for scientific research".[3] This proposed solution is very general and admittedly, does not automatically resolve the many dilemmas encountered in the field of genetics, especially the tensions between the interests of the individual and the interests of other individuals or of the community. In a recent Report on the "Proper Use of Human Tissue", the same Health Council gave the following scenarios of good practice: "A centre for clinical genetics stores identifiable (coded) DNA samples for use in diagnostic procedures involving relatives; the geneticist has discussed this with the patient. Agreements have been reached on what is to be done with any new findings and consent has been obtained. Later use for diagnostic purposes is permitted. Some of the material is sent abroad, in anonymous form, as part of a research project. The patients have received general information on the possible use of anonymous material in research. This use is permissible".[4]

These scenarios bring us to our topic of "looking back", that is, "future research or testing or even refinement of tests already consented to, (which) may result in a look back at a later date".[5] As with clinical genetics in its earliest stages, the main question remains about information which will be of interest to potentially at-risk relatives. Now, as then, one should say that the detection of hereditary diseases can reduce and prevent suffering, but that it can also cause suffering. The inaccurate interpretation of genetic information has caused a great deal of damage in the past.[6] Nowadays, it is morally imperative to make sure that "look back testing" is more than a potential blessing and, certainly, more than a mixed blessing.

As for the other focus of this paper, namely the duties to relatives, one must never forget that the position of relatives is often only a step away from the position of the screenee. For all practical purposes, relatives are bound to find themselves in exactly the same position as their affected family members. Relatives, in other words, are "virtual applicants" for screening. In the actual state of their knowledge (or ignorance) they are, so to speak, candidate-applicants.

Now, with respect to the very narrow topic of "looking back" techniques and duties to relatives, the literature on the European approaches is quite scant. Systematic studies of how duties to relatives have been addressed are still lacking. One clear exception is in the field of psychology with several national surveys, e.g. on the transfer of information about genetic transmission to brothers and sisters of parents with a CF child. Thus, it was shown that in Belgium about two thirds of the parents with a CF child inform their brothers and sisters about the genetic aspects of the disorder. Unfortunately, the information transfer from CF parents to relatives was far from perfect.[7] Apart from the field of psychology, little more than anecdotal and casuistic evidence is available. Case histories are, of course, of the greatest importance. They get one in touch with the real situation but, unfortunately, they seldom allow for generalization.

At the other end of the spectrum, that is on the side of basic principles, the literature reflects a consensus in many European countries (e.g. Denmark, Finland, Netherlands, UK) as well as in the Council of Europe. Almost all agree on the basic principle of respect for the autonomy of the individual governing all genetic testing and screening. Generally, they also agree that legislation and regulation concerning the use of human tissue ought to be guided by four sets of norms, namely the norms regarding information, patients' rights, the management of tissue storage, and the principle of non-commercialism.[8] What is missing is the practical "fleshing out" of these fundamental principles into agreements, codes of conduct and policies regulating the good clinical practice in genetics.

Specifically with regard to DNA sampling policies and agreements, neither Europe nor North America has defined the rights and obligations of persons from whom the DNA sample was taken. The results of a recent survey of 150 laboratories in the USA suggest that the rapidly growing activity of DNA banking is not accompanied by a corresponding concern for important social, ethical and legal aspects. The researchers conclude that "many DNA banks pay insufficient attention to the interests of consumers and do not adequately define their rights".[9] The question arising from this unsatisfactory state of affairs is whether self-regulation will be sufficient or whether regulation, possibly even legislation is indicated. Some sort of self-regulation seems to exist in, for instance, the "Concept guidelines for the molecular genetics predictive test in Huntington's disease", where several sections concern duties to relatives. The guidelines affirm the basic right of the individual to take the test as well as his ownership of the results. Here is what is said about the latter issue: "Ownership of the test results remains with the individual who requested the test. Legal ownership of the stored DNA remains with the person from whom the blood was taken".[10]

So, the first conclusion should be that European approaches to "looking back testing" ought to go beyond the initiatives of the past to define the proper use of human tissue. The simple reiteration of existing fundamental principles will not meet the new ethical challenges arising from the evolution of genetic technology.

The Screenee as the Gatekeeper of Information

The transfer of genetic information to relatives of the screenee has been a major problem for several decades and there appears to be no general consensus about how to proceed; when and what to tell relatives. At the Center for Human Genetics in Leuven (Belgium), it has been a long-standing tradition to rely heavily on the potential of existing family relationships, with the screenee at the helm. He/she is the one who commands and steers the communication process with the relatives. All information is his/hers and remains such until he/she decides to share it with others. Even after having been told that such information is important, of vital importance sometimes, to brothers and sisters or to distant relatives, the screenee is the only one to decide what will be transferred to which one(s) of the relatives. Normally he/she would be the one to make the first contact with relatives about available information which is of importance to them. The genetic counsellor, occasionally, will mention the screenee's duties but will exercise little or no pressure. This is no place for distribution of responsibility regarding the disclosure of genetic information in the sense mentioned by J.T.R. Clarke. Moreover, the acquired experience of 25 years of such policy seems to show that this is the best way to promote an optimal and maximal uptake in families affected by genetic disease. Scientific evidence confirms this impression: e.g. that the CF parents play a key role in informing relatives about their heightened risk of carrying the CF gene.[11]

This policy means that the responsibility to inform relatives never lies with the doctor, not even in cases where the information is essential to make choices on reproduction and career planning. Only the informed consent given by the patient will entitle a doctor to inform relatives. This approach allows the screenee to keep information about herself/himself secret even from relatives. The only possible exception would be a situation where vital information concerning life and death or serious damage would be involved, for example.

Recent developments in genetic screening have resulted in the possibility of a direct diagnosis of genetic mutations. This has at least two important consequences. On the one hand, the previous need to find affected individuals in the family circle is no longer present. Invasion of privacy of relatives can thereby be avoided. On the other hand, many new cases of direct diagnosis without family history can now be detected. Obstructive oligospermia, for instance, is known to occur more often in CF carriers. This brings the andrologist or gynecologist, who cannot find other etiologies for infertility, to refer a patient to the Center for Clinical Genetics and ask for a diagnosis of a possible genetic mutation for CF. Other examples known are in the field of Huntington's disease. Unexplained chorea in a fifty year old male, without any HD family history, may prompt the neurologist to add to other diagnostic investigations such as NMR scanning and eye testing, the request for genetic testing. It is also important to prepare these patients for the future possibility of informing relatives about the test results. Delicate and time consuming though this may be, and despite the occasional refusal by the patient, it is the doctor's duty to introduce the patient to the world of genetics. Understandably, the more remote a physician is from a genetics centre the more difficult it will be for him to properly inform the patient. Nevertheless, a patient ought to be told about such possible responsibilities from the earliest stages of genetic testing. A neurologist asking for such additional genetic testing cannot simply provide a general statement that a battery of various tests will be performed and thus run the risk, subsequently, of having to face a positive result for a genetic disease he left unmentioned to the patient.

Summarizing the screenee's responsibility as a gatekeeper of information, we might say that every new genetic patient by definition belongs to a cluster of potential other affected individuals. This network of "virtual applicants" should be brought to the patient's attention from the very start. Furthermore, good medical practice demands that the patient suffering from, let us say, chorea-like symptoms, greatly unexplained by the neurologist, be informed about a possible genetic test. In addition, the role of clinical genetic centres facing the increase of demands for genetic testing is to convince colleagues across the country of the necessity of well informing patients about such diagnostic methods, their implications and potential results. To offer genetic testing can be done only if we proceed with caution.

Informing Relatives

The Nuffield Report on ethical issues in genetic screening rejects the suggestion that there should be a legally enforceable duty of screenees to inform family members. However, two situations seem to allow for an exception: the first, "where the information would influence a decision having potentially damaging rather than merely inconvenient consequences for other family members"; and second, "if it can be determined that the reasons are malicious".[12]

The discussion of these exceptional disclosures is linked to the way a particular society looks at privacy. In other words, there is a multicultural dimension to genetic information. It has been said that it may be "appropriate to assume that certain genetic information should be passed on to other members of the family." Consistently, "appropriate privacy for genetic information is laid down by the norms of a particular society."[13]

It is, indeed, fair to say that the appreciation of genetic information is not the same across all cultures. Even in Western countries, genetic information is not perceived by everyone alike. For some it is neutral, for others it is hot stuff. A recent Report of the Health Council of The Netherlands illustrates how the perceptions of the individuals in one family may differ with regards to genetic information. The report sets out that "the hereditary nature of disorders means that any information obtained will also be of interest to other members of the family. This may lead to a stressful situation in which the person being tested wishes to be informed of the result, while one of his relatives does not wish to know, e.g. if a person wishes to know whether or not he is at risk of a hereditary form of cancer. Other members of the family may not wish to learn of this via screening."[14]

We found that the literature reflects this uneven approach to genetic information. Some believe that genetic information is like all medical information, whereas others see it as different and therefore, in need of tighter rules of confidentiality and secrecy.

Does Genetic Information Differ from Medical Information?

At first blush, one would think that genetic information is no different than other medical information. It originates from clinical situations where diagnosis and the possibility of treatment are the goals. The rule of confidentiality, as we all know, is quasi-absolute and valid in most cases. Exceptions have to be justified with serious arguments such as avoidable life-threatening situations. One would, therefore, expect that the same rule governs the handling of both genetic and other medical information. The previously mentioned Recommendation of the Council of Europe covers professional secrecy and states that genetic information is protected like other medical data. However, "in the case of a severe genetic risk in other family members, consideration should be given, in accordance with national legislation and professional rules of conduct, to informing family members about matters relevant to their health and that of their future children."[15]

But then again, the popular as well as some professional literature, leaves one under the impression that genetic information possesses distinctive qualities. Occasional remarks made on the sensitive nature of genetic information, on its penetrating, predictive, sometimes embarrassing nature illustrate this perception. Genetic information, it is suggested, deserves to more protection than other medical information. This is even more so wherever genetic information is used outside of health care situations, for instance in the work environment or in private insurance.

In line with this not uncommon presumption, we scanned the literature for characteristics attributed to genetic information that were distinct from other medical information. Three professional groups were thus surveyed: geneticists, lawyers and ethicists. Patients and patient organizations were also surveyed.

The results of our analysis of these groups showed that:

1. Geneticists handle genetic information carefully and with the greatest caution. Files are strictly controlled, especially when central registration is needed for clinical reasons. Caution, restraint, and thorough reservation are, if not universal, certainly common among geneticists.
2. Health lawyers speak about the predictive nature of genetic information, its intimate and sensitive character, and the possible societal and psychological consequences of its use. However, they do not set it apart, over and above other medical information.
3. Ethicists seem to think that the classical rules of medical secrecy will protect genetic information, even though they sometimes mention that the nature of the data necessitates greater caution and a stringent application of the rules of secrecy. Ethicists, moreover, point to the risk of abuse of genetic data, especially in the context of personal registers. Generally, ethicists formulate more serious objections against additional testing than against the use of already existing information. They are also concerned about the use of genetic information in a social context.
4. Patients and patient organizations warn against the already existing abuse, for instance the loss of health care insurance in the USA. They accuse society of giving in to a trend of discrimination against the genetically unfortunate individual. They point out that insurance policies already admit to such discrimination.

The outcome of our analysis shows that neither professional nor patient group clearly defines what intrinsic characteristics might be found in genetic information as opposed to medical information. They do, however, agree that the use of genetic information may degenerate into abuse and adverse social consequences of the unregulated access to and dissemination of genetic information.[16]

The Right Not to Know

In 1994, the Council of Europe adopted a recommendation "*On screening as a tool of preventive medicine*". This recommendation says that "the right to privacy requires that the results of tests as a general rule are not communicated to those who do not wish to be informed" and adds that "it is preferable not to screen individuals who do not wish to be informed of the results of the screening."[17]

The right not to know is, here again, justified by the negative effects such knowledge may entail. "Knowledge of future disorders ... can be most intimidating. It can have an effect on entering relationships, obtaining employment or obtaining approval for insurance coverage. A person's right to protection of their personal privacy means that they are not obliged to receive information in general. Health workers will have to respect the wishes of participants."[18]

In The Netherlands, the *Medical Treatment Agreements Act* (WGBO) describes the right not to known as follows "If a patient has indicated a desire not to be informed, then no information will be provided, except where the patient's interests in this regard are outweighed by the harm to the patient or others which could follow from this."[19] Since the situation under discussion is one of population screening in which the patient chose to participate, one may presume that the exercise of their right not to know would "only relate to chance findings or unexpected results."[20] The Report then recommends the following course of action: "it is therefore necessary to notify all participants in advance of the possibility of chance findings and to ask them if they wish to be informed about this. After due consideration, however, the health worker can decide to pass on certain information despite it (that is despite their wish not to be told)."[21]

How do Relatives Receive and Work with Genetic Information?

For over ten years now, a group of psychologists at the Center for Human Genetics in Leuven (Belgium) has carried out a number of studies on the psychological impact of autosomal recessive inheritance and genetic testing in cystic fibrosis. Out of the many publications generated by this team, several are of interest to the topic of duties to relatives. In the remainder of this paper some of those results will be presented. It may be noted that

Belgium belongs to the group of many countries where the general policy is not to offer CF carrier testing actively to large groups.

Self-Perception

In one study, the intention was to compare the impact of the news about CF carrier status to the impact of the news about non-carrier status and to the feelings they attributed to most carriers.[22] The researchers found that CF carriers suffered from some sort of self-stigmatization: they had significantly less positive feelings about themselves than non-carriers. Indications of social stigmatization were also found. Carriers as well as non-carriers attributed more negative feelings to most carriers of the CF gene than to most non-carriers. Moreover, carriers of the CF gene attributed more negative feelings to other carriers than to themselves. The conclusion was that CF carrier status seemed to carry negative connotations, but that it was not clear whether this self-stigmatizing effect was strong enough to change the self-concept of the tested individual. Perhaps the bias of "illusory superiority" was able to counterbalance the blow received from the bad news. It is noteworthy that an interesting hypothesis of this research remained unconfirmed, namely that "being identified as a carrier would be more traumatizing for people who live very close to a CF patient."[23]

A subsequent study was based on interviews taken at least one year after subjects had received the test result about their carrier status. The earlier suggestion of a stigmatizing effect of the CF carrier status was proven to have no lasting negative effect on anxiety and self-concept in interviews taken one year after receiving the test result. It is interesting to note that all carriers were CF relatives. They all said that they could cope well. "Nevertheless, an intriguing significant interaction was found: the group of sibs carrying the CF gene felt less integrated in the family than the group of non-carrier sibs. This effect of carrier status was not found in the more distant relatives."[24] The researchers felt it was important to pay sufficient attention to this problem during genetic counselling when brothers and sisters of a CF patient receive a test result.

Both studies reveal a slight potential for self-stigmatization and for social stigmatization in newly identified carriers who are also CF relatives. At the same time, they found that there was no significant effect on the participants' level of anxiety, and even less on their self-concept.

Transfer of Information to Relatives

The same researchers in Leuven studied the transfer of information about genetic transmission to brothers and sisters of parents with a CF child. They found that such information was only partially passed on to the relatives who had a high risk of being a carrier. The gaps in CF knowledge amongst relatives showed that explicit genetic counselling would be useful. They felt that spontaneous information transfer could be a good starting point but should be rounded out by an effort to detect those who "missed the boat" and by disseminating explicit risk information to those needing professional assistance. "Geneticists should take a more active stance in offering counselling to relatives with a heightened risk of carrying the CF gene, of course not directly but through patients or their parents."[25]

Family Planning

Clinical geneticists want to measure the impact testing and counselling have upon people's future decisions, for instance about reproduction and family planning. One important factor with regard to further reproduction is the perceived risk. This has been described for CF. In Belgium, studies of parents of children with CF revealed that for two thirds of them the risk involved in another pregnancy significantly influenced their planning. Many of them either postponed the next pregnancy or elected to have no further children. At least 53% of the parents of a firstborn with CF had no successive pregnancies within an average follow-up period of about seven years.[26]

The same group of researchers has just submitted another paper on "risk perception in a population tested for CF carrier status and on the impact of the test result on reproductive decision making".[27] The particular problem addressed is the correct interpretation of the results of a CF carrier test and the correct understanding of the risk of having a CF child. As is well known, both interpretation and understanding are complicated by the limited sensitivity of the DNA test. Moreover, the paper focused on the residual risk after a negative test result. It showed that knowledge about recessive transmission was weak. For instance, only half of the subjects knew that there is no risk when only one partner carries the CF gene. The researchers promptly concluded that "the current routine of offering CF carrier testing to CF families clearly underestimates the problems people have in understanding and remembering information about the recessive transmission of CF and the associated risks. The doctors who mediated for carrier testing seemed to rely too much on the process of information transfer within the families."[28] "In the case of both partners receiving a negative test result, more than half of the subjects were not aware of the restrictions of DNA testing, and were convinced that there was no residual risk. Two thirds of the subjects from the "carrier + negative test result couples" were aware of the residual risk. This risk did not hamper further reproduction. For the carriers who were single or whose partner was not tested, understanding of the risk was very difficult."[29]

Conclusion

1. The studies on the psychological impact of genetic information on relatives illustrate how important it is to pay sufficient attention to several

problems. First of all, genetic counselling should be available to relatives as well as to screenees. Second, health workers should look out for problems with the "self-perception" of relatives during genetic counselling when brothers or sisters of patients receive a test result. Third, since public knowledge about genetic transmission is limited, especially about recessive transmission, it seems only fair that geneticists call on society for better education and information in this field.

2. As for the European approaches to looking back techniques, it is fair to say that there is great concern about informed consent. However, the "fleshing out" of those concerns into concrete codes and rules of good clinical practice in genetics is very scant. To affirm that the old principles still prevail is a correct but wholly unsatisfactory approach to the rapid development of technologies. Thus, it remains unclear under what conditions duties to relatives would outweigh the rights of the screenee. The Nuffield Report's argument for overriding the screenee's right to confidentiality, namely "if it can be determined that the reasons (for refusing information to relatives) are malicious", seems so unusual that it hardly produces a generally applicable guideline. The same can be said about Recommendation R (92) 3 of the Council of Europe; while it acknowledges this dilemma, it then refers back to national legislation and professional rules of conduct. Perhaps the job of formulating new principles in this burgeoning field should rest with the geneticists and health lawyers. Meanwhile, it is hoped that the so-called Draft Convention on Bioethics,[30] once approved and ratified by the member states, will establish protocols in the field of genetics, among others. In such protocol, the duties to relatives in the use of looking back techniques should be outlined, in addition to the other outstanding issues in this area.

Acknowledgement

I am very grateful to Professor J.P. Frijns (Leuven) for his most helpful discussions on the screenee's responsibilities towards relatives.

Endnotes and References

1 Council of Europe, *Draft Convention for the Protection of Human Rights and Dignity of the Human Being with Regard to the Application of Biology and Medicine: Convention on Human Rights and Biomedicine*, Strasbourg, Directorate of Legal Affairs, 1996, p. 5.

2 Council of Europe, Committee of Ministers, Recommendation No R (92) 3, *On Genetic Testing and Screening for Health Care Purposes*, (adopted February 10, 1992).

3 Gezondheidsraad: Commissie Erfelkijkheidsdiagnostiek en gentherapie. *Advies inzake erfelijkheid: wetenschap en maatschappij*. Den Haag, Gezondheidsraad, 1989, publikatie nr 1989/31, p. 126.

4 Health Council of The Netherlands, *Proper Use of Human Tisue* (The Hague, 1994) at 82.

5 Knoppers B.M. and C.M. Laberge, "Research and Stored Tissues: Persons as Sources, Samples as Persons?" (1995), 274 *JAMA* 1806.

6 Health Council of The Netherlands, *Genetic Screening* (The Hague, 1994) at 13.

7 Denayer L., *Psychological Impact of Autosomal Recessive Inheritance and Genetic Testing in Cystic Fibrosis.* Doctoral Dissertation. (Dept. Psychology, Catholic University, Leuven, 1996) at 133. See also, Comité consultatif national d'éthique pour les sciences de la vie et de la santé, *La transmission de l'information scientifique relative à la recherche biologique et médicale. Questions éthiques.* Avis No. 45, Paris, 1995. See also, Marteau T.M., "The Genetic Testing of Children" (1994), 31 *J. Med. Genet.* 743. See also, Shickle D. and R. Chadwick, "The Ethics of Screening: Is 'Screeningitis' an Incurable Disease? (1994), 20 *J. Med. Ethics* 12.

8 Supra note 4, at 88.

9 McEwen J.E. and P.R. Reilly, "A Survey of DNA Diagnostic Laboratories Regarding DNA Banking" (1995), 56 *Am. J. Hum. Genet.*. 1485.

10 Concept Guidelines for the Molecular Genetics Predictive Test in Huntington's Disease (1994), article 2.7.

11 See Denayer, supra note 7, at 133.

12 Nuffield Council on Bioethics, *Human Tissue. Ethical and Legal Issues.* (London, 1995) at 51.

13 Shapiro D., "Report on Genetic Screening and Testing", in *International Bioethics Committee of Unesco.* Vol. 1. (Paris: Unesco, 1995) at 18.

14 Supra note 6, at 69.

15 Supra note 2.

16 de Wachter M.A.M., "Is er dan iets bijzonders aan genetische informatie?" In de Wachter M.A.M., et al., eds., *Genetica en levensverzekeringen: ethische en juridische aspecten* (Maastricht: Institute for Bioethics, 1991) at 39.

17 Council of Europe, Committee of Ministers, Recommendation No. R (94) 11, *On Screening as a Tool of Preventive Medicine* (adopted October 10, 1994), article 2.5.

18 Supra note 6, at 79.

19 Ibid.

20 Ibid.

21 Ibid.

22 See Shickle, supra note 7, at 12.

23 Evers-Kiebooms G., L. Denayer, M. Welkenhuysen, et al., "A Stigmatising Effect of the Carrier Status for Cystic Fibrosis?" (1994), 46 *Clin. Genet.* 336. See also, supra note 7, at 72.

24 Denayer L., M. Welkenhuysen, G. Evers-Kiebooms, J. Cassiman and H. Van den Berghe, "The CF Carrier Status is Not Associated with a Dimished Self-Concept or Increased Anxiety: Results of Psychometric Testing After at Least One Year", in supra note 7, at 75.

25 See Denayer, supra note 7, at 50 and at 133.

26 Evers-Kiebooms G., L. Denayer and H. Van den Berghe "A Child with Cystic Fibrosis: II. Subsequent Family Planning Decisions, Reproduction and Use of Prenatal Diagnosis" (1990), 37 *Clin.Genet.* 207.

27 Denayer L., "Risk Perception in a Population Tested for CF Carrier Status and Impact of the Test Result on Reproductive Decision Making", in supra note 7, at 105-126.

28 See Denayer, supra note 7, at 120.

29 See Denayer, supra note 7, at 105.

30 Supra note 1.

CHALLENGING THE PARADIGM: STORED TISSUE SAMPLES AND ACCESS TO GENETIC INFORMATION

KATHLEEN CRANLEY GLASS

RAPPORTEUR

Department of Human Genetics & Biomedical Ethics Unit

Faculty of Medicine, McGill University

The practice of medicine and medical research have traditionally been based upon a paradigm of the clinical encounter. In this paradigm, the autonomous patient receives information and makes a voluntary, informed choice about accepting treatment or participating in research. The activity within this doctor/patient or subject/investigator dyad is a private one, affecting, for the most part, only the two individuals involved.

Contemporary genetics challenges this paradigm in both clinical practice and research in a number of ways. The notion of the individual patient or research subject in a private encounter with the physician or investigator no longer holds true. Genetic information is essentially information not only about individuals, but about families, or even entire groups or communities. Traditional notions of confidentiality break down when dealing with genetic information. Providing individuals with information about themselves also tells them something about the genomes of family members. In some cases, this information may be very specific, as with the identity of obligate carriers in the construction of a pedigree for clinical or research use. Probands in such studies must be willing to share some information not only with the physician or investigator, but with family members as well.

Investigation of an individual's risk status also provides information about the risk status of other family members. If that risk is reducible or avoidable, for example, when early detection and prevention or treatment are available, is there any obligation to share information with other family members? If such an obligation exists, can it be reconciled with an individual's "right not to know" his or her genetic status? If an individual has no idea of family risk status, has not sought out information about it, or perhaps is aware of family history, but uses denial as a coping mechanism, what obligations do physicians or investigators have to other family members?

The family implications of genetics challenge the standard paradigm in other ways as well. In some cases, genetic testing may be required of one individual in order to diagnose the existence of the genetic status of other family members. Other problems may arise in addition to the potential for infringing on someone's "right not to know". Testing of children or mentally incompetent adults in the family may be the only way to diagnose, or rule out genetic disease for the patient. Is this appropriate when the testing has no intended benefit for those undergoing it?

Another challenge to the traditional paradigm arises from the fact that the model of an investigator/subject dyad is insufficient to support the impact of genetic research on entire communities. In the ordinary course of research, the potential risks for harm associated with participating in a protocol are disclosed to prospective subjects. Those who chose to participate do so knowing that the risks may (or may not) materialize. Some genetic research presents an entirely different situation. "Gene hunting" research, for example, may provide information about entire communities such as ethnic groups or genetic isolates, when most of the individuals in that community did not chose to participate in the research. They too, will bear the risks, such as the potential for stigmatization or discrimination, without having been given the opportunity to decide whether or not to accept them. Research looking for the genetic concomitants of alcoholism or breast cancer in an ethnic group are examples.[1]

Other challenges to the standard paradigm arise when non-family, non-community third parties are interested in information resulting from clinical consultation in genetics or from participation in genetics research. Much has been written about the interest in genetic information on the part of employers or insurers. A host of others may have interests as well. Prospective marriage partners, immigration officials, law enforcement agents, claimants in custody or paternity suits - are amongst those who could benefit from information about a person's genetic status.

Stored Samples as a Resource

All of these challenges affect how we view the use of our body substances by others. Traditionally, in health care institutions, tissues removed in the course of care were considered as "waste", to either be disposed of or made available for research. Tissue has been used in this way, and shared within and between institutions without having to be concerned that patients may be harmed by these practices. Genetic technologies have changed this situation. Whether stored in an investigator's DNA bank, in a pathologist's laboratory, or as part of a tumour registry system, tissue samples must now be considered as the equivalent of a personal medical record, requiring the same assurances and care concerning confidentiality.

Beyond being a static source of clinical or research data about an individual patient's or research subject's genome, stored samples have become a diagnostic resource with potential for current and future diagnostic utility for both the individuals concerned and their family members. Stored tissue is a valuable research and public health resource as well. Yet there is no consensus in North

America or in Europe on many important aspects of how to define the rights and obligations of those who are the source of the DNA samples, their family members and those responsible for their storage and maintenance. Given the difficulty in predicting future use for DNA samples, this situation is a cause for concern.

Choices/ Control/ Access

In Canada, as in many other countries, there is no federal, provincial or territorial legislation that deals specifically with genetic data. Issues of human research, including DNA sampling and storage follow general law. Consent to tissue sampling falls under medical law, although there is federal privacy legislation as well. Confidentiality laws are becoming more common at the provincial level.[2] Recently three federal research funding agencies have issued a draft *Code of Conduct for Research Involving Humans*[3] that has special provisions covering human genetic research and tissue banking. If adopted, this common *Code* will establish requirements for DNA sampling for research or for banking tissue that will be used for research funded by these agencies. Under the Code, all DNA sampling and data storage, including later uses of genetic information for purposes not disclosed at acquisition will normally require individual consent for nominative or identifiable data.[4]

In the United States, an important debate has been taking place regarding the issues of consent, choice and control over stored tissue samples. In terms of consent, the debate has focused on questions related to disclosures that should be made to patients and participants in research studies in order for these persons to make an informed choice concerning the uses of their stored biological materials. Issues of choice relate to whether patients and research subjects should be given an opportunity to express preferences about the uses of their stored DNA samples. Control is an issue because there is disagreement on the moral and legal status of stored DNA samples.[5] A number of suggested guidelines have been issued, which demonstrate a general consensus that protocols using samples which retain personal identifiers in most instances should require consent from the sources of the samples.[6] Areas of substantial disagreement remain concerning the use of anonymous samples, from which all identifiers have been irretrievably removed.[7]

There is basic consensus in many European countries concerning the principle of respect for the autonomy of the individual in matters of genetics. The *Declaration on the Promotion of Patient's Rights in Europe*[8] provides a set of common principles with respect to consent required for the preservation and use of human tissues and body substances. It has been accepted as guidance for national practices by 36 European countries. In addition, there is a general awareness that any legislation or regulations for the use of human tissue ought to relate to four sets of norms, regarding: 1) information; 2) the patient's rights; 3) the management of stored tissue; and 4) the principle of non-commercialism. Only a few countries have undertaken the practical "fleshing out" of these fundamental principles into agreements, codes of conduct and policies for dealing with ethical and legal aspects of the various uses of human tissue.[9]

France and the Netherlands are among those that have taken legislative action. France has adopted a law containing, among other things, a licensing system for the storage and use of human tissues. The Dutch Civil Code incorporates a provision on the use for medical research of anonymous human tissue obtained during treatment. This provision allows for such use unless a patient has objected. On the other hand, informed consent of the "donor" is required if identifiable tissue is stored to be used for purposes other than that for which it was originally obtained. In the United Kingdom, the Nuffield Council on Bioethics has proposed that the advice of a research ethics committee be required for any research involving human tissue, with the exception of DNA extracted from left-over or archived tissue where anonymity is assured.[10]

Looking Forward, Looking Back

The ability to store human tissue for significant periods is not new. Neither is applying new laboratory tests to add to information extracted from stored biological specimens. But the application of genetic techniques to stored material brings with it several new factors: a) the enormous scope of the information that is accessible through further analysis; b) the technical ease of extracting it; c) the rapid evolution and improvement in the precision of genetic testing; and d) the implications of such testing for both patients and their relatives. Technological advances in clinical genetics allow for reassessment of risks based on newer techniques that offer greater accuracy. More recently, calculated risk may be sufficiently different from the original to have implications for life or health choices. This raises difficult questions concerning when, on whom, and under what circumstances geneticists should perform newer tests on these specimens and communicate results to the patient or research subject.[11] More difficult still is the question of whether calculated risks affecting relatives should be communicated to them without either the permission of the individual who provided DNA or the prior agreement of the relatives to be contacted in such a case.

These situations challenge the standard paradigm of clinical decision making. Not unexpectedly, they generate different approaches to resolving the challenges. There is much agreement that prospectively, patients and research subjects can be made aware that genetic information may be of interest to other family members. At the time of original sampling, authorization can be sought for future tests on stored samples, with communication of results to the individuals from whom the DNA was obtained. While there are as yet no generally accepted guidelines defining the responsibilities of geneticists with regard to submitting stored DNA samples for more sophisticated testing as it becomes available,[12] evolving standards suggest that in advance of taking an initial sample, physicians ask patients whether they will be willing to have the sample retested in the future and whether they wish to be recontacted.[13] This would avoid at least some of the difficulties raised by retesting stored samples.

Other issues remain without resolution. Who should determine which risks are significant enough to merit recontact? Who will provide the resources necessary to undertake the retesting as well as the counselling required along with the recontact? These questions are of particular concern when samples are collected for research conducted outside of the doctor/patient context. Another factor requiring consideration is the fact that a thorough program of "look back" testing and counselling has the potential to overwhelm the health care system.

Significant disagreement remains about whether there is any obligation to disclose important genetic information to relatives. There is no clear legal obligation in Canada or the United States to inform relatives, although arguments have been made based upon existing case law in the areas of psychiatry or infectious diseases.[14] Ethical arguments have been offered which support a duty to inform relatives in circumstances where harm is preventable.[15] Yet there are important policy reasons not to require such disclosure to relatives, including the negative impact such a breach of confidentiality could have on the physician/patient relationship and the negative social, psychological or even financial impact that the genetic information could have on the relative who receives it.[16]

Conclusion

Consensus has evolved in North America about certain ethical principles relevant to clinical practice and human subjects research. They have provided a common framework for much of our ethical analysis. The existing paradigm at the foundation of much of clinical practice and research ethics is that of contemporary medicine - the doctor/patient dyad - where an autonomous individual makes a competent, voluntary and informed choice about treatment or participation in research. Full disclosure of material information, voluntary choice without coercion, pressure or undue influence, is fundamental to this model. Traditionally this choice has been considered to be essentially private, affecting each patient or subject individually.

New developments in genetics pose challenges to the accepted paradigm, and cause us to question whether it, and the normative standards, procedural mechanisms, guidelines and codes associated with it, are "robust" enough to accommodate them. New genetic technologies raise novel questions concerning the use and storage of information for clinicians and researchers alike. New emphasis on values such as responsibility to families and sensitivity to communities and collectivities are not easily addressed within the current paradigm.

The claims associated with new developments and values raise questions about whether the standard paradigm needs to be replaced, or whether it can be made more comprehensive and strengthened rather than eliminated. Respect for the autonomy of individuals and assurances of adequate disclosure, opportunities for informed choice and confidentiality of medical information have served us well, and continue to serve well the interests of patients and research subjects. They are an integral part of clinical practice and research, and cannot be discarded lightly. Given this situation, and the rapidity with which new genetic technologies are being developed, it is not surprising that consensus is not easily reached on all of the issues associated with the storage and use of tissue samples. The way in which clinical and research ethics respond to these new, but challenging, developments will be important not only to the medical and bioscientific communities, but as a precedent to the way in which the health care system itself adapts to new technologies.

Endnotes and References

1 Glass K.C., C. Weijer, R.M. Palmour, S.H. Shapiro, T.M. Lemmens and K. Lebacqz, "Structuring the Review of Human Genetics Protocols: Gene Localization and Identification Studies" (July-August 1996), 18(4) *IRB* 1 (*A Review of Human Subjects Research*).

2 Dickens B. in this volume at 71.

3 Tri-Council Working Group. *Code of Conduct for Research Involving Humans*. (Ottawa: Minister of Supply and Services Canada, March 1996).

4 Ibid., sections 15.6 and 17.

5 Weir R. in this volume at 91.

6 Hirtle M., "International Policy Positions on the Banking and Further Use of Human Genetic Material" in Knoppers B.M., T.Caulfield and D. Kinsella, eds., *Legal Rights and Human Genetic Material* (Toronto: Emond Montgomery Publications Ltd, 1996) at 149.

7 Clayton E.W. in this volume at 291.

8 World Health Organization, 1994.

9 De Wachter M. in this volume at 145.

10 Gevers S and Olsthoorn-Heim E. in this volume at 109.

11 Clarke T.R. and Ray P.N. in this volume at 121.

12 Ibid.

13 Andrews L.B. in this volume at 133.

14 Ibid.

15 Wertz D.C. and J.C. Fletcher, "Privacy and Disclosure in Medical Genetics Examined in an Ethics of Care" (1991), 5 *Bioethics* 212.

16 Andrews L.B., supra note 13.

GENETIC EPIDEMIOLOGY: INTRODUCTION

SÉGOLÈNE AYMÉ (CHAIRPERSON)

Director of INSERM SC11 Unit, Villejuif, France

Research in genetic epidemiology is very active in both the area of linkage studies to map genes involved in mendelian disorders, and in the area of identification of genetic susceptibility factors linked to common multifactorial disorders. Past experience now permits the identification of the major areas of concern:

1. **Safety and quality of the banks:** The competition in this area of research and the availability of efficient markers has lead to the multiplication of collections, some of them stored in well organized banks, others being kept in research laboratories where the facilities cannot guarantee either the safety of the biological material or of the computerized information. In private collections, funding is uncertain and there are many examples of lost collections. The usefulness of the stored material is dependent on the quality of the information on the phenotype. Very often the diagnosis as it is stored is very imprecise.

2. **Practice with regard to consent:** Information banks in genetic epidemiology include large groups of individuals, and in some cases, entire populations. Some individuals are patients, others healthy volunteers to be used as reference groups. All of them should have given their informed consent, but the primary goal of a bank is likely to evolve with time. Its cost and value is such that it is very tempting to make as extensive use as possible of the available data. How are we going to update the consent? Is it thinkable to study the biological material of healthy volunteers for any type of study?

3. **Deontology of access:** How to share the available materials with other research teams, in order to maximize the usefulness of the data collection? This is a major concern for lay associations. Conflicts of interest between research groups are often at the origin of the non-availability of biological materials.

4. **Freedom of research versus the protection of the individual:** Computerized record linkage is a very powerful tool in research.

Some countries authorize such an approach (Canada, Scandinavian countries), others do not (France), showing again an other important area of concern. How much should we protect privacy, knowing that we lose the power to detect important risk factors in doing so? Public opinion surveys show that people expect research to be as effective as possible and that the number of persons refusing to be registered when asked, is very small.

5. **Perception of genetic epidemiology research by the general population:** Research on population genetics and epidemiology of disease susceptibility factors among populations can be easily misconstrued as an attempt to prove scientifically the notion of race or to try to make use of the biological information for administrative or political purposes. This is why scientists have to be particularly careful in their approach.

REGISTRIES, RECORD LINKAGE, AND RESEARCH IN GENETICS: PROTECTING PRIVACY

PATRICIA A. BAIRD

University Professor, Department of Medical Genetics

University of British Columbia

Registries

A health related registry has been defined as a file, or list, that associates a name or other specific identifier, with a disease diagnosis, health related condition, or risk of condition.[1] Additional characterizing information is usually available on the individuals included, either in the registry itself or in the files of the parent health related organization. A registry may be assembled with either service, or research in mind, or both. There are many different kinds of health related registries, including registries related to transplantation, cancer, trauma, diabetes, child abuse, birth defects, occupational exposures etc.; genetic registries are one particular subset.

A genetic registry is one which contains data on individuals and their families with genetic disease or particular genotypes for the whole of a defined geographic or administrative entity. For ease of storage and retrieval of data, the records are usually computerized. Genetic registries are designed differently and contain different items of information depending on the goals for which the registry was set up. Common to all is the unique identification of the individuals on the registry.

There are many kinds of genetic registries - for example, chromosome registries, or registries dealing with particular genetic diseases such as neurofibromatosis or Huntington disease. In fact, in some ways the service files of a medical genetics department could be looked at as a registry.

If a registry is to be designed appropriately, it will contain different items of information depending on the goals for which it was set up. The goals, therefore, need to be very clear before development of a registry is embarked on. It is also worth asking at the outset whether it is necessary to set up a registry, or whether the same goals could be achieved in some other way. The current capacities in record linkage mean that many needs for specific registries could be met by using such methodology.

One goal for which a registry may be set up is the provision of direct services to individuals. For example, individuals with a particular disease, or particular exposures, may have access to counselling or treatment services and a register is kept to monitor them. Another goal for a registry may be to carry out research - a social goal which may not be of direct benefit to the individuals in it. A registry may be established to track the prevalence and incidence of a particular disorder over time, or to help uncover the etiology of a disorder, or to contribute knowledge on the impact of the conditions on affected individuals and on the health care system.

Many genetic registries combine both service and research goals. If DNA or tissue samples are kept, it is usually categorized as a bank rather than a registry. Registries may vary widely in scope - from national or even international, to quite local small entities as part of a funded research project. Unless there is some element of on-going functioning over time, these latter genetic "registries" are generally not thought of as such, however.

In essence, registries provide a mechanism by which data can be made available for genetic epidemiological studies. Information generated by such studies is helpful for planning for health and other special intervention programs or facilities, and in estimating medical, educational or other needs. Analysis of registry data may give valuable insights into the features and prognosis of various disorders - providing information that families, health care workers, and policy makers need to have.

Registries, Record Linkage, and Administrative Data Files

If the definition of a registry seems a little "blurry", this reflects reality. The concept of a clearly identifiable, independent, free standing registry has become even more uncertain in an era where linking data files of identified individuals kept in machine readable form is now possible. Files in Canada pertaining to vital events, hospital care, medical system contacts, etc. exist for virtually the whole population. Information from most of these social and health records is being transcribed routinely into machine readable form. The techniques of record linkage by high speed computer processing allows information from independently derived records relating to the same persons to be brought together. Provided enough identifying data are present in the source files to be linked, machine linkages can be done very quickly on extremely large data sets. The files can be linked into longitudinal event and outcome histories on individuals.

Record linkage means that analysis of data on far greater numbers of individuals is feasible. In the past, the labour and expense of data collection on individuals, or of manual linkage by clerks, did not allow truly large follow-up studies. It is only in the last decades that they have become common in epidemiology, made possible by computerized data sets and automated linkage that mimics the judgement of clerks.[2] For example in the 1960's, a search for induced cancer among 35,000 patients with thyroid disease treated either by radioactive iodine or surgery involved many field workers in follow-up, given the long lag time for disease expression. This was expensive, labour intensive, and intrusive to the people followed.[3] The same kind of study could be done today using record linkage methodology, far more cheaply and without personal intrusion, as individuals' histories can be tracked through their records of contacts with various medical facilities.

Many provinces in Canada are developing population based person-specific health information systems. Such files can have multiple uses - not only regarding measurement of health services and development of effective policies, but also playing an important role in epidemiological research. Such data bases could provide an increasingly powerful test bed for a range of hypotheses about the genetic factors that affect our health.

The technology needed to bring together fragments of individual and family health histories scattered throughout the routine files of vital and health events is available. Record linkage allows large quantities of follow-up data to be analyzed in a cost effective way, the Manitoba database being a very good example of what is possible. It is designed around information generated as part of administering the health care system, and documents every contact that the population has had with hospitals, nursing homes, and physicians over the last 25 years.[4] Many of the required elements are available in most Canadian provinces, many States and most European countries, so the approach could be duplicated elsewhere.

After initial investment in developing such a population based health information system, additional specific analyses can be done relatively quickly and cheaply. If there is a way of identifying those with a particular genetic trait of interest to genetic epidemiology, it would be possible to use these already assembled administrative and other data sets to answer research questions. As a concrete example, the Manitoba linked data files go from 1970 to the present and include such routinely collected data as hospital administration/separation records, physician services claims, the provincial drug insurance program, vital statistics files including deaths, physician registration, nursing home administration records. Unique identifiers permit linkage routines to be applied directly to the entire data bank so that multiple file and multiple year histories on individuals can be developed.

As discussed later, this database could theoretically be linked to specific genetic files or registries, for example, the prenatal diagnosis database of the Medical Genetics department. A data file of people with a particular characteristic (such as apoE genotype) could be linked to the population data files to evaluate outcomes in a far less expensive and less intrusive way than primary data collection through individual contact. The existence of routinely collected computerized files in Manitoba which are also linked makes it possible to document outcomes over time and permits the detection of long delayed harms or outcomes in a more accurate, less costly and intrusive way.

Computerized record linkage is not only able to build longitudinal health histories on individuals, but to link these into family groupings and sets of individuals with common parents (sibships). This allows detection of familial clustering of disorders. In light of these kinds of possible uses, the definition of registry becomes difficult. Can it be considered a file of individuals from whom a researcher has collected primary data with their consent?

Benefits of Using Data

Society clearly has an interest in using the information in medical records for research into patterns of illness or disability, and to evaluate the outcomes of treatment. Without the results of such research being available, the use of harmful procedures, or the use of harmful drugs could not be stopped, and improvements in medical treatment could not be made. Citizens rely on provincial and national government regulations to protect their safety, but these bodies can only do this if sufficient relevant information can be accumulated to guide policy. Therefore, access to information about the nature and results of treatment is one of the essential components in evaluating the quality of care and the responsible use of health care resources.

A substantial amount of research in Canada relies on such secondary uses of health information initially collected on individuals for administrative purposes. Administrative data relating to health encounters is an irreplaceable source of information for investigating questions of efficacy of medical care or questions of public health. The linkage of such data using unique identifiers has tangible benefits for the Canadian public.

It is also possible to use this information in genetic epidemiological research. For example, I carried out a study with my co-workers of individuals on a registry who had certain congenital heart defects - we were able to compare them with matched healthy controls from provincial birth files to see how often a paternal occupation of fireman occurred in the two groups.[5] We also did a study on life expectancy in individuals with Down Syndrome. We took registered individuals with Down syndrome and by linkage with the vital statistics death files were able to get a picture of life expectancy associated with this condition.[6] It is important to note that the data transfer on identifiable individuals was only one way, from the registry, and the format I received back was statistical.

The point I would like to make is that clever and imaginative uses of existing databases might achieve new understanding of the associations between genotype and long term health or illness. The health of individuals and populations unfolds through time, and the ongoing collection of data is needed to track this. A computerized record linkage approach could be very useful for those interested in these long term outcomes.

Privacy Concerns

So far, I have focused on the benefits of epidemiological research using registry data, and of using record linkage of data files on identified individuals. This is only part of what needs to be considered. Thoughtful consideration of the benefits is important but what are the harms? The existence of a registry, or a data file of personally identified individuals opens up the possibility that this information could be used in a way that violates individual privacy and causes harm or stigmatization.

There is agreement that privacy is a fundamental value in Canadian society and in most democracies. People have a legitimate interest in keeping information about themselves private. It is readily apparent that the use and misuse of personal data for research, commercial or political purposes raises important issues of confidentiality; issues that are part of the more general problems related to the protection of individual privacy in the face of ever-expanding information technologies.

Clearly, new ways of addressing these problems are called for. In setting up the needed protections, it is important to distinguish the statistical use of data sets, from the commercial or administrative use of data sets. An administrative use can be defined as any use of personal information about an individual, in a decision-making process that directly affects that individual. There is a fundamental distinction between an administrative linkage that can have a direct impact on a specific person, compared to a statistical linkage - which by definition does not allow the targeting of a distinct person for direct action. Research uses (with stringent protection regarding access to identified data, and publication of aggregated non-identifiable information only) should also be distinguished from administrative and commercial uses of personal data.

If the personal data given by individuals to primary researchers setting up a registry were linked without permission to other routinely collected administrative data files in a way that could violate the individual's right to privacy and autonomy; this would be a serious breach. The principles of respect for privacy and autonomy form the basis for fundamental human rights; they are not mere legal technicalities.

There is an inherent conflict between public interest needs and individual privacy protection. The potential benefits that could accrue to society and the health care system from setting up a particular registry, or allowing statistical research on administrative files, must be balanced against the dangers associated with the loss of privacy to the individuals involved. However, protection of privacy is not the only human value in the balance; although important, it should not take precedence over human life or the safety and health of the population. Protection of privacy is not an automatic "trump" - it needs to be weighed against other important human values and needs.[7] Citizens expect government to enact policy and legislation to protect them, to allow them to be free of harm. It is possible, through careful planning, to put in place processes and mechanisms that protect individual privacy yet permit the collection of information that yields public benefit.

Necessary Protections

What are the protections that exist today? In Canada, the data protection standards generally in use for administrative health data bases include the following:[8]

- all research must be reviewed and approved in advance by an ethics review board for compliance with confidentiality guidelines;
- the research must be judged scientifically valid by a competent peer review process;
- required data storage and protections include:
  - encryption techniques where appropriate
  - physical security of files and tapes
  - only authorized individuals are able to access identifying information e.g. through use of passwords;
- staff working with confidential data sign a formal agreement with regard to confidentiality protection procedures;
- individual identifiers (including personal health numbers, hospital record numbers etc.) are masked or scrambled before being released from the holder of the administrative data set to researchers;
- publications describing the research are not in such a form as to allow identification of individuals;
- information on individuals is not fed back to administrative bodies, although policy recommendations could be derived from research findings by the researcher.

Linkage across administrative files for statistical purposes should continue to be permitted without requiring the consent of each individual involved where there is significant justification and adequate protection in place. It should be possible to use health and administrative data for research purposes provided the above listed conditions for protection of data are met.

The regulations required to deal with commercial and administrative uses of administrative data files containing identified individuals differ from those required to deal with statistical research uses of such files. Employers and insurers are interested in named identifying information - that is, named information that is linked to a specific individual. By contrast, the specific identity of people receiving treatment is of no concern to researchers; what matters is the analysis of the aggregate results of many cases, which permits them to draw conclusions or suggest policies. There is a difference between information that reveals the personal identity of a specific individual, and coded information, which does not reveal an individual's identity. The latter assigns a code number to the individual, not a name. Coded medical data may contain information on an individual's diagnosis, treatment, and the results of treatment, as well as information about some personal characteristics (for example, age, sex, income, and general geographic location), but this information is not sufficient to permit the specific identification of the patient.

If coded identifiers are assigned to each individual covered by a province's programs, and these identifiers are used when information about individuals is recorded in various data files, it is possible to link the use of services over time by a given individual without researchers knowing the identity of the individuals involved.

The issue of consent should be balanced between individual privacy and research concerns. It would be impossible to identify all research purposes at the time of primary collection of administrative data. If a requirement for individual consent to use personal administrative information for secondary purposes were to be put in place, it would make it impossible to carry out epidemiological studies yielding aggregate data that do not identify individuals. It would be unfortunate if legitimate privacy concerns would lead to the introduction of policies which could impede the conduct of health research and the effective management of health care delivery systems. Our ability to understand disease processes, long term effects of medications, and health care in an increasingly sophisticated way would all be compromised.

Governments and holders of administrative data files should store and release data with coded person-specific labels that are adequate for research use, yet do not make possible the identification of the individuals themselves.[9]

Time limits imposed on the storage of administrative data as a protective measure would make it impossible not only to perform longitudinal analysis of trajectories of health and illness, but to investigate questions which may arise in the future. Blanket restrictions on the preservation, linkage, and use of such data go far beyond what is necessary to protect individual privacy, and would be contrary to the public interest. Regulation should be designed to accommodate the needs of society as well as the protection of privacy, as it may be feasible to achieve both goals.

The recommendations which have been discussed are relevant to administrative data sets where information is routinely collected as part of large societal systems. The situation is somewhat different with regard to genetic registries. Here, the researchers setting up such a registry have an ethical requirement to ask individuals for their permission to be included in such a registry. To give informed consent, potential registrants need to know what protections there will be for the data held, who will have access, whether it will be linked with other data sets, how long it will be kept, and how it will be destroyed.

In the United States, for example, it is possible for a researcher to get a certificate of confidentiality to protect the data in a genetic registry. This certificate protects researchers from being compelled, through subpoena, to reveal information about and the identities of subjects to insurance companies or employers.[10] To give an ethically valid informed consent, the individual needs to have a good understanding of the risks and benefits derived from being on the registry.

As mentioned earlier, it is possible to merge identified data from a genetic registry with administrative data sets. Unless permission had been given by the individuals in the registry for the link, any results from such linkage to administrative files should be released only in statistical terms to researchers outside the administrative data holders. For example, if a registry gave a list of 150 identified individuals with a particular genotype to administrative data holders - they in turn could release information that 120 of these had had hospitalizations for heart attacks, only not which individuals. In other words, personally identifiable data on individuals should only move one way with regard to administrative data sets - to administrative data set holders, not from them.

This is relatively new territory for genetic epidemiology and we need to move cautiously in order to achieve the balance that has already been discussed but cannot be overemphasized. That of the important societal interest in using individual-specific information to develop and improve knowledge of disease processes and put in place appropriate policies on the one hand, and the need to protect individual privacy on the other. With sufficient thought and care in developing policies for the collection, preservation, and use of such data, both objectives can be met.

Most researchers, in fact, strongly support the development of clear and concise guidelines and policies for data use and access. Researchers recognize that absent concrete rules, there is a very real risk that those responsible for administrative data sets may err on the side of caution going beyond any legislative requirements by simply refusing access regardless of the legitimacy and value of the proposed use. Or, when the rules are unclear, they may impose requirements for the deletion of data elements or the destruction of whole data sets "just in case", throwing away both research and managerial information. Unless protections are clearly in place, individuals may simply refuse to participate in any registry or data set used for research.

To summarize, privacy is a fundamental value in society. In view of the rapidly increasing capabilities of computer and information technology, as well as of identification of genotypes associated with various traits, there is a growing need for protection. In addition to the individual right to privacy, however, is a legitimate need for society to develop and improve policies with respect to health and illness. It is important to find a proper balance between protecting the privacy of individuals and allowing research that enhances our knowledge of the determinants of health and the effectiveness of medical interventions.

Privacy concerns and Population DNA Sampling

I have focused so far on privacy and access concerns with regard to registries and computerized data files of identified individuals. What are the implications of privacy concerns for population DNA sampling?

When a sample of a person's DNA is obtained - whether by plucking hairs, by finger prick to obtain blood, or scraping the cheek to get cells from inside the mouth, an enormous amount of genetic information on that individual is present in the sample. The long term stability of DNA means questions can be answered about that sample that weren't even envisaged when it was obtained. It could be tested for a wide variety of genes in the future.

This means taking and keeping the DNA of a person, differs from taking specific information about the self - such as testing urine for glucose, or examining blood for a white blood cell count. It is different because it is in essence taking a part of the self that can later be examined in a multitude of ways including testing for genes related to conditions where social stigmatization may be an issue. If personally identified research samples of DNA were to be later used to test for genes when the individual had not given specific consent for the additional testing, the individual's right to privacy and autonomy would be violated.

Additional issues include how should we perceive the DNA sample? Is it part of the person? Is it information about the person? If a DNA sample is perceived as an extension of the body of an individual then each examination and test of that DNA can be viewed as a medical act which inevitably involves obtaining the permission of the individual for each of those acts.[11] Thus, when a sample is obtained for one purpose and is stored, the question must be asked whether it is in fact possible to obtain informed consent for all other potential future uses. In cases where permission for unrestricted use of the DNA is requested, it is difficult to see how truly informed consent can be given if it is not known what will be done. In my view, should additional testing on personally identified samples be required that would not be covered by the initial consent, then further consent of the subject is necessary in all cases. Specifically, I do not think it is possible to give a truly informed, and therefore ethically based consent to an open ended "any future use the researcher deems appropriate".

The issue of permission for future uses becomes particularly relevant in light of the fact that DNA samples can now be taken in a non-invasive way. This fact has lead to discussion of the ways that population health surveys might be used to help elucidate the genetic components of common diseases. For example, it may be feasible to look at relationships between genotypes and particular disease categories on a population basis. It has been suggested that DNA samples might be taken in the context of a survey and then banked, along with information about the identities of the subjects, so that the samples could be used in further research. As knowledge is increasing very rapidly, the DNA samples may be more usefully examined at a later date - to see, for example, if those with particular genotypes are more likely to have particular diseases. DNA samples must be personally identified if the consequences of having particular genes are to be known as health consequences have to be allocated to the correct individual.

This type of population analysis would have to be approached with great caution. If tests were to be run in the future on the DNA that is held from a population sampling survey, some identified individuals would be found to be at high risk for particular disorders. Would they all be informed? Or would they only be informed in cases of a serious disorder and when there is something they can do about it? What ethical questions are raised by not informing anyone? Interpretation of the genetic information regarding a person's genotype may be very difficult, and may mean such genetic information may not be useful. Although the relationship of a genotype to an actual disease is very clear for some single gene diseases these are relatively rare; multifactorial disorders are much more common. Nor does the identification of a mutant gene necessarily translate into the manifestation of the disorder: that will depend on complex interactions with the rest of the individual's genetic background and environmental factors. In addition, the information may not be welcomed, particularly when it simply puts the person into a higher statistical risk group when there is nothing he or she can do to avoid this risk.

Clearly, the disclosure required to obtain informed consent in cases where a DNA sample is taken and kept for possible future testing of an unknown nature is very complex and perhaps impossible.[12] Individuals could be faced with choices that neither they, nor the researcher, envisioned at the onset. Knowledge regarding genetic status is not limited to the individual; this knowledge may have inevitable consequences for family members as well and these individuals may not have given permission. Informing individuals of a risk status because of genotype creates a category of people who are not ill but know they are susceptible to a particular condition. Knowledge of increased risk status in itself could be harmful to their self-image and relationships.

The potential for invasion of privacy and for harm is great with DNA sampling. This underscores the need to obtain appropriately informed consent for any use of the DNA sample. Requesting consent for unrestricted use of DNA samples is problematic, however, as it is impossible to see how consent can be truly informed if future uses cannot be defined.

Summary

In summary, I have described various categories and functions of registries, in particular genetic registries. I have outlined how data in such registries may be related to existing large administrative data files by computer based record linkage in order to carry out genetic epidemiology studies. As well, I have described how record linkage could be employed to mine the information valuable for developing policy or understanding disease that is contained in these administrative data files. I have also discussed the benefits of such studies stressing that they must only be carried out in the context of protecting the privacy of individuals. Finally, I have outlined some implications of privacy concerns for population DNA sampling.

Endnotes and References

1 Hook E.B., "Genetic Registers: Types, Goals, Methods and Limitations" in Emery A.E.H. and J.R.Miller, eds., *Registers for the Detection and Prevention of Genetic Disease* (Miami: Symposia Specialists, 1976).

2 Newcombe H.B., *Handbook of Record Linkage. Methods for Health and Statistical Studies, Administration, and Business* (New York: Oxford University Press, 1988).

3 Dobyns B.M. , G.E. Sheline , J.B. Workman, et al., "Malignant and Benign Neoplasms of the Thyroid in Patients Treated for Hyperthyroidism" (1974), 38 *J Clin. Endocrinology & Metabolism* 976.

4 "Health and Health Care. Experience with a Population-Based Health Information System" in Roos N.P. and E. Shapiro, eds., (1995), 33 (12) *Medical Care* Supplement.

5 Olshan A.F., K. Teschke and P.A. Baird, "Birth Defects Among Offspring of Firemen" (1990), 131 *Am.. J. Epidemiology* 312.

6 Baird P.A. and A.D Sadovnick, "Life Expectancy in Down Syndrome Adults" (December 1988), *The Lancet* 1354.

7 Letter from Dr. Martin B. Wilk, Former Chief Statistician of Canada, to Ms. A. Cavoukian, Assistant Information and Privacy Commissioner, Province of Ontario. April 1992.

8 "How Can Personal Privacy be Protected?" Position paper approved by Canadian Information Highway Advisory Council, Ottawa. Issue #10, March 25, 1995.

9 Letter from Dr. R.G. Evans and Dr. P.A. Baird to D.K. Martin, Secretary, Tri-Council Working Group on the Ethics of Research Involving Humans. January 1995.

10 Earley C.L. and L.C Strong, "Certificates of Confidentiality: A Valuable Tool for Protecting Genetic Data" (1995), 57 *Am. J. Hum. Genet.* 727.

11 Knoppers B.M. and C.M. Laberge, "DNA Sampling and Informed Consent" (1989), 140 *CMAJ* 1023. See also Knoppers B.M. and C.M. Laberge, "DNA Banking/Collecting: A Canadian 'Sample' of Consent Forms" in B.M. Knoppers, Caulfield T. and Kinsella T.D., eds, *Legal Rights and Human Genetic Material* (Toronto: Emond Montgomery Publications Ltd, 1996).

12 Baird P.A., "Identifying People's Genes: Ethical Aspects of DNA Sampling in Populations" (1995), 38 (2) *Perspectives in Biology and Medicine.*

GENETIC STUDIES IN POPULATIONS

HELENA KÄÄRIÄINEN

Department of Medical Genetics

The Family Federation of Finland, Helsinki, Finland

Introduction

The first step in characterizing a disease gene is usually to localize it to one of the human chromosomes. The strategy commonly used is positional cloning. This means that the gene is first mapped by linkage or association studies, which enables the researchers to physically locate and finally clone the gene. For these studies, blood samples of affected individuals and their healthy family members are obligatory. This implies that, in most hereditary diseases, the disease gene can never be found without the help and collaboration of the patients and their families.

The genes of most of the major monogenic disorders have already been located and the mapping effort is continuing with rarer monogenic disorders. The DNA samples are usually collected in collaboration with the clinicians treating patients with the disease concerned. The clinician contacts each individual patient or family, tells about the gene mapping project and asks for blood samples. At this point an informed consent is usually signed. Even the most common monogenic diseases are in fact very rare and thus the families usually regard themselves as a family with a very special problem. Generally, such families are interested in and well informed about the heredity of the disease concerned. When they are approached and asked to participate in a genetic linkage study, they usually are willing to help in solving the problems specific to their disease.

The focus of gene mapping is now turning towards the multifactorial diseases. Contrary to monogenic disorders, they are not rare. It is common knowledge that diabetes or allergies, for example, may "run in the family" but comprehensive information and counselling concerning the heredity of these disorders has often been neglected. Thus, when individuals and families affected with one of the common multifactorial traits are approached for genetic studies this may arouse a lot of questions and even worry. As the genetic background of the multifactorial diseases is usually very complex with several predisposing genes as well as exogenous factors, large collections of patients and families are needed in order to trace the predisposing factors. It is therefore seldom sufficient to base the sampling on individual families treated by selected clinicians but whole populations must be approached to obtain a sufficient amount of samples.

How to Approach the Subjects?

When investigating a trait in a population, different approaches can be applied depending on the different situations:

I. The study may be based on blood samples collected for another purpose, for example the samples of blood donors. This could be the method of choice when studying harmless genetic markers not associated with any symptoms or signs, for instance when comparing genetic polymorphisms in two different populations. In such a study, no medical or other data about the individuals would probably be needed and, in fact, the names on the individual samples could be permanently destroyed precluding identification. With such an approach there is no inconvenience to the subject, no risk of stigmatization or other adverse consequences. A written consent should nonetheless be obtained.

II. The samples may be collected by approaching a group of patients that may include subjects with the specific trait in question. If, for example, patients and healthy relatives are needed for investigating the role of predisposing genes in coronary heart disease, all patients attending a cardiology clinic could be approached. Sampling the patients is unlikely to create major difficulties but the sampling of apparently unaffected family members may cause confusion. They should be carefully informed as to why samples of healthy relatives are needed for gene studies. In cases of multifactorial diseases, they are usually needed for constructing the haplotypes; a complicated matter which is very difficult to explain to lay people. Even if this is understood, the fact that the family is needed for genetic studies naturally arouses fear of having inherited a harmful gene. Thus comprehensive background information should be given during the process of obtaining their consent.

III. The subjects may be chosen specifically by approaching all the known individuals with a certain diagnosis in a certain population, for example, everyone with adenomatous polyposis of the colon in Finland. With such an approach, clinicians familiar with the families are usually consulted. This usually helps to avoid any conflict in the initial contact. Moreover, patients having an infrequent disease running in the family are, as a rule, cooperative. This may lead to yet another problem encountered in genetic studies: an extremely strong family member may practically force the relatives to take part in DNA sampling.

What Should the Consent Include?

Legislation concerning research on human subjects does not exist in all countries. The legislation may also be in the process of being reformed due to the rapid development of medical research and especially molecular genetics. In Finland, the draft version of a law on medical research on human subjects has been introduced but not yet adopted. Even when it becomes law, the regulations concerning consent are rather imprecise.

Approval from an ethical review committee has to be obtained before a research project can proceed. Here again, however, detailed instructions for the drafting of a suitable consent form are seldom given. DNA sampling may appear to the members of an ethical committee as a simple, noninvasive procedure and the project may pass the review without real critical reflection.

It can be said that the legislation and the ethical committees define the general framework for genetic research and outline that which is unacceptable but they do not offer substantive guidelines. The ethical committees are primarily concerned with matters specifically defined by law like free choice and confidentiality. These principles, however, are often self-evident and naturally respected. Thus, the remaining problems concern the communication between the research group and the subjects as well as the quality of the information given.

Several good articles have discussed the DNA sampling and informed consent.[1,2,3] In my opinion, the subjects should get a 1-2 page leaflet together with the consent form. This should include information on the disease, its heredity and the goals of the project. It should tell how and why the subject was chosen and why the healthy relatives are needed. The type of the sample (usually 10-20 ml venous blood) should be mentioned and what will be done to it (creating a cell line, extracting DNA). When hospital files or other data are also needed, an explanation of the purpose should be provided. The research group should be defined, a contact person identified, and further use of the samples by other groups (e.g. international collaboration) discussed. The means for protecting confidentiality should also be explained. It should be stressed that the subject is free to join the project or not. Finally, what will happen upon project completion should be discussed. Will the subject get any personal results or a summary of the results of the project? Will the samples be stored or destroyed? Will the samples be used in other projects? Is there a possibility of commercial use of the results obtained with the help of the samples ?

It is a challenging task to convey a significant amount of information succinctly and in a manner which can be easily understood by lay people. In fact, one seldom sees really good examples of the art of producing information for research subjects. The ethical committee should read the text but, in addition, it would be wise to let several friends and neighbours evaluate it before the final use.

However well written and comprehensive the leaflet is, the subject should always be offered the possibility of discussing the project with someone in the research group.

To illustrate the previously mentioned problems, I will introduce two projects in which hundreds of subjects have been approached for DNA sampling. The first is directed at the mapping of genes predisposing to asthma in an isolated subpopulation in Finland. The second investigates prospectively the psychosocial consequences of the predictive genetic testing of hereditary colon cancer.

Genetic Studies of Asthma

The aim of the project is to map the gene(s) predisposing to asthma with the help of linkage disequilibrium mapping in an isolated subpopulation in Finland. The research group includes pulmonologists (Lauri Laitinen, Tarja Laitinen), molecular geneticists (Juha Kere), epidemiologists (Erkki Vauramo) and clinical geneticists (Jaakko Ignatius, Helena Kääriäinen) from the corresponding departments at Helsinki University or Helsinki University Central Hospital.

I) GENETICS OF ASTHMA

Asthma is a chronic inflammatory disease of bronchial mucosa and submucosa leading to permanent impairment of lung functions. In all industrialized countries, it is a considerable health problem and in Finland there are about 150,000 asthmatics (3% of the population) who need continuous medication or rehabilitation and thus get social benefits. Family studies[4] as well as twin studies[5] have suggested multifactorial inheritance with estimated heritability between 30% and 60%.

As linkage studies in asthma families have so far given controversial results about the possible genes predisposing to asthma we decided to collect samples from asthmatic patients and controls in a well-defined, isolated subpopulation in Finland. We believe that, due to our exceptional population history and the existence of isolated, genetically uniform subpopulations, such a collection of samples would be unique and extremely useful in the process of localizing the genes predisposing to asthma.

II) POPULATION HISTORY OF FINLAND

The 5 million inhabitants of Finland today are descendants from a small founding population from approximately 2,000-2,500 years ago. As Finland was surrounded by water and a sparsely populated wilderness, the population remained small and isolated for centuries. With the exception of the southern and western coasts, the country became permanently settled in the 16th century. The area chosen for collecting the samples (Kuhmo-Paltamo-Suomussalmi-Hyrynsalmi-Puolanka-Ristjärvi-region, FIGURE 1.) is sparsely populated (4.1 inhabitants/sq.km) and its population history has been extensively studied. Permanent settlements were totally destroyed during the Russian war of 1570-1595, and resettlement continued until the mid-17th century. Since that time, the original population has grown steadily and immigration has been very low. Thus, the great majority of the present population can be traced back through the well kept Church records to a handful of early settlers. The present population in these six communes is about 40,000 with about 2,000 asthmatics. The whole area is served by one central hospital.

FIGURE 1. The population in the sparsely populated area (indicated with black colour on the map) in eastern Finland is ideal for genetic studies as its well investigated population history suggests that the present population descends from rather few settlers.

FIGURE 2. Most of the HNPCC kindreds in Finland originate from two areas in middle and southeastern Finland. In the Figure (modified from Nyström-Lahti M: Genetic predisposition to hereditary non-polyposis colorectal cancer (thesis), Helsinki 1996) one dot marks the ancestral origin of one kindred.

III) COLLECTION OF THE SAMPLES

We decided to approach the patients by advertising in the local newspaper. Patients 16-40 years of age with asthma and originating from the study area were asked to contact research nurses on four simultaneous telephone lines during a weekend and the following Wednesday. The callers were interviewed by a nurse and those who were obviously not asthmatic were discarded. The hospital records of the rest were checked by a pulmonologist. If they fulfilled our criteria for asthma, they were contacted and invited to sampling sessions which were held in the central hospital and local health care centres. At least two first degree relatives of each asthmatic were needed to build the haplotype. If necessary, samples of the relatives were collected at a home visit. During the sampling session or home visit, each individual was given a leaflet on the heredity of asthma and the present project. At this time, they had the opportunity to discuss the project and then an informed consent form was signed. An article in the local newspaper and two programs on local radio were run concurrent with the advertisement which outlined the goals of the project and its background, including the mention of the special population history. The radio broadcasts were part of an "interactive" program where the public was invited to ask questions of the clinical geneticists and pulmonologists in attendance. A public lecture on the inheritance of asthma and the present project was organized by the local patient organization. In addition, information about the project was distributed two months before its start at a local training day for health care personnel. The appropriate permissions from ethical committees of the clinics and institutions involved and from the Ministry of Social Affairs and Health were secured before any sampling took place.

IV) INFORMED CONSENT

The informed consent form was accompanied by a two-page leaflet. They included information on the heredity of asthma, the goals of the project and the reasons for choosing this specific geographical region for the study. The sample type was explained as well as the fact that the subject would not receive any results. The issue of free choice was stressed and it was explained that refusing to give samples would have no effect on the individuals' future medical care. The form explained that the research group would not give any identifiable data to third parties but the group retained the right to use the samples for other medical research. Lastly, it introduced the study group (names, titles, affiliations).

V) DID THE SAMPLING SUCCEED?

Altogether, 811 individuals were sampled. Of these, 370 were asthmatics (including 57 affected sib pairs), 99 had other symptoms of atopy and the rest were healthy relatives. This constitutes less than a quarter of the asthmatics in the area. As the search for the gene(s) has progressed, it has become apparent that the number of individuals collected is not sufficient and so additional patients must be recruited.

Although our approach was positively accepted by patients, relatives, health care personnel as well as the media, it was not sufficiently effective. We had been afraid of negative reactions resulting from possible stigmatization of the region as a genetically distinct or even peculiar area, but such feelings did not emerge.

We asked the sampled individuals where exactly they had learned about the project. About one third mentioned the advertisement in the newspaper, another third the radio programs and the rest health care personnel, relatives etc. This indicates that several communication routes to the public must be used.

We have the impression that asthma is not a disease that people usually are ashamed of, hide or deny. This could be one of the reasons for the positive attitude towards the project. If we had collected samples for genetic studies in schizophrenia, learning disabilities or alcoholism, the reaction might have been very different. Yet, we believe that the vast amount of information distributed through different channels to the public, the issue of free choice, the ease of contacting the project group by phone, and, above all, the generally positive attitude towards health care and medical research, were all important in the acceptance of the project.

Predictive Genetic Testing in Hereditary Nonpolyposis Colorectal Cancer (HNPCC)

The aim of the study is to investigate the psychosocial consequences of predictive genetic testing in HNPCC. The research group includes gastroenterologist surgeons (Heikki Järvinen, Jukka-Pekka Mecklin), molecular geneticists (Albert de la Chapelle, Päivi Peltomäki, Lauri Aaltonen, Minna Nyström-Lahti), a psychologist (Antti Uutela) and clinical geneticists (Katja Aktan-Collan, Helena Kääriäinen) from Helsinki University, Helsinki University Central Hospital, and the Central Hospital of Central Finland.

I) GENETICS OF COLON CANCER AND HNPCC

Common cancers are not usually inherited, even though, on a cellular level, cancer is apparently always caused by genetic changes. However, in all types of cancer there are families in which it appears to be inherited. When it is, the mode of inheritance is usually autosomal dominant. This means that in such families, children of an affected person are at a 50% risk of having inherited the gene that predisposes to cancer. Of those who have inherited the gene, nearly 100% actually get the cancer in question and the onset of disease is usually earlier than cancers in the general population.

Of colon cancers, about 5% are believed to be hereditary. The two most common hereditary syndromes concerned are familial adenomatous polyposis (FAP) and hereditary non-polyposis colorectal cancer (HNPCC). The individuals in FAP-families who have inherited the predisposing gene, can be easily recognized by colonoscopy since they have hundreds of adenomatous polyps in the colon after the teenage years. In HNPCC, there are no clinical markers that would help in recognizing the family members who have inherited the gene. The recent description of the genes and mutations causing the susceptibility to HNPCC provided a tool for predictive testing in unaffected family members.

II) HNPCC IN FINLAND

Over the past 10 years, clinical and genealogical studies in Finland have led to the identification of about 90 putative or verified HNPCC families in Finland.

A mutation has been found by direct mutation analysis on two of the predisposing genes, MSH2 on chromosome 2p and MLH1 on chromosome 3p[6,7] in 86% of the Finnish kindreds meeting the stringent Amsterdam criteria for HNPCC.[8] Two founding mutations represented about 75% of these mutations.[9] Actually, the epidemiology of HNPCC in Finland (FIGURE 2.) had already suggested only one or two major mutations, as most of the HNPCC-families originated from two relatively sparsely populated areas in Finland. As it was possible to create a relatively simple screening test for those mutations, the situation for predictive genetic testing in HNPCC turned out to be exceptionally favourable in Finland.

III) PREDICTIVE GENETIC TESTING OF HNPCC

The impact of predictive genetic testing in cancer prevention and the emotional well-being of individuals is not known. We wanted to evaluate the acceptance and long term impact of such testing by offering predictive genetic testing to nearly 500 high-risk individuals in the HNPCC families. The study begins with an initial psychological assessment which includes items on sociodemographic background, life situation, social support, health status, illness attitudes and anxiety. During the first counselling session, information on the disease, mode of inheritance, gene test, and a follow-up plan is given. After a two-week interval, the person receiving the counselling is contacted and asked about the decision of whether to take the test or not. The counsellees, who wish to be tested, sign a consent and give a blood sample. The result of the test is disclosed at the second counselling session and the individual follow-up is planned as well as the genetic counselling of the other family members. The counsellees get their results in written form also. One month and one year after the disclosure of the results, the second and third psychological assessments are made. At the end of the study, the counsellees will receive a 15-page booklet about the inheritance, follow-up and gene testing in HNPCC.

IV) APPROACHING THE PATIENTS AND GETTING THE DNA SAMPLES

All 32 families chosen for the study have participated in organized follow-ups because of the cancer risk in the family. The cancer patients themselves and often their first-degree relatives, have been offered regular colonoscopies every two to three years to detect tumours when they are still small benign adenomas before they develop into malignant cancers. Two gastroenterologist surgeons and their secretaries have kept close contact with the families.[10]

For the present study, all 420 individuals at 50% risk of having inherited the predisposing HNPCC mutation in these 32 families were approached by the clinician who had been responsible for the follow-up in the family. First, a key individual in each nuclear family was contacted and asked permission to contact the other (adult) family members. Then these relatives were sent a letter telling them about a gene test that could help predict which family members had inherited the risk of early-onset colon cancer. They were offered the opportunity to take part in a study consisting of counselling and testing the family members at risk. If they wanted to participate, they were to sign a consent form and send it back to the research group.

V) INFORMED CONSENT

Two consents were obtained from the subjects during the study. First, they were briefly informed about the study and asked to consent to the first counselling session. During the counselling, which took about one hour, they were told in detail about the project and about the possible risks and benefits of taking the predictive test. Before asking for their consent to the DNA sampling, the subjects were given two weeks to consider their decision. The consent form for the sampling was short and simple as all the items had been discussed during the counselling. After receiving the results at the second counselling session, the subjects were asked permission to inform their clinicians of the results with the intent of planning the follow-up.

VI) DID WE SUCCEED IN APPROACHING THE SUBJECTS?

Of the 420 at-risk individuals in the 32 families chosen for the study so far, 361 (86%) consented to take part in the counselling program. While the program is still in progress, it appears thus far that practically all (96%) of those coming to the counselling also want to take the predictive test. This is a very high figure compared to the experience with Huntington families where only 10-15% of the relatives at risk have wanted the predictive testing. One reason for the disparity may be that the Huntington families have not been recruited as actively as in the HNPCC study. When comparing these diseases in this context, however, outcome is probably the most important determinant. In HNPCC, early detection and prevention of cancer can be offered to those at risk while for Huntington families no preventive measures are known.

Thus our approach was extremely effective and we could include a suprisingly large sample of HNPCC relatives in our research project. However, as the first contact came through the clinician who has been following the family for years already, it may well be that the family members felt obligated and found it embarrassing to refuse the offer in spite of the fact that free choice was stressed in the contact letter. During the counselling process, there was virtually no criticism of the program. The subjects appeared to be very pleased when learning that something new was finally available for their family. Even those who were tested and found to have the predisposing gene have taken a very constructive attitude. In the psychosocial assessment (which is ongoing) feelings of anxiety and confusion over taking the test have surfaced, but no regret.

Comparing the Different Methods of Approaching the Subjects

The above examples have illustrated two very different ways of approaching large numbers of patients and family members for DNA studies.

The first method was designed to generate interest in the study in a whole population living in a defined area, not to approach selected individuals. To summarize the experiences: the approach did not create anxiety or other adverse feelings but it was not very effective.

The second method was to approach individual families through the clinician responsible for the treatment of the disease concerned. Even though it was stressed that participation was totally voluntary, we have the impression that too few relatives refused. In spite of this, no adverse reactions were encountered.

It is not possible to say which approach was better. The choice of the method depends mainly on what is possible in a given situation. If a well informed group of patients treated by a few devoted clinicians is available, like in our HNPCC project, naturally the method of choice is to use the existing contacts. On the other hand, if we want to get all patients with a certain trait in a selected area, the whole population must be targeted. Both approaches can be carried out carefully and sensitively so that adverse reactions can be minimized.

Genetic Studies and Tests in Populations in the Future

More knowledge on relatively common gene defects is being uncovered all the time as the extensive molecular genetic projects in several countries are approaching their goals. The heterozygosity of recessive genes, which when homozygous cause serious illness, may be very common in some populations. The genes predisposing to common multifactorial diseases may also turn out to be very common. This may create the need to screen such genes in whole populations.

In Finland, testing for the heterozygosity for some of the most common recessive disorders belonging to the Finnish disease heritage is already being offered for all pregnant women in some parts of the country. Similarly, testing for carrier status in cystic fibrosis is offered to the public in many countries. Some of us believe that testing for the genes predisposing to the common diseases might have revolutionary effects on our health care by making it possible to focus the preventive measures on the right individuals.

In principle, this testing is no different than searching for carriers or predicting illness in families suffering from one of the rare diseases. This has always been done, in varying degrees, during the process of genetic counselling. In practice, however, testing for a trait in a family and screening for a similar trait in the population are two totally different tasks. The differences are the same as those encountered in research projects that approach selected individuals versus whole populations.

When a family makes a request for a genetic test this usually means that they are aware of a familial disease. They may or may not be well informed, nevertheless, they are already worried and anxious about the existence of the trait in the family. If testing and adequate counselling is performed, the family is likely to benefit from the process.

On the other hand, when a whole segment of the population is offered a test, for instance all pregnant mothers, the target population is probably not aware of any risk. The mere offering of the test in such circumstances, may cause anxiety and confusion. Thus, the information offered should be prepared with care so that it can educate people with no previous knowledge and cause as little anxiety as possible.

The acceptance of genetic studies in populations depends on the attitudes of the public towards health care and research in general. Whether these attitudes remain positive does not only depend on the public's basic knowledge of genetics and genetic research or the attitudes expressed in the media. It hinges on how accurately and sensitively these matters are dealt with in the course of these research projects. Moreover, if these projects are well executed, it may lead to positive attitudes and constructive discussion in preparing society for future applications of genetic testing or screening.

Endnotes and References

1 Knoppers B.M. and C.M. Laberge, "DNA Sampling and Informed Consent" (1989), 140 *CMAJ* 1023. Also Knoppers B.M. and C.M. Laberge, "DNA Banking/Collecting: A Canadian 'Sample' of Consent Forms" in B.M. Knoppers, Caulfield T. and Kinsella T.D., eds, *Legal Rights and Human Genetic Material* (Toronto: Emond Montgomery Publications Ltd, 1996). See also

2 Gold R.L., R.R. Lebel, E.A. Mearns, et al., "Model Consent Forms for DNA Linkage Analysis" (1993), 47 *Am.. J . Med. Genet..* 1223.

3 Harper P., "Research Samples from Families with Genetic Diseases: A Proposed Code of Conduct" (1993), 306 *BMJ* 1391.

4 Dold S., M. Wjst , E. von Mutius, et al., "Genetic Risk for Asthma, Allergic Rhinitis, and Atopic Dermatitis" (1992), 67 *Arch Dis Child* 1018.

5 Nieminen M., J. Kaprio and M. Koskenvuo, "A Population-Based Study of Bronchial Asthma in Adult Twin Pairs" (1991), 100 *Chest* 70.

6 Leach F.S., N.C. Nicolaides, N. Papadopoulos, et al., "Mutations of a MutS Homolog in Hereditary Nonpolyposis Colorectal Cancer" (1993), 75 *Cell* 1215. See also Bronner C.E., S.M. Baker, P.T. Morrison, et al., "Mutation in the DNA Mismatch Repair Gene Homologue HMLH1 is Associated with Hereditary Non-Polyposis Colon Cancer" (1994), 368 *Nature* 258.

7 Vasen H.F.A., J-P. Mecklin, P. Meera Khan, et al., "The International Collaborative Group on Hereditary Non-Polyposis Colorectal Cancer (ICG-HNPCC)" (1991), 34 *Dis .Colon Rectum* 424.

8 Nyström-Lahti M., Y. Wu, A-L. Moisio, et al., "DNA Mismatch Repair Gene Mutations in 55 kindreds with Verified or Putative Hereditary Non-Polyposis Colorectal Cancer" (1996), *Hum. Mol. Genet.* (in press).

9 Järvinen H., J-P. Mecklin and P. Sistonen, "Screening Reduces Colorectal Cancer Rate in Families with Hereditary Nonpolyposis Colorectal Cancer" (1995), 108 *Gastroenterology* 1405.

ETHICS FOR COMPLEXITY

DAVID J. ROY

Director, Centre for Bioethics, Clinical Research Institute of Montreal

Research Professor, Faculty of Medicine, Université de Montréal

Director and Coordinator, Quebec Network for Research in Clinical Ethics

GIULIA KRAMAR

Postdoctoral Fellow, Centre for Bioethics, Montreal

Assistant Professor, Pediatrics, Faculty of Medicine of Geneva, Switzerland

GHISLAINE CLERET DE LANGAVANT

Doctoral Candidate, Centre for Bioethics, Montreal

Département de sciences biomédicales, Université de Montréal

"If we wish to remain human, then there is only one way, the way into the open society. We must go on into the unknown, the uncertain and insecure, using what reason we have to plan as well as we can for both security and *freedom."*[1]

K.R. Popper

"... l'action se déracine de l'acteur..."[2]

E. Morin

The context for this presentation is genetic epidemiology and diversity; the title is as above; and the assignment is: introduce the application of current ethical norms to DNA sampling, and discuss the adequacy of these norms vis-à-vis the varied and complex questions raised by multifactorial disease.

Work in Ethics: Three Specializations

Rising to the challenge of this assignment requires a combination - the space for this article being insufficient for a full development - of three modes of ethical thought and reflection: normative ethics, horizon ethics, and practical ethics.

The organizers have directed this presentation to focus primarily on normative ethics, the specialty in ethics that works on the elaboration, in descending order of generality, of principles, norms and procedures. This activity is exemplified in the *Human Genome Organization (HUGO) Statement on the Principled Conduct of Genetics Research.*[3] The statement identifies four very general *principles*: the human genome as part of the common heritage of humanity; honouring international norms of human rights; respect for the values, traditions, culture, and integrity of participants; and upholding of human dignity and freedom. The *norms* needed to protect and honour these principles in practice are specified in 10 Cs (an echo of Moses redivivus?): competence, communication, consultation, consent, choice, confidentiality, collaboration, conflict of interest, compensation, continual review.

Principles and norms, left on their own, are still quite distant from the exigencies of action in a real world, so the finishing process of normative ethics turns to the crafting of detailed *procedures*. This activity is illustrated, for instance, in the work of the Human Genome Diversity Project (HGDP)'s North American Regional Committee on the conditions and requirements for obtaining groups consent or population-based consent for studies of variation in the human genome.[4]

Horizon ethics attends to the intellectual, cultural, social, and moral context or ecology within which normative ethics plies its craft. Horizon ethics deals with the limits and conflicts affecting what people believe, perceive, conceive, and what they seize upon as values to be maintained at all cost versus values that can be abandoned or compromised when circumstances so dictate.

The first notion of horizon is the line or the arc where the heavens and the earth seem to meet. Analogously, a horizon is a boundary, a limit, not only of vision and perception, but also of knowledge, of understanding, of deliberation, of foresight, and of appreciation of what is more and of what is less important in any domain of life and activity. The breadth and comprehensiveness of a horizon, whether it be that of an individual or the shared horizon of many people, vary proportionately to the height of one's standpoint or viewpoint, for these can be lower or higher. In general, any activity governed by a succession of higher viewpoints invites development while activities under the governance of a succession of ever lower viewpoints follow a curve of decline.[5]

Horizons can succeed each other as phases of a historical process of development or regression. With development, horizons widen as one thinker or a community of thinkers, standing upon the achievements of predecessors, sees and understands more than it was ever possible to see or understand before. With regression, triggered perhaps by the pressures and threats of all too rapid and unmastered change, individuals or groups may withdraw, hunker down, and lose sight of what had previously been seen and understood. Concentration on survival can both sharpen and constrict the mind.

Horizons can be specialized and complementary, and interdisciplinary collaboration, for example, illustrates the aligning and linking of limited horizons. Out of that alignment an integrated understanding of a complex whole can emerge, whereas within any one specialized horizon, only a portion of the parts are seen and understood.

Of course, the relationship can be quite complex, particularly when the horizon of one group is simply perpendicular, as it were, to the horizon of another group. Horizons are perpendicular when one simply cuts through another, such that what is seen, understood, or valued on one horizon is invisible, nonsensical, or unappreciated on another.[6]

The classical notion of culture and ethics assumed a single, universally shared horizon. There was supposedly one set of beliefs, ideals, principles, and norms and these were assumed to be the standard of civilized thought, word, and act for all human beings in all places and at all times. It was within a classicist notion of culture and ethics that Voltaire could claim that little more than a few hours of thought were needed for a wise *man* (note the cultural limitation!) to work out the difference between right and wrong, no matter what the area of activity involved.[7]

However, scientific work and public life in Western societies, and scientific research within a global society, is no longer conducted within a classicist mode of culture and ethics. We have passed from a supposedly integrated, universalist culture into a culturally, philosophically, and ethically fragmented and pluralist world. In this post-classicist world, ethics, with its systems of principles, norms, and procedures, is neither a ready-made achievement nor an inheritance stored in great books and great minds and awaiting universal application.

In this context of wide cultural, philosophical, and ethical diversity, principles and norms need to be complemented and activated by a continuing series of practical judgements about what has to be done, what has to be avoided, and what can be tolerated in specific concrete situations, whether these be in the laboratory, in the clinical arena, in the field of population studies, or in the domain of public policy for society at large.

The work of *practical ethics* is to produce judgements and decisions, not norms or arguments or analyses of conflicting moral and cultural systems. The immediacy of action in the real world is the workshop of practical ethics, and work in practical ethics requires comprehensive attention to the full particularity of specific cases and situations, whether these involve individuals or populations. The judgements and decisions of practical ethics are not precipitates of a deductive application of pre-fabricated principles and norms. Practical ethics, rather, works from the bottom upwards. The behavioural meaning of principles and norms, as well as their adequacy or need for correction or completion, emerges gradually across a complex series of interacting judgements about what is right, wrong, or tolerable in a range of unique situations.

Complexity as Method for Ethics

The work of normative ethics, the work of constructing principles and norms is a laudable and necessary effort to reduce the complexity of divergent and conflicting ethical systems, ethical imperatives, and ethical constraints to some kind of stable order capable of guiding the paths of behaviour away from chaotic movement.

If *algorithmic complexity* is the length of the concise description of the regularities of a system[8,9], then algorithmic complexity in normative ethics is low, since the tendency of normative ethics is to express an ethical-legal system's regularities in a concise, brief set of principles and norms, as noted above with respect to the *HUGO Statement*. One should note that *low* and *high* are descriptive characterizations of, not value judgements on, algorithmic complexity.

However, when we are dealing with the system of practical ethics, algorithmic complexity is necessarily of a higher degree. This system has to be described in terms of interrelated, interacting, and still emerging sets of practical judgements that have to be "worked out", not just "thought out"; worked out, tested, and modified, not just obtained by a linear process of deductive thought working on an unquestioned set of international norms and guidelines for genetic studies. The latter deductive approach, the approach of applied ethics, assumes that these practical judgements are, as it were, already contained within an established system of principles and norms. But they are not so contained, and they cannot be linearly and deductively so obtained.

In *The Broken Dice*, Ivar Ekeland mentions how each time we think we have found the ultimate component of reality, the fundamental building block of the universe, the particle breaks *downwards* into smaller pieces, like King Olaf's die.[10] Likewise for complexity as method in ethics. Each time we think we have fundamental, universal, and invariant principles and norms for human action, they tend to break apart *upwards* into an unfinished and emergent plurality and diversity of practical ethical judgements deriving from a related diversity of experiences, experiments, explorations.

Complexity as method in ethics exemplifies David Bohm's distinction between an implicate and an explicate order.[11] The order in normative ethics is explicate: the principles and norms of behaviour, their meanings and their relationships, are already worked out in advance of any applications made of them to concrete action. That order is explicate because it can be laid out, made explicit as a whole, and appeal is made to that order to justify conclusions about the ethical justifiability, unacceptability, or tolerability of actions and policies.

An implicate order cannot be made explicit as a whole. That order is manifested slowly and only partially as it takes shape across a sequence of historical instances, of practical ethical judgements. The order of an ethics for complexity cannot be laid out as a whole in advance of the practical judgements that have to be made on issue after issue in any domain of activity, in this case, in the domain of genetic epidemiology and studies of genetic variation in human populations. The practical judgements characteristic of an ethics for complexity emerge out of a comprehensive and detailed consideration of the full particularity of each ethically problematical situation in medicine, in the life sciences, and here more specifically, in genetic epidemiology and in population studies of human genetic diversity.

The approach of an ethics for complexity is in part inductive. The guidance for action and policy that it can deliver does not come most directly and initially from preestablished principles and norms, however important these are, but rather from a comparison and criticism of the practical judgements reached in cases and situations of a similar kind. One can find, though, over time that a series of such practical judgements display a recognizable drift away from norms and principles that are still proclaimed to be essential and fundamental for a profession or a society. So an ethics for complexity requires a constant interplay between practical ethics and normative ethics. While the meaning and the implications of principles and norms are unfolded gradually across a series of practical judgements brought forward to answer immediate questions about what is right, wrong, tolerable, or simply permissible, the series of such judgements may come to reveal what is not clear or perceptible in any one judgement of practical ethics considered in isolation from others dealing with similar matters. That revelation may be that the assumptions packed into widely proclaimed norms and principles need to be questioned, or even rejected. It may also be that individual or group behaviour, as evidenced in a series of practical ethical judgements, has so deviated from principles and norms as to be no longer compatible with a profession's, a group's, or a society's proclaimed moral identity. In either event, a point of crisis has been reached, calling for judgement of a higher order. A breakdown in the relationship, or in the order, between practical and normative ethics requires a return to horizon ethics; to a re-examination of principles, norms, practical ethical judgements, and behaviours in the light of the fundamental beliefs, assumptions, and perceptions that give rise to a moral order in the first place.

However, as noted above in the remarks about the breakdown in the classical notion of ethics, people and peoples diverge widely on the level of their basic beliefs, assumptions, and perceptions. So, while an ethics for complexity requires a continuing interaction between practical ethics, normative ethics, and horizon ethics, conflicts along this entire track are unlikely to be resolved in some comprehensive synthesis or consensus that will provide escape from the most difficult question: how can we live and work together when we differ so profoundly in our ideas about what matters most in human living?

Gaston Bachelard said: "If it's simple, it's been simplified." The Bachelard type of simplification here would be to suppose that any one of the three modes of thought and research in ethics mentioned so far — horizon ethics, normative ethics, practical ethics — can suffice while functioning independently of, and without continuing reference to, the others.

Normative ethics is concerned with the following general conditional statement: *if* genetic epidemiology, or the Human Genome Project, or the Human Genome Diversity Project, or the global study of genetic variation in human populations is to be undertaken at all, *then* only if a set of principles or norms are respected. It is the work of normative ethics to specify and formulate these principles and norms.

Normative ethics seeks to determine the principles and norms, that in their relationship to each other, can serve as something like an attractor in complexity theory. Attractors are states towards which dynamic systems converge and around which they eventually settle. Ethics is a dynamic system moving through practical judgements that eventually converge towards, and settle around, a set of norms. Norms may be formulated in thought experiments conducted prior to the actual run of a new course of action. However, these "thought" norms may not coincide with the "real" norms that emerge from the sets of practical judgements reached in real-life situations. A tension may arise between these "thought norms" and the "real" norms that are in fact serving as attractors in practical ethics.[12,13]

Normative ethics strives towards a general pattern that will both govern and order human behaviour along paths that do not diverge too widely from a centre of values considered to be essential to the identity of a community. Practical ethics, however, is governed by attention to particularity. Its genius is to understand a particular situation in its full uniqueness; to formulate practical ethical judgements tailored to match the unique combination of characteristics constituting this particular situation, and no other. That combination will inevitably demand comprehensive attention to the economic, political, social, cultural, scientific, religious and historical factors that create the uniqueness of any particular situation.[14] What may be right in one such situation may be quite wrong in another. What is imperative from the perspective of practical ethics, namely, respect for the full particularity of each unique case or situation, may appear to be reprehensible inconsistency from the point of view of normative ethics.

An ethics for complexity confronts the need to maintain tensions, tensions of the type mentioned above, between practical ethics and normative ethics. But there is also the tension that may arise between normative ethics and horizon ethics. A normative ethics working within the horizon of Western scientific culture seeks to determine the conditions for the ethical conduct of such undertakings as the Human Genome Project or the Human Genome Diversity Project, and the genetic studies required for, or made possible by, the achievements of these projects. Within the horizon of cultures which do not share, or perhaps even reject, the ethos of Western scientific civilization, such a normative ethics may appear to be little more than a subservient activity attempting to promote the doing better of what should not be done at all.[15]

Linkages of Genetic Epidemiology to an Ethics for Complexity

If the context of this paper is human genetic diversity and the genetic epidemiology of common and complex multifactorial diseases, the objective of this section is to identify links between genetic epidemiology, the study of human genetic diversity, and an ethics for complexity. This section is neither comprehensive nor definitive, but rather intends to be programmatic: a marking of pathways that will merit more persistent and rugged exploration. Two, among other, possible links between genetic epidemiology and an ethics for complexity will be highlighted: the place of history and evolution in the understanding and conduct of genetic epidemiology, and the potential impact of the genetic epidemiology of complex diseases on public health.

THE HISTORY — EVOLUTION LINKAGE

Genetic epidemiology, although initially discussed by James V. Neel and William J. Schull over forty years ago in their book on *Human Heredity*[16], is still looked upon as a relatively new scientific discipline — the journal, *Genetic Epidemiology*, having been launched in 1984, and the International Society for Genetic Epidemiology having been founded as recently as 1991.

Neel has sketched two faces of genetic epidemiology: one that seeks to tease out the genetic component from complex sets of family data; the other seeking a demonstration that some unique feature or experience of a population is reflected in one or more genetic endpoints.[17] If genetic epidemiology combines both the methods of epidemiology and genetics to study genetic variation in human populations, and to study the relationship of genetic variation to normal and pathologic phenotypic variation, it utilizes both population and family studies (with family studies ideally nested within population-based epidemiological studies)[18] to specify the role of genetic factors, and the interaction of genetic factors with environmental factors, in the causation of disease.[19]

Genetics and epidemiology intersect on at least ten plateaus of investigation,[20] and it is across these plateaus that genetic epidemiology pursues its three central and sequential questions regarding: the clustering of disease in families; the genetic or environmental or combined genetic-environmental-cultural explanation of that clustering; and the way genetic susceptibility is inherited.[21]

There is some disagreement, however, regarding the role of evolution and history in the understanding and practice of genetic epidemiology. Can an understanding of the evolutionary processes that have shaped the genetic composition of populations contribute anything decisive to explaining the frequency or causation of disease in contemporary population?[22] Could clarification of the selective pressures that might have prevailed in the past explain the high frequencies of some of the most common diseases prevalent in human populations today?[23] Or should one accept that genetic epidemiology, deriving from the primary division in population genetics between evolutionary inference and observations on contemporary health related problems should be broadly defined to embrace all aspects of population genetics *except evolution* (italics added)?[24]

It is far from clear or certain that genetic epidemiology, if it is concerned with the etiology, distribution, and control of disease in groups of relatives and with inherited causes of disease in populations today,[25] can afford to factor evolution and history out of its investigations. Kenneth Weiss has emphasized that evolution's natural selection operates on phenotypes, not genotypes, and that nature accepts any genotype of which the phenotype successfully runs the competitive gauntlet. A consequence of evolution by phenotypic rather than genotypic selection is a highly variable genetic basis for both simple and complex traits. People can have a similar disease caused or modulated by very different genetic causes.[26] The implication is that the impact of population history on the distribution of human genetic diversity is biomedically important for a genetic epidemiology attempting to explain the genetic causation of disease in contemporary families and populations. If recent studies have shown that most loci have many alleles, not just two, it is also the case that one of these many alleles is often found only in one population with other populations having their own different alleles for the same or clinically very similar diseases.[27]

The global distribution of the thalassemias, discussed by Weatherall and Clegg, exemplifies the point that each population in which the thalassemias are prevalent has its own set of mutations, with evidence now available that selection worked over a relatively short time to protect heterozygotes against malaria.[28] Evolution and history cannot be factored out of genetic epidemiology and population studies of genetic diversity.

Alan Templeton's work on cladistic analyses (clades signifying branches of the haplotype tree, and *haplotype* resulting from a combination of *haploid genotype*[29]) has shown that the phenotypic significance of variation in the human genome can be grasped when that variation is used to reconstruct an evolutionary history of the DNA region being studied. The lesson for genetic epidemiology is that the past is needed to understand the present. "The more accurate and detailed our reconstruction of the evolutionary past, the more accurate and detailed is our analysis of the present."[30] Genetic epidemiology can hardly do its work on disease in contemporary populations without attending to the biomedical significance of the trails of history etched into the genomes of both humans and other animals by a genetic evolution responding to the forces of contingency and chance.[31,32]

The principle that a reconstruction of our evolutionary past is critically important for understanding the genetics of disease in contemporary populations also relates directly to an assigned task of this paper, namely, to comment on the adequacy (or inadequacy) of the principles and norms currently proposed for the ethical governance of genetic epidemiology and population studies of human genetic diversity.

These principles and norms cannot be simply applied transculturally to the present, because the present mirrors and still harbours the extreme ethical and cultural diversity of the many civilizations, some extinct, others still vibrant, out of which the present has arisen. A breakthrough of this ethical and cultural diversity can be seen in the recent and still developing heated controversies about who owns and controls the past.

In Australia, the United States, and Israel, scientists are learning that governments are at times giving cultural traditions and religious beliefs of peoples higher value than scientific inquiry. Skeletons, bones, and hair, precious resources for anthropological and genetic studies, are being removed by law from the control and study of scientists and returned to peoples with cultural and religious traditions dictating that ancestral remains are to be respected by reburial rather than violated by scientific investigation.[33]

The Columbia River discovery of a 9,300 year-old skeleton offers a very recent example of the clash between an older civilization and contemporary Western scientific culture. The skeleton appears to be Caucasian and scientists would want to do DNA studies on bone fragments to carry out comparative DNA studies with other populations. However, the Umatilla tribe, whose reservation is across the Columbia river in Oregon, considers such DNA studies to be sacrilegious, disrespectful, and against its beliefs about how to treat the dead. The clash between the tribe and the scientists is not only over what is or is not in keeping with respect for ancestral remains. The statement of one of the members of the Umatilla Board of Trustees, "Our oral history goes back 10,000 years ... We know how time began and how Indian people were created. They can say whatever they want, the scientists...",[34] suggests that the clash is also profoundly about a scientific versus a culturally traditional understanding of a people's past and of their current identity.

Samuel Huntington has noted that a civilization is the highest cultural grouping of people and the broadest level of cultural identity people have, short of that which distinguishes humans from other species. The differences between civilizations are real and basic, basic because they affect beliefs and understandings about the most important things in human living, about the origins of humanity, the sacredness of the human body or even of all living creatures, the linkage of the body to the person both before and after death, the relationship of individuals to the community and of living persons to their ancestors. These differences are real because they govern laws, policies, and actions, and they can lead to more or less violent conflicts.[35]

If the unsecularization of the world should prove to be a dominant characteristic of the late twentieth century,[36] then the views of scientists and geneticists about the importance and urgency of genetic studies of populations may well clash with the views of peoples in civilizations that have not accepted, and perhaps never will adopt, the Western scientific *Weltanschauung*.

This is one juncture where the low complexity of the normative ethics devised for genetic epidemiology and for population studies of human genetic diversity may break out into the greater complexity of a practical ethics seeking to determine what should and should not be done, or what can be done, when peoples clash profoundly on the level of horizon ethics. A first general comment on the adequacy of current principles and norms for genetic epidemiology and population studies? This normative structure may well (over the coming years) be a testing site for the Huntington hypothesis:[37] that the great divisions among humankind and the dominating sources of conflicts at the end of this century will be cultural. The principal conflicts within global politics and global science may well arise between existing and diverse civilizations, regardless of whether nation states or transnational economic powers are the reigning masters of the world.[38]

THE PUBLIC HEALTH LINKAGE

Per Magnus has identified a link between genetic epidemiology, public health, and the need to develop an ethics for complexity. After stating that knowledge about genetic etiology in common diseases opens unwanted scenarios to many workers in public health, he asks: "What if modern societies, concerned with the high expenditures in health and social welfare, decide to discriminate on a genetic basis? Predictive medicine can be an unpleasant concept if private or governmental employees, insurance companies or health services choose to give their support only if a person has the right genes."[39]

Garrod's notion of biochemical individuality, the idea, as P. Baird and C. Scriver have expressed it, that "all of us are genetically unique, and all of us have weaknesses and strengths",[40] would be a basis for the position that genetic stigmatization and discrimination is universally unjust. For who could possibly be immune? Yet injustice has its degrees and these could rise if restrictions on rights, liberties, and entitlements ever come to be based on an ignorance of the genetic-environmental complexity of disease. The key idea underlying this complexity, as C. Sing has developed it, is that disease is not a simple consequence of variations in independent causal agents, and that health is a consequence of the complex organization of causal agents. Diseases, particularly the common multifactorial diseases, such as the cancers and coronary artery disease, emerge from interactions between the initial conditions on the genome and exposures over time to variations in environmental agents.[41] Direct linear extrapolations from the presence of disease susceptibility genes in individuals and populations will not permit accurate predictions of the time of onset, the progression or the severity of disease. Restrictive health care, employment, and insurance policies based upon inaccurate and false expectations will be inherently unjust.

The strong contemporary bias in public discourse today towards the simplification of the genetics of disease - a bias reflected in a steady flow of headlines about the discovery of an ever greater number of genes causally linked to an ever greater number of diseases, with explanations about the complexity and uncertainties of causation confined to the fine print if included in print at all[42] - could find its cultural mate in an ethics *cum* politics for simplification, a simplification that would base restrictive and possibly coercive policies on inadequately understood genotypes alone.

Genetic epidemiology, it has been stated, should provide a link between biomedical science and the public health consequences of its findings.[43] One consequence of the advances of DNA technology in identifying disease-related genes, it has been proposed, will be the need to reverse the traditional "inwards-outwards" approach that moved from an index case "outwards" to the identification of carriers. The "outwards-inwards" approach would involve population screening particularly when a simple test is available and where the public health burdens of a genetic disease are great. This population screening approach is presented as being possibly available in the future (unspecified) for common multifactorial diseases. The authors of this proposal admit that their proposed concept of clinical population genetics, organized under a common umbrella led by a public health physician, will require careful consideration, given the understandable ethical concerns.[44]

Although it may be understandable that there are ethical concerns, it is not so clear that the complexity of the ethical issues has been understood. While genetic screening, as contrasted with medical screening, is a relatively new instrument of public health,[45] and may come, indeed, to be used ever more widely, it is important to recall the Baird-Scriver observation that genetic consultation and counselling is complex and time-intensive and has not yet been well integrated into the clinical practice of medicine.[46] What will the complex ethical and social consequences be of introducing population screening programs for common multifactorial diseases if, as the authors of the "outwards-inwards" approach themselves estimate, the numbers of clinical geneticists and specialist counsellors will be inadequate to meet future needs?

The ethical and social complexity of using genetic epidemiology as a tool of public health has another dimension. It appears in D.J. Weatherall's and J.B. Clegg's discussion of thalassemia as a global public health problem. The problem is that "many thousands of children homozygous for ß thalassemia or with hemoglobin E thalassemia will require expensive treatment." And the solution? Well, "each individual country should decide on the way it wishes to approach this problem, either by counselling, marital advice or prenatal diagnosis, or by evolving adequate facilities for treatment."[47]

The choice between these solutions to the problem is where an ethics for complexity begins. The traditional family-oriented ethos for genetic counselling has emphasized "that genetic counselling is a health service offered to individuals and should not have population-related or 'eugenic' objectives."[48] Will that ethics and its related ethics of non-directive counselling hold true when the public health burdens of genetic diseases, whether they be as well characterized as the thalassemias or as complex and uncertain as the common multifactorial diseases, threaten national health budgets?

The challenge to an ethics for complexity arising from a potential ever wider use of genetic epidemiology for public health objectives is to identify the consequences of a choice between a logic of exclusion and a logic of inclusion, this latter being the logic of humanity.

DNA Sampling: From a Normative Ethics to an Ethics for Complexity

THE STEERING CHALLENGE

The central ethical challenge regarding the collection, banking, and use of DNA samples will require expert steering between the Scylla of ethical naïveté and the Charybdis of byzantine ethical scholasticism.

Samples of human blood and tissue have long been routinely collected and used for diagnostic and research purposes. Some doctors and scientists seem to follow the maxim, "business as usual", when it comes to collecting human blood and tissue samples for the purposes of extracting DNA that will be stored and used for a wide variety of basic and epidemiological studies. Some researchers have large collections of blood samples from persons with genetic disorders and little thought seems to have been given to the potential dangers to people arising from the existence of these DNA banks.[49] They seem to be unaware of, or if aware, insensitive to the fact that DNA samples, as P. Baird and G. Annas have emphasized, contain enormous amounts of information about people.[50,51] Some, perhaps much, of that information may come to be known and usable only after future studies have been completed, and that may be long after the DNA has been collected and banked. Individuals, families, populations as well as physicians, scientists, entrepreneurs, heads of companies, health care planners, insurance agencies and governments will all have their own interests in having access to and in using the information contained in DNA samples. It would be naïve to imagine that these interests will not intersect and clash at multiple points; naïve also to imagine that all who are keenly interested in this DNA-based information will be motivated by some putatively existent disinterested desire to advance knowledge that will be supposedly unlinked to social, economic, and political purposes.

Human blood and tissue samples, from which DNA can and will be extracted, stored, and used (for clinical, research, forensic, and a variety of other purposes), have moved beyond the ethical innocence, as it were, of the bedside and are now caught up on a dense network of intersecting and potentially conflicting purposes. Indeed, ethical norms are needed to govern the collection, storage, and uses of human DNA, and some of these norms may need legal backing.

However, as we steer away from the Scylla of ethical naïveté, we need constant vigilance to avoid drifting into chaotic currents of ethical-legal discourse that could potentially crash us all onto the Charybdis of mutual incomprehension and non-collaboration between the multiple scientific, professional and culturally diverse groups involved in DNA research and standing to be affected by it. Ethical-legal discourse can turn chaotic when it becomes entrapped in whirlpools of reflection and debate spinning ever further downwards into byzantine conceptual and procedural detail. Sight then is lost of the principles to be maintained, the values to be protected, the directions to be followed, and the practical judgements to be reached together if DNA research is to serve the needs and aspirations of humankind, and is not to divide people into those who have the power of DNA knowledge and those who are controlled.

AN EVOLVING NORMATIVE ETHICS

Currently there is ethical and legal uncertainty and controversy regarding: the nature of a DNA sample (part of the person? property? abandoned biological material?); the meaning of anonymity, the ways to achieve it, and its usefulness in research if DNA samples are to be stored anonymously; the scope of individual consent and the extent of its reach over future research carried out on stored DNA samples; about the ways to protect individuals, families, or populations from invasions of privacy, breaches of confidentiality, and exploitation; group consent when populations rather than individuals are the focus of studies of human genetic variation; patenting and commercialization of genes or of tests or treatments resulting from research on DNA samples.

Somewhat more broadly, the controversy centres on: the purposes and timeliness of DNA sampling for population studies and for genetic epidemiological studies, particularly of the more common multifactorial diseases; the kinds of regulation and legislation needed to protect human rights and dignity when DNA samples are collected, stored, studied, and used; on the interpretation and use of existing legislation when scientists and cultural traditions clash over studies conducted on ancestral remains.

There is also a methodological controversy within normative ethics. It has been described by Knoppers in terms of a diversity between private policy, public prospective, and interactive normative approaches to the devising of norms for the so-called new genetics. Emphasis is placed on the variety of norms (juridical, techno-scientific, socio-cultural, ethical) and on the dynamic rather than static, on the emergent rather than linear, nature of the normative process; these characteristics being particularly true of the interactive normative approach.[52]

Quite clearly, the norms - focus here being on ethical-legal norms - for DNA sampling, for genetic epidemiology, and for populations studies of human genetic diversity are in a state of evolution. The order between principles, norms, and procedures also seems to be evolving, and evolution does involve starts, stops, and shifts to new directions.

An emerging international consensus on norms for genomics and genetics has been observed. On one observation the five basic *principles* underlying this consensus are identified as: autonomy, privacy, justice, equity, and quality (of scientific and technical work).[53] In another later published observation, the four *principles* underlying norms, in this case for the Human Genome Project and the Human Genome Diversity Project, are stated to be: 1) recognition of the human genome as part of the common heritage of humanity; 2) adherence to international norms of human rights; 3) respect for the values, traditions, culture and integrity of participants; 4) acceptance and upholding of human dignity and freedom.[54]

The normative process, it would seem, still has to evolve towards a classification of the order and relationships between these two sets of principles.

The norms also appear to be in a state of flux, even of expansion. The seven C's of the Canadian consensus (communication and counselling, consent and choice, control, confidentiality, and competence)[55] have expanded to the somewhat different ten C's of the HUGO ELSI Statement (competence, communication, consultation, consent, choice, confidentiality, collaboration, conflict of interest, compensation, and continual review).[56]

One of these norms, competence, seems to be identical to what was called a principle (quality) in an earlier document specifying the five principles for the Human Genome Project.[57] Moreover, some of the ten C's seem to be procedures rather than norms, for example, the C for continual review.

The critique here is conceptual. A normative ethics should establish clear distinctions and a recognizable order between the principles, norms and procedures it is proposing for the governance of scientific research. The work has started, but is not finished. The deeper question still awaits its working out and response. Will an (putative) international consensus on the formulation of principles and norms be matched by a related consensus about what these principles and norms require or tolerate in practice?

THE LINK TO AN ETHICS FOR COMPLEXITY

A preceding section of this paper discussed two links, under the key words *history* and *public health*, between genetic epidemiology and an ethics for complexity. There are also links between a normative ethics for DNA sampling and the need for an ethics for complexity. We examine the issue of consent to illustrate this linkage.

Since a comprehensive methodological discussion of an ethics for complexity would exceed the boundaries of this paper and of any single article, we limit attention here to points discussed in the opening sections of this paper. An ethics for complexity, to recapitulate briefly:

1. emerges when real-life decisions have to be made at particular times and places in a world often marked by chaotic cultural and social diversity;
2. works with practical ethical judgements emerging from a detailed and comprehensive consideration of the full particularity of specific cases, situations, populations or societies;
3. unfolds the meaning of principles and norms across interacting series of such practical judgements;
4. operates in a tentative, probing, and experimental fashion, such that practical judgements considered justifiable for one place and time may

have to be corrected or radically changed for the same activity in another place and time;
5. acts as a braking force against premature universalization of any particular and concrete interpretation of principles and norms;
6. tolerates uncertainty while monitoring the unfolding of a course of action until consequences have become sufficiently clear to permit more definitive practical judgements that may differ from initial judgements;
7. accepts that evils and inequities are not all of one degree but are rather to be plotted along curves of greater to lesser to zero tolerability;
8. requires a continuing interaction between horizon ethics, normative ethics, and practical ethics such that each may undergo change through the interaction.

The normative ethics for DNA sampling, storage and use will probably call forth the development of an ethics for complexity every time each of the previously mentioned ten norms intersects with reality. Given the space limits, a brief consideration of the norm of consent will suffice to sketch this linkage.

Clinical investigators involved in multicentre and multicountry clinical trials have learned over the years that it is often impossible to impose Western societies' interpretation of the essential requirements of consent on other cultures that differ radically from Western societies in their understandings of illness, health care, autonomy, and the doctor-patient relationship, to mention only a few of the factors that shape the consent process.

Moreover, the norm of group consent for genetic epidemiological and population studies will remain extremely abstract until it is worked out over and over again in culturally, societally, and politically diverse populations. The practical ethical judgements about how that group consent can be achieved, if at all, will inevitably be as diverse as the populations from which that consent is sought.

These two very cursory considerations illustrate a point made earlier about an ethics for complexity. Each time we think we have basic, universal, and invariant principles and norms for human action, these tend to break open upwards into an unfinished and emergent plurality and diversity of practical ethical judgements that these attempts to implement pre-established norms call forth.

Another aspect of consent for DNA sampling opens onto the distinction between an explicate and an implicate ethical order, a distinction central to an ethics for complexity and already discussed briefly in a preceding section of this paper. Requiring people at the time of consenting to sampling to specify whether they want to be informed or not about information on health risks or benefits that could become available from future studies (in 3, 5, 7 years?) on stored samples, naively assumes that consent is part of an explicate ethical order. The value impacts of future studies and of the information these will produce are not in fact all laid out for inspection and for information. Moreover, the person consenting is not a finished and completed process. The biographies of the consenting persons are evolving and these persons may typically be quite different in three or five years than they are now. So consent cannot function like an arc extending from now, the time for consent to sampling, onto some future point of new information such that, what will be at stake in the future can be seen and consented to now.

The future risks of harm or benefits accruing from studies to be done on stored DNA samples at some future date, shifts consent into an implicate ethical order. That order emerges over time. It will be often illusory to imagine that people can, and it will often be meaningless to demand that people, *pro forma*, do specify now whether they want or do not want to be informed about some future event that neither they nor the investigators can pin down and describe.

This cursory consideration of the norm of consent sketches a linkage between a normative ethics for DNA sampling and an ethics for complexity. There are other such specific linkages for each of the ten C-norms mentioned above, and these will be worked out in a subsequent more comprehensive discussion of the ethics of complexity for DNA sampling in the context of genetic epidemiology and population studies of human genetic variation.

Two broader bonds of linkage between the normative ethics of DNA sampling and an ethics for complexity merit identification at the close of this section. First, an ethics for complexity will demonstrate that norms cannot be applied or implemented singly and sequentially, one after the other in some linear fashion. Each norm, when concretely interpreted in particular situations, tends to exert an impact upon the way the other pre-established norms will be interpreted and implemented in the same situation. So an ethics for complexity will require a detailed consideration of this mutual norm-feedback cycle.

Secondly, a consideration of this norm-feedback cycle in particular concrete situations cannot be accomplished as long as the cycle of normative ethics itself remains incomplete and unfinished. That cycle, as mentioned earlier, includes the working out of specific procedures to link norms and principles to particular real situations. Several of the most recent documents [58,59] that set out the normative ethics for DNA sampling for genetic epidemiological studies and for population studies of human genetic diversity clearly indicate that for many of the norms, the procedural phase of normative ethics is still at the workbench stage, and has not entered the experiment and implementation stage. Consequently, any judgement about the adequacy of these norms, which was one of the tasks assigned to this paper, would be premature.

An Ethics for Complexity vs an Ethics for Simplification

An ethics for simplification assumes what cannot be found or achieved in a complex real world. Such an ethics uses the linear principle of consequential containment to reach judgements about the ethical acceptability of a course of action or of projects, such as the Human Genome Project or the Human Genome

Diversity Project. An ethics for simplification would tend to conclude that a course of action should not be initiated if it is not consequentially contained, such that it can be ethically evaluated in terms of its perceived long-term consequences.

An ethics for simplification overlooks at least three utterly critical points. First, the long-term consequences of complex scientific-technological undertakings cannot be simply pre-conceived in thought experiments prior to the project's actual getting underway and demonstrating what is scientifically and technically possible.

Second, an ethics for simplification would try to escape the unavoidable dilemma deriving from the observation in point one above. That dilemma has been characterized as follows: "Die Wirkungen einer biotechnologischen Methode sind häufig erst absehbar, wenn sie nicht mehr vermeidbar sind; vorher aber lassen sie sich noch gar nicht definieren und daher auch nicht als erlaubt oder unerlaubt qualifizieren." Dilemmas of this sort require the development of an ethics for complexity.[60]

Third, an ethics for simplification, with its penchant for blocking projects that cannot be controlled by the principle of consequential containment, totally ignores the fact that the successful blocking of a scientific-technological undertaking will also have long-term consequences that cannot be governed by the principle of consequential containment. These consequences may prove to be ethically just as devastating, or even more so, than the consequences of the scientific-technological project itself.

When some people, including some scientists in the early 1970's, tried to launch a moratorium against the development of recombinant DNA technology until the purposes, hazards, and benefits of this technology could be worked out, they were involved in an ethics for simplification. They were assuming that these issues could be resolved without actually developing, and testing, working with, and living with this technology. In hindsight, the consequences of such a long-term moratorium, had it been successfully launched, would have been devastating. For instance, we would have lacked the knowledge and the molecular methods required to mount an attack on the HIV/AIDS epidemic. We would, in the early 1980s, have been scientifically and clinically helpless in confronting the virus, and we would probably still be so today.

A simplification ethics' quest for certainty via consequential containment is illusory. An ethics for complexity is based on quite different assumptions. This paper closes with a brief mention of two of these assumptions.

There is the Popper assumption contained in one of the opening quotations of this paper. The assumption is that the tension between freedom and security is enduring and any simplification - such as attempting to shut down a scientific project or, on the contrary, pushing ahead with such a project, but without procedures of vigilance - is doomed to failure or to produce evils as great as it is attempting to prevent.

There is the Morin assumption, also contained in the other opening quotation of this paper. The assumption is that courses of action, initiated with the best of intentions and for the highest of purposes can become radically separated from their initial agents; can, indeed, become totally diverted from their opening directions and made to serve purposes that the initiators of these actions would totally abhor.

Acknowledgements

We acknowledge with thanks Charles F.Sing, Professor Paul Bernard, Professor Guy Rocher and Dr. Jean Davignon for their assistance in the development of some of the key ideas presented in this paper. Work on this paper has been supported by the Canadian Genome Analysis & Technology Program (CGAT) - Grant # G0-12981.

Endnotes and References

1 Popper K.R., *The Open Society and its Enemies. Vol. 1. The Spell of Plato.* 5th Edition. (London: Routledge and Kegan Paul, 1966) at 200.

2 Morin E., *La Méthode. 2. La Vie de la Vie* (Paris: Éditions du Seuil, 1980) at 82.

3 The Human Genome Organization, "Statement on the Principled Conduct of Genetics Research", based upon Knoppers B.M., M. Hirtle, S. Lormeau, "Ethical Issues in International Collaborative Research on the Human Genome: The HGP and the HGDP" (1996), 34 *Genomics* 272.

4 HGDP North American Regional Committee, *Model Ethical Protocol for Collecting DNA Samples*, http://www-leland.stanford.edu/group/morrinst/protocol.html.

5 Lonergan B.J.F., *Insight. A Study of Human Understanding* (London: Longmans, 1957) at 13, 228 and 233.

6 Lonergan B.J.F., *Method in Theology* (New York: Herder and Herder, 1972) at 235.

7 Voltaire, "Dictionnaire Philosophique IV", in *Oeuvres Complètes de Voltaire* (Paris: Garnier Frères, 1879) at 195.

8 Gell-Mann M.,*The Quark and the Jaguar. Adventures in the Simple and the Complex* (New York: W.H. Freeman and Company, 1994) at 134.

9 Nicolis G. and Prigogine I., *Exploring Complexity* (New York: W.H. Freeman and Company, 1989) at 27.

10 Ekeland I., *The Broken Dice* (Chicago: The University of Chicago Press, 1993) at 28.

11 Bohm D., *Wholeness and the Implicate Order* (London: Routledge and Kegan Paul, 1980).

12 Kellert S.H., *In the Wake of Chaos. Unpredictable Order in Dynamical Systems* (Chicago: The University of Chicago Press, 1993) at 9.

13 Kauffman S.A., *The Origins of Order. Self-Organization and Selection in Evolution.* (Oxford: Oxford University Press, 1993) at 442, 467 and 482.

14 Berlin I., "On Political Judgment" (October 3, 1996), XLIII (15) *The New York Review of Books* 26.

15 This cycle of interaction has been captured in E. Morin's statement: "Il y a dans le phénomène hiérarchique deux mouvements de sens inverse: un mouvement du bas vers le haut (production d'émergences) et un mouvement du haut vers le bas (contrôle). Il nous faut considérer que ces mouvements sont les deux moments d'une même boucle: la production des émergences est un aspect du mouvement auto-producteur par lequel tout se constitue et se reconstitue sans trêve à partir des interactions de base; le mouvement descendant du contrôle hiérarchique est un aspect de la rétroaction du tout sur les interactions de base qui produisent son existence et dont il assure l'existence. Ainsi le mouvement du bas vers le haut et le mouvement du haut vers le bas sont à la fois le même et adverses." Morin, E., supra note 2 at 313.

16 Neel J.V. and W.J. Schull, *Human Heredity* (Chicago: The University of Chicago Press, 1954).

17 Neel J.V., "Problem of 'False Positive' Conclusions in Genetic Epidemiology: Lessons from the Leukemia Cluster Near the Sellafield Nuclear Installation" (1994) 11 *Genet. Epidemiology* 213.

18 Khoury M.J., T.H. Beaty and B.H. Cohen, "Scope and Strategies of Genetic Epidemiology: Analysis of Articles Published in *Genetic Epidemiology* 1984-1991" (1993), 10 *Genet. Epidemiology* 321.

19 Khoury M.J. and T.H. Beaty, "Applications of the Case-Control Method in Genetic Epidemiology" (1994), 16*Epidemiologic Reviews* 134.

20 Khoury M.J., T.H. Beaty and B.H. Cohen, "The Interface of Genetics and Epidemiology" (1986), 39 *J Chron. Dis.* 963.

21 King M.C., et al., "Genetic Epidemiology" (1984), 5 *Ann. Rev. Public Health* 1.

22 Supra note 20.

23 MacCluer J.W., "The Anthropological Perspective in Genetic Epidemiology" (1993), 65 *Human Biology* 1025.

24 Morton N.E., "Genetic Epidemiology" (1993), 27 *Ann. Rev. Genet*: 523.

25 Morton N.E., "Foundations of Genetic Epidemiology" (1986), 65 *J Genet.* 205.

26 Weiss K.M., "Introduction", in *Variation in the Human Genome*, Ciba Foundation Symposium 197 (Chichester: John Wiley & Sons, 1996) at 2.

27 Weiss K.M., "Is there a Paradigm Shift in Genetics? Lessons from the Study of Human Diseases" (1996), 5 *Molecular Phytogenetics and Evolution*: 259.

28 Weatherall D.J. and J.B. Clegg, "Thalassemia - A Global Public Health Problem" (1996), 2 *Nature Medicine*: 847.

29 Tomlinson I.P.M. and W.F. Bodmer, "The HLA System and the Analysis of Multifactorial Genetic Disease" (1995), 11 *Trends in Genetics*: 493. Reference 7 of this paper traces the origin of the term "haplotype" back to a 1967 publication of R. Cepellini on the HLA system.

30 Templeton A.R., "Cladistic Approaches to Identifying Determinants of Variability in Multifactorial Phenotypes and the Evolutionary Significance of Variation in the Human

Genome", in *Variation in the Human Genome*, Ciba Foundation Symposium 197. (Chichester: John Wiley & Sons, 1996) at 274.

31 Weiss K.M., *Genetic Variation and Human Disease. Principles and Evolutionary Approaches* (Cambridge: Cambridge University Press, 1993) at 179.

32 Cavalli-Sforza L.L. and F. Cavalli-Sforza, *The Great Human Diasporas.* Translated from the Italian by Sarah Thorne. (Reading, MA: Addison-Wesley Publishing Company, 1995) at 97.

33 Morell V., "Who Owns the Past?" (1995), 268 *Science* 1424.

34 Egan T., "U.S. Indians Block Study of Old Bones that Challenge History" (October 1: 2,1996) *International Herald Tribune.*

35/ Huntington S.P. "The Clash of Civilizations" (Summer, 1993) 72 *Foreign Affairs* 22.

36 George Weigel, cited in note 35, at 26.

37/ Supra note 35.

38/ *Les nouveaux maîtres du monde.* (Manière de voir 28. Le Monde Diplomatique, Novembre 1995).

39/ Magnus P., "Genetic Epidemiology - Possibilities and Problems" (1992), 4 *Scand J Soc. Med.* 193.

40/ Baird P.A. and C.R. Scriver, "Genetics and the Public Health" in Last, J.M. and R.B. Wallace, eds., *Maxcy-Rosenau-Last Public Health and Preventive Medicine.* 13th Edition. (Norwalk, Connecticut: Appelton & Lange, 1992) at 983.

41/ Sing C.E., M.B. Haviland S.L. Reilly, "Genetic Architecture of Common Multifactorial Diseases" in *Variation in the Human Genome*, Ciba Foundation Symposium 197 (Chichester: John Wiley & Sons, 1996) at 211.

42/ Supra note 27.

43/ Hopper T.L., "The Epidemiology of Genetic Epidemiology" (1992), 41 *Acta Genet Med Gemellol*: 261 at 270.

44/ Schickle D. and I. Harvey, "'Inside-Out', Back-To-Front: A Model for Clinical Population Genetic Screening" (1993), 30 *J Med. Genet*: 580.

45 Supra note 40.

46 Ibid.

47 Supra note 28.

48 Penchaszadeh V.B., "Genetics and Public Health" (1994), 28(11) *Bulletin of PAHO* 62.

49 Harper P.S., "Research Samples from Families with Genetic Diseases: A Proposal Code of Conduct" (1993), 306 *BMJ* 1391.

50 Baird P.A., "Identifying People's Genes: Ethical Aspects of DNA Sampling in Populations" (1995), 38 *Perspectives in Biology and Medicine* 159.

51 Annas G.J., "Editorial: Genetic Prophecy and Genetic Privacy - Can We Prevent the Dream from Becoming a Nightmare?" (1995), 85 *Am. J Public Health* 1196.

52 Knoppers B.M., "Professional Norms: Towards a Canadian Consensus?" (1995), 3 *Health Law Journal* 1. (Special Edition. *Professional Norms in the Practice of Human Genetics.* Health Law Institute, University of Alberta.)

53 Knoppers B.M. and R. Chadwick, "The Human Genome Project: Under an International Ethical Microscope" (1994), 265 *Science* 2035.

54 Supra note 3.

55 Supra note 52.

56 Supra note 3.

57 Supra note 53.

58 Supra note 3.

59 Supra note 4.

60 Kaufmann A., "Rechtsphilosophische Reflexion über Biotechnologie und Bioethik an der Schwelle zum dritten Jahrtausend", in T.D. Campbell , et al., eds. *Biotechnologie, Ethik und Recht im Wissenchaftlichen Zeitalter*, ARSP Beiheft 39. (Stuttgart: Franz Steiner Verlag, 1991) at 14. ["The consequences of a biotechnological project are often foreseeable only when they can no longer be avoided. Prior to their being so perceived, these consequences can be neither defined nor evaluated as being acceptable or objectionable."]

GENETIC EPIDEMIOLOGY: WHAT "IS" AND WHAT "OUGHT" TO BE?

ISABELLE PANISSET

RAPPORTEUR

Lecturer in Health Administration at Université de Montréal and Health Law at Universités du Québec à Montréal and Sherbrooke

Genetic epidemiology, in a broad sense, is the study of all the aspects of population genetics. More specifically, it is both the observation of contemporary health problems and the study of the evolution of gene expression and mutation. These two facets of population genetics pose different kinds of questions relating to the scientific knowledge of the genetic and environmental causes of common diseases, the distribution and effects of gene variation and mutations in a population, the possible causes of such diseases and the potential uses of this knowledge. It also poses questions about how, when and why populations and sub-populations should be approached for genetic studies and research purposes, in ways that will entail their collaboration while respecting not only individual autonomy, self-determination and privacy but also the cultural and religious beliefs of a community. Thus, it is in this perspective that the session was undertaken, while bringing to the fore the necessity of developing new paradigms to study the complex issues of genetic epidemiology.

The first paper, by Dr. Patricia Baird, presented the potential benefits and harms of genetic registries and population DNA sampling. In her opinion, information acquired through genetic epidemiology studies and research can benefit society as a whole when used to better public health. However, breach of privacy and of self-determination, as well as the stigmatization that may ensue from this research may nullify any potential benefit. More specifically, the subsequent research use of DNA samples of a population for purposes other than originally collected, brings to the fore the complex question of obtaining informed consent to a study for which most of the implications are unknown both by the investigator and the participant. Dr. Baird suggested that new policy models be developed with particular attention given to protecting the rights of the participants while allowing population genetic studies to take place.

The next paper, by Dr. Kääriäinen, gave two examples of population genetic studies in Finland, one in a familial setting, and the other focusing on a sub-population. In Dr. Kääriäinen's opinion, it is not only easier but less harmful to use at-risk families for genetic studies because they are aware of the genetic condition and they are generally well informed. The problem of confidentiality is not as important as the problem of free choice, particularly in a country such as Finland, where the population places a great deal of trust in the health care system and medical research. On the other hand, genetic research on entire populations is more difficult because the genetic components of common diseases is not their main concern and the people are not as well informed about the implications of genetic information. When you approach a population, the problem is one of communication and information to make people understand and enable them to make a free choice. She added that educating the public about genetic factors and the implications of the genetic information uncovered by population studies, must be done with great care and concern for the individuals, if future applications of genetic research are to be developed.

In contrast to the two previous papers, Dr. Charles Sing's oral presentation focused on the explanation of the scientific revolution and the paradigm shift that is reflected by the study of common multifactorial diseases. In these studies, there is a departure from the traditional models for explaining disease that is necessary to understand the complex nature of multifactorial common diseases, where the interaction of both genetic and environmental factors causes diverse phenotypes. Since no simple answer can be given to explain the complex systems of agents, then one must try to find the genetic answer through a new paradigm which takes into consideration invariant paradigms and context dependent paradigms. This is possible, in his view, by applying a theory of complexity. As he concluded, "this falls into a general view of nature that all successful adaptive complex systems are on the edge of chaos. These are combinations of the invariant global rules and the context dependent local rules."

While the concept of complexity and chaos were used to try to explain the relationship between genes, environment and phenotypes, Dr. Roy's paper focuses on the distinction between simplicity ethics and ethics for complexity in a manner that draws the inadequacies and adequacies of norms and ethical principles for genetic epidemiology and genetic studies of multifactorial diseases. His paper was articulated around four points within what he called a 'horizon ethics' perspective, which purports to take into consideration the environment (social, historical, cultural and political) within which projects of genetic epidemiology and the norm building aspect of ethics takes place.

First of all, it is assumed that past history gives the key to understanding the present. This is called the Templeton principle, which, in Dr. Roy's view, applies directly to the question of adequacy or inadequacy of ethical principles and norms proposed to govern genetic epidemiology and research. This leads to his second point, which is that "these principles and norms cannot be applied transculturally today because the present mirrors and still harbours the extreme ethical diversity of the many civilizations, some now extinct, others still vibrant, out of which our present has horizoned". The third point he put forward was that the formulation of principles and norms is the attempt of human intelligence to reduce ethical complexity and to steer away from chaotic ethical behaviour by identifying the ethical and legal attractors (e.g. the HGP 10 'C's). Algorithmic complexity being the length of the concise description of the regularities in a system, what he called normative ethics or simplicity ethics is an example of low complexity (e.g. the four principles of 'Principlism' and the 10 'C's), whereas, practical ethics would be an example of high complexity, where the norms confront the very diverse and contradictory ethical reality of antiethical beliefs and customs. The fourth and final point Dr. Roy made was that the emergence of norms, principles and ethical algorithms is an attempt for human intelligence to reduce uncertainty and to manage future behaviours. But simplicity ethics "assumes what cannot be found or achieved in a real complex world".

On the contrary, the ethics for complexity works with quite different assumptions. One of these assumptions is drawn from a quotation of Sir Karl Popper's book *Open Society* where he states: "If you wish to remain human then there is only one way. The way into an open society. We must go on into that unknown, the uncertain and insecure, using what reason we have to plan as well as we can for both security and freedom at the same time". The difficulty of maintaining a balance between security and freedom requires, in Dr. Roy's opinion, the development of an ethics for complexity. The second assumption is based on a quotation from Edmund Burk who said: "In my course I have known and according to my measure have cooperated with great men. And I have never yet seen any plan which has not been mended and bettered by the observations of those who are much inferior in the understanding to the persons who took the lead in the whole business in the first year". Dr. Roy draws from this the suggestion that scientists and geneticists must open to the views of the non-scientist, and draw upon their experience to better their projects.

From these papers, we can identify an underlying problem which is related to the epistemological distinction between what 'is' and what 'ought to be', and the question of the legitimacy of scientific knowledge. The first problem is related to the transition from the scientific explanation of how multifactorial diseases occur, to what ought to be done about them. The legitimizing force of scientific knowledge that somehow seems to justify crossing the line between what the facts are and what should be done about these facts, appears to be one of the most fundamental issues, and yet one that was ignored at the conference.

This comment is not meant to attack or diminish the work done by geneticists and other experts or what they believe in. But that criticisms of the legitimacy of expert knowledge to define what ought to be done is another element of the complex relationship between those who 'know' and those who should 'follow'.

Education, communication and information directed at the population are proposed solutions to encourage public collaboration. These may be instruments to convince the population of the true value of scientific knowledge. While it is necessary to establish the "facts", that is, what are current practices around the world, the authority of scientific experts as legitimate arbiters of what ought to be done in the interest of society remains to be examined.

GENETIC DIVERSITY: INTRODUCTION

ALAIN J. POMPIDOU (CHAIRPERSON)

Professor at René Descartes University, Member of European Parliament

Member of HUGO Ethics Committee

Studying the interaction between genetics, environment and culture offers promising results for the Human Genome Diversity Project (HGDP), which endeavours to help reconstruct the history, development, migration and expansion of the human populations.

Access to "exotic" gene pools worldwide is now possible with improved global communication in transport, information transmission and exchange of data.

Even if collections of DNA samples are more easily obtained, stored and analyzed, however, they are more difficult to protect and to manage from a political and ethical perspective. Stigmatization of the individual, family or ethnic group, population selection, abuse of natural human resources are all possible results of conflicts between populations or from the profit making orientation of an economy.

This implies that one must take into account not only the relationship between developed industrialized and developing countries but the attitude of emerging countries as well. Unfortunately, these latter countries do not place much importance on ethical concerns in their quest for successful commercialization.

As Ishwar C. Verma stressed in his paper, the intersection of anthropologic data and genetic based DNA analysis allows us to identify two scenarios:

- blood tested for diagnostic purposes in families affected by genetic disorder; and
- blood collected from a number of members of a community or a "tribe" and sent out for research, especially for genome mapping, using targeted markers.

The research on human genome genetic diversity raises different problems in terms of:

- individual selection and recruitment;
- modalities of consent respecting the autonomy and the freedom of choice;
- communication and information regarding:
  - the nature of research,
  - the modalities of storage and use of genetic materials,
  - the respect of confidentiality and the protection of anonymous data in repositories.

When approaching populations, researchers must make the terms and the general description of the project understood. Full disclosure of project details to local scientists or policy makers should be considered. The population consent must be obtained through local authorities as well as from individuals. Proof of this is given to the project leaders as well as the authorities responsible for maintaining the ethical standards of the research. Donors should be informed of any major change in the purpose of the research. In the case of individuals requesting access to their own information, special procedures must be established which include counselling particularly in cases that present a real pathologic risk to the individual or his family. A special concern is related to the proper management of existing biological samples.

Each protocol should comprehensively address the international standards of Human rights. This implies a collaborative effort among researchers to respect the rules proposed by international bodies, as well as between researchers and the individuals or populations tested. Such a collaboration should not serve scientific purposes exclusively but should also benefit the participants from the perspective of risk-benefit analysis, both present and future.

Consultation, informed consent and conflict of interest should be discussed **before** any agreement is reached. This should help to avoid any undue inducement through financial compensation to individual participants, families or populations. The collaborative nature of the agreement should provide for just reparation, however, in the form of public health and/or economic benefits.

These regulatory rules require **continual** review, oversight and monitoring to maintain the project imperatives which include the respect of human dignity and the non profit use of the human body. It is thus important that certain issues be addressed at different phases of the project such as informed consent, the misuse and misinterpretation of the data and the protection of intellectual property rights.

Research, as an essential activity of the mind, enables us to increase our knowledge. The aim of biomedical research is to relieve suffering for the well being of the individual, the improvement of public health and the promotion of mankind's welfare. The Human Genome Project deals with genetic screening and transmission of inherited characteristics. The Human

Genome Diversity Project is not linked exclusively to DNA sampling and sequencing but to the relationship between genetic diversity, evolution of populations, behaviour, language and sociocultural issues. Such a project necessitates a multidisciplinary approach and constructive exchanges between researchers, experts in bioethics and different segments of the society, including lay people.

Drawing a geographic map does not give one the right to appropriate the country but gives one the opportunity to visit and explore in detail the landscape and the socio-economic structure of each country. There is little difference, in terms of knowledge, between the map of a country and the human genome map but for the fact that the latter supports human identity and heredity. Nevertheless, Mother Nature is hostile to human interference. Aboriginal populations are equally sceptical about the advances of modern science as they see no acquired benefit from the mutual understanding process.

The human genome diversity project raises several questions:

- The consequences of the appropriation of the knowledge by humans of the genetic components supporting their identity and heredity.
- The use of scientific knowledge and of technological know-how and the risks and benefits inherent in that use.
- More generally, the consequences of the analysis of genetic diversity and of the determinant factors of the populations' sociocultural evolution.

One of the major ethical concerns is related to the conflict between public health priorities (related to the identification of genetic disorders or genetic predisposition to specific pathologies) and the scientific issue related to genetics of populations. This is relevant to geographic minorities identified through genetic screening in conjunction with anthropologic studies. This conflict arises from the necessity to fight disease and the desire to have better knowledge of the evolution of mankind:

- Where does it comes from?
- Where it is now?
- Where is it going?

Does scientific knowledge justify such an invasion of the privacy of individuals revealing their genetic identity? Does it justify the risk of misusing our knowledge to gain economic benefit, compromising the confidentiality of the data managed by the repositories, and resulting in possible stigmatization and discrimination?

In order to avoid such risks, it is necessary to promote pilot studies dealing with two major themes:

I. A scientific evaluation taking into account the feasibility of the project and the biological aspects in term of repositories management for data bank, choices of markers and identification of techniques for molecular biology;
II. An ethical evaluation taking into account the perception of the project by populations, and the proper evaluation of risk - benefit for each specific category of population studied.

The necessity of sustainable development for the Human Genome Diversity Project relies on three principles:

I. The principle of caution when seeking to prove the harmless nature of new technologies. It should strike a balance between complete non-intervention and excessive risk-taking. Choices have to be made and controlled risks need to be assumed.
II. The principle of learning from experience : pilot projects need to be supported.
III. The principle of vigilance, scrutinizing areas of weakness and allowing the opportunity to better anticipate the consequences of the risks based upon a permanent review and follow up.

The elaboration of specific rules based on a code of ethics should take into account the recommendations of the international committees involved in the European Convention of Bioethics and the International Bioethics Committee of UNESCO as well as the HUGO Bioethics Committee. The elaboration of international rules necessitates a multidisciplinary approach at a multinational and multicultural level. For example, the Occidental world has to pay attention to Asiatic perception and to Islamic rules. It is necessary to improve the perception of the risk involved and to ensure suitable and sustainable management which is based on appropriately adapted information and educational policy.

Society dictates that scientists be responsible for respecting the general principles of bioethics, internationally accepted and related to human values adapted to the evolution of the sociocultural contexts in each country. Scientists are, by and large, self-regulated in this context.

Today, advances in science and more specifically in medical science and in genetics, make it necessary to lay the foundations for **a new social contract**. Failure to do so will not only undermine the relationship of trust between doctor and patient, between scientist and public perception of science, but more broadly, that between man and society. The purpose of the HGDP is to rebuild the history of the populations with regard to their biological evolution. It will give us as well, the opportunity to enter a new biological era founded on the capacity of human beings to adapt themselves to the evolution of society.

HUMAN GENOME DIVERSITY: WHERE IS THE PROJECT NOW?

L. LUCA CAVALLI-SFORZA

Professor of Genetics, Stanford Medical School

The first bona fide human gene was discovered in 1900 and it determines the ABO blood group system. It took several years before it could be called a gene. The word itself was introduced later, but the essential step forward was the demonstration that the ABO variation is inherited and follows the rules of Mendelian inheritance. It was shown that the frequencies of the four ABO blood groups vary from one population to the other in 1919, and that same year can be considered the birth of human population genetics. Other blood group systems were described with immunological techniques similar to those used for the demonstration of the ABO blood groups, and of these, the Rh system discovered in 1940 was the most important clinically. Also immunological, at first, was the detection of the HLA system which occurred around 1970. This gene complex plays a major role in immunology, especially the immunological identity of individuals. Its study has therefore become of special importance in organ transplantation. Non-immunological methods using the electric mobility of protein molecules have been widely used since the first electrophoretic analysis of hemoglobin, in 1948, which proved the molecular nature of sickle cell anemia. This was the foundation of molecular pathology and, more generally, molecular biology.

Until the analysis of protein and DNA sequences became possible, genes had to be defined by the demonstration of individual genetic variation. About 250 genes were discovered in this way.[1] Variation of one gene, if sufficiently frequent, is called a polymorphism. Those discovered in the pre-DNA age are often called "classical." Their study in many different populations, and the theory developed to predict and explain these observations, have formed the beginning of human population genetics. After 1980, it became possible to study DNA directly, and since that time there has been considerable progress in analytical techniques. It is just a matter of a few more years before the sequence of the 3 billion nucleotides forming the entire human genome is known.

Research on classical polymorphisms has shown the usefulness of human population genetics for reconstructing the history of human evolution, for understanding the forces behind it, for proving the futility of race classifications, and the malignant nature of racism.[2] Today, molecular genetics has generated much more powerful research techniques, and we can start to feel their benefit in human population genetics as well. It is very unlikely, however, that the major conclusions reached through the analysis of classical polymorphisms will be changed. What we can expect is a considerable increase of precision and power, and we should gear up to make full use of it by providing the necessary material and expertise. This is what the Human Genome Diversity Project plans to do! It is not an alternative to the research that has been going on in Human Population Genetics but merely an extension of it, building on the knowledge acquired through new technology and past mistakes.

The total lack of coordination of the initiative has made it impossible to make full use of the knowledge already available, however, and this flaw should be remedied. Every researcher studying a new population has chosen, almost randomly, the markers he wanted to study. Some are counting different populations as those speaking different languages, even by an incomplete and rough estimate, they comprise in the order of 5,000 in the whole world. (The approximation is easily appreciated if one considers how many different populations speak English, Arabic, or Chinese as their primary language, but this limitation applies only to the few more widely-spoken languages). About 2,000 of these populations have been studied by classical polymorphisms. However, of the 250 loci known to date, the most frequent number of loci investigated per population is less than a dozen. This is not sufficient for evolutionary studies; a minimum of 30 to 50 would be necessary, and even this number would not give high resolution. What is worse, most researchers study a different set of polymorphisms. This limits enormously the power of population comparisons using available data, and compromises become necessary to make the analysis worthwhile. The outcome yields very patchy knowledge.

If nothing else, the Human Genome Diversity Project[3] should correct this obvious "original sin" of human population genetics studies. It can also greatly increase the number of useful polymorphisms, because many more are known today and the techniques are easier and usually cheaper. studies. Microsatellites are an example: they are polymorphisms arising when the number of repeats of a short sequence of nucleotides (e.g. 2-5) varies. There are over 5,000 polymorphisms known today, and tests are partially automated, cheap, and easy to use. They have other merits as well.[4] For instance, the variation in the number of repeats can be used to estimate the time of separation of two populations, by a method to some extent comparable to the radiocarbon dating of archeological events.[5] Both methods rely on an external measurement: the rate of disintegration of carbon 14 in the case of C14 use in archeology, and the rate of mutation of repeat numbers in the case of microsatellite evolution. This is the first example of what has been called genetic absolute dating. It differs from other methods of genetic dating of evolution in that all the others require a standard reference time, which in the case of human evolution is usually that of the evolutionary separation of humans and our nearest cousins, the chimpanzees. This is estimated at ca. 5 million of years by other procedures. It differs also because the other methods refer to the origin of single mutations, and not the time of separation of populations. Dates generated by the mutation rate method are bound to be more recent than the usual ones, by an unknown amount, and more relevant to population separations.

It may be worth reviewing some of the accepted conclusions that have already been established through classical human population genetics data and research, because they are important to understand both the enthusiasm and the fears expressed about the HGDP. Most fears have been voiced by people extraneous to the field who are generally afraid of any form of science, or have no real knowledge of the project. These people have strong prejudices resulting from a long history of negative contacts with colonial powers.

Some other obscure criticisms, independent of those advanced by anti-science activists, have been advanced by a few anthropologists who are rather unfamiliar with genetics, or whose political extremism seems to have impeded a fair analysis. On the whole, hostile anthropologists have been the exception and one should not confuse the extremism of a few with the positive attitude of the majority. This is fortunate, because the involvement of various groups including anthropologists, archeologists and linguists - can only benefit the Project. In fact, the beauty of the HGDP is that it can only be entirely successful if it involves rich and deep contacts and exchanges between a variety of disciplines including cultural and physical anthropology, archeology, paleontology, linguistics, history, geography to ecology and others. Some of the most exciting results so far have in fact been the product of such multidisciplinary studies. I believe that there has never been and there will never be a better opportunity for establishing a strong and wide bridge between the Two Cultures.

Human Population Genetics has helped clarify a new version of the origin of anatomically and behaviourally modern humans. It was generated by physical anthropologists/paleoanthropologists like Braeuer, Stringer and Klein,[6] and assumes that modern humans originated in Africa and spread from there to the rest of the world in a period dating between 100,000 and 50,000 years ago. This hypothesis is sometimes called Out of Africa 2, because it is generally accepted that there was an Out of Africa 1 when the first representatives of the genus Homo originated in Africa and spread from there to the Old World (but not to Oceania and America), at a time as long as one million years ago (dated by some at 2 million years). Paleoanthropological and archeological finds regarding the Out of Africa 2 hypothesis are limited in number, and thus statistical support coming from such data is scanty but increasing. This has fed a very lively, if not acrimonious debate among archeologists or paleoanthropologists. Some favour an alternative hypothesis, that after the first spread from Africa, this continent, as well as Asia and Europe, contributed more or less equally to the origin of modern humans throughout the last one or two million years (the "multiregional" hypothesis). An updated discussion is to be found in Foley and Lahr.[7]

A large fraction of genetic results, be they from classical polymorphisms, or from molecular markers - mitochondrial DNA, Y chromosome, autosomal chromosomes - favour the Out of Africa 2 hypothesis. The discussion at the purely paleoanthropological/archeological level continues unabated, however, and most theorists of the multiregional hypothesis do not seem to be interested in the genetic data. In all of science, and Out of Africa 2 is an outstanding example, one can expect that the level of debate is proportional to the difficulty of settling the issue, at least on the basis of paleoanthropological data alone. Here as elsewhere, it is only through multidisciplinary studies that progress is possible.[8]

We know that evolution depends on mutation, natural selection, drift, and migration. The effect of these factors is predicted by a mathematical theory, the basis of which was laid in the twenties. At the present time, it still continues to evolve and to become more and more sophisticated. Human population genetics has helped to prove the importance of random genetic drift as it can rely on estimates of population sizes, the major factor in the determination of drift. These estimates are much easier to obtain in humans than in animals. No biologist of sane mind would doubt the role of natural selection, but the relative magnitude of the role played by drift supports Kimura's contention that, in addition to the "survival of the fittest", one should always keep in mind the "survival of the luckiest".

I find the importance and multiplicity of effects of migration fascinating. Short range migration, for instance as is usual when husband and wife from different villages unite to form a new household, moderates or even suppresses the effect of drift in creating differences between local populations. Long range migration is, and used to be more frequently, the movement of a group of individuals in search of new environments, usually resulting in the foundation of a new colony which can be away from the place of origin. Long range migration has the opposite effect of the short range one: if the colony maintains scarce or no contact with its original source, it is a cause of differentiation among groups. Under these conditions, both genes and cultural traits, including language, will diverge, and usually they are found to be more different, the longer the separation. This is a cause of the correlations observed between linguistic and genetic evolution, a result which has been astonishing for some, but is reasonably well established today.

A special case of long range migration is that which accompanies population expansions.[9] These are usually tied, in humans, to cultural innovations which favour population growth. The combination of population growth and migration creates expansions, of which there have been many examples in archeology and history. The first expansion of the genus "Homo" was Out of Africa 1, and the much later one of modern humans, Out of Africa 2, was the first of "Homo Sapiens." Among the inventions of Out of Africa 1 must have been the first, very rough, tools (called Oldowan). From Out of Africa 2, came a more sophisticated new tool set (called Aurignacian, replacing the earlier Musterian) and also primitive navigation. This latter discovery was probably used to cross several straits of sea between Southeast Asia and New Guinea-Oceania and also for reaching Southeast Asia from Africa, along the southern coasts of Asia. Last but not least, a great innovation that must have been very useful in Out of Africa 2, was the development of a sophisticated language, like the modern languages we use today around the world.

The last of these major expansions brought Europeans to Africa, Southern Asia, America, and Australia starting with the fifteenth century, and was due to ocean navigation. In addition, the substantial overcrowding in Europe, a consequence of the growth of the European population in the long period between early Renaissance and the industrial revolution, must have played a role in the great expansion of Europeans. We are now witnessing the beginning of expansions in or from Africa, Central and South America, Southern Asia and Southeast Asia. They were probably brought about by the diffusion to those countries of hygiene and modern medicine. This diffusion is still incomplete but adequate to reduce by a factor of two or three the mortality prevailing in these parts of the world. In the absence of a reduction in birth rates, a major leap in the net rate of population increase occurs, and thus the population numbers.

The inadequacy of racial classification is easily proven by genetic geography: there are barriers to genetic exchange but they are easily overcome, and they have only a small effect in differentiating people. Physical barriers (mountains, seas, rivers, deserts) are of course important, and also linguistic barriers can prove to some extent effective.[10] These two types of barriers are highly correlated. Cultural differences like those due to religion and politics are probably also very important, but historically more unstable. In spite of physical and cultural barriers, isolation has not been enough of a determinant in the last hundred thousand years, and has become progressively less significant. The result is that no strong, clearly classifiable "races" exist, or have resisted the progression of human mobility. There are many isolated populations which differ somewhat from their neighbours and perhaps one might recognize, with highly sophisticated statistical tests, slight differences between many of the 5,000 linguistic groups in existence, but calling them "races" would be absurd. Geographic distance is sufficient to create genetic variation but not enough to generate discontinuity. Should any discontinuity result from barriers to marital exchange it is usually of trivial magnitude and can only be shown by powerful statistical tests. The classification of a continuum is perfectly arbitrary. Thus the number of "races" defined by various anthropologists varies from 3 to over 100. Darwin had already clearly perceived the futility of the effort.

Naturally, racists would feel deprived if they did not have race to think and talk about. And of course, it would be foolish to deny that there are differences between sub-Saharan Africans (or even Saharan ones) and Europeans or Asians. Real racism is not the acknowledgement of the existence of racial differences, but the belief of inferiority or superiority of some races due to inherited, stable characteristics. It is a cultural construct, probably generated by a social compulsion to see oneself surrounded by friends and potential helpers, and also by narcissism and xenophobia. The differences among groups living in different ecological regions are there for everybody to see, and they are there for good reasons: adaptation to climates, made necessary by the expansion to areas with extreme ecological conditions. If there is biological superiority or inferiority it is relative to the capacity to survive, unprotected, in different climates. We are moving towards an air conditioned climate equal in all the world, however, where this kind of ecological adaptation is becoming meaningless. The differences it has generated are easily perceived because, by their nature, they affect the surface of the body. They are the result of a small bunch of genes; random samples of genes show much more homogeneity across groups.[11]

In reality, we now know that differences among individuals are much greater than we thought, and those between groups are almost trivial in comparison.[12] We also know that many differences among groups (one would probably say most, if one could enumerate them) are cultural, and not genetic; easily reversible, at least potentially, and far from unchangeable. So, why is there so much insistence on, and intolerance of, "racial" differences? Clearly the spread of healthy genetic knowledge could help us to moderate them.

There is also considerable misunderstanding over the meaning and power of "eugenics." History has taught us some important lessons regarding this notion. One lesson is to mistrust eugenics which can be seriously abused for political motives. Another lesson is derived from population genetics which teaches us that eugenics is mostly ineffective, or impossible. Finally, that our judgement of what is good and bad, eugenically speaking, should be taken with a grain of salt; that the correct approach should be as much as possible euthenic, and not eugenic. The trouble is that most people, even those who should know genetics, and in particular its population aspects, aren't adequately informed. This lack of insight has generated unrealistic fears and hopes of what genetics can accomplish.

What does the Human Genome Diversity Project hope to achieve in the end? It is essentially trying to profit from the experience of almost eighty years of human population genetics, as well as the modern techniques of molecular genetics, to understand more about our diversity. It endeavours to complete its mission while adhering to the rules of anonymity and confidentiality of the scientific information accumulated which are fundamental to the dignity and rights of individuals and groups. These rules are correctly epitomized, for instance, in the HUGO ELSI document.[13] HGDP is, one may remember, an offshoot of HUGO, the International Human Genome Organization. Two years ago, I requested that UNESCO supervise our activities from the ELSI point of view, through their International Bioethics Committee. They have formed a committee for Human Population Genetics which has prepared a report on the HGDP. There is a direct connection between this committee and the HUGO ELSI Committee, in the person of our convener.

We in the HGDP believe that our regional organization, in existence since the first formal constitution, makes it easier to spread the task among all countries willing to participate in it. Our efforts are concentrated on ensuring the efficient collection, storage, and, above all, sharing of the information derived from the Project. Sharing the DNAs as well as the testing tasks among research scientists is the simplest way to achieve our goals. There are problems to be resolved relating to intellectual property, patents and the rights derived therefrom, but we have evidence that they can be overcome.

The regional organization of HGDP will eventually be extended to the whole world. Such presence will take time to establish, however, as one is only able to expand rapidly in areas where existing structure and development are in place. Creating empty, nonfunctional regional organizations would not be productive. Building on existing local forces and interests it has been possible to establish regional organizations in many parts of the world as set out in the following chronological order; a European region, a North American region, a Chinese region and a South American region. Regions in African, India, Russia and Southwest Asia are being developed. There are already examples of the beneficial effects, e.g. on chances of technology transfer to Southern countries. An International centre for the development and spread of Biotechnology and Genetic Engineering affiliated to UNIDO, the ICGEB, with main laboratories in Trieste and New Delhi, has held two hands-on courses of Human Genome Diversity, with participants from many Southern countries. This is just one of many activities of this Centre, which maintains a communication network with laboratories in some 40 Southern countries.

Interest in the HGDP among scientists has always been strong. Unfortunately, it is not the best of these times for obtaining financial support for new scientific developments, but there are many signs that the rate of progress of the Project is increasing. Among them, the National Academy of the Sciences of the U.S. has generated a National Research Council workshop which is examining the feasibility of the Project, and the National Science Foundation has promoted a Request for Grant Applications for pilot HGDP projects. Other major developments are coming from scientific centres which have already contributed in a major way to the study of human and medical genetics. There are important potential benefits for medical genetics that can come from the project.

It is inevitable that start-up is always slow. Paradoxically, a fast rate of development of the relevant technology is somewhat paralyzing. We know how to store DNA in relevant ways to create archives which can represent the world population. This part of the project can be effected in ways that are relatively cheap, compared to much more expensive biological projects. Material can be stored in two different forms: cell lines are easily obtained from small blood samples, and can supply renewable resources of DNAs. These are especially valuable for populations more difficult to reach for logistic reasons. One can store non-renewable sources of DNA from more easily accessible populations. This is not a difficult technical problem. The problem which needs to be resolved is the actual testing of these DNA samples. It certainly can be done today on the basis of existing knowledge. Many inexpensive tests on known DNA polymorphisms are available which could provide a very illuminating survey. To a certain extent, it has already begun in a haphazard fashion and not under the auspices of the HGDP. Unfortunately, the most comprehensive information can only come from a type of polymorphism which is especially important and most common in evolution called Single Nucleotide Polymorphisms or snips.[14] The number of snips known today is insufficient, but is growing rapidly and the techniques for testing them efficiently are practically ready, but need further refinement. Thus, we must wait a little longer before we can embark on large scale definitive testing. Comprehensive DNA collections have not been performed either, so the samples are still not there. Thus, it is clear that the first task should be the accumulation of DNA samples, knowing that final decisions on the details of testing may have to take a little longer. There are a number of markers that can already be used and, if one wants to start testing them, the knowledge thus acquired will not be lost. The final testing may start only a year or two from now. New methods may be so efficient that test results may be generated rapidly. At the moment, the best strategy is to collect DNAs from all world populations and begin working with the analytical means now at hand, even if we know that better ones will be soon available. In this first stage, we can learn how to best share and exchange material and information.

The Human Genome Project is distinct from ours because it aims at generating full knowledge on a single individual, and in fact on one half of it, because everyone of us receives an almost complete copy of the genome from the father and another copy from the mother. An army of researchers are active in that Project, and their work may be completed a few years from now. What will this army do at that time? Having learned a valuable set of techniques which are very likely to continue to be useful, it can take one of three paths: 1) extend the research to other organisms (this has already happened, especially on smaller ones like microorganisms, three of which have been fully sequenced, but there is a limit to the number of species - which are potentially millions - worth being examined in such detail); 2) begin an in depth study of the physiology of a gene, and there are nearly one hundred thousand of them whose function is sufficiently precise and understandable so that studying them could lead relatively easily to some tangible conclusion; 3) finally, study genetic diversity in detail in at least one species, namely, ours. We know that humans are becoming increasingly mobile and the present differences between groups are progressively diminishing. Human genetic variation will not disappear, in fact we know that it will remain approximately constant and the variation found between groups today will become even smaller than it is now. The loss of variation between groups will enhance that which exists within groups. Eventually, we will become a single heterogeneous group, even though there may remain small isolates here and there, true cultural museums. Some also consider these isolated groups biological museums and, although this may be an exaggeration, some - a very few - populations may yield genetic surprises. The inevitable loss of information accessibility due to the increased human mobility which we now face, is another reason to start the Human Genome Diversity Project as soon as possible.

Endnotes and References

1 Nei M. and A.K. Roychoudhury, *Human Polymorphic Genes: World Distribution.* (New York: Oxford University Press, 1988).

2 Cavalli-Sforza L.Luca, P. Menozzi and A. Piazza, *The History and Geography of Human Genes* (Princeton, NJ: Princeton University Press, 1994). See also, Cavalli-Sforza, L.Luca

and F. Cavalli-Sforza, translated from Italian by Sarah Thorne, *The Great Human Diasporas: The History of Diversity and Evolution* (Reading, Mass: Addison-Wesley, 1995).

3 Cavalli-Sforza, L.Luca, "Opinion: How Can One Study Individual Variation for 3 Billion Nucleotides of the Human Genome" (1990), 46*Am. J. Hum. Genet.* 649. See also, Cavalli-Sforza L.Luca, A. Wilson, C. Cantor, Cook-Deegan and M-C. King, "Call for a Worldwide Survey of Human Genetic Diversity: A Vanishing Opportunity for the Human Genome Project" (1991), 11*Genomics* 490. See also, Kidd J., K. Kidd and K. Weiss, "The Human Genome Diversity Initiative" (1991), 65 *Hum. Biol.* 1. See also, Weiss K., K. Kidd and J. Kidd, "Human Genome Diversity Project" (1992), 1 *Evolutionary Anthropology* 80.

4 Bowcock A.M., A. Ruiz-Linares, J. Tomfohrde, E. Minch, J.R. Kidd and L.L. Cavalli-Sforza, "High Resolution of Human evolutionary Tress with Polymorphic Microsatellites" 368 *Nature* 455.

5 Goldstein D.G., A. Ruiz Linares, L.L. Cavalli-Sforza and M.W. Feldman, "Genetic Absolute Dating Based on Microsatellites and the Origin of Modern Humans", 92 *Proc. Natl. Acad. Sci. (USA)* 6723.

6 Klein R.G. ,*The Human Career: Human Biological and Cultural Origins* (Chicago: University of Chicago Press, 1989).

7 Lahr M.M. and R. Foley, "Multiple Dispersals and Modern Human Origins" (1994), 3 *Evolutionary Anthropology* 48. See also, Lahr M.M., *The Evolution of Modern Human Diversity: A Study on Cranial Variation* (New York: Cambridge University Press, 1996).

8 Cavalli-Sforza L.Luca, "Genes, Peoples and Languages" (1991), 265 *Scientific American* 104.

9 Cavalli-Sforza L.Luca, P. Menozzi and A. Piazza, "Demic Expansions and Human Evolution" (1993), 259 *Science* 639.

10 Barbujani G. and R.R. Sokal, "Zones of Sharp Genetic Change in Europe are Also Linguistic Boundaries" (1990), 87 *Proc. Natl. Acad. Sci. (USA*) 1816.

11 Supra note 2, *The Great Human Diasporas: The History of Diversity and Evolution.*

12 Lewontin R.C., "The Apportionment of Human Diversity" in Dobzhansky T.H., M.K. Hecht and W.C. Steere, eds., *Evolutionary Biology* . Vol. 6. (New York: Appleton-Century Crofts,1972) at 381. See also, Lewontin R.C. *Human Diversity.* 1982. Scientific American Books. (San Francisco: W. H. Freeman and Company). See also, Nei M. and A.K. Roychoudhury, "Genic Variation Within and Between the Three Major Races of Man, Caucasoids, Negroids, and Mongoloids" (1974) 26 *Am. J. Hum. Genet.* 421.

13 The Human Genome Organization, "Statement on the Principled Conduct of Genetics Research", based upon Knoppers B.M., M. Hirtle, S. Lormeau, "Ethical Issues in International Collaborative Research on the Human Genome: The HGP and the HGDP" (1996), 34 *Genomics* 272.

14 Supra note 2.

THE HUMAN GENOME DIVERSITY PROJECT: A PERSPECTIVE FROM CULTURAL ANTHROPOLOGY

MARGARET LOCK

Professor in the Departments of Social Studies of Medicine and of Anthropology, McGill University

The Human Genome Diversity Project (HGDP) is designed to investigate biological difference among human populations, a subject which has been in effect been a taboo during the latter part of this century, particularly in North America, for fear of inciting racism. This silence is due, of course, to the long history of appalling discrimination and violence against peoples designated as biologically inferior, practices which were legitimized at the end of the 19th century, when racism was for several decades recognized as a scientific endeavour.

Paradoxically, we live in an era where the politics of difference is foremost in people's minds, despite concerted efforts to combat racism over the past quarter century. This was clearly evident in a recent American television program which revealed deep fissures along ethnic lines at Berkeley High school in California, even though a policy fostering integration among students has been in place for nearly thirty years. The hostilities which regularly erupt in connection with ethnicity at Berkeley High ensure that a vast amount of school time and student energy is put into creating and maintaining a sense of self based on a politics of difference. Black students stated repeatedly in the program that they are not American but African, and Hispanics cheered as one young woman proclaimed, "we are not Mexicana, Chicano, Latina - we are all La Raza (the Race)." White students usually appeared uncomfortable, sometimes angry participants in the program, the third major group by default, in the dividing of Berkeley High into these incommensurable camps. Chinese, East European immigrants, and other students who did not "fit" were left to join in as best they could, or else form dissenting factions of their own. Not surprisingly, there were no First Peoples present, no Pomo or Yurok left living to intrude on this post-colonial apportioning of power.

This particular television program made the violence associated with the politics of ethnicity very apparent; it was also clear that students are preoccupied with what they think of as immutable genealogies based on skin colour and geographical origins. There was not a single reference in the program to biological populations, to genetic diversity or, for that matter, to class and economic differences. The category that takes priority over all others is that of "race". The fact that this concept is freely adapted from the 19th century Spencerian theory of social evolution which placed the European white male at the apex of a progressive evolutionary development of races from primitive to "cultivated" is, it is no doubt safe to assume, not known to most of these students.

The Politics of Race

Of course, the trend to reify race is not found solely among the youth of California, on the contrary, the current politics of multiculturalism and of funding for health care encourage us all to "think" race and ethnicity. Publications such as the *Journal of Public Health Medicine,* which should know better, often use racial and ethnic categories as unproblematic independent variables, as though these categories are distinct entities which arise in nature. This is despite the fact that biologists have repeatedly argued that race is a political concept and not one which has any foundation in population biology.[1,2] Similarly, ethnicity - a term often used interchangeably with race - signifies a cultural and political entity. Both these concepts when understood as though they are immutable replications of the natural world have the potential to incite friction and violence among peoples. As epidemiological categories they have no meaning other than as self-reported descriptors by respondents to survey questionnaires. Since it is poverty which is the strongest predictor of ill health in human populations and not ethnicity, or gender for that matter, it would be more appropriate to make the distribution of wealth the focal issue for epidemiological analyses, but we keep returning to race, ethnicity, nationalism, and human difference these days. I believe this is because phenotypic difference, in particular that which constitutes physical appearance, remains in the cultural imagination as a seductive, perhaps indispensable folk categorization, in part because it is so readily subject to political manipulation.

One of the stated goals of the HGDP is to help "combat the widespread popular fear and ignorance of human genetics and make a significant contribution to the elimination of racism." Let me make it clear that in principle I strongly support research designed to investigate human genetic diversity, but that the publications and discussions which have taken place in connection with the HGDP thus far, with a few notable exceptions such as the UNESCO document (1995),[3] have left me with deep concerns. Claims that the HGDP will help eliminate racism are extravagant. To imagine that, if we were all better educated about our shared genetic heritage, we would eliminate racial discrimination and stop our warring over social and political boundaries smacks of a kind of naive reductionism. It is language usage, religion, individual and group behaviour, economics, and politics which drive these territorial disputes; physical appearance is made into one more powerful factor for use in the service of politics.

As the UNESCO subcommittee on population genetics has pointed out, exceptional caution is called for in outlining the methodology and goals of a project which takes up issues of genetic diversity, because of the dangers inevitably inherent in such research. Research used to support the eugenic practices of the early part of this century together with selective discrimination against peoples, had racist values built into its design. Eugenic practices were justified through appeals to a pseudoscience which set up alleged biological difference among humans as the fundamental reason why inequality is a "natural" condition of social life. The history of genetics throughout this century gives overwhelming testimony as to how easily this discipline can be corrupted, and to just how often policy making and health care practices have been driven by bad science.[4] Such research continues to this day, and the work of Philippe Rushton is one such Canadian example.

Extreme care was therefore necessary in setting up and implementing the HGDP, but this has not in reality been evident. Although the project organizers currently claim to have modified their original plans as a result of public criticism, they must now deal with the hostile feelings sent reverberating around indigenous communities throughout the world as a result of the original plans for the project as they have appeared in various communications and publications since 1991.[5]

Boundary Disputes: The Construction of Populations

The HGDP is designed expressly to focus on genetic diversity, on polytypic variation rather than on polymorphism. Ironically, it was the geneticist Earnest Hooton, a supporter of the eugenic movement of the 1920s, who first insisted that research in genetics should be directed to individual variation, to polymorphism, and not to difference between groups. The idea of polymorphism was not well recognized in the early part of this century, but Hooton's position contributed eventually to a shift in emphasis in genetic research so that attention moved away from the so-called "racial differences" characteristic of 19th century research. The significance of individual variation could not be appreciated while validation of difference remained the key paradigm, and it was not until well into the present century that it became widely recognized that almost all genetic diversity is found between individuals and within groups and relatively little difference is found among human groups. The HGDP seeks to direct attention once again to variation in the geographical distribution of genes among human populations, as did 19th century scientists, but now it is the nuances of molecular genetics, and not phenotypic anatomical and morphological features which are of interest. One important reason for undertaking this type of research is to counter the bias for uniformity built into the mapping of the human genome currently taking place under the auspices of HUGO.

The problem from the start with the HGDP has been that the idea of a human"population", far from being a readily definable natural fact, is a contested concept both politically and biologically. How, therefore, should one go about locating and specifying the boundaries of the populations to be sampled? One of the major difficulties is that almost all geographic variation in gene frequency is quantitative, or clinal -- that is, discrete demarcations cannot be established between one group of people and another on the basis of gene pools, because pools tend to grade off one into the other. Variations in the distribution of blood types is a case in point. We are almost always dealing, therefore, with **relative**, and not absolute difference.

Among the goals of the HGDP is one which aims to reconstruct the history of human development, migrations, and expansions of populations around the world, a mega-project which inevitably presents enormous problems. Four factors are believed to contribute to differences in human gene pools: length of time of separation of the populations under study; lack of subsequent genetic contact between them; genetic response to local conditions or history, and the restricted size of populations. Obviously, to reconstruct history it is the first of these variables which is of overwhelming interest. The third factor involves natural selection and is difficult to assess -- the gene pools of aboriginal American populations, for example, were probably altered in the 16th century through sudden contact with the smallpox virus among others, although it is not known exactly how this happened. Genetic drift is at work in the case of the fourth variable. It is the second variable which is of immediate concern to anthropologists since archeological and linguistic evidence suggests that subsequent contact among groups of people who may have migrated independently or initially drifted apart has been the rule, and not the exception, throughout prehistory and historical times. This has been the case even when culturally created barriers, such as rules of endogamy, have served to limit contact to some extent. In short, reconstruction of the points of separation of human groups one from another by creating phylogenetic trees based on protein allele or DNA sequencing is exceedingly problematic because of the complex inter-relationship of the four factors set out above.

Of even more concern to anthropologists is what in the social sciences is called a "category fallacy", namely the imposition of one set of data on another set of data of a different kind. For example, ephemeral socio-political human groupings as they are formed and dissolved through time tell one rather little about gene pools and visa versa. A "genetic isolate" list was composed in 1992 by HGDP planners of "unique, historically vital populations that are in danger of dying out or being assimilated." These populations were targeted as being those from whom blood should first be collected.[6] However, the San peoples of Southern Africa, placed at the top of the list, contain three different language groups, suggesting relatively recent formation as a single group and are therefore not as isolated as one might suppose. The "eta of Japan" were also placed on this list. The word *eta* is exceedingly pejorative and refers to outcast groups, composed primarily of people who worked with animal products. The origin of outcast groups is traced by some Japanese researchers to the 9th century; these groups have almost without exception been located within cities and have provided services such as butchery and tanning for urban dwellers.

They have never formed distinct linguistic groups, and although marriage outside the group was strictly prohibited, nevertheless there are records which document "mixed" liaisons of various kinds. The *burakumin*, in more polite language, ceased to be legally recognized more than a century ago in Japan, and clearly do not qualify as genetically distinct. Interest was also expressed by those organizing the HGDP in the founder populations of North America, but linguistic studies of such populations indicate enormous movement and extensive contact between groups, and there is no agreement as to how many separate migrations took place across the Bering Strait in the first place.

The image of isolated, exotic cultures is one from the days of 19th century colonialism, an era shaped by Spencer's theory of social evolution. We are finally recognizing that the "People Without History" as Eric Wolf has ironically called them, are not frozen in time, artifacts from the past, either culturally or biologically. When Time magazine reported last year on the HGDP it claimed, on the basis of discussion with one of the project's leaders, that "[a]ll Europeans are thought to be a hybrid population with 65% Asian and 35% African genes." As the biological anthropologist Jonathon Marks has pointed out, this statement is not actually false, but the way in which it is articulated is exceedingly misleading, for African and Asians are not a dichotomous pair, opposite from one another, homogeneous and pure -- this, in short, is an example of folk anthropology.

There are yet further difficulties in establishing what is to constitute a population depending upon whether one collects nuclear DNA inherited from both parents, or whether the focus is on mitochondrial DNA inherited only from ones mother. Mitochondrial DNA mutates much faster than does nuclear DNA, and does not recombine. Wilson, in his work, found that distinctive mitochondrial alleles are limited to fairly small geographical radii, eliminating the need to establish gene frequencies in populations in order to say something about genetic diversity. When the project was first discussed, it was argued by Wilson that the best way to go about mapping diversity was not to limit sampling to the so-called isolated populations, but to set up a grid across the globe and take representative samples at regular intervals.[7] It appears that this technique is now being given serious consideration by HGDP planners and would counter the bias built into the project as it was originally conceived, in which the uncovering of genetic difference associated with named groups was the primary objective.

In sum, a genetic population is a cultural construct, a product in part of the objects selected for analysis (mitochondrial or nuclear DNA), the selection of cut off points to create boundaries between human groups, the desired end results, and also in part by preconceived ideas about migration patterns. Goodman has characterized the HGDP as it is presently designed as having a "mechanistic and overly-deterministic approach to human biology," one in which "there is no built-in effort to examine interaction between genes, or between genes and the environment."[8] Like other critics of the project, Goodman is concerned that without accompanying information about the environment, phenotypic data, individual life histories, nutritional patterns, disease histories, and so on, it will be impossible to interpret the resultant genetic information as anything other than DNA sequences. It is hard, he concludes, "to envision how the project will do more than provide additional data on small and trivial polymorphic differences."[9] How best to reconstruct human prehistory and history remains a contentious issue, one deserving of much more debate in both professional and public forums. To my mind, it is misleading to suggest that, given the technology we have at present, one can indeed reconstruct the migratory history of a specific group of people. Meantime, local creation myths do a rather good job, I think.

Immortalization and Morals

For the 722 groups of people who, without consultation, found themselves in 1992 picked out of a larger group of 7000 to qualify as "genetic isolates" loud alarm bells started to ring. It is clear that deep concerns were created at that time among some leaders of the groups who found themselves targeted for sampling that although their blood was going to be immortalized, they themselves were to be allowed to continue on the road to "extinction".[10] It was in this climate of mistrust that questions of ethics were belatedly addressed.

Unless ethical issues are taken very seriously, the HGDP project will inevitably do considerable, long lasting social, political, and individual damage. The HGDP has been characterized as "resolutely non-commercial" by one of the organizers,[11] but one obstacle in the acceptance of this claim is that the HGDP becomes associated all too easily in the minds of many critics of the project with the "bleed and run" caravans sent out by Hoffman Laroche and other drug companies as they go about their gene prospecting. The diversity project has little chance of success until exploitation of indigenous populations by drug companies is brought under control, and second, project members make it explicit where they stand in relation to drug company initiatives.

In addition to concern about commodification of human cells and tissues, other legitimate worries have been expressed about several of the objectives of the HGDP, and associated ethical issues. For example, although the welfare and interests of indigenous peoples as been noted as of importance, no representatives of indigenous peoples have been included to date in the central planning process, despite requests to do so. Moreover, it remains unclear as to what extent, if any, local governments will be involved in facilitating the project and what recompense, if any, they would receive - an issue of grave concern for indigenous peoples. It has been suggested in HGDP publications that assistance may be given with training of local staff and developing research centres to aid in the collection of blood. This is seen as an opportunity for indigenous people themselves to become actively involved in the project and to promote development, but serious concern has been expressed by various communities that such initiatives may divert local finances away from the construction of urgently needed public health projects.[12]

It is frequently asserted that the HGDP will help provide information on the genetic patterning of disease susceptibility. This, however, is a false claim given the way in which the project is currently designed. As noted above, no contextualizing information will be gathered when blood samples are taken, and therefore no connections can be established between genotypes and the incidence of disease. Furthermore, people can be easily misled into believing that cures for diseases such as diabetes will be imminent as a result of the project, when in fact research into therapeutics are not among the objectives of the project. It has also been suggested that health care can be administered to people at the time when blood is drawn. This too is a misleading assertion since no responsible health care can take place without systematic follow-up, and with little or no knowledge of local nosologies of disease. This issue becomes confused because blood has, of course, often been given freely by indigenous peoples when health care is the primary purpose, but then on occasion it has been sent at a later date to the NIH for genetic analysis which was not part of the original plan, as appears to have been the case with the Hagahai of New Guinea.[13]

The draft ethical protocol put out by the North American Regional Committee of the HGDP states that it will be necessary to obtain consent not only from individuals, but also from community representatives in which all the proposed activities of project members are fully explained. The protocol goes to great lengths to explicate the difficulties of establishing what exactly can count as a given community when local and national boundary disputes are implicated. Under these circumstances, it is no straightforward matter to locate where the recognized authority resides.

Sensitivity is shown in the North American protocol to the pluralism of groupings present in most societies. However, even with both group and individual agreement, informed consent remains a problem, first because people simply cannot be made fully aware of what is involved in this project. Not only is it technically exceedingly complex and not amenable to easy simplification, but, as pointed out above, the involved concepts and methods are matters which cannot be agreed upon by the scientists themselves. Secondly, as things stand at present, the immortalized cells can be made available from the Washington storage site at any time in the future to researchers deemed as having legitimate objectives. No one knows, therefore, what may happen to these cells in the long run. Thus, consent can only be obtained from individuals and communities to draw blood on the understanding that in the future the resultant cells may be put to any number of unspecified and unforeseen uses. This may not present a difficulty, since some communities appear relatively untroubled as to what happens to their blood, but others are deeply concerned.[14,15]

In closing, I turn briefly to patenting. Planners of the HGDP have made it clear that they will not profit from any commercial use to which procured samples are put. The draft of the North American Model Ethical Protocol suggests that if any financial reward accrues from specific analyses then a system should be in place whereby individuals or populations who donated the blood should receive fair monetary compensation. The protocol also states that express permission must first be obtained from involved communities before any applications can be made for patenting, or the marketing of products, and a respected international body such as UNESCO should be made use of as a trustee. The right to withdraw samples, and the right to have them destroyed at a later date is also discussed. This draft protocol bears the mark of many hours of thoughtful discussion which may open some cooperative partnerships with indigenous peoples, something which it suggests is necessary if the project is to succeed. However, this document is still at the draft stage, and will only have a bearing on the North American part of the project, meanwhile blood collected proceeds on an ad hoc basis as has been the case for many years with little or no consideration given to ethical issues.

Incidents such as the patenting of a virus found in the blood of certain Hagahai individuals reverberate around the world causing consternation and resentment. The anthropologist Strathern suggests that claims that human cells can be owned through patenting arise because of their special status for, once manipulated in the laboratory, cells are no longer in their original form. Strathern argues that isolated segments of DNA are simultaneously cultural and natural products. Neither isolated cells nor the techniques by themselves could qualify for patenting, but only the hybrid, the DNA sequence, a product of cultural incursions into nature. Once the DNA is reproduced in the laboratory the original item, the cells to which an individual could lay claim as coming directly from their body, have been transformed into something different, partially artificial and no longer simply human in origin.[16] An added complication arises because in the Hagahai case it was a virus found in the blood sample which was patented, forcing us to pose the question of whether organisms housed in individual bodies belong to that body or not. We are rapidly entering an era where technological incursions into biology urgently require prolonged moral reflection and institutionalized monitoring systems, and it will not be sufficient for the HGDP to simply declare that it will not profit from the commercialization of cells and tissues. Since blood will be drawn by HGDP researchers and stored for potential use by many other unrelated researchers, then HGDP members must actively ensure that no door is left open for exploitation - the North American ethical protocol sets a very good example here.

The HGDP inadvertently blundered into a hotbed of political machination. A lack of foresight about these difficulties exhibited until recently by the planners suggests that they assumed scientific investigation to be a privileged enterprise, one which need only pay lip service to morals and to the welfare of the subjects to be investigated. One can only hope that such arrogance is on the wane, for we now have to turn our attention to a larger problem, the exploitation of individuals and communities through the commodification of body cells, organs, and tissues, an enterprise about which the HGDP must take up an unequivocal moral position.

Endnotes and References

1 Lewontin R.C., *Not in Our Genes: Biology, Ideology, and Human Nature* (New York: Pantheon Books, 1984).

2 Lock M., "The Concept of Race: An Ideological Construct" (1993), 30 *Transcultural Psychiatry Research Review* 203.

3 UNESCO IBC Population Genetics Subcommittee, *Bioethics and Human Genetic Research* (1995), Draft Report.

4 Kelves D., *In the Name of Eugenics* (Cambridge: Harvard University Press, 1995).

5 Roberts L., "A Genetic Survey of Vanishing Peoples" (1991), 252 *Science* 1614.

6 Roberts L., "Anthropologists Climb (Gingerly) on Board" (1992), 258 *Science* 1300.

7 Supra note 5.

8 Goodman A., *Glorification of the Genes: Genetic Determinism and Racism in Science* (London: Intermediate Technology Publications, 1996).

9 Ibid.

10 Lock M., "Interrogating the Human Diversity Genome Project" (1994), 39 *Social Science & Medicine* 603.

11 Greely H.T., "Genes, Patents and Indigenous Peoples: Biomedical Research and Indigenous People's Rights" (Summer1996), *Cultural Survival Quarterly* 54.

12 Baumann M., J.Bell, F.Koechlin and M.Pimbert, *The Life Industry: Biodiversity, People and Profits* (London: Intermediate Technology Publications, 1996).

13 Ibeji Y. and G.Korowai, "The Hagahai Patent Controversy: In their own Words" (Summer 1996), *Cultural Survival Quarterly* 33.

14 Liloqula R., "Value of Life: Saving Genes Versus Saving Indigenous Peoples" (Summer 1996), *Cultural Survival Quarterly* 42.

15 Mead A., "Geneology, Sacredness and the Commodities Market" (Summer 1996), *Cultural Survival Quarterly* 46.

16 Strathern M., "Cutting the Network" (1996), 2 (n.s.) *J. Royal Anthrop. Inst.* 517.

THE ETHICS OF THE HUMAN GENOME DIVERSITY PROJECT: THE NORTH AMERICAN REGIONAL COMMITTEE'S PROPOSED MODEL ETHICAL PROTOCOL

HENRY T. GREELY

Professor of Law, Stanford University

Member of the North American Regional Committee of the HGDP

Chair of HGDP Ethics Subcommittee.

There may be no other scientific project that has the capacity to touch so many lives and minds. At the beginning of this document, we set out its guiding principles:

- informed consent,
- respect for the sampled population's culture, and
- adherence to international standards of human rights.

If the Project is conducted according to these principles, it should enhance not only humanity's knowledge of itself, but also humanity's interest in, knowledge of, and confidence in science. If conducted poorly, without respect for and protection of the rights of those who participate, it may prove a disaster - not for humanity, but for science. Researchers participating in this Project, and those who review their proposals for funding or ethical compliance, bear an enormous responsibility both to participating communities and to science. This document is an effort to help them discharge those responsibilities well.

The Proposed Model Ethical Protocol for Collecting DNA Samples, North American Regional Committee, Human Genome Diversity Project [1]

The Human Genome Diversity Project ("the HGDP") was first proposed in 1991.[2] Although the Project remains, at this writing, only a proposal, it has evolved in the past six years into an ambitious effort to collect, preserve, and analyze the genetic variation spread throughout all of the Earth's 5.5 billion human genomes. The Project wants to collect, preserve, and analyze DNA from hundreds of human populations. The samples and the data derived from them are to be collected and prepared in standard ways and are to be generally available to interested scholars. In essence, the HGDP seeks to create an efficient and useful reference library for a large sample of humanity's genetic diversity.

The scope of the Project has been rivalled by the breadth and complexity of the ethical problems it has raised. The fullest discussion of those problems - and their solutions - is found in the proposed Model Ethical Protocol for Collection DNA Samples ("the Model Protocol"), prepared by the HGDP's North American Regional Committee ("the NAmC") and released by it for public comment.

The Model Protocol is a detailed examination of the issues the Project raises and an ambitious and innovative effort to resolve those issues. It is the primary document and should be read by anyone interested in the ethical questions of research into human population genetics. This chapter is really a commentary on the Model Protocol, written by its principal author. It begins by describing the history of the Model Protocol and the process through which it was produced. In so doing, it provides, in summary form, one perspective on the history of the HGDP's consideration of ethical, legal, and social issues. The chapter then highlights the most important aspects of the document, particularly its provisions requiring group consent and governing control over commercialization. Finally, it discusses the problems, practical and political, that the Model Protocol confronts.

The History of the Model Protocol

After the initial proposal for a Human Genome Diversity Project, Sir Walter Bodmer, then president of the Human Genome Organisation, appointed a committee to study the idea. The American members of that committee[3] received funding for planning workshops from a combination of the United States National Science Foundation, National Institutes of Health, and the Department of Energy. That funding was used to hold three workshops: one on population genetics in July 1992, one on anthropology in October 1992, and one on a variety of issues, including ethical questions, in February 1993. The committee then used its funding to co-sponsor an international planning workshop in September 1993 near the city of Alghero in Sardinia, Italy, which became the organizing meeting for the HGDP.[4]

My own involvement with the proposed HGDP began in early December 1992, when Professors Luca Cavalli-Sforza and Marcus W. Feldman asked me to organize and moderate a full-day session on ethical and human rights issues for the February 1993 workshop. We quickly reached a preliminary determination that the ethical issues fell into three broad categories: sample collection issues (mainly but not entirely those of informed consent), intellectual property, and racism.[5] On February 17, 1993, a set of 14 experts discussed these issues at the National Institutes of Health in Bethesda, Maryland. The all-day discussions took place through three panels, one on each major topic.[6] I wrote a summary of the workshop's discussions and, in a separate memorandum, a set of recommendations to the American organizers of the Project. For me, the panel discussions confirmed that we had focused on the proper three issues and that each raised complicated, but ultimately tractable problems.

In early September 1993, a four-day international workshop in Sardinia discussed, and ultimately organized, the HGDP. Ethical issues were discussed at many points in that meeting and were the subject of a special panel discussion. The panel was chaired by Dr. Colin Renfrew and included presentations by myself, Dr. Anne Cambon-Thomsen of France, and Dr. Partha Majumder of India. During and after the workshop, work proceeded on a statement of ethical principles for the proposed HGDP, which was incorporated in the eventual report of the Alghero meeting. This report identifies four major areas of concern: collection issues; intellectual property rights; racism, xenophobia, and hyper-nationalism; and public fear and misunderstanding about genetics.[7]

The Alghero report contains ten proposed ethical guidelines, which stress the following issues:

- respect for the humanity of sampled individuals and the cultural integrity of sampled populations;
- informed consent;
- providing appropriate benefits for research participants;
- individual and, in some cases, community confidentiality;
- financial returns to the participating populations in the unlikely event that the Project resulted in any commercial products;
- responsibility to combat racist or nationalistic misuse of Project results;
- public education about human genetics;
- continual review of ethical issues in the Project;
- technology transfer to the developing world;
- feed-back of results to participating populations.[8]

In Sardinia, the organizers recognized that these guidelines were only general principles, which would have to be made more specific in the future. In overall organization, the HGDP adopted a regional model, with an international executive committee that would coordinate and oversee regional committees that would actually implement the Project. An international executive committee was created with thirteen members: five from the United States, five from Europe, and one each from Africa, India, and Japan.[9]

The Alghero report provided that the international executive committee would have two standing subcommittees, one on databases and informatics and one on ethics. As to the ethics subcommittee, the organizers agreed that it "should be subject to the overall guidance of HUGO's standing committee on Ethics."[10] In addition, the report "recommended that each regional committee consider appointing a subcommittee on local ethical issues."[11] The executive committee immediately created the informatics subcommittee, but, for more than three years, it took no action to create an international ethics subcommittee.[12]

Within two months of the meeting in Alghero, the NAmC was organized. I was one of the founding members of the NAmC and was appointed chair of its ethics subcommittee. The NAmC's initial eleven, and then thirteen, members were scattered throughout the United States and Canada.[13] The logistics of full meetings were daunting. A partial meeting was held in November 1993, followed by the first full meeting in January 1994.

Also shortly after the Alghero meeting, at its meeting in January 1994, the Human Genome Organization Council endorsed the HGDP and agreed, in some unclear respects, to oversee it. HUGO eventually appointed a committee of three to maintain liaison with the Project: Sir Walter Bodmer of the United Kingdom, Dr. Victor McKusick of the United States, and Dr. Sergio Pena of Brazil.

It soon became clear that, at least in North America, the HGDP would be a controversial project, largely for ethical and political reasons. In late 1993, almost as soon as it was organized, the NAmC began discussions with the John D. and Catherine T. MacArthur Foundation about funding organizational, communications, and ethical planning for the Project. The NAmC received a grant from the Foundation for those purposes in May 1994. The grant application included a request to fund what it called a "Model Protocol," which it said would be "a 50- to 150-page document that would serve as a reference and a guide to investigators and IRBs that were concerned about how the special ethical problems raised by the project should be approached."[14]

NAmC members began a serious discussion of what would become the Model Ethical Protocol at their second full meeting, held in August 1994 at Stanford. The Ethics Subcommittee initially included John Moore, Mark Weiss, and myself as chair. At the Stanford meeting, we were joined in discussions of what would become the Model Protocol by Kenneth Kidd, Emöke Szathmary, and Catherine Twinn. We drafted a rough outline of the document and asked various NAmC members to contribute ideas and language to the different sections.

At and after the same August NAmC meeting, the regional committee expressed concerns about what it perceived as a lack of action by the international executive committee. The immediate spark for the concern was the long-standing desire of the NAmC to release a document explaining the Project, which was being blocked by objections from some members of the international executive committee.[15] The concerns escalated beyond that point, however. The international executive committee had a meeting scheduled for London in mid-September 1994. The continuation of the NAmC's discussions through electronic mail led to the creation of a set of framework issues (sometimes referred to as "the seven pillars") that the

NAmC representatives on the international executive committee were to ask that committee to resolve on behalf of the entire Project.

The international executive committee met very briefly in London and neither accepted nor rejected the NAmC's request for decisions on these points. The international executive committee has not met since that time, largely if not entirely because of its lack of funding. Its main subsequent activity has been the publication in early 1995 of the report of the Project's founding meeting at Alghero.

The failure of its efforts at the September 1994 meeting made the NAmC less willing to wait for the international executive committee to propose solutions to the ethical issues raised by the HGDP. It determined to press ahead with its own planning for the HGDP on a regional basis, in the hope that the international executive committee would eventually largely accept the NAmC's work. This led to a renewed commitment to the production of the Model Ethical Protocol, channelled through a "Model Protocol Working Group" made up of Drs. Kidd, Moore, and Weiss, Ms. Twinn and myself.

On March 4 and 5, 1995, four members of this Working Group met for a weekend at the University of Florida to advance the writing of a first draft of the Model Protocol. This meeting began with some detailed outlines and a few pages of draft. It ended with a much more complete and detailed outline and a firm sense of agreement on the underlying principles of the document. With help on some sections from my colleagues, I completed a draft of the document after returning to Stanford.

The first draft was finished in April 1995; the second, somewhat longer, draft circulated to the entire NAmC on June 16, 1995. NAmC members made numerous thoughtful and substantive comments through June, July, and August. The most critical comments concerned the idea of "group consent." After making many corrections and changes, including a substantial rewriting of the discussion of group consent, the revised version circulated to the NAmC at the beginning of September 1995. This version, modified a few days later by some typographical changes, is the draft of the proposed Model Protocol that has since circulated widely. The NAmC authorized its circulation as the NAmC's *proposed* Model Ethical Protocol. The NAmC has been quite clear both that the Model Ethical Protocol speaks, at this point, only for the North American Regional Committee of the Project and that even the North American Committee is, at this time, only circulating this version for comments. It had not in September 1995 and has not now finally adopted the Model Protocol.

Nonetheless, the NAmC found it quite useful to be able to circulate an authorized version of a *proposed* Model Protocol widely in September 1995, as ethical issues in the HGDP were being examined in several different ways. The International Bioethics Committee of the United Nations Educational, Social, and Cultural Organization (UNESCO) had appointed a subcommittee to consider ethical issues in human population genetics research. This subcommittee, chaired by Dr. Darryl Macer, made a report to the International Bioethics Committee in late 1995.[16] It did receive and review the Model Protocol, of which it said: "[t]he North American HGDP regional ethical committee has produced detailed guidelines, which has progressed the ethical review of future population genetics studies conducted within their auspices."[17]

In August and September 1995, Bartha Maria Knoppers, a law professor at the Université de Montréal and a member of both the UNESCO subcommittee and HUGO's Ethical, Legal, and Social Issues ("ELSI") Committee, was writing her own report for the HUGO committee on ethical issues in human genetics research. She received both an early version of the Model Protocol and the authorized September draft.

Professor Knoppers' report[18] formed the basis for an important discussion at the HUGO ELSI Committee meeting in mid-October 1995. Kenneth Kidd and I were asked to make a presentation to this committee about the HGDP and the ethical issues it raises. We discussed both the science of the Project and the Model Protocol, which had been sent to the committee in advance. The Model Protocol was the subject of extensive and mainly friendly discussion by the committee.

Professor Knoppers then presented her paper, which concerned both the HGDP and other research in human genetics. The Committee, relying heavily on Prof. Knoppers, then drafted a shorter statement of ethical principles, abstracting ten "commandments" from Prof. Knoppers' paper. This shorter paper was eventually approved by the HUGO Council in March 1996 and released as HUGO's general position on ethical issues in human genetics research.[19] In extensive discussions at the committee meeting, Prof. Knoppers and I agreed that the Model Protocol was almost entirely consistent with those principles.[20]

The Model Protocol was released more broadly in the fall of 1995 and thereafter to those involved in the HGDP, to scholars with a particular interest in the topic, and to anyone who requested it. By mid-1996 it was placed on a home page on the World Wide Web, where it has been freely available. Several of the groups or individuals who have reviewed the document have made useful comments on it. Those comments were considered in producing a revised version in August 1996. This version, which remains only a "proposed" protocol, was published in the Houston Law Review in February 1997[21] and replaced the September 1995 version on the Web in early 1997.

The Key Provisions of the Model Protocol

The NAmC's goal in preparing the Model Protocol was to provide useful information to researchers, institutional review boards, funding agencies, and populations about the ethical issues that collection of DNA samples for the HGDP raises. It was not intended to answer all questions, but to make sure they were all considered and to give some guidance to groups thinking about the answers.

After an overview, the Model Protocol has nine substantive sections. These cover a wide variety of difficult issues, from the necessary preparation before approaching a population, providing benefits to participating populations, provisions for privacy and confidentiality, and the importance of education. It ends with a discussion of the importance of creating partnerships with participating populations. This aspiration embodies the document's emphasis on respect for populations that choose to participate – researchers show deep respect for a population by treating it as an equal partner rather than as a "subject" to be studied from the outside.

Of all the issues discussed in the Model Protocol, however, two stand out for their novelty and importance: group consent and control over commercial uses. In these respects, the NAmC believes that it has broken important new ground.

The Model Protocol requires researchers to obtain not just the informed consent of individuals who participate in the research, but, wherever possible, the informed consent of the population. This group informed consent must be obtained from the authority or authorities that are appropriate within the population's culture - whatever authorities the people involved find meaningful. The group must in all instances be obtained from the local community in which the research is to be done. For many populations, group consent also will be required from broader-based authorities, such as tribal governments or religious organizations.

The group consent provisions of the Model Protocol stem from the nature of much of the research the HGDP expects to support - research not about individuals, but about populations. Both points deserve comment. The HGDP is not about individuals and it is about populations. In most research, an individual's participation primarily affects himself. It may have secondary importance for his family or friends, but it provides information about him. The HGDP, like other population genetic research, is not seeking information about individuals except as they contribute to an understanding of their group. The data produced by the HGDP will report the frequencies with which standardized genetic markers are found in particular populations, not in individuals.

Of course, most research involves populations of one kind or another. But study populations for clinical research generally are created for the purposes of the research. The populations to be studied as part of the HGDP long predated the project and often have tremendous importance.[22] They are communities, large and small, that have social meanings because of the culture and the history they share. They deserve, and demand, the respect of researchers for them as groups and not just as collections of individuals.[23]

One can argue for group consent in a straightforward manner. Ethical research generally requires the informed consent of the subject of the research. When the subject of the research is a meaningful group and not an individual, the group's consent should be sought. And, in fact, many scholars who do field work among groups, from ethnographers to epidemiologists, do seek such collective consent. It is important to show respect to the group with which they work; it is also often crucial for actually doing the research.

For the HGDP, group consent is particularly appropriate. The HGDP's research concerns biological, almost genealogical, relationships, both within a group and between it and other groups. The research may bring significant findings about the group's culture and history, findings that might affect the entire group. In that context, the NAmC concluded that the group must give its consent, as a group. Informed consent from a few individuals in the group should not be sufficient to allow the collection and publication of this kind of information.

For many of the populations that the HGDP would like to study, this conclusion is even stronger. The Project has been widely misunderstood, in part as a result of some its own initial statements, as focusing on the world's indigenous populations, particularly small populations in danger of disappearing as separate cultures. In fact, the Project is interested in samples from almost any population that has not been the subject of intensive research. The Han of China make up nearly a quarter of our species but have been little studied. They, and many other large populations, are as important to the HGDP as much smaller populations.

Nonetheless, the HGDP would not have a representative sample of human DNA without material from many smaller populations. Many of those smaller populations, as well as some quite large populations, have been the victims of oppression by larger groups. Certainly, almost all, if not all, the populations native to the Americas have been robbed, exploited, and mistreated by the invading Europeans; many were exterminated, culturally or even physically. To recognize this background is not political correctness; it is to take note of an important reality.

Cultures that have survived this onslaught are understandably wary of researchers from the dominant culture. (In many cases, they are also weary of being studied and restudied by fascinated non-Natives.) In this historical context, the HGDP must be particularly careful to understand, listen to, and respect the wishes of these populations. The group consent requirement respects the autonomy of these cultures and forces researchers to interact meaningfully with them. It is the linchpin of the Model Protocol.

It is also likely to be complicated in practice. For many populations, particularly in North America, defined tribes with recognized governments will provide a starting place for seeking group consent. But not all groups have clearly recognized structures of authority. There may well be no "culturally appropriate authority" to give group consent for some populations. Who could consent for Irish-Americans or Scottish Canadians? Even when a recognized authority does exist, it may not be the only important authority within the population. A tribal government might have less real authority in the community than a social or religious organization. Seeking group consent will require sensitivity and expertise – and a lot of time. In many cases, the process of seeking group consent will take months or even years.

The Model Protocol provides advice to researchers about group consent, but it recognizes that the process will often be difficult and messy. Taking other people seriously often is, even within the same culture. In some cases, taking the group's decision seriously will mean walking away from research with particular populations, even if a sufficient number of individuals want to take part. This commitment to group consent is both new and stringent. The NAmC believes that, for the HGDP, it is also essential.

The Model Protocol's second important innovation deals with control over the patenting or commercial use of the samples or data collected as part of the HGDP. As discussed above, this was not initially seen as a major issue, for two reasons.

First, it is not clear that the HGDP will produce information of commercial value. Although the organizers hope the project will provide helpful background information for medical researchers, it does not intend to hunt for disease genes. It will not collect the kind of detailed and carefully authenticated medical data on participants and their families that such research would require. Even if the Project did lead to the discovery of a genetic disease in a participating population, commercialization – and hence, unfortunately, development of a medical intervention – would likely only occur if the population constituted a substantial market.

In any event, the HGDP is not a commercial project. It has had, and will have, no commercial funding or sponsorship. In fact, at the Alghero meeting it expressly disclaimed any financial interest in the samples and data it would collect. It further resolved that, in the unlikely event the Project's samples or data led to a commercial product, it would seek to ensure that fair financial returns went back to the relevant participating populations.

In spite of these facts, the HGDP was accused of "biopiracy".[24] Cooler critics were willing to accept that the Project organizers meant what they said but they asked how the HGDP could keep commercial organizations from profiting from access to the HGDP's materials and databases. And, for many critics, the issue of the HGDP was swallowed up in the broader debate about patents on human genes.

The NAmC decided to try to create a workable plan for controlling third party commercial use of HGDP materials. The proposed plan, as laid out in the Model Protocol, seeks to protect the interests of the populations that take part in the Project while avoiding two major unresolved issues.

The first of the unresolved issues is that of patenting. Controversy over gene patenting continues, particularly in Europe. The opposition to such patents features many very different arguments. The arguments include, among others, religious concerns about claiming to own "life", claims that patent protection is inappropriate because genes are "discovered" and not "invented" and fears that patents on genetic sequence encourages sequencing too much and development of therapies too little.

HUGO has taken a position on gene patenting, in which it supports some patenting.[25] The HGDP has not taken a position on the issue. Members of the NAmC held many different views, with many, and perhaps most, opposing such patents. No one on the NAmC, however, was eager to take a position that was both far from our expertise and of little relevance to the HGDP.

The second unresolved issue is a legal question – the property status of human biological material. If the participating populations would continue to "own" their samples and data, even when it is in the hands of the HGDP, they could stop unauthorized commercial use. Similarly, if the HGDP owned the samples and data, it could limit their use.

Unfortunately, whether human biological materials are "property" and, if so, to whom they can belong, is not clear. There is one major court decision on the topic, *Moore v. Regents of the University of California*.[26] In that case, the California Supreme Court held that a patient whose spleen had been surgically removed could not claim a property interest in a cell-line developed from the spleen. Whether that decision will reach beyond cell-lines, which are substantially different from cells found in the body, to DNA is not clear.

Neither is it clear whether the decision will reach beyond California. Although the *Moore* case has sparked more fifty articles in law reviews, there have been no comparable cases in California or in other American jurisdictions. The application of *Moore* outside the United States is even more doubtful, as commentators in many other nations reject the idea of treating such materials as property at all.

The Model Protocol proposes a system that takes no position on gene patenting and avoids reliance on property concepts. It offers a two step contractual alternative. First, as part of the group consent process, participating populations would decide how they wanted to deal with patenting and commercialization. They could choose to allow both, ban both, or allow one but not the other. Or they could permit patenting or commercial use but on their own terms, such as a license fee or, more generally, a requirement that anyone seeking to commercialize a discovery based on their materials obtain their written permission first. The Project would therefore not impose its views on patenting on anyone, but would allow each group to reach its own decision.

The group's agreement would be enforced through a second contract, between the HGDP and researchers using its materials or data. The HGDP would allow access to its materials and data only to researchers who agreed, by contract, to abide by certain restrictions. The contracts would be materials transfer agreements and database access agreements. Each such agreement would require the researchers to accept the restrictions placed on samples and related data by the populations that provided them. This contractual obligation could be enforced in court by the HGDP or by the population concerned.

This solution largely avoids questions of property. Whether or not the samples are "property" (and, if so, whose property they are) need not be answered. The parties should be able to enter a binding agreement creating contractual rights even where no property rights existed.

Materials transfer agreements and database access agreements are quite common. Their fine print rivals the license agreements for personal computer software. One might well question whether those documents would even be read. Fortunately, the context for these concerns provides its own assurance. Pharmaceutical products are extremely expensive to develop and test. Although an individual researcher may not pay much heed to these contracts, they could threaten the right of a pharmaceutical firm to develop a drug. As a result, any record that a pharmaceutical company had used the HGDP resources should inject enough uncertainty to lead the firm to negotiate with the relevant populations.

The possibility that a participating population will choose to profit financially from its participation marks the one significant area of tension between the Model Protocol and the HUGO's *Statement on the Principled Conduct of Genetics Research* . The HUGO Statement provides:

> That undue inducement through **compensation** for individual participants, families and populations should be prohibited. This prohibition, however, does not include agreements with individuals, families, groups, communities or populations that foresee technology transfer, local training, joint ventures, provision of health care or of information infrastructures, reimbursement of costs, or the possible use of a percentage of any royalties for humanitarian purposes.[27]

The HUGO guidelines would thus limit the uses to which a population could put financial returns from its participation, notably to "humanitarian purposes". The NAmC has not been willing, as yet, to try to limit the uses that participating populations want to make of any such returns. It seems to us unreasonable for outsiders to tell a community what it should need or want. On the other hand, the HUGO position could serve as a useful check on corruptly used or unfairly distributed benefits. In the unlikely event that there were substantial returns, the NAmC certainly would not want the proceeds to go directly to numbered Swiss bank accounts. The tension between the two statements remains, at this point, unresolved. It does not, however, seem insoluble.

The Problems of the Model Protocol

The Model Protocol is an ambitious effort to protect and extend the rights and protections of groups that participate in population genetics research. It remains a work in progress and is subject to change. Even at this point, the NAmC knows that it is not free of problems. These can be put into two categories: practical and political.

The practical problems revolve around the fact that the Model Protocol is innovative. Its provisions, particularly for group consent and control of commercial use, are untested. As noted above, the NAmC foresees a number of difficulties with group consent. Defining the "group" whose consent is sought, as well as identifying culturally appropriate authorities, will often be complicated. Researchers will need to be careful in evaluating the relevant authorities, as well as to avoid being pulled into internal power struggles. Similarly, the NAmC remains uncertain whether participating populations will be able effectively to discuss and decide issues concerning commercialization and patenting, particularly groups whose lives are far removed from the world of biotechnology and intellectual property.

Fortunately, many of these issues can be studied in pilot projects, before the entire Project begins. In June 1996, the U.S. National Science Foundation released a Request For Applications, announcing that it intended to grant $600,000 for pilot projects studying two important aspects of the proposed HGDP. One aspect concerned improving techniques for collecting, preserving, amplifying, and selecting DNA markers. The second dealt with ethical, legal, and social issues. The Request stated that:

> The pilot projects should investigate what is important to populations in their decision process about cooperating with studies involving collection of tissue samples and cultural information. A field component is desirable but not required. Projects should address culturally relevant concerns, such as identifying culturally appropriate contacts, maintaining continued interaction, negotiating contracts, and identifying participant concerns regarding use of data and samples.[28]

The NSF expects to issue the grants under this program in February 1997.

Even if the Model Protocol proves to be workable, at least one major concern remains: enforcement. The best document is merely fine words if it is not used. The NAmC does not contemplate that "ethics auditors" will review all collection for the HGDP. It does expect that researchers will certify that they have followed the Model Protocol if they seek funding from the HGDP or when they seek to deposit samples in the HGDP repository.[29] At the same time, it plans to distribute the final version of the Protocol widely.

Institutional Review Boards, other researchers, non-governmental organizations, and members of participating populations should all have access to the document. Each should be able to provide some oversight as to the Protocol's enforcement.

The Model Protocol and its concept of special ethical rules for population genetics research face political obstacles as well as practical problems. These political problems come from three very different directions.

First, a few researchers have opposed the group consent requirement as a matter of principle. These researchers argue that the group into which a person is born should not be able to veto his or her choice to participate in research. The decision to participate in research, they urge, should remain personal, in spite of the fact that the research is intended to provide information about groups. At least two members of the NAmC have held this position, but accepted that the Committee as a whole preferred group consent. Those who have taken this position agree that research in population genetics raises special ethical issues and agree with the remainder of the Model Protocol, including its constraints on commercialization.

Second, some researchers have rejected the idea that the HGDP should be held to any higher ethical standard than other research. These scientists contend that the only significant ethical requirements for the Project are individual informed consent plus confidentiality of the data.

In my experience, this position has been expressed in conversation more often by European researchers. It may well stem from a different set of social and political issues surrounding ethnic populations in Europe. Alternatively, this difference may stem from more general differences between North America and Europe in the social constraints on research. The NAmC feels that the special provisions of the Model Protocol are important for the ethical treatment of participating populations. Whatever the merits of the ethical argument, however, in many areas the status quo position is impracticable. Sufficient concern has been raised about the Project - among populations, non-governmental organizations, and the press - that in much of the world, traditional research methods would not work. Without useful safeguards, including group consent, no one will participate.

The third challenge to the Model Protocol comes from the groups that have raised those concerns through their vigorous opposition to the HGDP, notably a Canadian non-governmental organization called the Rural Advancement Foundation International, or RAFI. RAFI was started in the mid-1970s as a public interest group concerned about developing world agriculture. In general, RAFI has supported small scale and indigenous farming techniques and has opposed the adoption of more uniform and industrial farming practices. It has also long expressed concern about "biopiracy", in the form of "genetic prospecting" by Western pharmaceutical and seed companies in the developing world.

RAFI first inquired about the proposed HGDP in early 1993. RAFI asked for information about the HGDP, which was provided. It then blasted the Project in mid-1993 as a human version of the biopiracy it had earlier decried.[30] Since that time, it has consistently attacked the Project and has successfully helped mobilize opposition to it among groups interested in indigenous peoples.

RAFI's campaign may have reached its peak in October 1995 when it issued a "communiqué" denouncing a patent the U.S. government had received on a cell-line derived from a blood from a member of the Hagahai people of Papua New Guinea.[31] The press release did not stop at the patent, however, but also attacked the HGDP.

> "'The thin veneer of the HGDP as an academic, non-commercial exercise has been shattered by the US government patenting an indigenous person from Papua New Guinea,' said Edward Hammond, Program Officer with RAFI-USA in North Carolina."[32]

RAFI's press release failed to note that the HGDP was still only in the planning stages, that HGDP had nothing to do with the Hagahai patent (which was applied for before the HGDP was even conceived), or that the patent (as they described it) appeared to be inconsistent with the HGDP's position on protecting the interests of populations that participated in research.[33]

RAFI and other groups opposed to the HGDP have had a remarkably consistent reaction to the Model Protocol – they have ignored its existence. Rather than discuss its weaknesses or suggest improvements, they have refused to engage it. Perhaps they fear acknowledging the Model Protocol would weaken the picture they have tried to paint of the HGDP. Whatever the reason, the result has been that the groups that have expressed the most concern about the ethical issues raised by the HGDP have not taken the opportunity to comment on, and improve, the HGDP's most complete effort to address those issues. Their insights and criticisms have not been expressed. And that seems a loss, both for them and for the HGDP.

Conclusion

The HGDP is nearing a crossroads. In early 1996 the United States National Research Council appointed a committee to study the scientific and ethical aspects of the proposed HGDP. Several ethicists are members of the committee, including Professor George Annas, Dr. Eric Juengst, and Dr. Katherine Mosely. The committee held several public meetings in 1996 at which the ethical issues raised by the Project were prominently discussed. The Committee's report is expected in the spring of 1997. If the report is favourable, the chances for funding from the United States government are good. If the report is unfavourable, at least the American part of the HGDP, and most probably the NAmC, are likely to disappear. With it may disappear the Model Protocol.

The problems it addresses will not disappear. Research in human population genetics has been ongoing for more than eighty years and will continue. With this research will continue the special ethical issues that go with it, particularly the problems of the relationship between communities and scientists who want to study them. Whatever the fate of the HGDP, I hope the Model Protocol will improve that relationship and, in its own small way, thus advance the interest of both science and humanity.

Endnotes and References

1 32 *Houston Law Review* (forthcoming, Feb.1997). The Proposed Model Ethical Protocol is also available on the World Wide Web at or http://www.leland.stanford.edu/group/morrinst/ HGDP.hmtl. (Two other useful documents about the HGDP are also available at that web site: the summary report of the Project's organizing meeting in Alghero, Sardinia, in September 1993 ("the Alghero report"), released in spring 1995; and Frequently Asked Questions about the HGDP, prepared by its North American Regional Committee. Hard copies of any of these documents may be requested from the North American Regional Committee of the Human Genome Diversity Project ("HGDP") by electronic mail at morrison@forsythe.stanford.edu or by mail at the Morrison Institute for Population and Resource Studies, Stanford University, Stanford, California 94305-5120.

2 Cavalli-Sforza L., et al., (1991), 11 *Genomics* 490.

3 These members were Dr. L. Luca Cavalli-Sforza, a geneticist from Stanford; Dr. Marcus W. Feldman, a population biologist from Stanford; Dr. Kenneth K. Kidd, a geneticist from Yale; Dr. Mary-Claire King, a geneticist then at the University of California at Berkeley (and now at the University of Washington); and Dr. Kenneth M. Weiss, a physical anthropologist at Pennsylvania State University.

4 This four day meeting was also supported by funds from the Porto Conte Research and Training Laboratories Foundation, the European Commission, the Soros Foundation, and HUGO Europe. The Alghero report, the summary document from this meeting, is available at http://www-leland.stanford.edu/ group/morrinst/HGDP.hmtl.

5 In retrospect, it seems ironic that the early organizers of the Project saw no reason to include intellectual property issues in this discussion. Both Dr. Cavalli-Sforza and Dr. Feldman believed that the HGDP and its data and samples would engender little if any commercial interest and that, therefore, the intellectual property issues were not substantial. I did not think the issues would prove to be very important, either ethically or politically, but I did think they were potentially substantial enough to warrant inclusion.

6 Drs. Cavalli-Sforza and Feldman provided background information on the proposed HGDP and on the scientific issues. The panel on collection issues included Drs. Gary Ellis and Joan Porter, director and deputy director respectively of the National Institutes of Health's Office for Protection from Research Risk; Dr. Rachelle Hollander, director of the Ethics and Values Studies Program of the National Science Foundation; and Dr. Kenneth Weiss from the HGDP Committee. The panel on intellectual property issues included Dr. Val Giddings, an official with the U.S. Department of Agriculture and a United States

negotiator of the Biodiversity Convention, and Dr. Walter Reid of the World Resources Institute. Dr. Jason Clay, then of Cultural Survival, Inc., had been scheduled to attend but was prevented by a snowstorm that closed Boston's Logan Airport that morning. (One of my colleagues had suggested I invite either Dr. Clay or Pat Mooney of the Rural Advancement Foundation International ("RAFI") as an advocate of indigenous people's property rights; I reached Dr. Clay first and, as a result, did not invite Mr. Mooney.) The panel on racism featured Drs. Diane Paul, of the University of Massachusetts at Boston; Dr. Robert Murray, of Howard University; Dr. William Schneider, Indiana University-Purdue University at Indianapolis; and Dr. Eric Juengst, then director of the Ethical, Legal, and Social Issues program of the National Center for Human Genome Research.

7 *The Alghero Report* at 33.

8 Ibid., at 32.

9 The membership of the international executive committee has not changed since its creation. The members from the United States are Drs. L. Luca Cavalli-Sforza (chair), Marcus W. Feldman, Kenneth K. Kidd, Mary-Claire King, and Kenneth M. Weiss. The European members are Sir Walter Bodmer, Dr. Julia Bodmer, Dr. Svante Pääbo, Dr. Alberto Piazza, and Dr. Marcello Siniscalco. The remaining members are Dr. Takashi Gojobori from Japan, Dr. Partha Majumder from India, and Dr. Onesmo ole-MoiYoi from Kenya.

10 Ibid. at 37.

11 Ibid. at 38.

12 Within the past year, some international oversight has been provided by HUGO's Ethical, Legal, and Social Issues Committee. In addition, in January 1997, Dr. Cavalli-Sforza, chair of the International Executive Committee, took steps toward the appointment of such an ethics committee.

13 The NAmC's initial members were Drs. Cavalli-Sforza, Feldman, Kidd, King, and Weiss (all members of the international executive committee), plus Dr. Georgia M. Dunston, a molecular biologist from Howard University; Dr. John H. Moore, an ethnographer then from the University of Oklahoma (and now at the University of Florida); Dr. Emöke Szathmary, a physical anthropologist then at Western Ontario University (and now president of the University of Manitoba); Dr. Ryk Ward, a geneticist and anthropologist, then at the University of Utah and now at Oxford; Dr. Mark Weiss, a physical anthropologist at Wayne State University; and myself. In the spring of 1994, the NAmC added two members: Catherine Twinn, a Canadian barrister and member of the Sawridge Indian Band in Alberta, specializing in Native American rights issues; and Dr. Russell Thornton, an anthropologist and expert in pre-Columbian North American populations, then at the University of California at Berkeley and now at UCLA. Dr. Mark Weiss left the NAmC in the summer of 1994 before taking a temporary position at the National Science Foundation; Dr. Ward ceased to be a member of the NAmC at the time of his permanent move to Oxford in 1996.

14 Grant application to the John D. and Catherine T. MacArthur Foundation, (Nov. 1993).

15 The document in question is the NAmC's document entitled Frequently Asked Questions about the HGDP, eventually released in October 1994 and now found at the HGDP Web Site.

16 *Bioethics and Human Population Genetics Research* UNESCO International Bioethics Committee Subcommittee on Bioethics and Population Genetics (Nov. 15, 1995), available at http://www.biol.tsukuba.ac.jp/~macer/PG.html.

17 Ibid., at Section 4.1. See also Macer D., et al., "UNESCO and Population Genetics" (1996), 377*Nature* 11.

18 Knoppers B.M., M. Hirtle and S. Lormeau, "Ethical Issues in International Collaborative Research on the Human Genome: The HGP and the HGDP" (1996), 34 *Genomics* 272.

19 "HUGO Statement on the Principled Conduct of Genetics Research" (May1996), *Genome Digest* at 2 (available at http://hugo.gdb.org:80/conduct.htm.)

20 Commercialization is the area where the two documents could most easily be viewed as inconsistent. See the discussion at the end of the "provisions" section.

21 "North American Regional Committee of the HGDP, Proposed Model Ethical Protocol for Collecting DNA Samples" (Feb. 1997), 32 *Hous. L. Rev.* (forthcoming).

22 Kurt Vonnegut many years drew a parallel distinction in one of his early novels between "real groups", thrown together unknowingly to fulfil a purpose, and people who were connected only in superficial ways. The first group he called a "karass", the second was a "granfalloon". His examples of the latter included Hoosiers (people from the state of Indiana) and graduates of Cornell University, as well as "any nation, anytime, anywhere". Kurt Vonnegut, *Cat's Cradle* at 67(1963). Most biomedical research creates granfalloons; the HGDP intends to study what the people involved (though perhaps not Vonnegut) would consider karasses.

23 The importance of group participation in human genetics research is discussed more fully in Greely H. T., "The Control of Genetic Research: Involving the "Groups Between"" (Feb. 1997), 32 *Hous. L. Rev.* (forthcoming).

24 Rural Advancement Foundation International, *Communiqué: Patents, Indigenous People, and Human Genetic Diversity* (May 1993) (available at RAFI's web site: http://www.charm.net/~rafi.

25 *HUGO Statement on the Patenting of DNA Sequences* (Jan. 1995) (available at http://hugo.gdb.org:80/patent.htm.)

26 *Moore v. Regents of the University of California*, 51 Cal. 3d 120, 793 P.2d 479, 271 Cal. Rptr. 146, (1990), cert. denied, 111 S. Ct. 1388 (1991).

27 "HUGO Statement on the Principled Conduct of Genetics Research "(May 1996), *Genome Digest* at 3.

28 National Science Foundation, *Pilot Projects for a Human Genome Diversity Project (Program Guideline)* document NSF 96-112 (June 19, 1996).

29 Whether the HGDP's current committee members and structure have a strong role in the eventual Project remains to be seen. If oversight of the Project moves to another organization, perhaps a federal funding agency, the NAmC hopes that such an organization would also adopt, and enforce, the Model Protocol.

30 Supra note 24.

31 Rural Advancement Foundation International, Press Release, *Indigenous Person from Papua New Guinea Claimed in US Government Patent* (Oct. 4, 1995).

32 Ibid.

33 See the electronic mailing list discussions on this topic, archived at a Native-L mailing list site, http://bioc09.uthscsa.edu/natnet/archive/nl/hgdp.html. This site includes a separately indexed set of exchanges directly concerning the HGDP and this patent. Apart from its unwarranted attack on the HGDP, RAFI's press release was also grossly in error concerning the patent itself and the Hagahai's interest in it. This controversy was the

subject of an entire issue of *Cultural Survival Quarterly*, which presented a number of different perspectives on the matter. (Summer 1996), *Cultural Survival Quarterly* 20. (I represented Dr. Carol Jenkins, an anthropologist in Papua New Guinea who was a named inventor on the patent, in negotiations with the National Institutes of Health to assign the patent to a trust for the benefit of the Hagahai. These negotiations were ultimately successful in that the N.I.H. agreed to such a transfer, but Dr. Jenkins and others in Papua New Guinea decided that the patent was not worth the cost of establishing the trust or making the regular maintenance payments on the patent. As a result, in late 1996 the United States disclaimed its interest in the patent, effectively destroying it. See Lehrman S., "US Drops Patent Claim to Hagahai Cell Line" (Dec. 12, 1996), *Nature* 500.

ETHICAL CONCERNS IN GENOME DIVERSITY STUDIES IN DEVELOPING COUNTRIES

ISHWAR C. VERMA

Professor of Pediatrics, Head of the Genetics Unit, Department of Pediatrics

All India Institute of Medical Sciences

Introduction

India provides an ideal setting for human genome diversity studies. It has an enormous population of 918.6 million comprising 4,635 caste groups.[1] The people of India project, (POI), launched by the Anthropological Survey of India (1985-95), with its 43 volume output, is recognized as a major exercise in the exploration of diversities.[2] Ethnographically, this project has generated information about 3,000 communities, 28,000 "endogamous" groups, and about 80,000 units of identities. On languages, the POI has collected information on 325 "functioning" languages and 25 scripts. For biological variation in Indian populations, material has been collected on about 900 communities or mendelian populations.

TABLE 1. Primitive Tribal Groups in India (n=43)

State	Tribe
Andhra Pradesh	Bondo, Gadaba, Khonds, Thoti
Bihar	Birhor, Asur, Birjia, Soura
Gujarat/Maharashtra, MP	Kathodi, Siddi / Muria gond
Orissa	Didayi, Mankideas, Lodha, Pandi, Bhuyan
Karnataka	Jenu Kuruba, Koraga
Kerala	Cholanaikan, Kadar, Kurumba, Kattunaikan, Koragal
Manipur/UP	Marram / Raji, Buxa
Tamilnadu	Kota, Toda, Irula, Kurumba, Paniyan
Andaman & Nicobar Islands	Great Andamanese, Jarwa, Sentinalese, Onge, Shompens

The constitution of India divides caste groups into scheduled castes (751, 16.2%), scheduled tribes (635, 13.7%), and general castes (3,249, 90.1%). These communities comprise eight major religious groups. Of special interest are 43 "primitive" or "pre-agricultural" tribal groups (TABLE 1). These communities are diminutive having small numbers varying from 100-1,000 and most of them face a demographic decline.[3] Some of them, for example the negrito tribal communities in the Andaman & Nicobar islands face extinction.[4] A similar situation regarding the great diversity of populations and the representation of "ancient" cultures prevails in many other developing countries, although on a smaller scale.

Special Features in Developing Countries Which Raise Ethical Issues?

In addition to a large population, the per capita income in India is US$ 300 as compared with US$ 19,970 in Canada, and US$ 31,490 in Japan. The adult literacy rate is also low (48%) as compared with >97% in Canada and Japan.[5] The situation is even worse for the tribal communities who live in remote and inaccessible areas, often untouched by modern civilization, health care and developmental activities of the Government of India. They live on forest produce which is often inadequate as the forests are being denuded resulting in malnutrition and scarcity of resources. They are also scourged by mosquitoes and malaria. It is not surprising, therefore, that poverty combined with low literacy become major determinants of unethical practices when a study of these groups is undertaken.

Benefits of the Human Genome Diversity Project

The benefits of the diversity project to the scientific community and the world at large are well known.[6] The overall goal of the project is to define the precise origins of different world populations by integrating genetic knowledge, derived by applying the new techniques for studying genes, with our knowledge of history, anthropology and language. It plans to investigate the variation occurring in the human genome by studying samples collected from populations that are representative of all of the world's peoples, and ultimately, to create a resource for the benefit of all humanity and for the scientific community worldwide. The resource will exist as a collection of biological samples that represents the genetic variation in human populations worldwide and also in an open, long-term, genetic and statistical database on variation in the human species that will accumulate as the biological samples are studied by scientists from around the world.

The Department of Biotechnology, Government of India has recognized the tremendous diversity of human populations in India and has allocated a substantial sum of money for this research. The Indian program, the Genomic Diversity in Indian Populations Project,[7] hopes to achieve the following: First, improve the understanding about the causes of human evolution in India - the nature of adaptation to different stresses, ecological, clinical, etc. This understanding will help identify factors contributing to susceptibility and predisposition to diseases. Second, it will help to better define the origin and dispersal of human populations, and shed light on the epidemiology of diseases. Third, assist in identifying important genetic and environmental factors contributing to the etiology of diseases. Identification of these factors will promote better health care management and contribute to the improvement of medical care at both the individual and the population levels.

The Indian initiative plans to (i) establish a network of laboratories in the country for studying genomic diversities of anthropologically well-defined populations from the four regions - north, west, south and east - following a uniform set of protocols for collecting information, and testing an agreed set of genomic markers; (ii) organize regional and national repositories of biological samples (DNA, cell lines, etc.); and (iii) set up regional and national statistical databases comprising genomic, epidemiological, cultural and linguistic data.

However, considered dispassionately, the benefits of such an exercise are not of significant relevance to the tribal communities themselves. These communities are so engrossed in making both ends meet in their day to day life that tracing their biologic origins to remote ancestors is of little consequence to them. Possibilities of finding genes which confer resistance/predisposition to disease largely have not materialized into realities, apart from the identification of and hemoglobinopathies and thalassemia providing resistance to falciparum malaria when present in the heterozygous state.[8] In India, we also observed that there were less antibodies to malaria in subjects with HbAS (carriers of sickle cell gene) as compared to normal subjects with HbAA.[9] Moreover, as the "genes" cannot be changed, even identification of a "harmful gene" in these communities does not result in any significant benefit, apart from the general recommendation of protection or prophylaxis against malaria.

Effect of Participation in Diversity Studies on the Local Population

Many aboriginal groups around the world are literally "up in arms" against diversity studies. They say "they took away our lands and our forests. Now they want to take our blood". This has not happened so far in India, although these groups suspiciously question the motives of the investigators before consenting to participate in a research study. Nevertheless, there is some merit to this argument. Participation in diversity studies causes these community members to experience inconvenience, loss of their time which they would have used to plough their land or search for food, loss of wages and expenses on travel to the location where the studies are being done or blood is being collected.

The scientist has the narrow, single-minded objective of obtaining blood in order to conduct his/her studies. To this end and to avoid possible failure, it is easy to see how proper ethical procedures may be bypassed during the conduct of such research. Certainly, the scientist has some obligations to the community which is to be studied.

Obligations of the Scientist to the Community

No one would deny that such obligations exist, although there can be disagreement regarding the content and extent of these obligations. Certain universal elements have been identified by the Human Genome Diversity Project set up by HUGO.[10] The researcher must always respect the humanity of the sampled individuals and the cultural integrity of the sampled populations. Informed consent is considered both an ethical imperative and a legal requirement. The researcher should actively seek ways in which participation in the diversity project can bring benefits to the sampled individuals and their communities.

We have, ourselves, used this approach successfully in our studies. For example, in Bihar we combined the diversity studies with investigating the cause of hypersplenomegaly syndrome among the Sunderpaharia tribals, Kondhs in Orissa, Muria gonds in Madhya Pradesh and Paniyans, in Kerala we linked diversity studies with testing them for sickle cell disease and in Andaman islanders we concurrently investigated the causes of their demographic decline. Protecting the confidentiality of those sampled is of paramount importance. All those involved in the Project must accept a responsibility to strive, in every way possible, to avoid misuse of the project data for promoting racism, xenophobia and hypernationalism.

It is generally agreed that the subjects who participate should be compensated for their loss of wages or earnings resulting from their participation. The cost of travel should be reimbursed. Should they get any monetary reward? This can prove embarrassing for both the scientist as well as the community members. The latter often consider it demeaning that they "sold their blood" or "agreed to participate because of money offered to them". Less contentious is the issue regarding the giving of "gifts". The puritan may consider these gifts as "bribes" or "inducements" to participate but gifts which are likely to be useful to the members like clothes or utensils of daily use, or ornaments, or nutritional supplements should be permissible.

The offer of a medical examination to the individuals to detect any health problem should be mandatory. It not only establishes immediate rapport with the group, but also provides them a positive, tangible benefit.

The old vision of the anthropologist coming to live with the community being studied is fast disappearing, or has almost disappeared, as the pace of modern life and the fast moving scientific advances preclude such a leisurely approach. Although this process of living among the group being studied does generate a deeper understanding of the culture and customs of the group and a knowledge of their needs and aspirations. It is frequently a two way process of learning from each other. The anthropologist or the scientist has much to give in the way of knowledge of modern ways and medicines. He has much to gain from the local wisdom regarding forest and other resources. Very often, these communities have been using plant resources as medicines for their ailments - what may be termed as "traditional remedies". This knowledge could have commercial potential. The scientist should ensure that, if such knowledge is exploited for commercial purposes, the interests of the local community in the profits which may flow from such purposes are protected. This fact is also acknowledged by the HGDP.[11]

International Collaboration on What Terms?

It is of importance to note that, while a majority of the most interesting communities from the point of view of diversity studies live in developing countries, the resources and expertise for such studies lies in the developed countries. Collaborations between scientists in developing countries and those from developed countries working abroad is thus desirable, and should be established so as to be mutually beneficial. However, there has been an uproar in the local press that this is a means of pillaging natural genetic resources of the country by the west. There are reports of removal of innumerable plants and other natural products illegally out of India. This has extended to the removal of blood samples/leukocytes/DNA out of the country. There was a recent report highlighted in "Nature" that blood samples of patients with eye diseases had been taken abroad without the proper consent of the authorities. The Government of India has appointed the Indian Council of Medical Research (ICMR) as the agency to approve, in selected cases, the sending of blood samples abroad.[12] Generally, permission is granted easily where a sample is being sent abroad for a diagnostic test. Often, no permission is secured for this purpose by the doctors concerned. When large numbers of samples are to be sent abroad for research purposes, however, ICMR will only allow such exportation if the proposed research cannot be performed in India.

At times, international collaboration involves the trial of drugs, vaccines or appliances manufactured abroad on patients in developing countries. This is often done to bypass stringent rules and regulations in force in the developed countries. It is claimed that manufacturers frequently try to test their products in developing countries in return for financial support being provided to the local collaborator and patients. There is no doubt that such practices are undesirable, to say the least. The Drug Controller of India, whose permission is required before introduction/trial of any drug in India is quite strict about giving permission for such trials. It requires that all trials involving human subjects be cleared by the ethics committee of the host institution, and the drug has been tested in another country to show its beneficial effect and freedom from major side-effects. With the exception of a few top institutions, however, ethical committees do not exist in this country. Furthermore, in a vast country with numerous problems, it becomes almost impossible to monitor all scientists except those working in the larger, high profile institutions.

Most collaborations between scientists in developing and developed countries are one sided, the one in the developed country getting the major share of the benefits of the project. The researcher in the developing country often only gets his name included, or rather submerged, in a long list of authors, or occasionally under acknowledgements. Although financial help is provided to the local laboratory, ideally, there should also be a component of technology transfer and training. This is rightly acknowledged as an important component by HGDP.[13] An ideal situation is where the local scientist takes the samples to work in the laboratory abroad and carries out the analysis. Eventually, the collection and typing of samples should be done by local scientists in laboratories in their own country.

Consent Form

The informed consent of all subjects participating in the study should be mandatory. Our own experience suggests that contact with a community leader or leaders is important, often through an intermediary who is well-known to the group. The nature of the study and its objectives should be explained in simple language. A written statement, in a language the community members can understand, should be provided. The voluntary nature of the participation in the study should be stated, as well as the option of refusing to participate. No false hopes of research benefits should be held out.

Some investigators have opined that in communities which are illiterate a formal consent is not required, and only a verbal consent may be taken. I disagree with this view. Such communities should be explained the contents of the consent form and their thumb impression recorded. If only a verbal consent is taken then no objective proof remains that consent was actually obtained.

It should be explained to the subjects that the DNA sample will be stored in a repository, and may be used by many investigators for a long period of time. The anonymity of all individuals participating in the diversity project must be preserved in order to provide protection against any possible abuse of the results of the study.

Local Ethical Committees

It is desirable that all hospitals, medical and research institutions in India should form ethical committees.[14] There must be some members who are from outside the medical profession, or from a discipline outside that of the research institute in question. There must always be 1-2 female members. All clinical trials or research studies involving human subjects should be cleared by the local ethical committee. The committee should periodically monitor the work done to ensure that it is being conducted as proposed and planned. The local committee should function within the guidelines set out by national ethical committees.

They have a major role to play in ensuring that ethical practices are followed in the conduct of diversity studies.

Endnotes and References

1 UNICEF, *The State of the World's Children* (Oxford: Oxford University Press, 1996).

2 Singh K.S., "People of India-An Introduction" (Anthropological Survey of India, Calcutta, 1992).

3 Patel M.L., "Awareness of Tribal Health and Medical Care in Madhya Pradesh" in Singh B., N. Mahanti, eds., *Tribal Health in India* (New Delhi : Inter-India Publications, 1995) at 139.

4 Verma I.C., "Health Problems of Tribal Communities in Andaman and Nicobar Islands" (1976), 19 *Journal of Social Science Research* 16.

5 Supra note 1.

6 The Human Genome Diversity Project, Summary Document, (HUGO Europe, London, 1993).

7 Department of Biotechnology, Government of India, Genomic Diversity in Indian Populations Project, Government of India, 1996.

8 Alison A.C., "Protection Afforded by Sickle Cell Trait Against Subtertian Malarial Infection" (1954), 1 *BMJ* 290.

9 Thakur A, I.C. Verma, "Malaria and Abnormal Hemoglobins in Muria Gonds of Madhya Pradesh" (1992), 10 *Indian Journal of Hematology & Blood Transfusion* 123.

10 Supra note 6.

11 Ibid.

12 Indian Council of Medical Research, Office Memorandum "Transportation of Biological Samples out of the Country For the Purpose of Analysis, Diagnosis and Research Work" (New Delhi: Indian Council of Medical Research, 1992).

13 Supra note 6.

14 Pandya S.K., "Hospital Ethical Committees" (1996), 4 *Issues in Medical Ethics* 51.

BIOETHICS AND GENETIC DIVERSITY FROM THE PERSPECTIVE OF UNESCO AND NON-GOVERNMENTAL ORGANIZATIONS

DARRYL R.J. MACER

Institute of Biological Sciences, University of Tsukuba

Tsukuba Science City, 305, Japan

Introduction

Where are your roots? I come from Japan, Nihon. It is my home. I have another home, New Zealand, Aotearoa. I wonder how many generations back your roots go back in the place you call home? In the Isle of Montreal, Hochelaga, in the so-called new World maybe many of you are new to your home too?

In this paper, I attempt to build harmony between the views of the UN and all NGOs, however big or small, from RAFI to HUGO. Harmony is considered, in my home, Asia, to be one of the basic principles of bioethics. I believe that much of ethics and culture is universal. The important word is not so much universal, but universally diverse. The need to support diversity is well recognized in international law, but not always in ethics or practice.

The work in drafting the UNESCO report gave me the privilege to meet and contact sincere individuals on both sides of the debate. Friendship, I believe comes from what I consider to be the first principle of bioethics-love. Love includes all the traditional bioethics principles, autonomy, justice, do no harm, and try to do good. Friendship is a relationship, and relationships are another language of bioethics.

How many generations link you to your home? Is it related to the definition of who is indigenous? How many generations does it take? The question actually may not seem to be so important, however in ethics I think the concerns that someone has, and the respect for people, mean that we need to consider and answer all fears that people have. Minority groups may have valid reasons to be more afraid of abuses than those of a majority. The alleged abuses of genetics that they raise are relevant to us all, as they raise questions of how the knowledge will be used as well as how the research will be conducted. They raise the important question of who has control.

Current population genetics research is under the oversight of different layers of control which vary widely around the world. This oversight ranges from the discretion of individual researchers, consent from the persons who provide the tissue samples, consent from the groups being studies, to several layers of ethical committees. International regulations on research involving human subjects clearly state that informed consent is needed. Some funding agencies require ethical review, such as NIH-funded research in the USA. Some universities in the world also require ethical review, and the trend is to increase review. There have been some abuses under the current system of control and a call has been made for the inclusion of other representatives in the oversight, especially community members. The spirit of friendship is one which should be added to that of professional ethical conduct in decisions about participation in research.

Some of the ethical issues of population genetics research need to be further addressed and they include: Consent from individuals; Consent from population groups; How to obtain free and informed consent; Selection and participation; Use of the knowledge gained; Return of benefits to participants; Clash of world-views; Does the right not to know apply to communities? Who speaks for a community? Ownership of genes and derived knowledge; Public understanding and racism or eugenics; Stigmatization and genetic reductionism; International oversight of anthropologists & geneticists.

The UNESCO International Bioethics Committee Report

Given the transnational nature of population genetics studies, the issues raised were the subject of a study by the UNESCO International Bioethics Committee. The report has been available on the Internet since completion in November 1995.[1]

Key points of the UNESCO report were:

1. no endorsement of a particular population genetics project;
2. call for establishment of a separate ethical committee that is available to all population genetics researchers;
3. discussion of a variety of ethical, ethnic and social issues.

There are many issues of population genetics research that were raised in general in the report that apply to the whole of genetics research. One of the issues is commercialization and use of the results of the collected DNA and cells. This controversial issue is discussed in the report, to the extent that it should be addressed by those involved in the collecting of samples and be part of the consent and cooperation agreements. The resolution of biotechnology patents and "genetic prospecting" was not a subject for the subcommittee to resolve, but we urged the clarification of this issue by a global body.

Financial returns are not the only form of benefits of resulting from research which could be returned to the subjects of research. The feedback of results to the communities concerned should also help to foster a greater sense of community identity in the face of aggressive cultural imperialism by industrial superpowers. But perhaps the most poignant problems of many populations involved in population genetics research is in the realm of public health. The provision of health and medical care, however, should be appropriate to the cultural and social context of the community and should be sustained. In this regard, the principles of primary health care, as contained in the Alma-Ata Declaration (WHO/UNICEF) of 1978, should serve as appropriate guidelines to follow.

At the community level, the health data could be utilized for the improvement of local community health. Thus, benefits should also flow back to the groups and communities in the form of contributing to the formulation and implementation of local and national health care policies that would enable communities to better their positions. Commercial benefits could be expressed in other ways. While there could also be provision for a one-time gift of cells or blood with no conditions, as is found in some tissue donation forms for blood and body tissues, can one individual sign away commercial rewards to future research knowledge for the population to which they belong? It may be technically possible to conduct population genetics research among students of an international university, with them giving their cells to science, and whether they like it or not, they represent their population.

Genetic screening and genetic testing have been discussed in another report of the UNESCO International Bioethics Committee, and by numerous other persons and organizations over the last twenty years.[2] Many of the issues in current genetic screening programs are relevant to population genetics research, but some significant issues are different, such as the notion of group consent (as discussed by H. Greely in the North American Protocol of the HGDP). Moreover, while at present we are focusing on research we should also foresee the applications and benefits flowing from the Human Genome Project that could well apply to whole populations. The ethical considerations must therefore be carefully addressed since whole groups of asymptomatic individuals are the targets rather than single individuals who come forward themselves.

The application of the ethical principle of informed consent and respect for integrity is a complex process at the population level. In order to ensure that potential subjects understand the goals of research, the risks involved, the potential uses of research results and the rights of the groups and individuals under study, careful consideration is needed. The lines between genetic testing of individuals, genetic screening within one's own population, and population genetics research of other populations and groups, are not always clear. We do not ethically require group consent for most genetic testing, though society may draw the line at the freedom of choice to use genetic probes for non-therapeutic purposes (e.g. sex selection is banned in several countries, and would be banned under the European Convention on Bioethics). The fact that some recent population genetic studies may involve investigation of several hundred genes between single individual representatives of different populations makes the question of group consent extremely difficult.

There are various levels at which consent may need to be obtained for studies of population groups. High level governmental approval is, in many countries, mandatory for studies on specific populations of persons. Such official clearances need in every instance to be complimented by consent from the individuals and the local groups/communities selected for study-whether the consent is obtained directly or through formal/informal leadership, group representatives, or trusted intermediaries.

It is important to identify the most appropriate persons with whom to communicate, the persons from whom clearance should be obtained, and the appropriate content and media of communication. For example, communication via protest is not ideal as both parties need to be in dialogue. Research will need to take into account the group's social organization, goals and aspirations, cultural values, and laws (both statutory and customary). If the research methods involve the use of saliva, skin, hair, or blood samples it is necessary to ensure that the collection of these body samples does not violate cultural norms and concepts relating to the human body and its functions.[3]

The ways of approaching the communities must always take into account the particular social and cultural organization and laws. Sometimes the leader or the individual chief of a family or familial group is the person who gives consent for the other members of the community to participate in the inquiries and biological sampling. These persons may be difficult to identify. Of course, the most difficult group consent question is who can give group consent for the genome project itself - a question that no one has been able to answer.[4]

Various groups of indigenous peoples have expressed their dissatisfaction with past population genetics research which they claim has been conducted without prior consultation and in a way where consent was obtained in terms inconsistent with their cultural norms. Practitioners of contemporary science do not always understand that the goals and aspirations of scientific projects may not always coincide with the goals and aspirations of particular cultures. It may not be ethically acceptable to some people to cooperate in the collection of samples for the purpose of storage and the establishment of "transformed cell lines", samples which would be basically identical to the individual of origin which are then made available for study to scientists around the world. Therefore many representatives of indigenous peoples have expressed strong concerns about the HGDP.

The planners of the HGDP got off to a bad start with misunderstandings and fears widely expressed among indigenous peoples. Because the HGDP was planning to collect blood samples some groups called the HGDP the "Vampire project"[5], while other groups were angry because they believed that they were possible target populations even though no community representatives had been contacted about the Project. The Mataatua Declaration on Cultural and Intellectual Property Rights of Indigenous Peoples of June 1993[6] called for a halt to the HGDP until its impact had been discussed. Article 3.5. of the Declaration calls "for an immediate halt to the on-going 'Human Genome Diversity Project' (HUGO) until its moral, ethical, socio-economic, physical and political implications have been thoroughly discussed, understood and approved by indigenous peoples". The Declaration is actually not anti-science, and includes a call in recommendation 2.11 for involvement in scientific research to "Ensure current scientific environmental research is strengthened by increasing the knowledge of indigenous communities and of customary environmental knowledge".

In fact the HGDP included all populations, not only indigenous populations. Since that time, the HGDP goals have shifted somewhat, but there has been a series of Declarations directed against this project.[7] The HUGO HGDP *Summary Document* includes ethical guidelines which do address the question of participation, consent, and commercialization.[8] Nevertheless, the controversy continues. In February, 1995, a forum of Indigenous Peoples in Asia (ARCW) issued a statement to the European Parliament in which they strongly opposed the HGDP and called for it to be stopped. The Beijing Declaration of Indigenous Women formulated at the United Nations Fourth World Conference on Women (30 August - 8 September 1995) demanded "that the Human Genetic Diversity Project be condemned and stopped" and that their "intellectual community rights" be recognized.

The open letter that was circulated against this conference included four demands or requests of scientists. The first was a moratorium on the HGDP and population genetics. Unfortunately, it is beyond the control of any group to stop population geneticists who do not want to abide by ethics, although international pressure can help ensure that practice is not so distant from international norms of ethics and consent. The second was that researchers should investigate the samples that they have and show whether they were obtained using informed consent. This seems a worthy fact to reveal, and documenting this would provide some fresh data into the alleged abuses of the past. The third demand was that those samples that did not show evidence of being gathered with consent be destroyed. Already, the accounts of many scientists suggest there are many samples in this category, especially those taken in past decades when consent was only vaguely recognized, if at all. Whether they should be destroyed is a question for debate, but it is not without precedent, and one could at least place restrictions on the input of data into a global database should that be formed. The fourth request was against sharing of data scientists with commercial or military researchers. The suspicions raised about past sharing of data make this another concern of research and documentation. The cases of data sharing need to be recorded and documented, and I suggest a database be established of what has been done in the past - it seems ethically more urgent than the database of cell lines.

DNA collected from population groups would present analogous problems relating to the adequate protection of privacy,[9] but the meaning of privacy could vary across cultures. Furthermore, it is important to note that in population genetics research confidentiality issues have to be considered at the community level as well as at the individual level. The past examples would shed light on the likely future uses.

An issue which was dismissed by an editorial in *Nature*,[10] is eugenics and racism. Although there is scientific evidence to suggest that there will be little population genetic diversity found that is unique to one particular group, there is also a logical possibility that there may be distinct genetic features that make one genetic group distinct from others. The fact is that, while eugenics (cf. Galton) was founded on racism, eugenics today does not have to be linked to racism.[11] Those who continue to associate eugenics with racism will not be dissuaded by scientific evidence, since racism is a state of mind, or prejudice. People who tenaciously hold to such prejudices are not usually susceptible to the voice of pure reason and may even misappropriate scientific data to "prove" the truth of their own prejudices.

One of the fundamental points of opposition of indigenous groups towards genetic studies of human history is that the results may contradict indigenous people's views of oral and traditional history, and the meaning of genes and genealogy. For example, Maori people have two words to describe the human gene, one meaning "life spirit of mortals" (Iratangata) and the other genealogy (Whakapapa), which connects Maori with themselves and others.[12] The gene and genome are not the property of individuals but, rather, are part of the heritage of families, communities, tribes and entire indigenous nations. In this regard, the UNESCO position on the human genome being part of the common human heritage is more compatible with the views of indigenous persons, than the view supporting patents on genes.

The UNESCO report did not endorse any particular population genetic project, but this is not a critique of the HGDP. It was, rather, our personal view that the role given to us by UNESCO could better be served, as could science, by the establishment of a separate ethical committee that is available to all population genetics researchers. Rather than being exclusively linked with one particular project and focusing attention solely on it, we want a wider selection of scientists to feel able to seek an international ethical committee, and we invited scientists to contact us.[13] Several have, but the progress towards such a committee is currently in limbo.

In the UNESCO Declaration on the protection of the Human Genome and Human Rights there is a paragraph in the preamble also discussing diversity, "*Bearing in mind also* the United Nations Convention on Biological Diversity of 2 June 1992 and emphasizing in that connection that the recognition of the biological diversity of humanity should not give rise to any interpretation of a social or political nature which could call into question the fundamental principle of equal dignity inherent in all members of the human family." The role of the UN organizations is to work consistently for the dignity of humankind.

HUGO Code of Ethics

The Human Genome Organization (HUGO) Ethics Committee has endorsed a Code of Ethics for genetic sampling, based on a report prepared by B.M.

Knoppers, M. Hirtle and S. Lormeau. It stresses issues similar to those raised by the UNESCO subcommittee. It starts from the same principles: Recognition that the human genome is part of the common heritage of humanity; Adherence to international norms of human rights; Respect for the values, traditions, culture, and integrity of participants; and acceptance and upholding of human dignity and freedom.

The HUGO-ELSI Committee Code of Ethics was endorsed by HUGO in March 1996. It recommends principles for genetics research based on: scientific competence, understandable communication (two way), consultation with participants, free and informed consent, respect for the choices of those involved, confidentiality, international collaboration, avoidance of conflict of interest, undue inducement through compensation, and continual review of the research.

There are other non-governmental studies of population genetics underway, and especially of the HGDPThese include a study in progress by the US National Academy of Sciences, and work of the UNDP on indigenous populations.

Conclusions

International research projects raise the issue of how universal bioethics are, and whether different standards can be applied to different population groups and peoples. Results of an International Bioethics Survey conducted in more than a dozen countries since 1993 suggest the same diversity of opinions on issues raised by genetics is found within each society.[14]

There are two ways to think of the term "bioethics",[15] one is as descriptive bioethics - the way people view life and their moral interactions with and responsibilities to living organisms in life. The other is prescriptive bioethics - to tell others what is good or bad, what principles are most important; or to say something/someone has rights and therefore others have duties. Both of these concepts have much deeper roots, which we can trace to religious and cultural patterns that may share some universal ideals. If this descriptive bioethics study is correct, then the work of prescriptive bioethics in providing universal guidelines can proceed with more confidence.

While all admit that the function of the United Nations system is to protect the Universal Human Rights of all persons, another function of international organizations may be to foster studies into how best to protect the interests of different groups, which can best be done after finding out what their interests are. We need to ask whether, if in the same way that our genetic diversity suggests the word "race" is inappropriate, our ethical and cultural diversity also does? The data suggests the answer is yes although our prejudices may deny this.

It is ethically and scientifically desirable to have regulatory oversight of research involving sampling of human populations. This would mean a certain degree of scientific and ethical review prior to acceptance of a research protocol and, once accepted, ongoing monitoring and surveillance (although not usually assured). Can there be sanctions? Disciplinary measures including for example, suspension, withdrawal of privilege and fines, constitute the usual avenues of professional measures. In addition, where research subjects have been harmed, civil and criminal sanctions are also possible. Funding bodies may withdraw funds, sometimes even retroactively. If researchers are to become more accountable and actual practices more transparent, other forms of sanctions or at least of publicity, should be envisaged. Stricter, standardized reporting requirements, on a regular basis and publication of such reports are one such possibility. The UNESCO committee considered the latter to be a basic ethical obligation that should be universally applied.

If researchers are to be subject to greater scrutiny, the same holds true for the media whose duty of honest, scientific reporting and preservation of privacy, needs to be underscored. Whole populations, communities and the researchers themselves have often been wrongly depicted and misrepresented with the resulting unjust labelling and discrimination. Such practices only serve to undermine public confidence and participation in research.

Population genetics is not simply a multiplication of the individual ethical and legal issues already raised by genetic research. There are different concerns and traditions in each group under study, and even among individuals within any group. The degree of information, consultation and cooperation must reflect such differences in participants. Likewise, the role and responsibilities of the researchers and of the local and national authorities, as well as the societal implications, will differ. For the future, we need consultation with populations; individual and group consent mechanisms; ongoing ethical review; inclusion of representatives of populations in decision-making; communication, education, benefits, and feedback strategies at the population level; confidential data and sample banking; continual scientific review and monitoring; and appropriate sanctions. We also need to start systematically gathering the examples of use and abuse of DNA and cell sampling, to give us the necessary knowledge to better predict the future. Above all, we need to have anthropologists and scientists who seek ethical sampling.

Endnotes and References

1 Chee H.L., L. El-Hamamsi, J. Fleming, N. Fujiki, G. Keyeux, B.M. Knoppers and D. Macer, "Bioethics and Human Population Genetics Research", Report of the UNESCO International Bioethics Committee Third Session, 1995, from the subcommittee on bioethics and population genetics <http://www.biol.tsukuba.ac.jp/~macer/PG.html>.

2 Recent reviews include: Chadwick R. , et al., *Ethical Implications of Human Genome Analysis for Clinical Practice in Medical Genetics with Special Reference to Genetic Counseling* (Cardiff: Centre for Applied Ethics, 1993); McCarrick P.M. , "Genetic Testing and Genetic Screening" (1993), 3 *Kennedy Institute of Ethics Journal* 333; Murray T.H.,

"Genetics and Just Health Care: A Genome Task Force Report" (1993), 3 *Kennedy Institute of Ethics Journal* 327; *Nuffield Council on Bioethics,Genetic Screening: Ethical Issues* (London: Nuffield Council, 1993); Nielson L. and S. Nespor, *Genetic Tests, Screening and Use of Genetic Data by Public Authorities in Criminal Justice, Social Security and Alein and Foreigners Acts* (The Danish Center for Human Rights, 1994).

3 Supra note 1.

4 Macer D.R.J., "Whose Genome Project?" (1991), 5 *Bioethics* 183.

5 Lock M., "Interrogating the Human Diversity Genome Project" (1994), 39 *Social Science & Medicine* 603.

6 Mataatua Declaration on Cultural and Intellectual Property Rights of Indigenous Peoples of June 1993 (From the First International Conference on the Cultural and Intellectual Property Rights of Indigenous Peoples, 12-18 June, 1993, Whakatane, Aotearoa, New Zealand).

7 Mead A. "Genealogy, Sacredness, and the Commodities Market" (Summer 1996), *Cultural Survival Quarterly* 46. Declarations against the HGDP include: Karioca Declaration (June, 1992, Brazil); Mataatua Declaration (June, 1983, Aotearoa New Zealand); UN-Working Group on Indigenous Populations, 10th Session (July, 1993, Geneva); Maori Congress (1993, Aotearoa New Zealand); National Congress of American Indians (3 December, 1993, Resolution NV-93-118); Maori Congress Indigenous Peoples Roundtable (June 1994); Guaymi General Congress (1994, Panama); Geneva IPR Workshop (August, 1994); Latin & South American Consultation on Indigenous Peoples Knowledge, Santa Cruz de la Sierra, Bolivia (September, 1994); Asian Consultation on the Protection and Conservation of Indigenous Peoples Knowledge, Sabbah, Malaysia (February 1995), Pan American Health Organisation Resolution (15 April, 1995); Pacific Consultation on the Protection and Conservation of Indigenous Peoples Knowledge, Suva Statement (May, 1995).

8 HGD Committee of HUGO, "The Human Genome Diversity (HGD) Project" (1994), Summary Document.

9 Annas G.J., "Privacy Rules for DNA Databanks. Protecting Coded 'Future Diaries'" (1993), 270 *JAMA*: 2346-50. See also, (1992), 267 *JAMA*: 2158.

10 (1995), 377*Nature* 372.

11 Macer D.R.J., *Shaping Genes: Ethics, Law and Science of Using Genetic Technology in Medicine and Agriculture* (Eubios Ethics Institute, 1990) <http://www.biol.tsukuba.ac.jp/~macer/SG.html>.

12 Supra note 7.

13 Macer D.R.J., J. Fleming, G. Keyeux and B.M. Knoppers, "UNESCO and Population Genetics" (1996), 379 *Nature* 11.

14 Macer D.R.J., *Bioethics for the People by the People* (Eubios Ethics Institute, 1994) <http://www.biol.tsukuba.ac.jp/~macer/BFP.html>.

15 Macer D.R.J., "Bioethics: Descriptive or Prescriptive?" (1995), 5 *Eubios Journal of Asian and International Bioethics* 144.

GENETIC DIVERSITY - A CLASH OF WORLD VIEWS?

LORI LUTHER AND MARIE HIRTLE

RAPPORTEURS

Research Associates, Centre for Public Law Research (CRDP)

Université de Montréal

Advances in biotechnology and genomics have provided valuable insight into the biological makeup of humanity. This will eventually lead to the mapping of the entire human genome, to the identification of disease related genes and eventually to therapeutic applications. As a result, it is now possible to study the diversity of the world's populations at its most fundamental level - its DNA, its mutations and alleles.

Genetic diversity, at its simplest, suggests that the human gene is variable and that DNA sequences vary with each individual. Scientific research indicates that such variation is far greater amongst individuals than populations, leading to the conclusion that we are all part of the family of humanity. As Kenneth Weiss has commented: "[t]he study of human genes provides us with a wonderful opportunity to define ourselves at the most fundamental biological level. But we can only do that accurately if we view ourselves as a variable species, the world over."[1] Despite this inclusive backdrop of genetic diversity research, opposing views on the suitability of genetic testing emerges. The first official proposal - the Human Genome Diversity Project - to study human genetic diversity systematically has been met with a plethora of views and positions.

The aim of the Human Genome Diversity Project (HGDP),[2] originally conceived in 1991 as a comprehensive study of human genetic diversity, is to collect blood samples from the world's populations in order to study human evolution, the history of human migrations, genetic epidemiology, the predisposition of certain groups to genetic disease, and the essential unity of our entire species. The overall goal of the Project is thus to increase our understanding of the common heritage of humanity. Ultimately, the Project hopes to create a data resource for the benefit of all humanity and for the scientific community world-wide. The resource will exist not only as a collection of biological samples representative of the genetic variation in human populations but also as an open, long-term, genetic and statistical database on variation in the human species accessible over and over again and for many years to come to legitimate researchers around the world.

While the Human Genome Project (HGP) currently underway, seeks to identify all human genes as well as map and sequence the entire human genome, it is largely euro-centric in nature. Concepts of variation are therefore skewed since the HGP focuses on only one genome largely ignoring genetic variation in about 85% of humanity.[3] The HGDP, conversely, seeks to rectify this inadvertent lacuna by collecting, studying and making available, genetic information from a representative sample of the world's population - European and non-European, indigenous and non-indigenous - in order to examine human variation in our whole species. As such, small, large, linguistically special, and culturally endangered groups may be sampled to ensure that the full spectrum of humanity is included.[4]

The shift from indigenous and isolated populations to representative world samples has seemingly done little to abate the fears of those populations who believe that they are the focus of the Project's research. A number of issues remain persistent roadblocks to the successful commencement of the Project. As discussions surrounding this controversial Project continue, it remains, for the most part, in its initial planning stages and is still largely unfunded. Some of the Project's main concerns include consent and choice, compensation for participation, return of benefits to participants, use of information gained, ownership of human genetic material and knowledge or inventions derived therefrom, discrimination and stigmatisation, and finally, effective oversight.[5]

Given the international and co-operative nature of many population genetic studies these important issues require continuing attention and discussion to ensure that all concerns, from both participants and researchers, are properly addressed. Many of the concerns, particularly with regard to consent, discrimination and racism, are not novel in the field of genetic research. What is novel, however, is the all encompassing global dimension of the scientific and ethical issues raised by genetic research on populations or collectivities, issues that need to be addressed and adapted according to varying cultural backgrounds.

In the case of the HGDP, this global dimension of ethical issues must also be addressed in the light of multimedia attention prompted by various interest groups. Indeed, even though the HGDP is still at the proposal stage, there have been few genetic research studies which have prompted such world-wide attention in the form of scientific and popular press coverage, extensive and lively discussion on the Internet, and a range of declarations and positions from non-governmental organizations and various population or peoples.[6]

Despite the multiplicity and breadth of the issues raised by the HGDP, the plenary discussion focused primarily on two essential aspects of population genetics: free and informed participation in genetic research and the potential misuse or misinterpretation of information gained.

The ethical principle of voluntary and informed participation in research, over the past few decades, has been, and continues to be, widely acknowledged. The scope of informed consent and its practical implementation has continually evolved according to emerging criteria of ethical appropriateness. In the field of genetic research the principle of informed consent has been translated not only into the requirement that individual consent be obtained for the procurement of a sample but for subsequent research uses as well. With population genetics research, the notion of free and informed participation has been widened to include the population's right to self-determination and to decide if it will participate in genetic research endeavours. Hence, the notions of self-determination and autonomy have moved beyond individuals to groups or populations.

Although an attractive means of addressing many of the consent issues raised by population genetics and the HGDP, the concept of population consent is fraught with uncertainties and difficulties. For example, despite the fact that both the proponents and the critics of the HGDP are strongly committed to respecting whether or not a particular population will choose to participate or not, important disagreements persist at the level of its implementation.

The North American Regional committee for the HGDP, has developed a lengthy Proposed Model Ethical Protocol which addresses population consent and which would necessarily have to be followed by researchers involved with the project.[7] On the issue of free and informed consent for participation, this protocol proposes that two levels of consent be obtained: population and individual consent. Population consent, obtained through the population's recognized leader, would be necessary in order to initiate contacts with individuals in that population. Accordingly, the North American Protocol provides that if a population leader refuses to consent, then individual participation is denied. If the leader on behalf of the group agrees to pursue the ongoing consent process then individuals may be approached in order to obtain consent. Individuals always retain the right to refuse to participate even if the group to which they belong decides otherwise. Ultimately, by requiring both of these levels of consent, the North American Regional Committee hope that groups and individuals who choose to participate in the HGDP will consider their participation as a partnership with researchers. It is considered that some groups will choose to participate and others will not. But, if one tenth on the world populations decide to participate then main aims of the HGDP could be fulfilled.

There are many more difficulties with regard to this position. For example, who determines the initial selection criteria of populations to be approached? How is a group or population defined and whence, how is the appropriate community leader identified? Additional concerns also arise with respect to the disclosure of information to the population leader during the consent process. Controversy persists over the scope of disclosure and the interpretation of the risks and benefits inherent to participation. Proponents of the project have maintained that good knowledge is better than no knowledge at all. This, however, presupposes that the knowledge derived from the Project will be empowering and beneficial to all. Indigenous and minority populations, and those who speak on their behalf, however, question and in many cases, deny the usefulness of the information derived from such a project.

The consent process will also need to consider the issue of control over blood samples once they are collected and stored. Consensus to the effect that control should remain with the participating individuals and populations appears to be gelling. Nonetheless, pressing concerns remain over how such individual and population control can be effectively implemented. More importantly, however, the issue of control is intimately linked to deep-seated fears of discrimination and racism given the historical experiences of minority and indigenous populations at the hands of a dominant culture.

Indeed, the HGDP, which seeks to discover the differences amongst human populations smacks of racism, eugenics, exploitation, and paternalism particularly within minority populations. Human genetic diversity research has ostensible and inherent racist overtones. Beyond these issues, critics of the Project are concerned about how the information obtained will be used. Will it be used against indigenous or endangered populations and ultimately result in genetic reductionism? Or, will it be used to alter their endangered status or ensure their identity and culture? Clearly proponents of the HGDP must prove that the project is good science and that those who are sampled will benefit from their participation.

The HGDP claims that it will make a significant contribution to the elimination of racism insofar as it will demonstrate the commonality of humanity. The human species, it is argued, is genetically quite homogeneous. Genetic variation within human populations is far greater than variation between populations. Differences are considered to be almost entirely phenotypic in nature and as such, largely superficial.[8] No one population can, or should, be considered genetically advantaged or disadvantaged. Accordingly, the enormous diversity among individuals will, according to Cavalli-Sforza[9], render the whole concept of race at the genetic level, meaningless.

Proponents of the project contend that the information obtained from the HGDP will lead to the conclusion that we are all part of the human family and will (optimistically) result in a general sense of inclusiveness. However, the history of human genetic research evokes considerable fear in indigenous populations because it is replete with the extermination of minority populations and scientific racism. The general feeling is that the dominant culture stole their bodies, land, and resources, and are now trying to steal their blood.[10] Past exploitation therefore continues to resonate.

Racism, even "scientific" racism has existed for a long time. Fear that genetic data will be used to oppress a particular group is not exclusive to the HGDP. It is a factor which those who support the project claim they are willing to grapple with. Their desire to create a partnership relationship so that those sampled are partners not subjects to the project,[11] is an attempt to step away from paternalistic tendencies which tend to lead to misinterpretations along discriminatory, racist, and eugenic lines.

Beyond issues of racism and discrimination, other concerns of advocacy groups with regard to misuse of the data collected from the Project, are the privatisation of the indigenous population's genetic heritage through the patenting of DNA and the commercialisation of the human body through the buying and selling licenses on those patents. The goals of indigenous populations are to protect their life, culture, identity, knowledge, and resources. The prevailing belief is that the HGDP is only concerned with profit and not with the status of endangered or indigenous people. Those who are involved in initiating the project resolutely maintain that no profit will be derived from any commercial uses of samples it gathers or knowledge it derives therefrom. Should any economic value ensue, the sampled population will get a fair share of the benefit. Further, access to the project's samples would be subject to the adherence of contractual rules as set out by the varying populations.

Issues of misuse and misinterpretation require education and oversight. As a result, the initiators of the HGDP have proposed the establishment of a rapid action task force which would provide ready responses to any cases of misuse. However, others provide that such a remedy while beneficial is itself insufficient in that pervasive education - to scientists, academics, journalists and the general population - is essential not only to the establishment of a true partnership with the HGDP but also to overcoming notions of racism.

Despite an ostensible clash of world views, there appear to be a number of points of common understanding between the proponents and the critics of the HGDP. For example, both agreed that populations must choose whether or not to participate in the HGDP, or in any other genetic research project. Moreover, there is consensus on the importance of fighting misuses and misinterpretations of collected information, be it information that will eventually be collected through the HGDP or already available from other research settings. Agreement has yet to be reached on whether and if so, how, such misuse can be overcome.

It must be recognized that there is a complexity and diversity of values and beliefs amongst different populations and different individuals. Furthermore, not only must this diversity of views be recognised but it must also be respected by all interested whether they be scientists, individuals or groups who decide, or conversely refuse, to participate in this or any research initiative.

If appropriate safeguards are put in place which will protect the rights, beliefs, and self-determination not only of indigenous peoples and their communities but of all human participants throughout the world, then perhaps the HGDP can go forth. It is the manner, or perceived manner, in which the project is proceeding, which seems to offend. Perhaps once the moral, ethical, socio-economic, physical and political implications of the project are discussed and appropriately dealt with in true partnership, the project will be able to proceed.

The title of this paper reflects the radically different views of indigenous peoples who desire to protect their integrity and valued resources on the one hand and the scientific values of the Western world on the other. Indeed, it is questionable whether this clash of world views will ever merge in a unifying global perspective.

Endnotes and References

1 Weiss K.M., "Biological Diversity is Inherent in Humanity" (Summer 1996), *Cultural Survival Quarterly* 26 at 27.

2 For more information on the HGDP see L.L. Cavalli-Sforza in this volume at 219; H.T. Greely, in this volume at 239; See also: Cavalli-Sforza L.L., "The Human Genome Diversity Project" in International Bioethics Committee of UNESCO, *1995 Proceedings Vol. II*, at 71.

3 Greely H.T., Presentation at the Post Congress Symposium - *Studying Human Genetic Diversity: Can We Do It Right?*, III World Congress on Bioethics, San Francisco, Monday, November 25, 1996.

4 For a discussion on endangered groups see I.C. Verma in this volume at 257.

5 As summarized by D.R.J. Macer in this volume at 265. See also Lock M., "Interrogating the Human Genome Diversity Project" (1994), 39 *Soc. Sci. Med.* 603; UNESCO International Bioethics Committee - Sub-committee on Bioethics and Population Research, *Bioethics and Population Genetics Research*, November 15, 1995 [available on the Internet at : http://www.biol.tsukuba.ac.jp/~macer/PG.html].

6 Genes, People and Property - Furor Erupts over Genetic Research on Indigenous People (Summer 1996), *Cultural Survival Quarterly*, the entire issue.

7 See H.T. Greely in this volume at 239. See also North American Regional Committee - Human Genome Diversity Project, "Proposed Model Ethical Protocol for Collecting DNA Samples" (1997), *Houston Law Review* [forthcoming].

8 See M. Lock in this volume at 229.

9 L.L. Cavalli-Sforza in this volume at 219.

10 See I.C. Verma in this volume at 257.

11 Supra note 7.

GENETIC SCREENING AND RESEARCH: INTRODUCTION

JUDITH G. HALL (CHAIRPERSON)

Professor and Head of the Department of Pediatrics

University of British Columbia and British Columbia's Children's Hospital

Developed countries have come to think of screening and research as an integral part of health care and the health care system. Inherent in this acceptance is the assumption that both the individual and society will benefit from these processes. The discussions at this conference make it clear that the issues are very complex. Societal changes and new knowledge require an ongoing review of how screening programs are run, how samples may be used and how research on these samples should be conducted.

Inherent in the development of screening programs is the expectation that there will be some benefit derived for those individuals who are screened. A part of newborn screening programs is the availability of a therapeutic modality and access to a treatment program if an abnormality is found. That type of individual benefit is not quite as clear when screening occurs for a predisposition or a carrier status since, in these situations, therapies and options are not always as obvious or straightforward. Carrier and predisposition screening may require additional monitoring and testing as well as avoidance of some situations or changes in the individual's environment. The age of the individual being screened converts into quite different types of options and therapies.

Prenatal screening, newborn screening and adult screening reflect different values. In general, prenatal screening is aimed at terminating affected pregnancies or, at the least, handling them in a quite different manner. Newborn screening, in general, is aimed at providing therapy that allows a child to reach near or full potential. Adult screening involves, because of the adult individual's assumed autonomy, the "affected" individual's right to make decisions for themselves regarding the utilization of various treatment and reproductive options.

As human genetic research and the human genome project have progressed, much has been learned both from the examples of specific disorders and from public input. Because genetic information is not owned by a single individual (i.e., relatives share bits and pieces), the identification of "at risk" individuals by genetic techniques has implications for other family members. In the past, screening was aimed at individuals (at risk or affected) but it has become quite clear that genetic screening has implications for all members of the family.

As the public has become involved in screening programs, they have demanded information on which to make appropriate decisions. Thus, within newborn screening programs, education about and consent for newborn screening is expected or required. Informed consent means educating the permission giver as to what the test is that is being offered, how samples might be used in the future, and what the implications of positive and negative results are for the individual and family. Counselling about the implications of positive or carrier testing are becoming a required part of most screening programs. This, of course, requires greater resource allocation.

In general, when individuals take part in research projects, it is not anticipated that they will necessarily benefit from the project. It is recognized that participants must sign some type of consent form in order to be part of a research project. In the past, the exception was that stored screening samples and old pathologic samples could be considered anonymous. However, with the recognition that no DNA sample is really anonymous (since it can be uniquely identified by its DNA), the concept of anonymization of samples has evolved. This process has been developed in order to protect the individual, whose sample it is, from unwanted information and intrusion into their personal life. This attempt to preserve their autonomy, however, may also deny them access to any new information.

With the development of DNA technology, a whole range of new safeguards are being put into place. Most of them have arisen because each disease presents different types of problems. Thus, as a particular disorder is studied in depth, concepts and models are developed which often apply to other diseases but need modification to the unique aspects of the next disorder. The individual and societal ramifications of various types of research must be considered within an ever changing context of information, understanding and social values.

There are many types of research including hypothesis-driven, basic, laboratory, clinical, therapeutic trials, pilot studies, natural history studies, perspective, retrospective, metanalysis, information review - just to mention a few. Each type of research requires somewhat different considerations just as each specific disease has different ramifications. An important part of the discussion of screening and research is whether there are any fundamental principals that can apply to all forms of screening or to all forms of research.

Perhaps the most important consideration has to do with the stigmatization of carrying or having a genetic disorder. Not very long ago, having tuberculosis or developing cancer had a major societal stigmatization associated with the diagnosis. Fortunately, as those disorders have become treatable, the stigmatization has been replaced by a sense of sympathy and a desire to undertake appropriate therapy as rapidly as possible. At this time, genetic diseases still carry a sense of abnormality. Unfortunately, that sense of abnormality reflects on other family members as well as occasionally raising the issue of nonpaternity or rejection by the family.

Part of the reason for safeguards regarding research as it relates to screening is to help with this problem of stigmatization. Some of the safeguards which are now available include institutional review boards, ethics committees, institutional research offices, granting agency councils, federal and local laws, policy and position papers, the media and public opinion. Nevertheless, disadvantaged and disenfranchised individuals still occur among the unborn, children, adolescents, the legally incompetent, the poor, the geographically isolated, and individuals at high risk. These groups need special consideration and protection as policies are developed.

Societal changes, new knowledge and population differences require an ongoing review of how screening programs and research related to screening programs are run. This requires thoughtful consideration by researchers and their institutions, input from the public and adjustment to various jurisdictions. It can be anticipated that there will continue to be many changes in policy and procedures over the next few decades as new perspectives are learned from experience with particular disorders.

In the discussion that follows, let us consider:

1. How to build into various systems a mechanism for review and evolution of the policies and models related to screening and research.
2. Will there ever be some core principles that can be applied to all types of screening or all types of research involving humans?
3. How can public input into policies take place so that policies really reflect the values of a particular society?
4. How can the stigma of genetic disorders be dealt with most effectively?
5. Is it possible to really anonymize samples which involve DNA, since the DNA of each individual is unique and recognizable?
6. Is there a need to have an international code of ethics with regards to research since many research projects are international in scope?
7. What groups need to be excluded or given special consideration as policies are developed for screening and research?

IMPACT OF FRENCH LEGISLATION ON NEONATAL SCREENING

JEAN-LOUIS DHONDT
JEAN-PIERRE FARRIAUX
Association française pour le dépistage et la prévention des handicaps de l'enfant
Paris, France

For the last 25 years, neonatal screening programs have been considered as public health programs aimed at preventing the burden of metabolic diseases. However, dried blood samples collected by neonatal screening programs represent an attractive material for genetic studies since the collection of these samples is usually systematic, the analytes remarkably stable and DNA extractable.

History of Neonatal Screening

The history of Neonatal Screening can be divided into three periods:

THE "GUTHRIE AGE"

In the sixties, pediatricians recognized the enormous advantage of setting up neonatal screening programs for the early diagnosis and treatment of metabolic diseases. The simple, robust and cheap method developed by Robert Guthrie for Phenylketonuria (PKU) screening has been the foundation for the development of this new form of preventive medicine.

Most of the programs were initiated on the presumption that screening was inherently good, insofar as the concerned diseases were frequent, treatable and detectable at birth by a test with good/excellent sensitivity and specificity (TABLE I). In this regard, the model of PKU has long been considered the standard. In such routine screening programs, obtaining an individual consent from every parent has not been and is not current practice.

TABLE I. Accepted criteria for inclusion of a disease in basic neonatal screening program.

1-	the disease will result in severe morbidity (mental and physical) and/or mortality if not diagnosed in the neonatal period;
2-	clinical screening by simple physical examination is not totally effective to identify the disease;
3-	an effective treatment is available;
4-	there is a significant improved prognosis with early treatment;
5-	the disease has a relatively high incidence;
6-	there is a simple rapid, reliable, inexpensive screening test.

THE "ECONOMIC AGE"

In the eighties, efforts were concentrated on cost-benefit analysis. The concept of a "screening system" had emerged, which describes the overall organization of the neonatal screening program, and ensured the systematic screening of all newborns and the appropriate follow-up of all detected patients.

From the perspective of costs and benefits, this approach introduced the notion that complete treatment and follow-up services could be provided effectively and that the costs of such legislatively mandated programs could be economically justified.

The addition of a new test to an ongoing program was thus regulated by the necessity of demonstrating the feasibility and efficiency of all components of the new program (technical, medical and financial). The term "pilot studies" was coined for such a purpose, but it failed to address the issue of ethical guidelines applicable to research.

THE "ETHICS AGE"

In the nineties, considerable advances in biochemical technologies offered the possibility of extending the field of investigation to areas not initially envisioned by screening, from preventive to predictive medicine.

In particular, methods derived from molecular biology technologies began to be used as:

- confirmatory methods in existing programs (i.e.: two steps strategies of CF screening: immunoreactive trypsin (IRT) then ΔF508 mutation);
- means to detect heterozygoty and avoid recurrence of a disease in families and descendants (reproductive counselling);

- tools for genetic population studies/research (whatever the genotype traced);
- identification of persons at higher than average risk for the development of a variety of disorders.

Such developments have moved the field of neonatal screening into that of Genetics, with all its inherent ethical and legal considerations with respect to the rights of the individual. These considerations, however, may create situations where the need to follow procedures required by the law will be at cross-purposes with the public health goal of systematic screening of the population.

Ethics and Law in France

Even if Jean Bernard, the president of the French National Ethical Committee, had initially claimed that it was difficult to introduce ethical considerations into a Law, the actual trend is that described by Braibant:

> "Science once obliged man to pass from faith to ethics, it obliges him today to pass from ethics to law."[1]

Ethical considerations in the French Law have been progressively introduced since 1978, but major additions were made in 1988 and 1994 concerning the respect of human rights in health activities.

In January of 1978, Law 78-17 was enacted concerning the processing of nominative data, data banks and individual liberty. This law created a national agency (CNIL, Commission nationale de l'informatique et des libertés) whose mandate is to oversee computerized systems organization as it relates to health activities. To this end, all systems involving data processing or data banks must be disclosed and approved by CNIL.

This law also set out that "persons whose health data is likely to be used must be informed of the purpose of such usage."

Enacted in December 1988, Law 88-1138 is concerned with human rights and biomedical research/experimentation. This law was initially drawn up for drug experimentation, but its breadth has been considerably extended to include biological or medical research. This law also defined the role of the Advisory Committee for the Protection of the Individual (Comité consultatif de protection des personnes dans la recherche biomédicale) which must be consulted before undertaking any biomedical research. These committees must evaluate the scientific validity, the actual need for nominative data and the pertinence of such data with regard to the final use. This law also sets out a specific definition for free, informed and written consent of the person.

Law 94-548 (July 1 1994) concerning the use of nominative data in medical research, extended the systems requirements set out in the 1974 law, added restrictions to the storage length of nominative data and set out the circumstances requiring written consent:

- the use of data banks with nominative data requires a procedure of application for approval by the CNIL;
- data must not be stored in nominative form information beyond the length of time required by the research;
- if the research requires identified biological samples, written consent from subjects has to be obtained before data acquisition.

Law 94-653 (July. 29 1994) concerning the respect of "human body" and Law 94-654 (July. 29 1994) concerning the use of part or products of the human body, medical assisted procreation and prenatal diagnosis both address the issue of consent:

- the study of genetic characteristics of an individual can be performed only for medical or research purposes. Informed written consent has to be obtained before testing;
- exceptionally, when the study is performed for a direct medical purpose, the consent of the patient may not be required.

Neonatal Screening in France

In France, neonatal screening is not legally mandated, but by the virtue of an agreement between the CNAMTS (National Fund for the Medical Insurance of Salaried Workers) and the "French Association for the Detection and Prevention of Metabolic Diseases and Handicaps in Children" the screening is systematic and free of charge for the family. Until recently, the program has been limited to the screening of PKU and CH (congenital hypothyroidism), diseases that meet the criteria for public health activity (the "PKU model").[2] Parental consent is thus not required, but information on the program is available, distributed to professionals with the recommendation to distribute it to parents.

The principles of the program are in accordance with those set out in the "Guidelines for Policy in Newborn Genetic Screening", established in conjunction with a consensus meeting held in Quebec in 1989 and "founded on the respect of human rights and on the protection of individuality and difference."[3]

This screening program is tentatively stepping into the sphere of modern genetics. New programs are also being considered. Sickle cell disease screening, for example, which is able to detect healthy heterozygotes, could be a possible addition. For reasons of efficiency and economy, this screening should be restricted in France to the at risk population. Cystic fibrosis screening is also being considered. This disease cannot be screened efficiently by indirect markers alone (i.e. Immuno Reactive Trypsine) and requires DNA typing.

With recent technical advances, it is clear that a dried blood sample from a given individual represents the key to their most intimate secrets. It must therefore be protected as securely as the person himself.[4]

Such programs (existing or future) and the introduction of ethical considerations into French law have forced the French Association for Neonatal Screening to evaluate the consequences of the legal changes in the practice of neonatal screening and to establish new guidelines.

Recommendations of the Ethical Committee of the French Association for Neonatal Screening

The ethical committee of the French Association for Neonatal Screening has made the following recommendations:[5]

1. A clear distinction has to be made between well established screening programs known to be efficient ("routine screening") and pilot studies aimed at exploring the feasibility and efficacy of a new screening test or for epidemiological studies.
2. Neonatal screening for disease with an obvious and immediate benefit for the child can be implemented if parents are informed and do not refuse the test. In other words, the absence of a written refusal is considered as a tacit consent.
3. Experimental programs for which the benefit is not yet evaluated or ascertained need a formal decision from the competent ethical committee and have to follow the principle of informed consent of parents.
4. In order to prevent any deviant use of stored samples for research, it is recommended that sample cards be destroyed as soon as the routine analytical process is completed.

Endnotes and References

1 Braibant G., et al., *Rapport du groupe de travail interministériel du Conseil d'état: Bioéthique et droit*. Avant-projet sur les sciences de la vie et des droits de l'homme. (Paris, 1989).

2 Dhondt J.L., J.P. Farriaux, M.L. Briard, R. Boschetti and J. Frézal , "Neonatal Screening in France" (1993), 2 *Screening* 77.

3 Laberge C.M. and B.M. Knoppers, *Genetic Screening: From Newborns to DNA Typing* (Amsterdam: Elsevier, 1990) at 379.

4 Mattei J.F., "Ethical and Legal Issues Associated with the Conservation of Blood Samples" in Farriaux J.P. and J.L. Dhondt, eds., *New Horizons in Neonatal Screening* (Amsterdam: Elsevier, 1994) at 41.

5 Association française pour le dépistage et la prévention des handicaps de l'enfant - Comité d'éthique, "Les prélèvements de sang sur papier pour le dépistage néonatal. Recommandations pour leur collecte, leur traitement et leur conservation" (1995), 2 *Arch. Pédiatr.* 3.

PROSPECTIVE USES OF DNA SAMPLES FOR RESEARCH

ELLEN WRIGHT CLAYTON

Associate Professor of Pediatrics, Vanderbilt School of Medicine and Associate Professor of Law, Vanderbilt School of Law

In recent years, problems posed by the use of human tissue samples for biomedical research have been discussed by commentators around the world. Within this broader analysis, substantial attention has been devoted to the issues arising from the use of DNA samples for genomic research. A fundamental tension underlies all these discussions. On the one hand is the desire to promote research for its own sake and to improve health. On the other is the recognition that research can pose risks to the participant/subjects and that individuals whose tissues are used may have concerns about research. This debate has been further complicated by the nature of the risks posed by this sort of research for the individual. These risks are primarily psychosocial and so, until recently, have received little attention. There exists a largely unspoken fear that, in some instances, increased knowledge may not be beneficial to individuals, particularly in the short run.

This paper addresses the policy issues raised in this debate and focuses on determining who should control how and whether samples collected in the future are used in research. The possible loci of control, in general, are four: the person or institution who holds the tissue or DNA, the researcher, the patient, and external bodies such as scientific or institutional review boards (IRBs). This examination of some of the recent discussions about who should have decision making authority over the use of tissue samples demonstrates the rather large areas in which there is substantial consensus and explores in greater depth the areas in which significant disagreement remains. The examination of these areas will serve as a basis for setting forth possible solutions.

Current and Proposed Guidelines for Using Tissue Samples for Research

THE UNITED STATES

In the United States, the use of tissue samples is governed primarily by the federal policy for the protection of human subjects, which focuses on defining the roles of IRBs, researchers, and patients in deciding how research is to be conducted. Under the federal regulations, protocols that involve "existing data, documents, records, pathological specimens, diagnostic specimens, if these sources are publicly available or if the information is recorded by the investigator in such a manner that subjects cannot be identified, directly or through identifiers linked to the subjects" are generally exempt from this policy (45 CFR § 46.101(b)(4)). If protocols fall within this exemption, neither review by an IRB nor consent of the person from whom the tissue was obtained is required by federal law.

Whether the research can proceed is determined only by the researcher, subject perhaps to the concerns of the entity holding the samples or the funding agency. The current debate is not the first time that the desirability of retaining this exemption from IRB oversight or individual consent has been examined. The Office of Technology Assessment explored this issue in its 1987 report on the related issue of the ownership of human tissues and cells but did not reach a definitive recommendation.[1]

The prerequisites for obtaining this exemption mean that two types of protocols that use stored tissue samples are subject to the requirements of the federal policy. The use of the term "existing" means that proposals to collect new data or samples to be used for research in the future are not exempt, no matter how widely the samples and data are made available or how thoroughly their identifiers are removed. In addition, protocols that code already existing samples and information and then remove identifiers while retaining a "key", whether in the possession of the investigator or someone else, that permits samples to be reconnected with the patient or donor do not qualify for the exemption.

The federal regulations require that protocols falling within the federal policy be reviewed by IRBs to ensure that the risks to subjects are minimized and are appropriate in relation to the benefits that can be expected from the research, that the selection of subjects is equitable, that appropriate informed consent is obtained and documented, and that adequate provisions are made to protect privacy and confidentiality (45 CFR § 46.111). Written informed consent, however, is not required in all cases. Instead, IRBs can limit the information that must be disclosed or even waive the requirement of consent altogether if they find that:

1) the research involves no more than minimal risk to the subjects;
2) the waiver or alteration will not adversely affect the rights and welfare of the subjects;
3) the research could not practicably be carried out without the waiver or alteration; and
4) whenever appropriate, the subjects will be provided with additional pertinent information after participation. (45 CFR § 46.116)

The debate in the United States about guidelines for protocols using stored tissue samples for genetic research has been informed by these regulations. On some points, remarkable consensus has been achieved among the groups that have published formal position papers. All these groups agree, for example, that informed consent must be sought in projects that propose to study samples that are or can be linked to particular individuals.[2,3,4] This necessarily includes all protocols in which investigators plan to do long term follow up of individuals' health because such projects require retention of identifiers must decide what sort of consent must be obtained. It is generally acknowledged, however, that the language typically contained in operative consent forms fails to provide adequate protection of the interests of patients. Admittedly, not all groups, even within the United States, applaud this analysis, as some groups have expressed concern that requiring even nominal consent will stifle epidemiological research.[5]

One promising response to the conclusion that greater attention must be given to obtaining consent has been the effort by the National Action Plan on Breast Cancer (Plan) to develop a Model Consent Form for Biological Tissue Banking. The members of the Plan believe that patients strongly support research but wish to have some voice in the process. This form allows patients who are undergoing surgery for cancer to decide whether they are willing to have residual excised tissue used to study cancer or other diseases, whether they are willing to allow investigators to have access to their medical records in the future, and whether they are willing to be contacted at a later time to participate in other studies. Field tests will be conducted to determine whether patients who use this form feel that their concerns have been met and whether patients ultimately permit their tissue to be used for research. If successful, this form as well as that proposed in 1989 by Knoppers and Laberge[6] could provide a model for the future.

Broad based recognition exists for the notion that the use of tissue samples in research can raise substantial issues of ethics and policy. As a result, it has been recommended that all such protocols be reviewed by an IRB or other similarly constituted body. There is also growing agreement that research results often are too preliminary to be of clinical utility and so should not be disclosed routinely to subjects. This policy of nondisclosure, when adopted, should be conveyed to subjects prior to their entry into the study.

Areas of substantial disagreement remain. The most notable surrounds the use of samples that will be collected in the future, either without any identifying information (anonymous samples) or with identifiers that subsequently will be irretrievably removed (anonymized samples). The American Society of Human Genetics (ASHG) has opined that informed consent is not required for the use of such samples in research.[7] The American College of Medical Genetics (ACMG), by contrast, has recommended that whenever samples that may be used for genetic analysis are collected in the course of either clinical care or research, permission should be sought to use such samples without identifiers in research.[8] Similarly, Clayton, *et al*, suggest that permission be obtained whenever it is likely that samples will be used in research.[9] The latter two positions are based on the premise that people should generally be allowed to decide whether to permit their tissue to be used in research.

None of these proposals for the role of consent in the use of anonymous and anonymized samples directly parallels the requirements of the federal regulations. On the one hand, the ASHG's formulation would suggest that informed consent is not required even when the use of unidentifiable samples is planned at the time the samples are collected, a posture that contravenes both law and policy. The exemption from IRB review exists only for projects that propose to use samples that are already "on the shelf". It is almost unthinkable, for example, that the recent project in the Washington, DC area to obtain blood samples from Ashkenazi Jews to establish the prevalence in that population of the 185 delAG mutation in BRCA1 would have been undertaken without the informed consent of the participants.

At the same time, the positions taken by the ACMG and Clayton, *et al*, go beyond the literal requirements of the federal regulations, particularly if one were to argue that consent must always be sought when samples are collected because it is possible or likely, respectively, that essentially any tissue sample could be used in research. Such a broad interpretation truly would alter current practice. What is more likely to evolve is a policy of seeking consent at the time of collection when there is a significant chance that clinical samples will be used in research. The efforts of the Plan to draft a model consent form to be used at the time of surgery for diagnosis or treatment of cancer can be understood in this light.

The policies discussed previously were strongly shaped by the current federal regulations for the protection of human subjects. In 1994, George Annas, Leonard Glantz, and Patricia Roche published the *Genetic Privacy Act*, a far reaching proposal to establish guidelines for the use of genetic information in ways that require significant changes in current law.[10,11] In their proposal, identifiable samples are treated very differently from unidentifiable samples. The authors proposed that all identifiable samples, whether collected for research or clinical care, be destroyed after use unless either the source expressly consented to their being retained or all identifying information is irretrievably destroyed. This proposal represents a significant change from current practice, particularly since pathological and other clinical specimens are often stored for long periods of time after the initial diagnosis is made. The call for routine destruction of samples that contain DNA has been met with heavy criticism from pathologists who argue that retention of samples often is needed to ensure that patients receive appropriate care.

On the other hand, these authors would permit free use for research of samples from which identifiers had been removed. People are permitted to object to such use at the time samples are collected, but these authors do not require that people be asked about the use of their tissue once identifiers have been removed. As a result, very few people would be expected to act affirmatively to limit use of tissues removed from them.

The *Genetic Privacy Act* is a very complex proposal, with the provisions regarding the use of samples for research representing only a small part. Efforts to enact a closely related bill into law in Maryland met with resounding failure.[12] The fact that the Act has not become law, however, does not mean that it has had no effect. The Act has already generated substantial public and academic response,[13,14,15,16] which doubtless will become more heated because a bill entitled the "Genetic Confidentiality and Nondiscrimination Act," which parallels the *Genetic Privacy Act* in many ways, was introduced for consideration in the United States Congress earlier this year.[17]

THE UNITED KINGDOM

In 1995, the Nuffield Council on Bioethics published a comprehensive analysis of the ethical and legal issues posed by the use of human tissue for a whole host of purposes extending far beyond research.[18] In the course of its analysis, the Nuffield Council discussed the policies of numerous members of the European Community, devoting particular attention to the report of the Health Council of the Netherlands on the *Proper Use of Human Tissue.* As a result, their report is valuable not only for its own analysis but also as a source of information about the policies of these countries.

The Council set forth tentative guidelines for deciding which proposals to use human tissue in research should be considered by research ethics committees. The authors set forth early on the general principle that "[w]here there is any doubt whatsoever in the mind of the research investigator or collaborators on the ethics or propriety of the research to be undertaken, recourse to a research ethics committee is advised. This will be particularly important in instances where the relationship between research investigator and subject, whether patient or healthy volunteer, is close and trusting".[19]

The Council went on to recommend that ethics committees review a wide array of protocols, including those "that require the identity of patients and healthy volunteers to be made known to the research investigator even if the research is retrospective and the tissue has been stored and archived"[20] as well as those "that require prospective collection of tissue over and above that strictly necessitated by diagnosis or treatment of disease. Here, the specific consent of the subject to the research procedure must be secured."[21].The omission of a statement regarding consent in paragraph 3.1 suggests that the Council did not believe that consent was always required for the use in research of previously collected, but still identified samples.

Earlier in their Report, the Council discussed when and what people need to be told about the possibility that tissue taken from their bodies would be used in research. In the Council's view, an important factor in determining the sort of consent required from the person whose tissue was obtained is whether the tissue is collected routinely as part of the individual's clinical care.

They opined that the patient should be considered to have abandoned any tissue that is left over after its use in clinical management and so recommended "that when a patient consents to medical treatment involving the removal of tissue, the consent should be taken to include consent also to the subsequent use or storage of the tissue and to any further acceptable use provided that this is regulated by appropriate ethical, legal and professional standards."[22]

The Council nonetheless suggested that consent forms should refer in general to the possibility that such samples could be used for research in the future and recommended that hospitals and other such bodies consider whether any changes in current forms were warranted.[23] These provisions apparently permit the use of identified samples with no more than typical surgical consent as long as the tissue was obtained in the course of clinical care.

By contrast, the Council concluded that people who either have more tissue than necessary for treatment or diagnosis removed during their clinical care or who give tissue as healthy volunteers should be regarded as making a donation. In such cases, the Council recommended that "those involved in the removal of tissue from donors should ensure that the explanation given to the donor is explicit about the range of intended uses of the tissue and about any risks the donor may incur either in having the tissue removed or as a consequence of its removal".[24]

Finally, the Council opined that protocols using anonymized leftover samples generally do not even warrant review by an ethics committee.[25] Although the term "anonymized" is not defined in the document, it is evident that the authors considered samples to be anonymous whenever the particular investigator did not know the person's identity. In addition, the Council believed the later communication of research results to patients to be permissible. For example, the authors stated that pathological samples are anonymous since they are stored under a laboratory number not the person's name. They reasoned that "if the material is to be used for research purposes anonymity is readily assured, but patient identity can be established by the pathologist from the confidential diagnostic records, if the research reveals information of relevance to the treatment of the patient".[26]

CANADA

Some of the earliest work on developing guidelines for the use of DNA samples in research was published by Bartha Maria Knoppers and Claude Laberge in 1989.[27] These authors focused their attention on defining the information that must be disclosed when DNA samples are obtained specifically for the purposes of DNA banking, genetic testing, and/or research. They developed a model consent form as well as a later, expanded table.[28,29] These authors would give patients a wide array of choices, including whether or not their samples may be shared under conditions of confidentiality with other investigators for either the disease that initially led to the sampling or for other diseases and whether or not they wish to be informed of research results. Patients are also informed about the limitations of testing and treatment, where and under what conditions their samples will be stored, their rights to withdraw, as well as the obligations they must assume if they wish to ensure future communication with the holders of the DNA samples.

Although their focus in 1989 was on testing performed in genetics centres, these authors recognized at that time that the consent forms typically used when tissue samples are obtained in the course of routine clinical care are woefully inadequate if the samples are to be used for genetic testing or research. Their more recent editorial in the *Journal of the American Medical Association* brings more clearly into focus the problem of the use in research of samples obtained in the course of clinical care. These authors object to the proposal that people be asked at the time of testing whether they are willing to have samples obtained from them stripped of identifiers and used for research, arguing that:

> Access to residual tissues is essential to the understanding of disease, the development of new therapeutic modalities and tools, genetic epidemiology research to establish, for example, allele frequency in populations, and surveillance research to determine incidence and prevalence. This can be undermined by the "secularization" of the sample. The anonymous-anonymized, altruistic contribution of the citizen to general well-being, the public health, and the advancement of science for the benefit of all members of a society is slowly being supplanted.[30]

They are concerned that requiring consent to use unidentifiable samples for research promotes reductionism, rather than human values. Despite their concerns about asking patients about the use of unidentifiable clinical samples for research, these authors affirm the need for IRB review of protocols that propose to remove identifiers from currently identifiable samples as well as the need "to obtain a separate consent for use of a research sample for other research purposes."[31]

Where are the areas of disagreement and how, if possible, can they be resolved?

What is "anonymous ?" One question involves the meaning of the term "anonymous". If the term means that samples and data are anonymous only when identifiers have been irretrievably removed, several consequences follow. The first is that one cannot obtain follow-up or other information about specific individuals whose earlier data and samples have been made anonymous. As a result, particular attention must be devoted to deciding which information must be collected prior to the removal of identifiers. It is also difficult to conceptualize how one might do long term prospective epidemiological studies using truly anonymous data.

The second consequence is that protecting anonymity limits the amount of information that may be connected to any particular sample. This is not only true for rare disorders, in which a test result and a family tree may be all that is needed to identify specific individuals, but also for large populations in which large amounts of information are collected about specific people, this is true of the NHANES study. At a minimum, adhering to the implications of this definition, which is widely understood to be the appropriate one in the United

States and Canada and is required under U.S. federal regulations, would require a substantial rethinking of current research practice.

The more open understanding of the meaning of "anonymous" that appears to be in use in the report of the Nuffield Council of Bioethics report is more in line with current practice but violates current notions of the protection that ought to be afforded to privacy and confidentiality.

One response to this dilemma is to encourage debate about how fully to address people's potential concerns about research participation. Some people are interested in the preservation of privacy; people generally do not want others to have information about them. A requirement of absolute anonymity meets this concern, while retention of linking information opens up the possibility of breach of privacy, which can only be reduced but not entirely eliminated.

Another concern some people have is avoiding the use of tissue for research that is objectionable to them. Women, for example, may not want their tissues to be used to find a "gene" that "explains" poor mathematical ability. That some types of research are controversial is clear, as experience with fetal research has demonstrated, for example. Nonetheless, IRBs in the United States are specifically prohibited from considering the social harms that might follow from certain types of research.

The question is whether people who provide tissue ought to have any say in what type of research is done or whether that type of decision making ought to proceed elsewhere. If patients/donors ought to have some voice in this process, then retaining any exemption from seeking consent would seem impermissible as it would eliminate any role for the individual patient. If one decides that exemptions are inappropriate, one is then left to consider only whether people ought to be required to agree to the use of samples or whether the ability to "opt out" will suffice to protect their interests.

If it is decided that the concerns of patient/donors about the use of stored, delinked samples do not always need to be heard then, in the United States, decisions about which projects proceed will reside solely with the investigator; subject, as a practical matter, to the concerns of funding bodies and institutions that hold samples. One step that might be taken in the United States would be to amend the regulations to permit IRBs to consider the potential for research to cause group harms.

Should people from whom tissue is obtained have control over whether samples can be made anonymous and used in research?

The second large issue is defining when it is appropriate to ask, at the time samples are obtained, for consent to use the samples in future research after identifiers are removed. On this subject, opinions diverge markedly and depend in part on what is meant by anonymity. Annas, *et al.*, and the ASHG state that anonymized samples can be used freely for research unless the person from whom the sample was obtained specifically objects to such use. Objection is unlikely to occur because patients need not be informed of the possibility of research. Perhaps the argument for allowing researchers free access to prospectively collected samples that are subsequently anonymized is that such research presents no risks because there is virtually no chance that information about a specific individual would be revealed.

An intermediate position is taken by the Nuffield Council on Bioethics and by Knoppers and Laberge. For these groups, it matters greatly whether the samples were obtained as part of a research project or routinely in the course of clinical care. If the former, both agree that the person must be asked for permission to use the sample for any other type of research. In the eyes of the Nuffield Council, such consent is required because the person who agrees to provide tissue for research is making a gift over which he or she is entitled to retain control. Another argument that could be made is that, given the detail typically provided in consent for participation in research, it would be unacceptable to forgo discussion of such foreseeable uses.

At the same time, both groups oppose routinely seeking consent from patients for use of samples obtained in the ordinary course of clinical care for research. The Nuffield Council takes the position that even if patients are unaware of the use of samples for research, patients have nonetheless abandoned their residual tissues to such uses. The distinction in choices to which research participants and patients are entitled is problematic. It seems unjust to say that research participants can limit their participation in similar types of projects because they are volunteers, but that patients who seek health care have no control over whether tissues obtained from them are used in research.

The need to protect human subjects grew in part out of a recognition that one does not automatically give oneself up to research by seeking medical care. The fact that the Council advocates that patients be given general information about use of samples for research suggests that they have at least some degree of uneasiness about the use of clinical samples. Finally, the loose notion of anonymity used by the Nuffield Council provides very little protection to patients.

The reasons for the objections of Knoppers and Laberge to seeking permission from patients are less clear, but include at least some concern that valuable research would be impeded by seeking consent, particularly if too many people said no. Other concerns might include the burdens of record keeping, particularly if it was unlikely that a particular sample would ever be studied in a research protocol.

Finally, the ACMG and Clayton, *et al.*, argue that there are occasions when consent should be obtained at the time clinical samples are obtained. They urge that the uses of tissue samples should conform with patients' expectations in order to show respect for them and to maintain the integrity of the health care system. In the United States, for example, many people are reluctant to seek health care because they do not want to be treated as guinea pigs, which they believe will occur regardless of their wishes.

Conclusion

The early debates about ethical issues in research focused on protocols in which individuals were asked to undergo specific interventions, a paradigm that does not fit many epidemiological and genetic studies. The emerging importance of the latter types of research has revealed new issues that only recently have become the object of formal analysis and debate.

Although all the issues have not been resolved, certain points can now be made. Perhaps investigators used to feel free to use stored tissue samples for research without any sort of formal oversight or patient consent. If so, those days should be over. At a minimum, individuals other than the investigators themselves, should review protocols for their scientific merit and for their broader implications for individuals and for society.

In addition, consent must be obtained whenever there is a chance that the individual can be identified, as is true in any study using identified or identifiable samples. Securing consent is particularly important when it is possible that a person will be contacted for further information or to be given research results. Reaching consensus on whether individual patients should have any role in deciding whether residual tissues are used for research after removal of identifiers or whether such decisions appropriately are made elsewhere, however, will require further analysis and public discussion.

Endnotes and References

1 Office of Technology Task Force, *New Developments in Biotechnology: Ownership of Human Tissues and Cells* (Washington, D.C.: Congress of the U.S., Office of Technology Assessment, 1987).

2 American College of Medical Genetics Storage of Genetics Materials Committee, "Statement on Storage and Use of Genetic Materials" (1995), 57 *Am. J Hum. Genet*: 1499.

3 "American Society of Human Genetics Statement on Informed Consent for Genetic Research" (1996), 59*Am. J Hum. Genet.* 471.

4 Clayton E.W., K.K. Steinberg, M.J. Khoury, E. Thomson, L. Andrews, M.J.E. Kahn, L.M. Kopelman and J.O. Weiss, "Informed Consent for Genetic Research on Stored Tissue Samples" (1995), 274 *JAMA* 1786.

5 "Pathologists Enter Debate on Consent for Genetic Research on Stored Tissue" (1996), 275 *JAMA* 503.

6 Knoppers B.M. and C. M. Laberge, "DNA Sampling and Informed Consent" (1989), 140 *CMAJ* 1023.

7 Supra note 3.

8 Supra note 2.

9 Supra note 4.

10 Annas G.J., L.H. Glantz, and P.A. Roche, *The Genetic Privacy Act and Commentary* (Boston: Health Law Department, Boston University School of Public Health, 1995)

11 Annas G.J., L.H. Glantz, and P.A. Roche, "Drafting the Genetic Privacy Act: Science, Policy, and Practical Considerations" (1995), 23 *J L Med. & Ethics* 360.

12 Holtzman N.A., "The Attempt to Pass the Genetic Privacy Act in Maryland" (1995), 23 *J L Med. & Ethics* 367.

13 Clayton E.W., "Why the Use of Anonymous Samples for Research Matters" (1995), 23 *J L Med. & Ethics* 375.

14 Supra note 12.

15 Parmet W.E., "Legislating Privacy: The HIV Experience" (1995), 23 *J L Med. & Ethics* 371.

16 Reilly P.R., "The Impact of the Genetic Privacy Act on Medicine" (1995), 23 *J L Med. & Ethics* 378.

17 Genetic Confidentiality and Nondiscrimination Act, S. 1898, June 24, 1996

18 Nuffield Council on Bioethics, *Human Tissue Ethical and Legal Issues* (London: Nuffield Council on Bioethics, 1995).

19 Ibid., Appendix 6, ¶ 2, at 148.

20 Ibid, Appendix 6, ¶ 3.1, at 148.

21 Ibid., Appendix 6, ¶ 3.2, at 148.

22 Ibid., ¶ 13.12, at 126.

23 Ibid., ¶ 13.13, at 126.

24 Ibid., ¶ 13.16, at 127.

25 Ibid., Appendix 6, ¶ 4, at 149.

26 Ibid., ¶ 5.25, at 37.

27 Supra note 6.

28 Knoppers B.M. and C.M. Laberge, "Research and Stored Tissues: Persons as Sources, Samples as Persons?" (1995), 274 *JAMA* 1806

29 See Knoppers B.M. and Laberge C.M., "DNA Banking/Collecting: A Canadian 'Sample' of Consent Forms" and Knoppers B.M. "Human Genetic Material - Commodity or Gift?" in Knoppers B.M., T. Caulfield and T.D Kinsella, eds., *Legal Rights and Human Genetic Material* (Toronto: Emond Montgomery Publications Ltd., 1996).

30 Supra note 28, at 1807.

31 Ibid.

ADDITIONAL REFERENCES

Weir R.F. and J.R. Horton, "DNA Banking and Informed Consent: Part 1" (1995), 17(4) *IRB* 1.

Weir R.F. and J.R. Horton, "DNA Banking and Informed Consent: Part 2" (1995), 17(5) *IRB* 1.

Frankel M.S. and A.H. Teich , *Ethical and Legal Issues in Pedigree Research* (Washington, D.C.: American Association for the Advancement of Science, 1993).

USE OF STORED SAMPLES FROM THE DANISH PKU REGISTER

BENT NØRGAARD-PEDERSEN

Professor, Department of Clinical Biochemistry

Statens Serum Institut, Copenhagen Denmark

Danish Health Information Banks

Recently, representatives from the Danish Council of Ethics (DCE), the Danish Medical Research Council (DMRC) and the Central Scientific - Ethical Committee for Denmark (CSEC) published a report on "Health science information bank -Biobanks".[1] The purpose of the report was to give an overview of the large number of health science information banks in Denmark, and to describe the legal status and the control of these banks, especially with respect to the necessary personal protection against unauthorized scientific research.

The report was initiated by the national and international debate concerning protection of the individual, and the right to prohibit any use of personal biobank material for any other purpose than originally planned. The report describes how a definite claim of this kind will impede many research projects which are of importance for prevention, diagnosis and treatment of many different diseases. The working group describes the different attitudes regarding the existence of biobanks and their use and also includes a general consensus among the authors on present control measures such as the *Public Registers Act*[2] and the *Scientific Ethical Committees Act.*[3]

There has been no report to date in Denmark concerning unacceptable use or misuse of biobank material, however. This is an important point to consider before introducing additional control measures. A claim of informed consent in all scientific projects based on biobank material could severely inhibit health research.

Public debate on the Danish PKU register

One of the reasons behind the publication on biobanks was a long debate in the news media involving the Danish PKU register, e.g. stored filter paper blood samples from all newborn infants in Denmark which have been examined for phenylketonuria (PKU) and congenital hypothyroidism (CH).

It all started on October 10th, 1991 with a question in the Danish Parliament to the Health Minister regarding the legal right to store the filter paper samples. The next day, "the story" was on the front page of most Danish newspapers and was also the lead story on Danish national television news, where I had to explain the testing, the potential use and storage, and to show the storage facilities. In addition, a detailed report was drawn up for the Health Minister and the Director of the Danish National Board of Health.

Fuelled primarily by the members of the Ethical Council, the debate continued over the next two years. The primary goal of the Council was thus achieved with the ensuing public debate on health care issues.[4] Finally, an "on site" inspection was arranged at Statens Serum Institut on September 27th, 1993 for members of the Ethical Council and selected members of the Danish Parliament. At this meeting, a detailed written description was provided together with an explanation of routine and research related to the PKU specimens. In addition, a general consensus was reached on the use, storage and current rules and regulations governing the Danish PKU biobank.

The Danish PKU register and biobank

The purpose of this register is to store laboratory and clinical data from the newborn screening program in Denmark for PKU and CH, and also to store the filter paper PKU samples. The stored information and biobank are used for:

1. Diagnosis and treatment of phenylketonuria and congenital hypothyreosis.
2. Control and documentation of previously performed analyses for PKU and CH should suspicion of these diseases arise later in life e.g. repeated analyses.
3. Quality assurance of the screening program and the development of new and better assays for PKU and CH.
4. Non-individual based statistical analyses of the screening program.
5. Specific disease testing if unexpected events occur during the newborn infant's first year of life or later.
6. Research projects using biochemical, genetic and environmental marker analyses on the stored samples.

The register has been approved by the Health Ministry with Statens Serum Institut as responsible authority. It offers a detailed description of the content of the register including input and output data and the information available to public and private authorities. The security rules are very strict, and no unauthorized person has access to the system. Only departmental staff members authorized by the Director of the Institute have access to the register. Permission has to be obtained for registry use in research projects from both the Danish Data Surveillance Authority and the Scientific Ethical Committee system. Individuals in the register can, on request, receive information concerning registered data and have a particular PKU card removed from the bank.

Routine Screening for PKU and CH

Nationwide screening for PKU and CH has been carried out in Denmark since 1975 and 1978 respectively using filter paper blood samples from newborns taken 5-7 days after birth. The screening is not mandatory but very few of the approximately 70,000 newborns per year in Denmark are not tested. The samples are examined using the Guthrie test for PKU, and TSH immunoassay for CH. Each year, 20-30 newborns are found with either PKU or CH. Since 1982, more than 1 million samples have been stored at -20^{0}C after analyses.

By using some of these stored samples in 1985, we have been able to improve the TSH assay significantly.[5] Initially, the screening for CH was performed with a somewhat complicated and less reproducible radioimmunoassay (RIA). The new TSH sandwich immunoassay can be completed within 6 hours compared with 6-7 days for RIA, and the necessary filter paper blood sample is approximately 10 times smaller. Furthermore, the number of false positive samples with elevated TSH values have been reduced from about 1 percent to around 0.04 percent. This is, therefore, an example of how important the stored samples are for improving the newborn screening program.

Specific Disease Testing Using Stored PKU Cards

If unexpected events occur during the newborn infant's first year of life or later, the stored PKU blood sample can be used for specific testing for various inborn errors of metabolism by metabolite identification and DNA analyses using the polymerase chain reaction (PCR-technique). In most cases of infant death such as Sudden Infant Death Syndrome (SIDS), no tissue sample or blood sample is available for analyses except the PKU blood sample.

Certain diseases may be suspected which can be retrospectively tested using the stored filter paper sample. It is usually the local pediatrician, with written informed consent of the parents, who requests examination of the PKU sample. This examination may not only clarify the diagnosis, but may also be important for parents contemplating future pregnancies. What is the recurrence risk, and can prenatal diagnosis be performed early in pregnancy etc.? The number of samples from the PKU bank examined in this category is still less than ten per year, but with the new mutational analyses the number will definitely rise in coming years.

Research projects using PKU cards

All research projects (anonymous or otherwise) using biochemical, genetic and environmental markers are carried out with approval of the Regional

Scientific Ethical Committee, sometimes with involvement of the Central Scientific Ethical Committee for Denmark.

The Data Surveillance Authority should also give permission for specific projects. As a general rule, projects can be said to be implemented with parental permission. In concrete cases, however, the Scientific Ethical Committee may feel it unnecessary or even outright inappropriate to approach parents for informed consent.

The following research projects have been carried out with approval of the Scientific Ethical Committee System:

1. THE FREQUENCY OF A DISEASE-CAUSING POINT-MUTATION IN THE GENE CODING FOR MEDIUM-CHAIN ACYL-COA DEHYDROGENASE (MCAD) IN SUDDEN INFANT DEATH SYNDROME (SIDS)[6]

MCAD is a defect of the fatty-acid metabolism producing a tendency for low blood sugar levels. The disease has therefore been focused on as a potential cause of some cases of SIDS. By means of a specific mutation, G-985 for MCAD, it is now possible to determine the frequency of the mutation on filter paper blood samples using the polymerase chain reaction (PCR). The frequency was determined using PKU cards, partly from healthy newborns (anonymous) and from 170 SIDS infants. It was not possible to confirm earlier reports of an association between MCAD and SIDS. The study was carried out without informed consent.

2. AN ANONYMOUS PILOT STUDY IN NEWBORN SCREENING FOR CYSTIC FIBROSIS USING IMMUNOREACTIVE TRYPSIN (IRT) AND ΔF508 MUTATIONAL ANALYSES[7]

Several studies have shown that quantification of IRT in PKU samples from newborns can be used in screening for CF. However, elevated IRT levels are found in about 1 percent of all newborns (false positives), in which event additional testing should be carried out. It is now possible to use a specific mutational analysis (ΔF508) for those samples with elevated IRT values, especially in Denmark where the ΔF508 mutation is present in 88 percent of Danish CF patients. With this two-tiered IRT and DNA approach, only true positives will be identified with no false positives, and the number of false negatives will be very low. In another Danish pilot study, primary ΔF58 screening was offered to pregnant women in first trimester screening for CF.[8] The study showed that it is possible to perform a screening of this kind from an analytical point of view, and that the patient acceptance was high. It has not yet been determined whether routine screening should be offered prenatal or neonatal.

3. NEONATAL SCREENING FOR CONGENITAL TOXOPLASMOSIS[9]

In 1992, a prospective screening study for Congenital Toxoplasmosis was started using filter paper samples from newborns and testing for toxoplasma IgG antibodies. If a sample is IgG positive, a stored first trimester sample from the mother is also tested. If this sample is IgG negative, a maternal infection has taken place, and the infant may be infected. These infants are at high risk of having an asymptomatic infection and should, therefore, be further examined and even treatment may be justified. The study has been completed but not yet published. The study was carried out with informed consent.

This study is an example of how important information can be obtained by testing corresponding maternal and newborn samples. This kind of storage of mother/child samples should be routine in the future and would allow testing for other diseases (e.g. other infections, carrier status, toxins etc.). These samples can also be used for anonymous surveillance of HIV, Hepatitis B, vaccination status, or parvovirus B19 infection.

4. PARVOVIRUS B19 INFECTION IN PREGNANT WOMEN

This project examines about 50 000 corresponding mother/ child samples for parvovirus B19 infection during pregnancy in order to identify a possible relationship to abortion, intrauterine fetal death and malformations.

The study has been approved as a Register project using laboratory data and different register data in encryption forms.

The study will have no consequences for the mother or child, but may offer new possibilities for better prenatal care and possibly vaccination.

5. DIFFERENT MUTATIONAL ANALYSES BASED ON PCR AMPLIFICATION OF DNA FROM THE FILTER PAPER

The purpose of these studies is to determine anonymously the incidence of different mutations in a random selection of the Danish population. We have determined the incidence of apolipoprotein B-3500 and the factor V (Arg 503 Glu) Leiden mutation in Denmark. This information is important when the different mutational analyses are used in daily clinics. In the near future, newborn screening could use DNA typing as a test procedure when genetic heterogeneity in populations becomes technically interpretable.

Improvement in filter paper technology

There are several advantages associated with the use of filter paper blood samples compared to liquid blood technology. The sampling, the mailing and the laboratory testing are much simpler. In addition, most blood constituents, including RNA, seem to be very stable in samples dried on absorbent paper[10] and long term storage is much easier.

The volume may be problematic, since a dried blood spot corresponds to only a few ml. of whole blood and the amount of blood absorbed will also differ from sample to sample. Therefore, the different filter paper assays are only semi-quantitative, although it is possible to use sodium in the eluate as a volume marker and thereby make marker determination quantitative when needed.[11] It is also possible, in some situations, to make the determination by measurement of two independent markers in the filter paper eluate, e.g. apolipoprotein B/A-1 ratio in screening for familial hypercholesterolemia (FH).[12] A high ratio, above 0.83, indicates a high risk for FH, but may also be a false positive due to the instability of apolipoprotein B. However, blood collection on filter paper impregnated with ascorbic acid increases the stability significantly.[13]

Filter paper technology will certainly be used much more in the future. This is primarily attributable to significant progress in assay technology and the fact that most procedures involved are simpler and much cheaper than liquid blood technology.

Discussion and conclusion

Before introducing a new screening service, a much more cautious approach will be taken today than was taken in the past.[14,15] This caution is mainly attributable to a greater awareness in the community of the problems involved. As described by Gray, there are four basic needs of the community for effective and efficient screening, namely; adequate resources must be available, an open discussion of relevant ethical problems should take place, there should be good communication to those who receive the service, and finally, the service must be under continuing evaluation.[16] Most of these needs require extensive intervention and problem resolution can be quite difficult. The ethical issues may be especially difficult to resolve completely, but the decisions should be based on a moral consensus between the community and the professionals involved in the screening process.

In recent Danish publications on biobanks, the Ethical Committee has stated that the establishment and scientific use of such health science information banks should continue to be subject to public scrutiny and control. The information should be intensified and all banks should be reported to the Danish Data Surveillance Authority. An annual list of registered biobanks should be published, describing in a few lines the nature and purpose of the individual banks. Maintaining public control over the scientific exploitation of biobanks will be achieved through the coordinated effort of the Data Surveillance Authority, as set out in the Registry legislation,[18] and the legislatively established Scientific Ethical Committees.[19] The recommendations by these bodies and the current practice of omitting scientifically unnecessary personalized data in health science research projects should be continued. Wherever possible complete anonymization should be adopted or alternative encryption.

Internationally, there have also been many publications related to biobanks especially DNA banking.[20,21,22] The Council of Europe has just prepared a draft *Convention on Human Rights and Biomedicine*[23] and a recent publication describes the problems involved in "Stored Guthrie Cards as DNA Banks".[24]

Attempts have been made to formulate new guidelines for running newborn screening programs in the 1990's (TABLE 1).[17] Such guidelines should serve as a framework for analyzing the pros and cons for a particular screening program in a given country.

TABLE 1. Amended guidelines for newborn screening (Buist 1991)

1. Newborn screening is a public health act of preventive medicine.
2. Tests should be of immediate health benefit to the infant, i.e. intervention should prevent or ameliorate symptoms
3. Tests should be universally available for the target population.
4. Tests should not be done if facilities for evaluation, treatment and counselling are not available.
5. Tests should be done with appropriate methods for the population being tested and the methods should have appropriate sensitivity and specificity.
6. Pilot studies should be done to demonstrate efficacy and benefits in the population to be tested.
7. Screening programs should inform parents and the public of the goals, scope and objectives of the tests being performed.
8. Screening test results should be confirmed by specific assays.
9. No tests should be introduced until matters of quality control in the laboratory, a follow-up treatment program and screening practices have been identified and addressed.
10. Use of anonymous samples for disease surveillance is acceptable provided that a) voluntary access to such testing is also available, b) the test results are unlinked and c) that sample or program requirements for the anonymous testing do not impinge upon the primary reasons for screening the samples in the first place.
11. Newborn screening programs could use DNA typing as a test procedure when genetic heterogeneity in populations becomes technically interpretable.

Certainly, many ethical problems and moral issues are involved in DNA banking and testing. It is important, however, not to overregulate the area so that patients, society and future generations can still benefit from its availability. From a technical point of view, the analytical performance of the testing is far superior today than in the past. Increased financial support is thus important not only to the support of ethical issues but also to sustain the research efforts which improve technology and raise the overall level of public health.

Endnotes and References

1 Almind G., L. Nielsen , N.S. Pedersen and P. Riis, *Health Science Information Banks - Biobanks* (1996), Danish Medical Research Council, Danish Council of Ethics, Danish Central Scientific-Ethical Committee.

2 *The Danish (Consolidation) Act on Public Authorities Registers*, L 1992-05-14 No. 337, L 1994-06-01 No. 430 and L 1994-12-21, No. 1093.

3 *The Act on the Scientific Ethical Committees*, L 1992-06-24 No. 503, L 1994-12-21 No. 1133, and L 1996-06-12 No. 499.

4 *The Act on the Danish Council of Ethics*, L 1987-06-03 No. 353, L 1990-05-16 No. 315 and L 1992-06-24 No. 503.

5 Arends J. and B. Nørgaard-Pedersen, "Immunofluorometry of Thyreotropin from Whole-Blood Spots on Filter Paper to Screen for Congenital Hypothyroidism" (1986), 32 *Clin. Chem* 1854.

6 Lundemose J.B., N. Gregersen, S. Kølvraa, B. Nørgaard-Pedersen, M. Gregersen, K. Helweg-Larsen and J. Simonsen, "The Frequency of a Disease-Causing Point-Mutation in the Gene Coding for Medium-Chain Acyl-CoA Dehydrogenase (MCAD) in Sudden Infant Death Syndrome (SIDS)" (1993), 82 *Acta Paediatrica* 544.

7 Nørgaard-Pedersen B., E. Høgdall, A. Iitiä, J. Arends, P. Dahlen and J. Vuust, "Immunoreactive Trypsin and a Comparison of Two DF508 Mutation Analyses in Newborn Screening for Cystic Fibrosis: An Anonymous Pilot Study in Denmark" (1993), 2 *Screening* 1.

8 Schwarts M., N.J. Brandt and F. Skovby, "Screening for Carrier of Cystic Fibrosis Among Pregnant Women" (1993), 1 *Eur. J Hum. Genet* 239.

9 Lebech M. and E. Petersen, "Neonatal Screening for Toxoplasmosis in Denmark: Presentation of the Design of a Prospective Study" (1992), 84 *Scand. J Infect. Dis. Suppl.* 75.

10 McCabe E.R., "Utility of PCR for DNA Analysis from Dried Blood Spots on Filter Paper Blotters" (1991), 1(2) *PCR Methods Appl.* 99.

11 Arends J. and B. Nørgaard-Pedersen, (Technical Note), "Increased Analytical Precision for Filter Paper Technology Using Sodium for Blood Volume Correction" (1995), 4 *Screening* 101.

12 Skovby F., S. Micic, B. Jepsen, S.O. Larsen, B. Hansen, L. Tegllund and B. Nørgaard-Pedersen, "Screening for Familial Hypercholesterolaemia by Measurement of Apolipoproteins in Capillary Blood" (1991), 66 *Arch. Dis. Child.* 844.

13 Micic S. and B. Nørgaard-Pedersen, "Improved Stability of Apo-Lipoproteins A-I and B in Filter Paper Blood Spots Impregnated with Ascorbic Acid" (1995), 41 *Clin. Chem.* 1042.

14 Wilson J.M.G. and G. Jungner, *Principles and Practices of Screening for Disease* (Geneva: World Health Organization, 1968).

15 Gray J.A.M., "Needs of the Community" in *Antenatal and neonatal screening* (Oxford: Oxford University Press, 1984) at 1.

16 Ibid.

17 Buist N.R.M., "Whither and Whence of Filter Paper Technology" in B. Wilcken and D. Webster, eds., *Neonatal Screening in the Nineties* (New South Wales, Australia: The Kelvin Press, 1991) at 3.

18 Supra note 2.

19 Supra note 3.

20 McEwen J.E. and P.R. Reilly, "A Survey of DNA Diagnostic Laboratories Regarding DNA Banking" (1995), 56 *Am. J Hum. Genet.* 1477.

21 Harper P.S., "Research Samples from Families with Genetic Diseases: A Proposed Code of Conduct" (1993), 306 *BMJ* 1391.

22 Knoppers B.M. and C.M. Laberge, "Research and Stored Tissues - Persons as Sources, Samples as Persons" (1995), 274 *JAMA* 1806.

23 Council of Europe, *Draft Convention for the Protection of Human Rights and Dignity of the Human Being with Regard to the Application of Biology and Medicine: Convention on Human Rights and Biomedicine*, Strasbourg, 6 June 1996.

24 McEwen J.E. and P.R. Reilly, "Stored Gutrie Cards as DNA Banks" (1994), 55 *Am. J Hum. Genet.* 196.

SAMPLING ISSUES IN CLINICAL IMPACT OF GENETIC TESTING AND COUNSELLING STUDIES

ELIZABETH J. THOMSON

Assistant Director, Clinical Genetics Research

Ethical, Legal and Social Implications Research Program

National Center for Human Genome Research

As new genetic technologies are moving rapidly from research into the clinical practice arena, concerns have been raised that, in some cases, not enough is known about the impact of these technologies and this new knowledge on people's lives and health. Furthermore, questions have arisen as to whether health professionals have been adequately educated about genetics, genetic technologies and the ethical, legal, and social implications surrounding their use in order to optimally provide genetic services to their patients.

To respond to these urgent concerns, the Ethical, Legal, and Social Implications (ELSI) program of the National Center for Human Genome Research (NCHGR) has focused much of its efforts in attempting to study alternative ways to provide genetic testing and counselling services and to examine the impact of these new genetic technologies on people's lives. Research projects have been funded to establish a better understanding of the current state of knowledge by health professionals, to examine the impact of integrating genetic technologies into health care practice, and to develop recommendations about how best to improve knowledge and incorporate these technologies into health care practice. The focus of work in this area has been on basic research to study clinical ethical issues and professional issues and standards, and on applied research designed to examine the impact of genetic testing and counselling.

In addition to funding individual investigator-initiated research, the ELSI program has sponsored two special initiatives in this area. The first, in 1991, was a Request for Applications (RFA) which solicited applications to study issues surrounding genetic testing and counselling for cystic fibrosis (CF) mutations. The second RFA, released in 1994, was designed to stimulate the study of issues surrounding genetic testing and counselling for heritable breast, ovarian, and colon cancer risks.

Shortly after the discovery of the CF gene in 1989, concerns were expressed that there would likely be an increasing demand for such testing and that inadequate numbers of health professionals were prepared to provide such testing.[1] Further, concerns were expressed that not enough was known about how such testing could best be carried out safely and with appropriate pre-test education and post-test counselling. As a result, in the first year of its existence, the ELSI Program of the NCHGR, along with the National Institute of Child Health and Human Development, the National Institute of Nursing Research and the National Institute of Diabetes and Digestive and Kidney Diseases released an RFA titled, "Studies of Testing and Counselling for Cystic Fibrosis Mutations," to solicit applications to examine alternative approaches to genetics education, testing and counselling in order to help establish practices that improve professional interpretation and patient understanding of CF testing.[2]

The results of these projects have been published in the peer-reviewed literature[3] and presented at numerous professional and scientific meetings. NCHGR and several other sponsoring Institutes and other federal agencies are now planning an NIH consensus development conference[4] so the empirical information gained from these and other related projects can be used to inform policy development regarding genetic testing for cystic fibrosis.

A second major initiative was undertaken in 1994 by the NCHGR in anticipation of the discovery of a number of cancer predisposing genes. This initiative (also an RFA) was co-sponsored by the National Cancer Institute, the National Institute of Mental Health and the National Institute of Nursing Research.[5] It solicited application for studies designed to examine the psychosocial and clinical impact of using gene-based diagnostic tests in families with heritable forms of breast, ovarian, and colon cancer. The studies are designed to identify those individuals who have an increased risk of developing cancer within a high risk family and those who do not. Knowledge and attitudes about genetic testing for cancer risks are being assessed and information is being gathered to establish clinical protocols for the optimum use of these risk assessment technologies in the future. These projects are now in their third year and preliminary results are becoming available. Once completed, these projects will provide valuable experience-based guidance for genetic testing for cancer susceptibility genes.

In the above two activities, NCHGR sponsored the formation of research consortia (the Cystic Fibrosis Studies Consortium and the Cancer Genetics Studies Consortium) in order to promote collaboration among individual research projects and to reduce duplication of efforts. Other goals were to increase the likelihood of interstudy comparisons, to jointly develop guidance for informed consent and laboratory and sampling issues, and, in the case of the cancer genetics studies, to develop follow-up recommendations for those found to have inherited breast, ovarian, or colon cancer mutations. These follow-up recommendations will be published in the coming year and will provide interim guidance to researchers and others who provide genetic testing for cancer risks.[6]

In each of these activities, members of both Consortia grappled with what to do with the samples that were obtained as a part of these projects. Although the sampling and laboratory issues were considered to be somewhat peripheral to the overall goals of these studies, they were nevertheless an integral part. The ultimate goal for these projects related to sampling and testing was to have high quality laboratory testing services for an optimal number of mutations at an affordable price. This had to be considered since the NIH-funded studies had thousands of laboratory tests associated with them.

Alternative methods of collecting specimens (e.g. blood, saliva, buccal brush) were discussed and there were discussions about what to do with the samples collected once these studies were complete. For a variety of reasons, (the peripheral nature of these laboratory tests to these studies and the fact that the tests in some cases were being carried out by laboratories that had no direct association with the research participants) it was determined in the CF studies, that obtaining consent for the specimens to be used for purposes unrelated to these projects would have been difficult, if not impossible, particularly when how and by whom the samples might be used in the future was unknown. In addition, the samples obtained as a part of these studies would, for the most part, be obtained from members of the general population and the vast majority of samples would not have been found to have a CF mutation. Therefore, for this set of projects, a decision was made that the specimens would be destroyed at the end of these studies. This conclusion has not been enthusiastically received by all researchers, however, in order to increase the likelihood of adequate informed consent, it was determined to be the best option at that time.

In the case of the breast, ovarian, and colon cancer studies, investigators came to a different conclusion. Many of the investigators in this consortium were affiliated with a laboratory in which research regarding inherited cancer mutations was being conducted. In addition, the samples were to be obtained from individuals who had an increased risk to have a mutation in one of their cancer predisposing genes. As a result there was much greater interest among investigators to request permission to store tissue samples for future related research purposes.

While some investigators ultimately determined that they would not request permission for the samples to be used for other research purposes, others preferred to obtain consent for future research. Such a decision, however, did complicate even further an already extremely complicated informed consent process. NCHGR's hope was that the additional consent needed for storing samples for future uses would not jeopardize participation in the currently funded projects.

There has been limited evidence published that some researchers store samples for future research purposes, without obtaining adequate informed consent.[7] Staff at the NCHGR communicated to its investigators that if they were intending to store samples, they would need to request permission to do so and that participation in this research should not be dependent on whether participants agreed to store their samples for research for other purposes. While obtaining informed consent, investigators were encouraged to clearly spell out the following issues[8]:

- whether their samples could be used for either identifiable or anonymous research;
- whether they were willing to have their samples shared with other researchers and other institutions; and
- whether they wanted to impose any limitations on the type of research that could be done using their samples.

Research involving identifiable samples carries with it some known risks including potential anxiety, altered family relationships, social stigmatization and discrimination. In the case where researchers were proposing that the samples be used in the future in identifiable research, in addition to the usual required elements of consent[9] they were asked to emphasize the following issues in their consent discussions:

- assurance that refusal to participate in other research projects in no way jeopardized their ability to participate in this research project;
- he risks and benefits of research to be carried out on their samples;
- the extent to which confidentiality can realistically be maintained;
- under what circumstances, if any they would be recontacted;
- and their ability to withdraw their sample at a future date.

NCHGR remains committed to assuring that individuals whose samples are stored for future related or unrelated research know and give permission for such secondary uses of their samples. It is crucial that participants be given an opportunity to understand the risks and benefits of such research participation and that they be protected as much as possible from unanticipated, unintended, and undesired consequences of research participation. Finally, it is crucial that the request to store tissues for secondary research purposes not interfere in the conduct of the research project for which the participant has volunteered.

Endnotes and References

1 American Medical Association, Council on Ethical and Judicial Affairs, "Ethical Issues in Carrier Screening of Cystic Fibrosis and Other Genetic Disorders", Reports of the Council; No. 36. Chicago: American Medical Association; 1991 Jul:89-106. American Society of Human Genetics, "American Society of Human Genetics Statement on Cystic Fibrosis Screening" (1990), 46 *Am. J Hum. Genet.* 393. American Society of Human Genetics, "Statement of the American Society of Human Genetics on Cystic Fibrosis Carrier Screening" (1992), 51 *Am. J Hum. Genet.* 1443. U. S. National Institutes of Health, "Workshop on Population Screening for the Cystic Fibrosis Gene Statement

from the National Institutes of Health Workshop on Population Screening for the Cystic Fibrosis Gene" (1990), [Special report] 323 *New England Journal of Medicine* 70.

2 National Institutes of Health, "Studies of Testing and Counseling for Cystic Fibrosis Mutations", *RFAHG* 91-01.

3 Publication list available from the Ethical, Legal, and Social Implications Research Program, National Center for Human Genome Research, National Institutes of Health, Bethesda, MD.

4 NIH Consensus Development Conference: on Genetic Testing for Cystic Fibrosis, sceduled to be held April 14-16, 1997, National Conference Center, National Institutes of Health, Bethesda, MD.

5 National Institutes of Health, "Studies on Genetic Testing for Heritable Breast, Ovarian, and Colon Cancer Risks", *RFA HG* 94-01.

6 Burke W., G. Petersen, P. Lynch, J. Botkin, M. Daly, J. Garber, M. Kahn, A. McTiernan, K. Offit, E. Thomson, and C. Varrichio, "Recommendations for Follow-up Care of Individuals with an Inheritied Susceptibility to Cancer 1. HNPCC Mutations", (submitted for publication). See also, Burke W., M. Daly, J. Garber, J. Botkin, M. Kahn, P. Lynch, A. McTiernan, K. Offit, J. Perlman, G. Petersen, E. Thomson, and C. Varricchio, "Recommendations for Follow-up Care of Individuals with an Inheritied Susceptibility to Cancer 2. BRCAl and BRCA2 Mutations", (submitted for publication).

7 Weir R. and J. Horton, "DNA Banking and Informed Consent-Part 1" 17(4) *IRB* 14. See also, Weir R. and J. Horton, "DNA Banking and Informed Consent-Part 2" 17(5&6) *IRB* 1.

8 Adapted from recommandations in Clayton E., K. Steinberg, et al, "Informed Consent for Genetic Research on Stored Tissue Samples" 274 *JAMA* 1786.

9 DHHS's Protection of Human Subjects, Title 45 Code of Federal Regulations Part 46 and DOE's Protection of Human Subjects Title 10 Code of Federal Regulations Part 745.

TECHNICAL AND SOCIAL ASPECTS OF ß-THALASSEMIA SCREENING IN EUROPE AND DEVELOPING COUNTRIES

ANTONIO CAO

Istituto di Clinica e Biologia dell'Età Evolutiva

Università degli Studi di Cagliari

The inherited hemoglobinopathies are among the most common autosomal recessive disorders affecting human beings. Under this definition are included ß-thalassemias, α–thalassemias and the sickling disorders.

The ß-thalassemias are inherited anemias characterized by absent (ß°-thal) or reduced ($ß^+$-thal) production of the ß-globin chains of hemoglobin.[1,2] The homozygous state most commonly results in a severe anemia, associated with marked spleen enlargement and characteristic skeletal modifications due to the enormous bone marrow expansion because of the marked ineffective erythropoiesis (thalassemia major). The hematological features are microcytosis, anisocytosis, presence of a large number of nucleated red blood cells in peripheral blood, an hemoglobin electrophoretic pattern characterized by absent to low amount of HbA, and high percentage of HbF, which in ß°-thalassemia is practically the only Hb present in peripheral blood, and unbalanced α/nonα globin chain synthesis. Without treatment patients with thalassemia major die from 2-6 years with one of the complications resulting from severe anemia. Patients with homozygous ß-thalassemia may be cured by bone marrow transplantation, which, however, even in the best condition, is associated with a high rate of mortality (5-8%).[3] Nowadays, however, the present sibship size severely limits the use of this procedure. Present management consists in regular blood transfusions and iron chelation with nightly subcutaneous infusion of desferroxamine B.[4] Life expectancy with this regimen is not yet established, but presumably extends beyond the third decade (5). A proportion of patients homozygous for ß-thalassemia develop a mild disorder, referred to as ß-thalassemia intermedia, which is a mild to severe anemia for which continuous transfusions are not necessary.[6,7] Heterozygotes for ß-thalassemia are clinically healthy but could be identified by hematological analysis. The principal hematological characteristics are low mean red blood cell volume (MCV), low mean red blood cell Hb concentration (MCH), high HbA2 and slightly unbalanced α/nonα globin chain biosynthesis. These hematological features are today the object of the analysis in ß-thalassemia carrier screening.[8]

In the last fifteen years the molecular bases of ß-thalassemias have been elucidated. The disease proved to be very heterogeneous at the molecular level, since resulting from more than 150 different mutations. In spite of this marked heterogeneity in each at-risk population, a limited number of mutations are prevalent, a finding which makes prenatal diagnosis technically easy to perform.[9-11]

Prenatal diagnosis in the management of ß-thalassemia has been introduced in the late seventies,[12-14] and was initially carried out by globin chain synthesis analysis on fetal blood and later on by the direct detection of the mutations on fetal DNA.[15,16,9,17-19]

Frequency and Distribution of ß-thalassemias

ß-thalassemias are widespread, occurring with a high frequency in a belt extending through the Mediterranean littoral and islands, the Middle East and the Indian subcontinent as far as South Asia.

However, through the emigration occurred in the last three centuries, ß-thalassemia spread worldwide in Northern and Southern America, Oceania, and Northern Europe (TABLE 1).

TABLE 1. Heterozygous ß-thalassemia in different regions[35]

Region	ß-thalassemia carrier (in % of population)*	ß-thalassemia carrier born per year (thousands)*
Africa	1	327
Americas	0.8	134
Asia	3.7	3,347
Europe	1.12	117
Oceania	1.8	...**
Total	2.62	3925

* including HbE, which is a mild ß-thalassemia mutation. ** not known

Worldwide there are at least 70 million heterozygotes and at least 25,000 homozygotes are born per year. As shown by the world distribution, the large part of patients are born in developing countries.[20] The health burden created by these disorders is enormous and will obviously steadily increase because of the rise of life expectancy following introduction of modern supportive measures in those places where they are not presently available.

Prevention of ß-thalassemia

Prevention programs based on pilot heterozygote screening and counselling with the aim to decrease the mating between carriers or the number of children born from couples at risk before prenatal diagnosis was available, have been totally ineffective, as it is indicated by the minimal influence of these programmes on the reproductive performance of couples, who had an affected child, no significant difference in the proportion of marriages between heterozygotes from that expected by random mating and no change in the incidence of thalassemia major.[21-23] The development of antenatal diagnosis gave a new dimension in genetic prevention of ß-thalassemia and since 1975 has led to the introduction of preventive programs based on heterozygote detection, genetic counselling and fetal diagnosis in several high risk areas of the Mediterranean basin, namely Cyprus, Greece, Sardinia and later on Continental Italy.[24-27] A program with a similar design directed to immigrant couples mostly of Cypriot, Asian Indian and Pakistan origin has been introduced in Great Britain since 1977.[14]

In this paper I shall review the characteristics of these programs and their effectiveness in reducing the incidence of thalassemia major, mostly concentrating on those operating for a long time (Sardinia, Cyprus, Greece) and for which more data are available. I will then discuss the measures for prevention of ß-thalassemia in Northern Europe and in developing countries, focusing on those populations for which data have been published or are available.

Prevention of ß-thalassemia in Mediterranean At-risk Populations

In Sardinia, Greece and Cyprus, both the Turkish and Greek part of the island, the prevention program was carried out by a central reference center responsible for the organization, fetal testing and identification of atypical heterozygotes, and by several satellite units, which were responsible for local carrier screening.[26-28]

Prevention of autosomal recessive disorders could be retrospective or prospective, namely after or before the birth of an affected proband. Retrospective diagnosis, although very useful for individual families, has however a very limited effect on the reduction of the number of affected children in the target population.

All the programs started with retrospective diagnosis and later on moved to prospective prevention. A critical issue deriving from these experiences is that before embarking in large scale prospective prevention it is necessary to organize adequate facilities to meet the continuous increase of the demand for screening and prenatal diagnosis. For a successful program, indeed, a critical prerequisite in order to avoid disaffection is a careful calculation of the projected workload increase and proportional expansion of the laboratory facilities.

All these programs were preceded and accompanied by intensive and large scale educational campaigns. Population education on ß-thalassemias and its prevention was achieved by means of mass media, namely local newspapers, radio, TV and magazines, posters and informative booklets. In all these at-risk areas where ß-thalassemia is common, the population at large at the beginning of the program were informed about this disease because of the striking appearance and body build of the patients. Today, however, this sensitizing factor does not exist anymore, since with modern treatment thalassemic patients cease to be recognizable among other people.

In addition more personal approaches through lectures and discussions with the community leaders and/or the population at large in clubs and rural communities have been largely used to convey the educational message. In Sardinia (TABLE 2) the large majority of the spouses were informed about thalassemia via mass media, general practitioners or obstetricians, indicating that these types of information channels are the most efficient to date available.

TABLE 2. Channels of information to couples requesting screening in Sardinia

Information channel	%
Mass Media	44
General practitioners	31
Obstetricians	23
Midwives	2

In the Greek part of Cyprus, an annual thalassemia week is organized and a magazine and numerous pamphlets are issued. Another very critical step in the educational campaign have been meetings with physicians, particularly pediatricians and obstetricians, family planning associations, nurses and social workers, in order to inform them about the program and the progress continuously made in prenatal diagnosis procedures.

Informative leaflets, which included details on when and how to get examined, have been made available to prospective couples at several critical places, for instance marriage registry offices, general practitioners' offices and family planning clinics. These booklets emphasized three main messages, namely the carrier state has no disadvantage, the homozygous state is a very severe and eventually fatal disease for which there is for most patients no definite cure but only palliative measures, and thirdly, fetal diagnosis can be carried out and is highly reliable and safe for the mother.

A major role in the implementation of the preventive programs was played by health care workers and paramedical staff. In addition, consultation with the parents' associations was periodically organized in order to prepare the educational message to be given for the population education, taking into account the presence of many patients in the population, who could eventually be harmed by the message.

Lately, education on thalassemia by using educational videotapes was introduced in the school curriculum in secondary schools in all these Mediterranean populations.

The position taken up by the religious leaders in the preventive program varied markedly according to the different countries. The Orthodox Church, particularly in Cyprus, contributed substantially to the overall success by encouraging carrier testing. In Cyprus, indeed, in order to discourage heterozygote marriages, the Church requests a premarital certificate attesting that carrier testing has been carried out[26] although the Church will not refuse to carry out the marriage between spouses both carriers of ß-thalassemia.

In Sardinia and Continental Italy, the Catholic Church did not take up an adverse position against the program, essentially because the couple in case of prenatal diagnosis of thalassemia major was left free to decide whether to interrupt or not the pregnancy. In the meantime a campaign against abortion for any reason, including genetic disorders, was implemented.

Carrier screening

Carrier screening was carried out voluntarily. The message conveyed by the educational campaign was conceived to allow individuals or couples to request testing, when they are best prepared to absorb the information, namely before or at marriage or conception. In Cyprus and Sardinia at the outset the target population were women at early pregnancy. In all these populations, however, many spouses had requested testing when pregnancy was relatively advanced. Late testing may produce dramatic emotional stress on couples and pressure on the laboratory staff to expedite the examinations.

In Cyprus as well as in Sardinia, however, in the past few years the number of singles or couples without a pregnancy in progress requesting screening has been continuously increasing (TABLE 3).

TABLE 3. Population requesting screening in the Sardinian program

Population	1980	1996
Pregnant women	65%	52%
Couples	15%	32%
Singles	20%	16%

In Cyprus as well as in Sardinia the main emphasis today has shifted to school leavers. This will prove to be an efficient approach, as seems to be indicated by a very long-dated experience in the Italian province of Latium.[29]

Screening in the Army in Greece has not proved to be successful as the examinees were little interested and failed to absorb the information provided. An informed consent by the screnee was not requested. In Sardinia, however, prior to testing, an effort was made to inform each person about the nature of the illness, the meaning of "carrier", the implications of being a carrier and the alternatives available to individuals found to be carriers.

Counselling

Genetic counselling was carried out in a non-directive manner, usually to both members of the couple at risk, according to internationally accepted guidelines,[30] namely accurate diagnosis, truth and confidentiality. Any mandatory measure, restricting the individual freedom was carefully avoided. During the counselling sessions details on the natural history of thalassemia major, its management and complications are given. Because of the quite good results of BMT, we recently added information on this procedure. The information provided were directed at giving an informed basis upon which to make reproductive decision, i.e. birth control procedures, mate selection, adoption, fetal testing and artificial insemination by donor. Particular emphasis has always been given on details of fetal testing, including sampling procedures, risk to the fetus, failure to obtain appropriate material for analysis and risk of misdiagnosis. An explanatory booklet illustrated by picture is usually provided to the spouses. Counselling for those couples at risk for the common genotypes of ß-thalassemia is relatively simple and this can be done by well trained social workers or paramedical staff. When pregnancy is in progress or in the presence of uncommon genetic combination, which may lead to mild disorders, a senior member of the staff is usually involved.

In Sardinia, once identified, each carrier was also informed on the implication of his/her carrier status for close relatives and simple clearly written educational material was provided for them. Relatives were informed in this way and were given the option to contact the Center if they desired further information or wanted to be screened. This strategy, as we will see later on, multiplies the efficacy of the screening. A similar approach has been used in the other Mediterranean at-risk populations.

Efficacy of the screening

The Sardinian program was very effective, as it is indicated by the large percentage of couples at risk detected of those expected on the basis of the carrier rate by screening a very limited proportion of the population (13%). This efficacy is most likely related to the magnifying effect obtained by heterozygote testing of relatives of known carriers (inductive screening). In addition, relatives of patients were certainly highly motivated to request screening (TABLE 4). Similar results have been reported in Greece, where screening of less than 1% of the population resulted in the identification of a large number of couples at risk.

TABLE 4. Overall results of ß-thalassemia carrier screening in Sardinia

Subjects tested	212,899
% of population tested	13
Carrier detected	36,389
Prospective at-risk couples detected	2,310

Carrier detection methods

The purpose of these programs is the identification of couples in which both spouses carry ß-thalassemias (including rare genotypes such as ∂ß-thalassemia and Hb Lepore) or the sickle cell trait. The compound heterozygous state for a carrier of a sickling disorder and ß-thalassemia should indeed be detected because results in sickle cell anemia.

A strategy adopted by several programs, which may reduce the cost, is to test only one member of each couple, the other member being tested if his/her test disclaims a carrier state.

Some programs, for instance those running in Greece or in Latium, make an initial screening using either MCH or osmotic fragility test combined with blood film examination and carry a complete hematological assessment only on those samples which show an abnormal result in the first screening. These strategies may miss double heterozygotes for α– and ß-thalassemia, who tend to have a normalization of their blood red cell indices including MCH.[31-33] Since in Sardinia, in addition to ß-thalassemia, α–thalassemia is also common and thus double heterozygosity for α–and ß-thalassemia is obviously not rare, we included in the initial set of examinations HbA2 quantitation in addition to MCH-MCV determination (FIGURE 1).

The most frequent problem in carrier identification arose in the counselling of those couples in which one member is a typical ß-thalassemia carrier with a raised HbA2 and the other has thalassemia like red cell indices, no iron deficiency and normal HbA2 and F levels. This phenotype in fact may result from α–thalassemia, mild ß-thalassemia alleles, γ∂ß-thalassemia or double heterozygosity for ß- and ∂-thalassemia, which by decreasing the output of ∂-chains may reduce the increased HbA2 levels resulting from the ß-thalassemia carrier state. In these cases family studies, globin chain synthesis analysis, eventually in combination with α– and ∂- globin gene analysis, should be carried out in order to define the genotype and give appropriate counselling. In spouses found to be carriers, the ß-thalassemia mutation is defined either by dot blot hybridization or primer specific amplification using oligonucleotide probes or primers complementary to the most common ß-thalassemia mutations in each population. In those rare cases in which the mutation is not defined by this approach, we carry out denaturing gradient gel electrophoresis followed by direct sequencing on amplified DNA. In a proportion of the cases, homozygous ß-thalassemia results in a mild clinical phenotype not requiring transfusions, which is referred to as thalassemia intermedia.

A molecular mechanism responsible for these mild forms is inheritance in homozygosity of a mild ß-thalassemia mutation, i.e. a mutation associated with a consistent residual output of ß- chains. On the other hand compound heterozygosity for a mild and a severe mutation leads to a very heterogeneous clinical picture. Other ameliorating factors are co-inheritance of α–thalassemia, which by decreasing the output of a chains reduces the α/nonα chain imbalance, or co-inheritance of genetic determinant(s) able to sustain a continuous production of γ– chains in the adult life, such as mutations in the Aγ or Gγ promoters. The compound heterozygous state for a typical ß-thalassemia and a ß-thalassemia mutation associated with high HbF production may also lead to a mild disorder. However, of these modifying factors only the presence of homozygosity for a mild ß-thalassemia mutation leads consistently to a mild phenotype, and thus may be used for improving the counselling. The effect of the other factors mentioned is not sufficiently consistent to be used to predict the phenotype.

In couples with a previous normal child, we offer the possibility to carry out HLA typing in the fetus in order to check whether he has inherited the same HLA genotype of the brother/sister, making eventually possible in the future bone marrow transplantation from the HLA identical sibling.

Prenatal Diagnosis

In the late 70s and early 80s prenatal testing was carried out by globin chain synthesis analysis using fetal blood obtained by placental aspiration or fetoscopy.[12,14] As soon as the molecular bases for ß-thalassemia in the Mediterranean populations had been defined, the ß-thalassemia mutations were directly detected on fetal DNA. At the beginning each specific mutation was defined by hybridization of allele-specific oligonucleotides to electrophoretically separated restricted non amplified DNA fragment and later on by allelic specific probes or primers on enzymatically amplified DNA.[15-17,34,19] The fetal DNA is obtained by transabdominal or vaginal chorionic villi biopsy. Globin chain synthesis analysis has been shown to be a very reliable procedure. In our series two misdiagnoses (0.2%) had occurred out of 1,131 cases monitored (TABLE 5). The procedure is, however, associated with a high risk (~ 5-6%) of fetal mortality.

TABLE 5. Overall Results of Prenatal Diagnosis of ß-thalassemia in Sardinia

	FETAL DNA		FETAL BLOOD
	PCR-based Analysis	Enzymatically Restricted DNA with ASO Probes	
Pregnancies monitored	1,666	1,171	1,131
Homozygous fetuses	416	321	268
Failures		7 (0.6%)	10 (0.9%)
Misdiagnosis		1 (0.09%)	2 (0.2%)

Direct detection of the mutations on fetal DNA gave very reliable results. In our Unit we observed only one case of misdiagnosis resulting from maternal contamination. In order to limit the incidence of diagnostic errors, we have adopted the following guidelines: careful dissection of maternal decidua from fetal trophoblasts under the inverted microscope, request of a minimal amount of chorionic villi (~ 3mg) to limit the effect of maternal contamination; use of a limited number of amplification cycles which may reduce the chances to co-amplify DNA from maternal decidua, analysis in duplicate by using two different but overlapping DNA fragments, amplification of a previously selected suitable polymorphism to monitor for the presence of maternal contamination. The introduction of first trimester prenatal diagnosis led to a dramatic increase in the uptake of this procedure following non-directive counselling. In our Center, for instance, the percentage of spouses opting for prenatal testing has increased from the figure of approx. 92% of the time when only fetal blood analysis was available to the present value of approx. 99%. The trend indicates that prenatal diagnosis is more acceptable when it is carried out earlier in the pregnancy. Following prenatal diagnosis of an affected fetus, the majority of the couples decided to interrupt the pregnancy. The limited proportion, approx. 0.1% in our Center, deciding to continue the pregnancy were motivated by ethical reasons. This finding clearly indicates that counselling was not carried out in directive way.

Evaluation of the programs

The programs were evaluated by monitoring the birth rates of thalassemia major. In all the Mediterranean populations with ongoing preventive programs a consistent and progressive decline in the incidence of thalassemia major was noted. In Sardinia, before prevention, 1 newborn in every 250 was affected by thalassemia major. On the basis of the carrier frequency and considering the present total number of newborns, the expected number of homozygous newborns per year should be 65. Today, only 4-5 cases arise per year (1:4,000 live births) with 94% of the cases effectively prevented. The fall in the birth rate of thalassemia major in the Mediterranean countries indicates a marked effectiveness in the delivering to the target population of education, screening and counselling in such a way that individuals and families at risk were fully informed about the choices available to them. The main reasons for residual cases of thalassemia major in these populations were lack of parental knowledge about ß-thalassemia and the procedure for its prevention, mistake in carrier identification or prenatal diagnosis, option for continuing pregnancy and false paternity.

Adverse effects

To date, stigmatization or psychological adverse effects of discovering to be a carrier has not been detected. Nor has any consequence for employment or insurance of disclosing the carrier status been noted. The only exception regards the recruitment in the Army in Italy, where ß-thalassemia heterozygotes are exempted from carrying out military service when their Hb levels are lower than 2DS from mean.

Following this policy, those ß-thalassemia heterozygotes with low Hb are not admitted to work in any military corp.

Conclusions

The results described herein indicate that the programs based on carrier screening, genetic counselling and prenatal diagnosis are very effective for the control of an autosomal recessive disorder, such as ß-thalassemia, at the population level.

From the ethical point of view, it should be noted that these programs were carried out by very competent and motivated staff. However, communication was accurate and delivered in understandable way by taking into account the sociocultural context. Consultation with parents' associations and community leaders preceded the educational campaign and was continuously repeated. Counselling was carried out before and after the screening procedure. This counselling was voluntary and non-directive and offered the various options available. Confidentiality of the genetic information was fully preserved. All the procedures were carried out free of charge in the context of the Public Health System and the program was subjected to a continual critical review.

Populations with a different religion, including Roman Catholic (Italians), Orthodox Christian (Greeks and Greek Cypriots) and Muslim (Turkish Cypriots) were the target of these preventive programs. This indicates that programs carefully designed and appropriate for each context may be successful independently of religion.

NORTH-EUROPEAN POPULATION

Population migrations in Europe have brought thalassemia major into all the Northern industrialized countries, where today ß-thalassemia represents a significant health problem. The information available on the delivery of carrier screening and prenatal diagnosis in these countries is quite limited. The only exception, due to the continuous commitment of Bernadette Modell,[35] is the United Kingdom. To the best of our knowledge retrospective counselling and prenatal diagnosis is available in all European countries. In the United Kingdom, Belgium, Holland, and France genetic screening is offered to at-risk immigrant populations. However, the delivery of information, screening and counselling to the ethnic minorities in these countries was much less efficient as compared to the Mediterranean populations and thus there has been an increase in the number of patients. For example, a retrospective analysis from Bernadette Modell has shown that many of the parents either had not been screened or they had not been adequately counselled. Furthermore, a wide inequality in service delivery to different groups was observed, with the Asians and especially the Pakistans being the less privileged immigrant population in the United Kingdom. In Germany, although prenatal diagnosis and selective abortion are largely available, the fear of "eugenics" most likely precludes the use of prospective genetic screening.

The suggestions made by B. Modell to improve the delivery of a preventive program to the ethnic minorities in U.K. include the promotion of information, screening and counselling in primary health care, appropriate genetic counselling using a language the parents are familiar with, different screening policies in the different areas according to the prevalence of at-risk populations with universal screening in districts with high prevalence of at-risk populations (15%) and selective screening on the bases of ethnic origin in low prevalence areas. In the future, however, because of population mixing, the ethnic origin will be progressively less useful for risk prediction.

MIDDLE EAST AND DEVELOPING COUNTRIES

In many countries of the Middle East including the Gulf States and Saudi Arabia, ß-thalassemia is very common, and the resources and infrastructures to carry out genetic screening and prenatal diagnosis are largely available. However, the religion and legal position and the social attitudes versus prenatal diagnosis and interruption of pregnancy preclude at the present time the introduction of a genetic preventive program. In the large majority of the developing countries where ß-thalassemia is prevalent, the infrastructures or resources to provide screening and prenatal diagnosis at the level of populations via the Health System are not available. Screening and prenatal diagnosis are effective in some areas of Turkey, India, Thailand and Malaysia, Southern China and Hong Kong, Taiwan and Singapore.[35,36] In most countries, however, (Turkey, Azerbajan, Pakistan, Iran, India, Thailand) prenatal diagnosis is carried out mainly on a private basis.

The greatest challenge for the future in ethical terms is, in my opinion, the reduction of the inequities in the delivery of genetic services to the world population in such a way to introduce education, screening, and prenatal diagnosis in those populations where ß-thalassemia is largely prevalent but where the level of infrastructures and resources do not favor the development of such a program. We do hope that such programs, even if adapted to each social and religious context, will follow the most important ethical requisites including competence, proper consultation, communication and counselling, voluntarism, confidentiality, and continual reviewing.

References

1. Weatherall D.J. and J.B. Clegg, eds, *The Thalassaemia Syndromes*. 3rd ed. (Oxford: Blackwell Scientific Publications, 1981).
2. Bunn H.F. and B.G. Forget, eds, *Hemoglobin: Molecular, Genetic and Clinical Aspects.* (Philadelphia: W.B. Saunders, 1986).
3. Lucarelli G., Giardini C., Baronciani D., "Bone Marrow Transplantation in Thalassemia" (1995)*Semin. Hematol.* 32:297-303.
4. Modell B. and V. Berdoukas, eds, *The Clinical Approach to Thalassemia.* (London: Grune and Stratton Ltd, 1984).
5. Olivieri N.F., Nathan D.G., MacMillan J.M., et al., "Survival in Medically Treated Patients with Homozygous ß-thalassemia" *N. Engl. J. Med.* (1994) 331:574-578.
6. Wainscoat J.S., Thein S.L., Weatherall D.J., "Thalassemia Intermedia" (1987) *Blood Reviews* 1:273-279.
7. Cao A., Gasperini R., Podda A., Galanello R. "Molecular Pathology of Thalassemia Intermedia" (1990) *Eur. J. Int. Med.* 1:227-236.
8. Cao A. & Rosatelli MC. "Screening and Prenatal Diagnosis of the Hemoglobinopathies" in *The Haemoglobinopathies,* D.R. Higgs and D.J. Weatherall, eds. (London: Clinical Haematology, Bailliere Tindall, 1993) pp. 263-286.
9. Kazazian H.H. Jr., "The Thalassemia Syndromes: Molecular Basis and Prenatal Diagnosis" (1990) *Semin. Haematol.* 27:209-228.
10. Huisman T.H.J., "The ß- and ∂-thalassemia Repository" (1993) *Hemoglobin* 17(5):479-499.
11. Cao A., Gossens M., Pirastu M., "ß-thalassemia Mutations in Mediterranean Populations" (1989) *Br. J. Haemat.* 71:309-312.
12. Kan Y.W., Golbus M.S., Trecartin R.F. et al., "Prenatal Diagnosis of Homozygous ß-thalassemia" (1975) *Lancet ii*:790-792.
13. Kan Y.W., Golbus M.S., Trecartin R.F., et al., "Prenatal Diagnosis of ß-thalassemia and Sickle-cell Anemia: Experience with 24 Cases" (1977) *Lancet* 1:269-271.
14. Modell B., Petrou M., Ward R.H.T. et al, "Effect of Fetal Diagnostic Testing on Birth-rate of Thalassemia Major in Britain" (1984) *Lancet ii*:1383-1386.
15. Rosatelli C., Falchi A.M., Tuveri T. et al., "Prenatal Diagnosis of ß-thalassemia with the Synthetic-oligomer Technique" (1985) *Lancet i*:241-243.

16. Ristaldi M.S., Pirastu M., Rosatelli C. et al., "Prenatal Diagnosis of ß-thalassemia in Mediterranean Populations by Dot Blot Analysis with DNA Amplification and Allele Specific Oligonucleotide Probes" (1989) *Pren. Diagn.* 9:629-638.

17. Kan Y.W., Lee K.Y., Furbetta M. et al., "Polymorphism of DNA Sequence in the ß-globin Gene Region: Application to Prenatal Diagnosis of ß-thalassemia in Sardinia" *N. Engl. J. Med.* (1980) 302:185-188.

18. Pirastu M., Kan Y.W., Cao A. et al., "Prenatal Diagnosis of ß-thalassemia. Detection of a Single Nucleotide Mutation in DNA" (1983) *N Engl J Med* 309:284-287.

19. Maggio A., Giambona A., Cai S.P. et al., "Rapid and Simultaneous Typing of Hemoglobin S, Hemoglobin C, and Seven Mediterranean ß-thalassemia Mutations by Covalent Reverse Dot-blot Analysis: Application to Prenatal Diagnosis in Sicily" (1993) *Blood* 81:239-242.

20. World Health Organization, "Report on the Community Control of Hereditary Anemias. Memorandum from a WHO meeting" (1983) *Bulletin of the WHO* 61:63-80.

21. Barrai I. and Vullo C., "Screening for ß-thalassemia Heterozygotes" (1980a) *Lancet ii*:1257.

22. Barrai I. and Vullo C., "Assessment of Prospective Genetic Counselling in the Ferrara Area" (1980b) *Am. J. Med. Genet.* 6:195-204.

23. Angastiniotis M., "Prevention of Thalassemia in Cyprus", Personal Communication.

24. Cao A., "Results of Programmes for Antenatal Detection of Thalassemia in Reducing the Incidence of the Disorder" (1987) *Blood Reviews* 1(3):169-176.

25. Cao A., "1993 William Allan Award Address" (1994) *Am. J. Hum. Genet.* 54:397-402.

26. Angastiniotis M.A. and Hadjiminas M.G., "Prevention of Thalassemia in Cyprus" (1980) *Lancet i*:369-370.

27. Loukopoulos D., Karababa Ph., Antsaklis A. et al., "Prenatal Diagnosis of Thalassemia and HbS Syndromes in Greece: An Evaluation of 1500 Cases" (1985) *Ann. N.Y. Acad. Sci.* 445:357-375.

28. Cao A., Furbetta M., Galanello R. et al., "Prevention of Homozygous ß-thalassemia by Carrier Screening and Prenatal Diagnosis in Sardinia" (1981) *Am. J. Hum. Genet.* 33:592-605.

29. Bianco I., Graziani B., Lerone M. et al., "Prevention of Thalassemia Major in Latium (Italy)" (1985) *Lancet ii*:888.

30. Milunsky A., ed.,*The Prevention of Genetic Disease and Mental Retardation.* (Philadelphia: W.B. Saunders Co., 1975)

31. Kanavakis E., Wainscoat J.S., Wood W.G. et al., "The Interaction of α–thalassemia with Heterozygous ß-thalassemia" (1982) *Br. J. Haemat.* 52:465.

32. Melis M.A., Pirastu M., Galanello R. et al., "Phenotypic Effect of Heterozygous α– and b°-thalassemia Interaction" (1983) *Blood* 62:226-229.

33. Rosatelli M.C., Falchi A.M., Scalas M.T. et al., "Hematological Phenotype of the Double Heterozygous State for α– and ß-thalassemia" (1984) *Hemoglobin* 8:25-35.

34. Old J.M., Fitches A., Heath C., et al., "First Trimester Fetal Diagnosis for the Haemoglobinopathies: Report on 200 Cases" (1986) *The Lancet* ii:763-766.

35. Petrou M., Modell B., "Prenatal Screening for Hemoglobin Disorders" (1995) *Pren. Diagn.* 15:1275-1295.

36. Verma I.C., "ß-thalassemia in India - Molecular Biology to Community Control", Personal Communication.

GENETIC SCREENING AND RESEARCH REVISITED

MARIE HIRTLE

RAPPORTEUR

Research Associate, Centre for Public Law Research (CRDP)

Université de Montréal

In her opening statement for the session on genetic screening and research, the president, Judith Hall, set out an impressive agenda. An agenda that is impressive because of the distinct and broad topics to be addressed and because of the pressing issues she identified. In this paper, I shall underscore the points of consensus and of disagreement that emerged from the presentations and discussions in an attempt to address one particular issue: are there any fundamental principles that can be uniformly applied to all forms of genetic screening and to all forms of genetic research? From the experience gained from screening programs and genetic research projects from a number of countries, the fundamental principle of informed consent emerged as the primary contentious issue. One of the consequences of this, as described below, is the uncertain lot of samples upon completion of the purpose they were collected for.

Individual informed consent has long been a recognised component of genetic screening programs with the widely accepted exception of routine screening of newborns that uses an informed refusal model. At least two developments have prompted a reassessment of consent requirements in screening programs. The first is the possibility that collected samples will be stored for further uses, and the second is the potential for expansion of neonatal screening programs to include predictive and carrier testing.

A strong point of consensus was quickly identified on the requirement to obtain informed consent for the future uses of residual identifiable tissue in genetic research and other types of research. Indeed, an increasing number of experts refer to "expanded consent requirements" when determining the ethical requirements for genetic research on stored samples that have retained identifiers. Consensus crumbled, however, on the issue of the consent requirements for further use of anonymous or anonymized samples.

Before highlighting certain aspects of the presentations and discussion as they relate to these issues, it is important to recall two fundamental tensions that underlie the topics addressed in this plenary. The first is the fundamental tension that exists between the interests of society and populations, on which public health programs are based, and the interests of individuals expressed in terms of autonomy and integrity of the person. The second fundamental tension exists between the desire to promote valuable research and the recognition that research may pose risks to individuals who participate hence the need to protect, to obtain consent and to recognise the concerns of participants. Working towards identifying fundamental principles for genetic screening and research will require a balancing of these competing interests.

The session opened with a presentation on newborn screening programs, a topic that clearly demonstrates how advances in human genetics offers new potential to an established procedure. The re-evaluation of the underlying principles that guide the ethical conduct of neonatal screening is timely. For the past quarter of a century, as Professor Dhondt pointed out, neonatal screening programs have been considered a routine public health program and the choice of diseases included in the programme followed clear and widely, if not universally, accepted criteria.[1] As this is a routine test, and a "public health activity", most classical neonatal screening programs do not require the individual consent of the parents but rather function with an informed refusal model of consent. Neonatal screening programs have, however, entered a new era as predictive or carrier status tests could be added to classical screening programs and bloodspots stored for use in genetic studies.

These developments disrupt the delicate balance maintained so far in classical screening programs between the interest of the individual and the interest of society. The recommendations of the French Association for Neonatal Screening[2] in reaction to the new French "bioethics" laws requiring informed consent for the taking of any specimens, are an important step in reassessing the issues raised by neonatal screening programs. Nonetheless, several points warrant further clarification. Firstly, the recommendation that experimental programs need to receive ethical review and individual informed consent of parents prior to testing is clearly in line with current expanded informed consent requirements. However, what constitutes an experimental program, and thus submitted to the more stringent legal and ethical requirements, remains unclear. Is a pilot program experimental? If a predictive test is added to a classical screening program (for example including CF testing) does this inclusion qualify as an "experimental program"?

Secondly, the recommendation that newborn bloodspots be destroyed as soon as routine testing is completed in order to prevent inappropriate use of stored samples is in stark contrast with practices in other countries. In fact, it is recognised that newborn bloodspots are valuable for research that ultimately could benefit society. Such a categorical rejection of all research and destruction of samples is certainly arguable especially if it is founded on the fear of possible misuse. Experience in other countries demonstrate that individuals may be protected from research risks through various security mechanisms while not impeding research completely. It remains controversial, however, if in addition to the protection offered by stripping identifiers from the sample, it is ethically required that individual consent be obtained for the anonymous uses of newborn bloodspots.

The Danish example, presented by Professor Bent Nørgaard-Pedersen, demonstrates a number of beneficial uses of a neonatal screening bloodspot register. Addressing this issue in the broader context of biobanks, that are comprehensively defined,[3] the Danish experience has the unique feature that its reflection on these issues started with a debate involving the general public and the press over the legal right to create a register of newborn bloodspots collected in screening programs. A consensus was reached about the accepted uses of the stored material that included quality assurance, anonymous statistical studies and genetic research. The Danish register also serves as a resource for paediatricians for studies, with parental consent, on unexpected disease or mortality (e.g. sudden infant death) in the infants' first years of life. As DNA mutation analyses increase, it is expected that the register will serve increasingly for this purpose.

Given the public debate and the enactment of specific legislation on registers, the Danish model for the further use of stored bloodspots presents some interesting features. In addition to legislation, specific administrative rules for the register were elaborated guided by principles such as ensuring protection of individuals, transparency and respect for the best interests of the child.[4] Parents also retain control over their newborns' stored bloodspot as they have a right to information, to ask that specific tests be done, to opt out of storage and to consent to specific research uses on nominative samples. The regional ethics committee must review and approve research projects and in some cases the parental consent requirement will be waived even if identifiers remain. In anonymous research, parental consent is not required since anonymity of samples protects the individual.

The outcome of samples is also an issue in some carrier or predictive screening programs or studies. Interestingly, in three cases discussed during the plenary there were three different outcomes for the collected samples: one program stores samples but no research is conducted, a study decided to destroy samples, and yet another opted to store them for prospective research.

The first program is the ß-thalassemia carrier and prenatal testing in southern Europe. As discussed by Antonio Cao, it is an example of a program that is successful in many different populations. Indeed, in contrast to the controversial carrier screening initiatives for diseases like cystic fibrosis and sickle cell, the ß-thalassemia program has succeeded in reducing the number of births affected per year from one hundred to five. This program may thus serve as an interesting model for other carrier screening programs. Some of its main features are the extensive information and education campaigns adapted to each population with respect to aspects such as language and religion, testing is voluntary and is carried out primarily on relatives of identified carriers who are encouraged to notify their families of the risk. Samples collected from these screening programs are stored but serve only for follow-up testing. Hence, no research is currently carried out on these samples, a situation that appears to be acceptable.

Greater concern was raised by two carrier and predisposition testing studies carried out in the US, as described by Elizabeth Thomson. The decision of the US government funding agency, the National Centre for Human Genome Research (NCHGR), with respect to the outcome of samples upon completion of these two studies were totally different although both were based on the principle that informed consent was required for storage and further use of samples. In the first study of population carrier screening for cystic fibrosis[5] it was decided, although not without opposition, that the 20,000 samples would be destroyed upon completion of the study. The decision to destroy the samples was based on a number of factors including the fact that it was almost impossible to re-contact participants to get their individual informed consent for storage.

In the second study, for predictive testing for breast, ovarian and colon cancer, samples were considered very valuable for future research. NCHGR similarly decided that if samples collected in the course of the study it funded were to be subsequently stored for further use, the informed consent had to be obtained at the time of sampling. Despite the fact that this measure further complicated an already complex consent process, NCHGR recommended that consent cover an important number of items, as presented by E. Thomson. As the cancer study is ongoing, the effect of these requirements are still unknown.

It is clear that the NCHGR requirement that informed consent of research participants be secured prior to banking residual tissue was intended to give individuals control over the outcome of their removed tissue samples. This decision of the NCHGR also demonstrates that funding agencies have an impact on the outcome of samples.

The issue of prospective uses of DNA samples for genetic research is examined by E.W. Clayton. She approaches this issue from the perspective of who should control the samples and whether and how samples collected in future are to be used in research.[6] A review of several recent policy positions has confirmed what the different examples cited above have demonstrated: control of the prospective uses of tissue samples does not lie exclusively with the researcher. Wide consensus exists to the effect that informed consent is necessary prior to use of identified or identifiable tissue sample in research, a position that detaches itself from past practices and should be commended. The role of ethics committees in the scientific and ethical review of research protocols is also becoming more widely accepted as, according to Clayton, considerable consensus exists to the effect that no matter how identifiable or non identifiable samples are, research protocols should receive ethical review.

Substantial disagreement and contrasting practices remain with respect to consent requirements for the future use of anonymous tissue. At the outset, the very definition of anonymous tissue remains ambiguous. In some cases, tissue is considered anonymous if the researcher does not have access to identifiers, while others consider that tissue is anonymous only if identifiers are irretrievably removed. Irrespective of these differences, Clayton considers that the exemption from informed consent and ethical review of the use of anonymous tissue raises concern. In the absence of at least ethical review, the control of whether and how research is conducted on these anonymous tissue samples resides principally with the investigator.

The question of whether informed consent should be sought at the time of collection for samples to be anonymized for research remains controversial. This issue will require further discussion as views are significantly divergent and may be based on different rationales as discussed below.

The plenary discussion following these presentations focused primarily on two themes: information and consent requirements for newborn screening and how expanded consent requirements will be implemented especially as regards previously stored tissue.

Distinct differences between jurisdictions were manifest on the issues of disclosure of information and requirement for consent in neonatal screening programs. Whereas some European experts think that parents can be over informed and caused unnecessary anxiety, the situation in the United States was definitely depicted as moving towards requiring the disclosure of much more information to parents.

The most common consent requirements for neonatal screening programs remains the informed refusal model. The newborn will be screened unless parents decide to opt out of the test. The primary justification for not obtaining individual informed consent was reconfirmed for programs in which tests are only for early onset treatable diseases such as PKU that are considered routine. Concern was expressed, however, over the experience in a number of countries showing that the information crucial in the informed refusal model, is not being assimilated by the parents so that, in fact, the informed tacit consent may indeed be more a "non-informed non-dissent".

In many jurisdictions where neonatal screening for treatable early onset diseases is considered routine, either explicitly through legislation or through standards of practice, a distinction is made with respect to new tests, such as carrier testing, that could be added to the program but which do not offer the same benefits to the infant. Individual informed consent for the new tests becomes a necessary condition as it is not a routine procedure. The addition of carrier testing to routine neonatal screening does not appear to be current practice, except in the US.

In the United States, there appears to be no consensus that the informed refusal model should continue to prevail. In at least one state, Maryland, the law requires that screening be offered rather than performed. This issue is becoming increasingly controversial in the US as new tests for carrier screening are added to classical screening programs. Carrier testing of newborns for diseases such as hemoglobinopathies, thalassemia or the breast cancer genes, provides information that goes beyond the immediate benefit of the child. Serious concern was raised regarding the need to offer parents the opportunity to reflect on the implications of receiving predictive information about their newborn., as increasing numbers of tests are being included in neonatal screening programs. These concerns should also be addressed by policy makers and health care professionals who make the decisions to include particular tests.

Several conclusions may be drawn from this discussion. First, there is considerable consensus that if testing is limited to early onset treatable diseases, then it is appropriate to use an informed refusal model of consent as this testing is in the newborn's best interest. Second, as soon as additional tests are to be included in the screening program under the same conditions for participation (informed refusal), then it is imperative that the new diseases screened for correspond to the criteria set out for classical screening programs.[7] As carrier testing provides information that is of little or no immediate benefit to the newborn, it seems difficult to justify its inclusion without re-evaluating the consent requirements. In these cases, not only should the individual informed consent of parents be obtained, but it may be appropriate to follow the more stringent requirements applicable to research involving children in order to ensure proper protection of newborn infants. Finally, in keeping with the best interests of newborns, it should be considered essential that routine screening programs not be jeopardised by the inclusion of additional tests that do not offer the same proven benefits to newborns that justify an informed refusal approach.

The second main topic of discussion was informed consent requirements for further use of stored tissue. Although the principle of an expanded informed consent for research uses of residual tissue obtained during medical care is widely accepted, its implementation raises several important, previously discussed, issues. A first and very practical concern regards the costs for researchers, institutions and ultimately governments, to conform to the expanded consent requirements in maintaining existing tissue banks. As it is almost impossible to get informed consent for already stored tissue, this raises a second related issue of the outcome of existing tissue repositories in which the samples are not stored according to emerging informed consent standards.

The field of research on pathological specimens emerged as an area facing important concerns. Pathology laboratories have been using identifiable slides of tissue for years to conduct extremely valuable research. Obtaining informed consent for storage of these identifiable samples in registries, such as tumour banks, and for research has not been the standard of practice. It is not clear if research projects using pathology samples need to obtain ethical review by an ethics committee. These repositories could be a valuable resource for genetic research but the emerging consent requirements would exclude the use of these samples.

It was clearly stated by several experts on the panel, that if in past practice pathology laboratories were not obliged to conform to ethical and legal research requirements, this practice must change as it is considered ethically and legally unacceptable. Despite these critical conditions, any intention of destroying stored samples was strongly disavowed. Nonetheless, all research projects intending to use biological samples should comply with the minimal ethical requirement of undergoing external review for scientific merit and ethical compliance. In addition, individual consent must be obtained for research on already stored tissue that is identifiable. Despite non-compliance in the past by pathologists, obtaining consent for the use of identifiable tissue has been an ethical and a legal requirement, at least in the US, for a number of years in the absence of waiver by an IRB. It was further recognised that requiring informed consent for the storage of residual tissue will entail substantial costs, evaluated at several million dollars in the US. It is foreseeable that such costs may be problematic and even prohibitive in certain situations or countries.

Several possible solutions to the problem of already stored pathological tissue were proposed. First, identifiers should be removed from the samples. Second, research on the stored tissue should be limited to diseases related to the disorder for which the sample was initially removed. Third, the protocols should be reviewed by an ethics committee for scientific merit and ethical appropriateness. Ultimately, it is the ethics committee that should decide, on a case by case basis, if consent can be waived.

Reflecting upon the exchanges of the participants in this plenary, one may conclude that the opinions regarding research on stored residual tissue obtained during medical care are diverse. The spectrum of positions ranges from the French example that recommends that valuable research material be destroyed for fear of misuses, to some practices in pathology where residual nominative tissue have been used without consent for years. Despite these divergent practices, a point of consensus is forcefully emerging: in a number of countries, the common understanding of the scope of informed consent has expanded to include the individual's right to consent to uses of her/his identifiable tissue samples other than those for which the sample was initially collected. In other words, it is widely recognised that individuals have the right to control identifiable bodily samples removed from the body and stored for further uses.

As for the consent requirements for research on anonymous or anonymized tissue, there are two competing positions. The first frames the issue primarily in terms of autonomy and individual control, hence, the need to obtain consent in order to anonymize tissue is absolute. The second position may be described as considering the issue in terms of solidarity and protection of participants from research risks. Informed consent is the primary mechanism for ensuring the protection of the individual. Using anonymous or anonymized samples is another mechanism of protection that is deemed sufficient for the protection of individuals in some cases.

Against this backdrop of controversy, and given the increasing international and collaborative nature of genetic research, further discussion will be required to develop a common ethical framework necessary for the conduct of ethical genetic screening and research.

References

1 See Dhondt J.L. and Farriaux J.P. in this volume at 285.

2 Id.

3 See Nørgaard-Pedersen in this volume at 303.

4 The Danish Medical Research Council, the Danish Central Scientific-Ethical Committee and the Danish Council on Ethics, *Health Science Information Banks - Biobanks* (The Danish Medical Research Council, the Danish Central Scientific-Ethical Committee and the Danish Council on Ethics: Denmark, 1996).

5 See Thomson E.J. in this volume at 313, for a complete discussion of the studies.

6 See Clayton E.W. in this volume at 291.

7 Supra note 1, TABLE 1.

COMMERCIALIZATION/PATENTS: INTRODUCTION

PETER LOWN (CHAIRPERSON)

Professor, Faculty of Law, University of Alberta

Many legal systems have had great difficulty translating moral issues into rules of law. Similarly, creating legal principles that can show some longevity against a backdrop of rapid technological change, had been a daunting task.

Combine both these factors, basic moral issues and rapid technological change, and legal policy makers have been at their most uncomfortable.

What creates this discomfort is the need to identify criteria or factors; to do so in a context in which the relevance and weight of those criteria vary; and to anticipate the relevance of those criteria over the course of a reasonable time period.

Usually, we accomplish the latter by generalized statements of principles from which specific applications can be drawn. We also feel comfortable working incrementally from a known context to a novel situation.

The scope and rate of change in genetic research is such that we have few, if any, readily available models from which to work. Nor do we have a clear consensus of the effects, short or medium term, of the few models we can use. For example, what processes can be patented, how wide should the claims be, and how will improvements be handled.

A good starting point is to lay out some general policy issues:

1. At what point do we draw a line separating prohibited from permitted activity? Is "control of life forms" the appropriate standard of demarcation?
2. If an activity is to be permitted, does it need to be specifically regulated, and if so how will the "public interest" be introduced and protected?
3. Can the requisite degree of research activity be generated without a significant private investment ? If private investment is necessary:
    - Will the industry develop guidelines or principles for the conduct of the activity and the control of the benefits from it?
    - What form will the return on investment take?

4. Are existing property and intellectual property regimes adequate to regulate the relationship among commercial participants, individual users and contributors, and other potential users of information and products? For example:
    - Is it possible to distinguish between research and diagnostic purposes?
    - Do current rules on ownership of source materials adequately respect privacy issues?
    - Are current methods of collection and usage consistent with principles of privacy?

Genetic research represents a quantum leap in methods and benefits. It holds out incredible promise for the future, but raises profound moral and legal issues.

The challenge to this conference and its participants is to assess the propriety and adaptability of existing regimes to an area rife with uncertainty. We should neither be frightened nor beguiled by the promise of pioneering activity, and we should try to bridge the gap between those on the frontier and those in the mainstream.

PATENTING OF HUMAN GENETIC SEQUENCES IN CANADA

RANDALL W. MARUSYK

MBM & Co./ Marusyk Bourassa Miller & Swain, Ottawa, Canada

ARIADNI ATHANASSIADIS

Candidate of McGill University's National Program

Introduction

Ever since the United States Supreme Court ruled that life forms can 'be invented', genetic engineering has been fuelling the growth of the biotechnology industry. However, the concomitant patenting of the resulting products, especially human based products, has also stimulated debate regarding the extent to which scientific enquiry and commercialism should be allowed to flourish where human genetics is concerned.

In Canada, the recent *Intellectual Property Improvement Act*[1] effected significant changes to the *Patent Act.*[2] Some of these changes affected the filing requirements for patent applications that claim as their inventions nucleotide sequences. Fulfilling these formalities and the basic disclosure requirements under the *Patent Act* form the cornerstone of human DNA sequence patentability. The current position of the Canadian Patent Office (CPO) is that such sequences, whether they comprise cDNA or genomic (native) DNA, are patentable in the same way as any other chemical compound.[3]

This paper outlines the legal framework in Canada that allows for the patenting of nucleotide sequences derived from human sources. The additional point addressed is that patentability should not be confused with the possible existence of property rights in human nucleotide sequences.

Policy Issues

The patentability of biotechnology products derived from living matter has not been subjected to the same kind of judicial and perhaps ethical scrutiny as has the patentability of whole living organisms. The key rests in the fact that once a component of living matter is extracted from its natural state, it must be the subject of some manipulation to be novel, nonobvious and of patentable utility. This may entail, for example, coating a seed with a herbicide, stabilizing a biomacromolecule in the appropriate buffer system, or establishing the appropriate delivery concentration of a substance for experimental or therapeutic purposes. Irrespective, the patent distinction is made that a substance derived from living matter is no longer in its natural state once it has been combined or treated with new substances, transformed morphologically, or simply isolated from substances it may have normally been associated with *in vivo.*

Policy issues arise with respect to the patenting of products derived from living matter when such products have their origins in human tissue. The argument against patenting in these instances has, however, only served to technically misinform the question of the inherent patentability of genetic material, instead of focusing on the underlying ethical argument of common heritage for the human species. The confused debate is clearly manifest in the predicament of patent applicants who have developed cell lines from the tissue of aboriginal peoples and consequently been accused of bioprospecting.[4] In particular, a discussion of patent rights in human tissue or components thereof often simultaneously and confusingly invokes the separate issue of traditional common law property rights in such substances.[5] Patents and ownership rights in living matter, however, should not to be confused. Obtaining a patent does not give one the right to own a tangible thing, but rather the right to stop others, for a limited period of time, from making, working or selling a patent holder's invention without permission.

The Canadian *Patent Act*

A Canadian patent can only be granted under the *Patent Act* and this statute is intended to encourage economic development which benefits the public. The rights embodied by a patent flow entirely, exclusively and solely from the statute, including the patent holder's right to exclude others from making, using or selling the patented invention for 20 years after the patent application's filing date.[6]

Canadian patents can be obtained for a product, a process of manufacture or a method of use. In general terms, these types of patents may cover tangible objects, new ways of arriving at products and new uses for already known products. Common examples of product patents involving human genetic sequences include cell lines established from carcinomas or human tissue, non-human cells containing human genes, or the nucleotide sequences themselves. Gene therapy is an example of a method of treating the human body, whereas the biosynthesis of human insulin using bacteria containing the recombinant insulin gene is an example of a patentable process.

REQUIREMENTS FOR OBTAINING A CANADIAN PATENT

The *Patent Act* states that "...any inventor...may, on presentation to the Commissioner of a petition setting out the facts...obtain a patent granting to the applicant an exclusive property in the invention."[7] The proposed subject of the patent must, therefore, meet the definition of an **invention** under section 2 as follows:

> "invention" means any new and useful art, process, machine, manufacture or composition of matter, or any new and useful improvement in any art, process, machine, manufacture or composition of matter;

A patentable invention must be, by definition under the *Patent Act, novel* and useful. Case law has imported a requirement for ingenuity[8] as well as general policy considerations regarding the inherent patentability of the subject matter in question. All four conditions **must** be satisfied in order to obtain a patent in Canada. The following paragraphs present a review of the four conditions for patentability and how claims to human derived nucleotide sequences can be framed to meet these standards.

SUBJECT MATTER

Under the *Patent Act*, the patentability of subject matter that has passed the tests for novelty, nonobviousness and utility is circumscribed by two statutory exceptions. The first of these relates to the now defunct situations involving foods and medicines. Under subsection 39(1), no claim could be made for food or medicine if derived from a naturally occurring substance prepared or produced or significantly derived from microbiological processes. However, since 1991 this provision has not been operative so that foods or medicines have had the same access to patent protection as other inventions. The second exception, provided for under subsection 27(3), specifies that if an invention constitutes a scientific principle or abstract theorem, it is not patentable.[9]

Moreover, the scope of unpatentable subject matter has been expanded by the CPO, upon reflection of Canadian case law dealing with patentable subject matter. Their express position as stated in the Manual of Patent Office Practice (MOPOP)[10] reflects the CPO's interpretation of the *Patent Act* and case law. Chapter 12 of the MOPOP stipulates what kinds of subject matter they consider to be patentable under section 2 of the *Patent Act*. With regard to living matter, medical treatments, diagnostic methods and intellectual matter, section 12.03.01 of the MOPOP provides:

a) Plants and animals are not patentable subject matter.

b) Subject matter being a process of treating living humans or animals by surgery or therapy is excluded by Section 2. The exclusion does not cover methods of testing which do not relate to any step of actual treatment or vital function of the body. Articles or apparatus designed for use in the treatment of humans or animals may be patentable...

In relation to living matter, specifically, section 12.03.02 further states that:

> Inventions for new microbial life forms such as bacteria, yeast, moulds, fungi, actinomycetes, algae, cell lines, viruses and

> protozoa may be patentable. Processes for producing and utilizing microbial life forms may be patentable. To be patentable, such inventions must fully satisfy Section 34(1) and all other requirements of the *Patent Act.*
>
> Inventions for new plants and animals are not patentable. Processes for producing plants and animals which require significant technical intervention by man may be patentable. Traditional biological breeding processes used for the production of plants and animals are considered essentially natural biological processes and are not patentable.

The recent amendments to the *Patent Rules* now allow for the deposit of biological material to supplement the general disclosure requirements of a patent application. This significantly enhances the ease of obtaining meaningful patent protection for biotechnology inventions since the deposit of biological material increases the chances of meeting the statute's patentability requirements.

Therefore, at the very outset there is no outright prohibition under the statute case law, or in the policy practice of the CPO, restricting the patentability of human nucleotide sequences or suggesting that such sequences are improper subject matter.

The recent decision by the Commissioner of Patents to reject the patent application for the 'Harvard Mouse' supports this conclusion.[11] Canadian patent application number 484, 723 (class 195-1.22), filed on June 21, 1985 [hereinafter 'Harvard Mouse'].[12] In the Examiner's Final Action it was posited that "the Commissioner has both the right and an obligation to consider the public interest in the granting of a patent."[13] The implication that "the Commissioner can decide that a particular invention can be found unpatentable as a matter of policy or discretion rather than as a result of an interpretation of the provisions of the Act," was, however, rejected by the Commissioner of Patents.[14] On a plain reading of section 42 of *Patent Act,*[15] there is no issue of discretion; the Commissioner must justify refusing a patent application by indicating that it is clearly without substantial foundation based on an interpretation of the *Patent Act* and any applicable jurisprudence.[16] This duty arises from the Supreme Court decision in *Monsanto Co.* v. *Commissioner of Patents*[17] which concluded that there is no residual discretion on public policy.

The Commissioner of Patents' review of the "Harvard Mouse" patent application was informed primarily by the *Pioneer Hi-Bred* decision[18] Despite the deliberate refusal of the Supreme Court in *Pioneer Hi-Bred* to decide whether a soybean plant resulting from artificial cross-breeding was a patentable invention, the Commissioner of Patents placed greater stock on the preceding Federal Court of Appeal ruling[19] that a cross bred variety of soybean was not a manufacture or composition of matter within the meaning of 'invention' under section 2 of the *Patent Act.* In short, the distinction between a process of nature constituting a mere discovery and the degree of intervention necessary to constitute an invention was used to defeat the applicant's appeal. Although the Commissioner of Patents was prepared to construe the meaning ascribed to a 'composition of matter' broadly to include genetic engineering techniques, the *Abitibi* decision[20] was revisited to apply the criterion of reproducibility. The narrow view of the line drawn by *Abitibi*, that any 'human' matter more complex than unicellular or undifferentiated cellular life cannot be patented, was maintained. That is, whereas sperm and eight-cell embryos,[21] cell-lines derived from human sources or transformed with human DNA may be patented, in the "Harvard Mouse" application the inventors did not "have full control over all the characteristics of the resulting mouse."[22] As such, a composition of matter could not include a non-human mammal, because human intervention in this instance only ensured that reproducibility extended "***as far as the cancer forming gene.***"[emphasis added][23]

What does this mean with regard to whether human genetic material is proper subject matter under Canadian Law? Although the decision of the Commissioner of Patents illustrates the reluctance of Canadian patenting practice to admit the patentability of higher life-forms under the relevant case law, the same decision accepts the patentability of nucleotide sequences as commonplace and not affected by their origins.[24] Therefore, there is no basis to 'read in' restrictions on the patentability of either human or non-human nucleotide sequences under CPO practice, statute, or case law.

NOVELTY, OBVIOUSNESS AND UTILITY

The test for *novelty* examines disclosure of the invention *as claimed in the petition* and not as disclosed in, for example, existing scientific publications which constitute prior art. However, novelty may be manifested by reference to prior art which helps to identify the presence, absence or improvement of any and all elements relevant to a claim. This last point, therefore, admits claims to improvements on patented inventions, as long as such improvements meet the basic requirements of patentability and do not embrace that, which on a fair construction of the specification, is already within the public domain.[25]

The test of *obviousness* attempts to determine whether a person skilled in the relevant art would have been inexorably led to the invention without undue experimentation, on the basis of common knowledge and other specified prior information. The test asks whether a person with no scintilla of imagination would be capable of creating the invention.[26] If the answer is 'yes', the invention is obvious and, therefore, not patentable.

Finally, for the purposes of patentability an invention must either be useful for solving a practical problem or have commercial value. If someone skilled in the relevant art can take a patent specification and apply it to such benefit, then the invention has *utility*. There is no formal obligation upon the patentee to establish the utility of the invention. Utility is a question of fact that stands to be decided, on the basis of the disclosure, by those having the technical skill and knowledge to understand the subject of the patent application. However, reducing an invention to practice, especially where biotechnology products are concerned, is often critical since this may be the only way that an invention's utility may become apparent.

A commonly held view is that human nucleic acid sequences are said to be part of our 'common heritage'; the isolation and knowledge of the sequences themselves is seen as having no immediately apparent commercial use. How then, can such sequences, technically speaking, be patentable under the *Patent Act*? The answer, as revealed by case law, rests in what constitutes a discovery versus an invention.

Patents may not issue for a disembodied idea or a simple disclosure resulting from the mere use of one's observational and analytical skills.[27] In essence, a discovery cannot be patented unless it is an element of a method of practical application. This is simply an approach to inventiveness asserting that just 'stumbling' upon something lacks the requisite expenditure of effort and creative input to warrant proprietary protection.[28] The distinction between an invention and a mere discovery has been imported from English case law,[29] but its conceptualization has nonetheless been difficult for the judiciary.[30]

In *Continental Soya Company Limited* v. *J.R. Short Milling Company (Canada) Limited*[31] the Supreme Court of Canada allowed claims to a naturally occurring enzyme isolated from the soybean plant for use as a flour bleaching agent. The discovery of the soybean enzyme as it existed in nature was held to be the starting point for the development of methods for extracting the enzyme and preserving its activity for use as an effective bleaching agent in the manufacture of bread. It was concluded that the production of a naturally occurring enzyme in a stabilized, purified state constituted an invention that was patentable, both as a product and as a process that was new and useful in the patent sense. Commenting on the distinction between a discovery and an invention Sir Lyman P. Duff C.J.C. quoted the following from Luxmoore, Moulton and Boyer J.J.:[32]

> [I]t has been laid down that a patent cannot be obtained for a discovery in the strict sense. If, however, the patented article or process has not actually been anticipated, so that the effect of the claims is not to prevent anything being done which has been done or proposed previously, the discovery which led to the patentee devising a process of apparatus may well supply the necessary element of invention required to support a patent. This is certainly the case if it can be shown that, apart from the discovery, there would have been no apparent reason for making the variation in the former practice.[33]

Therefore, if the practical application of a discovery can be patented, then 'discovery', as a "concomitant creature of invention,"[34] may reveal the ingenuity that went into the development of a new and inventive use for a 'natural' product.

This reasoning was further refined in the decision of *Shell Oil Company* v. *Commissioner of Patents*[35] wherein a patent on a plant growth regulating composition, consisting of previously known compounds combined with an appropriate adjuvant, was at issue. Although the claims did not refer to the composition's new use, but to the new combination alone, the claims were allowed. The Court held that the inventive step resided in the new use for the compounds as taught in the disclosure.[36] It was acknowledged on all sides of this case that there was nothing inventive about the actual act of mixing the compounds with the plant growth regulating properties with an adjuvant commonly used in compositions applied to plants. In fact, the patent had previously been denied because the composition claims had not been inventively distinguished from the existing compound claims. However, in the end, the claims to the new composition were the practical embodiment of the knowledge; they were "a new and useful art" because the knowledge had been applied to effect a desired or intended result, with an undisputed commercial value. The Court stated that "the combination [was] simply the means of realizing on the newly discovered potential of the compounds" and that beyond the discovery, "no further inventive step [was] required in the application of the compounds to that use."[37]

The classic distinction in respect of this matter has been extracted from the English decision of *Reynolds* wherein Buckley J. stated that:

> Discovery adds to the amount of human knowledge, but it does so only by lifting the veil and disclosing something which before had been unseen or dimly seen. Invention also adds to human knowledge, but not merely by disclosing something. Invention necessarily involves also the suggestion of an act to be done, and it must be an act which results in a new product, or a new result, or a new process, or a new combination for producing an old product or an old result.
>
> [T]he idea that leads to an invention is ... not part of the invention. The idea must stimulate the inventor to do something else. It is the something further which he does which is the invention.[38]

In this way, case law dictates that although a nucleic acid sequence may not be 'new' in nature it can be 'new' in the patentable sense. Therefore, a patent application just describing the discovery of a naturally occurring gene would fail. If on the other hand, the patent application described a method of isolating and purifying the gene, in addition to a new and inventive use for the nucleotide sequence, the threshold for patentability should be met.

With regards to obviousness, what may be obvious today, however, was not so obvious at some point in the past. By extension, then, today's invention may at some point become the future's routine. The evolution of 'the obvious' where biotechnology is concerned is necessarily a matter to be extracted from case law. For example, the U.S. decision of *Ex Parte Erlich*[39] is the culmination of Cetus' unsuccessful ten year attempt to patent monoclonal antibodies specific to human fibroblast interferon. Whether this decision of the U.S. Patent and Trademark Office to deny the patent was soundly rationalized or not, it nonetheless illustrates how the straight application of certain methodologies may be insufficient for procuring patent rights without some inventive element or result to such application.[40] This and other American decisions are relevant to Canadian law because the tests for obviousness are very similar in both countries. In all instances such matters will turn on the facts as revealed by the disclosure of the invention in the patent application. Whereas a disclosure of routine hybridoma technology to produce a monoclonal antibody against a known antigen may be obvious, the disclosure of an application of the same technology to produce a monoclonal antibody against a previously unknown antigen or with a novel specificity may reveal a patentable invention.[41]

This same sort of reasoning could conceivably be extended some day to the patenting of genetic sequences. The automated refinement and improved efficiency of sequencing has not changed the technology in any fundamental respects. Today's general sequencing is "a useful but straightforward extension of a technique that has been in use on a smaller scale for years."[42] If the upshot of this is that the patentability of nucleic acid sequences is utility based,[43] then the novelty and nonobviousness of a nucleic acid sequence claimed as an invention will likely hinge upon and, therefore, will likely only be fully disclosed upon the manifestation of patentable utility. At the same time, however, although the utility of a genetic sequence remains a question of fact, it will likely not exclusively entail, nor at a minimum require, establishing the actual biological function of the gene to which it maps.[44]

FORMAL DISCLOSURE REQUIREMENTS

The amendments brought about by the *Intellectual Property Improvement Act* will now require a patent application that includes either amino acid or nucleotide sequences to disclose such sequences in both paper and electronic form. The regulations under the *Patent Rules* will closely reflect WIPO Standards ST.23 and ST.24 and a version of the computer program "PATENTIN" will be adopted as the official formatting program with which to meet the electronic sequence requirements.

The amendments to the *Patent Act* also allow for the deposit of biological material to supplement the general disclosure requirements of a patent application. This significantly enhances the likelihood of obtaining meaningful patent protection for biotechnology inventions since the deposit of biological material increases the chances for meeting the statute's patentability requirements.

These amendments were enacted, in part, as a response to the Supreme Court of Canada's decision[45] in *Pioneer Hi-Bred.* In this decision, the *Abitibi* decision allowing a biological deposit to serve as a substitute for an incomplete s. 36(1) disclosure requirement was rejected. However, the Court did appear to appreciate the negative impact such a decision could have on scientific research in Canada, as manifest by the following reasoning by Lamer J.:

> I would simply say that my observations should not be taken as directed at patent applications for micro-organisms, though such practice had never been endorsed by Canadian courts ... the practice of a deposit is simply intended to require the applicant submitting a process involving a micro-organism unknown and inaccessible to the public as a necessary part of reproducing the invention to deposit a culture of the micro-organism with the authorities.[46]

This statement is qualified by the suggestion that "[i]t might be in certain circumstances, that the deposit may contribute to complete the description" even though this was not "applicable to the case at bar."[47] Therefore, the introduction of section 38.1 of the *Patent Act* is consistent with the depository situation found in earlier case law and brings Canada's patent laws dealing with the deposit of biological material in line with the laws of other countries that are signatories to the *Budapest Treaty on the International Recognition of the Deposit of Microorganisms for the Purposes of Patent Procedure.*[48] Use of the word "shall" in subsection 38.1(1), signals Parliament's intent to permit biological deposits to supplement the disclosure requirements under the *Patent Act* as follows:

> Where a specification refers to the deposit of biological material and the deposit is in accordance with the regulations, the deposit shall be considered part of the specification and, to the extent that subsection 27(3) cannot otherwise reasonably be complied with, the deposit shall be taken into consideration in determining whether the specification complies with the subsection.

This provision does not, however, create a presumption that such a deposit is required if reference to one is made in a patent application. A written description in an application will likely to continue to be sufficient to meet the disclosure requirement for a patent.[49] However, when the text of a patent application does not "enable any person skilled in the art or science to which it pertains, or with which it is most closely connected, to make, construct, compound or use" an invention, the CPO **must** take the deposit of biological material, such as a plasmid containing a given genetic sequence, into consideration when determining whether a petition's disclosure requirements have been met.

DISTINGUISHING PATENTABILITY FROM PROPERTY RIGHTS IN HUMAN GENETIC MATERIAL

The biotechnology industry relies heavily on human source material, especially at the sub-cellular level, to develop new products and procedures. But what property rights, if any, exist in human tissue and bodily substances that are used by the industry?[50] More generally, if the biotechnology industry already operates on the premise that human tissue and bodily substances can be owned *vis-a-vis* patents, then what property rights, if any, exist in the actual starting material.[51]

The strong resistance of the Canadian legal system to recognize property rights in the human body has been based largely on an understandable distaste to confront issues of human objectification or threats to the integrity of human dignity. Viewed in the harsh light of historical context, the courts have only directly addressed such issues when slavery was legal, or when the sexual and physical assault of one's wife was merely considered a property violation.[52] However, the same concerns underlying this property debate should not by some misapplied (although not necessarily misplaced) extension, be used to negatively affect the administration of the current patent regime. Any ambiguity or controversy surrounding the distinct issue of according property rights in human matter should not confuse the technical application of the *Patent Act* to biotechnology products derived from human matter, including those inventions encompassing human genetic sequences.

Irrespective of whether tissue donation and transplant statutes in Canada adequately serve their primary purpose,[53] they provide only a rudimentary legal framework to address what, if any, rights exist in human matter, as used in research or by the biotechnology industry.[54] As biotechnology companies continue to secure patents over new products derived from human matter, even if one assumes that such patents are valid, the enjoyment of any rights flowing therefrom could be affected if the donors of the original human sources asserted ownership rights down the road.

In dealing with the question of property rights in human tissue or bodily substances and any consequent problems securing unencumbered patent protection, the assumption is that no matter by what means the human matter was procured, consent for such procurement was properly and legally obtained.[55] Without proper legal consent the possibility exists that any property rights that could exist in the tissue or bodily substances remain vested in the original donor. In such a situation, there is risk of exposure to legal action based on, for example, breach of a duty to disclose facts material to the donor's consent or the abuse of another individual's property.[56]

Does the common law allow for property rights to be recognized in human tissue and bodily substance acquired by *inter vivos* transaction? The paucity of case law in Canada forces us to look towards other common law jurisdictions for guidance. The Supreme Court of California decision in

Moore[57] leads us to conclude that, at common law, no property rights exist in tissue and bodily substances obtained by *inter vivos* transaction. Partial support for this position is found in recommendations expressed in the report by Canada's Royal Commission on New Reproductive Technologies.[58] In this report, it was urged that such tissue and bodily substances acquired from "reproductive material should never be characterized as property, because terms such as 'ownership' and 'property' suggest that human zygotes can be treated as objects, which is contrary to principles such as respect for human life and dignity and non-commercialization of reproduction."[59] However, it would appear that under the various provincial human tissue statutes it is possible to create some form of property rights in blood and blood constituents, and in regenerative tissues, including blood, skin, hair, bone marrow, a variety of body fluids, possibly the liver and in other limited circumstances, human growth hormone.[60]

The *Human Tissue (Gift/Donation) Acts*,[61] and in Québec the *C.C.Q or* C.C.L.C.,[62][hereinafter *C.C.L.C.*],[63] [hereinafter *C.C.Q.*],[64] are the major pieces of legislation that govern the use and control of human tissues and substances.[65] In short, care must be exercised in determining the type and degree of property rights that have been created in such tissue and bodily substances based on: (1) the method, (2) the jurisdiction, and (3) the date of acquisition. In all Canadian jurisdictions, provisions pertaining or applicable to human tissue statutes are not retroactive.[66] Therefore, the procurement of human matter that occurred prior to any statute coming into force will continue to be lawful.[67] Care must be taken, therefore, to ensure that any tissue obtained prior to the enactment of the current statute is not still governed by an earlier human tissue statute.

Other statutes that touch upon the use and control of human tissue and bodily substances, include the respective provincial versions of the *Anatomy Acts*,[68] the *Coroners Acts*,[69] and the *Cemeteries/Burials Acts*.[70] The underlying mechanism employed by these statutes is the grant of temporary possessory rights in the cadaver to facilitate its prescribed use under these laws.[71] This entails either permitting the executor of the deceased to dispose of the body in a proper manner,[72] or the cadaver's use in research and teaching.[73] No property rights are created under these statutes. It is likely that this 'no property rule' applies equally to any tissue or bodily substances, including cellular material or genetic material that may be directly obtained from cadavers. In Québec, the *Public Health Protection Act* and *An Act Respecting the Determination of The Causes and Circumstances of Death*,[74] operate as Québec's equivalent to the common law provinces' *Anatomy Acts* and *Coroners Acts*, respectively.

Conclusions

The issue of patentability must not be confused with the possible existence of property rights in nucleic acid sequences, especially in the human context.

In contrast to patent rights, the question of property rights existing in human DNA will be determined by the source, time and place of its procurement, and is largely grounded in provincial legislation and case law that focuses primarily on a non-proprietary regime of tissue procurement for transplantation. From a biotechnological standpoint, this is currently the only available legal framework from which to address the application of proprietary rights to human tissue, procured *inter vivos*, as an initial source for the isolation of nucleic acids.

The relevance of the foregoing considerations rests in whether the biotechnology industry can be legally prevented from using certain human tissues as a source of genetic material, irrespective of any patents held. The important first step is to determine what, if any, rights exist in the particular tissue and bodily substances. If a legal determination is made that no rights exist, then any other's claims of ownership or proprietary interest in that tissue are likely without legal foundation. However, if one suspects that some form of property rights exist in a given tissue or substance, the key elements in the determination of such rights are: (1) the source of the tissue or substance, (2) the jurisdiction of its acquisition, and (3) the date of its acquisition.[75] When the source of tissue or substances is acquired from an *inter vivos* transaction that originated outside of Canada, private international law dictates what laws govern and what rights exist in such tissue and bodily substances.

Once a determination is made that some form of property rights may exist in a given tissue sample or bodily substance, it is necessary to determine who owns those rights and whether proper legal consent to use such tissue or bodily substances has been or can be obtained. Full and informed consent should be obtained from the actual donor, the donor's trustee, or executor.

The importance of obtaining full and informed consent was recently illustrated when the U.S. Centers for Disease Control and Prevention filed a patent application for an immortalized human cell line that originated from the blood sample of a Panamanian tribeswoman.[76] Despite the fact that oral consent had been obtained from the woman, the Canadian-based Rural Advancement Foundation International (a group that supports the rights of indigenous people) launched a complaint that the patent application amounted to "bio-piracy". This case scenario and others like it illustrate that even with informed consent larger policy issues remain to be resolved regarding the attachment of proprietary rights to human tissue and bodily substances.[77]

Once it is determined that no proprietary rights exist in a given human genetic sequence, attention is then shifted towards ensuring that a full and adequate disclosure of the invention is provided for in a patent application on such a sequence.[78] Nucleic acid sequences, whether they have their origins in human sources or otherwise, are patentable subject matter in Canada like any other chemical substance. Sequences so claimed must meet the *Patent Act*'s and case law's requirements of patentable subject matter, novelty, nonobviousness, and utility. The occurrence of nucleic acids in nature and the somewhat routine or predictable character of the recombinant DNA technologies used to facilitate their isolation and elucidate their sequences, make adequate disclosure a matter which will likely increase the importance of establishing patentable utility.

Endnotes and References

1 S.C. 1993, c.15 [hereinafter *Intellectual Property Improvement Act*].

2 R.S.C. 1985, c. P-4 as am.[hereinafter *Patent Act*]; C.R.C. 1978, c.1250 as am. [hereinafter *Patent Rules*]. The new regulations came into force on October 1, 1996.

3 Discussion with Canadian Patent Office; also see McMahon E., "Nucleic Acid Sequences and Other Naturally Occurring Products: Are They Patentable in Canada" (1993), 10 *C.I.P.R.* 11.

4 Anderson C., "While CDC Drops Indian Tissue Claim" (1993), 262 *Science* 831 where the patenting of a cell line derived from a tissue sample of a Panamanian tribeswoman was said to amount to "bio-piracy"; RAFI,"Following Protest, Patent Claim Withdrawn on Guaymi Indian Cell Line" (1994), 9 *GeneWATCH* 6 and RAFI, "New Questions About Management and Exchange of Human Tissues at NIH" (1996), 10 *GeneWATCH* 14.

5 Marusyk R.W. and M.S. Swain, "A Question Of Property Rights in the Human Body" (1989), 21. *Ottawa L Rev* 2; Swain M.S. and R.W. Marusyk, "An Alternative to Property Rights in Human Tissue" (1990), 20(5) *Hastings Center Report* 12; Marusyk R.W., "Biotechnologie, Tissu Humain et le Nouveau Code Civil du Québec"(1993), 6 *Les cahiers de propriété intellectuelle* 99 and Swain M.S. and R.W. Marusyk, "Biotechnology, Human Tissue and the Civil Code of Québec" (1995), 55 *R. du B.* 419; Litman M. and G. Robertson, "The Common Law Status of Genetic Material" and Hirtle M., "Civil Law and the Status of Human Genetic Material" in Knoppers B.M., T. Caulfield and T.D. Kinsella, eds., *Legal Rights and Human Genetic Material* (Toronto: Edmond Montgomery, 1996) at 51 and 85, respectively.

6 Inventions for which patents were filed prior to October 1, 1989 are governed under an earlier regime of the *Patent Act*, enjoying 17 years of protection from the date of grant.

7 Supra note 2 at s.27(1).

8 The judicial interpretation that established a requirement for inventiveness has now been codified into the *Patent Act*.

9 *Patent Act* as amended by *An Act to Implement the North American Free Trade Agreement*, S.C. 1993, c.44, s.192. Prior to this time section 27(3) also prohibited the patenting of anything that was "for an illicit purpose."

10 Canadian Patent Office, *Manual of Patent Office Practice* (Ottawa: Supply and Services Canada, 1989).

11 In 1988 the United States became the first country in the world to grant a patent for higher life forms. A U.S. patent was granted to Harvard University for a genetically engineered (transgenic) mouse, used in breast cancer research.

12 This recognition of a genetically engineered animal as an invention has since been accorded elsewhere. In Canada, the Final Office Action of the Examiner rejected the patent application and consequently the issue was put before the Commissioner of Patents which upheld the Examiner's decision on August 4, 1995. The case has been appealed to the

Federal Court, Trial Division, (Notice of Appeal, Ct. No. T-275-96, filed 2 February 1996).

13 Commissioner of Patents, ibid., at 2.

14 Ibid.

15 Section 42 of the *Patent Act*, supra note 2, reads: Whenever the Commissioner is satisfied that an applicant is not **by law** entitled to be granted a patent he shall refuse the application and, by registered letter addressed to the applicant or his registered agent, notify the applicant of such refusal and of the ground or reason therefor. [emphasis added]

16 See *Vanity Fair Silk Mills* v. *Commissioner of Patents*, [1938] 4 D.L.R. 657, [1939] S.C.R. 245 at 246 and Commissioner of Patents, supra note 12 at 3.

17 [1979] 2 S.C.R. 1108, 42 C.P.R. (2d) 161 at 177.

18 [1989] 1 S.C.R. 1623 [hereinafter *Pioneer Hi-Bred*].

19 *Pioneer Hi-Bred Ltd.* v. *Commissioner of Patents* (1987) 14 *C.P.R.* (3d) 491 (F.C.A.).

20 *Re: Application Abitibi* (1982), 62 C.P.R. (2d) 81 [hereinafter *Abitibi*].

21 The embryo is undifferentiated up until this stage.

22 Commissioner of Patents, supra note 12 at 7.

23 Commissioner of Patents, supra note 12 at 7. The Commissioner of Patents put the matter as follows: Since the plasmids and the transgenic unicellular material are produced under the full control of the inventor and are reproducible, I am satisfied that they are a "manufacture" or a "composition of matter" under Section 2 of the Act. I note that no objections, based on Section 2, were raised against such claims in the instant application.

24 Ibid. Although the claims at issue only included the genetic construct incorporating the murine c-*myc* gene used to develop the oncomouse, the petition's summary of the invention presented the process being claimed as one capable of being performed with, amongst others, a number of listed human oncogene sequences, see Notice of Appeal, supra note 12 at 3-4.

25 *White and Toms* (1868), 37 L.J. Ch. 204; *Acetylene Illuminating Co. Ltd. v. United Alkali Co. Ltd.* (1905) 22 R.P.C. 145; *Waterhouse's Patent* (1906), 23 R.P.C. 55; *Crost waite Fire Bar Syndicate Ltd. v. Senior* (1909), 26 R.P.C. 713 at 730; *Sherbrooke Machinery Co. v. Hydraulic Machinery Co.*, [1927] Ex. C.R. 114; *Bergeron v. De Kermor Electric Heating Co.*, [1927] Ex. C.R. 181; *Electric Telegraph Co. v. Brett* (1851), 10 C.B. 838.

26 *Baxter Travenol Laboratories of Canada Ltd. v. Cutter (Canada) Ltd.* (1983), 68 C.P.R. (2d) 179, 45 N.R. 393 (F.C.A.); *Farbwerke Hoechst A.G. v. Halocarbon* (Ont.) Ltd., [1979] 2 S.C.R. 929, 42 C.P.R. (2d) 145; *Ernest Scragg & Sons Ltd. v. Leesona Corp.*, [1964] Ex. C.R. 649, 45 C.P.R. 1; *Beloit v. Valmet* (1986), 8 C.P.R. (3d) 289 (F.C.A.); *Beecham v. Proctor & Gamble* (1982), 61 C.P.R. (2d) 1 (F.C.A.).

27 See *Reillo Canada Inc.* v. *Lambert* (1986), 3 F.T.R. 23 (FCTD). This case provides a concise overview of the key decisions and tests addressing the distinction between a discovery and an invention.

28 The distinction between discovery and invention is especially pertinent to inventions involving human body components where the medical research has previously elucidated the structure, function and role of the component. Given the requirement that an invention be a 'new composition of matter,' it could be argued that a patent should not

issue, or is invalid for a naturally occurring (especially previously described) product of the human body.

29 *Reynolds v. Herbert Smith & Co., Ltd.* (1903), 20 R.P.C. 123 (Ch. D.) [hereinafter *Reynolds*]; *Hickton's Patent Syndicate v. Patents and Machine Improvements Co.* (1909), 26 R.P.C. 339; *In re May & Baker Ltd. and Ciba Ltd.* (1948), 65 R.P.C. 255.

30 Fox H.G., *The Canadian Law and Practice Relating to Letters Patent for Inventions*, 4th ed., (Toronto: Carswell, 1969) at 88. Confusion arises "when discovery is contrasted with invention in the sense of those words as involving mental acts," and not in reference "to subject matter as it affects the content of a patent grant." For example, reference in some case law to an invention realized by "mere accidental discovery," see *Smith v. Goldie* (1883), 9 S.C.R. 46 at 60, directly conflicts with doctrine establishing that a discovery alone does not amount to invention.

31 [1942] S.C.R. 187, 2 C.P.R. 1, 2 D.L.R. 114 (S.C.C.) [hereinafter *Continental Soya* cited to S.C.R].

32 Luxmmoore Lord Justice, H. Fletcher Moulton and A.W. Bowyer, *Treatise on Patents and Inventions*, 24 Hals. (2d), para. 1123, p. 591.

33 Supra note 31 at 190.

34 Fox, supra note 30.

35 [1982] 2 S.C.R. 536, 67 C.P.R. (2d) 1 (S.C.C.) [hereinafter *Shell Oil* cited to S.C.R].

36 Ibid., at 538-542. This was based on the case law of *Commissioner of Patents v. Farbwerke Hescht Aktiengesellschaft Vormals Meister Lucius & Bruning* [1964] S.C.R. 49 [hereinafter *Farbwerke*]. In *Farbwerke*, the essential inventive feature of the anti-diabetic drug composition was in the medicinally active chemical compounds and not in the commonly applied dilution practice using a given carrier. By extension the proposition that there is no inventive ingenuity in the mixing of a compound with a carrier was derived. This case may be distinguished from *Burton Parsons Chemicals Inc. v. Hewlett Packard* (Canada) Ltd. [1976] 1 S.C.R. 555 where an electrocardiogram cream composition and its process of manufacture were patentable because the inventive ingenuity was in the decision to combine the components in question. See also, *Jules R. Gilbert Ltd. v. Sandoz Patents Ltd.* (1970), 64 C.P.R. 14 (Ex. Ct.), aff'd [1974] S.C.R. 1336 and *Agripat S.A. v. Commissioner of Patents* (1977), 52 C.P.R. (2d) 229.

37 Supra note 35 at 548-549.

38 *Reynolds*, supra note 29 at 126-127.

39 (1986) 3 U.S.P.Q. (2d) 1011, (1992) 22 U.S.P.Q. (2d) 1463.

40 McGough K.J. and D.P. Burke, "The End of Monoclonal Patents?" (1993), 12 *Biotechnology Law Report* 6. The key decision which supported Cetus's contention that monoclonal antibody technology was unobvious was that of *Ex Parte Old*, (1981) 229 U.S.P.Q. 196.

41 Carton J.K., "The Fate of Patenting Hybridomas and Monoclonal Antibodies in Canada" (1993), 10 *C.I.P.R.* 35 at 40.

42 Caskey T., R.S. Eisenberg and J. Straus, "HUGO Statement on Patenting of DNA Sequences" (April 1995), *Genome Digest* at 7.

43 Ibid. at 9. See also, Anderson, "NIH Drops Bid for Gene Patents" (1994), 263 *Science* 909. However, despite the PTO's rejection of the NIH patent applications, private companies are continuing to pursue such patent rights. In Europe, after the NIH decided

not to appeal the PTO's rejection, the MRC in the United Kingdom formally took the position that such patent applications if admitted could only "hamper research collaborations" globally, see Gershon D., "US and British Reseachers Agree not to Seek Gene Fragment Patents" (1994), 367 *Nature* 583.

44 Calia K.G., "Patentability of Expressed Sequence Tags: A Study of the Venter Application" (1992), 11 *Biotech. L.R.* 540 and the accompanying Office Action at 578.

45 Supra note 18 at 1643.

46 Ibid. That is, the distinction was made between a biological deposit which was the subject of a patent application (*i.e.*. embodied the invention) and one which was necessary as part of a patented process. It was following *Pioneer Hi-Bred*, that section 12.03.02 of the MOPOP was revised to reflect the Court's ruling regarding the status of biological deposits submitted as part of a petition's disclosure requirement.

47 Supra note 18 at 1643.

48 Supra note 2 and April 28, 1972, U.K.T.S. 5 (1981), Cmnd No. 8136, T.I.A.S. No. 9768 [hereinafter *Budapest Treaty*]. Canada acceded to the treaty September 17, 1996.

49 The CPO has indicated that it may be sufficient to describe an organism with reference to characteristics such as its taxonomic description, method of isolation and selection, morphological properties, availability, etc, see Maher E., "Patenting Life Forms" (1985) 2 *C.I.P.R.* 125.

50 One of the main concerns is the challenge faced by the courts to resolve disputes between the donors and users of human tissue and bodily substances. The classic US embodiment of this very issue is to be found in the case law of *Moore* v. *The Regents of the University of California*, *infra* note 56.

51 Gilmour J.M., "'Our Bodies: Property Rights in Human Tissue" (1993), 8 *C.J.L.S.* 113.

52 Hardiman R., "Towards the Right of Commerciality: Recognizing Property Rights in the Commercial Value of Human Tissue" (1986), 34 *U.C.L.A. Law Review* 207 at 224. See also *Miles Inc.* v. *Scripps Clinic and Research Foundation*, 8100 F. Supp. 1091 (S.D. Cal. 1993).

53 Federal laws focus primarily on the safety and effectiveness of tissue replacement technology and provincial laws focus on obtaining informed consent and other tissue donation procedures or options. For a review of these laws, see Law Reform Commission of Canada, *Procurement and Transfer of Human Tissues and Organs: Working Paper 66* (Ottawa: Canada Communication Group, 1992) at 117.

54 Transplantable tissue is tissue that is taken from one part of the body to another, or to another individual while remaining in its natural condition.

55 Somerville M.A., "Structuring the Issues in Informed Consent" (1981), 26 *McGill Law Journal* 740; Knoppers B.M. and C.M. Laberge, "DNA Banking/Collecting: A Canadian "Sample" of Consent Forms" in *Legal Rights and Human Genetic Material*, supra note 5 at 33 and the case law of *R.* v. *Dyment* [1988] 2 S.C.R. 417.

56 This occurred in the case of *Moore* v. *The Regents of the University of California* 249 Cal. Rptr. 494 (Cal App. Dist. 1988) and 793 P. 2d 479 (Cal. 1990), cert. denied 111 S.Ct. 1388 [hereinafter *Moore* cited to S.Ct., 1990] at 150. In total, there were twelve separate causes of action. Although, the present discussion is not meant to be a review of the possible actions available in circumstances where there is a defect in consent, the reader should be aware that claims under the common law tort of negligence and art. 1457 *C.C.Q.* under Quebec's civil law jurisdiction are accessible.

57 Ibid.

58 Royal Commission on New Reproductive Technologies, *Proceed With Care* (Ottawa: Canada Communications Group, 1993) at 643 and 1002.

59 Ibid. at 597.

60 See provincial *Coroners Acts*, infra note 68 with respect to human growth hormone procurement and Marusyk and Swain, supra note 7 regarding the general conclusions. For alternative approaches to the same issue see also, Baudouin J.-L. and C. Labrusse-Riou, *Produire l'Homme: De quel droit* (Paris: Presses Universitaires de France, 1987) at 190-191 and Kouri R.P. and S. Phillips-Nootens, "L'utilisation des parties du corps humain pour fins de recherche: L'Article 22 du *Code Civil du Québec*" (1994-95), 25 *R.D.U.S.* 359.

61 The legislative titles used for the purposes of the following discussion reflect the subject matter of the statutory instruments in question rather than the actual short titles enacted by the jurisdictions in question.

62 Up until December 31, 1993, Québec was governed by the *Civil Code of Lower Canada.*

63 On January 1, 1994 this Code was replaced by the new *Civil Code of Québec*, S.Q. 1991, c.64.

64 The transitional provisions under *An Act Respecting the Implementation of the Reform of the Civil Code*, S.Q. 1992, c.57, s.2., clearly provide that the laws of both codes still govern their respective time periods; the *C.C.L.C.* governs all transactions that occurred before January 1, 1994 and the *C.C.Q.* governs all transactions that occurred on and subsequent to January 1, 1994. Consequently, when determining what, if any, rights exist in human tissue and bodily substances, the time of the tissue's acquisition determines whether the *C.C.L.C.* or the *C.C.Q.* applies.

65 *Human Tissue Gift Act*, R.S.B.C. 1979, c.187; *Human Tissue Gift Act*, R.S.A. 1980, c. H-12; *Human Tissue Gift Act*, R.S.S. 1978, c. H-15; *Human Tissue Act*, C.C.S.M. c. H-180; *Human Tissue Gift Act*, R.S.O. 1990, c. H-20; *Human Tissue Act*, R.S.N.B. 1973, c. H-12; *Human Tissue Gift Act*, R.S.N.S. 1989, c.215; *Human Tissue Donation Act*, S.P.E.I. 1992, c.34; *Human Tissue Act*, R.S.N. 1990, c. H-15; *Human Tissue Gift Act*, R.S.Y.T. 1986, c.89; *Human Tissue Act*, R.S.N.W.T. 1988, c. H-6.

66 Côté P.A., *The Interpretation of Legislation in Canada*, 2nd ed., (Cowansville: Les Éditions Yvons Blais, 1992) at 115.

67 The effective years for each jurisdiction are: British Columbia, March 30, 1972; Alberta, 1973; Saskatchewan, 1973; Manitoba, 1987; Ontario, 1971; Québec, January 1, 1994; New Brunswick, June 18, 1986; Nova Scotia, April 6, 1973; Prince Edward Island, May 6, 1992; Newfoundland, 1971; the Yukon, April 6, 1980; the Northwest Territories, 1974.

68 *Anatomy Act*, R.S.B.C. 1979, c.15; *Universities Act*, R.S.A. 1980, c. U-5, ss.55-59; *Bodies of Deceased Persons Amendment Regulations*, Alta Reg. 298/86; *Anatomy Act*, R.S.S. 1978, c. A-19; *Anatomy Act*, C.C.S.M. c. A-80; *Anatomy Act*, R.S.O. 1990, c. A-21; *Anatomy Act*, R.S.N.B. 1973, c. A-8; *Anatomy Act*, R.S.N.S. 1989, c.13; *Human Tissue Act*, R.S.N. 1990 c. H-15, ss.11-15. The collection and use of unclaimed or donated cadavers for anatomical research and teaching purposes by university medical schools is provided for under the *Anatomy Acts*. Prince Edward Island, the Yukon and the Northwest Territories do not have analogous versions of the *Anatomy Acts* since these jurisdictions do not have medical schools.

69 *Coroners Act*, R.S.B.C. 1979, c.68; *Fatality Inquiries Act*, R.S.A. 1980, c. F-6; *The Coroners Act*, R.S.S. 1978, c. C-38; *The Fatality Inquires Act*, C.C.S.M. c. F-52;

Coroners Act, R.S.O. 1990, c. A-37; *Coroners Act*, R.S.N.B. 1973, c. C-23; *Fatality Inquires Act*, R.S.N.S. 1989, c.164; *Coroners Act*, R.S.P.E.I. 1988, c.25; *Summary Proceedings Act*, R.S.N. 1990, c. S-30; *Coroners Act*, R.S.Y. 1986, c.35; *Coroners Act*, R.S.N.W.T. 1988, c.20. These statutes empower a coroner or medical officer to take control of a cadaver for the purposes of examination in order to determine whether an inquest is necessary, and if so, to follow through with such an inquest.

70 *Cemetery and Funeral Services Act*, S.B.C. 1989, c.21; *Cemeteries Act*, R.S.A. 1980, c. C-2; *Cemeteries Act*, R.S.S. 1978, c. C-4; *Cemeteries Act*, C.C.S.M. c. C-30; *Cemeteries Act*, R.S.O. 1990, c. C-4; *Cemetery Companies Act*, R.S.N.B. 1973, c.1; *Cemeteries and Funeral Services Act*, R.S.N.S. 1989, c.62; *Cemeteries Act*, R.S.P.E.I. 1988, c. C-2; *Cemeteries and Burial Sites Act*, R.S.Y.T. 1986, c.18. Newfoundland and the North West Territories do not have comprehensive legislation specifically directed to this matter. However, under the Northwest Territories' *Human Tissue Act*, subsection 2(1) and subparagraph 2(2)(e) provide that a coroner or funeral director cannot direct the use of body or part thereof for donation. These statutes regulate the final destination of cadavers. Where public legislation is absent, there is likely to be provision for these matters under ecclesiastic legislation.

71 A similar possessory right is created under other statutes as well; for example, Ontario's *Crown Administration of Estates Act*, R.S.O. 1990, c. C-47, allows a public trustee to possess a body for purposes of burial.

72 The obligation for proper disposal is also alluded to under section 182(b) of Canada's *Criminal Code*, R.S.C. 1985, c.C-46, which states that "[e]very one who ... improperly or indecently interferes with or offers any indignity to a dead human body or human remains, whether buried or not, is guilty of an indictable offence punishable by imprisonment for a term not exceeding five years."

73 Skegg P.D.G., "Human Corpses, Medical Specimens and the Law of Property" (1975) 4 *Anglo-Am. L Rev.* 412. This conclusion was confirmed by the Ontario decision of *Abeziz* v. *Harris Estate*, (17 June 1992), Toronto RE1171/92 (Ont. C.G.D.) where Farely J. stated that "I understand that there is not legal right in a corpse (absent possibily some interim element under the *Anatomy Act*, R.S.O. 1990, c.A.21 for medical research)."

74 *Public Health Protection Act*, R.S.Q. c. P-35; *An Act Respecting the Determination of the Causes and Circumstances of Death*, R.S.Q. c. R-0.2.

75 See Marusyk and Swain, supra note 5.

76 C. Anderson, supra note 4.

77 The U.S. Centers for Disease Control and Prevention has apparently chosen to abandon the patent application rather than argue for ownership rights in the original material, see RAFI, "Following Protest, Patent Claim Withdrawn on Guaymi Indian Cell Line" (1994), 9(3-4) *geneWATCH* 6. See also, "Patent Blather" (1995), *The Economist* 87, where a patent was granted to the National Institutes of Health (NIH) over a cell line derived from a member of the Hagahai people in New Guinea. The man, whose blood was procured, was infected with the human T-cell leukemia virus 1 but showed no signs of the disease normally associated with this infection. The Rural Advancement Foundation International, which objects to the patent granted, opposes in general the extension of any form of proprietary rights over genetic material.

78 McMahon, supra note 3 at 21. The "Canadian Patent Office Record", May 9, 1989 at v, under the heading "Chemical Patent Practice", enumerates the format of claims it is prepared to accept. In all instances reference to the 'use', new or otherwise, of the chemical compound is an integral part of the formats listed.

THE PATENTABILITY OF THE HUMAN GENOME: A EUROPEAN PERSPECTIVE

JEAN-CHRISTOPHE GALLOUX

Professor of Law, University of Versailles

Patent law is relatively uniform throughout the European Union as each of the fifteen member states have ratified the European Patent Convention (EPC), commonly known as the Munich Convention of 1973. This Convention provides for a patent which is valid within all the applicable countries noted and requested by the applicant in accordance with a unique and centralized procedure which is carried out at the European Patent Office (EPO). The national offices continue to grant national patents on the basis of their legislation patterned after the EPC; their activities differ little from the activities of the divisions of the EPO.

Until the registration application at the U.S. Patent and Trade Office for several EST sequences by Craig Venter, the patentability of human genetic sequences had never raised any particular controversies within the EPO, apart from those normally evoked in dealing with biotechnological inventions. The number of Venter's applications, the broad interpretations made of patent law and the likelihood that, if accepted, they would extend patent protection in the realm of scientific research, created a shock within the European scientific community. This issue has been taken up by lobby groups representing the extreme left and the ecology movement who had not been able to mobilize public opinion as to intellectual property rights on organic, living matter before this time.

Political groups have been contacted, including, in particular, community institutions which are more responsive to lobbying than national institutions. In response to lobbying pressure, the European Union Commission was obliged to modify and limit its proposed directive on biotechnological inventions that it had prepared over a period of years. The French parliament anticipated the position of the European authorities along these lines in 1994. The EPO, an entity totally independent from the European Union, was obliged to take into account the growing ethical concerns within its examination of patent applications.

In 1995, the controversies subsided as political and scientific authorities became better informed about patent law. The most recent decisions of the EPO reflect a greater tendency to allow patents for genetic sequences of human origin. However, it is difficult to anticipate what will develop in light of the European texts being drafted. Looming in the horizon, such proposals are casting a shadow over biotechnology development in Europe and creating uncertainty.

To better understand this technical subject, we will examine the requirements for patenting inventions in light of current European laws and texts which deal with particular inventions. We will compare the objective conditions for a patent (subject to patentability, novelty, inventive activity and industrial application) with the rather subjective European conditions which must be fulfilled for a patent grant (conformity with law and order, respect for morality and human dignity).

I. Objective Criteria for Patentability

The objective criteria for patentability in Europe can be summarized accordingly:

- The EPO, like most of the member state patent offices, does not differentiate the purpose of the invention according to its biological origin. The EPC has no provisions whatsoever that would permit such a distinction to be made. Thus, a gene, cell or protein of human origin are evaluated in the same way that one evaluates an animal gene, a vegetable cell or a protein secreted by a microorganism.
- Inventions relating to human genes run up against the same difficulties as to principles as do other types of biotechnological inventions. Indeed, the EPC drafted various articles much too narrowly during a period where the "*biological revolution*" had not yet emerged and the consequences were not foreseeable (the 1960's) so that today one encounters significant problems of interpretation.

For an invention to be patentable in accordance with the rules of the EPC, it must, following article 52:

1. be an invention;
2. be novel;
3. present an inventive activity;
4. have an industrial application.

The above conditions form the basic criteria for patentability. We will skip over the questions of form (in particular the description of the invention) for the sake of brevity.

1. AN INVENTION

In European patent law, there are several categories of inventions (a), however, the idea of the invention is not defined (b), one simply notes that a discovery is not an invention (c).

(a) There are product inventions (a material object having a form or special characteristics which distinguishes it from any other object); procedural inventions (from which one can realize a material object, a product, an immediate effect or a result); and inventions for the use of a product and for the use of an apparatus to initiate a procedure.

Within these categories of inventions, product inventions have raised the greatest number of problems with regard to the patentability of human genes in Europe. Indeed, it is where one claims rights as to a product - a human gene, a DNA sequence, etc. - "*per se*", for themselves, which certain people find shocking. The patentability of procedures and methods, in and of itself, is less criticized, like inventions for the use of a product or apparatus. This does not mean that all procedural inventions dealing with human genes are patentable. Rather, article 52(1) EPC provides: "*Methods for treatment of the human body by surgery or therapy and diagnostic methods practised on the human body shall not be regarded as inventions which are susceptible to an industrial application within the meaning of §1*". For example, one may conclude that the genetic therapy methods applied to humans are generally excluded from the field of patentability in Europe.[1] This applies to the therapeutic methods themselves and not to the products that these methods use: the products used in gene therapy are thus not targeted by this exclusion.

In order to get adequate protection, one must patent not only the procedures for obtaining a product through a genetic engineering method, but also the initial product and the result achieved. This is the reason why in patentability "*per se*", in so far as the product invention is concerned, one must have the human genetic sequences.

(b) An invention may be carried out on "*living*" matter within European law. This principle is enunciated in the decision T 19/90 rendered October 3, 1990.[2] The EPC has no provisions whatsoever excluding such objects from the scope of patentability.

As to genetic sequences, human or otherwise, the Opposition Division of the EPO held on December 8, 1994, that one does not look at "*life*" but "*a chemical substance carrying genetic information, which substance may serve as an intermediary in the production of proteins usable in the medical field*".[3] To patent a gene is not to patent life. Genes are, in this context, only molecular chemicals.

(c) Are human genes invented or discovered? The latter case states that they are not patentable because under European law, discovery by definition is not invention (article 52(2) a) EPC). The distinction between the two

concepts is narrow. It is not the object of the discovery that in and of itself is excluded from patentability but the object in so far as it is developed in a certain manner for certain ends. The mere fact that one finds something in nature that has existed before, something which was unknown, does not constitute an invention. By the same token, this does not prevent one from "*realizing*" an invention. A discovery may form the basis of an invention, as was held by the British Patent Court on Appeal in *Genentech v. Wellcome* (October 31, 1989).[4] The intervention of an inventor must go beyond the simple revelation of the object, arising within the context of a technical problem.

Thus, an unknown human genetic sequence may be claimed in the context of a patent if it addresses a technical solution to a technical problem. The act of isolating and characterizing a fragment of DNA does not necessarily constitute a discovery if the gene facilitates the coding of a given protein for a particular use in an industrial application. In these conditions, European law does not distinguish between the original element drawn from the human body, the genomic DNA, and its "*biological reflection*" which is complementary DNA (cDNA).

2. A NEW INVENTION

In European patent law, the requirement for novelty is more strictly applied than in North American law (Canadian or U.S.): any invention is novel that is not, at the registration date for the patent application, present within the state of the art. This means that novelty disappears when an invention is accessible to the public before this date, without regard for time or place. This requirement does not prevent the patent offices in Europe from viewing the DNA sequences as novel although these sequences may have "*existed*" from the beginning of time.

As in the distinction between discovery and invention, the requirement for novelty is independent of the natural/artificial distinction. Indeed, although the DNA sequences exist in nature, they are not necessarily part of the "*state of the art*", which means accessible to the public, particularly if no one knows of their existence. In accordance with standard jurisprudence in the field of chemical products, a substance is considered novel if it is isolated for the first time and if its existence has not been previously known.[5] Synthetically developed DNA or DNA in its pure state are equally subject to patent application.

One may also affirm that although there is no jurisprudence available from the EPO on this point, that a sequence of DNA coded for a known polypeptide may be considered as novel. In fact, once a series of amino acids is known, all the DNA sequences which code for this sequence may be theoretically "*known*"; yet they do not necessarily form part of the state of the art. In the decision T 301/87 of February 16, 1989,[6] the EPO court of appeal decided that the mere presence of a DNA sequence among numerous clones of a gene pool, coding for a given polypeptide, did not automatically mean that the polynucleotide was part of the state of the art.

It should be noted that the novelty of a process for obtaining or manufacturing does not confer novelty to known resulting organisms or products: these may not benefit from "*product-by-process*" claims.

3. INVENTIVE ACTIVITY

> "An invention is considered as having the attribute of inventive activity if, for a person knowledgeable within the field, the invention does not obviously follow from the state of the art" (article 56 EPC).

Because of the rapid evolution of knowledge and technique in the realm of genetic engineering, it is difficult to anticipate the practical criteria for inventive activity in the field of DNA sequences. It is likely that the development will be parallel to that within the field of chemistry.

Thus, the difficult isolation of a gene, the fact that it codes for an "*inventive*" protein, the advantageous qualities which are as yet unknown or unanticipated when the gene is inserted into a new organism: these are all means for determining an inventive activity. For the EPO, the corresponding reverse transcription of the RNA messenger (mRNA) is not a routine operation. By contrast, the substitution of certain equivalent codes or the determination of a particular DNA sequence from a sequence of amino acids is not invariably characteristic of an inventive activity. For inventions resulting from the isolation of genes, specifically human genes, inventive activity is often confused with novelty.[7]

4. INDUSTRIAL APPLICATION

According to article 57 EPC, "an invention is considered as having an industrial application when its object may be manufactured or used in a some field of industry, including agriculture."

The application of this provision to fundamental research in the domain of human genetics poses certain problems in Europe. As to DNA sequences, the use as such of an intermediary product in obtaining a final product fulfils the requirements for an industrial application. By contrast, the mere use of a genetic sequence in the course of research without anticipation that this research will yield an industrial application does not appear to fulfil this condition. Thus, a claim put in for EST sequences without indication as to the function of the corresponding genes would not be considered as having (as of yet) an industrial application.

A liberal interpretation of the text might enlarge the field of patentability since articles 52 and 57 of the EPC only require that the invention be "likely" to have an industrial application: merely the possibility of such an application is thus sufficient, and modifications on this point may be made to the request for a patent up to the point of publication (which takes place within a period of 18 months from the date of submitting the request).

On the basis of these objective conditions for patentability, the EPO has granted, as of June 1996, 303 patents on genes coding for human proteins out of 2,000 patents granted in biotechnology.

This situation may be called into question by the application of "bioethical" criteria which arise largely in the context of a subjective evaluation of the invention.

II. Subjective Conditions for Patentability

Certain ecological and religious organizations have decided to oppose the patentability of human genetic sequences in Europe, under the presumption that such patentability is contrary to ethical principles. The debate was initiated when applications were filed by the NIH and Craig Venter on the EST sequences and, oddly enough, died down with the rejection of these applications by the Patent and Trademark Office (PTO) and the EPO, on the basis of the objective conditions outlined previously.

The attack developed on three fronts:

1. in the ethical committees, where its success was mitigated;
2. within the EPO, on the basis of a predisposition against granting patents, touching on article 53 (a) of the EPC, where its success was moderate;
3. within the European and French parliaments, where it was politically successful.

We shall see, in a fourth point that will be brought up in our conclusion, how this conflict may (or might) be resolved.

1. THE OPINION OF THE ETHICAL COMMITTEES

The arguments advanced pell-mell by those who oppose the patentability of human genes are diverse due to their philosophical and metaphysical bases. These arguments arise from a form of fundamentalism, often religious or ecological in nature, which views nature as something sacred, eternal and not possessing an intrinsic value, historically.

Of all the ethical bodies advancing an opinion on this question, the National Ethical Committee of France was the most clear. In an opinion from December 2, 1991,[8] it determined that the patentability of human genes was in and of itself unethical since it was contrary to the principle of non-ownership of the human body.

The Counsel Group for Bioethics before the European Commission gave an opposing opinion on September 30, 1993. For this body, "*there is no ethical objection to the patentability of biotechnological inventions "per se"; however, genes and the partial sequences of genes where the functions are unknown must not be patented in order to end international uncertainty on the matter*". The same question was presented to the GCB in the beginning of 1996 and it should render a second opinion sometime this year.

The International Bioethics Committee of UNESCO, in the context of preparing an "*international convention on the protection of the human genome*" designated the human genome as a "*common human heritage*". However, the Committee did not draw any conclusions as to the patentability of inventions relating to human genes. This patentability, in any case, does not conflict with the international position as officially presented.

In light of all this, it is rather difficult to define a rational ethic as to the patentability of human genes.

2. UNCLEAR JURISPRUDENCE FROM THE EPO

Article 53(a) EPC excludes from patentability "inventions the publication or exploitation of which would be contrary to public order or morality, provided that exploitation shall not be deemed such merely because it is prohibited by law or regulation in some or all of the Contracting States."

The arguments introduced by the opponents to the patentability of living matter gave the EPO an opportunity to present its opinion on this matter in three separate cases, one case involving a human gene. These cases highlight the tentative position of the EPO and the appearance of some important elements of subjectivity in the evaluation of the morality of inventions.

In the 1989 "*Harvard transgenic mouse*" case,[9] concerning the invention of a genetically modified animal, the Examining Division of the EPO refused to apply article 53(a) EPC to refuse the application. It noted, "the present invention might have a beneficial effect on mankind" and that "the patent law is not the right legislative tool for regulating problems which may arise, such as economic and ethical questions, with the production and the use of transgenic animals." The Board of Appeal[10] ordered the Examining Division to consider, on further examination, whether article 53 (a) EPC is a bar to patenting the invention. This would appear to be dependent upon a careful weighing of the suffering of animals and the possible risks to the environment versus the invention's usefulness to mankind. This examination must be carried out on a case by case basis.

The above case was an instance where foreign concepts of "morality" were applied. In fact, this case was interpreted in a traditional manner, notably as to patent law by the European continental jurisdictions, as preventing the patentability of "inventions appearing so offensive to our contemporaries that it would be impossible to patent them". Whether or not an invention conforms to "morality" does not, therefore, depend on an "ethical balancing" of the advantages and disadvantages since this is not the definition of ethics. Morality refers to a minimum standard of public morality; it is impossible to find such a balance in a significant and rational manner, e.g. a weapon may be used to kill someone's wife yet also be used in a case of self-defence. Slipping down a slope of total subjectivity was an error to be avoided.

In the 1994 *Relaxine* case,[11] the "Opposition Division" of the EPO returned to the traditional concept of public order and good morals. Controversial ideas are not automatically considered contrary to good morals: such is the case with the debate over abortion. The position of the general public as to the patentability of genes is complex and varied and is frequently dependent upon the manner in which a question is asked. This diversity is not reflected in the opinions of those select groups who view a publication or use of such an invention as immoral.

In the 1995 case of *Plant Genetic System*[12] relating to the patentability of transgenic plants, the "Opposition Division" gave a surprising definition of public order. The Board stated that its duty was to assess the hazard stemming from the exploitation of a given technology. The Board opined that it should apply its own value judgements on the technology involved, instead of using national laws and the Directives of the European Union as yardsticks which would regulate the use of genetic engineering techniques and tools as well as their resulting products.[13] The EPO's actions and opinions continued to provide important doses of subjectivity in the examination of patentability of biotechnology inventions the result of which remain unforeseeable.

3. NEWER, MORE RESTRICTIVE LAWS

Several initiatives have been undertaken throughout Europe to limit the patentability of genes or genetic sequences, with legislators being responsive to lobby groups, not understanding the nature of intellectual property rights. These initiatives have come to an end in France and are presently blocked at the European level.

In France, in the context of the bioethics laws of July 29, 1994, parliament has adopted provisions stating that inventions with the object of "*the human body, its elements and its products, as well as the knowledge of the total or partial genetic structure... as such...*" would be qualified as contrary to public order and good morals. The term "*as such*" defines a state of nature which definition would only interfere, under an broad interpretation, with the patentability of inventions claiming DNA or DNA fragments absolutely identical to those existing in the human body. Yet, DNA or DNA fragments presented in patent applications are often complementary DNA or DNA in a different form than that existing within the human body (for example, these often have no exons). It would be practically impossible to prove the similarity or differences of such with the natural elements.

The European authorities have followed a path parallel to that of the French. In 1988, the Commission decided to harmonize patent law in the realm of biotechnology along the lines of a directive.[14] The 1988 proposition made no reference to the non-patentability of human genes; however, in 1989, the Economic and Social Counsel which was dealing with this text, inspired by the EPO jurisprudence on the "*Harvard transgenic mouse*" requested that the patentability of "*human beings*" be excluded.[15] In 1992, the Parliament introduced a modification of the initial text excluding "*the body or parts of the human body*" from the field of patent law, advocating a cost benefit analysis in the application of concepts of public order and morality.[16]

In 1994, following a lively debate, the common position of the Council and the European Parliament faltered on the convoluted drafting of a provision on "*the body or the elements of the human body as such*" as well as "*the means of modifying the genetic identify of the human person contrary to the dignity of the human person*",[17] where such action would be considered against public order and good morals. Even though the text was amended, the European Parliament rejected the proposed directive on March 1, 1995, essentially because the text's wording authorized the patentability of human genes in certain circumstances. A new proposal was published at the beginning of 1996.[18] The drafting of the contested provision was modified as follows:

> "the human body and its elements in their natural state may not be patented. Notwithstanding... the object of an invention which may have an industrial application and which touches on an isolated element of the human body or other product by a technical procedure may be patented, even if the structure of this element is identical to that of a natural element".

The interpretation of this text is not clear and under any interpretation, the debate is not over. A French parliamentary commission has just examined the text and has demanded new modifications to exclude patentability for products of the human body as well as partial or total knowledge of the genes, requesting, above all, that the expression "*in their natural state*" be more narrowly defined in order to designate the elements and products of the human body which are found in their original, bodily context.[19]

The parliamentary uncertainties and the divergence between the European authorities and the EPO have had a disastrous effect on European industry and research. One sole figure may give a hint as to the extent of these problems: 70% of the patents granted by the EPO on genetic sequences are of U.S. origin. Is this the cost of "*bioethics*" interrogation?

4. OUTLINES OF A SOLUTION

The European example is not one to follow Opposition to the patentability of human genes arises from ignorance of the legal concepts and public perception of the human body. The first must be eliminated and the second taken into account.

As to the issue of ignorance, one may aver:

- A patent does not grant rights on a physical thing, as in property rights, but rather on an abstract creation, an invention. The patents covering human DNA do not confer on their proprietors any right whatsoever to individual human beings, no more than a patent directed at other human products such as proteins. Thus, the principle of non commercialization of the human body does not apply here.
- The principle of "*non-commercialization of the human body*" is deceptive. It does not mean "*free of cost*" but "*the impossibility of applying a legal act*" to the specified object. Thus, a donation is already a form of commerce. The laws, particularly the French bioethics laws, seek to prevent the sale of parts of human bodies for "*consideration*". These laws never totally forbid such elements from being collected, verified and packaged and then transferred for a "*consideration*". Why, then, forbid the patentability of human genes - when the conditions for patentability are fulfilled - in view of a principle (non-commercialization) which does not apply? Which, moreover, is clearly not applicable to trade touching on the elements and products of the body?
- Bioethics should not be confused with the law, with public order or with morality, even if though there be some connecting link.

It should be emphasized that "*Bioethics*" is only ethics and is not intended to impose restrictive behavioural norms, but merely propose options. The law does not seek to make people "good". A system of law applies norms which may serve as ethical rules but only in cases where the absence of such rules would foster injustice or social disorder.

In reality the only question that one must pose, from an ethical point of view, is the following: To what extent would the patentability of human genes threaten the freedom or dignity of humanity, that is to say, to what extent would the rights granted by a patent be antagonistic to these rights?

Apart from a case of infringement, patent law is not concerned with the material object which incorporates the patented invention. As to any possible violation of human dignity, such violation would arise from public perception, both of the human body and of the notion of industrial property.

If one truly sees the act of integrating human biological matter into a patentable invention as contrary to the dignity of humanity, one must first determine if this offence arises from the industrial or technical ***use*** of this invention, or from the patentability in an of itself.

It seems to me that it is rather the industrial or technical use and the modalities that this use assumes which are found offensive, instead of the assertion of a right of industrial or intellectual property which is a natural and logical consequence of a liberal "*property rights*" oriented society.

Consequently, it is at the level of gathering biological samples and at the level of application of any inventions that social and moral control must be imposed, rather than at the level of patenting techniques or products. The debate over patentability is seemingly only a red herring which was designed to divert the debate from more pointed topics.

Whatever the outcome of the debate on the patentability of human genes in Europe, however, one must never forget the words so aptly expressed by Radbruch: "As law makes morality possible, it inevitably makes immorality possible as well."[20]

Endnotes and References

1 Decis. T820/92, OJ EPO 1995, p. 113.

2 Decis. T19/90, Oct. 3, 1990, PIBD n° 494, II, p. 96; OJ EPO 1990, at 476.

3 Decis. Dec. 8, 1994, Recueil Dalloz 1996, p. 44, with commentary J.C. Galloux.

4 *Genentech v. Wellcome*, Sup. Ct. of App. (UK), Oct. 31, 1989, EIPR 1989, 2, at 66.

5 Supra note 3.

6 Fowlston B.J., "Biotechnology Patents in Europe", Vol. 6 *Biotechnology* at 912.

7 Supra note 3.

8 Galloux J.C., "Ethique ou brevet ou le syndrome bioéthique" (1993), Recueil Dalloz, chronique at 83.

9 Dossiers Brevets, 1989, IV.4.

10 Supra note 2.

11 Supra note 3.

12 Dec. T356/93, Feb. 21, 1995, Recueil Dalloz 1996, Sommaire at 290, commentary J.C. Galloux.

13 Straus J. ,"Patenting Human Genes in Europe - Past Developments and Prospects for the Future", IIC Vol. 26, n° 6/1995, at 920.

14 Doc. COM(88) 196 final - SYN 159, Oct. 17. 1988, OJ n° C, 12 Jan. 1989.

15 89/C159/05, OJ n° C 159/10, June 26, 1989.

16 Doc. A3.0286/92, Oct. 5, 1992.

17 OJ. n° C101, April 9,1994, art. 65.

18 Doc. COM (95) 661 final.

19 Mattei J-F., *Breveter la matière vivante? Propositions pour une réponse Européenne: Rapport d'information sur la proposition de directive du Parlement Européen et du Conseil relative à la protection juridique des inventions biotechnologiques* (Paris: Assemblée Nationale, 1996).

20 "Aphorismen zür Rechtsweisheit" Göttingen 1969 n° 5.

GENOMIC PATENTS AND PRODUCT DEVELOPMENT INCENTIVES

REBECCA S. EISENBERG

Professor of Law, University of Michigan Law School, Ann Arbor, MI.

Patents on human genetic information have been controversial among different groups for different reasons. The purpose of a patent system is to motivate the commercial development of new technologies; it is thus unsurprising that those who have fundamental misgivings about commercial biotechnology would oppose gene patents. More intriguing is the controversy over gene patenting among those who welcome the commercial development of biotechnology products by private firms. While many proponents of commercial biotechnology assert that gene patents are essential to motivate product development, some have expressed more nuanced views, endorsing patents under some circumstances and condemning them as unnecessary or even counterproductive in others.

The most striking example of this ambivalence has been the opposition -- some of it from industry trade groups and entrepreneurs -- to patent filings on cDNA fragments (expressed sequence tags or ESTs). Perhaps it was this outspoken opposition, from sources beyond the usual suspects, that provoked the U.S. Patent and Trademark Office (PTO) to take the extraordinary measure of calling for public comments on the question of "[whether] the patenting of human genome fragments [would] inhibit rather than promote advancement of the biotechnology arts[, and] if so, why?"[1] The PTO promptly repented of its unwonted foray into open-ended questions of public policy and cancelled the request for comments within two weeks,[2] it subsequently issued a revised request for comments that was more narrowly focused on the administrative burden and costs associated with examining applications containing large numbers of sequences or excessively long sequences, with no mention of broader policy questions.[3] Yet the question the PTO originally posed remains important and unanswered.

More recently, as human genomic sequencing gets underway, the National Center for Human Genome Research (NCHGR) has taken the unusual step of discouraging grantees from patenting "large blocks of human primary DNA sequence", advising that it considers "raw human genomic DNA sequence, in the absence of additional demonstrated biological information ... inappropriate material for patent filing" and that patent applications on such sequences "could have a chilling effect on the development of future inventions of useful products." While acknowledging that the Bayh-Dole Act gives grantees the right to elect to retain title to inventions made with federal funds and to apply for patents, NCHGR has admonished its grantees that it "will monitor grantee activity in this area" and that it may consider making a determination of "exceptional circumstance" (required under the Bayh-Dole Act before an agency may restrict the right of grantees to retain patent rights to discoveries) in the future if necessary "to ensure that sequence generated by these grants is maximally useful to the research and commercial sectors."

Given that pharmaceutical and biotechnology firms are big users of the patent system, it may seem surprising that they do not join together in an equivocal endorsement of gene patents. What can we make of this debate? Are gene patents good for business or bad for business? More specifically, how will the existence or absence of patents on human DNA sequences affect the incentives of private firms to develop commercial products that emerge from knowledge of such sequences?

The answer to this question is likely to vary depending on the type of product at issue and the type of firm whose incentives are under consideration. Most firms involved in the development of biotechnology products are both consumers of technology developed by others and producers of technology embodied in products and processes that they hope to sell to their own customers. Firms are more likely to view patent rights as essential to their incentives when they cover the technology they sell to their own customers than when they cover technology that they need to acquire from others.

This is entirely unsurprising given the function of patents. A patent confers a monopoly in a new invention for a limited term, allowing sellers of products embodying new technologies to charge higher prices by excluding competitors from the market. This is how patents motivate firms to invest in R&D, an investment that might be unprofitable if free riders were permitted to enter the market for new technologies that prove successful without having shared in the initial cost and risk. But what makes patents attractive to firms is the prospect of *charging* monopoly prices - not the prospect of *paying* them. When R&D is conceived not as a single-firm enterprise culminating in the creation of a patented end product for sale to consumers, but rather as a more complex stream of successive innovations, in which firms use the discoveries of others in the course of making their own discoveries, it is easy to see how firms might disagree about the impact of patents at different points in the stream on their own R&D incentives. Thus firms welcome the patents that allow them to charge higher prices, while cursing the patents that require them to pay higher prices. At any given point in the stream, downstream patents motivate R&D, while upstream patents make it more costly.

Patents on DNA sequences are thus likely to have different impacts on firms that occupy different market niches in the biotechnology industry. Firms that specialize in identifying novel DNA sequences are likely to be motivated by patents on such sequences, while firms that use DNA sequences in their research as targets for drug discovery are more likely to be indifferent or hostile to such patents. Thus a firm like Merck, that makes its money primarily from the sale of small molecule drugs, is willing to dedicate new DNA sequences to the public domain, while DNA-sequencing firms like Human Genome Sciences and Incyte hold them as proprietary resources. One firm's research tool is another firm's end product.

A complicating factor that changes the alignment of incentives somewhat in the case of DNA sequences is government sponsorship of the Human Genome Project. Governments presumably do not require patents to motivate them to sponsor research in the public interest; one might therefore expect that publicly-funded contributions to the stream of innovation could safely be dedicated to the public domain to reduce the costs to firms of downstream R&D. The prevailing wisdom is otherwise: since passage of the Bayh-Dole Act[4] and the Stevenson-Wydler Act[5] in the U.S. in 1980, recipients of government research funds have generally been encouraged to patent their inventions in order to promote their development as commercial products. By discouraging its grantees from patenting raw genomic sequence data, for the avowed purpose of averting "a chilling effect on the development of future inventions of useful products", NCHGR is challenging the validity in this particular setting of the ordinary presumption in favour of patents as a mechanism for promoting product development. For better or worse, a likely consequence of this move is that a considerable amount of DNA sequence data will enter the public domain through the Human Genome Project.

Is this good or bad? In the absence of patents on DNA sequences, are we likely to lose out on the development of new products? Or can firms be expected to welcome free access to DNA sequences generated with government funds as a subsidy for their own research? There is no simple, obvious answer to this question, but we can engage in a bit of cautious speculation. In all likelihood the bottom line will be uneven, favouring incentives to develop some types of products, while diminishing incentives to develop others.

Most likely to suffer from the absence of patents on DNA sequences are therapeutic products that are closely related to the sequences (such as therapeutic proteins that the sequences encode). Such products require costly clinical testing before they may be brought to market, and firms have rarely been willing to make such an investment in an unpatented product. A patent on a DNA sequence encoding a therapeutic protein (which would typically include claims to any recombinant vector or host cell incorporating the sequence) allows the patent holder to exclude competitors from making the encoded protein by recombinant means. In some case, process patents on methods of using proteins for particular therapeutic purposes may be adequate to ensure market exclusivity, but process patents are generally considered less advantageous than product patents (and therefore provide less motivation to invest in clinical testing). One problem with relying on therapeutic process claims to protect a pharmaceutical product is that such a patent does not prevent competitors from making and selling the unpatented product for other purposes, and thereby bringing down the price of the product. In theory the owner of the process patent could still enjoin the particular use of the product described in the patent claims, but it is impractical to monitor what individual consumers are doing with a product that is available from multiple sources for multiple uses. A patent on the DNA sequence encoding the protein provides a direct remedy against any competing firm that uses the sequence to manufacture the protein and thus is a much more effective means of securing market exclusivity even after new uses are found for the product.

As a general rule, incentives to develop diagnostic applications of DNA sequences are likely to be less sensitive to the absence of patents on the sequences themselves than incentives to develop therapeutic proteins. For one thing, diagnostic products are less extensively regulated, and therefore considerably cheaper to bring to market, than therapeutic products, reducing the need for exclusive rights to recoup development costs. Second, process patent claims may offer more effective commercial protection for diagnostics than for therapeutics. While therapeutic products are widely distributed to individual consumers whose activities are difficult to monitor, DNA diagnostic services are typically supplied by a more limited number of laboratories that a patent holder can more readily keep an eye on. Diagnostic laboratories might be able to infringe a process patent surreptitiously, but so might they infringe a product patent on a DNA sequence used in a diagnostic test. Thus in contrast to the therapeutic setting, in the diagnostic setting product patents do not clearly offer a more efficacious remedy than process patents. Moreover, a DNA diagnostic product may be less likely than a therapeutic protein to have multiple uses that would leave the patent holder vulnerable to competition from other suppliers.

Nonetheless, some DNA diagnostic products may be quite costly to develop, and the absence of patent rights on DNA sequences may undermine incentives to develop such products. For example, developing tests for genetic susceptibility to certain diseases may require identification of numerous mutations, particularly in the case of complex polygenic disorders. Moreover, the use of such tests has been controversial, and it is entirely possible that ethical concerns raised by genetic susceptibility testing may ultimately lead to further regulatory measures that increase the risks and costs associated with commercial development of such products. Patents on DNA sequences may help motivate firms to develop diagnostic products in the face of these risks and costs.

Least likely to suffer from the absence of patents on a DNA sequence are incentives to develop products that are only indirectly related to the DNA sequence (such as a small molecule drug for which the DNA sequence, or the peptide it encodes, is a target). Such products are far enough downstream from the identification of the DNA sequence itself that a patent on the DNA sequence is unlikely to provide innovating firms with a source of exclusive rights in the products they ultimately bring to market, yet DNA sequence patents could impose royalty obligations on innovating firms that make R&D more costly. More important to the profit expectations of the firms that bring these products to market is the prospect of obtaining patents on their own end products the small molecules that they hope to sell to consumers.

The impact on product development incentives of placing DNA sequences in the public domain thus depends in part on what type of product is at issue, and whether other patent rights are likely to preserve for an innovating firm an exclusive position in the market for that product. In addition, the presence or absence of patents on DNA sequences may be more or less significant to different types of firms.

Both established pharmaceutical firms and younger biotechnology firms are likely to be sensitive to patent incentives, but their interests in the patent system are not exactly the same. Young biotechnology firms typically have a problem that established pharmaceutical firms don't need to worry about: if they are not yet earning significant revenues by selling products to consumers, they need to raise funds from other sources to keep their research operations moving forward. For these firms, a patent portfolio may be critical at an early stage in their R&D efforts in order to attract financing from investors or research partners; otherwise they will lack the resources to continue the effort, and they will never have any products to sell. But the discoveries available for patenting at this early stage may be far upstream from a final product.

Established pharmaceutical firms are also very sensitive to intellectual property rights, but for different reasons, and at a different stage in the R&D process. Pharmaceutical firms typically have no need to go to the capital markets to fund their research; they are already selling products and can fund their next generation of research projects out of profits on existing products. They are therefore less likely than cash-poor biotechnology firms to require patent rights on early stage research discoveries that are far-removed from the marketplace, so long as they anticipate a strong enough patent position further downstream to ensure them of an effective commercial monopoly in the products they sell to consumers at the end of the day.

Thus although both big pharmas and smaller biotech firms want patent rights in the products they sell to their consumers, biotech firms are more likely to require patents on discoveries made further upstream in the R&D process as well in order to attract research funding. For this reason, the absence of patent rights on DNA sequences may undermine the incentives of smaller, younger firms to develop products that would still be attractive to larger, more established firms. The presence or absence of patents on DNA sequences may thus determine not only what type of product is profitable to develop, but also what type of firm is able to summon the resources for product development.

Endnotes and References

1 U.S. Dep't of Comm., Pat. & Trademark Off., Notice of Hearings and Request for Comments on Issues Relating to Patent Protection for Nucleic Acid Sequences (Nov. 8, 1995), 60 Fed. Reg. 57223 (Nov. 14, 1995).

2 60 Fed. Reg. 58601 (Nov. 28, 1995).

3 U.S. Dep't. of Comm., Pat. & Trademark Off., Notice of Hearings and Request for Comments on Issues Relating to Patent Protection for Nucleic Acid Sequences (Mar. 6 1996), 61 Fed. Reg. 9980 (NIar. 12 1996).

4 Pub. L. No. 96-517, 94 Stat. 3014 (1980) (codified as amended at 35 U.S.C. §§ 200-11, 301-07 (1994).

5 Stevenson-Wydler Technology Innovation Act of 1980, Pub. L. No. 96-480, 94 Stat. 2311 (1980) (codified as amended at 15 U.S.C. § 3701 et seq. (1994).

GENE PATENTS AND DRUG DEVELOPMENT: THE PERSPECTIVE FROM MERCK

CHRISTOPHER P. AUSTIN

Department of Human Genetics

Merck Research Laboratories, West Point, PA

JACK L. TRIBBLE

Patent Counsel - Biotechnology, Merck and Co., Inc., Rahway, NJ

The rapid and accelerating pace of human gene discovery, together with advances in the understanding of gene regulation and delivery, promise to usher in a new era in the treatment of human disease. Fulfilment of this promise will, however, require resolution of a fundamental question: whether the patenting of genes will influence the direction and pace of future research involving genetic information, and the development of new therapies for disease. A balance between the patenting of genetic technologies and access to these technologies must be achieved. Any result must reward investigators for novel discoveries, while maximising opportunities for the entire research community to use the information to develop new therapeutics.

Historical Perspective

The current debate over gene patents and access to genomic technologies reflects a relatively recent change in the methods of gene discovery. The first genes to be cloned (i.e., isolated and characterised) were those whose proteins were well understood physiologically. From a therapeutic perspective, the reason for cloning these genes was often to provide unlimited sources of proteins which were difficult or impossible to obtain in large quantities by any other method; examples are the genes for erythropoietin, growth hormone, and human insulin. As genes were isolated only after their function was known, patenting was straightforward because the genes were novel, nonobvious and immediately useful.

In the early 1990's, a new method of isolating human genes was developed that allowed the isolation of genes based solely on distinguishing characteristics of their structure, without regard to function. Of the 10^9 base pairs of DNA in the human genome, only about 2% are "expressed" (i.e., translated into a protein that may have some function); this 2% is divided into approximately 80,000 genes. The rest of the DNA in the human genome regulates when and where each gene is expressed, or is "junk" DNA with no known function. Though the regulatory regions of DNA are of interest, most of the initial DNA sequencing efforts have focused on the 2% of the genome that is expressed, for these promise to have the most direct therapeutic potential. These expressed sequences can be identified and isolated from the rest of human DNA using characteristic modifications at one end of the cDNA made from the expressed mRNA's. By sequencing the DNA starting at this modification, unique sequences are generated which identify, or tag, the gene. These sequences are known as Expressed Sequence Tags, or EST's. EST's are unique in DNA sequence, but they are not genes. Based on unique DNA sequences, the U.S. National Institutes of Health (NIH) filed patent applications covering several hundred EST's in 1991, in an attempt to preserve a proprietary position for presumed valuable DNA sequences.[1] Following an international outcry and an inability to overcome rejections from the U.S. Patent and Trademark Office, NIH allowed the applications to go abandoned. Shortly thereafter, J. Craig Venter, who had led the EST sequencing effort at NIH, left NIH to start The Institute of Genome Research (TIGR), a private non-profit organisation devoted to large-scale sequencing, and Human Genome Sciences, Inc. (HGS), a for-profit corporation to patent and commercialise the genes identified by TIGR. Other companies, including Incyte Pharmaceuticals, Sequana Therapeutics, Millennium Pharmaceuticals, and Genset Corporation, are also generating EST data and sequencing DNA derived from EST's and positional cloning efforts, and attempting to patent these sequences. These genome companies are restricting access to the technology, thus preventing the scientific community from pursuing full-length sequencing, mapping and gene-based discoveries that would fulfil the promise of genomic based therapies.

In addition to this intense activity in the private sector to sequence and patent expressed human genes, the academic and non-profit sectors are continuing their efforts to sequence not only EST's, but the entire human genome, as part of the Human Genome Project.[2] The Human Genome Project is an international effort begun in 1989, coordinated in the U.S. by the NIH and the Department of Energy, and includes major efforts with governmental funding in the United Kingdom (U.K.), France, Canada, Japan, Italy, Australia, and Russia. Non-profit organisations such as the Wellcome Trust, the Howard Hughes Medical Institute, and Généthon have also funded a tremendous amount of basic work in gene mapping and sequencing of DNA in man as well as in several model organisms. DNA sequence data from governmental and non-profit organisations has generally been placed rapidly in World Wide Web-based public databases such as GenBank and the EMBL database, whereas private companies' databases have remained proprietary. NIH has recently issued a condition of funding which requires rapid depositing of sequence data into public databases.

An effort that represents a hybrid of these two approaches - directed EST sequencing by the private sector and broader genome sequencing by the public and non-profit sectors - is the Merck Gene Index Project, a multicenter academic effort funded by Merck and Co., Inc.[3] The purpose of this effort is to sequence EST's and deposit them immediately into public databases, so that the genetic information that will be most useful in developing novel therapeutics will be freely available to all researchers, in the public and private sectors. In the last two years this sequencing effort, performed principally at Washington University in St. Louis, has placed over 350,000 partial gene sequences, representing 40,000 genes, into the public databases.

Gene Patents

When the gene for the blood protein globin became the first human gene to be cloned in 1980[4], no patent was filed, and the primary interest was in the prodigious technical feat it represented. Human genes cloned shortly thereafter also encoded proteins, like globin, whose function and potential therapeutic value were well understood. These latter gene discoveries were patented, but there was little disagreement about this at the time because each of these genes had an immediately obvious therapeutic utility because of the prior work on the proteins they encode. Patents on the human genes for insulin, erythropoietin, tissue plasminogen activator, and growth hormone have all led to remarkable therapeutic and commercial successes.

As a result of the gene isolation and sequencing efforts in the private and public sectors over the past 15 years, gene patent application filings have accelerated rapidly. To date, over 4,000 gene patent applications have been filed. The private sector has filed over 80% of these patents, and it is clear that unless major changes occur in the direction of genetic research in the public sector, the vast majority of gene patents will be held by private U.S. companies. A large number of applications have been filed by genomic companies that are in the business of selling the technology. The importance of this trend is that private companies generally do not allow all researchers unlimited access to the information, or if they do they charge unreasonable fees for this information. This contrasts with the free exchange of information that characterises the scientific efforts in the public sector, exchange that has allowed the rapid development of genomics as a science and gene therapy as a discipline. There is real and legitimate concern that the patenting of the majority of human genes by private companies will significantly slow the development of novel therapeutics based on genetic information. It has been stated that differences of opinion among private companies concerning gene patents depends on whether the company is a developer or user of the new genetic information,[5] but this distinction is overstated. Though genome companies must have gene patents because their products are DNA sequences, most biotechnology and pharmaceutical companies are involved in both gene discovery and therapeutic development, so are both producers and consumers of genetic information.

Objection to the patenting of human genes has come principally from two sources: first, those fundamentally opposed, for philosophical or religious reasons, to gene patents under any circumstances, and second, from scientists who support gene patenting but fear that broad patents will be granted without a beneficial utility being demonstrated. In the U.S. and most other countries, an invention must be novel, non-obvious, and have utility to be issued a patent. Many of the current gene patent applications concern DNA sequences that are novel, but have no demonstrated utility. Any sequence of DNA greater than 16 bases is identifiable as unique, but even the complete coding sequence of a gene has no utility if its function is not known. To put this issue in perspective, it is helpful to review the process by which the genetic information is obtained. EST DNA is isolated by widely used techniques, and the majority of DNA sequencing then done by robotically operated automatic sequencers. New DNA sequences are assigned putative functions by comparison to the DNA sequences of other genes with known functions in the public databases. In this paradigm, function is not assessed directly, but rather is inferred from genes that are similar according to computer-based comparison algorithms. Utility may therefore be only speculative, not demonstrated.

Implications for Biomedical Research and the Public Health

Because of these concerns, the Human Genome Organisation (HUGO)[6], the U.K. Bioindustry Association, and others, have urged that patent offices worldwide employ the same stringent requirements to gene patent applications as they do to other inventions. This means that a gene must have a demonstrated utility before it is patentable. The European Patent Office (EPO) appears to be moving in this direction.[7]

Merck supports this view.[8,9] Neither the interests of ongoing research nor the development of new therapeutics will be served by the indiscriminate issuing of patents on DNA sequences for which a practical utility has not been demonstrated. Such patents would seriously slow the development of whole classes of new therapies, because companies could not responsibly invest the $350 million currently required to develop a new drug[10] if uncertainty existed as to its patent status.

Several solutions have been suggested.[11,12,13] First is the patenting of genes only if a full length sequence and practical utility have been demonstrated. Second, a distinction should be made between genes whose function and role in disease is understood, and which therefore leads directly to a therapeutic (e.g., erythropoietin), and "research tools", such as cDNA clones, transgenic animals, screen assays, and most antibodies, that do not represent or suggest a therapeutic utility, but are useful because of their ability to discover such utility. Even if patented, these genomic research tools should be available to the entire research community, through nonexclusive licensing with reasonable terms.

Conclusions

While we are very early in the process of discovery of human genes and their function, the current pace of discovery will accelerate over the next five years with continuing EST sequencing efforts and the start of the high-throughput sequencing stage of the Human Genome Project. The process of finding and sequencing novel human DNA sequences is now straightforward given robotic and computer-assisted technologies. Elucidation of a novel gene's function and role in disease remains, in contrast, difficult and far more demanding of ingenuity and insight. The development of novel therapeutics from novel DNA sequences will be facilitated by the placement of sequences into the public domain, or non-exclusive licensing under reasonable terms. Such a balanced paradigm will best serve the public interest, rewarding truly novel discoveries, while facilitating biomedical research needed to translate the promise of human gene discoveries into therapies to address the health needs of society.

Endnotes and References

1 Olsen M.V., "A Time to Sequence" (1995), 270 *Science* 394.

2 Ibid.

3 Williamson A.R., K.O. Elliston and J.L. Sturchio, "The Merck Gene Index: A Public Resource for Genomics" (1995), 7 *J NIH Research* 61.

4 Fritsch E.F., R.M. Lawn and T. Maniatis, (1980), 19 *Cell* 959.

5 See R.S. Eisenberg in this volume at 373.

6 Caskey C.T., R.S. Eisenberg, E.S. Lander and J. Straus, "HUGO Statement on Patenting of DNA Sequences" (1995), 2 *Genome Digest* 6.

7 See J.C. Galloux in this volume at 361.

8 Caskey C.T., "Gene Patents: A Time to Balance Access and Incentives" (1996), 14 *Trends in Biotechnology* 298.

9 Elliston K.O. and J.L. Tribble, "Access to Genomic Inventions" (1996), 6 *Expert Opinion on Therapeutic Patents* 543.

10 "Pharmaceutical R&D: Costs, Risks and Rewards" (1993), *Office of Technology Assessment.*

11 Supra note 6.

12 Supra note 8.

13 Supra note 9.

COMMERCIALIZATION/ PATENTS

KATHY CHERNIAWSKY

RAPPORTEUR

Lawyer, de Villars Jones, Edmonton, Alberta

Introduction: Consensus and Divergence

This plenary session of the First International Conference on DNA Sampling focused on the commercialization of human DNA through the provision of patent protection over human genetic materials and over inventions indirectly involving human genetic materials and information to varying degrees. The panellists came from diverse backgrounds to discuss the Canadian, American and European approaches to patenting human genetic materials and related inventions under each jurisdiction's current legal regime. The panel included a Canadian lawyer specializing in intellectual property law and pharmaceutical innovations, two law professors and two American industry representatives. The application of traditional principles of patent law in the field of human genetics can and has been be problematic. These problems have been exacerbated by the fact that patent law tends to treat the industry as if it were a homogeneous enterprise; however, the industry has in fact evolved into a divergence of interests.

In each jurisdiction, patent rights are determined by reference to various national statutes and to international treaties. Under patent laws an inventor receives the exclusive right to prevent others from practising his/her invention for a limited period of time in exchange for disclosing how the invention may be replicated. The patent holder is therefore free to charge monopoly prices and to recoup the development costs during the exclusivity period. Through this economic incentive, patents encourage technological advancement and continued research and development of new and useful products. In the absence of such a monopoly, competitors would be able to copy the invention at much lower costs, which ultimately could discourage the development of innovations with high research and development costs.

The legal threshold criteria of patentability and the rights encompassed in a grant of patent are quite similar in all jurisdictions. Inventions are patentable if they are novel, non-obvious (or inventive) and useful (or possess an industrial application). Together these three criteria ensure that only certain types of inventions can be protected and that patent protection is commercially meaningful. Patentable inventions are not necessarily limited to inventions comprised of products; patents may also issue over processes, means of manufacture, uses, or products produced by particular processes. Some jurisdictions permit the issuance of patents over methods of treatment of human beings, while other jurisdictions specifically prohibit this practice.

Neither animacy nor biological origin are recognized grounds of distinction in patent law. In many jurisdictions, human DNA is treated like any other chemical substance. Patents have been issued over human genes, human genetic material and other related inventions out of the European Patent Office, the Canada Patent Office and the United States Patent Office, often without any special consideration of their origin or social implications. Over time, some opposition to the issuance of such patents has arisen; frequently this opposition is based upon the view that such patents represent an unacceptable recognition of property interest in life or life forms. This traditional opposition (and indeed some novel opposition) was heightened in the early 1990s by patent applications which laid claim to human DNA fragments, specifically hundreds of expressed sequence tags ("ESTs") of unknown specific utility beyond research applications.

There was a high degree of consensus amongst panellists about several key issues including certain issues which remain contentious in other sectors. While each panellist provided a unique academic or industry perspective, they all endorsed a pro-patent stance. They also agreed that an appropriate intellectual property regime is an essential incentive to attract firms willing to invest huge amounts into the research and development required to reduce human genetic information to marketable therapeutic and diagnostic products. According to the panel, patent law is not the most appropriate locus for arguments over the propriety of scientific advances involving human genetic materials, nor is it an appropriate vehicle to control the underlying commercial activities.

However, a consensus did not readily emerge about how to split the intellectual property spoils amongst the chain of inventors whose contributions build cumulatively, and sometimes culminate in a commercially valuable therapeutic or diagnostic product or process. As some pointed out, individual views on this issue are likely to be influenced by the comparative advantages available to those individuals which in turn depend upon their position in the internal research and development process which begins with isolation of raw genetic material and ends in the marketing of pharmaceuticals to consumers. Not surprisingly, the potentially adverse effects of diluting the traditional rigorous conditions of patentability, particularly the utility or industrial application criterion, was a key issue for the industry representatives. They argued that monopolistic control inherent in patent protection of basic research tools could create an inequitable division of property rights and undermine the development of useful therapeutics. While none of the panellists suggested that the current patent system should (or even could) be replaced, some advocated the implementation of modifications to the existing regime. According to some, the merits of compulsory nonexclusive licensing or even the outright denial of patent protection over "basic research tools" (such as DNA sequences of unknown utility) are two fold. First, it would preserve the rigorous preconditions essential to commercially meaningful patent protection. Second, it would create a clear pathway for the efficient advancement of the science and in particular the continued promulgation of beneficial pharmaceuticals.

The Canadian Experience

The Canadian perspective on patenting human DNA was sketched out by Mr. Marusyk. He explained some basic technical aspects of domestic patent law with regard to three areas: types of patents, patentability of genetic materials and the impact of public disclosure of genetic sequences. In Canada, there are three basic categories of patents which include genetic material: product patents covering genes and genetic material, process patents covering processes of manufacturing having little connection to genetic materials and use patents covering the use of particular products for particular purposes. Human genes and genetic material are patentable regardless of their form and without reference to any unique ethical or social issues. New patent rules are expected shortly which will include specific provisions governing the patenting of amino acid or nucleotide sequences. Canada is currently less sensitive than the United States about prior publication and therefore the disclosure of partial sequences will not necessarily defeat all subsequent patent rights in genetic materials and genetic related inventions.

The European Experience

In stark contrast to the Canadian position, the patentability of human genetic material has been a live political issue in Europe. Debate was heightened by the failed attempts to patent human DNA fragments, and has since continued with varied success before the European and French parliaments. While France has passed some restrictive laws, legislative initiatives brought before the European Parliament to prohibit the patenting of genes and genetic sequences have been defeated.

European patent law is standardized by international treaties. Patents issued through the European Patent Office ("EPO") are valid throughout all member nations. There are both objective (inventive, novel, industrial application) and subjective (legal, and not contrary to morality or human dignity) preconditions to the issuance of European patents. Some of the most vocal opposition to the issuance of patents covering inventions involving human genetic material specifically has centred upon the subjective preconditions which integrate ethical considerations into the European patent paradigm. This opposition has been evident in several EPO patent applications.

Professor Galloux provided a technical review of the EPO assessment of both the objective and subjective criteria of patentability in relation to inventions involving human genetic material. The objective criteria have been applied to human genetic material in a traditional manner. For example, the industrial application criterion precludes the issuance of patents of EST sequences or genes with unknown utilities. The EPO has issued contradictory rulings with respect to the subjective criteria encompassing morality and public order. These criteria traditionally precluded the issuance of patents over a small group of inventions considered so offensive to contemporaries that it would be impossible to patent them. With respect to genetic inventions, however, the EPO initially expanded the ethical exception by suggesting that the subjective criteria are satisfied only after a careful weighing of the benefits and costs of the particular proposed invention. The EPO has since reinstated the traditional stance and come into step with other jurisdictions by issuing patents of inventions involving human genes.

For Professor Galloux, the patentability furore misses the key point that patenting genetic material is not the same as patenting life because patents do not grant positive rights on a physical thing. As patents over human DNA do not confer any right to individual human genes, ethical prohibitions against the commercialization of human beings simply do not apply to the situation. In his view, it is certain industrial uses, not exclusionary patent rights, that can be offensive. Accordingly, substantive regulation should be directed at the levels of gathering samples and of industrial application, rather than within the intellectual property paradigm. However, for many other Europeans the issue is not so clear. Patenting genes remains a controversial practice.

The American Position

The three remaining panellists (Professor Eisenberg, Dr. Austin and Dr. Galas) proceeded upon the presumption that the patentability of inventions involving human genetic material was quite simply an irrevocably done deal. For them, contention now centred upon a secondary distributive issue: how to best resolve the clash between the legal principles of patent law and the economic realities involved in developing commercially viable products from raw genetic information. In other words, how should the patent system be designed to ensure the appropriate division of patent rights amongst a chain of connected and successive inventors in a way that secures future commercial innovation. All three agreed that patent applications claiming DNA sequences highlighted this distributive issue and were the impetus for new opposition to issuance of patents over genetic materials and for calls to re-evaluate the standard threshold conditions of patentability and the quid pro quo embodied in the issuance of patents over basic research.

Professor Eisenberg described the various players and forces within the biotechnology industry and the impacts of patenting human DNA sequences, particularly large blocks of sequences, upon certain sectors within this industry. She noted that despite the fact that the American government has generally encouraged and required the agencies it funds to obtain patents as a means of promoting further commercial development, it has adopted the opposite position with respect to raw genomic sequences. Because of this exceptional stance, sequence data is being assimilated into the public domain, rendered unpatentable and therefore made freely available for subsequent commercial exploitation. Amongst proponents of the patent system, support for this policy is affected by two factors: the type of product that the firm produces and the financial strength of the firm.

In this field, research and development involves a stream of successive innovations, in the words of Professor Eisenberg "[o]ne firm's research tool is another firm's end product". If firms at the beginning of the innovation chain are allowed to exploit patent rights over raw genetic information and genes, they will do so at the expense of other firms further down stream, who require those materials to complete the cumulative invention process. If patents of DNA sequences are not obtained, then products most related to those sequences (such as therapeutic proteins that the sequences encode) are most likely to be rendered unpatentable or patentable only through limited process claims. The loss of robust patent protection makes recapturing the development costs of these products difficult. In contrast, inventions directed towards diagnostic applications may be less affected because they currently involve less development costs and are more conducive to protection by process patents. At the opposite end of the spectrum, those who invent products only indirectly related to DNA sequences will benefit if DNA sequences enter the public domain because these developers will still be able to secure patent protection. At the same time, they will be released from any compensation obligation with regard to the use of the sequence information. Finally, the nature of the firm is also a key factor. The more stringently the threshold criteria of patentability are set, the more the system will favour established firms at the expense of less established and less well capitalized innovators who are more dependent upon early receipt of the enhanced profit stream generated by patent protection.

Dr. Austin further elaborated upon current research and development processes in the pharmaceutical industry and the optimal distribution of intellectual property rights from the perspective of a well established pharmaceutical firm. While pharmaceutical firms depend upon the public sector to provide basic knowledge, the issuance of intellectual property rights over basic research tools would severely hamper the development process for these firms. He argued that the upstream fruits of basic research should be viewed as tools, not as patentable products in and of themselves, because the more costly and innovative work occurs later. Originally, isolation of genetic sequences was a great innovation involving much ingenuity, but sequencing is now fairly routine. Therefore genes isolated as research tools should not be patented; DNA sequences should be patentable only if they satisfy the traditional stringent patent law preconditions. Finally, he suggested that if intellectual property rights are granted over DNA sequences in the absence of a known therapeutic ability, the sequences should be made available for further research and development through non-exclusive licensing arrangements.

With powerful examples, Dr. Galas in his oral presentation affirmed the undeniable value and importance of genetic information discovered at the upstream level of innovation. In his view, as the line between basic and applied science has been irretrievably blurred, assessing the commercial implications of patent law has become more difficult. While public research fuels the science; it is the commercial sector that brings the direct social realization of benefit from human genetic research to the consumer. While patents are indispensable, something more than patents is needed to secure the pathway to full commercial realization. An industrial code of conduct is that something extra which will ensure that when human genetic material is involved in any way, the medical realization should be diligently pursued (by the original intellectual property right holder or by another party if necessary).

Conclusion: Debate and Lost Opportunity

According to the panel, the patent paradigm has been irrevocably placed upon inventions involving human genetic materials. Developments in human genetics over the next 20 years are likely to be as unpredictable as the previous 20 years, but it seems clear that these developments and derivative property disputes will continue to be played out within the patent regime. The high level of consensus amongst the panel precluded a robust discussion of the merits and steering effects of patents per se, and of the best means of ensuring that patents encourage rather than retard the progress of genetic science and realization of tangible social benefit. Unfortunately, there was no one to represent the interests of the genetic source materials or of ultimate consumers. However, it was revealed that the patent debate is an evolutionary process in different stages of development in different jurisdictions around the world. While Europe remains focused upon the basic propriety of patents, America is attempting to reconcile economic and industry realities within the confines of the traditional patent system. The discussion illustrated how difficult it can be to create legal principles of general application which retain the qualities of relevance and justice over time. This is particularly so in the sensitive area of human genetics, which involves rapid and often unpredictable technological change in addition to unique moral and social challenges.

INTRODUCTION

T. DOUGLAS KINSELLA (CHAIRPERSON)
Professor and Director, Office of Medical Bioethics,
Faculty of Medicine, University of Calgary

Internationally, the ethical and legal status of human DNA as property, remains uncertain and controversial. The practices and procedures used in the banking of human DNA are similarly surrounded by ethical and legal uncertainty and controversy. This situation requires urgent international redress because of the potential harms it can bring to both society and genetic research. Because DNA banking is the entrance to most contemporary genetic research, clarification of, and commitment to international ethical and legal precepts to guide human DNA banking would help to allay suspicion and fears, and avoid scientific misadventure.

In the course of our session, we were presented with a variety of issues relevant to human DNA banking in Canada, the United Kingdom, France, the United States, and Europe. From these presentations we can verify that the ethical and legal deficiencies of at least several current practices and procedures used in human DNA banking are, indeed, international in their scope. For some, verification of these deficiencies will prompt a censorial response. For others, presumably most of those attending this conference, verification of these deficiencies will excite the challenges necessary to ensure that these practices and procedures are reconfigured so as to protect the genetic status of humanity.

The survey data presented by Professor Verhoef and her colleagues catalogue some of the relevant deficiencies reported by Canadian DNA bankers, researchers, regulators and administrators. Although potentially capable of fostering misadventure, it is salutary to note that the majority of respondents recognized the "problems", and opted for remedial regulatory initiatives. The report by Professor McEwen echoes this theme in the United States and, further, brings our attention to millions of DNA samples collected for purposes other than scientific research, but which will likely eventually find their way into this stream of inquiry. Similarly, Professor Aymé in her oral presentation reminds us not to neglect both RNA and DNA samples which have found their way to industrial and commercial banks and, at this time, remain outside the ethical and legal purview of academic regulation, imperfect though the latter is. Likewise, in his oral presentation, Professor Prembrey gave us some practical examples from the United Kingdom where researchers and services providers have attempted to inform DNA donors concerning sample linkage and potential breaches of confidentiality. The final presentation in our session, by Professor Quintana, explored some of the existing European ethical and legal paradigms concerning organ transplantation and medical devices which might serve to inform our decisions about human DNA banking.

In summary, somewhat meagre though it is, the existing evidence reveals converging concerns among researchers, ethicists and jurists about the current lack of *formal* ethical and legal regulation of human DNA banking. This convergence of opinion, as it progresses, will no doubt be stressed by those tensions which always exist between and among science, ethics and the law in many areas of science. Hopefully, in the area of human DNA banking, our deliberations at this conference will lessen these tensions and help to create regulation which will respect our genetic heritage and protect our genetic future.

ETHICAL ISSUES CONCERNING CURRENT HUMAN DNA BANKING PRACTICES IN CANADA: THREE PERSPECTIVES†

MARJA J. VERHOEF

Associate Professor, Department of Community Health Sciences

Faculty of Medicine, University of Calgary

RAYMOND M. LEWKONIA

Professor, Departments of Medicine and Medical Genetics

Faculty of Medicine, University of Calgary

T. DOUGLAS KINSELLA

Professor and director, Office of Medical Bioethics

Faculty of Medicine, University of Calgary

Introduction

Few data are available to guide patients, physicians, researchers, research subjects and participants with respect to their ethical and legal obligations concerning human DNA banking.. Although guidelines have been published to assist investigators in some national jurisdictions[1,2], at present no international consensus exists concerning the form or content of ethical, legal, or scientific regulations for human DNA banking.[3] This is disturbing in view of the ethical, legal and social issues that derive from contemporary molecular genetics.[4]

From the perspective of research ethics,[5] DNA banking procedures subserve the ethical propriety of subsequent research. Thus, "getting the DNA sample" precedes and involves recruitment and informed consent which, in turn, engages the ethical principles of respect for persons and virtue.[6] Similar relationships can be constructed between the other procedural components of banking, such as ownership/control, sharing, storage and linkages, on the one hand, and the ethical principles of beneficence, non-maleficence and justice, on the other hand.[7] In effect, the procedural components of the banking of human DNA provide unusually substantive issues and opportunities to analyse the ethical status of human genetic investigation and research.

We investigated the awareness of current policies and practices concerning human DNA banking among three groups of stakeholders: Canadian geneticists and researchers involved in human DNA banking, Canadian Research Ethics Boards and senior administrators of Canadian research institutions. As will be shown, the surveys which we undertook not only reveal deficiencies in current actual practices but also illustrate the perceived need for formal national policies.

Methods

In this paper, we report data obtained in three simultaneous surveys conducted in Canada in mid-1995:

I. A survey of Canadian geneticists and researchers involved in human DNA banking to assess their actual practices and their awareness of and satisfaction with current policies regarding to the collection of, and research with human DNA genetic material in Canada;

II. A survey of Canadian Research Ethics Boards (REBs) to assess their opinions about current and desired policies regarding human DNA banks and collections; and

III. A survey of senior administrators of Canadian research institutions to assess their perceptions of current policies concerning the regulation and commercialization of human DNA banks and collections in their institutions.

In our surveys and in this chapter, we have used the term *DNA bank* to denote a physical location for storage of DNA-containing human material or tissue. Specifically, a DNA bank and/or collection was defined as one that "stores human DNA so that it can be preserved for the purposes of research and/or diagnosis of human genetic disease". We have used the term *DNA banker* to denote persons who store DNA specimens for purposes of service-related investigation, or for basic research, or both. The term *institution* we used to denote the place where service-related DNA-based testing, or basic research, or both, is performed. This may be at a university or an affiliated hospital laboratory. The term *DNA work* we used to denote all varieties of laboratory investigation and research in which human genetic analysis is done, utilizing techniques that examine the DNA of identifiable persons. The term *DNA donor* denotes a person who is asked to provide blood or tissue specimens for investigation or research that will reveal aspects of the genetic constitution of themselves or their relatives.

TABLE 1 includes an overview of the three studies with respect to the surveyed populations, their size and response rate, and the topics which were addressed. Details of each survey will be discussed in the following sections.

TABLE 1: Overview of the three surveys

Survey Population	Size	Response Rate	Questionnaire Topics
Canadian Researchers and Geneticists	473	230(49%)*	Sociodemographics.
- involved in human DNA work	230	132 (57%)	Perception of and satisfaction with existing policies, and practices regarding DNA banking and/or collections.
- involved in human DNA banking	75	75 (57%)	
Canadian Research Ethics Boards (REBs)	156	106 (67%)	Existing policies concerning DNA banks and/or collections. Perceived need for national policies.
Canadian Senior Administrators	91	69 (76%)	Existing policy guidelines concerning DNA banks and/or collections, and commercialization resulting therefrom.

* It emerged that many of these were not involved in human DNA work (see Methods).

I. SURVEY OF RESEARCHERS, BANKERS AND CONTRIBUTORS

Because there is no central or national registry of researchers and others involved in human DNA research in Canada, we compiled a list by searching the mailing lists of agencies funding such research. The resulting list included recipients of grants from the Medical Research Council of Canada (MRCC) and/or the Fonds de la Recherche en Santé du Québec (FRSQ), the mailing list of the Canadian Genetic Diseases Network, the Canadian Genome Analysis and Technology (CGAT) Program's Networks of Centres of Excellence, and Canadian-based members of the American Society of Human Genetics (ASHG). The membership list of the ASHG rather than the Canadian College of Medical Geneticists (CCMG) was used because the former has a more diverse membership of physicians as well as non-physicians. These lists were screened for duplicates and generated a composite list of 473 names.

A questionnaire mailed to each person on the composite list asked whether the recipient was involved in human DNA work, and, if so, whether as a researcher, banker, and/or contributor. The questionnaire also ascertained their sociodemographics, the respondents' perceptions of existing policies guiding ethical aspects of human DNA research in Canada, their satisfaction with these policies, and, finally, their own current practices regarding recruitment, informed consent and sample ownership (including sample sharing, storage, and linkages). Non-respondents were sent one reminder. Some respondents were sent an additional request for clarification if it was not clear from their initial response whether they were involved in *human* DNA research, rather than non-human DNA research.

Results

SOCIODEMOGRAPHICS

Of the 473 potential respondents, 230 (49%) returned the questionnaire. Sixty-eight percent of the respondents were male, and 32% female. Their mean age was 47 years, with a range of 26 to 79 years. Fifty-seven percent (132) were personally involved in *human* DNA work. Numerous cross-activities were reported by the latter: 110 (83%) as researchers, 75 (57%) as bankers, and 70 (53%) as contributors to banks. Seventy-two percent held research grants from various national, provincial and local granting agencies.

OPINIONS ABOUT POLICIES

Thirty-four percent (45/132) of those involved in human DNA work acknowledged familiarity with the 1991 policy statement of the Canadian College of Medical Genetics (CCMG) concerning DNA banks/collections.[8] Of those who were familiar with the CCMG policy statement, 61% were physicians and 38% were not, a result reflective of the CCMG membership which identifies approximately 75% as physicians.

TABLE 2 shows the perceptions of those who responded affirmatively to the question about whether their institution had a policy concerning DNA banks and/or collections.

TABLE 2. Perceived of policies concerning DNA banks and/or collections at the respondent's own institution

	Yes	No	Uncertain	No Response
All Respondents (n=230)	16%	54%	18%	12%
Involved in Human DNA work (n=132)*	23%	62%	8%	6%
DNA Researchers (n=110)*	24%	64%	8%	5%
DNA Bankers (n=75)*	24%	67%	4%	5%
Contributors to banks (n=70)*†	36%	50%	6%	9%

* Many respondents pursue one or more self-selected roles; all numbers rounded to nearest percentage.

† "Contributors" excludes index cases and family members; it is restricted to those who recruit/solicit samples for human DNA banks.

From all groups, at least 50% indicated they believed there were no applicable policies in their institutions. Twenty-seven (12%) respondents left this question unanswered. Of those involved in human DNA work (132), only 31 (23%) indicated that in their estimation, policies existed. These individuals were asked whether they were satisfied with their institution's policies concerning recruitment, informed consent, ownership/control, sample sharing, sample storage and nominal linkage (TABLE 3). Actual numbers are also shown in this table because of the small size of the relevant respondent group. Satisfaction was highest with policies regarding recruitment and informed consent (74% each), and lowest with policies regarding sample sharing (45%) and nominal linkage (42%). Except for the responses concerning recruitment and consent, substantial percentages of respondents were "not satisfied, "uncertain", or did not answer questions concerning ownership, sharing, storage and nominal linkage of samples.

TABLE 3. Satisfaction with their own institutional policies among those involved in human DNA work (n=31)

Policy	Satisfied	Not Satisfied	Uncertain	Missing
Recruitment	23 (74%)	3 (10%)	2 (6%)	3 (10%)
Informed Consent	23 (74%)	3 (10%)	2 (6%)	3 (10%)
Ownership/Control	16 (52%)	5 (16%)	7 (23%)	3 (10%)
Sample Sharing	14 (45%)	5 (16%)	8 (26%)	4 (15%)
Sample Storage	16 (52%)	5 (16%)	6 (19%)	4 (13%)
Nominal Linkage	13 (42%)	2 (6%)	11 (35%)	5 (16%)

CURRENT PRACTICES

Respondents involved in human DNA work were asked who usually solicited DNA samples from index cases and/or family members for their current DNA research. Twenty-three percent (30/132) indicated that genetic counsellors (medical and non-medical) usually recruited participants, 60% (79/132) indicated clinicians, and 20% (27/132) 'other' (e.g. personnel from their own institutional DNA bank and other institutional DNA banks). Some respondents indicated more than one source of recruitment. Twenty percent (27/132) did not answer this question.

Thirty-three (43/132) percent reported that informed consent for specimen banking was obtained by themselves, 30% (40/132) by clinicians, 28% (37/132) by genetic counsellors (medical and non-medical), 13% (17/132) by a research assistant or technician, and 8% (11/132) reported that no informed consent was obtained. As will be obvious, multiple answers were possible given the multiple roles of some respondents, such as physicians, in the recruitment and consent processes. Thirty percent (40/132) did not answer the consent question.

Those who maintained a human DNA bank were asked whether their informed consent form specified ownership/control options for banked samples. Twenty-one percent (16/75) answered 'yes', 56% (42/75) 'no', and in 23% responses were missing. Those whose consent forms specified ownership/control options (n=16), reported that in 56% (9/16) the consent forms specified ownership/control options for index cases, 56% (9/16) for family members, 44% (7/16) for principal investigators, and 19% (3/16) for institutions. In none of the consent forms were ownership/control options specified for sponsors of research.

With respect to storage conditions, only 15% (11/75) of the bankers indicated that the duration of storage was specified in their consent form, and 8% (6/75) that consent for the destruction of samples was specified. Large percentages (23% and 25%, respectively) did not answer the questions regarding consent by donors for duration and storage of samples.

Sixty-one percent (46) of the bankers reported they shared samples with other laboratories, 25% (19/75) did not share, and 13% (10/75) did not answer the question. Of those 46 who shared samples, 89% shared nationally, 87% internationally and 2% commercially. Of those who shared, 48% (22/46) obtained consent to share from each index case and/or family member, 46% (21/46) did not obtain consent, and 6% (3/46) did not answer the question. However, four of the 19 bankers who reported they did not share samples, and one of the bankers who did not respond to the question, nevertheless reported they obtained consent for sharing, giving an overall value of 47% (27/75) who obtained consent to share samples. Of the respondents who obtained consent to share, 63% (17/27) indicated that the consent was restricted to research about the donor patient's own disease/problem.

It was reported that, on only 48% of the consent forms (13/27), donors were advised that linkage of clinical data with their samples was disclosed to sharing banks. Anonymous donor linkage was used by 63% (17/27) of respondents who shared samples and obtained consent to share, one did not use anonymous linkage, and 9 (33%) did not answer the question. Nominal (nominative) donor linkage was used by 15% (4/27) of the respondents, 6 (22%) did not use nominal linkage, and 63% (17/27) did not answer the question about the use of nominal linkage.

TABLE 4 shows the percentages of DNA bankers who reviewed the regulations of the external institution with which they shared samples. Thirty to forty percent did not review any of the external regulations, and at least one third did not answer the relevant questions.

TABLE 4. Review of external institutional regulations prior to sharing samples with external banks (n=46)

	Yes (Always, Sometimes)	Never	Missing
Recruitment	11 (24%)	18 (39%)	17 (37%)
Informed Consent	13 (28%)	17 (37%)	16 (35%)
Ownership/Control	12 (26%)	18 (39%)	16 (35%)
Sample Sharing	18 (39%)	14 (30%)	15 (33%)
Sample Storage	16 (35%)	15 (33%)	15 (33%)
Nominal Linkage	11 (24%)	16 (35%)	19 (41%)

COMMENTARY

Our findings indicated that, according to those involved in human DNA work, very few of their own institutions have an explicit policy concerning DNA banking. This does not necessarily mean that policies do not exist, but could mean that many of those involved in human DNA work are not aware of existing institutional policies. It might also indicate lack of institutional effectiveness in communicating policies. Clarity of awareness and satisfaction among respondents was highest concerning institutional policies for recruitment and informed consent.

Consent for DNA research was obtained from DNA donors by a large percentage (92%) of the respondents. However, our data reveal major concerns with respect to the quality of the informed consent process, a major component of which is the recruitment process. Ownership/control issues were only specified in the consent forms of 21% of DNA bankers, and mainly for index cases: Family members and principal investigators were less frequently considered, and institutions and sponsors seldom or not at all. Storage conditions were specified in less than 16% of consent forms. Forty-eight percent of consent forms disclosed linkage of clinical data with DNA samples. The banking policies of external institutions were reviewed by, at most, 39% of those 46 bankers who shared samples.

The percentages of missing answers to the various questions in our survey were unusually high for mailed survey questionnaires. This may be an indication of either lack of knowledge of policies and/or lack of clarity of existing policies and procedures. However, it could be that policies were clear, but that respondents did not wish to adhere to these policies. Whichever are the relevant answers, it seems that more precision concerning banking policies is needed to enhance the ethical status of DNA donors in Canada.

II. Survey of Research Ethics Boards (REBs)

A composite listing of REBs was created from those known to the MRCC, those included on the Canadian list of paediatric teaching hospitals and affiliated institutions, and those listed as REBs or Ethics Committees by the Association of Universities and Colleges of Canada. These listings were screened for duplicates and generated a final list of 156 REBs. The chairpersons of the latter were asked to respond for their own REB. The one-page questionnaire asked whether formal ethical policies for DNA banks and collections currently existed in their institutions, and whether it was believed that national policies were required. One reminder was sent to REB chairpersons who did not respond after the first mailing.

RESULTS

Sixty-seven percent (106/156) of the questionnaires were returned. Of those responding, 29 (28%) indicated that their REB reviewed research protocols which required DNA banks and/or collections for research. Of these, only 9 respondents (31%) indicated that their REB required specific informed consent forms for research requiring DNA banks or collections.

REB chairpersons whose REBs currently reviewed research protocols which required DNA banks or collections for their research were asked whether their REB had formal policies regarding specific issues with ethical implications and whether their REB believed that Canadian policies for DNA banks or collections should be developed. Figure 1 illustrates that for each of the issues included less than one third of the respondents believed that the issue was included in their institution's accepted policies. Major differences exist between the awareness of existing policies and the perceived need for policies regarding these issues. Expect for the issue of nominal linkage, policies were deemed needed by at least 65% of the respondents. The percentages of missing data with respect to these questions were minimal except regarding nominal linkage (24%). The question concerning the perceived need for Canadian policies was answered both by chairpersons whose REBs had, and those whose REBs did not have formal policies regarding these issues: most believed that formal policies were needed including those who already had policies in place in their institutions.

FIGURE 1

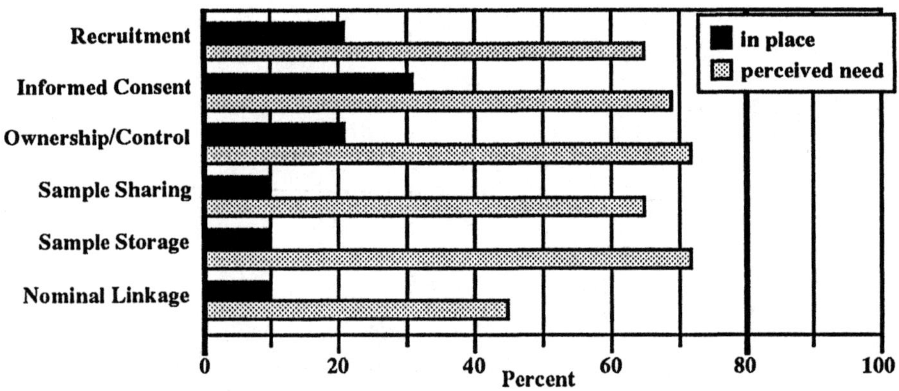

Commentary

Only a small proportion of Canadian REBs review research protocols which require DNA banks and/or collections and, of those, few have formal policies regarding DNA banking. From this perspective, these results might not indicate an urgent need to establish regulatory policies and their attendant bureaucracies. However, from the perspective of patients, index cases and family members, our results do indicate a need for relevant national policies, a conclusion deemed desirable by the great majority of REBs, including those currently lacking formal policies (FIGURE 1). This figure also demonstrates large discrepancies between the extent of policies actually in place in 1995, and perception of desirable policies.

Although the current need for such policies might seem a minor matter in view of the small number of REBs reviewing relevant research, it is certain that DNA-based investigation and research will increase over the next decade in Canada and elsewhere. From this perspective alone, it would seem reasonable to create appropriate policies to anticipate and accommodate, where possible, future requirements for the ethical protection of DNA donors, investigators, institutions and sponsors.

It is interesting to note that major differences appear to exist between researchers and REBs with respect to satisfaction with current policies (Table 5). Researchers tend to be much more satisfied than REBs.

Table 5:. Comparison of satisfaction with their own institutional policies among those involved in human DNA work (n=31) and REBs (n=29)

Policy	Researchers % Satisfied	REBs % believe that policies do not need to be developed
Recruitment	74%	24%
Informed consent	74%	21%
Ownership/control	52%	17%
Sample sharing	45%	21%
Sample storage	52%	14%
Nominal linkages	42%	21%

It should be noted that three of the REB chairpersons indicated that they answered only for themselves and not for their REBs. However, given the large majorities who perceived a need for formal policies, as well as the authoritative status of chairpersons in REB decision-making, it seems reasonable to accept the generalizability of our findings.

III. Survey of Senior Administrators

A list of senior administrators of medical schools and teaching hospitals was compiled from institutional directories, including those at paediatric hospitals and research institutes, and the Association of Universities and Colleges of Canada. In total, 91 senior administrators were surveyed. A one-page questionnaire asked whether the respondents' institutions had, or contemplated, policy guidelines concerning human DNA banks and/or collections, and whether they had, or contemplated, policy guidelines for the commercialization of research outcomes which involved human DNA and/or other genetic materials.

RESULTS

Seventy-six percent (69/91) of the questionnaires were returned. Of those responding, 31 (45%) indicated that clinical and/or research activities which required DNA banks were currently conducted at their institution. Only those at whose institutions these activities took place were asked to respond to the remaining questions. Eight (26%) respondents replied that their institution had policy guidelines for research requiring human DNA banks or collections, 18 did not have guidelines, one was uncertain, and 4 did not answer. Only two of the 18 respondents who replied that their institution had no guidelines reported that such a policy was under consideration, 9 that it was not, 2 were uncertain, and 4 did not answer.

Policy guidelines concerning the commercialization of research outcomes which involved research with human DNA and/or genetic materials were confirmed for 5 of the 31 institutions. Two of the 21 respondents who indicated that no policy concerning commercialization existed in their institution but that it was under consideration.

COMMENTARY

In the opinions of senior administrators, policy guidelines exist or were under consideration in approximately one third of Canadian institutions where clinical and /or research activities requiring human DNA banks or collections are conducted. It is of interest that, with respect to opinions about the existence of current policies, there is close agreement between the responses of administrators (26%) and those involved in human DNA work (23% - Table 2) and REBs (31%).

IV. Discussion

Increasing concerns are being expressed in many countries about the adequacy and ethical sufficiency of policies and practices relating to human DNA banking.[9,10] These concerns derive, in part, from the concern that human molecular genetic investigation, diagnosis and therapy is dependent upon, and conditioned by the ethical policies and practices of such banking. Thus, as reflected in literature from the ethics, legal and social sciences communities, there is apprehension that current regulatory policies are not sufficiently precise to promote ethically sufficient practices in human DNA banking.[11,12]

In our studies we have obtained quantitative survey data about the status of existing policies and practices concerning human DNA banking in Canada, as well as the need for future policies. Our data reveal that, in the opinions of the majority of research administrators, REBs and those involved in human DNA work, most Canadian academic centres do not have formal policies to regulate human DNA banking, although in particular REBs agree that such policies are needed. In addition, the majority of REBs and those involved in human DNA work report current banking practices in which there are obvious ethical deficiencies.

The shortcomings observed in current human DNA banking practices in Canada are many and varied, and are similar to those identified elsewhere.[13,14]Many seem obvious and amenable to correction. For example, despite their admission of an absence of specific banking policies at their own institutions (TABLE 2), most Canadian DNA workers express satisfaction with their own recruitment and informed consent practices for banking (TABLE 3). On the other hand, these practices which engage the ethical principles of respect for persons, justice and virtue, are seen as inadequate by about two-thirds of their own REBs (FIGURE 1). A national policy framework informed by the consensus of those involved in human DNA banking could address the relevant ethical issues, most of which are probably unintended.

Conflicting ethical opinions between researchers (and others) and REBs are not unusual. In our studies, however, the expressed discrepancies between DNA workers and REBs seem to reflect some degree of ethical naiveté. For example, although 45% of DNA workers express satisfaction with their own policies for sample sharing (TABLE 3) - policies which engage the ethical principles of respect for autonomy, confidentiality, justice and virtue - the majority do not actually review the corresponding policies of external institutions with which they share samples (TABLE 4). Under this circumstance it is difficult to comprehend "satisfaction" with a policy when those who are satisfied are largely unaware of the terms and conditions of that policy. Such inconsistency in what is inherently an ethically derived practice clearly can bring moral and other disadvantages to all participants in human DNA research, and, therefore, favors the formation of relevant national, and international DNA banking policies.

Canada has a relatively small, but technically sophisticated, human genetics research community whose opinions about the actual and ideal practices of DNA banking were expected to be readily available to our surveys. This expectation was met with respect to senior administrators and REBs, with 67% compliance from both populations. Unfortunately, in the absence of a national registry, we cannot be certain that we adequately sampled the whole population of researchers, bankers and/or bank contributors. Based on our knowledge of this community, however, we believe that the 132 respondents (57%) were representative of those "involved in human DNA work" in Canada (TABLES 1 and 2). Caution should be exercised in generalizing the responses from those respondents to their reference population for the reasons and limitations that we have discussed.

In summary, our results reveal widespread and substantive deficiencies concerning policy and practice for human DNA banking in Canada. Most institutions, as judged by administrators, REBs and DNA workers, do not have banking policies in place. In addition, our results show that most of the major ethical implications which derive from current banking practices, such as sample ownership, sharing, storage and linkage, are not adequately addressed in local policies. Fortunately, however, these undoubtedly undesirable omissions were counter-balanced by equally strong indications from DNA workers and REBs that formal national policies are desirable.

To some extent the need for formal national policies in Canada is currently being addressed by the draft Canadian Code of Conduct for Research Involving Humans.[15] However, as noted in the Code, greater precision in policy and practice is required to preserve and promote the ethical integrity of human genetic research. As we and others have shown[16,17],ethically-grounded policies and practices in human DNA banking are imperative to achieve this worthwhile goal.

Acknowledgements

The technical assistance of Carole Craig and Kathy Fitch, the secretarial assistance of Lydia Riddell, and the contributions and suggestions of Professor Bartha Maria Knoppers, Dr. Claude Laberge and Dr. Ron Worton are gratefully acknowledged. These studies were supported by a grant from the Canadian Genome Analysis and Technology Program. Requests for reprints should be sent to Dr. T.D. Kinsella, Office of Medical Bioethics, University of Calgary, 3330 Hospital Drive NW, Calgary, Alberta, T2N 4N1.

Endnotes and References

† Supported by a grant from the Canadian Genome Analysis and Technology Program. Reprinted, with modifications, with permission of Emond Montgomery Publications Limited, Toronto, from: *Legal Rights and Human Genetic Material*, Knoppers BM, Caulfield T, Kinsella TD (eds), Chapter 1. Ethical Implications of current practices in human DNA banking in Canada. Verhoef MD, Lewkonia RM, Kinsella TD, 1996

1 Canadian College of Medical Geneticists (CCMG), "Policy Statement Concerning DNA Banking and Molecular Genetic Diagnosis" (1991), 14 *Clin. Invest. Med.* 363.

2 American College of Medical Genetics Storage of Genetics Materials Committee, "Statement on Storage and Use of Genetic Materials" (1995), *57Am. J Hum. Genet.* 1499.

3 UNESCO *Study Concerning the Possibility of Drawing up an International Instrument for the Protection of Human Genome* (27C/45). General Conference, (Paris: September 30, 1993).

4 Beauchamp T.L. and J.F Childress. (eds). *Principles of Biomedical Ethics.* (Oxford: Oxford University Press, 1994).

5 Ibid.

6 Ibid.

7 Knoppers B.M. and C.M. Laberge, "Research and Stored Tissues. Persons as Sources, Samples as Persons?" (1995), 274 *JAMA*: 1806.

8 Supra note 1.

9 Supra note 7.

10 Clayton E.W. , K.K. Steinberg, M..J. Khoury et al. "Informed Consent for Genetic Research on Stored Tissue Samples" (1995), 274 *JAMA* 1786.

11 Wilfond B.S. and K. Nolan, "National Policy Development for the Clinical Application of Genetic Diagnostic Technologies" (1993), 270 *JAMA* 2948.

12 Rüs P. "The Danish Brain Collection and Its Important Potential for Future Research" (1993), 15 *IRB* 5.

13 Weir R.F., J.R. Horton, "DNA Banking and Informed Consent-Part 2" (1995), 17 *IRB* 1.

14 McEwen J.E., P.R. Reilly, "A Survey of DNA Diagnostic Laboratories Regarding DNA Banking" (1995), 56 *Am. J Hum. Genet.* 1477.

15 *Code of Conduct for Research Involving Humans.* Draft prepared by the Tri-Council Working Group. Ottawa: March 1996.

16 Supra note 13.

17 Supra note 14.

DNA SAMPLING AND BANKING: PRACTICES AND PROCEDURES IN THE UNITED STATES

JEAN E. McEWEN

Boston College Law School and New England School of Law

Ongoing advances in our understanding of human genetics are leading us into a new era: an era of DNA banking. DNA banking typically involves the routine collection and storage of DNA (or of biological samples from which DNA may be extracted in the future), typically with individual identifiers.

Although DNA banking in the United States had its inception in the context of medical research and clinical medicine, these applications of the technology are quickly becoming eclipsed by the storage of DNA in the forensics context. There, government agencies specifically, state crime laboratories and the United States Department of Defence are establishing large repositories of biological samples (and of the data derived from their analysis) to assist in the identification of individuals. In the state law enforcement arena, DNA data banks are being used to identify suspects in crimes of violence; in the military, stored DNA will be used to identify soldiers missing in action in war.

A large and growing number of DNA samples also continue to be collected and stored for research or clinical purposes. For example, many university and hospital-based labs and biotechnology companies store samples for gene mapping studies or other research use. Some biotech companies, for a fee, offer DNA storage as a service to researchers, or as a clinical service to physicians, genetic counsellors, or individuals in families at risk for particular genetic disorders.

This paper outlines the current status in the United States of these DNA collection and storage activities. It also describes various "inchoate" DNA "banks": repositories of samples originally obtained for reasons unrelated to DNA analysis, but from which DNA could potentially be extracted in the future.

DNA Banking in the Law Enforcement Context

By mid 1996, 42 states had enacted statutes to establish forensic DNA data banks (and associated DNA banks), and several other states had relevant bills pending. These laws authorize or require law enforcement agencies to collect blood (and in some cases saliva) samples from various categories of criminal offenders, either at the time of sentencing or prior to their release from prison.[1] State crime labs will then extract DNA from these samples and, using what is becoming a nationally standardized set of enzymes and probes, create for each offender a unique DNA identification profile. These profiles will then be entered onto computer in digitized form, and the samples themselves placed in storage. Should biological material of unknown origin (such as semen or blood) be found at the scene of a future crime, investigators will be able to compare the DNA profile derived from analyzing that sample with the reference profiles already in the data bank. A "match" so attained may then lead to apprehension of the perpetrator and resolution of the case. DNA profiles from samples collected at the scenes of as-yet unresolved crimes will also be entered into the data bank and compared with each other in an effort to detect linkages.[2,3,4]

Nationwide, by mid 1996, almost 300,000 samples had been amassed around the country for forensic DNA data banks. Although only about 65,000 of these samples had been tested, the rate at which crime labs (or the private labs with which they contract) will be able to process samples should increase markedly over the next few years, as the technology becomes less expensive and better automated and as more DNA analysis resources become available. The federal DNA Identification Act, passed in 1994, will make $40 million in grants available to states for DNA work over a five year period to states that adhere to specified uniform standards.[5] This law also formally authorizes the Federal Bureau of Investigation (FBI) to establish a national computer network (called "CODIS") to facilitate the exchange of DNA data between crime labs in different states.[6,7] A proposal to set up a *federal* DNA data bank (consisting of samples and profiles from persons convicted of certain offences in federal or military courts) is also under consideration.

State forensic DNA data banks (and their associated DNA banks) hold much promise for the resolution of violent crime cases, especially sexual assault cases, where rates of recidivism are known to be exceptionally high. By mid 1996, data banks around the United States had already achieved "cold hits" (matches to a known offender whose profile was in the data bank as a result of a prior conviction) in at least 28 cases. In 45 other instances involving more than 100 crime scenes, data banks had been used to link two or more as-yet unresolved cases to the same (still unidentified) perpetrator.

The National Academy of Sciences, in a 1992 report, recommended a "go-slow" approach to the expansion of forensic DNA data banks, cautioning that massive data banks launched too hastily could soon find themselves "locked in" to an outmoded technology.[8] Nevertheless, a rapid expansion has already occurred in the range of offenders many states' laws are designed to target. Originally drafted to cover primarily persons convicted of rape or other violent offences, many statutes now require samples from non-violent felons or even from those convicted only of specified misdemeanours.[9]

For example, Virginia, which maintains the nation's largest DNA data bank, now requires samples from *all* convicted felons (including those convicted of "white collar" crimes).[10] South Dakota takes samples from those who have merely been *arrested* for an otherwise covered offence.[11] States increasingly are moving to extend their data banks to cover juvenile offenders, mentally institutionalized offenders, and specified plea bargainers and prison transferees.[12] In addition, most states are now requiring samples not only from offenders incarcerated after the enabling statute's effective date, but also from those already in prison.[13] These trends have raised concerns that DNA data banking requirements, over time, will fall into the same pattern as conventional fingerprinting requirements, which in the United States are increasingly being extended to cover certain segments of the *non-criminal* population.[14]

As of this writing, the American courts that have entertained challenges to state forensic DNA data banking laws have consistently upheld the laws. Although not always without dissent, courts have upheld even some laws that sweep quite broadly in scope as against the claim that they violate the constitutional (Fourth Amendment) prohibition against unreasonable searches and seizures.[15] Courts have also upheld statutes that require samples from offenders already in prison on the law's effective date (and not just from those convicted thereafter), rejecting the argument that they violate the constitutional protection against *ex post facto* laws.[16] In addition, courts have rejected arguments that forensic DNA data banking laws violate due process, equal protection, freedom of religious belief, the prohibition against cruel and unusual punishment, and the right to the effective assistance of counsel.[17]

Privacy concerns associated with state forensic DNA data banks

Understanding the unique *privacy* concerns associated with forensic DNA data banks requires an appreciation of the difference between the DNA *data* stored in such data banks and the *samples* from which those data are obtained.[18] DNA identification *profiles* raise only limited privacy concerns because they are (at least currently) derived through restriction fragment length polymorphism (RFLP) analysis, a technique that merely examines so-called "junk DNA" (areas that do not code for structural proteins).[19] For this reason, DNA profiles contain only limited information relating to individual identity and no health related information. Although this is beginning to change somewhat as forensic data banks move increasingly toward PCR-based analysis methods (which focus directly on portions of genes, and not just on spacer material), the profiles generated are still, for the most part, likely to have quite limited informational value.[20]

Stored DNA *samples*, however, raise much greater privacy concerns, because they contain a potential *wealth* of genetic and other information, some of which may be highly personal, sensitive, or stigmatizing to individuals.[21] Moreover, such information may be of interest to a range of persons and institutional entities, from insurance companies to employers, school systems, and other public agencies.[22] The practical extent of the risk of unauthorized dissemination to such third parties has occasionally been overstated (for example, an insurance company interested in learning an applicant's predisposition to genetic disease could just as easily request a blood sample from the applicant and test it directly, without seeking recourse to the samples in a state crime lab). Nevertheless, concerns persist about the potential for stored samples to be used for purposes different from those for which they were initially collected.[23] For example, a particular concern is that the unique composition of *forensic* DNA banks (with large numbers of samples from violent felons) will make those repositories a nearly irresistible source of samples for *behavioural* genetics research or testing (for example, on genetic predispositions to violence)-without the informed consent of those from whom the samples were taken.[24]

The National Academy of Sciences, in recognition of the special risks to privacy that samples collected for forensic DNA data banks may implicate, has recommended that samples be destroyed "promptly" after being analyzed-at least once the data banks are "up and running."[25] However, a 1994 survey of state crime labs that house DNA data banks revealed that the labs, without exception, were planning to retain their samples indefinitely (except in situations where expungement is necessary, such as where the conviction in connection with which the sample was drawn is reversed on appeal).[26] Crime labs cite a need to save samples in order to ensure their availability to defendants in future cases, for re-testing if new and improved testing technologies become available, and for quality control purposes.

Although state forensic DNA data banking laws are somewhat uneven in the privacy protections they provide,[27] the federal DNA Identification Act, which all states will be required to comply with to receive federal DNA analysis funds and participate in the CODIS system, incorporates several privacy provisions. It requires crime labs to limit the disclosure of stored samples (at least in their individually identifiable form) to criminal justice agencies for "law enforcement identification purposes" (and for use in court proceedings if otherwise admissible and to defendants in connection with the cases in which they are charged).[28] It also provides criminal fines of up to $100,000 for the knowing, unauthorized *obtaining* of DNA *samples* and for the knowing, unauthorized *obtaining or disclosure* of DNA *data*.

The DNA Identification Act does not, however, speak directly to the unauthorized disclosure of DNA *samples*, nor does it address the question of the precise circumstances under which *anonymous* samples may be used for genetic or other *research*. Interestingly, Alabama's DNA data banking law specifically authorizes the use of samples collected for its data bank for "educational research or medical research or development"[29] - an authorization that would presumably encompass a range of non-law enforcement applications.

DNA Banking by the United States Military

Since June of 1992, the Armed Forces Institute of Pathology of the United States Department of Defence has required all military inductees and all active duty and reserve military personnel to provide both blood and saliva samples for a DNA repository.[30] These samples, which are collected at the time of enlistment, re-enlistment, or preparation for operational deployment, are intended to be used for humanitarian purposes: to help identify soldiers missing in action in future wars so that their remains can be returned to their families. In an era of increasingly destructive weaponry, DNA identification analysis has become in some cases the only reliable means of identifying human remains left at the battlefield.

Although DNA analysis was first used to identify war casualties during Operation Desert Storm, those identifications pre-dated the establishment of the DNA *repository* and thus required comparing DNA from remains with DNA from samples provided by the missing soldier's relatives. Having a reference sample on file from each service member will make possible for *future* wars the *direct* comparison of DNA from remains and banked DNA known to have come from the missing service member. This will permit positive identification even where paternity is uncertain or where no biological relatives are available for testing.

The military stores the samples collected for its repository in a large warehouse located just outside of Washington, DC. Samples are kept in two forms: blood stain cards (vacuum-sealed and placed in large freezers); and buccal swabs (preserved in vials with isopropanol at room temperature). By the middle of 1996, almost 1,500,000 samples had already been collected. More than 4 million are expected to be in storage by the year 2001, and at full capacity, the repository will hold some 18 million samples. The current policy of the Department of Defence calls for extracting DNA from these samples only as the need arises (in the event that a soldier is missing in action), although DNA is also being extracted from a limited number of samples for quality assurance and research purposes.

The military's DNA collection program was challenged in 1995 by two marines who were subjected to court-martial proceedings as a result of their refusal to provide samples. A federal district court upheld the program, rejecting the service members' claims that it violated the constitution and the terms of existing military contracts or was inconsistent with military regulations governing the protection of human research subjects.[31] The court also upheld the military's initial plan to retain all samples for a period of 75 years. This decision was appealed, however, and during the pendency of the appeal, the Department of Defence amended its policy so as to permit service members to request the destruction of their samples when they leave the military.[32] It also reduced to 50 years the period of time the samples will be kept and clarified its policy regarding the range of permissible uses of samples. Under the revised policy, samples cannot be used without consent for any purpose other than remains identification (and routine quality assurance), except where subpoenaed for the investigation or prosecution of a felony.[33]

DNA Banking for Clinical and Research Purposes

DNA banking in academic institutions and commercial labs, while still a relatively novel activity, appears to be on the increase. A 1992 poll of eleven biotechnology companies that examined the extent of *commercial* DNA storage going on at the time suggested that fewer than 10,000 samples were then being banked in the United States, and that many of those were being kept for research investigators rather than for individual patients.[34] However, a 1994 survey of 148 North American DNA diagnostic labs--both commercial and academic--showed that 90% had begun to bank DNA in at least some form or forms, and that over half of those already had 500 or more samples in storage.[35] Moreover, almost one-third of the labs in the survey indicated that they planned to develop DNA banking further as a service over the next two years.

United States biotechnology companies and university or hospital-based labs that store DNA generally do so for one of two purposes. Some labs, particularly in the commercial arena, bank samples as a service to individuals or families believed to be at risk for particular genetic conditions; such persons are often interested in making their samples available for family-based linkage testing in the future. These samples are frequently, although not always, stored at the request of an intermediary, such as a physician or genetic counsellor. Other facilities bank DNA for research purposes, such as for gene mapping studies, which typically require samples from many family members over a span of several generations. The line separating these two types of banking is sometimes murky; for example, a sample initially provided for purposes of linkage testing might later (in the absence of any agreement to the contrary) be used for genetic research - perhaps on an unrelated condition. A very small number of samples banked in commercial DNA facilities are stored for identification purposes; these are typically reference samples from children stored by parents who want to ensure that the child's DNA will be on hand for identification profiling in the (however unlikely) event of a future abduction. However, most DNA samples stored in commercial and academic facilities are being kept for medical rather than identification purposes.[36]

The forms in which DNA is banked vary.[37,38] Seventy labs in the 1994 survey indicated that they were storing multiple samples in more than one form, with 25% stating that they kept samples in four or more forms. In addition to keeping the extracted DNA, many labs were also keeping transformed cell lines, cryopreserved or unprocessed blood or other tissue, paraffin blocks, fibroblast lines in culture, non-transformed isolated lymphocytes, or DNA in some other form or forms.[39]

Policies and Procedures of Clinical and Research Banks

Only four percent of the labs in the 1994 survey that banked DNA indicated that their labs had never become involved in a dispute with family members involving their DNA banking activities.[40] However, few entities that bank DNA appear to have developed comprehensive written depositor's agreement, written internal procedures, or other documentation designed to minimize the potential for misunderstandings with depositors that could lead to such disputes.[41,42] Although large commercial DNA banks are more likely than small academically-based banks to have developed such written policies, 35% of all labs in the 1994 survey that banked DNA indicated that they had no written internal policies regarding any aspects of DNA storage, and more than half were without any type of written depositor's agreement.[43] Many labs take the position that it is the responsibility of the entity or person who draws the sample and submits it for storage to communicate to the depositor the applicable storage policies and conduct the necessary follow-up.

A number of labs, however, have informal *unwritten* policies regarding various operational matters. In addition, research-oriented DNA banks, although they do not technically use written "depositor's agreements", generally employ more general informed consent forms, sometimes with accompanying information summaries provided to potential participants in their studies.[44,45] However, many of these informed consent forms merely explain the research to be done on the samples and do not specifically mention the fact that the samples will be *stored* (or that transformed cell lines will be created). In addition, both the 1994 survey and another study that comprehensively examined more than 100 informed consent forms used for DNA banking throughout the country showed that many consent forms that do explicitly discuss sample storage tend to do so in a very cursory manner.[46,47]

Protocols for maintaining the privacy of samples banked for research or clinical use (and for communicating those protocols to depositors) vary widely among banks. Most simply inform depositors or research subjects that their "privacy will be maintained", without further describing how this will be accomplished. Only about one of every six labs in the 1994 survey that banked DNA had a written internal policy or written depositor's agreement that specified what actions were necessary before the bank would release an aliquot of stored DNA to the depositor or his or her physician; even fewer had documentation outlining the conditions under which samples could be released to the depositor's family members or to other third parties. In addition, only about one in every six banks had documentation stating the conditions under which samples could be disseminated (anonymously) to others for research purposes. Yet, 53% of the banks in the 1994 survey stated that they had, in fact, at least on occasion, shared anonymized samples for research purposes with investigators at other institutions.[48]

Another area in which most DNA banks have not yet developed clear policies relates to their procedures for maintaining contact with depositors or research subjects and/or for recontacting them in the future concerning the availability of a new or improved test or treatment for the disorder in question. In addition, among the banks that have developed such policies, few convey them by way of a depositor's agreement or other written communication at the time the sample is collected.[49,50]

The above-mentioned study of consent documents used in conjunction with research-oriented DNA banking found none stating that persons who provide samples retain any ownership interest in those samples, or may be entitled to future profits should the research someday result in the development of commercially valuable products (such as diagnostic tests, drugs, or other therapies).[51] In fact, very few DNA banks convey to depositors or research subjects any reference at all to even the *possibility* that some commercial benefit may result (to the researcher) from studying the stored samples.[52,53] This silence is striking because a leading 1989 case of the California Supreme Court, *Moore v. Regents of the University of California*, suggested that significant liability may attach when a DNA bank fails to address issues of potential commercialization with those who provide DNA samples for study.[54] In *Moore*, a physician and various researchers used a patient's cell lines to obtain a patent without the patient's authorization. The court declined to recognize the existence of a property right of the patient in the cell lines and thus did not hold them liable for conversion; however, it held that the patient could state a claim for breach of fiduciary duty or lack of informed consent based on their actions. The court reasoned that a physician, in obtaining a patient's consent to medical treatment, must disclose personal interests (whether research or economic) unrelated to the patient's health that may affect his or her professional judgement.

The fact that most entities that bank DNA have developed little written documentation regarding these and other potentially problematic aspects of their storage activities may be due in part to the fact that some labs, while technically banking DNA according to a broad definition of the term, collect samples only sporadically or on special request. Some, for example, may simply have accumulated a number of samples from patients and families over time in the course of studying a particular genetic disorder. Nonetheless, there has been a growing recognition of the importance of developing written agreements to anticipate and address potential ethical and legal problems attendant to this activity--even for entities that store DNA on a relatively small scale basis, secondary to their study of disease.[55,56] To this end, several model consent forms have been drafted that address various aspects of DNA storage in there search and clinical contexts.[57]

Inchoate DNA "Banks"

Many collections of biological samples that were originally obtained and archived for reasons unrelated to DNA analysis may in the future be sought to be used for DNA testing or research, and for this reason can be viewed as inchoate DNA "banks." For example, the Armed Forces Institute of Pathology, separate and apart from its above-described DNA repository, houses a collection of pathological and surgical specimens from some 2.5 million cases, accessioned and coded since 1917 by pathologic diagnosis.[58] Most hospital pathology labs in the United States likewise keep pathology specimens embedded in paraffin tissue blocks as a matter of routine, frequently for an indefinite period of time.[59]

Although these samples are kept primarily for medico-legal purposes, they hold obvious appeal to research investigators as a resource for retrospective genetic research studies (for example, the correlation of genotype to pathogenesis and prognosis).

DNA "banks" could also be developed from placental blood cryopreserved for bone marrow transplantation,[60] from blood in ordinary blood banks, or even, potentially, from residual (surplus) blood or tissue samples initially obtained from patients in the course of ordinary medical care. For example, the Centers for Disease Control (CDC) has archived tens of thousands of individually identifiable blood samples drawn from the participants in its National Health and Nutrition Examination Surveys (NHANES) - a longitudinal study to monitor and track the health status of persons from various demographic groups.

Other examples of large inchoate DNA "banks" in the United States reside in the collective repositories of blood spots on newborn screening cards ("Guthrie cards") that have been amassed over the years in state public health labs. Every state in the country has a mandatory newborn screening program, which requires taking a small sample of blood from all babies and spotting it on a card, so that it can be tested for PKU and other treatable inborn errors of metabolism. A 1993 survey of all United States newborn screening labs found that in 75% of the states, these cards were being retained after the testing is complete-at least for a short period of time.[61] Three states indicated that they saved all their cards for a period of 20-25 years, four others stated that they planned to keep their cards indefinitely, and several others said they were considering moving to permanent retention.

Although most states that keep their newborn screening cards have systematically begun to do so only in recent years, eleven have been saving them since the 1960s. As a result, eight labs in the survey indicated that they had in their possession cards dating back more than ten years, with two having cards dating from 1967 and 1970, respectively. While most labs had accumulated less than 500,000 cards over the years, seven had amassed more than 500,000--with four of those reporting collections of between 1 and 5 million cards and one reporting a collection of 6 million. The number of cards collected over the twelve month period immediately preceding the survey ranged from less than 10,000 in four states to more than 500,000 in two of the most populous states.[62] Thus, while it is difficult to estimate precisely the total number of newborn screening cards retained in United States newborn screening labs, it appears to be at least in the tens of millions.

The conditions under which the cards are maintained varies widely among labs; some keep them in boxes at room temperature, some keep them in boxes or folders in freezers, refrigerators, or climate controlled rooms, and some keep them in basements or warehouses. However, it appears that the blood spots on the cards may remain remarkably stable even when the cards are stored in less than optimal conditions. For example, in one state a card released to a forensic lab was introduced as a critical piece of evidence in a murder trial; the lab was able to extract from the blood spot sufficient DNA to create an identification profile of the victim even though the card had been stored at room temperature for more than ten years.[63]

Only 13% of the labs in the 1993 survey indicated that their state departments of public health had issued written regulations on third party access to newborn screening cards, and only 19% said that they had developed written internal protocols on this matter. Although the labs were not asked how many requests for cards they had received from research investigators or from other third parties, several volunteered that they had recently begun to receive more such requests, and one predicted that such requests would soon begin to multiply.[64]

Proposals to Regulate Clinical, Research, and Inchoate DNA Banks

Research and clinical service-oriented DNA banks, unlike their counterparts in the forensics context, are essentially unregulated in the United States. The same is true of most "inchoate" DNA banks of the type described above-at least insofar as concerns issues of privacy and access. This situation, coupled with the fact that few DNA banks to date have engaged in formal self regulation, has led some to call for strict laws governing DNA storage, [65] it was also major impetus behind the drafting of the proposed Human Genome Privacy Act (HGPA).[66]

The HGPA, if enacted, would alter existing practice by presuming the destruction of samples provided for a particular purpose following the completion of the authorized analysis unless otherwise directed by the sample source. It would also give individuals the right to prohibit the use of their samples for future research, even if such research is to be conducted anonymously. Although prospects for whole enactment of the HGPA at the federal level remain uncertain, the Act has had considerable influence on portions of other relevant bills introduced in Congress.[67] In addition, the HGPA has served as a model for genetic privacy legislation that has passed or is pending in several states.[68]

The publication in 1995 of a major consensus statement on informed consent for genetic research on stored tissue samples has also begun to sensitize those who bank DNA (or other tissue samples from which DNA could someday be extracted) to the potential ethical and legal problems involved with the long-term storage of genetic material.[69] For *newly collected* samples (which will become the stored samples of tomorrow), the guidelines recommend giving those who have provided the samples the ability to choose whether they wish to make their samples available for research, and if so, whether the samples may be used in identifiable or linked (as distinct from purely anonymous) research. In order to enable subjects to make this decision, the guidelines recommend informing them about the risks and benefits of participation, the extent to which confidentially can realistically be maintained, under what (if any circumstances) they will be recontacted, and their ability to withdraw from the study at any time. The guidelines also state that subjects should be given the opportunity to decide (among other things) whether or not their samples may be shared with other researchers (either inside or outside the institution) or used only to study certain disorders.[70]

For samples that have *already* been collected and that are identifiable or can be linked, the guidelines would require recontacting the person who provided the sample to obtain such consent, *except* where it can be determined that the person who provided the sample previously agreed to its use for genetic research or where the standards for the waiver or alteration of informed consent under existing research regulations have been satisfied. The guidelines also outline a series of detailed recommendations regarding the treatment of research protocols that propose to "anonymize" existing identifiable samples analysis so that they can be used for genetic research.[71]

The American Society of Human Genetics (ASHG) and the American College of Medical Genetics (ACMG) have both issued sets of voluntary guidelines on DNA banking; these guidelines reflect strongly the principle that those who provide samples for banking have a right to control what happens to those samples in the future.[72,73] However, there remains little agreement on when, if ever, stored biological samples collected for purposes unrelated to genetic research may be used for such future research without the specific and renewed informed consent of those from whom they were taken.[74] Many pathologists have decried the call for heightened informed consent requirements for genetic studies using anonymous stored samples as being overly rigid and as unduly impeding the progress of important epidemiological studies, many of which cannot be done except with large numbers of archived tissue samples.[75] The guidelines in the consensus statement have also been criticized as encouraging the very reductionism they were ostensibly meant to prevent, by according to samples such life of their own as to make them more akin to the "persons" in the research, and rendering the persons themselves mere "sources".[76]

Acknowledgements

The research for this work was supported by Boston College Law School, New England School of Law, the Eunice Kennedy Center for Mental Retardation, and a grant from the Ethical, Legal, and Social Implications Program of the Human Genome Project (Department of Energy Grant DE-FG02-91ER61237).

Endnotes and References

1 Ala. Code §§36-18-20, et seq. (1994); Alaska Stat. §44.41.035 (1996); Ariz. Rev. Stat .Ann. §31-281 (1993); Ark. Acts 922 (1995); Cal. Penal Code §§290.2, 3060.5, Cal. Govt. Code §76104.5 (1994); Colo. Rev. Stat. Ann. §17-2-201(5)(g)(1) (1988); Conn. Gen. Stat. Ann. §54-102g (1994); Del. Code Ann. tit. 29, §4713 (1994); Fla. Stat. Ann. §943.325 (1994); Ga. Code Ann. §24-4-60 (1992); Haw. Rev. Stat. §706-603 (1992); Ill. Ann. Stat. ch. 730, ¶ 5/5-4-3 (1992); Ind. Code Ann. §10-1-9 (1996); Iowa Code Ann. §13.10, Iowa Admin. Code

§§61-8.1(13), et seq. (1991); Kan. Stat. Ann. §21-2511 (1991); Ky. Rev. Stat. Ann. §§17:170, 17:175 (1992); Me. Rev. Stat. Ann. tit. 25, §1571 (1996); Md. Ann. Code art. 88B, §12A, Md. Code Ann. Cts. & Jud. Proc. §10-915 (1994); Mich. Comp. Laws Ann. §750.520m (1994); Minn. Stat. Ann. §§299C.155, 609.3461 (1993); Miss. Code Ann. §45-33-15 (1995); Mo. Ann. Stat. §§650.050, 650.055 (1991); Mont. Code Ann. §44-6-101 (1995); Nev. Rev. Stat. Ann. §176.111 (1989); N.J. Stat. Ann. §§53:1-20.17, et seq. (1994); N.H. Laws ch. 177 (1996); N.Y. Exec. Law Art. §§995, et seq. (1994); N.C. Gen. Stat. §§15A-266, et seq. (1993); N.D. Cent. Code §§31-13-02, et seq. (1995); Ohio Rev. Code Ann. §§109.573, 2151.315, 2901.07 (1995); Okla. Stat. Ann. tit. 22, §§751.1, 991a, tit. 57, §584, tit. 74, §§150.27, et seq. (1996); Or. Rev. Stat. §§137.076, 181.085 (1991); 35 Pa. Cons. Stat. §§7651.101, et seq. (1996); S.C. Code Ann. §§23-3-600, et seq. (1995); S.D. Codified Laws Ann. §§23-5-14, et seq. (1990); Tenn. Code Ann. §§38-6-113, 40-35-321 (1991); Tex. Code Ann. §§411.141, et seq. (1995); Utah Code Ann. §§53-5-212.1, et seq. (1994); Va. Code Ann. §19-2-310.2 (1993); Wash. Rev. Code §§43.43.752, 43.43.754 (1990); W. Va. Code §§15-2B-1, et seq. (1995); Wis. Stat. Ann. §§165-76, 165.77, 973047 (1993).

2 National Academy of Sciences, National Research Council, Commission on Life Sciences, Board of Biology, *DNA Technology in Forensic Science*, (Washington, DC: National Academy of Sciences,1992).

3 United States Congress, Office of Technology Assessment, *Genetic Witness: Forensic Uses of DNA Tests* OTA-BA-438, (Washington, DC: United States Government Printing Office, 1990).

4 Ballantyne J., G. Sensabaugh, and J. Witowski, eds., *DNA Technology and Forensic Science*, Banbury Report 32, (Cold Spring Harbor, NY: Cold Spring Harbor Laboratory Press, 1989).

5 DNA Identification Act, 42 U.S.C. §§14131, *et seq.*, §§379kk, *et seq.* (1994).

6 Ibid.

7 Technical Working Group on DNA Analysis Methods (TWGDAM), "The Combined DNA Index System (CODIS): A Theoretical Model" in Kirby L.T., ed., *DNA Fingerprinting: An Introduction* (New York: Stockton Press, 1989) at 279.

8 Supra note 2.

9 McEwen J.E. and P.R. Reilly, "A Review of State Legislation on DNA Forensic Data Banking" (1994), 54 *Am. J. Hum. Genet.* 941.

10 Va. Code Ann. §19-2-310.2 (1993).

11 S.D. Codified Laws Ann. §§23-5-14, et seq. (1990).

12 Supra note 9.

13 Ibid.

14 Bereano P.L., "DNA Identification Systems: Social Policy and Civil Liberties Concerns" (1990), 1 *Int'l J. Bioethics* 146; Shapiro E. D. and Weinberg M.L., "DNA Data Banking: The Dangerous Erosion of Privacy" (1990), 38 *Clev. St. L. Rev.* 455.

15 *Rise v. Oregon*, 59 F.3d 1556 (9th Cir. 1995); *Jones v. Murray*, 962 F.2d 302 (4th Cir. 1992), *cert. denied*, 113 S. Ct. 472 (1992); *Ryncarz v. Eikenberry*, 824 F. Supp. 1493 (E.D. Wash. 1993); *Sanders v. Coman*, 864 F. Supp. 496 (E.D. N.C. 1994); *Vanderlinden v. Kansas*, 874 F. Supp. 1210 (D. Kan. 1995); *People v. Calahan*, 649 N.E.2d 588 (Ill. App. 1995); *State ex rel. Juvenile Department v. Orozco*, 878 P.2d 432 (Or. App. 1994); *Washington v. Olivas*, 856 P.2d 1076 (Wash. 1993); *People v. Wealer*, 636 N.E.2d 1129 (Ill. App. 1994), *cert. denied*, 642 N.E.2d 1299 (Ill. 1994); *Gilbert v. Peters*, 55 F.3d 237 (7th Cir. 1995).

16 *Rise v. Oregon*, 59 F.3d 1556 (9th Cir. 1995); *Ewell v. Murray*, 11 F.3d 482 (4th Cir. 1993), *cert. denied*, 114 S. Ct. 2112 (1994); *Vanderlinden v. Kansas*, 874 F. Supp. 1210 (D. Kan. 1995); *Sanders v. Coman*, 864 F. Supp. 496 (E.D. N.C. 1994); *Ryncarz v. Eikenberry*, 824 F. Supp. 1493 (E.D. Wash. 1993); *Washington v. Olivas*, 856 P.2d 1076 (Wash. 1993); *People v. Calahan*, 649 N.E.2d 588 (Ill. App. 1995); *Gilbert v. Peters*, 55 F.3d 237 (7th Cir. 1995).

17 *Rise v. Oregon*, 59 F.3d 1556 (9th Cir. 1995); *Gilbert v. Peters*, 55 F.3d 237 (7th Cir. 1995). *Jones v. Murray*, 962 F.2d 302 (4th Cir. 1992), *cert. denied*, 113 S. Ct. 472 (1992); *Vanderlinden v. Kansas*, 874 F. Supp. 1210 (D. Kan. 1995); *Sanders v. Coman*, 864 F. Supp. 496 (E.D. N.C. 1994); *Ryncarz v. Eikenberry*, 824 F. Supp. 1493 (E.D. Wash. 1993); *People v. Calahan*, 649 N.E.2d 588 (Ill. App. 1995); *State ex rel. Juvenile Department v. Orozco*, 878 P.2d 432 (Or. App. 1994); *People v. Wealer*, 636 N.E.2d 1129 (Ill. App. 1994), *cert. denied*, 642 N.E.2d 1299 (Ill. 1994); *Washington v. Olivas*, 856 P.2d 1076 (Wash. 1993);

18 American Society of Human Genetics (ASHG), "Ad Hoc Committee on Individual Identification by DNA Analysis, Individual Identification by DNA Analysis: Points to Consider" (1990), 46 *Am. J. Hum. Genet.* 631.

19 Supra note 2.

20 Ibid.

21 Reilly P.R., "Reflections on the Use of DNA Forensic Science and Privacy Issues", in Ballantyne J., G. Sensabaugh and J. Witowski , eds., *DNA Technology and Forensic Science* (Cold Spring Harbor: Cold Spring Harbor Laboratory Press, 1989) at 43.

22 Bereano P.L., "The impact of DNA-based identification systems on civil liberties" in Billings P.R., ed., *DNA on Trial: Genetic Identification and Criminal Justice* (Cold Spring Harbor: Cold Spring Harbor Laboratory Press, 1992) at 119; DeGorgey A., "The Advent of DNA Databanks: Implications for Information Privacy" (1990), 16 *Am. J. L. & Med.* 381.

23 Andrews L.B., "DNA Testing, Banking and Individual Rights" in Knoppers B.M. and C.M. Laberge, eds., *Genetic Screening: From Newborns to DNA Typing* (Amsterdam: Excerpta Medica, 1990) at 217.

24 Scheck B., "DNA Data Banking: A Cautionary Tale" (1994), 54 *Am. J. Hum. Genet.* 931; Wilker N.L., S. Stawski, R. Lewontin and P.R. Billings, "DNA Data Banking and the Public Interest" in Billings P.R., ed., *DNA on Trial: Genetic Identification and Criminal Justice* (Cold Spring Harbor, NY: Cold Spring Harbor Laboratory Press, 1992) at 141.

25 Supra note 2.

26 McEwen J. E., "Forensic DNA Data Banking by State Crime Laboratories" (1995), 56 *Am. J. Hum. Genet.* 1487.

27 Supra note 9.

28 Supra note 5.

29 Ala. Code §§36-18-20, *et seq.* (1994).

30 Assistant Secretary of Defense (Health Affairs) Memorandum and Policy Statement, "Establishment of a Repository of Specimen Samples to Aid in Remains Identification Using Genetic Deoxyribonucleic Acid (DNA) Analysis" January 5, 1993.

31 *Mayfield v. Dalton*, 901 F. Supp. 300 (D. Hawaii 1995).

32 Assistant Secretary of Defense (Health Affairs), Memorandum, "Policy Refinements for the Armed Forces Repository of Specimen Samples for the Identification of Remains" April 2, 1996.

33 Ibid.

34 Reilly P.R., "DNA Banking" (1992) 51 *Am. J. Hum. Genet.* 1169.

35 McEwen J.E. and P.R Reilly, "A Survey of DNA Diagnostic Laboratories Regarding DNA Banking" (1995), 56 *Am. J. Hum. Genet.* 1477.

36 Weir R.F. and J.R. Horton., "DNA Banking and Informed Consent" (1995), 17(4) *IRB* 1 (Part 1); 17(5-6) *IRB* 1 (Part 2).

37 Ibid.

38 Supra note 35.

39 Ibid.

40 Ibid.

41 Ibid.

42 Supra note 36.

43 Supra note 34.

44 Supra note 35.

45 Supra note 36.

46 Supra note 35.

47 Supra note 36.

48 Supra note 35.

49 Ibid.

50 Supra note 36.

51 Ibid.

52 Supra note 35.

53 Supra note 36.

54 *Moore v. Regents of University of California*, 51 Cal.3d 120, 271 Cal. Rptr. 146, 793 P.2d 479 (1989).

55 Supra note 35.

56 Supra note 36.

57 Gold R.L., R.R. Lebel, E.A. Mearns, R.B. Dworkin, T. Hadro and J.K. Burns, "Model Consent Forms for DNA Linkage Analysis and Storage", 47 *Am. J. Med. Genet.* 1223; Knoppers B.M. and C.M. Laberge, "DNA Sampling and Informed Consent" (1989), 140 *CMAJ*. 1023.

58 Peterson M.R., "The Armed Forces Institute of Pathology: An Underutilized Repository of Case Material" (1996), 86 *Am. J. Pub. Health* 592.

59 Grody W. W., "Molecular Pathology, Informed Consent, and the Paraffin Block" (1995), 4 *Diagnostic Molecular Pathology* 155.

60 Sugarman J., E.G. Reisner. and J. Kurtzberg, "Ethical Aspects of Banking Placental Blood for Bone Marrow Transplantation" (1995), 274 *JAMA* 1782.

61 McEwen J.E. and P.R. Reilly, "Stored Guthrie Cards as DNA 'Banks' " (1994), 55 *Am. J. Hum. Genet.* 196.

62 Ibid.

63 Ibid.

64 Ibid.

65 Annas G.G., "Privacy Rules for DNA Databanks: Protecting Coded 'Future Diaries" (1993), 270 *JAMA* 2346.

66 Annas G.G., L.H. Glantz and P.A. Roche, *The Genetic Privacy Act and Commentary* (Boston: Boston University School of Public Health, 1995).

67 Genetic Privacy and Nondiscrimination Act of 1995, H.R. 2690, 104th Cong., 1st Sess., S. 1416, 104th Cong., 1st Sess. (1995); Medical Privacy in the Age of New Technologies Act of 1996, H.R. 3482, 104th Cong., 2d Sess. (1996).

68 Lin M.M.J., "Conferring a Federal Property Right in Genetic Material: Stepping Into the Future with the Genetic Privacy Act" (1996), 22 *Am. J. L& Med.* 109.

69 Wright-Clayton E., K.K. Steinberg, M. J. Khoury, E. Thomson, L. Andrews, M.J. Ellis Kahn, L.M. Kopelman and J.O. Weiss, "Informed Consent for Genetic Research on Stored Tissue Samples (Consensus Statement)" (1995), 274 *JAMA* 1786.

70 Ibid.

71 Ibid.

72 American Society of Human Genetics (ASHG), "Ad Hoc Committee on DNA Technology, DNA Banking and DNA Analysis: Points to Consider" (1988), 42 *Am. J. Hum. Genet.* 781.

73 American College of Medical Genetics (ACMG), "Storage of Genetic Materials Committee, Statement on Storage and Use of Genetic Materials" (1995), 57 *Am. J. Hum. Genet.* 1499.

74 Marshall E., "Policy on DNA Research Troubles Tissue Bankers; Centers for Disease Control and Prevention Develops Ethical Standards for Genetic Research on Archived Blood and Tissue Samples" (1996), 271 *Science* 440; Stephenson J., "Pathologists Enter Debate on Consent for Genetic Research on Stored Tissue"(1996), 275 *JAMA* 503.

75 Supra note 59.

76 Knoppers B. M. and C. M. Laberge, "Research and Stored Tissues: Persons as Sources, Samples as Persons?" (1995), 274 *JAMA* 1806.

HUMAN TISSUE BANKS IN EUROPE

OCTAVI QUINTANA

Advisor on biotechnology to the President of the European Commission

We are entering a new age of biotechnology and genetics. One aspect of the rapid advances in biological and medical research is that human tissue is being used in an increasing variety of ways.

The various purposes for which human tissue is collected and stored may include DNA sampling, research and transplants. Transplants of human tissue, though less familiar to the public than organ transplants, have become increasingly frequent and successful in recent years, a trend which is sure to continue.

Many of these developments have unquestionable benefits but using human tissue in different ways also raises new ethical dilemmas. These ethical dilemmas are similar to those related to organ transplants because both are substances of human origin which will be used for the benefit of other human beings.

There are, however, features which differentiate organs and tissue:

- Human tissues do not involve emergency procedures as compared to organs.
- There is no shortage of human tissues. Shortages are due to lack of organization.
- Tissues may be cultured and stored for a long time.

Regulation

This last feature has fostered the creation of human tissue banks in many countries. The similarities and differences are very relevant when considering the possibility of regulation. From a juridical point of view it is worth mentioning that most countries have legislation covering organ transplantation with the significant exceptions of Germany, Holland and Switzerland. Most countries have no legislation regarding human tissue, however, with the understanding that either the norms governing organs apply or that no norm is needed. The countries which have enacted legislation concerning human tissue include Belgium, France, Spain, Macedonia and Australia as well as the Council of Europe. In addition, some tissues have long been covered by specific regulation, e.g. blood and its derivatives, corneas and tissues related with reproductive functions such as sperm, ova and embryos.

Legislation is needed to deal with ethical issues which are particularly relevant in the case of human tissue banks. The absence of legislation opens the door for possible abuses. The straight application of existing organ transplant rules to tissue banks leaves unresolved problems as some important differences exist. Moreover, there are no physical organ transplant banks because organs cannot be stored.

Most countries prohibit tissue collection for commercial purposes but very few regulate its processing, preservation or distribution, effectively leaving the door open to commercialization.

In Europe, it is now possible to obtain tissue from non profit and for profit banks, stocked with samples from around the world with no clear indication of origin or proof of examination carried out on donors (no guarantees for public health).

Health care professionals are able to contact a tissue bank or a commercial organization in Europe or the US and place an order, as for any other product. These centres import tissue from around the world and distribute it on request at prices they deem appropriate (with a profit margin) with no guarantees in terms of allocation criteria or transparency.

The European Union has adopted a Directive on medical devices on the grounds that measures were required in the context of an internal market in which goods, services and capital are guaranteed free movement. The Directive does not apply to:

- Human blood, human blood products, human plasma or blood cells of human origin or to devices which incorporate at the time of placing on the market such blood products, plasma or cells. (Article 1 (5)(e))
- Transplants or tissues or cells of human origin nor to products incorporating or derived from tissues or cells of human origin.

However, industry is pressing for the Directive to be amended to include tissues and cells of human origin as well as medical devices. This would, of course, lead to trade in tissues and national health authorities would no longer be able to maintain control over health guarantees. Nor would it be possible to provide proper donor tissue recipient monitoring which enables recipients to be traced and any necessary measures taken.

The Group of Advisors on Ethical Implications of Biotechnology of the European Commission is preparing an opinion on this matter since we believe that the Directive should not be amended and that human tissues should be regulated separately.

For ethical and health safety reasons, the opinion will contain recommendations that the following activities should be standardized:

- accreditation and registration of tissue banks
- accreditation and registration of collection and implant Centres
- donor-tissue-recipient tracing
- procedural quality control
- health authority monitoring
- monitoring of the fees charged by the Centres.

In the end, it is important to decide whether there is a need for specific legislation on human tissues. Two reasons may support this notion; firstly, there is increasing intervention of public authorities in matters concerning human health, even in the USA (FDA). Secondly, there are specific ethical matters that are difficult to resolve with other legislation.

If norms are to be established, what direction should be adopted? Should human tissues be considered equivalent to medical devices, especially those with no live cells, or should the rich experience acquired from two decades of organ transplants be used as a guide?

In my opinion, the latter alternative better fulfils the ethical requirements. Legislation on human tissue should cover the following topics, at least:

- Informed consent of the donor, including incompetent persons and cadavers
- Non-commercialization of the human body
- Quality standards for the obtention, preservation, storage and distribution of human tissues
- Confidentiality and anonymity of the data
- Responsibility

Whatever the intended use of human tissue, it all comes from the same source and it is used to the same end, which means we must apply common principles to guarantee public health and provide an ethical framework.

The use of DNA samples raises somewhat different problems. In fact, the use of and the information which may be derived from a DNA sample may be not known, not even by the researchers. Thus, the consent is not so well informed and flexibility is needed to implement the waiving principle.

In the case of minors and incompetent individuals, the issue of consent is interpreted strictly for human tissue transplantation and is much more restrictive than that applied to DNA sampling. Admittedly, the risk of the latter procedure is much lower. Consent is nonetheless required from the legal representative for any collection of human tissue.

DNA sampling is not specifically addressed in the proposals to regulate human tissues and there is no legislation in Europe regarding this area (that I am aware of). There are some facts, however, worth mentioning.

In practice, there are three ways of obtaining samples:

1. As a procedure under a research project (e.g. markers for certain breast cancer), subjects have to provide a written informed consent.
2. As a result of a diagnostic test; these samples may be stored but no informed consent is obtained for storage.
3. Using any human body part (usually serum from blood tests) for purposes of research or screening in which the subjects are the general population. No one other than the researcher knows the results and their use.

Legislation is needed to preserve the confidentiality and the use of stored DNA. One should be aware, however, of the great difficulty of controlling unethical practices since it is very easy to obtain human specimens and to isolate DNA.

The Group of Advisors on Ethical Implications of Biotechnology is planning to draft an opinion paper addressing the issues germane to the use of human tissues for research and transplant purposes and then, formulate guidelines concerning human tissue for DNA sampling.

The proposal of the Group of Advisors is to require authorization from the public health authorities for the extracting centre. The competent authorities will check that the qualification requirements for the health professionals performing these extractions are met, as well as the resources supplied, and the adequate procedures for tissue transport. It is also the responsibility of the authorizing body to check conditions related to consent, non commercialization issues and confidentiality.

The second principal item of the proposal of the Group of Advisors regarding collection of human tissue, is to make controls on substance safety. It includes all the tests and controls on donors to prevent problems due to infections, neoplasms and inmunological conditions.

A very important issue related to tissue banking is to promote public awareness, enhancing the importance of donation and the solidarity implied in it. Professional training on these matters has to be emphasized.

Endnotes and References

1 Council of Europe, *Recommendation R(94)1 on Human Tissue Banks.*

2 WHO, Human Organ Transplantation, pages 21 and 23, Geneva 1991.

3 Belgium, Crown Order in Council of 15 April 1988 regarding Tissue Banks

4 France, *Loi 94-654*,juillet de 1994.

5 Spain, Real Decreto Actividades con Tejidos Humanos, 1 marzo 1996.

6 Macedonia, Law on Human Tissues, June 1995.

7 Australia, 1989, Therapeutic Goods Act.

8 Health Council Of Netherlands, *Proper Use of Human Tissue*, Publication 1994/01 E, The Hague 1994.

9 European Association of Human Tissue Banks, *Ethical Rules for Tissue Banking*, 1994.

10 The Nuffield Council of Bioethics, *Human Tissue, Legal and Ethical Issues*, London 1995.

11 Englert, Y, ed., *Organ and Tissue Banking in the EU.* (London: Martinus Nijhoff, 1995).

DNA SAMPLING AND BANKING: PRACTICES AND PROCEDURES

BÉATRICE GODARD

Research Associate, Hôtel-Dieu de Montréal

T. DOUGLAS KINSELLA

Professor and Director, Office of Medical Bioethics,

Faculty of Medicine, University of Calgary

RAPPORTEURS

Introduction

Research in the field of human genetics continues to advance rapidly and DNA sampling has become an increasingly common medical act. No other procedure intrudes more intimately upon the individual and nowhere is informed consent more sensitive. No practice in classical epidemiology carries such implications for personal autonomy, beneficence and harm, the protection of the vulnerable, nor even for social justice. Moreover, the expanded collection of DNA samples and the subsequent use of genetic information has heightened public concern about confidentiality and privacy. Consequently, right-to-privacy legislation is being enacted in many countries. But administrative or statutory provisions may both help and hinder DNA banking, for example, privacy laws may make banking of identifiable data impossible or allow DNA sample donors to refuse banking.

This plenary's presentations suggest that any statement of principles and guidelines, no matter how carefully established and far reaching, requires a vast effort of educating the lay public as well as the medical and other professions concerned in order to insure implementation. At the same time, if the acceptance of research on population genetics depends on public attitudes towards health care and research in general, it also depends on how appropriately and sensitively genetic research projects are carried out.

It appears that the issue of informed consent has become more complex as it has become easier to use DNA samples for purposes quite different from those for which they were originally obtained as Professor McEwen states and also far into the future, long after the donor's death. A consensus seems to be emerging, however. At the beginning of any project, investigators should inform the subjects as to the following: definition of the purposes for which the samples or the results will be used, which research groups will have access to the samples, and what results, if any, the subjects can expect to receive as presented orally by Dr. Aymé. Dr. Pembrey's oral presentation also reminds us that principles of data protection and professional secrecy are to be discussed to avoid breaches of confidentiality. Likewise, the lack of formal ethical and legal regulations in current DNA banking practices, as illustrated in Dr. Verhoef's study, underscores the urgency of remedial regulatory initiatives. Citizens rely on governments to protect them and promote their health, but governments can do this only if sufficient knowledge has been acquired to guide policy. The Government in the U.K., Dr. Pembrey notes, has seen fit to intervene in the area of genetic testing with the creation of a Parliamentary Select Committee which will study, in particular, aspects of consent to testing and the protection of personal genetic data. At an international level, guidelines can carry a moral rather than a legal weight by virtue of the authority and competence of the body establishing them and they could command wide respect as Dr. Quintana points out.

In a survey of DNA banking practices in Canada, Dr. Verhoef and her colleagues examined the details of sample collection. Local institutional policies to regulate DNA banking exist, but they are not always known. Policies on ownership/control options, duration of storage and sample destruction seem to be less well known. A majority of researchers practised anonymous linkage of donors with shared samples. Most academic research centres agree that formal policies to regulate human DNA banking are desirable. Dr.Pembrey avers that in the U.K., the majority of DNA banking grew out of and was greatly facilitated by the National Health Service (NHS); most banking in the U.K. is tied to NHS clinical services which is comprised of 14-15 Regional Genetic Centres within which clinical molecular labs are found. The NHS link has allowed the DNA banking system to carry on under the umbrella of the old system, where patient information could move around quite freely, without much thought given to guidelines or regulation. Things are changing, however, creating standards for those performing the banking function as well as protecting the individual whose DNA is banked (the Parliamentary Select Committee referred to above). To assist professionals involved in banking, the Molecular Genetics Society was formed in 1988. This organization drafted guidelines in 1989 for service labs including what is now a well established quality assurance scheme. As for the United States, Professor McEwen reports that human DNA is stored for many reasons: as a service to genetically at-risk individuals or families, who may later wish them to be available for family-based linkage testing; for research purposes, such as gene-mapping studies that may require samples from many family members over several generations; for reasons unrelated to contemporary DNA analysis but potentially useful for future testing, or, still, as a matter of routine. In France, there are many different kinds of human DNA banks established with either service, or research in mind, or both. Of the 150 known banks, however, only 2 (Généthon and Cassini) are able to provide service to external users, the balance consist of private DNA collections. DNA banking has been largely unregulated but this may change. The French government, in response to increasing numbers of budget requests from hospitals and research labs for banking facilities, set up a Working Party two years ago to study the ethical, regulatory, practical and technical issues related to this area. The recommendations addressed the need to obtain informed consent from the patients (this requirement being largely ignored under the auspices of clinical care, as opposed to research) and the lack of quality assurance in the labs i.e.. reliability of information, operational organization. Additionally, the Working Party proposed options for the reorganization of the banking system in France. The most likely scenario would be the creation of a National Council of Banks and a small number of national DNA banks. The Council would take on the role of overseeing bank audit, activity follow-up, monitoring practices, establishing a database for information sharing, advise on political issues relating to sampling and banking, and negotiate with the government for funding. In essence, Dr. Aymé relates that the use of personally identified data in the banks and in private collections raises important issues of storage, quality, safety, practice with regard to consent, ethics of access, and freedom of research versus protection of individuals. While some banks are well organized and pose little problem, others are in research labs where the facilities cannot insure either the safety of DNA samples or of computerized information. In private collections, funding is uncertain and there are many instances of lost samples. The establishment of an overarching Council could help to correct these shortcomings and establish some degree of uniformity with regard to practice and procedures.

Similarly, Dr. Quintana notes that European human tissue banks are being used in a variety of new ways. Many of these developments have unquestionable benefits but they also raise new ethical dilemmas. If these dilemmas parallel those related to organ transplants, they differ from a legal point of view. Their similarities and differences are very relevant when considering the possibility of regulation. It is worth mentioning that if most countries have legislation on organ transplants, they less often have laws regarding tissues, with the understanding that either the standards governing organs apply, or that standards aren't necessary. Some biological materials have long been covered by specific legislation, e.g. blood and its derivatives, corneas or, more recently, materials related to reproduction such as sperm, ova, and embryos. Is there a need for specific legislation on human tissues, wonders Dr. Quintana? Human health is being increasingly legislated, yet there are specific ethical matters that are difficult to solve without targeted legislation. How then should the latter be formulated? Should it build on the experience of two decades of organ transplants? Or should it view human tissues as medical devices? Dr. Quintana believes the first alternative better fulfils ethical requirements. It would seem that public awareness regarding the collection of human tissues needs to be stimulated. It is important to note that the ease with which human specimens can be obtained and DNA isolated makes the control of unethical practices correspondingly difficult.

Current banking practices have deficiencies. These point to multiple ethical and legal questions, surrounding the nature of the information given to patients, their degree of autonomy, or still the communication gaps existing between different levels of institutional decision-makers. The primary rationale for DNA banks is likely to evolve over time. Their present aim is to make aggregate and individual data accessible for medical, statistical, and research purposes. To be of value, data must be accurate, reliable and as complete as possible. To maximize their usefulness, it is sometimes essential that donors be identified, which in itself may lead to problems. Accuracy and completeness can be achieved only if the donor and the investigator are confident that the data collected are indeed necessary for the aims of the bank and that they will be safeguarded, that is, both secured against unauthorized access and not used for purposes other than those for which they were collected. To that end, formal national DNA banking policies are necessary. In the absence of explicit guidelines, the protection of individuals (and their anonymity) remains uncertain.

Informed consent: paralogism or sophism? Is it possible to obtain informed consent for all potential contemporary and future uses of a DNA sample? The explosive growth in genetic applications raises questions that were unforeseen when samples were first obtained. Moreover, it may be very useful to keep these samples: for instance, when a donor dies or, still, for retrospective studies. At the same time, asking for unrestricted use of DNA samples will render informed consent irrelevant. Due to costs, it is tempting to make as extensive a use as possible of available samples and related data. How then to update the consent? Dr. Aymé wonders whether it is ethical to study the biological material of healthy volunteers for any type of study. How then to share the material with other research teams, with a view to maximizing its usefulness? Its relative non-availability is often a consequence of conflicts of interest between research groups. Yet sharing is a major concern for patient advocacy groups. To what extend should privacy be protected, if by the same token the power to detect important risk factors drops dramatically?

The right to control information about oneself is a fundamental value in most democracies, and means for protecting privacy are in order. Human genetic research is growing and it is recommended that the collection of DNA samples within research projects take place within the framework of laws pertaining to confidentiality and research on human subjects. Whatever the protective measures decided upon for human DNA banks, they will have to strike a balance between the dictates of privacy, and the need for a better understanding of health determinants.

In the case of forensic DNA banks Professor McEwen indicates that in the United States, DNA samples are stored for a variety of reasons. Likewise, most hospital pathology labs keep paraffin embedded tissue blocks for legal purposes. Forty states have enacted statutes that authorize or require the collection of blood from convicted sex offenders and some other types of criminals. These samples are tested for their unique identification characteristics; the resulting profiles are then stored to be used to help identify suspects in future crimes that involve biological evidence. These practices have led to a growing societal awareness regarding questions such as 1)Who can be included in forensic data banks; 2)Who should be in charge of these banks? 3)How long should labs keep DNA samples? The consent forms do not come close to covering these issues. Proceeding with limited consent or without any at all may be appropriate in some circumstances such as crime scene investigations or in health emergencies.

Informed consent involves choices and possible control by the participants over time and even after death. There are ongoing obligations for DNA bankers in this continuum, from the time of obtaining samples and testing through to identifying markers and genes with other researchers or economic partners.

Dr. Pembrey raises other problems with DNA banking, i.e. potential breaches of confidentiality and invasion of privacy. In the United Kingdom, much human genetic research is closely integrated with medical services. This close link between service and research has certain advantages. The dual responsibilities of the medical profession to both "care for" and "learn from" the families who seek help is well understood, in particular as regards the disclosure of information and the use of DNA samples for clinical services or for research. However, the link also highlights the need to distinguish between research, service, and clinical audit because of the potential consequences. For example, in regard to the health and the daily life of individuals, being informed that one has specific genotypes associated with common diseases will mean very little in practice for a long time.

Greater caution is necessary in population wide screening than in high risk group testing. But even if one recommends that research results not be disclosed and that DNA samples collected for research not be used for clinical services, Dr. Pembrey notes that not everyone accepts this and that there is no standard practice. For example, in a service setting there is no agreement on the need to obtain specific consent from a person for their DNA analysis result to be communicated to another clinical genetics centre in order to facilitate testing of a different branch of the family. Whilst mindful of the need for confidentiality within the family, information may be transferred within the National Health Service under the umbrella of "professional duty of care" to the whole family. The problem is that individuals could be faced with information they do not wish to have, or with choices both the investigators and themselves were unaware that they may have to face. Also, knowledge regarding genetic status is not limited to individuals: this knowledge has consequences for family members, especially those in the next generation. Dr. Pembrey therefore recommends "to move away from general to more specific confidentiality" in any remedial regulatory initiatives to come.

Conclusion

The issues of practices and procedures of DNA sampling and banking revolve around what safeguards should exist for the collection and the use of

DNA samples, as well as the disclosure of information. To whom does a DNA sample belong? How can DNA banking be done in an ethical and beneficial manner, given the dangers to individual privacy and autonomy, given the lack of defined beneficial goals at this stage of our knowledge? Under what circumstances and which government agencies should allow access to DNA samples without individual consent? What do the choices mean in terms of respect for the donors, the scientific freedom of researchers, and the legal and ethical obligations of ethics boards or government agencies? These questions have become all too familiar.

The particularities of legal safeguards (or lack thereof) will continue to differ from country to country. However, most people recognize that it is time to re-examine their parameters, given the context of a rapidly expanding capacity for genetic identification and because genetic information raises issues that go beyond strict medical information. Whether it be in North America or in Europe, the lack of clear protocols for DNA banking may heighten the potential for future misunderstandings with depositors or for unforeseen legal liability. The dangers of DNA sample misuse or third-party access to information are real and likely to increase as more disease genes are isolated. A change in the regulatory framework governing genetic testing could influence the attitudes and help modify the practices of DNA bankers. Pressures for a wider commercialization of genetic testing could increase from private companies. There is a reasonable enough expectation of growth in DNA banking to justify setting up mechanisms to protect users as well as donors. The growing recognition of the banks' existence and a keener understanding of the need for DNA banking by diverse stakeholders will challenge and ultimately transform the social perception of human genetic research.

THE VIRTUAL LIFE OF A GENETIC SAMPLE
CONCLUSION TO THE CONFERENCE

CLAUDE M. LABERGE

Professor of Medicine and Pediatrics, Laval University, Quebec

President of the Quebec Network of Applied Genetic Medicine

Introduction

In concluding the First International Conference on DNA Sampling and Human Genetic Research, we must first thank all the speakers from around the world who have attended. The speakers have covered the gamut of subjects under DNA sampling and banking and have exposed the legal, ethical and policy issues that such practices generate. We must also thank the Chairpersons, the Rapporteurs and especially the participants (15% of them students) who contributed greatly to the comments and discussion at each session of the Conference.

In concluding a full two and a half days of profound and thoughtful presentations and discussions it is evident that only impressions are possible.

First Level Impression

If we rely on the official title of this meeting, the first impression may have been that, although technical and fraught with ethical and legal issues, the problem to be confronted and studied was somewhat simple, like the view of DNA sampling as shown in FIGURE 1.

However, any participant perusing the conference materials, including the speakers' abstracts and reference material, would have understood immediately that the matter was much more complicated and broad than first thought. The sessions, the personal presence of different experts in their fields, the discussion, the logic of the program, all contributed to create a wonderful world of ideas, of problems known and unknown, of new issues emerging from the confrontation of different viewpoints and areas of expertise, of entirely new perspectives from unsuspected frontiers, of languages, of semantics, of translation into different cultures, etc.

Another first impression at the end of the Conference is that it was indeed a real meeting place, a significant multidisciplinary congregation of ideas as well as a peer and public forum of exchange of ideas and information. A rare magic took place and kept hold of the participants until the end.

FIGURE 1: Simplified view of genetic sampling

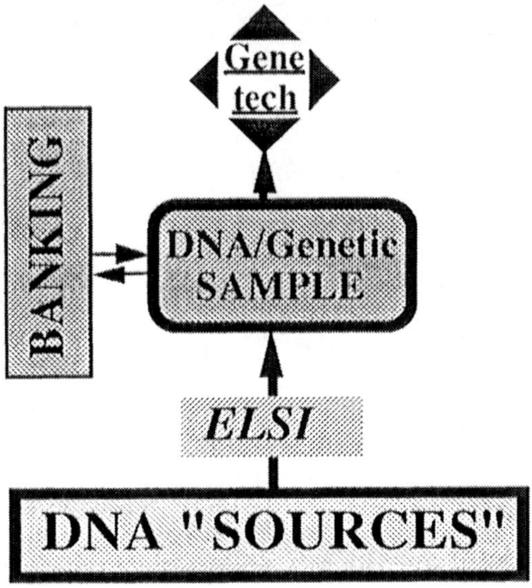

Second Level Impression

Beyond the appearances, another impression emerged as the Conference was progressing: that of complexity in the loops of concepts, facts, discussions and positions as well as in the different perspectives and representations brought to the theme of the Conference. DNA sampling and banking (or at least keeping the sample for a certain amount of time) were not as simple as presumed. Banking involves all kinds of processes and procedures depending on the finalities and the justifications inherent to genetic research, to the clinical application (individual, families, populations), and even to the large scale sequencing phase of the human genome.

To complement this secondary impression, another one became immediately evident. Genetic research cannot proceed without genetic samples to analyze and study (an undisputed premise and fact). Persons should know and choose to participate in genetic research. Thus, no personalized human genetic material can be procured and banked for genetic research without the informed consent and choices of the donor, and this also for samples procured during medical care unless anonymized. Simply, the general rule is:

- "No sample without consent!"

But is it as simple as that? Or is it so complex and full of specific exceptions and rules? Or can there be order, categories, levels, fields, areas, sub-systems in this second level impression?

Can the complexity of human DNA/genetic sampling and banking in research (fundamental, clinical, epidemiological, anthropological) be simplexified?

The Simplexity of Sampling and Banking Human DNA

The Conference, in its internal logic, touched base with the history and update of modern human and medical genetics in the Introductory lecture by Professor McKusick. On this fresh background, presentations and discussion included practices and procedures of sampling and banking genetic material, in those countries involved in large scale human genetics studies. Once sampled, the status of genetic material becomes essential to its processing and its finalities. Thus, the basic legal theories of property, gift and *sui generis* were reviewed.

Acquiring genetic material for clinical and research purposes entail procedures attached either to the sample and/or to the information derived or constructed from it. Basically, these procedures must include consent, confidentiality, access, look back and accompanying duties.

In addition to sampling in clinical and familial situations, the uses for both genetic epidemiology or for the proposed Human Genome Diversity Project of genetic material and information at the population level were examined. These applications were further analyzed in areas of genetic screening.

Finally, since knowledge issued from genetic material and information may have commercial applications and patentability, these questions were reviewed both as to the different legal approaches to patentability and as to the pharmaceutical industry approaches to research and development of useful products.

Thus, from the beginning of the Conference, a logical diagram ensured that a large spectrum of issues and problems would be presented and discussed. This approach worked in exposing the larger complexity of the international field of sampling and banking genetic material. In this way, the global geography of ELSI (ethical, legal, and social issues) related to the field of DNA sampling was surveyed and a preliminary map of this complexified field emerged from the weekend survey.

The major components of the complex self-organizing open system of sampling and banking genetic material can be identified and constructed from the simplified view as: DNA "sources", the consideration of the ELSI, then the sample itself as well as the sampling procedures, banking (or collection, or processing for testing), the creation of "genetic information" through the use of genetic technologies and its transit through databases. Peripheral, but nonetheless important, complementary areas are informatics and genomic research.

FIGURE 2: The complexified view of genetic sampling

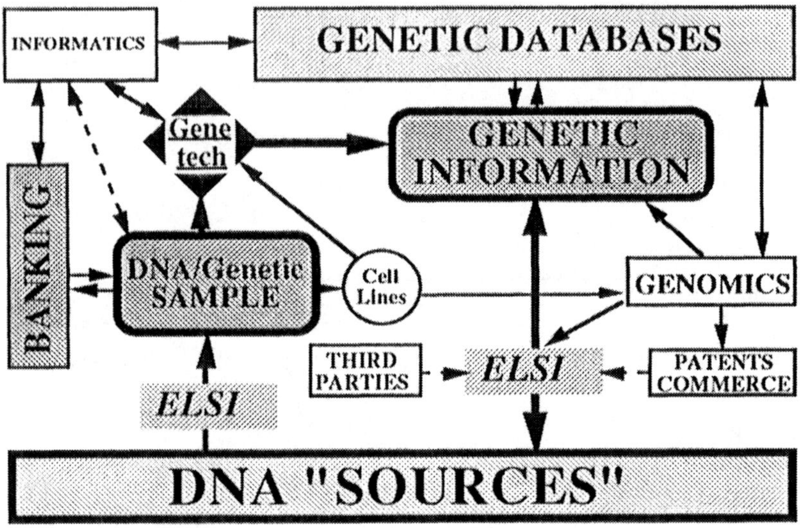

We can thus define the minimal component of the system as in FIGURE 2, albeit in condensed boxes. For example, DNA "sources" may vary from patients (competent or incompetent), families, demes, communities of interest, populations, abandoned samples, clinical samples, pathological samples and survey samples. Banking may be interpreted as the step before analysis of samples and this could be pure banking for future use, collection of interesting samples, or even the delay between extraction of DNA/RNA and uses by technology. There are yet no DNA "stick tests" available!

However, it is the construction of information, the added "plus-value" to a material sample that really constitutes the "main-frame" activity of genetic research and services. Procuring samples does not in itself advance knowledge. No production of information content can be envisaged without "containers" which can be viewed generally as databases.

This complexity (or rather "complicity"[1]) model shows that ethical, legal and policy issues stemming from sampling and banking of genetic material are positioned at the input and output points of genetic information. All the other interactions between components of the system should be seen as upgrading, quality control, validation, professional norms and backup procedures. These do not have immediate connections with the ethical, legal and policy issues that may directly affect the "sample sources", although the quality and finalities of the inner production system must be filtered through the ELSI environment that provides "open" access to those DNA "sources" that feed the system.

In the complementary way by which a complex system must be viewed, simplexified[1] and analyzed, identification of the "attractors" that are specific to the means and ends of such a system becomes the way to construct the looking-glass (if not the hour-glass) by which both sides of their gateways must constantly be observed, evaluated and corrected.

Two Attractors into One

If we consider the genetic material in itself, then the ethical interactions are not with the "material" but with the "individual" whence it comes.

Thus, if the ethical phase of transition of the "gene-tech" system is the individual (as the basic unit of DNA "source"), then it follows that the commerce of ethics entails judicial and legal "contracts" with these individuals.

The ELSI are central to knowledge in human genetics. They best modulate the system at the two points which constitute the two "attractors" that define the potentials and the limits accorded to the input of genetic material feeding it (DNA "sources") and to the output (the same DNA "sources") using its production as genetic information. However, in practice, these two "attractors" can be viewed as a single gateway, a kind of swing-door.

We can thus "renormalize" the view of the system as in FIGURE 3, if we focus on the compounded attractor of MELSI (medical, ethical, legal and social issues). It has now become MELSI because most of the justifications for human genetic programs are couched in terms of eventual or actual medical understanding and/or applications. The most evident addition to the first diagram of FIGURE 1 is that of "genetic information", which for a more comprehensive understanding of the "sampling system" becomes an obligate twin to genetic material.

A) THE SAMPLING (INPUT) PART OF THE MELSI ATTRACTOR

Since samples have to come from an individual, and since the finality of this input is to process the samples into genetic information, it is clear that in order to respect the human dignity of the donor (the term participant would be better), we must admit and accept the first rule of the DNA sampling system, otherwise there is no input. That first rule is simple, often cited and obvious but must be restated in the perspective of "complexity":

- "No use of samples without consent (**if** identifiable genetic information can be derived from it)".

This is more comprehensive than the "no consent, no sampling" general guideline. It permits under due review, and in certain circumstances, the use of anonymous and anonymized samples for aggregate and non-identifying genetic information, thus preventing discrimination and stigmatization. Thus, it is a consent based on informed choices.

Samples must be adequate and adapted to the genetic information that it will provide in the "gene-tech" sub-system.

FIGURE 3: Simplexified view of genetic sampling

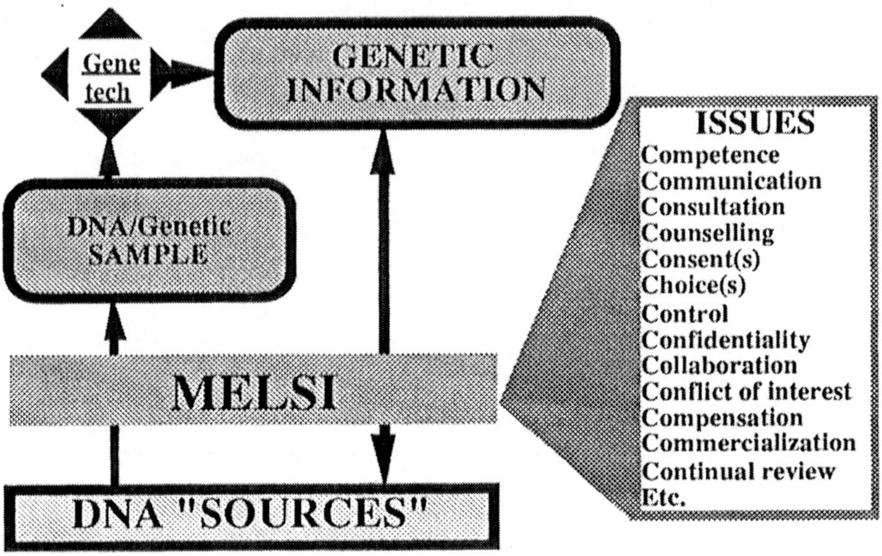

B) THE INFORMATION (OUTPUT) PART OF THE MELSI ATTRACTOR

Production, transfer, explanation, linkage and use of genetic information, when involving the individuals who procured the samples, requires respect for their choices and their human dignity, whatever the levels of interaction, be they medical, ethical, legal or social ("policy"). The basic and simple rule is then:

- No unauthorized release of genetic information should be given concerning an individual (or collectivities if appropriate).

At the social level, uses of genetic information in commercialization and patenting are subsumed in the output part of this attractor and thus should also be viewed within the integrated system of acquisition and utilization of human genetic information.

Beyond this First Conference

After two and a-half days of intense presentations and discussion, the evident conclusion is that sampling/banking cannot be isolated and studied in itself without including the inherent "human" quality of the material which feeds the system of genetic research for information and utilization.

This fact brings home the evidence that we do know what we do not know. In a "complexity" mode, we will probably never know all about genetics and human genetics in particular. We are evolving within a science which is both biological and social, which integrates the human person both as observer and observed, and consequently must essentially be a "science with conscience".[2]

Evolving knowledge, evolving technologies, evolving needs, evolving benefits, evolving costs and disadvantages, evolving social perceptions, evolving goals, all contribute to make human genetic information one of the most complex living communication "systems" in our universe. We will have to keep on working at simplifying the complexity or better still, in a complementary way, to simplexify the complicity. In human genetics, humans are observers while observed, participants while recipients, actors while auditors.

These issues are of sufficient medical, ethical, legal and societal importance to warrant meeting again at intervals to re-examine this fundamental triad of genetics — sample * technology * information — in human affairs. The Conference just ended and already there are new problems. The organizers only wish that this meeting in Montreal is a "transition phase" for an emergent community. This community should see to it that open and factual discussions on these issues central to all humanity continue and expand. If so, the organizers will have realized their goals.

Who, when and where will be the next "attractor" for an eventual follow-up Conference? Will the sewing and construction of the "DNA Quilt" continue to comfort the world?

Endnotes and References

1 Cohen J. and I. Stewart, *The Collapse of Chaos: Discovering Simplicity in a Complex World.* (New York: Viking, Penguin Group, 1994) at 3 and 396. Simplexity and complicity are two new concepts combining content and context to complement the more classical concepts of simplicity and complexity. "Simplexity is the tendency of simple rules to emerge from underlying disorder and complexity, in systems whose large-scale structure is independent of the fine details of their substructures. Complicity is the tendency of interacting systems to coevolve in a manner that changes both, leading to a growth of complexity from simple beginnings - complexity that is unpredictable in detail, but whose general course is comprehensible and foreseeable."

2 Morin E., *Science avec Conscience* (Paris: Seuil, 1990).

INDEX